How to Remove a PC's Case

1. Turn off the computer, monitor, and peripherals. Make sure that everything normally attached to your computer is turned off *and* unplugged. Your computer's easier to move around that way.

2. Unplug your computer from the wall or Uninterruptable Power Supply. (Unplug the power cord from the back of your PC, too.)

3. Remove the screws from your PC's back or outside edges. Many PCs use two large thumbscrews along one edge, as shown in the figure. Some new models have sides that simply flip down when you depress a release.

4. Remove the PC's cover or side panel. On some computers, the cover slides toward the front; others come out the back. You might need to pull pretty hard.

5. While the case is off, take your PC outside and use a can of compressed air to blow out all the dust from inside. Clean away the dust balls clinging to any outside vents, as well.

To replace the cover, reverse these steps.

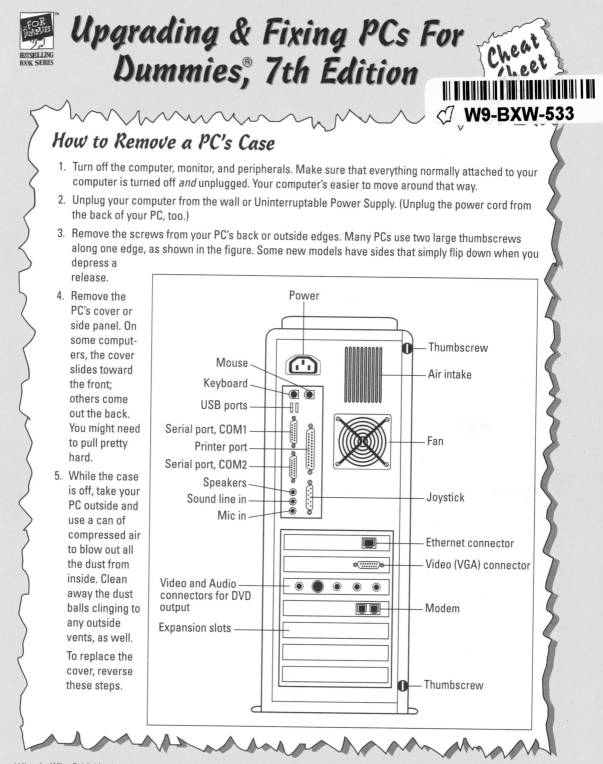

For Dummies: Bestselling Book Series for Beginners

What Vista Needs for Each Version

	Vista Home Basic	Vista Home Premium	Vista Ultimate
Fast CPU	X	X	X
Powerful video		X	X
5.1 or 7.1 sound		X	X
TV tuner/TV out		X	X
Large hard drive		X	X

See Chapter 6 for detailed explanations.

Steps for Adding a New Part to Your PC

1. Copy any important information on your hard drive to a CD/DVD, another computer on your network, or a portable hard drive for safekeeping. (To be really safe, back up the entire hard drive.)
2. Read any instructions that came with your new part.
3. Exit any running programs, turn off your PC, and unplug it from the wall.
4. Clean off the desk or table space next to your computer.
5. Put your tools next to the computer.
6. Remove your PC's cover.
7. Touch an unpainted part of the computer's case to discharge any static electricity that might have built up. This keeps static electricity from damaging your computer's sensitive internal parts. (If you work in a particularly static-prone environment, buy a wrist strap or grounding mat from your computer store to help discharge static.)
8. Remove the old item and insert the new one.
9. Plug in the PC, turn it on, and carefully test the new part to see whether it works.
10. Turn off the PC, unplug it, and put the case back together.
11. Plug in the PC and put away your tools.

Your First Lines of Defense in Windows

- Always install the "Critical" updates listed by Windows Update. (Chapter 1)
- Use System Restore to repair problems caused by damaged settings or software; return to your prior settings if it doesn't help. (Chapter 1)
- Install a new driver to fix problem parts. (Chapter 19)
- Invite a computer-literate friend to fix your computer using Remote Assistance. (Chapter 21)
- Make daily backups using Windows Vista's Backup and Restore Center or a more full-featured third-party software. (Chapter 9)
- Turn on Windows Vista's firewall. (Chapter 18)
- Vaccuum dust from your computer's fan area and vents often to prevent overheating. (Chapter 24)

Always Remember These Things

Turn off and unplug your computer before taking off its cover. Please. This one's the most important step. You can damage both yourself *and* your computer if you forget to turn off and unplug the computer.

Install parts one at a time. Always make sure the first one works with Windows before installing the next.

Read a USB part's instructions before installation. Sometimes you must install the drivers *before* plugging in the part. Other times, you install the drivers afterward.

The red (or colored) wire is positive. The red (or colored) wire often plugs into the pin or socket marked by a little + sign.

The positive/red wire connects to Pin 1. Look for little numbers printed along the edge of a socket. Can't see the number 1? Then push the plug into the socket with the red wire facing toward the *low* numbers on the socket.

Upgrading & Fixing PCs

FOR

DUMMIES®

7TH EDITION

by Andy Rathbone

BICENTENNIAL
1807
WILEY
2007
BICENTENNIAL

Wiley Publishing, Inc.

Upgrading & Fixing PCs For Dummies,® 7th Edition

Published by
Wiley Publishing, Inc.
111 River Street
Hoboken, NJ 07030-5774

www.wiley.com

Copyright © 2007 by Wiley Publishing, Inc., Indianapolis, Indiana

Published by Wiley Publishing, Inc., Indianapolis, Indiana

Published simultaneously in Canada

For general information on our other products and services, please contact our Customer Care Department within the U.S. at 800-762-2974, outside the U.S. at 317-572-3993, or fax 317-572-4002.

For technical support, please visit www.wiley.com/techsupport.

Wiley also publishes its books in a variety of electronic formats. Some content that appears in print may not be available in electronic books.

Library of Congress Control Number: 2007924227

ISBN: 978-0-470-12102-3

Manufactured in the United States of America

10 9 8 7 6 5 4 3 2

WILEY

About the Author

Andy Rathbone started geeking around with computers in 1985 when he bought a boxy CP/M Kaypro 2X with lime-green letters. Like other budding nerds, he soon began playing with null-modem adapters, dialing up computer bulletin boards, and working part-time at RadioShack.

In between playing computer games, he served as editor of the *Daily Aztec* newspaper at San Diego State University. After graduating with a comparative literature degree, he went to work for a bizarre underground coffee-table magazine that sort of disappeared.

Andy began combining his two main interests, words and computers, by selling articles to a local computer magazine. During the next few years, he started ghostwriting computer books for more-famous computer authors, as well as writing several hundred articles about computers for technoid publications like *Supercomputing Review, CompuServe Magazine, ID Systems, DataPro,* and *Shareware.*

In 1992, Andy and *DOS For Dummies* author/legend Dan Gookin teamed up to write *PCs For Dummies.* Andy subsequently wrote the award-winning *Windows For Dummies* series, *TiVo For Dummies,* and many other *For Dummies* books.

Today, he has more than 15 million copies of his books in print, which have been translated into more than 30 languages.

Andy lives with his most-excellent wife, Tina, and their cat in Southern California. Feel free to drop by his Web site at www.andyrathbone.com.

Dedication

To that sense of satisfaction felt when you fix it yourself.

Author's Acknowledgments

Thanks to Jean Rogers, Matt Wagner, Heidi Unger, Andy Hollandbeck, Lee Musick, and Steve Hayes.

Publisher's Acknowledgments

We're proud of this book; please send us your comments through our online registration form located at www.dummies.com/register/.

Some of the people who helped bring this book to market include the following:

Acquisitions, Editorial, and Media Development

Associate Project Editor: Jean Rogers

(Previous Edition: Nicole Haims)

Senior Acquisitions Editor: Steven Hayes

Copy Editors: Heidi Unger, Andy Hollandbeck

Technical Editor: Lee Musick

Editorial Manager: Kevin Kirschner

Media Development and Quality Assurance: Angela Denny, Kate Jenkins, Steven Kudirka, Kit Malone

Media Development Coordinator: Jenny Swisher

Media Project Supervisor: Laura Moss-Hollister

Media Development Associate Producer: Richard Graves

Editorial Assistant: Amanda Foxworth

Sr. Editorial Assistant: Cherie Case

Cartoons: Rich Tennant (www.the5thwave.com)

Composition Services

Project Coordinator: Lynsey Osborn

Layout and Graphics: Brooke Graczyk, Joyce Haughey, Stephanie Jumper, Barbara Moore, Laura Pence, Ronald Terry

Proofreaders: Aptara, Cynthia Fields

Indexer: Aptara

Anniversary Logo Design: Richard Pacifico

Publishing and Editorial for Technology Dummies

Richard Swadley, Vice President and Executive Group Publisher

Andy Cummings, Vice President and Publisher

Mary Bednarek, Executive Acquisitions Director

Mary C. Corder, Editorial Director

Publishing for Consumer Dummies

Diane Graves Steele, Vice President and Publisher

Joyce Pepple, Acquisitions Director

Composition Services

Gerry Fahey, Vice President of Production Services

Debbie Stailey, Director of Composition Services

Contents at a Glance

Table of Contents

Introduction

. . . .

*Y*ou're no dummy; we both know that. But something about computers often makes you feel like a dummy. And that's perfectly understandable. Unlike today's kids, you probably didn't grow up with a computer in your kindergarten class, living room, or on the palm of your hand. With this book, you'll no longer feel helpless when you're faced with a computer that refuses to work the way it should.

This book doesn't help you replace your computer's motherboard or build a PC from scratch using custom-selected parts. Plenty of more advanced titles out there can help you with those chores.

No, this book helps you with the types of upgrade and repair tasks that you're most likely to encounter today: Upgrading an older PC to run Windows Vista, for instance, and making sure that everything works correctly. Adding a larger hard drive. Upgrading that video card to satisfy the needs of Windows Vista or a new computer game. Making sure your PC's firewall is turned on and working correctly. Turning on the security option for your wireless network.

Simply put, this book discusses the most common upgrading and repair problems facing computer users today. It explains what to buy, where to plug it in, and how to make sure that your computer knows what to do with it.

What's New in This Edition?

Welcome to *Upgrading & Fixing PCs For Dummies,* rejuvenated for its seventh edition, and celebrating more than a decade in print. Aimed at people who want to upgrade to Windows Vista or spice up their computers to take advantage of today's latest technology, this book contains several helpful new chapters and updated sections:

- ✔ You'll find a full-color 16-page insert with photos depicting exactly how you're supposed to remove your PC's case, install a card, connect a new hard drive, and perform other operations described in this book.

- ✔ This book includes an updated visual Appendix that explains how to use *all* the ports on your computer and add any ports you might need.

- ✔ Chapter 17 includes a network installation guide that helps you configure a network with both wired and wireless devices.

- ✔ Chapter 20 provides details on installing or upgrading to Windows Vista — even onto a newly installed hard drive.

✔ Computer parts need *drivers* — special software that helps Windows understand how to talk with them. Without a proper driver, Windows Vista probably won't know how to talk to some parts of your computer. Chapter 19 contains everything you need to know about how Vista treats drivers: When you need them, where to find them, and how to install them successfully.

✔ Windows Vista's Home Premium edition lets you record TV shows onto your PC for later viewing or burning to DVD. The catch? Your PC needs a TV tuner, a device I explain how to buy and install in Chapter 12.

✔ DVD burners are the rage today, and I've explained their odd format terminology and incompatibilities in Chapter 15.

Plus, this edition continues to include the information that hundreds of thousands of people have relied on for 14 years: information about upgrading and fixing video cards, hard drives, CD/DVD drives, memory chips, monitors, modems, printers, scanners, hard drives, and other popular computer parts.

Where to Start

Jump in anywhere. Each chapter is a self-contained nugget of information, keeping you from flipping back and forth between different sections.

Chapters start by defining the buzzwords surrounding each new upgrade; they also offer tips on making hardware purchases. A step-by-step installation guide follows, complete with screen shots, color photos, or line drawings, where appropriate.

Each chapter ends with a troubleshooting guide for those awful moments: when you turn on the computer, but the new part stays turned off.

Read These Parts

If you're lucky (and your computer is fairly healthy), you don't need to read very much of this book; just skim the step-by-step instructions. But when something weird happens, this book helps you figure out what went wrong, whether it's repairable, or whether you must replace it.

Along the way, you might find helpful comments or warnings to help you out.

You find tips like this scattered throughout the book. Take a look at them first. In fact, some of these tips might spare you from having to read more than a paragraph of a computer book — a worthy feat indeed!

Don't Read These Parts

Okay, I lied a little bit. I did stick some technobabble in this book. After all, you sometimes need to decipher the language on a computer part's packaging. Luckily for you, however, I have neatly cordoned off all the technical drivel.

Any particularly odious technical details are isolated and posted with this icon so that you can avoid them easily. If a computer nerd drops by to help with your particular problem, just hand him or her this book. With this icons, the computer nerd knows exactly which sections to look for.

How This Book Is Organized

This book has six major parts. Each part is divided into several chapters. And each chapter covers a major topic, which is divided into specific sections.

The point? Well, this book's indexer sorted all the information with an extra-fine-tooth flea comb, making it easy for you to find the exact section you want when you want it. Plus, everything's cross-referenced. If you need more information about a subject, you can figure out exactly which chapter to head for.

Here are the parts and what they contain.

Part I: Boring, Basic Repairs

You find the boring, basic stuff in here. If you read the first chapter, for instance, you discover all those boring programs you can set up to make your computer *repair itself*. The other chapters cover those day-to-day parts that must be replaced: keyboards, mice, monitors, and printers. Yawn.

Part II: Beefing Up Your PC for Windows Vista, Games, and Video

Microsoft's latest version of Windows, Vista, will soon march onto most of the world's PCs. This part of the book explains how to make sure your PC's ready when Vista arrives. It explains how to find out whether your current PC can run Vista, what parts need to be replaced, and how to add Vista essentials, such as better graphics, more memory, and a larger power supply.

By the way, upgrading your PC for the graphics-intensive Vista also makes it a prime PC for playing the latest computer games.

Part III: Teaching an Old PC New Tricks

Flip here quickly for the fun stuff. Rather than focusing on the boring, necessary repairs and upgrades, this part of the book explains the luxuries. You can transform your PC into a home theater, for example, by upgrading its sound, speakers, and adding a TV tuner. Another chapter explains how to transform your camcorder footage into an edited movie, stored on an easily viewed DVD. No DVD burner yet? Another chapter explains how to choose and install a DVD burner to take advantage of Vista's new DVD-burning programs.

Part IV: Communications

Computers running Windows Vista don't like to be alone. This part of the book shows how to hook your computer up to the Internet with a dialup or broadband modem. Because many households now sport two or more computers, a chapter in this part explains how to create a home or small office network, enabling all your computers to share the same Internet connection. If you're worried about hackers breaking into your computer, head to this part to make sure Windows Vista's firewall works as it should.

Part V: Introducing Parts to Windows

If anybody's a dummy here, it's your computer. Even after you've stuck a new part in its craw, your computer often doesn't realize that the part is there. If Windows refuses to deal politely with the newly installed device, check out the chapter on finding and installing the right *driver* to make Windows behave. Turn to this part also when you're ready to upgrade to Windows Vista or install it onto a brand new hard drive.

Part VI: The Part of Tens

Some information just drifts away when it's buried deep within a chapter — or even within a long paragraph. That's why these tidbits are stacked up in lists of ten (give or take a few items). Here, you find the cheap fixes you should try first, a list of handy upgrade tools, and other fun factoids.

Icons Used in This Book

This book's most exceptional paragraphs are marked by icons — little eye-catching pictures in the margins:

This icon warns of some ugly technical information lying by the side of the road. Feel free to drive right by. The information is probably just a more complex discussion of something already explained in the chapter.

Pounce on this icon whenever you see it. Chances are that it marks a helpful paragraph worthy of a stick-on note or highlighter.

If you've forgotten what you were supposed to remember, keep an eye toward the margins for this icon.

Better be careful when you're about to do stuff marked by this icon. In fact, it warns you about dangerous activities you *shouldn't* be doing, like squirting WD-40 into your floppy drive.

Not everybody is rushing off to buy Vista, and this book doesn't forget Windows XP owners. This icon alerts you to instructions particularly applicable to the Windows XP holdouts.

This icon flags areas of special importance to Windows Vista owners. After all, everybody uses Windows Vista these days — or at least that's what the newspaper inserts say.

Laptops aren't nearly as upgradeable as desktop PCs. This icon alerts laptop owners to the laptop parts that *are* upgradeable.

Auto mechanics can find the most helpful sections in their manuals by just looking for the greasiest pages. So by all means, draw your own icons next to the stuff you find particularly helpful. Scrawl in some of your own observations as well.

Where to Go from Here

If you're clamoring for more basic information on Windows, check out one of my *Windows For Dummies* books, published by Wiley Publishing. They come in several flavors, including Vista, XP, Me, 98, 95, and earlier.

Also, be sure to check my Web site at www.andyrathbone.com. It contains a complete and updated list of all the Internet sites mentioned in this book, collected for your point 'n click convenience. Any corrections, heaven forbid, appear there, as well.

Ready to go? Then grab this book and a screwdriver. Your computer is ready whenever you are. Good luck.

Part I
Boring, Basic Repairs

The 5th Wave   By Rich Tennant

"I bought a software program that should help
us monitor and control our spending habits, and
while I was there, I picked up a few new games,
a couple of screen savers, 4 new mousepads, this
nifty pullout keyboard cradle..."

In this part . . .

This part of the book doesn't cover those exciting new toys that make you whip out the credit card. You don't find wireless network cards, digital cameras, home theater computers, or DVD burners in this part. No, this part of the book covers the boring, basic computer things that you *have* to do. And sometimes repeatedly.

The first chapter explains how to find out exactly what's inside your PC — how much memory it has, for example. It walks you through making sure your computer's System Restore and Windows Update features work correctly, for instance, so that Windows can keep itself running smoothly.

Spilled a Coke on the keyboard? Keyboards are covered here, as well as mice, monitors, and printers. Except for adding two monitors to a single PC (Chapter 3), nothing new and exciting has happened with these types of parts for quite some time. But chances are that this is the stuff you'll find yourself needing to fix or replace the most often.

And if you've just walked home with a new Windows Vista PC, check out Chapter 5: It explains how to move your files, bookmarks, and program settings off your old PC and onto your new one.

Chapter 1

Start Here First

*Y*ou picked up this book for any of several reasons. You might be eyeing the power-hungry Windows Vista, Microsoft's newest version of Windows, and want to upgrade your PC's video to meet Vista's stringent needs. Perhaps one of your PC's parts died, and you're looking to replace it with a better one. Or maybe your PC simply needs some fine-tuning. Whatever your reason, this is the right chapter to read first.

This chapter explains what Windows expects out of a PC and how to replace the outdated parts that no longer work. It explains how to know what parts currently live inside your computer's case, so you can see if your computer meets those fine-print System Requirements listed on the side of many software boxes.

And for the fix-it folks, this chapter points out where Windows Vista and Windows XP have the power to repair themselves — if those powers are turned on and running correctly, that is. You find complete instructions on making sure those self-healing abilities are up to snuff.

Any time you're not sure what plugs in where, check out this book's Appendix. It's a visual directory of all your computer's ports and the plugs and gadgets that fit into them.

Determining When to Upgrade

Your computer usually tells you when it wants an upgrade. Some warning signals are subtle, others more obvious. At worst, they can be downright annoying.

In any case, keep track of the following when you're deciding whether it's time to open the wallet and grab the toolbox:

- **When your operating system demands it:** Everybody's using Vista, the latest version of Windows. (Or at least that's what the folks at Microsoft say.) If you've caught the "latest and the greatest" fever, it's easy to find out if your computer is up to snuff; Microsoft lists Vista's System Requirements at www.windowsvista.com, and I dissect them in Chapter 6.

- **When you keep waiting for your PC to catch up:** You press a key and wait. And wait. When you're working faster than your PC, give your PC a boost with some extra memory and maybe a faster video card. (Of course, if you want a bigger and faster hard drive too, it might be time to throw in the towel and buy a new computer.)

- **When you can't afford a new computer:** When a new PC's out of your price range, upgrade your PC one part at a time. Add that memory now, for example, and then add a new hard drive with your holiday bonus. Time each purchase to match the lowest prices. When you finally buy a new computer, save costs by salvaging your old computer's monitor and recently added parts.

- **When you want a new part in a hurry:** Computer repair shops aren't nearly as slow as stereo repair shops. Still, do you *really* want to wait four days for some tech head to install that hot new video card — especially when you have a nagging suspicion that you could do it yourself in less than 15 minutes?

- **When there's no room for new software:** When your hard drive constantly spits up Disk Full messages, you have three options:

  - Uninstall programs you no longer use and copy unneeded files to CDs or DVDs.

  - Replace your PC's hard drive with a larger one or add a second internal hard drive.

  - Buy a removable drive to serve as a parking garage for files and programs. Most external drives plug into your PC's USB port, a chore as simple as plugging in a mouse.

- **When you're afraid to open the case:** Fear of opening your computer's case is no longer an excuse to put off upgrades. Many new computer parts now live on the *outside* of the computer. You find external CD-ROM drives and burners, hard drives, floppy drives, memory card readers, sound boxes, and much more. None of these devices require popping open the case to install them.

Determining When You Shouldn't Upgrade

Sometimes, you shouldn't upgrade your own computer. Keep your hands off during any of the following circumstances:

- ✔ **When a computer part breaks while under warranty:** If your computer is under warranty, let the manufacturer fix it. In fact, trying to fix or replace a part sometimes voids the warranty on the rest of your computer. Some manufacturers void the warranty if you simply open your computer's case. Read the warranty's fine print before touching anything.

  Keep track of your warranty expiration date; it's usually listed on your sales receipt. Lost it? Some manufacturers (Gateway, Dell, and a few others) provide access to your warranty information through their Web sites, as described in Chapter 22.

- ✔ **On a Friday:** Never try to install a new computer part on a Friday afternoon. When you discover that the widget needs a *left* bracket, too, many shops will be closed, leaving you with a desktop full of detached parts until Monday morning.

- ✔ **When you're working on a deadline:** Just like kitchen remodeling, computer upgrading and repairing occasionally takes twice as long as you originally planned. Some parts install in a few minutes, but always allow yourself a little leeway.

- ✔ **If your computer is *old*:** Not all computers can be upgraded. If you bought your PC before 2001, you're pouring money into a sinking ship.

Before upgrading a computer, check these numbers: Add the cost of needed parts (more memory, a bigger hard drive, a faster video card and/or monitor, a DVD burner, networking card, and updated software) and compare it with the cost of a new computer. Chances are, a new computer costs much less. Plus, it already comes with Windows Vista and parts guaranteed to be compatible.

Finding Out What Parts Your Computer Has

Computers come in a wide variety of makes and models pieced together with parts made by variety of manufacturers. So how do you know who made what part?

Luckily, Windows takes pity on its users and tells you exactly what parts lurk inside your computer's case — if you know how to ask it politely. The first step is finding out your Windows version, your PC's Central Processor Unit (CPU), and its amount of Random Access Memory (RAM).

And why should you care, you might ask, shifting impatiently in your chair? Because when you buy computer software or parts, the box's fine print lists the System Requirements, followed by lots of details about what your computer must have to use the software or part. If your computer doesn't meet those detailed requirements, the software or part won't work very well — if at all — on your computer.

To add insult to injury, many stores don't let you return software — even if it won't run on your computer. Some stores even refuse to accept *unopened* software. Check your store's return policy before opening your wallet.

Locating your version of Windows, CPU, and RAM

Windows comes in many different versions, each with its own set of requirements, problems, and personalities. Luckily, all versions reveal their version numbers when you follow this simple step.

1. **Right-click the Computer or My Computer icon on your desktop and choose Properties.**

   If you don't see the Computer or My Computer icon on the desktop, click the Start menu, and then right-click the Computer or My Computer icon.

   In both Windows Vista (see Figure 1-1) and Windows XP (see Figure 1-2), that step reveals basic information about your PC's power.

   - **Windows version:** Chances are yours says Windows XP Home, Windows XP Professional, Windows Vista Home Basic, Windows Vista Home Premium, or Windows Vista Ultimate.

   - **CPU:** Short for Central Processing Unit, this big chip drives your entire PC. Windows lists the chip's model and speed.

   - **RAM:** Short for Random Access Memory, these upgradeable chips enable Windows to open many programs at once without lagging.

   That's it — a one-step guide to seeing your PC's most important parts, and how well they match the requirements listed on a box of software.

   ✔ If you'd rather not write down all that system information, you can print what's on your screen by following these steps:

   Press the PrtScrn key, open Paint, paste the screen into a new image by pressing Ctrl+V, and then send it to your printer by choosing File, and then Print. That gives you a quick reference guide to take to the store when shopping for software or a new PC.

✔ Vista lists the PC's Windows User Experience in Figure 1-1, which rates how well your PC runs Windows Vista. Click the User Experience Index to see ratings on each of your PC's parts, a quick way to see what parts need upgrading. (The higher the rating number, the better the part's rating.)

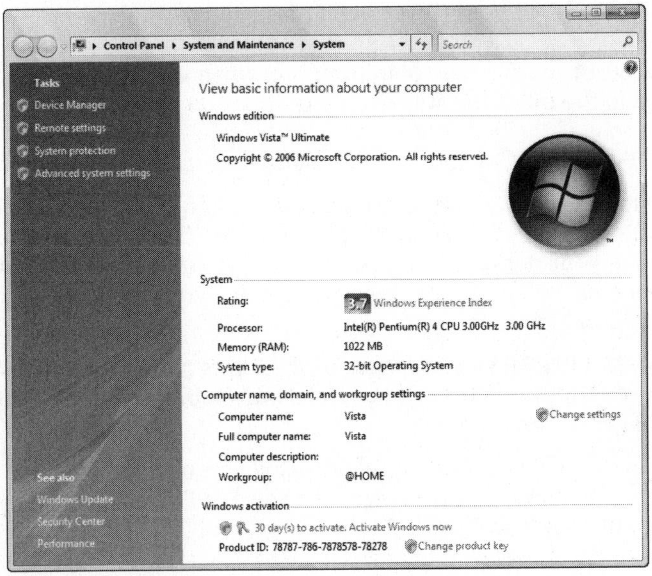

Figure 1-1:
This PC runs Windows Vista's Ultimate version on a 3 GHz Intel Pentium 4 with 1022MB of RAM.

Figure 1-2:
This PC runs Windows XP's Professional version on a 3.40 GHz Intel Pentium 4 CPU with 1GB of RAM.

Identifying the parts inside your computer

The big three — Windows version, CPU, and RAM — usually have the most influence on which software and parts your computer can handle. But sometimes you need more detailed information — your video card's driver version, for instance, or your DVD drive's make and model.

Windows burps up this type of information when you push a little deeper, as described in the following steps:

1. **Right-click the Computer or My Computer icon and choose Properties.**

   Windows Vista's Computer icon and Windows XP's My Computer icon live on the Start menu. (You might also have the Computer/My Computer icon on your desktop.) Choosing Properties unleashes the System Properties dialog box, as shown earlier in Figure 1-1 (Vista) and Figure 1-2 (Windows XP).

2. **In Vista, click Device Manager in the Tasks pane along the window's left. In Windows XP, click the Hardware tab, and then click the Device Manager button.**

   No matter which version of Windows you're using, the Device Manager dialog box jumps to the screen, as shown in Figure 1-3, displaying your computer's parts.

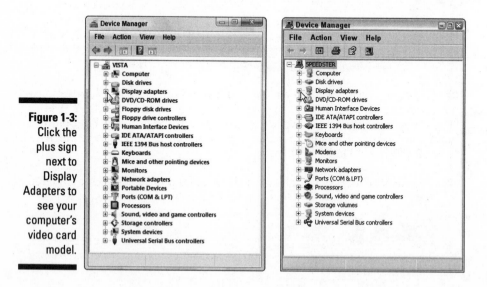

Figure 1-3:
Click the
plus sign
next to
Display
Adapters to
see your
computer's
video card
model.

3. **To see the make and model of a specific part, click the plus sign next to its name.**

   For instance, to see what type of video card sits inside your PC, click the plus sign next to Display Adapters — a Windows term for a PC's video circuitry. Windows shows your video card's model and manufacturer, invaluable information when the part stops working.

When a particular part stops working, look for its make and model in the Device Manager. Then head to the manufacturer's Web site and download that part's latest driver, a chore covered in Chapter 19.

Please! Before You Do Anything Else!

Wouldn't it be nice to push a button and have Windows fix itself? Well, you can. That is, if you make sure you've set up the two things that I describe next. Sit up straight and plow onward.

Turning On Windows Update

Bored youngsters work late nights probing Windows to locate programming problems. When they discover a new problem, they write a *virus* or *worm* (a small, malicious program meant to do damage, such as erasing important files) to take advantage of it. These hooligans release the virus, and it begins damaging people's computers as it spreads worldwide. (Remember that virus that infected your computer when you merely *opened* an e-mail?)

When hackers uncover a new *security exploit,* as they're called, Microsoft programmers scratch their heads and wonder what's wrong with today's youth. Then they release a special piece of software to fix the problem. But before your computer can find and install that special tool, usually called a *patch* or *update,* you need Windows Update.

The Microsoft Windows Update program automatically scans your computer to see if it's vulnerable to any newly found security problems. If so, the program automatically grabs the patch that cures them.

Microsoft released a patch to fix that ugly mail preview virus a long time ago. Because many people don't know about Windows Update, their computers remain vulnerable.

The Windows Update Web site (www.windowsupdate.com) organizes patches into several categories. Always install the ones in the Critical category, as they contain patches for security problems. You needn't install updates from any other categories unless you think they'll correct problems you're currently experiencing with your PC.

Here's how to make sure Windows' Windows Update feature automatically grabs any new patches so that you may install them:

1. **Open Windows Security Center.**

   Windows Vista: Click the Start button and choose Control Panel➪Security➪Security Center.

   Windows XP: Choose Control Panel and open Security Center. Windows Security Center opens in both versions.

2. **In Vista, if Automatic Updating is turned off, click Change Settings.**

   In Windows XP, simply click Turn on Automatic Updates, and you're done. If you're running Windows Vista, move to Step 3.

3. **Choose Install Updates Automatically (Recommended).**

   In Vista, you might need to click the Continue button in a permission screen to turn on Automatic updating.

In both Windows versions, these steps tell Windows to automatically visit the Windows Update site whenever you're online. (It does this in the background.) When your computer finds a new security fix, it downloads the software and either installs it automatically, or it places a little pop-up window near your clock, reminding you to install your new patch.

✔ Even if you're using Windows' automated Windows Update program, feel free to visit the Windows Update Web site on your own. Sometimes Windows waits a few days before checking the site, leaving your computer open to the latest problems.

✔ In the Recommended Updates section, Windows Update sometimes offers to check for patches on other Microsoft programs on your PC. Take it up on its offer to keep them patched, as well.

Making sure System Restore is working

System Restore, built into Windows Vista and Windows XP, often works miracles for problematic computers. If your computer suddenly stops working correctly, System Restore often enables you to bring your computer back to a time when everything worked fine.

When it's working correctly, System Restore automatically creates restore points that save important settings when Windows is up and running smoothly. The more restore points you have available, the further back in time you can travel to find a place when your computer was running strong and lean.

To make sure System Restore's running — or to fix it if it's not working correctly — follow these steps:

1. **Click the Start button, right-click the Computer or My Computer icon, and choose Properties.**

   The Device Manger dialog box, shown earlier in Figure 1-1 (Vista) and Figure 1-2 (XP), appears.

2. **Open the System Properties dialog box.**

   Windows Vista: Click System Protection in the Tasks pane along the window's left side.

   Windows XP: Click the System Restore tab.

   The System Properties dialog box, shown in Figure 1-4, opens to show System Restore's settings. The figure shows the settings for Windows Vista (left) and Windows XP (right).

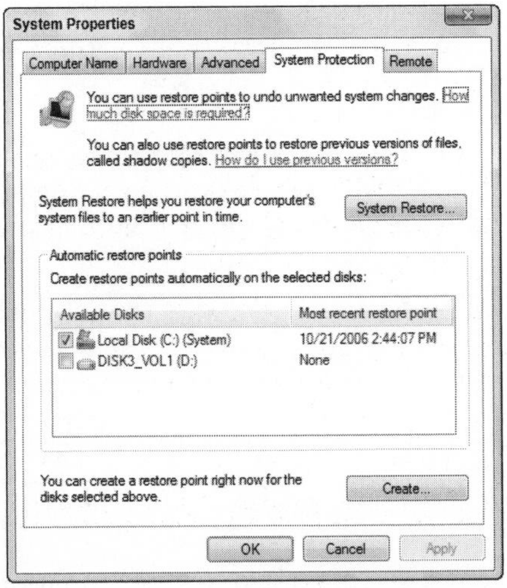

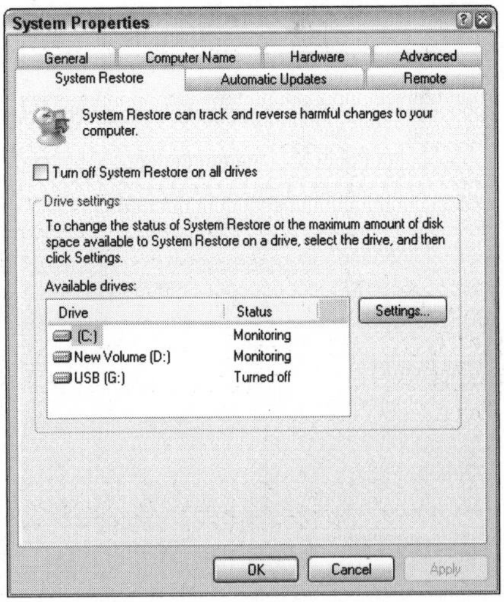

Figure 1-4:
In Windows Vista (left), System Restore is working correctly on drives with check marks next to them. In Windows XP (right), System Restore is working correctly on drives displaying the word Monitoring next to them.

3. **Make sure System Restore is turned on.**

Windows Vista: Make sure a check mark appears next to the first drive on the list. For example, Figure 1-4 (left) shows a check mark next to the words Local Disk (C:) (System). Vista also lists the date of the last Restore Point. Vista automatically turns off System Restore if your hard drive falls below 300MB of storage space. (That's when it's time to upgrade to a larger hard drive.)

Windows XP: Look for the word *Monitoring* next to each drive, as shown in Figure 1-4 (right). If you don't see the word *Monitoring,* System Restore is turned off. To turn it back on, check these things:

• Make sure that there's no check mark in the box next to the Turn Off System Restore on All Drives option. If there is, click the box to remove the check mark.

• If System Restore says that your hard drive is too full to create any Restore Points, it's time for housecleaning: You need at least 200MB of free space for System Restore to work. Open My Computer from the Start menu, and then right-click your C drive and choose Properties. Click the Disk Cleanup button on the General tab and follow the instructions to make Windows delete any unnecessary files — including old Restore Points, if you check that box.

If you're itching to run System Restore right now, flip ahead to Chapter 23 for the rundown.

Chapter 2

Keyboards, Mice, and Joysticks

- -

In This Chapter

▶ Understanding keyboards, mice, and game controllers

▶ Replacing keyboards, mice, and game controllers on new and old computers

▶ Configuring wireless keyboards, mice, and game controllers

▶ Repairing keyboards, mice, and game controllers

- -

*Y*ou push them, and they prod your computer into doing something. This chapter deals with the ultimate push/prodders: the keyboard and the mouse. Because that stuff grows boring pretty darn quickly, you find game controllers (game pads and joysticks) served up at the end of this chapter.

Updating Your Keyboard

Talk about moving parts — most keyboards have more than 100 of 'em, moving up and down hundreds of times during the day.

Keyboards don't die very often, but when they start to go, the problem is easy enough to diagnose. A few keys start to stickkkk or stop working altogether. And when almost any type of liquid hits a keyboard, every key stops working at the same time.

This section explains the types of keyboards on the market, where each plugs in, which works best in different situations, and how to fix them when they're heading down the wrong road.

Understanding keyboard buzzwords

For years, keyboards remained the simplest part of your computer. They mimicked the typewriter's keyboard that had served so well over the years. With the advent of wireless keyboards, numeric keypads, and other dedicated keys, that's unfortunately no longer the case. Today's keyboards have never been more complicated.

Here's a list of the buzzwords to decipher when diagnosing your keyboard's problems — or pitching it and buying a new one.

 Standard 101 key: Most keyboards today sport at least 101 keys, including the usual typewriter layout, a numeric keypad along the right, and a row of function keys (F1, F2, and so on) along the top. The standard keyboard even includes a few keys added by Microsoft — most importantly, the Windows key. Shown in the margin, the Windows key offers quick access to Windows commands, as described in Table 2-1.

Table 2-1	Windows Key Shortcuts
To Do This	*Press This*
Display Windows Help	<Windows Key>+F1
Display the Start menu	<Windows Key>
Display Windows Explorer	<Windows Key>+E
Find files	<Windows Key>+F
Minimize or restore all windows	<Windows Key>+D
View System window	<Windows Key>+Pause/Break
Lock PC	<Windows Key>+L

Gaming/multimedia/multifunction keyboard: Some companies figure that 101 keys aren't enough. So they stuff their own specialized keys along the keyboard's top or sides. Often devoted to single jobs, some keys simply change the volume or skip to the CD's next song. Gaming keyboards offer programmable keys: One key press lets you open a chat window in *World of Warcraft,* for example.

 Specialized keyboard keys require special drivers. Those specialized keys won't work until you install the keyboard's bundled software.

USB versus PS/2: These words describe the plug on the end of a keyboard's cord. The newest keyboards sport USB (Universal Serial Bus) connectors, ready to slide into your PC's rectangular USB port. Older keyboards use round, PS/2-style connectors. All PCs work with either type. The PS/2 keyboards work better for troubleshooting (Chapter 21), but only USB keyboards can be plugged in and unplugged while your PC's turned on — if that matters to you.

Ergonomic keyboards: Ergonomic keyboards like the one shown in Figure 2-1 resemble a thick boomerang. Some folks say the shape helps them spend hours on the keyboard; others find it awkward and gimmicky. Most computer stores offer display models, so definitely try before you buy.

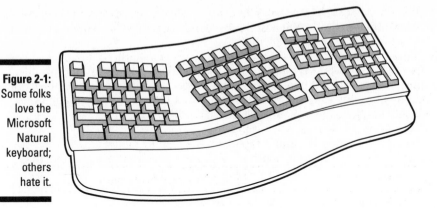

Figure 2-1:
Some folks
love the
Microsoft
Natural
keyboard;
others
hate it.

Wireless: Wireless keyboards bear no cords, making for tidy desktops. Most come in two parts: the keyboard and a receiving unit, which plugs into your PC's USB part. Unfortunately, they're battery hogs.

Media Center keyboard/mouse/remote: Windows Vista now comes with Windows Media Center, software which automatically records and plays back TV shows. To keep you rested firmly on the couch across from the TV, several companies offer special remote controls and wireless keyboards for channel changing and living room Web surfing.

Most of these new Media Center keyboards, remotes, and mice use Bluetooth, the same wireless technology that links cell phones with headsets. Because few PCs come with Bluetooth, most of these come with a tiny Bluetooth receiver that pushes into your PC's USB port.

Installing a new keyboard

Difficulty level: Easy

Tools you need: One hand; possibly a flashlight if your PC is in a dark spot

Cost: From $15 for a basic, no-frills keyboard, to $100 or more for elaborate ergonomic and wireless models

Stuff to watch out for: Look at the connector on the end of your old keyboard and buy one that matches it. Keyboards with round connectors on the ends of their cables, like the one in the margin, are known as PS/2-style keyboards. Keyboards with rectangular connectors are USB keyboards.

Look for a USB keyboard that's bundled with a *PS/2 adapter* — a tiny gadget that plugs into a USB connector to give it a PS/2 connector. That lets you plug the keyboard into either type of port.

Although some USB keyboards sport an extra USB port or two on the side, those USB ports aren't *powered* — they work only with small, low-power gadgets such as tiny USB flash drives. They won't charge an iPod or any other device that draws power through the USB port.

Don't buy a keyboard without typing on the display model at the store. You'll work closely with that keyboard for years to come, so don't pick one that feels too hard, too spongy, or just plain unfriendly.

To install a new keyboard, follow these steps:

1. **Save your current work, close your programs, and turn off your computer.**

   Don't ever unplug your PS/2 keyboard when the PC is turned on. Your computer might freeze and not recognize a new keyboard. (If your PC's frozen, its mouse can still click the Start button to restart your PC.)

   You don't need to turn off your PC to install a new USB keyboard.

2. **Remove your old keyboard by pulling the cable's plug from its socket on your computer.**

   When you're unplugging any type of cord, pull on the plug, not the cord, to save the cord a little wear and tear.

   Examine the end of the cord. (The Appendix explains connectors in detail.) A rectangular plug with a pitchfork symbol on it is a USB plug. A smaller, round plug is an older-style, PS/2 plug.

3. **Buy a replacement keyboard.**

   Buy one that fits your computer, either USB or PS/2. If a keyboard says it works with both types of ports, it's a USB keyboard with a tiny adapter. To plug it into the PS/2 port, slip the adapter onto the USB plug.

   Bought a wireless keyboard? Insert its batteries before plugging it in.

4. **Carefully insert the new keyboard's plug into the correct port.**

   USB: These slide in pretty easily. Doesn't fit? Turn over the plug and try again, as it fits only one way. If the USB keyboard is wireless, plug its receiver into the USB port.

   PS/2: This plug fits only one way, so you need to match up the pins in the plug with the notches of the port. Most PCs have two PS/2 ports, one for the mouse and the other for the keyboard. They won't do any harm plugged into the wrong port, but they won't work until pushed into the right port. Push firmly until it's all the way in.

5. **Turn your computer back on.**

   If the computer doesn't complain and your new keyboard works, your computer found the keyboard and liked it.

6. **Install your keyboard's software, if required.**

   Some fancier keyboards use special drivers or installation software to set up their specialized keys. Insert the CD and run the Setup program, if necessary, to install it.

   Or, if Windows asks for drivers after you turn on your computer, insert the CD into your drive and click OK. (Plenty of information about drivers awaits in Chapter 19.)

7. **Adjust your keyboard's settings in Windows.**

   Choose Control Panel from the Start menu and continue with the instructions for your operating system that follow:

   Windows Vista: Open the Hardware and Sound area, and double-click the Keyboard icon.

   Windows XP: Open the Printers and Other Hardware area, and double-click the Keyboard icon.

The Keyboards area lets you change options such as a key's repeat rate — how long it waits before repeating when you hold down a letter. Your keyboard's manufacturer might have tossed in a few options for your specific model, as well.

   ✔ If a PS/2 keyboard connector's little pins become bent, they won't fit into the hole, no matter how hard you push. A little care and needle-nose pliers should set things straight.

   ✔ Using a wireless keyboard? Plug the keyboard's receiver unit into your computer, just as if it were the keyboard itself. Check the batteries in your wireless keyboard and install any required software; the receiver should pick up its signals right away. A few models use infrared signals, requiring a clear line of sight between the keyboard and receiver. The majority use radio waves — you can put the receiver anywhere nearby. Some wireless keyboards also have a button you must push before being recognized by the receiver.

A *wrist pad* — a piece of foam or a gel-filled pad that your wrists rest on as you type — sometimes helps deter typing soreness or carpal tunnel syndrome. To see whether you can benefit from one, make a test model from a thin, rolled-up magazine taped shut. Put it along the front of the keyboard and see whether your arms feel better when the magazine lifts your wrists slightly.

Fixing keyboard problems

Although it's tempting to throw out the keyboard and grab a new one at the first sign of evil, you can fix some problems. This section walks you through some simple, do-it-yourself repairs. If these fixes don't work, buy a new keyboard. It's almost always cheaper to buy a new one than to repair an old one.

Fixing the Keyboard Not Found error

Chances are that your keyboard's cord isn't plugged all the way into its socket. (And pressing F1 won't do anything, no matter what the message on-screen says.) Fumble around in the back of your computer until you find the keyboard's cable. Push it into its socket a little harder.

After you fasten the keyboard's cable more securely, you might need to push your computer's Reset button. Some computers look for keyboards only once — and that's when they're first turned on. The Reset button forces the computer to take a second look. Or, if there's no Reset button, turn off your computer, wait 30 seconds, and turn it back on again.

Also, make sure that nothing is sitting on any of the keys — such as the corner of a book, or a small furry animal. If any of the keys are pressed when you first turn on the computer, the computer assumes the keyboard is broken.

Still doesn't work? If you're using a wireless keyboard, check the batteries or make sure the keyboard is within range of its receiver.

If your keyboard *still* doesn't work, check to see whether something might have been spilled on it. (See the following section.)

Cleaning up spills on your keyboard

Your keyboard is probably a goner if you spilled prune juice or coffee on it. But here's the Emergency Keyboard Preservation Procedure: Save your work if possible, turn off your computer, and unplug the keyboard.

With a sponge, wipe off all the spilled stuff you can find. Then sit there and feel foolish for the 24 hours or so that it takes for the keyboard to dry in the sun or a warm room.

If you spill only water, your keyboard might still work the next day. But if you spill anything containing sugar — soda pop, coffee, margaritas, prune juice, Tang — you probably coated the inside of your keyboard with sticky gunk. This gunk then attracts dust and grime, and your keyboard starts a slow decline and dies sooner or later, depending on the tragedy level of the spill.

Luckily, new keyboards are pretty cheap, ranging from the $15 specials to the $100 deluxe wireless models.

- ✔ If you have lots of spare time and little spare change, pry off all the key-caps one by one with a small screwdriver. (Don't bother trying to remove the spacebar because it has too many gizmos holding it on.) When the keys are off, sponge off any stray gunk, dry off the moisture, and try to put all the keycaps back in their right locations. (Figure 2-2 might help.)

- ✔ Some people report success (and sometimes odd stares) by immediately taking their wet keyboard to the gas station and squirting it with air from the tire pump to loosen debris. Other people have successfully used a hair dryer. If you're lucky enough to have a can of compressed air on hand, use that.

- ✔ Wait at least 24 hours before giving up on your keyboard. You can salvage many wet keyboards, but only after they are *completely* dry.

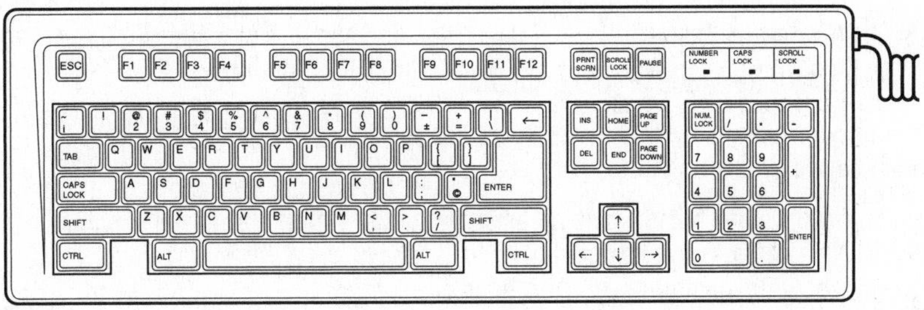

Figure 2-2:
Use this replacement guide to help you replace keys you've removed to clean the keyboard.

Don't give up hope too early. Erik writes in from Portugal with an old college story about a basketball player who borrowed his computer to play video games. Unfortunately, the sportster knocked a cup of spit and tobacco juice onto the keyboard. Figuring he had nothing to lose, Erik rinsed off the keyboard at the nearby gym's shower and toweled it off. When the keyboard dried, Erik plugged it in, and the machine rose from the dead.

Replacing keys on your keyboard

If your rapidly moving fingers have worn off the printed letters, you've probably already memorized all the locations. But if you still want labels, salvage the keycaps from a dead keyboard or ask your local computer store if it sells replacement keycaps. (The Key Connection at www.customkeys.com sells them online, as well as thin plastic keyboard covers for clumsy, caffeinated gamers.)

The legacy of USB and you

Normally, Windows Vista and XP recognize USB keyboards without problem. But when troubleshooting, sometimes you're not running Windows normally. You might be running disk utilities, or editing your PC's BIOS (Basic Input-Output System), which is a collection of hardware settings. If your USB keyboard stops working during these times, the fix is to change a setting in your PC's BIOS by following these steps:

Warning: Choosing the wrong settings on your computer's BIOS can cause serious problems. When in doubt, choose Exit Without Saving Changes and start over.

1. **Shut down your computer.**

2. **Connect a PS/2 keyboard to your computer.**

3. **Turn on your computer and enter System Setup before Windows starts.**

   Computers use different ways of accessing their BIOS settings. Watch the screen when you turn on your computer. It often says,

`Press F1 for Setup`, or something similar. Press that key quickly to enter your BIOS settings area.

4. **Find the USB Legacy Support setting, usually on the Advanced menu.**

5. **Select USB Legacy Support and change the setting to Enabled.**

   Please don't fiddle with anything else, no matter how tempting. And if you should yield, write down the setting you changed. Even System Restore can't save you when you change your BIOS settings.

6. **Choose Save the Settings and exit the BIOS, quickly.**

No USB Legacy Support setting? Stick with a PS/2 keyboard and mouse, or a USB keyboard with a PS/2 adapter attached. (Most computer and office supply stores sell inexpensive adapters.) They both work fine.

If you give up and buy a replacement keyboard, coat the new keyboard's keycaps with a thin layer of clear nail polish. That often helps protect the lettering from finger damage, extending the key caps' lives.

Making Way for a New Mouse

Mice all tackle the same computing chore. When you nudge your mouse, a little arrow called a *mouse pointer* moves on your computer's screen. By pointing the arrow at buttons on the screen and pushing buttons on the mouse, you "push" the buttons on the screen.

For years, all mice looked like a beige bar of soap with two buttons and a long tail. Now, mice come in many varieties and colors. Both Microsoft and Logitech each sell more than 20 different models.

Understanding mouse buzzwords

When mice burst into the PC world in the early '80s, Macintosh models had one button. PC models came with two buttons. Then somebody introduced a three-button mouse for PCs, and the world went wild. Today, zillions of mouse models try to separate you from your money.

Here's a handy translation for the Language of the Mouse.

Mouse ball: A little rubber ball rests in the belly of a mouse; when you move the mouse, you also roll the little ball. The movement of the ball tells the computer the direction and speed to move the on-screen pointer. Ball mice work best on a mousepad, a rubbery surface that clings to the rolling ball as it moves, giving it the best accuracy. Ball mice have mostly given way to optical mice, described next.

Optical: Optical mice ditch the ball/roller mechanics for a small glowing light and a sensor. As you move the mouse, the optical sensor takes little snapshots of your illuminated desk, hundreds of times each second. By comparing differences between snapshots, the mouse knows how fast and far you're moving it, and it updates the pointer accordingly. An optical mouse still requires a mousepad over glass or shiny laminate desktops, as the reflections confuse the sensor.

Trackball: Trackballs are, in essence, upside-down mice. Rather than roll the ball around your tabletop, you roll the ball directly with your fingertips. They're popular with laptops, although some desktop keyboards also include trackballs for convenience.

The early laptops aboard the space shuttle *Discovery* used the Microsoft Ballpoint trackball. The trackball clipped to the laptop's edge to keep it from floating away.

TrackPoint/AccuPoint: Found on some laptops, this pointing device looks like a pencil eraser protruding from the middle of your keyboard. Nudge the little joystick with a fingertip to move the mouse pointer. Desktop keyboards have been slow to embrace the technology.

Touchpads: Found on many laptops, this square pad lets you move the cursor by dragging your finger across its surface. If you love your laptop's touchpad, pick one up for your desktop: External touchpads plug into a USB port. (Trivia: Windows calls a touchpad a "Human Interface Device.")

Scroll wheel: This little wheel protrudes from the mouse's back, usually between the two buttons. Spin the wheel with your index finger, and your computer scrolls up or down the on-screen page, accordingly. Push down on the wheel to make it click; most scroll wheel mice let you program the wheel click to do just about anything you want.

Wireless: Wireless mice work just like their keyboard counterparts; in fact, some share the same receiving unit, which plugs into your computer's USB or mouse PS/2 port. The mouse sends signals to the receiver, which sends them to your computer. You can find more information about wireless technology in this chapter's "Updating Your Keyboard" section.

PS/2: An older mouse comes with a PS/2-style connector, which still works fine. Just don't ever unplug the mouse while the computer is turned on, or the mouse will stop working — even after you frantically plug it back in. (Restart the computer, and the mouse will begin working again.)

Installing or replacing a USB or PS/2 mouse

Difficulty level: Easy to Medium, depending on your computer's setup

Tools you need: One hand; possibly a flashlight

Cost: Anywhere from $10 to $100

Stuff to watch out for: If you're buying a fancy mouse for your Windows Vista computer, visit the manufacturer's Web site to see if it offers downloadable Windows Vista drivers. (You rarely find up-to-date drivers in a new product's box.)

A mouse comes with its own software, if needed, and cord. You needn't buy any extras. And Windows can use pretty much any old PS/2-style mouse. Just plug it in, turn on your computer, and Windows knows it's there.

To replace or add a mouse, follow these steps:

1. **Turn off your computer.**

   Be sure to exit any of your currently running programs first.

2. **Examine where you currently plug in your mouse (and buy a replacement mouse that uses the same type of plug).**

   USB: Most computers come with several of these squat, rectangular ports.

   PS/2: Most desktop computers have two of these small, round, black ports, one with a little mouse icon and the other with a little keyboard. Feel free to upgrade to a USB variety, if your computer has a spare USB port.

3. **Push the plug from the new mouse into the correct port on your computer.**

   USB: These slide on in pretty easily. Doesn't work? Turn it over. USB connectors fit only one way.

   PS/2: Use the small, round PS/2 connector with the little mouse icon next to it; the adjacent keyboard port won't work. Make sure the notches and pins line up and push firmly until it's all the way in.

4. **Run the mouse's installation program, if necessary.**

   Windows usually provides a basic driver for your newly installed mouse. To use the mouse's fancier features, though, stick its CD into your drive. If the installation program doesn't start automatically, browse the drive's contents for a program named Setup to start things rolling.

✔ Mouse cord isn't long enough? You can find extension cables for USB and PS/2 mice at most office supply and electronics stores.

✔ Some mice plug into either the USB or PS/2 ports. Plug them into the PS/2 port unless the USB port offers additional features.

✔ You might want to disable your laptop's touchpad or TrackPoint after plugging in a mouse, especially if you keep touching it accidentally. This task varies with different laptops, unfortunately. Sometimes the touchpad's Disable setting appears in the Control Panel's Mouse area. Other times, it's located in the PC's BIOS, a settings area described in this chapter's "The legacy of USB and you" sidebar.

✔ Left-handed users can switch their mouse buttons through the Buttons tab in the Control Panel's Mouse area:

   • *Windows Vista:* Click Start⇨Control Panel⇨Hardware and Sound⇨Mouse.

   • *Windows XP:* Click Start⇨Control Panel⇨Printers and Other Hardware⇨Mouse.

Fixing mouse problems

If your mouse just died, here's the magic set of keystrokes to shut down Windows in a gentle way, without reaching for your computer's Off button.

Press your Windows key (or press Ctrl+Esc). Then press the right-arrow key three times and press the letter U.

Press your Windows key (or press Ctrl+Esc). Press U. When the Turn Off Computer menu appears, press U.

If your mouse isn't completely dead, though, these fixes might revive it.

Cleaning your mouse to fix a jerky cursor

If your cursor is jumpy when you move your mouse, you probably need to clean your mouse. If you're using an optical mouse, use some screen wipes to clean the shiny lens on its undersurface. A pair of tweezers can remove a stuck cat hair or small fiber that's confusing the sensor.

Mechanical mice occasionally need their balls removed and gunk scraped from the rollers by following these steps:

1. **Turn the mouse upside down and remove the little square or round plastic plate that holds the ball in place.**

   You usually find an arrow indicating which way to turn a round plate or which way to push a square plate.

2. **Turn the mouse right-side up, and let the mouse ball fall into your hand.**

   Two things fall out: the plate holding the ball in place and the ball itself.

3. **Set the plate aside and pick all the hair and crud off the mouse ball. Remove any other dirt and debris from the mouse's ball cavity, too.**

   If you have a Q-tip and some rubbing alcohol handy (or even some mild soap and warm water), wipe any crud off the little rollers inside the mouse's ball cavity. Roll the little rollers around with your finger to make sure that there's no stubborn crud you can't see hiding on the sides.

   Mouse balls give off a very disappointing bounce. Don't waste too much time trying to play with them.

4. **Drop the mouse ball back inside the mouse and replace the plate. Turn or push the plate until the mouse ball is locked in place.**

   This cleaning chore cures most jerky mouse cursor problems. However, the mouse ball stays only as clean as your desk. Computer users with cats or shaggy beards might have to pluck stray hairs from their mouse ball frequently.

Telling your computer how to find your mouse

If your computer doesn't seem to recognize your mouse, make sure that the mouse is plugged in firmly. Grope around until you're sure that the plug on the end of its cable fits snugly into the little socket on the back of your computer. Plugged in tight?

If so, reboot your computer. Check the batteries on a wireless mouse and make sure the receiving unit is pushed firmly in place. As a last resort, try installing newer drivers (explained in Chapter 19).

Fixing a wireless mouse that's acting strangely

If your wireless mouse is acting funny, try replacing the batteries. Some batteries fit in the mouse's receiving unit as well as the mouse itself.

An infrared wireless mouse needs a clean line of sight between itself and its *receiving unit,* the thing that plugs into your computer. But because that clean line of sight is probably the only clean spot on your desk, that's the first place you might tend to set down books and junk mail. Try moving your books and junk mail out of the way to calm down the mouse.

Other wireless mice use radio signals. These mice don't need to point in any particular direction. (Except for the battery drawer, unfortunately. These little critters feast on batteries.)

Weird Tales Department: One woman wrote to me that she kept seeing *two* mouse pointers on the screen. The problem? Her ailing wireless mouse was sending a ghost image, similar to the one you see on a TV screen with a bad signal.

Upgrading Joysticks and Game Controllers

Many computer games make do just fine with the keyboard and mouse. Keyboards can handle both online chats and direction: Resting the fingers on the W, A, S, and D keys often lets you tell the PC whether you're moving up, left, down, or right, respectively. That leaves the mouse free for shooting or other activities.

But for advanced gaming, many people prefer dedicated game controllers, described in this section.

Understanding game controller buzzwords

Easy to install, most game controllers come with a flat, rectangular plug that fits directly into your USB port. Here are a few terms you encounter when shopping or reading software boxes:

 USB port: Most game controllers plug into the USB port. If your PC lacks a front-mounted USB port, pick up a *USB hub* — a small, USB-port-filled box with a cable that plugs into your PC's awkwardly placed USB port.

 Game port: Very few controllers still plug into a PC's game port, so many PCs no longer come with the 15-hole port, shown in the margin. If you find yourself needing a game port, examine your computer's sound card, where you plug in the PC's speakers. Many sound cards still come with game ports because musicians use them for plugging in their MIDI instruments.

Joystick/game pad: Joysticks hail from the older school of gaming and use a movable stick for controlling on-screen action. Game pads skip the joystick in favor of a flat surface and many buttons. Some controllers combine both: a joystick surrounded by buttons.

Analog: Analog game controllers measure the direction the joystick moves on a scale of 0 to 255. They send the number to the game, which interprets the joystick's direction and speed, moving the machine gun accordingly.

Digital: Digital models, by contrast, work on an on/off basis. Most simply inform the game which of nine directions the joystick is moved: top, top-right corner, right, bottom-right corner, bottom, and so on. The ninth direction? Centered, meaning it's not being moved at all. Game pads, with their many on/off buttons, usually hail from the digital camp.

Both types of controllers have their advantages and problems. Analog controllers can drift, requiring calibration. Their moving parts might wear out. Digital controllers offer more accurate control, but more limited direction movements.

Different games work better with different types of joystick, so your best bet is to own one analog and one digital model. If possible, try out a friend's controller before you buy. Although some game controllers support both digital and analog modes, they don't always do that very well.

 Some games work better with one kind of game controller over another, and not all controllers work with every game. Serious gamers acquire a serious collection of controllers.

Calibrate: Game controllers all have their own particular feel. When you tell the computer to calibrate the controller, the computer measures the device's movements and corrects its settings to allow smoother and more accurate game play.

Installing a game controller

Windows XP and Vista recognize most controllers as soon as you slide the plug into the USB port. Remember, the plugs fit in only one way. If it doesn't fit, turn it over and try again.

If you're using an old-school game port, push the joystick's plug into the joystick port on the back of your computer.

Fixing game controller problems

Computer games cause the most grief for technical support people. Games push a PC to its limits, and game programmers often tweak the PC to make it work slightly faster.

Because angry gamers can be difficult to placate, many game controller manufacturers provide detailed Web sites explaining how to troubleshoot problems. Often what works for one game doesn't work for the next. Look for the specific game on the site and tweak your settings accordingly.

For the best results, see which game controller your favorite games support, and then buy that game controller.

Solving USB game controller problems

Sometimes games don't recognize a USB game controller or know which one to use for which game; other controllers need periodic calibrating. To access Windows' limited settings for game controllers, follow these steps:

1. **Quit your current game, and choose Control Panel from the Start menu.**

   The Control Panel, Windows' collection of switches and settings, rises to the screen.

2. **Double-click the Game Controllers icon.**

   Windows Vista: The Game Controllers icon lives in the Hardware and Sound category.

   Windows XP: Hides the icon in the Printers and Other Hardware category.

3. **Choose your default game controller and access your particular controller's settings.**

   Click your controller and choose Properties to access its settings.

Chapter 3

Replacing a Monitor, Adding a Second One, or Connecting to a TV

. . . .

In This Chapter

▶ Understanding video vocabulary

▶ Upgrading to an LCD flat-panel monitor

▶ Understanding digital connectors

▶ Installing one or two monitors to a PC

▶ Matching monitors with video cards

▶ Fixing monitors that don't turn on

▶ Eliminating weird monitor noises

. . . .

*M*ost computer terms sound dreadfully ho-hum: *high density. Device driver. Video adapter.* Yawn.

But the engineers had apparently just returned from a science-fiction flick when they started coming up with monitor terms: *Electron gun! Cathode ray! Liquid crystal!*

This chapter talks about the thing everybody stares at and puts stick-on notes all over — the computer monitor. It explains how to upgrade to a nicer, larger monitor — or even connect two of them to your PC to double your desktop. It explains how to connect your PC to your TV set for the ultimate gaming experience.

Along the way, I toss in a few digestible tidbits about your *video card,* that almighty gadget responsible for pitching everything onto your monitor.

Understanding Monitor Buzzwords

Your PC's video circuits send images to your monitor, where you can see the action. Because monitors and your PC's video circuits (known as *video cards* or *display adapters*) work as a team, this chapter's stuffed with twice as many bothersome buzzwords than usual. When you shop for either a monitor or video card, these words show up on newspaper ads, showroom signs, and the fine print of product boxes.

This section deciphers the terms surrounding the monitors and their plugs, ports, and cables.

Monitor buzzwords

Monitors come in two types, each described below.

- **LCD:** The most popular monitor today, LCD *(Liquid Crystal Display)* monitors look much like large laptop screens mounted on a stand. LCD monitors, like the one shown in Figure 3-1, are also called *flat-panel* monitors.

- **CRT:** Fading fast from the marketplace, CRT *(Cathode Ray Tube),* shown in Figure 3-2, monitors resemble small (but expensive) TV sets. Although some CRT monitors call themselves "flat screen," that merely means their glass screens are relatively flat. They're not flat *panel* monitors, an honor belonging only to LCD monitors.

- **TV set:** TV sets are designed for moving images, not text, so they make lousy computer monitors. Their low resolution can barely display an icon. So, why bother hooking up a PC to a TV? Because their large screens excel at showing digital photos, movies, computer games, or TV shows recorded in Windows Vista's new Media Center. (Computer monitors make great TV sets, though, especially widescreen LCD monitors, described next.)

- **Widescreen:** Just like the movie theaters, these LCD monitors boast a wide screen, making for more realistic movie viewing. (If you've upgraded your PC with a TV tuner, described in Chapter 12, you can watch *The Simpsons* reruns in a corner of your extra-large desktop.) Some widescreen monitors can even be turned upright on their stand, letting you see an entire page on-screen, not just a choice between the page's top or bottom half.

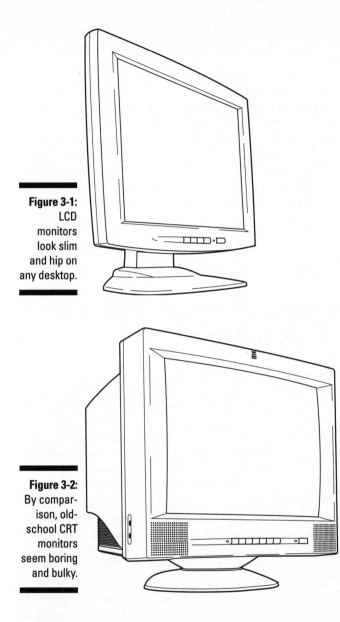

Figure 3-1:
LCD monitors look slim and hip on any desktop.

Figure 3-2:
By comparison, old-school CRT monitors seem boring and bulky.

Neither Windows Vista nor Windows XP supports swiveling widescreen monitors. That requires software made for your PC's video card. If your swivel monitor displays your desktop only sideways — not vertically — drop by your video card manufacturer's Web site and download the latest drivers (a chore covered in Chapter 19). You might need to upgrade your video card to match your new swiveling monitor.

If you're sold on those cool, flat LCD monitors, don't forget these important points:

- LCD monitors cost more to create than CRT monitors, so some manufacturers cut corners in quality, shipping some with a handful of dead pixels that don't light up or that display the wrong colors. Manufacturers rarely cover dead pixels under the monitor's warranty, leaving you stuck with them. Check the return policy before buying.

- Check the connector on the LCD monitor's cable, as some connectors are digital, others are analog. The analog ones often plug directly into standard VGA video cards found on almost all PCs. The digital ones require a video card with a special connector like the one shown in the margin.

- Technically, *all* LCD monitors are digital. However, some use a built-in digital-to-analog converter that transforms an analog signal into the required digital one. The converter built in to LCD monitors labeled as *analog* or *analog/digital* lets them plug into regular VGA cards.

Shopping buzzwords

Much as a sticker on a new car's side window breaks down the car's features into a few words, monitors sum up their features with these buzzwords:

- **Screen size:** A diagonal measurement from one corner of a monitor to the other. Don't be fooled, though: A TV-style monitor's screen size *includes* the plastic surrounding its edge; an LCD monitor's size measures the actual screen you see. That's why a 17-inch LCD monitor will have more usable space than a 17-inch CRT monitor.

- **Pixel:** A single, little, square dot on your screen. Computer pictures are merely collections of thousands of little, colored dots. You need to know about pixels mostly in connection with *dot pitch.*

- **Dot pitch:** The distance between pixel dots on-screen. The smaller the dot pitch, the clearer the picture. Magic number: Buy a monitor with a dot pitch at .28 or smaller.

- **Resolution:** Your monitor stacks pixels across the screen in a grid, like tiny bottles in a wine rack. The more rows and columns your monitor and video card can display, the higher its *resolution* and the more images you can crowd onto your screen. Resolution is adjustable through the Windows' Control Panel, so choose the highest available resolution that still reads comfortably.

  A 1024-x-768 monitor displays a maximum of 1024 columns x 768 rows of pixels. If your video card can display at a higher resolution, such as 1280 x 1024, the monitor still displays a maximum of only 1024 x 768 pixels.

- **Video mode:** A combination of resolution and color. Most cards and monitors display several different modes. For example, some cards can display Windows in 800-x-600 resolution with zillions (32-bit) of colors. Or you can switch to 800-x-600 resolution with fewer (16-bit) colors. Your video mode depends largely on your personal preference and the type of computing you're currently doing.

Here's how to adjust the resolution and color in Windows Vista and Windows XP:

Windows Vista: Right-click a blank part of your desktop and choose Personalize from the pop-up menu. Choose Display Settings from the Personalization Appearance and Sounds window, and adjust the resolution with the sliding control. You can also choose the color from that page's Colors drop-down box.

Windows XP: Right-click a blank part of your desktop and choose Properties from the pop-up menu. Click the Settings tab in the Display Properties dialog box, and adjust the resolution with the sliding control. You can also choose the color from that page's Color Quality drop-down box.

✔ **Refresh rate:** How fast your CRT monitor and card can repaint a picture. The bigger the refresh rate number, the less flicker you see on the CRT's screen. You rarely want more than 60 or 80 hertz (Hz).

Windows Vista and Windows XP let you adjust the refresh rate in slightly different ways:

Windows Vista: Right-click a blank part of your desktop and choose Personalize from the pop-up menu. Choose Display Settings from the Personalization Appearance and Sounds window, click that page's Advanced Settings button, and click the Monitor tab. Then choose one of the refresh rates listed in the Screen Refresh Rate drop-down list.

Windows XP: Right-click a blank part of your desktop and choose Properties from the pop-up menu. Click the Settings tab in the Display Properties dialog box, click the Advanced button, and click the Monitor tab. Then choose one of the refresh rates listed in the Screen Refresh Rate drop-down list.

The plugs and ports

Monitors come in two types, analog or digital, and you can tell which type of monitor you have by ogling the plug at the end of its cord. (Monitors with two cords are both analog *and* digital.) The plug on the end of that cord must fit into the video port on the back of your PC or TV, if you're using your TV as a monitor.

Here are the plugs and ports you're likely to find on your monitor and TV:

✔ **Analog (VGA):** The most common ports found on PCs and monitors, these look like the ones shown in the margin. They're also called VGA *(Video Graphics Array)* ports, and most monitors can plug into them.

✔ **Digital (DVI):** Digital monitors plug into special DVI *(Digital Video Interface)* ports, which resemble the one shown in the margin. Many digital monitors come with both VGA and DVI ports, letting you connect whichever one fits into your PC's video port or cable. Some high-quality TV sets have this port, as well, for connecting to a PC.

If your monitor can plug into either a digital (DVI) or an analog (VGA) port, plug it into your PC's DVI port for the sharpest picture. If your PC's video card doesn't have a DVI port, plug the monitor into the VGA port, instead. (You can also upgrade your video card, which I explain in Chapter 7, for a sharper picture.)

Some monitors don't come with any cable, but offer two ports, VGA and DVI. That lets you buy whichever type of cable that fits with your PC's video port. (DVI cables cost about twice as much as VGA cables, but the sharper picture is worth it.)

Installing One or Two Monitors to a PC or Laptop

Difficulty: Easy

Tools you need: A screwdriver

Cost: Anywhere from $150 to $2,000

Stuff to watch out for: Monitors display only what your PC's video card sends it, so make sure that the card and monitor can communicate. A flat-panel LCD monitor with digital *and* analog inputs will connect with the widest variety of cards. Similarly, video cards with both a VGA port *and* a DVI port support the widest variety of monitors.

Connecting a second monitor to your PC

Hooking up a second monitor to your PC takes two steps: Plug the second monitor into a second video port on your PC, and then tell Windows about your second monitor. Specifically, you must tell Windows which monitor is *default*, meaning which of the two monitors should display your Start button and taskbar:

Windows Vista: Right-click a blank part of the desktop and choose Personalize. Then choose Display Settings, click the picture of your default monitor, choose This Is My Main Monitor, and then click OK.

Windows XP: Right-click a blank part of the desktop, choose Properties and click the Settings tab. Select the Extend My Windows Desktop onto this Monitor check box, and then click OK.

Some newer video cards come with two video ports, making adding a second monitor a snap: Plug one monitor into each port. But if your video card doesn't have two ports, your only solution is to buy and install a second video card or upgrade to a video card with two ports, one for each monitor.

I explain how to install a video card in Chapter 7.

Some manufacturers test your patience by claiming their monitor has a *15-pin mini D-SUB connector.* That's a fancy term for *VGA plug.* The most common plug, it connects to nearly every PC and laptop.

If you're installing a new video card along with your new monitor, flip to Chapter 7 first for instructions on installing the card. After the new card rests inside your PC, head back here to hook up the monitor.

To install a new monitor, perform the following steps:

1. **Shut down Windows, turn off your computer, and unplug your old monitor.**

   Unplug your old monitor's power cord from the wall before you unplug the monitor's video cable from its little port on the back of your computer's case.

2. **Remove the old monitor from your desktop.**

   Don't throw your old monitor into the trash can because monitors contain noxious chemicals. Check Chapter 5 for tips on finding recycling programs.

3. **Remove the new monitor or monitors from the box.**

   Some monitors come with different cables and adapters for different video card connectors.

4. **Place the monitor on your desk and connect a cable between the monitor's port and the matching port on your PC.**

   The cable should fit into only one port on both your PC and your monitor. If the cable doesn't fit right, you're either trying to plug it into the wrong port, or your monitor isn't compatible with your PC. If the monitor's not compatible, you need to upgrade your PC's video card to match your monitor, a chore tackled in Chapter 7.

   If you have one of those cool swivel stands, leave a little slack on the cables so that you don't pull a cable loose when turning the monitor.

5. **Plug the monitor's power cord into the wall outlet or a power strip.**

6. **Turn on your monitor and then turn on your computer.**

   Can you see words on the screen as the computer spews its opening remarks? If so, you're done. Hurrah! If it doesn't work, however, go through some of the fixes in the section, "Fixing Your Monitor" later in this chapter.

   If you bought a fancy monitor with speakers, cameras, or other goodies, you have to perform two more tricks: Plug the cords from the speakers or camera into their ports in the back of your computer. (The Appendix shows pictures of all your PC's ports and what plugs into them.) Then, if Windows doesn't recognize your new monitor's special features, you probably have to install the drivers that came on the CD that came with the monitor. (Your monitor *did* come with a CD, didn't it?) Either way, Chapter 19 can help out.

Watching Your PC on a TV

When connecting a PC to a TV, success depends on your PC, not your TV. Unfortunately, not all PCs can send video to a TV. To see if your TV and PC can become friends, look on the back of both your TV and your PC, specifically the spot where your monitor currently plugs into your PC. You need to find a matching pair of any of these jacks on both your PC and your TV:

- ✔ **S-Video**: This appears on high-quality TV sets and some PCs, and carries a very good picture. By connecting an S-Video cable between the two ports, your PC can send high-quality video to the TV.

- ✔ **RCA**: Found on most TV sets and some PCs, this sends lower-quality video to the TV. If you spot one, connect an RCA cable between the yellow RCA port on the TV and the PC's RCA port.

- ✔ **DVI**: Many HDTV sets come with a DVI port — the same one found on most LCD monitors and PCs. That makes the connection as easy as with an LCD monitor: Just connect a DVI cable between your PC's DVI port and the HDTV set. (You might need to unplug your PC's monitor when you plug in the TV.)

When you've found matching ports on both your PC and TV, I explain how to connect the two and adjust the settings in the "Connecting Your PC's Video to a TV" section of Chapter 12.

Fixing Your Monitor

Can you fix the old one? Probably not. Nobody takes apart monitors these days and repairs them. You might be able to solve the following problems, though.

Monitors not only attract your attention, but they also attract dust. Thick, furry layers of dust that coat your monitor on a weekly basis. Clean your monitor regularly as follows:

- ✔ **For CRT monitors:** Spray a glass cleaner onto a soft cloth (not on the monitor itself) and wipe away the dust. Keep the cleaner out of the monitor's vents.

- ✔ **For LCD monitors (and laptop screens):** Don't use any ethyl alcohol or ammonia-based cleaners on these types of screens. Those types of harsh cleaners can yellow the screen over time. A slightly damp soft cloth towel does the trick for me with no ill effects. (This book's editor, Jean Rogers, avoids moisture problems by cleaning with dry static wipes.)

Fixing a monitor that doesn't turn on

If your monitor doesn't turn on, check to make sure that your monitor is plugged in. Actually, your monitor has four plugs that you need to check:

- ✔ Check to make sure that you plugged the power cord securely into the wall or power strip and make sure that your power strip is turned on.

- ✔ Wiggle the connection where the monitor's video cable plugs into the back of your computer.

- ✔ Check where the video cord plugs into the back of your monitor. Some cords aren't built into the monitor, leading to loose connections. Push the cord hard to make sure that it's plugged in tight.

- ✔ Check where the power cord leads to the back of your monitor. Like video cables, some power cords plug into the monitor.

Finally, make sure your monitor's power button is turned on. Some monitors don't turn themselves back on after a power outage.

Checking a monitor that makes weird noises

Almost all monitors make little *popping* sounds when first turned on or while warming up. That's nothing to worry about. But after they're turned on, they're never supposed to whine or buzz.

Monitors are usually one of the quietest parts of your PC. If your monitor ever starts making noise, something is wrong. If those noises are ever accompanied by an odd smell, don't wait for smoke: Turn off your monitor immediately.

If you install a new video card and the monitor screams, the card is trying to make the monitor do something cruel and unnatural. Chances are that the two aren't compatible. Before giving up, try changing the *refresh rate* of your monitor, a task I explain in this chapter's sidebar, "Shopping Buzzwords." (Look in that sidebar's "refresh rate" section.)

Chapter 4

Choosing a New Printer

Windows Vista makes installing a printer easier than ever. Plug in a new USB printer, and Windows automatically recognizes it, installs the driver, and introduces the printer to all your programs. At least, that's the way it's supposed to work.

And if Windows greets your printer with a puzzled stare, it's still fairly easy to inform Windows of your printer's brand name and model. After dispensing with those formalities, Windows plays gracious host once again, spreading the printer's name and settings to all Windows programs that drop by.

Yep, printers are easier than ever to install. Now, today's printing problems center on those *little* things. You know, when the margins run off the side of the page, the angry letter to the phone company prints out with odd birthmarks, or the printer runs out of ink — and you don't have another ink cartridge handy.

When your printed pages look funny — or the paper won't even come out of the printer — this is the chapter you want.

Understanding Printer Buzzwords

Like most computer toys, printers come with their own secret vocabulary. The first few entries here describe the most common types of printers sold today. The second set describes more esoteric words found in printing menus and the printer's dreaded technical specifications area.

Commonly encountered printer breeds

You encounter the following types of printers most often when you're shopping. You're almost certain to find yourself choosing among inkjet, laser, photo, and "all-in-one" printers.

Inkjet: Popular for their low price and high quality, inkjet printers (shown in Figure 4-1) squirt ink onto a page, creating surprisingly realistic images in color or black and white. Although the printers come cheap, their expensive ink cartridges wear out much faster than the typewriter ribbons of yesteryear. For low-to-medium level work and digital photography, these versatile printers often provide the best buy for the buck.

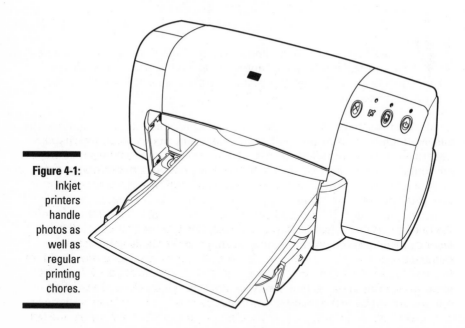

Figure 4-1:
Inkjet printers handle photos as well as regular printing chores.

Laser: Laser printers might sound dangerous, but these printers (shown in Figure 4-2) use technology similar to their ho-hum equivalent, copy machines; they sear images into the paper with toner. Black-and-white laser printers cost a little more than inkjet printers; double that price for color laser printers. Although laser printers can't print digital photos, they're cheaper in the long run for general office paperwork.

Figure 4-2:
Laser
printers
provide
better quality
than inkjet
printers but
at higher
prices.

Laser printers are *supposed* to heat up. That's why you shouldn't keep dust covers on laser printers when they're running. If you don't allow for plenty of air ventilation, your laser printer might overheat. After you're through using your laser printer, let it cool off; then put on the dust cover to keep out lint and small insects.

All-in-one (AIO): Popular with small offices, this type of printer combines a laser or inkjet printer, copy machine, scanner, and a fax machine into one compact package. (Sorry, no coffee maker.) The quality of all-in-one machines has risen dramatically in the past few years. As shown in Figure 4-3, they're great for small, one-person offices; they're not so great when you want to spread the equipment around. They're also a drag because if one component stops working — the scanner, for example — you've lost your copier and fax machine, as well.

Photo Printer: Many color inkjet printers do a fair job at printing digital photos, but photo printers contain extra colors, letting them print with more finesse. Some photo printers print directly from your camera's memory card, letting you print without firing up your PC. Photo printers work best as a second printer, keeping you from wasting your expensive ink on shopping lists, schoolwork, and Web pages.

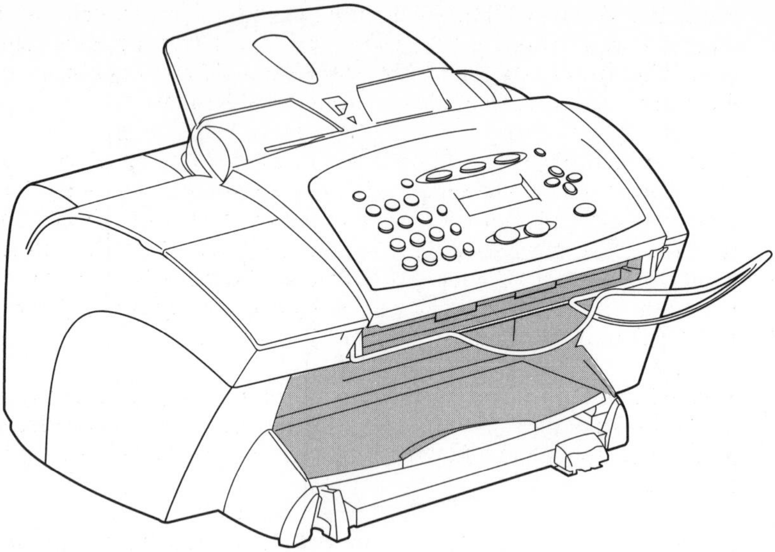

Figure 4-3:
This all-in-one printer combines an inkjet printer, a scanner, a fax machine, and a copy machine into one package.

If you're a digital photography enthusiast and you're considering buying a photo printer, keep the following tips in mind:

✔ Pick up some photo-quality or glossy inkjet paper. It's not cheap, but it makes all the difference when printing photos. (Check out the section, "Choosing the right paper," later in this chapter for more on choosing paper.)

✔ Although they offer the utmost convenience, photo printers can't compete with professional developers for both quality and price. Drop by your local photo developer with a memory card or CD full of photos and compare the difference.

✔ Because of printing costs, the vast majority of pictures taken with digital cameras never see print. To share them with friends, consider posting them on one of the Internet's many photo-sharing Web sites, like Flickr (www.flickr.com). You can find similar sites by searching for the words *photo sharing* on Google (www.google.com).

The Sweet Art (www.sweetart.com) company in Lenexa, Kansas, sells a printer that prints digital images onto cakes and cookies using edible food coloring.

Awkward printer terms

These terms often appear on a printer's box, in advertisements, or when you're trying to figure out the software's menu.

Pages Per Minute (PPM): The number of pages a printer can squirt out in one minute. Careful, though: That's when you're printing the *same* page over and over. When you're printing a series of several different pages, as required by most printing jobs, the PPM rate drops considerably.

Dots per inch (dpi): The number of dots a printer can pack into one square inch. The more dots per inch, the better your printed stuff looks. Photographers looking to print high-quality photos want printers with at least 2880 horizontal x 720 vertical dpi. (Some photo printers fudge it, though, and still look good with less dpi.) Compare the same photo printed on several printers before buying. (A 360 dpi color printer works fine for printing party invitations, birthday cards, and Web pages.)

Parallel and USB ports: For years, all printers attached to a standard printer port (also known as a *parallel port*) on your PC. Today, many plug straight into the USB port. (The Appendix contains a pictorial reference on ports and plugs.)

Driver: Software that tells Windows how to talk to your printer. Because different printers come with different features, they almost always require custom drivers. When you're printer shopping, make sure that the printer you choose comes with drivers written specifically for Windows Vista or your current version of Windows. (Check out Chapter 19 for more information about drivers.)

Point size: The size of a single letter. This word uses a bigger point size than this word.

Typeface: Describes a letter's distinctive design style. `Courier` is a different typeface than Times New Roman.

Font: A typeface of a certain size and characteristic. For example, Times New Roman is a typeface, and **Times New Roman Bold** and *Times New Roman Italic* are different fonts within that typeface family.

Cartridge: Expensive, replaceable plastic boxes inside printers that hold ink or other chemicals used for printing. Inkjet printers use ink cartridges, as shown in Figure 4-4; laser printers require toner cartridges. Keep several cartridges on hand because printers consume them quickly. Most color printers have two or more cartridges, one for black ink and the other(s) for color inks.

Portable Document Format (PDF): A special file containing a printable picture of a document, often a manual or form. PDF files require the freebie Adobe Acrobat Reader program for viewing.

To view information stored as a PDF file, download a freebie version of Adobe Acrobat Reader from www.adobe.com. To create your own PDF files, buy Adobe Acrobat's *full* version from the same Web site.

Figure 4-4:
A Hewlett
Packard
inkjet
cartridge.

PostScript or Encapsulated PostScript (EPS): The Adobe Systems Incorporated programming language that describes images to printers.

PostScript Printers: Mostly used by design professionals, these expensive printers can read PostScript files directly and print them to exacting standards. NonPostScript printers rely on software interpreters or drivers to translate PostScript files into something printable.

Installing a Printer

Difficulty level: Easy

Tools you need: One hand and installation software

Cost: Anywhere from $100 to $2,500

Stuff to watch out for: When you're shopping for a printer, compare the same letter and/or photo printed from several different printers. For example, one printer might be better for photos but lousy for letters. Other printers might be just the opposite. Consider your personal printing needs and compare several printers that meet those needs before making a final decision.

No matter what kind of printer you choose, you might have to buy a printer cable, as many printers don't include one. Check the box to see if you have a *parallel* or *USB* printer, and choose the correct cable accordingly. (The Appendix offers solutions if your computer lacks enough USB ports to accommodate your new printer.)

Before you install a USB printer, be sure to read the installation instructions. Some USB peripherals prefer that you install their Windows drivers *before* you plug them in and turn them on.

To install a printer, follow these steps:

1. **Remove the new printer and accessories from the box and install its software, if necessary.**

   Remove the printer's cover and extricate any packaging from inside the printer. Many printers come taped up and with cardboard or plastic holders to protect moving parts during shipping. Check the manual to be sure you've located and removed them all. Also, make sure that you can account for any installation CDs, cables, paper, and cartridges that came with the printer.

2. **Find the printer cable and the appropriate ports on your computer and printer, and then connect the cable between them.**

   a. *First, plug the cable into your PC. It fits into one of these two ports, both of which I describe in detail in this book's Appendix:*

   Parallel port: The parallel port looks the same on any PC, no matter what era, model, or manufacturer.

   USB port: This rectangular hole looks like no other on your PC.

   b. *Next, plug the cable's other end into your printer. Your printer probably has one of these two ports:*

   Centronics: Resembling a robot's mouth, this connector accepts the other end of the cable that's plugged into your PC's parallel port. (Unlike *USB cables,* which use the same type of plug on each end, *parallel cables* end in different plugs.)

   USB: Slide the plug into the printer's USB port, the hole with the pitchfork symbol next to it. (Some printers accept the larger, square type of USB port.)

3. **Plug in the printer, turn it on, and install the printer's cartridge or cartridges.**

   • *Inkjet:* Pull off the plastic strip that protects the cartridge's ink nozzles and electrical contacts. Before you may install the cartridge, most inkjet printers must be turned on, so their cartridge-bearing arm slides out of its hiding place. Finally, raise the printer's cover and check the manual for your model's exact cartridge-installation instructions.

   Done? Close the cover and turn off the printer.

   • *Laser:* Be careful here, as spills are messy. Rock the new toner cartridge (shown in Figure 4-5) back and forth gently to loosen the toner and spread it around evenly inside. When you've evenly distributed the toner, gently remove the plastic protective strip from the cartridge. Avoid tipping the cartridge, as toner sometimes spills out. Check the manual for your model's exact cartridge installation instructions.

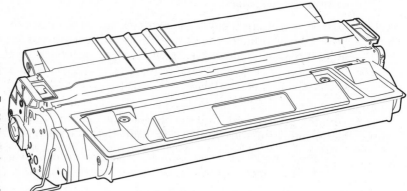

Figure 4-5:
A toner
cartridge
for a laser
printer.

4. **Add paper.**

   Add about 25 sheets of plain old office paper because you don't want to waste your expensive photo paper on the first few test runs you make. When you're ready to add better paper, read the section later in this chapter, "Choosing the right paper."

   Some printers make you attach trays to hold incoming or outgoing paper. Always rustle the paper to get some air between the pages before placing it in the tray. That reduces paper jams and expletives.

5. Turn on your monitor and PC, if you'd turned them off.

As your PC awakens, Windows notices that you've attached a new printer. Give Windows time to sniff your printer thoroughly and add the printer's name to your programs' printer menus.

- Many printers come with special drivers and fancy programs. Install them now, with the printer turned on, if the printer's manual didn't require you to install them before you plug in the printer for the first time.

- Windows usually offers to print a test page when it notices a newly plugged in printer. Take it up on its offer, as the test page will contain information important to tech support people should things not go well.

Fixing Common Printer Problems

No matter how carefully it's installed, sometimes the printer just doesn't work right. These sections show how to fix the most common problems you might encounter during your printer's lifespan.

Replacing an inkjet printer is often more cost-effective than repairing it, unfortunately. The more expensive laser printers, by contrast, require servicing to ensure a long lifespan. Some printers simply need to be cleaned in the right places, so get an estimate on repairs before giving up.

All-in-one printers vary widely in price and quality, so there's no clear answer about the cost-effectiveness of repairing versus replacing. When in doubt, get an estimate.

To test whether it's your computer or your printer that's acting up, plug the printer into a friend's computer or laptop or test it on a computer at work. (Have a coworker blindfold the network administrator first.) If the printer doesn't work with other computers, either, your printer is dead. If it works fine everywhere else, your computer is the culprit. Try installing a new driver, a task covered in Chapter 19.

Reuse your paper when things don't print correctly. Place it in your printer tray so that the printer can use the blank side. Don't use scrap paper for important stuff, of course, but it's great for printing tests, drafts, or things nobody else will see.

Fixing a printer that doesn't print anything

Are you *sure* that the printer is turned on, plugged in to the wall, and a cable connects it securely to your computer?

Check to see whether the printer's little power light beams merrily. If not, plug a lamp into the outlet to make sure that the outlet works. If the lamp works in the outlet where your printer doesn't, the printer is most likely suffering from a blown power supply. Head for the printer repair shop for an estimate.

If the printer's power light comes on, though, keep reading.

- Does the printer have paper? Is the paper jammed somewhere? Some printers have a little readout or blinking light that announces a paper jam when the paper is stuck. With other printers, you have to ogle the paper supply yourself.

- Do you have a switch box that enables two computers to connect to one printer? Check to make sure that the switch box is switched to the right computer. While you're there, give the cables a push to make sure that they're firmly attached. Still doesn't work? Try connecting the printer directly; some printers don't work correctly with a switch box.

- Sometimes the problem lies with the printer's driver. It's fairly easy to make sure that your printer is using the most up-to-date driver, and it's all explained in Chapter 19. (That chapter also explains how Windows can return to your older driver if your new driver makes things even worse.)

- Windows comes with drivers for most printers, but they often lean toward the generic, meaning that they don't support a printer's more advanced features. Upgrading to the manufacturer's current printer driver that's written for your particular model often fixes major problems.

How two computers can share one printer

Many folks solve the problem of having two computers and one printer with an *A/B switch box*. The printer plugs into the box's printer port. One computer plugs into the box's A port, and the other computer plugs into its B port. (Before shopping, check your printer's manual to make sure it works with a switch box.)

When you want to print from one computer, flip the switch to A. When you want to print from the other computer, flip the switch to B. Or better

yet, look for a switch box with *automatic* sensing. Those fancier boxes sense where the information comes from, and automatically route the incoming page to the printer.

A *network* — a group of connected computers described in Chapter 17 — enables all the computers to share a single printer, or each other's printers. Before buying an expensive A/B switch, check out Chapter 17, as networks are easier than ever to set up inexpensively.

Playing the replacement ink cartridge guilt game

Printer cartridges wear out all too quickly. Color printers are the worst culprits, as each cartridge often contains several colors, each color in its own separate tube. When one color is used up, the printer usually considers the entire cartridge to be empty, even if the other tubes still contain some colored ink.

Those expensive replacement cartridges create huge business opportunities, and manufacturers practically give away the printers in the hopes of making back the money on the cartridges. Cartridges are easy to find. In an emergency, local drugstores often carry replacement cartridges for the most popular printers. Office supply stores offer lower prices and a larger selection. Internet outlets carry the lowest prices and widest selection.

Now, the problem: Printer manufacturers say to buy *only* their Official Manufacturer-Approved Cartridges. Unfortunately, these official cartridges often cost more than twice as much as the compatible cartridges sold by competing manufacturers.

To add another layer to the confusion, people selling refill kits, like the one in Figure 4-6, say that *everybody* is saving money by refilling their empty cartridges. Which cartridges should you buy?

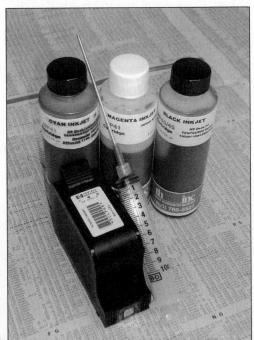

Figure 4-6: Many companies sell refill kits to extend the life of inkjet cartridges.

When you're deciding how to handle the situation, weigh the following facts, and then come to your own conclusion. There's no right or wrong answer here; different folks have different needs.

- ✔ Some manufacturers patent their ink chemicals, ensuring that any replacements created by competing manufacturers have colors that differ slightly. Some people notice the difference in color, drying time, and print longevity. Others don't have any problems.

- ✔ Quality varies among different manufacturers. Don't give up on all generic cartridges because of one bad experience.

- ✔ When something goes wrong with a compatible or refilled cartridge, it often leaves a nagging question: "Did this happen because I didn't use the manufacturer's cartridges?"

- ✔ Official replacement cartridges usually cost from $10 to $50 or more. Refilling an empty cartridge costs anywhere from $1 to $5.

- ✔ Refilling cartridges is messy. It involves filling syringes with ink, injecting the ink into the cartridges' sealed chambers, and then placing tape over the broken seals. Wear gloves or buy refilled cartridges online. Injecting any air causes problems. And you must buy the right ink to match your cartridges.

- ✔ Cartridges can be refilled only a certain number of times because they're designed to work only once. You must decide when your cartridge is past the point of no return. Lower print quality often signals that the end is near. Leaking cartridges signal that the end is already here.

- ✔ Check your printer's warranty carefully. Refilling cartridges might not void your warranty, but most warranties don't cover any damage caused by refilling.

- ✔ If you find yourself buying black ink cartridges often, consider buying a laser printer, as its cost-per-page is much lower.

Installing a new toner or ink cartridge

Printers need ink or toner to place images onto a page. When your pages start to look blotchy or faint, you probably need a new cartridge.

Various printers work differently, but here's the general rundown:

1. **Turn off the printer and open its cover.**

   Printers usually have a hood-release type of latch that pops up the cover. You might need to remove the paper tray first.

If your laser printer has been turned on, let it cool off for 15 minutes. Laser printers get hot enough inside to brand a steer. The parts that seem hot *are* hot, and they can burn your fingers.

2. **Pull out the old cartridge.**

   The cartridge usually slides straight out. While the cartridge is out, wipe away any dust or dirt you see inside the printer. The printer's manual tells you the most appropriate places to clean. A little rubbing alcohol on a soft rag usually works well. Check your printer's manual first to make sure that alcohol won't damage any parts inside.

   Color printers usually come with two ink cartridges, one for black and the other for colored ink. Because they're often completely enclosed in black plastic, they're usually labeled to avoid confusion. If you're in doubt, the smaller cartridge probably holds the black ink.

3. **Slide in the new cartridge.**

   Before sliding in a laser printer's toner cartridge (refer to Figure 4-5), gently rock it back and forth to evenly distribute the toner that lurks inside. Don't turn the cartridge upside down or completely on one end.

   Some toner cartridges have a protective plastic strip you must remove before you install the cartridge. Better check your printer's instruction manual on this one.

4. **When the new cartridge snaps in place, close the printer's cover and turn it back on.**

   You might need to put the paper tray back on the printer.

5. **Run your printer's software, if it has any.**

   Some inkjet printers, for example, come with software that aligns a newly installed cartridge. The software prints several coded designs, and then asks you to examine them and choose the best-looking ones. The printer then knows the best way to print.

✔ You should check your laser printer's manual for mention of any fuser pads or corona wires that need to be changed or cleaned when you replace the toner cartridge.

✔ New toner cartridges are sometimes blotchy for the first few pages, so don't print any résumés right off the bat.

✔ If you run into trouble, take the printer to the repair shop for an opinion. The printer probably needs a good cleaning anyway.

Fixing printing smears and blotches

When you begin seeing smears or blotches on your printouts, start diagnosing the problem by checking the toner or inkjet cartridge. Many inkjet printers let you check cartridge ink levels directly from Windows; you can also perform tests for nozzle clogs, print head cleaning, and alignment.

To see if your printer offers these options, follow these steps:

1. **Open the list of all printers attached to your PC.**

   Windows Vista: Click the Start button, open Control Panel, select the Hardware and Sound category, and then choose Printers.

   The list of printers includes Vista's phantom Microsoft XPS Document Writer. (It's not a real printer.)

   Windows XP: Click the Start button, open Control Panel, choose the Printers and Other Hardware category, and finally select View Installed Printers or Fax Printers.

2. **Right-click your printer's icon and choose Properties.**

   The Properties window appears.

3. **Click the Printing Preferences button.**

   A window appears, as shown in Figure 4-7. In this case, it shows the levels of ink left in the printer's black and color cartridges. My printer currently has plenty of color ink ($29.95 per cartridge). The black ink ($24.99) is still half full.

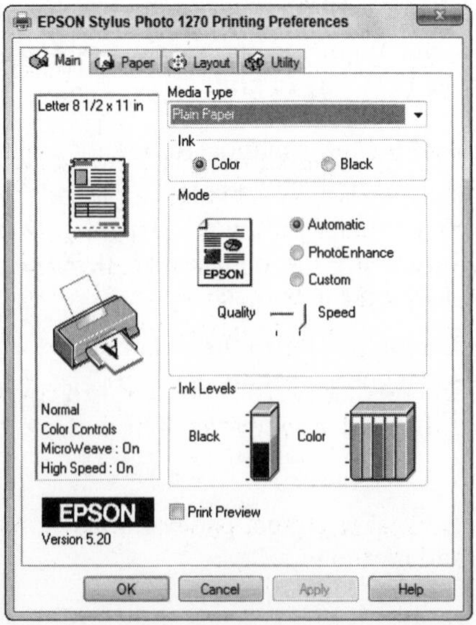

Figure 4-7: Some printers let you check the cartridge's ink level directly from Windows.

EPSON Stylus Photo 1270 Printing Preferences

Main | Paper | Layout | Utility

Letter 8 1/2 x 11 in

Media Type
Plain Paper

Ink
◉ Color   ○ Black

Mode
EPSON
◉ Automatic
○ PhotoEnhance
○ Custom

Quality ——— Speed

Normal
Color Controls
MicroWeave : On
High Speed : On

Ink Levels
Black   Color

EPSON
Version 5.20

☐ Print Preview

OK | Cancel | Apply | Help

4. **Click the Utility tab.**

   Not all printers offer this tab; your particular printer might offer a differ-ent menu option for testing your printer for clogged nozzles and other problems.

5. **Run your printer's built-in diagnostics.**

   Look for a test that checks the nozzles for clogging, as that's the number-one cause for print quality problems. If the test proves positive, look for a head cleaning utility to fix it. Head alignment tests make sure the car-tridge is seated properly.

   ✔ If your printer has built-in utilities, keep fiddling around in the printer's Properties window until you find it. Or you can dig out the manual, just to make sure your printer *does* include those utilities and to find out exactly where they're located. Check the printer's front panel, as well, as they might be hidden there.

   ✔ Don't clean the nozzles unless you notice something wrong with your printer's quality. It wastes ink (and often several sheets of paper).

Laser printers often require poking, prodding, cleaning, and billing by a pro-fessional. The next few paragraphs describe some laser-printer-specific prob-lems and how to fix them.

Black streaks: This problem can mean that you need a new photoconductor — a big, expensive thingy inside the laser printer. You might get lucky and dis-cover that the repair shop can just clean the photoconductor to bring your laser printer back to life. Or maybe you just need a new toner cartridge — an increasing number of printers now put the photoconductor inside the cartridge. If your photoconductor is done for good, get a repair estimate to compare with the cost of a new printer.

Faded print: You probably need a new toner cartridge. Before buying a new one, try this tip:

When your print looks faded, your printer is probably running out of toner. Open the lid to the laser printer and look for a big black plastic thing. Pull it straight out, and then gently rock it back and forth. (***Warning:*** Don't turn the cartridge upside down unless you want to make an incredible mess!) Then slide the cartridge back in the same way. This procedure sometimes lets your laser printer squeeze out a few dozen extra pages.

Creased paper: Keep paper stored in a dry place and not in a corner of the garage or near the coffee machine. Moist paper can crease as it runs through a laser printer.

A Tupperware lasagna container makes a great paper storage container for sealing out air, cockroaches, and moths.

Choosing the right paper

Inexpensive yet powerful, color inkjet printers spit out some incredibly beautiful color pictures, provided you use the right paper. When you use ordinary office paper, the paper's fibers soak up the ink. Usually, that means that ink bleeds and blurs. On specially designed (and especially expensive) color inkjet paper, the colors stay put, creating a crisp image that looks almost as if it was created by a standard film camera and processed at a photo-processing lab.

Some paper comes with its application listed right on the packaging: Premium Inkjet Paper, for instance. Others aren't nearly as clear. Here are some papers required for different applications:

- **Junk:** Always keep a supply of cheap or scrap paper for running printer tests, printing quick drafts, making grocery lists, and printing other things not intended for others. You can always use the other side of paper from botched print jobs, as well.

- **Legal:** Created mainly for boring legal documents, these longer sheets of paper measure 8½ x 14 inches instead of the standard 8½ x 11 inches.

- **Letter quality:** The words *premium* or *bright white* are the clues for this higher-quality paper that's good for nearly everything.

- **Photos:** You can print photos on nearly any paper, but only waste your ink on the good stuff: special paper bearing the word *photo*. Insert this paper into the paper tray carefully so that the printer uses the glossy side. Also, look for a loading support sheet to place beneath some photo papers; it helps the paper glide smoothly off the tray and into the printer.

  Matte photo paper works well for brochures and newsletters, where the glossy look isn't necessary.

- **Labels:** I love the Avery Wizard for printing Avery labels with Microsoft Word. Available at www.avery.com, the free, downloadable software places preconfigured templates in Word for nearly every size of Avery label. Just type your information into the template for your label, slide the labels into the printer, and the information prints neatly onto the individual labels. (Avery's Web site also carries templates for Avery business cards, CD labels, mailing labels, dividers, greeting cards, and more.)

- **Transparencies:** For overhead presentations, buy special transparent plastic sheets designed to be used with your type of printer.

Be sure to buy paper specifically designed for your type of printer: inkjet or laser. Laser printers use heat to fuse the ink onto the paper, so they require paper designed to hold up to the heat.

Keeping the print from running off the page

Sometimes an image or document refuses to align itself onto a single page: The printer cuts off lines or images along the right side. To avoid this problem, always use a program's Print Preview mode before you actually print the page. The computer displays a picture of the paper with your image or text printed on it. If the image doesn't fit onto the page, try these things to fix the problem:

- ✔ **Switch to Landscape mode:** Printers usually print onto paper in Portrait mode: The paper is positioned vertically. If you're printing a spreadsheet or something that extends off to the right, look for a place in the Preferences or Page Setup area to switch from Portrait to Landscape mode. Then the printer prints the information horizontally, like a landscape. (Get it? *Landscape*?)

- ✔ **Reduce to fit page:** Some printers and programs offer an option to shrink the image so that it fits onto the page. This works nicely for photos, but not so well for things with lots of fine print. Give it a test on cheap paper or the back of your page that didn't print correctly.

- ✔ **Use templates:** Avery and other manufacturers offer free templates from their Web sites. By calling up the template in your software and printing in the templates boxes, your program positions the text perfectly on the page. It works great for labels, greeting cards, certificates, and other hard-to-configure spots.

- ✔ **Change margins:** Use your program's Page Setup area and make sure you've set the margins to within a half-inch of the paper's edge. You might need to move out the right margin until everything fits.

Fixing paper jams

Sounds like you need to get your printer cleaned by a professional. In the meantime, open the printer's top and carefully remove the offending sheet of paper. Keep your eyes peeled for little shreds of paper that might be getting caught in the printer's gears.

When you're adding paper, hold the paper stack loosely at the bottom, and flick the top edges as though they were one of those little flip-page cartoons. This loosens up the paper and makes it flow through the feeder easier.

Never run labels through a laser printer unless the labels' box specifically states that it's okay. The heat inside the printer can make the labels fall off inside the printer and gum up the works. Inkjets handle labels okay.

Keeping your printer happy

Your printer generally prefers Authorized Service Technicians with white coats to perform repairs. Feel free to perform any of the appropriate tasks listed next, however, to keep your printer happy:

- ✔ **Download the latest software and drivers.** When your printer is acting too weirdly to ignore, head to your printer manufacturer's Web site and download the latest drivers and software. Sometimes the two come in one package. Other times the *driver* enables Windows to communicate with your printer when sending pages; the *software* is a utility program that allows you to adjust your printer's settings.

- ✔ **Run your printer's software.** Some printers come with troubleshooting programs (occasionally built right into their drivers) that offer suggestions when things go wrong. They also align your printer whenever you replace the ink cartridges, carefully ensuring optimal quality.

Turn off your printer when you're not using it. Inkjet printers, especially, should be turned off when they're not being used. The heat tends to dry the cartridges, shortening their lives.

Don't unplug your inkjet printer to turn it off. Always use the on/off switch. The switch ensures that the cartridges slide back to their home positions, keeping them from drying out or becoming clogged.

Chapter 5

Moving from the Old PC to the New One

. . . .

In This Chapter

▶ Using the Files and Settings Transfer Wizard

▶ Migrating by using a home network or portable hard drive

▶ Transferring from an old computer to a new one

▶ Migrating by using a direct cable connection, a network, or CDs

. . . .

Moving to a new house might be a lot of work, but the process takes just a few logical steps. You grab everything you want from the old house, toss it in the moving truck, and unload it at the new place. And the stuff you *don't* want goes to family, friends, charity, the neighbors, the curb, and the dumpster — usually in that order.

Moving to your new Windows Vista computer, by contrast, isn't as clear-cut. For one thing, who can possibly find everything that's important on their old Windows XP computer? The My Documents folder is a natural place to start packing, but what about *other* things you use? Your list of favorite Web sites in Internet Explorer, for example? Your e-mail addresses, mail account settings, and Outlook Express messages? How about all the other settings you've painstakingly set up in your favorite programs?

Windows XP's solution, the Files and Settings Transfer Wizard, only lets you move things to another Windows XP computer, so it can't help you move things to your new Vista PC. Windows Vista's equivalent, Windows Easy Transfer, handles that job, and this chapter explains how to put it to work.

Understanding File Transfer Buzzwords

After years of intense brow furrowing, Microsoft realized that Windows owners often purchase new computers. And those people need a quick and easy way to migrate all Windows' convoluted settings — as well as all their files — from their old computers to their new ones.

Windows Vista helps you make the move as painless as possible. Here's the type of language you hear tossed about by the moving crew:

Windows Easy Transfer: The backbone of the moving process, this program enables you to choose what files, settings, and folders to transfer, and how to transfer them. When you've made your desires known, the wizard carries out your request, copying everything you've selected over to the new computer. Unfortunately, the program doesn't work with Windows Me and Windows 98, only Windows XP, Windows 2000, or from another Windows Vista PC.

Transfer: The wizard doesn't really *move* your desired files and settings from your old computer into your new one. The transfer process only *copies* them, leaving the originals on your old computer. Before disposing of your old PC, be sure to delete your personal information, a chore I tackle in the sidebar, "Can't I just throw the darn thing away?"

Can't I just throw the darn thing away?

Several years ago, many organizations accepted donations of old PCs. Charities are more reluctant to accept PCs today, however, for several reasons. First, most old PCs cost more to refurbish than to buy new. Second, many states now consider PCs to be hazardous waste, making their disposal more costly.

So what do you do with all this stuff? Here are some ways to safely dispose of old computers and parts, either through recycling or donation programs. Also, when you buy your new computer, ask your dealer about any recycling programs.

Before getting rid of your old PC, buy a data destruction program, available in the Utilities section of most computer stores. These specially designed programs fill up your hard drive with random characters, wiping out your files in the process. Formatting the hard drive isn't enough to thwart dedicated thieves. Only a data destruction program can keep potential thieves away from your passwords, financial records, and other information commonly found on PCs.

Here are a few options for disposing of an unwanted PC:

IBM's PC Recycling Service

www.ibm.com/ibm/environment/ products/pcrservice.shtml

IBM accepts any manufacturer's PCs (including monitors, printers, and peripherals) from consumers and businesses. (The program costs $29.99, including shipping.) IBM's worldwide program saves anything refurbishable for philanthropic organizations and recycles or safely disposes of the rest. It's a great way to kick your karma points up a few notches.

Dell's Recycling

www.dell.com/recycle

Buy a Dell PC, and Dell will recycle your old PC for free, regardless of its manufacturer. The company also recycles any old Dell PCs or products for free.

Freecycle

www.freecycle.org

A grassroots, community-based mailing list, Freecycle lets you post items you no longer want in the hopes somebody else will pick them up for free and give them a new life. Students, hobbyists, and repair technicians might still find some value in your old PC.

Settings: This refers to any changes you make to a program: Entering your e-mail address into a mail program, for example, or telling Internet Explorer how to connect to the Internet. Windows Easy Transfer copies settings from many of your old computer's programs to the programs on your new computer. It doesn't copy the actual programs, mind you. You still need to install those on your new computer. But the wizard saves you from tweaking those programs' settings to make them work the way they worked before.

Preparing to Move into Your New PC

Like any other moving day, Windows Easy Transfer's success depends on your preparation. Instead of rummaging for boxes and duct tape, you must do these two things to prepare the move:

✔ Choose how to transfer the information between PCs

✔ Install your *old* PC's programs onto your *new* PC

The next two sections explain each topic in more detail.

Choosing how to transfer your old information

PCs are very good at copying things, much to the concern of the entertainment industry. For example, Windows Easy Transfer offers *four* different ways to copy your old PC's information onto your new PC. Each method works at a different speed and level of difficulty. You must choose one of these four:

✔ **Windows Easy Transfer Cable:** Every PC comes with a handful of USB ports, so an "Easy Transfer Cable" is the fastest and simplest solution. Often sold in stores as Easy Link, Direct Link, USB Bridge, or simply Linking USB cable, this special cable resembles a regular USB cable that's swallowed a mouse: The cable bulges in the middle, as shown in Figure 5-1. These cables cost less than $30 at most electronics stores or online.

✔ **Network:** If you've already created a network between your new and old PCs, Vista can transfer your information that way. Creating a network requires *much* more work than plugging in an Easy Transfer cable, but I tackle the job of linking your PCs into a network in Chapter 17.

✔ **DVDs or CDs:** If both PCs have CD or DVD burners, you can transfer information by burning boatloads of discs. But be prepared for a *long* evening's work feeding discs to your PCs. Unless you're transferring a handful of files, this method is your slowest and most labor-intensive option.

✔ **Portable hard drive:** Costing between $100 and $200, a portable hard drive works well for transferring information from one PC to another. Most portable drives plug into both a wall outlet and your PC's USB port. (An empty iPod will work as a portable hard drive, in a pinch, if you already know how to store files on it.) 512 MB or larger Flash drives, those little memory sticks, also work for small transfers.

When your PCs live more than a cable's reach apart, a portable hard drive is your best transfer option. Choose one that's almost as large as the hard drive inside your PC. After transferring the files, put the portable hard drive to work backing up your files each night, an extremely prudent task I describe in Chapter 9.

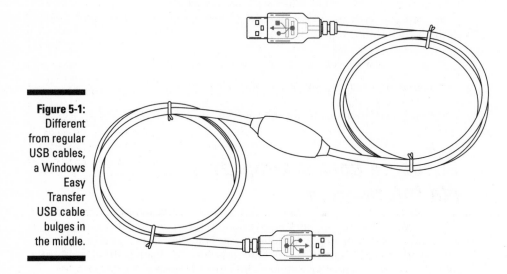

Figure 5-1:
Different from regular USB cables, a Windows Easy Transfer USB cable bulges in the middle.

Installing your old PC's programs onto your new PC

Although Windows Vista transfers your PC's data and settings, it doesn't copy the *programs* themselves. You must install all of your old PC's programs onto your new PC the old way — by installing them with their installation CDs or downloading their installation programs. And you need to install those programs *before* running the Easy Transfer program. That way, the programs will be ready to accept their incoming settings.

To install the old programs, dig out their installation CDs and any copy protection codes you might need to reenter. The codes are usually printed on the CD itself, the CD's packaging, or a sticker on the program's manual. (If you purchased a program online, you might be able to retrieve the copy-protection code from the manufacturer's Web site.)

Copying Windows Easy Transfer to your old PC

Copying Windows Easy Transfer onto your Windows XP PC is fairly easy — if your PC has a DVD drive, that is. Insert Windows Vista's installation DVD into your Windows XP PC's DVD drive. At the opening screen, choose Transfer Files and Settings from Another Computer, and Windows Easy Transfer hops onto the screen.

But if your decrepit Windows XP PC lacks a DVD drive or you lack a Vista DVD, install the Windows Easy Transfer program by following these steps:

1. **Open Windows Easy Transfer on your Vista PC and click Next at the program's opening screen.**

   Click Start, choose All Programs, click Accessories, click System Tools, and click Windows Easy Transfer. If asked, click Close All to close any currently running programs.

2. **Choose Start a New Transfer.**

   Vista asks whether you're running the program on your new PC or your old one.

3. **Choose My New Computer.**

   Vista asks whether you have an Easy Transfer cable.

4. **Choose No, Show Me More Options.**

   Choose this counterintuitive option even if you *do* have a Windows Easy Transfer cable.

5. **Choose No, I Need to Install It Now.**

   Vista offers to copy the Windows Easy Transfer program to a CD, USB flash drive, external hard drive, or shared network folder.

6. **Make your choice, and Vista creates a copy of the program to run on your old PC.**

   Vista stores the program in a folder named MigWiz. To run the program on your Windows XP PC, navigate to the MigWiz folder, open it, and double-click the program's cryptic name: migwiz or migwiz.exe.

Be sure to run the program's update command, if it has one. That tells it to connect with the Internet and install any updates or patches released since your purchase.

Transferring Information between Two PCs with Windows Easy Transfer

Depending on how you plan to transfer your files, Windows Easy Transfer works in just a few steps or a lengthy string of steps. But no matter how you choose to transfer the files, you'll move through these three basic procedures:

1. You tell the program how to transfer your information, be it through a single cable, a larger network, or on discs.

2. You tell Vista what information to collect from your old PC — everything from your user account? From *everybody's* user accounts?

3. You tell Vista which pieces of information should go into which user account.

After dispensing with those details, the program gets to work, grabbing everything you've chosen from your old PC and stuffing it into the appropriate places inside your new Vista PC.

The steps in this section describe how to make Windows Easy Transfer shuffle the information from your old PC to your new Vista PC.

Windows Easy Transfer requires an Administrator account. If you're stuck with a lowly Limited account, you won't be able to copy any files. And although some of the program's choices might seem confusing, don't fret: If you make the wrong choice, you can return to the previous screen by clicking the blue arrow in the window's top-left corner.

By far, the easiest way to transfer information between two PCs is with a Windows Easy Transfer Cable. It's cheap, built for the job, and limits your work to a few short decisions.

1. **Start both PCs and log on to each PC.**

   If you plan to transfer information through a USB Easy Transfer Cable, install the Easy Transfer Cable's bundled software onto your Windows XP PC now.

   Those particular cables are new to Windows XP, and the software lets Windows XP figure out how to use them. (Don't install the Easy Transfer Cable's bundled program on your Vista PC, as Vista already knows how to use a USB Easy Transfer Cable.)

2. **Run Windows Easy Transfer on your Windows XP PC, and click Next.**

   Insert Windows Vista's installation DVD into your Windows XP PC's DVD drive. At the opening screen, load the program by choosing Transfer Files and Settings from Another Computer.

   No DVD drive on your Windows XP PC? Then read this chapter's sidebar, "Copying Windows Easy Transfer to your old PC." It explains how to copy the program to your old PC.

3. **On your Windows XP PC, choose how to transfer files and settings to your new Vista PC.**

   The Easy Transfer program offers three options, as shown in Figure 5-2:

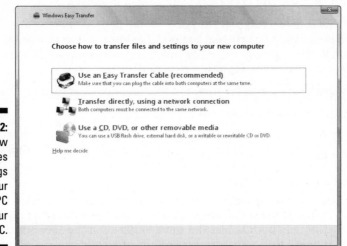

Figure 5-2:
Choose how
to copy files
and settings
from your
old PC
to your
new PC.

- *Use an Easy Transfer Cable (Recommended).* If you choose this quick 'n' easy option, connect the Easy Transfer Cable between USB ports on your Windows XP PC and your Windows Vista PC. When Windows Easy Transfer opens automatically on your Windows Vista PC, jump *way* ahead to Step 11.

- *Transfer Directly, Using a Network Connection.* If you choose to transfer through your PC's network, move to Step 5.

- *Use a CD, DVD, or Other Removable Media.* If you choose this option, move to the next step.

4. **Choose how to transfer your files and settings.**

   The program offers three options:

   - *CD or DVD:* This option works if your old PC can burn CDs or DVDs *and* your new PC has a CD or DVD drive for reading them. Be prepared to spend a long evening in front of both PCs, though, copying discs and feeding them to your new PC.

   - *USB Flash Drive:* Much quicker than CDs or DVDs, USB flash drives work for transferring smaller files. If you have lots of digital photos or other large files, though, be prepared to shuffle information back and forth with the flash drive.

   - *External Hard Disk or Network Location:* External hard disks (also called *portable hard drives*) plug into your PC's USB port to give it a big dose of storage space. They're your fastest and most reliable choice. If both PCs can connect to the same network location — a Public or Shared Documents folder on a third PC — you might choose that option, as well.

After making your choice, choose the drive letter of your CD/DVD burner, USB flash drive, external hard disk, or the path to your network location, and then create an optional password to keep your information secure. (You'll need to reenter that password on your Windows Vista PC to access the information.) Click Next and jump to Step 11.

5. **Choose how to transfer files and settings over a network.**

   The program offers two options:

   - *Use a Network Connection:* The most likely choice for small home networks, this option pipes the information straight from your Windows XP PC to your Windows Vista PC. If you choose this one, move to Step 6.

   - *Copy to and from a Network Location:* Choose this option for more esoteric networks where your PCs can't communicate directly, but they can both access the same location on the network. If you choose this, select the network location, choose an optional password, and move to Step 11.

6. **Choose whether or not you have a Windows Easy Transfer key.**

   Choose No, I Need a Key and then write down the key on a piece of paper. You'll need to enter that key later on your Vista PC. (Vista's *very* security conscious.)

7. **Move to your Windows Vista PC, run Windows Easy Transfer, and click Next.**

   Just as with Windows XP, Windows Vista lets only Administrator account holders use Windows Easy Transfer.

   Vista's Easy Transfer program asks whether you want to start a new transfer or continue one that's in progress.

8. **Choose Continue a Transfer in Progress.**

   The program asks whether the computers are connected to a network.

9. **Choose Yes, I'll Transfer Files and Settings Over the Network.**

   Vista might ask permission to let the Easy Transfer Program connect through your firewall. Click Yes to overcome this security hurdle. The program then asks you to type your Easy Transfer Key.

10. **Type the key you received in Step 6, click Next, and return to your Windows XP PC.**

    Don't have the key? It's still displayed on the monitor of your Windows XP computer. Type the key, and click Next. Vista connects to your Windows XP PC.

    Then return to your Windows XP PC and move to Step 11.

11. **On your Windows XP PC, choose which accounts and information to transfer to the new Vista PC.**

Windows Easy Transfer offers three ways to transfer your old PC's information, as shown in Figure 5-3:

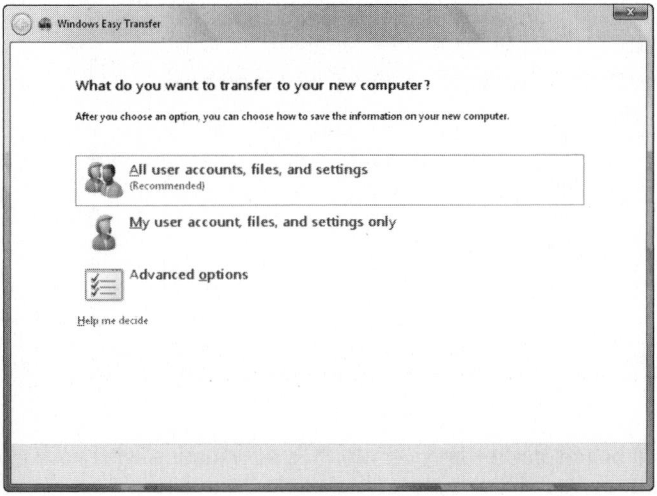

Figure 5-3:
Choose
which
information
to move
to your
new PC.

- *All User Accounts, Files, and Settings:* The best and simplest option for families moving to a newer PC, this option transfers information from every user account to the new PC.

- *Only My User Account, Files, and Settings:* This choice copies only information from your *own* user account. This option works well if you shared a PC with others, but now want to move your information to your own shiny new laptop or new PC.

- *Advanced Options:* Tossed in for the techies, this option lets you pick and choose exactly which files and settings to move. Today's PCs contain an overwhelming amount of files and settings, so it's not for the faint of heart.

If you're piping your information into your Windows Vista PC through an Easy Connect cable or network cable, sit down at your new Vista PC and jump to Step 16.

But if you're transferring your information in the other, more labor-intensive methods, move to the next step.

12. **Review your selected files and settings and click Transfer.**

The program lists all your selected files and settings, as shown in Figure 5-4. Note the size of your transfer, listed above the Transfer button. Click Customize to jump back to Step 11 for further fiddling; otherwise, click Transfer to keep the ball rolling.

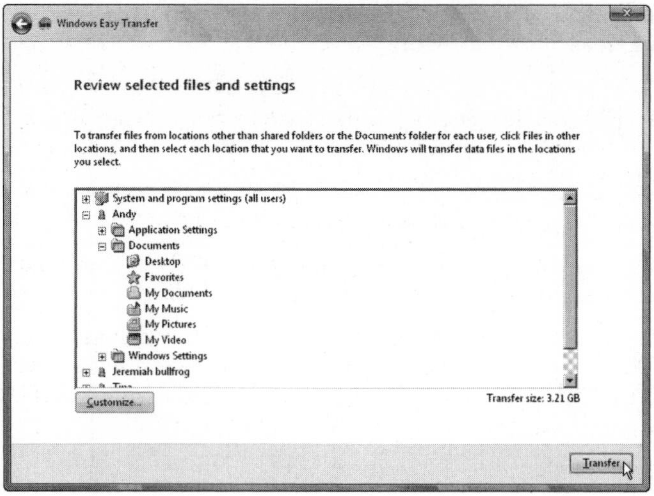

Figure 5-4:
Click
Transfer to
copy all your
selected
files and
settings.

Vista begins gathering your old PC's information with your chosen method:

- *Direct Network Connection:* If you chose this method, jump to Step 17.

- *CDs or DVDs:* Vista leads you through burning discs on your old PC to insert, in order, into your new PC. As you create each disc, write a number (CD1, CD2, CD3 . .) on its printed side with a felt-tip pen.

- *Drive:* Insert your portable hard drive or flash drive, if necessary, to store your precious data.

- *Network Location:* The program begins moving the information to the network location for your Vista PC to grab it.

When your PC finishes stashing that last bit of information, move to the next step to copy it all to your new PC.

13. **Go to your new Vista PC, open Windows Easy Transfer, and click Next at the opening screen.**

    If the program complains about any open programs, choose Close All to close them. The program then asks whether it should Start a New Transfer or Continue a Transfer in Progress.

14. **Choose Continue a Transfer in Progress.**

    Vista asks whether you're transferring the files through a network.

15. **Choose No, I've Copied Files and Settings to a CD, DVD, or Other Removable Media.**

    Vista asks where you've stored the incoming files.

16. **Choose the location of the disc or drive containing the files and click Next.**

    Tell the program the incoming files' exact location: the letter of your CD or DVD drive, for example, the drive letter of your USB flash drive or external hard drive, or, if you've saved the information someplace on a network, the path to the network location.

    Enter your password, if you password-protected the files.

    When you make your choice, Vista immediately begins looking in that spot to make sure that the information's there.

    If you choose CDs or DVDs, Vista leads you through inserting CDs or DVDs, in order, into your new PC. If you're using a flash drive, Vista leads you through collecting information on the old PC and shuffling it to the new one. (You might need to take several trips.)

17. **Choose names for the transferred accounts and click Next.**

    Vista needs to know where to put the incoming user account information. The window lists the names of the incoming user accounts on the left, and the PC's existing user accounts on the right, as shown in Figure 5-5. That leaves you three possible scenarios:

    • *Same user account names:* If you've used the same user account names on both your old and new PCs, this step is easy: Vista automatically lines up the accounts on the two PCs so that they go to the right places.

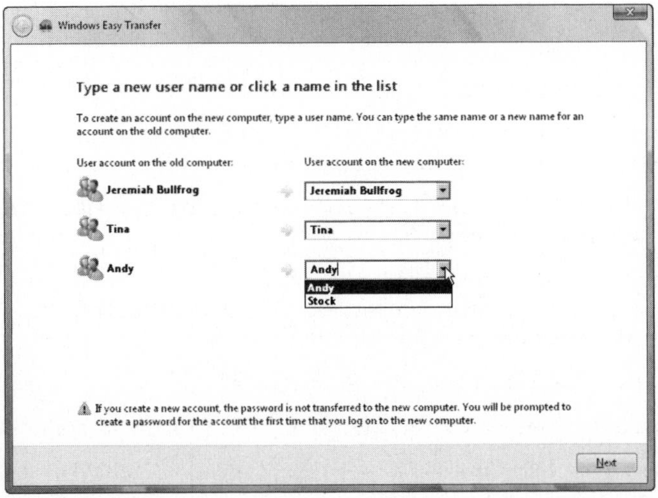

Figure 5-5: Match the existing user account on the left with its new destination on the right.

• *Different user account names:* If some or all account names are *different* on both PCs, tell Vista which information goes into which account. Use the drop-down menus to match up the old PC's user account name with the new user account names on the new PC.

• *New user account names:* To transfer a user account's files to a brand-new account, type that new account name into the top of the adjacent drop-down menu. The Easy Transfer program creates that new account on your new Vista PC.

18. **Review your selected files and, depending on your transfer option, click Next or Transfer.**

    Vista begins copying your chosen information into your new PC, creating new accounts as needed. Depending on the amount of information, your transfer method, and your PCs' processing power, the job can take from minutes to several hours.

    The program ends by summing up all the information it moved, leaving you wondering how you'd ever get by without it.

If you transferred your information with CDs or DVDs, stash the discs in a safe place so they can serve as emergency backups. If some disaster befouls your new PC, you'll at least have your old PC's information safe.

Part II

Beefing Up Your PC for Windows Vista, Games, and Video

The 5th Wave   By Rich Tennant

"Well, the first level of Windows Vista security seems good—I can't get the shrink-wrapping off."

In this part . . .

*V*ista's the latest version of Windows, and this part
of the book helps you get your PC in shape for
Microsoft's most powerful Windows version yet.

You start by finding out whether your old PC's able to run
Vista at all and where its weak spots lie. The subsequent
chapters each tackle those weak spots.

For example, one chapter explains how to meet Vista's
biggest demand: a powerful new video card. It walks you
through choosing the right card, putting it in the right slot
inside your PC, and fine-tuning its picture.

The next two chapters show how to add more memory
and a larger hard drive — perhaps even a second one —
to your PC.

After beefing up your PC's power, it might be time for
another upgrade covered here: your power supply. All
those new parts might overwhelm your old one.

Chapter 6

Discovering How Well Your PC Will Run Windows Vista

In This Chapter

▶ Understanding Vista's hardware requirements

▶ Running Vista's Upgrade Advisor

▶ Identifying parts that need upgrading

▶ Buying the right parts from the right place

*I*f your current PC is less than two years old and already runs Windows XP, your PC should be able to run Vista with only a few upgrades. The problem is finding out exactly which ones.

To make things easier, Microsoft offers the Vista Upgrade Advisor, a freebie program offered for download on Microsoft's Windows Vista Web site. The program probes your PC, examines its parts and programs, and lists exactly what items will and won't work under Vista.

This chapter explains how to find and run Vista's Upgrade Advisor, understand its advice, and buy the right parts for your PC from the best vendors.

Understanding Vista's Hardware Requirements

Although Microsoft released Vista in early 2007, Microsoft didn't design Vista to run perfectly on the current crop of PCs. Instead, Microsoft's engineers envisioned the PCs we'll all be running a year or two down the road and designed Vista around those powerhouses. Indeed, some Vista features support parts that weren't even available when Vista's boxes first hit the store shelves.

To help you see what Vista expects out of a PC, Table 6-1 lists the bare minimum of oomph your PC needs to run Vista, as well as what it needs to run Vista *well*.

Table 6-1	Vista's System Requirements
Microsoft's Recommended Requirements	**What You Really Need**
Processor running at 800MHz or faster	1 GHz or faster
512MB memory (RAM)	1GB memory
DirectX 9 compatible with 32 MB of video memory	128MB video memory (Video RAM) and DirectX 9 compatible
At least 20GB hard drive with 15GB free	At least 40GB hard drive with 15GB free
DVD drive	DVD burner

Vista comes in several versions, each with its own slightly different requirements. Table 6-2 explains the extra parts to consider if you want to run everything Vista has to offer.

Table 6-2	Requirements for Vista's Programs
The Part	**The Vista Feature**
TV tuner	Vista's Media Center
DVD burner	DVD Maker
Hybrid hard drive	Windows ReadyDrive

Running Vista's Upgrade Advisor

Windows Vista comes in four main versions: Home, Home Premium, Business, and Ultimate. And each of those four versions requires slightly different things from your PC. To help you choose the right version for your PC, Microsoft's Windows Vista Upgrade Advisor lets you see how well Vista will run for each of those four versions.

The program displays a list of problems — perhaps your PC needs more hard disk space or memory, or some of your computer's parts need Vista-compatible drivers. Then the Windows Vista Upgrade Advisor finishes up with a list of tasks you must perform both before and after slipping that Vista installation DVD into your PC's drive.

Follow these steps to install the Windows Vista Upgrade Advisor, find out its recommendations, and understand what they mean to your particular PC.

1. **Download and install Microsoft's Windows Vista Upgrade Advisor software.**

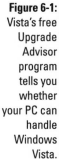

Download the software from Microsoft's Web site at `www.microsoft.com/windowsvista/getready/upgradeadvisor` and save it onto your PC. Double-click the program's icon, shown in the margin, to install it onto your PC. Let it leave a shortcut icon on your desktop for easy loading.

During installation, don't be surprised if the program asks to download some additional Microsoft programs in order to carry out its mission.

2. **Start the Upgrade Advisor program.**

Double-click the Windows Vista Upgrade Advisor program icon (shown in the margin), and the program appears on the screen, as shown in Figure 6-1.

Figure 6-1: Vista's free Upgrade Advisor program tells you whether your PC can handle Windows Vista.

3. **Plug in and turn on all your PC's accessories, and then click Start Scan.**

Plug them *all* in: Your printer, MP3 player, scanner, external hard drive, webcam, microphone, speakers, PDA, cell phone, and anything else you can find. Make sure everything's turned on so the Upgrade Advisor program can find them all.

The program takes a few minutes to scan your PC and identify its parts and software. Then it heads for the Internet to check its database, seeing if they'll play nicely with Vista.

 4. **When the scan completes, click the See Details button to view the program's recommendations.**

 When it's through scanning, the Upgrade Advisor recommends one of Vista's four main versions for your particular PC. The Upgrade Advisor usually recommends Vista's Business version on PCs running Windows XP Professional; if you're running Windows XP Home Edition, the advisor usually recommends Vista's Home Premium version.

 But no matter which version the Upgrade Advisor initially recommends for your PC, the dirt's in the three See Details buttons, shown along the window's bottom in Figure 6-2. There, the advisor spells out exactly how your PC fared in these categories:

 • *System Requirements:* Here, Vista lists the items you need to add, upgrade, or replace in order to run a particular version of Vista. If the advisor recommended Vista Home Premium, for instance, the Upgrade Advisor will check to see if your PC has a Vista-compatible TV tuner.

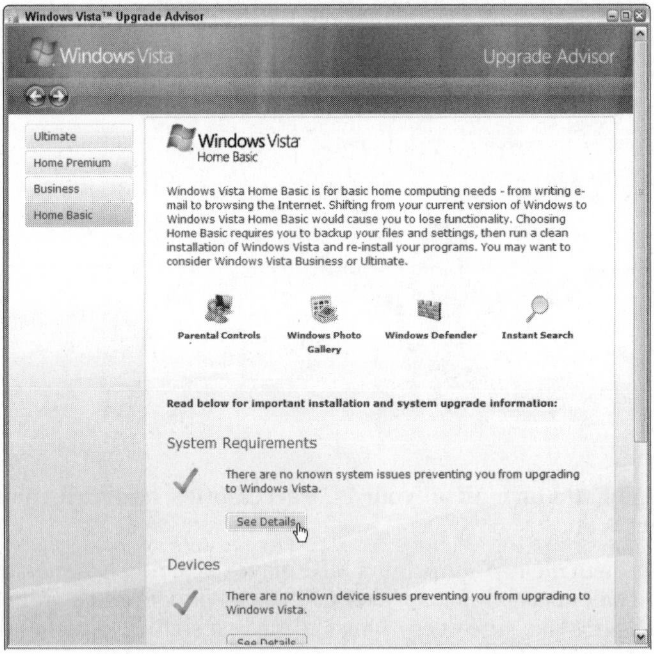

Figure 6-2:
Click the Show Details buttons in each category to see how well your PC will handle that particular version of Vista.

 • *Devices:* In this category, Vista lists your PC's parts that don't work with Vista. These parts usually don't need to be replaced, however. Instead, you can make them work by finding and installing a Vista-compatible *driver* — tech talk for a certain type of software. I cover finding and installing Vista-compatible drivers in Chapter 19.

If the Upgrade Advisor program says you need updated drivers for your *network adapter*, *modem*, or *wireless network card*, find and download those drivers while you're still running Windows XP. Then burn them to a CD. Later, after you upgrade to Vista, Vista can install those drivers from your handy CD. That extra legwork on your part lets Vista connect to the Internet immediately.

• *Programs:* This category lists any programs that won't run under Vista. Visit the program manufacturer's Web site to see whether they offer free upgrades or force you to buy new Vista-compatible versions.

The Upgrade Advisor usually finds a few problems or incompatibilities with every PC. Don't be surprised to see some flagged items.

5. Click other Vista versions you're interested in running.

Although the Upgrade Advisor initially recommends one version for your PC, you're certainly not limited to that version. Click any of the other Vista versions listed along the window's left, shown in Figure 6-2, to see how your PC would fare with Ultimate, Home Premium, Business, or Home Basic. Each version requires slightly different things from a PC; Vista Ultimate is the most demanding, and Vista Home Basic isn't very picky at all.

Although Vista Home Basic works fine for basic Web browsing and word processing, most people will want Vista Home Premium, with its built-in photo editor, DVD slide-show creator, and digital video recorder. Be sure to see how well your PC runs that version.

6. Create a printout of your PC's Tasks page.

After clicking one of the See Details buttons, shown in Figure 6-2, click the Task List, shown in Figure 6-3, to see what you need to do to run that Vista version on your PC.

At the top of the Task List in Figure 6-3, the program shows my PC's current configuration — that's what my PC *has*, not what it needs. Below that, the program lists things I need to do before installing that particular Vista version. Usually, the suggestions start by saying to run Windows Update, which often finds drivers for the parts listed in the Devices category. You may need to uninstall some incompatible programs, as well, before upgrading to Vista.

Be sure to click the Print Task List link in the top right corner. (See Figure 6-3.) That creates a handy list of everything you need to upgrade or fix before installing Vista.

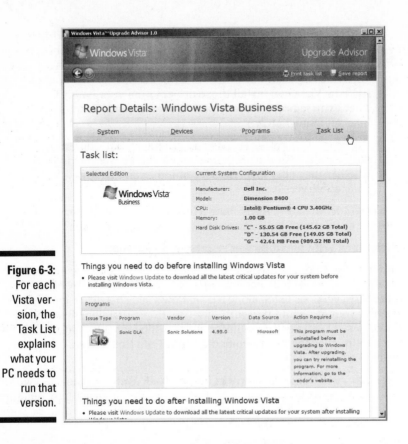

Figure 6-3:
For each Vista version, the Task List explains what your PC needs to run that version.

Understanding Parts That Need Upgrading

Although Microsoft's charts and tables spell out exactly what your PC needs to run Vista and its many programs, some of the Upgrade Advisor's recommendations sound more like techtalk than advice. Here's the breakdown on the specific items the Upgrade Advisor flags most often.

TV tuner card/TV output

Microsoft's hoping that Vista will sneak into your living room. Unlike Windows XP, Vista comes with a built-in *digital video recorder* – a device that automatically records your favorite TV shows so you can watch them later. Vista records TV shows through its *Windows Media Center* software. (Don't confuse Media Center with Windows Media *Player,* the music and video playing software Windows has had for years.)

Before Media Center can record your TV shows, it needs a TV tuner to grab specific shows. The best TV tuners come on little cards that fit inside your PC. If you're not ready to pop open your PC's case, buy a TV tuner that plugs into one of your PC's USB ports.

When Vista says you need a TV tuner card, it also says you also need a *TV output* — a port for you to pipe your PC's video into your TV set. Luckily, most TV tuners include TV output, so you needn't worry about this one. (I cover TV tuners, TV output, and connecting your PC to your TV set in Chapter 12.)

Only Vista *Home Premium* or Vista *Ultimate* include Windows Media Center; the other Vista versions leave it out.

CPU (Central Processing Unit)

This one's a make or break deal. If the Upgrade Advisor says your CPU isn't powerful enough to run Vista, you're stuck. A CPU is often the most expensive part of a PC. When your CPU needs upgrading, many of your PC's other parts should probably be replaced, too, to bring your PC up to speed. Buying a new PC is usually less expensive.

When shopping for a new PC, make sure it's either running Vista or has a Microsoft-approved "Windows Vista Capable" or "Windows Vista Premium Ready" sticker. The budget models may run Vista *slowly*, but Vista *will* still run.

DVD or DVD R/W (Digital Video Disk Read/Write)

Vista comes on a DVD, so your PC needs a DVD drive simply to install Vista. But if you're aiming to store information or movies onto your *own* DVDs, make sure your DVD drive can also write to DVDs.

Most DVD drives sold today can write as well as read from DVDs. Installing a DVD R/W drive is a fairly simple and inexpensive upgrade I cover in Chapter 15.

RAM (Random Access Memory)

If Vista says your PC needs more memory, there's some good news: Memory is fairly inexpensive. Unfortunately, installing memory requires opening your PC's case — there's no way around that one. Once you've popped open the case, though, installing memory is fairly simple. I describe how to buy and install the right type of memory for your PC in Chapter 8.

Don't confuse *system* memory with *graphics* memory, as they're two different things. Your PC's graphics adapter, described in the next section, needs its own memory to create graphics. Shadows must be calculated, curves must be smoothed, all as quickly as possible.

Graphics adapter

Your PC's graphics adapter translates Vista's numbers into pictures that it displays onto your monitor as your Windows desktop. Chances are your current monitor will still work fine with Vista. The problem is your PC's graphics adapter, often called a *video card*.

Your PC can display graphics either of two ways:

- ✔ **Onboard video:** Inexpensive computers drop the price tag by tossing a few inexpensive graphics chips inside your PC. Onboard video works fine for word processing and office work, but it doesn't pack enough oomph for graphics-intensive programs: PC games, movie making, and much of Windows Vista.

  Affixed to your PC's motherboard, onboard video chips usually share some of your PC's RAM, keeping the PC's price low.

- ✔ **Video card:** More expensive computers devote a large amount of power entirely to graphics. Video cards are separate boards that push into a slot inside your PC. Video cards come with their own circuits, memory, and cooling systems. All those things drive their price upwards from $50 to several hundred dollars. Sliding a video card into your PC lets you upgrade your PC's graphics as far as your wallet extends.

To see whether your PC has onboard video or a video card, look at where your monitor's cord plugs into your PC. If the cord plugs in next to ports for your speakers, USB gadgets, and printer, your PC has *onboard video*. If it plugs in a more isolated port that lives on a long silver strip, your PC has a *video card*. I explain how to upgrade your PC's video card in Chapter 7.

Hard drive

Vista installs on any hard drive that has at least 15GB of free space. But if that's all the room your hard drive has left, don't bother installing Vista. You need room for your programs and files, as well. Even 100GB of space can fill up fairly quickly, especially if you're saving lots of digital photos, music, or movies.

When upgrading, buy the largest hard drive you can afford. And if you don't want to install one inside your PC's case, buy an external hard drive that plugs into one of your PC's USB ports. I cover hard drives in Chapter 9.

Choosing the Right Parts from the Right Place

When your PC needs a new or replacement part, you're left with two problems. You need to choose a particular brand and model, and you need to decide where to buy it for the best price.

There's no right or wrong answer for either dilemma, so this section explores how to narrow your choices to arrive at a decision that works for your budget and time frame.

Choosing the right brand and model

There's no "perfect" or "best" part. And even if there was such a thing, the fast pace of technology guarantees that a better part will replace it within a few months. So instead of spending your time looking for that mythical best part, look for one that simply meets your current needs. Here's how to narrow your choices.

- ✔ **Ask the opinions of others.** Start by asking your tech-savvy friends what they recommend. No tech-savvy friends? Then drop by online shopping sites like Amazon (www.amazon.com) and Newegg (www.newegg.com) and read the reviews left by other customers. You might not understand everything somebody says about a particular item. But you'll be able to stay away from the lemons, and that's half the battle.

- ✔ **Check your budget.** The newest and most powerful items command a premium price, but their price drops a few months later, when the more powerful replacement enters the market. Instead of buying the latest and greatest, buy what *was* the latest and greatest a few months ago.

- ✔ **Read professional reviews.** Lots of computer magazines and Web sites review new parts when they come out. Pick up a copy of *PC World* magazine, for instance, or drop by its Web site (www.pcworld.com) to read reviews. Tom's Hardware (www.tomshardware.com) also reviews products regularly.

As you read the reviews, keep in mind which brands receive consistently bad reviews. Then, when faced with a dizzying array of choices on the store shelves, you'll know which brands to avoid.

Buying locally versus buying online

When you need something immediately, buy locally. You'll pay a higher price than shopping online, but you'll have the part in your hands as soon as you drive to the store. You'll pay a premium price, but the extra cost lets you buy something quickly, with all its packaging, and without any shipping charges. And if the part's defective or you've purchased the wrong one, you can return it for a refund fairly easily.

When you're in no particular hurry, though, buy your parts online. Instead of choosing from a shelf or two of items, you can browse quickly through dozens of stores, all with large inventories, with prices that beat what you'll find locally.

Don't shop online by price alone, though, or you may face shipping delays or outright scams. Instead, find an online vendor you can trust and stick with them. Before ordering, check the shipping charges and return policies, as well.

Chapter 7

Beefing Up Your PC's Video

. . . .

. . . .

*W*hen engineers sat down at their poker table many years ago to design computers, they decided on a quick and easy way to add and upgrade them. Upgrades would come on *cards*, they decreed. To upgrade the computer, owners simply slide the card into one of several standard-sized slots built into every computer. Simple.

And today, that's still how you upgrade your PC's video: You slide a card into a slot inside your PC. This chapter covers that specific task in minute detail:

   ✔ Finding out what type of video slot lives inside your PC

   ✔ Buying a more powerful video card to match that slot

   ✔ Pushing the card into that slot

Dig in.

Understanding Video Buzzwords

Few parts inside your PC generate as many buzzwords as its *video* — the circuits that create the visuals you see on your monitor. Here's the rundown on the fine print you'll see living on computer sales sheets, requirement lists, and boxes lining the store shelves.

Video card: The most powerful (and expensive) video circuitry lives on a little *card*. Cards are small replaceable circuit boards that slip into slots inside your PC. By adding or replacing a card inside your PC, you can upgrade its video fairly easily.

Video slot: One of three specially designed slots built to accept a video card. Video cards come in three types, and each fits into a slightly different video slot.

Video memory: This memory is dedicated entirely to your PC's video circuits — nothing else inside your PC can borrow any of it. The more detail the video card can display, the more memory it needs to create the images. Vista runs best with at least 256MB of video memory.

Don't confuse *video* memory with your *computer's* memory. Video memory comes with the video card to help it generate and display pictures. Your PC's regular memory is filled with your programs and files.

Driver: A piece of software that lets Windows talk to your hardware — in this case, your video card. Without the right driver, your part won't work properly. Chapter 19 covers drivers in excruciating detail.

Port: A computer buzzword for *connector,* this is one of many little stubs on your PC where you plug in cables. The plug on the end of your monitor's cable must match your PC's video port.

TV Out Port: This sends a signal not to your PC monitor, but to a regular TV set.

 VGA (Video Graphics Array) port: Created in the mid-'80s, this early standard for displaying graphics lives on today. Most PCs come with a VGA port, and most monitors still plug into them. (VGA ports are almost always blue.)

Digital video port: A newer type of video port, this sends numbers to a flat-panel monitor, which displays them as pictures. (To keep things simple, many flat-panel monitors also plug into VGA ports.)

DirectX: Software that programmers use to create advanced visual tricks with video circuitry. Many games use DirectX to display three-dimensional fire-breathing dragons and other spectacular effects. Vista requires video that can handle DirectX version 9, known as *DirectX 9c.*

Discovering What Video Circuitry Is inside Your PC

Microsoft refers to video circuits as *video display adapters,* but the rest of the world usually calls them *video cards*. Video cards can plug into either of three different types of slots, so your first job is to find out which video slot lives inside your PC.

You may need to open your PC's case, a simple chore explained on the Cheat Sheet in the front of this book. After you're inside your PC's case, look at Figure 7-1: It shows the motherboard, the flat bed of circuitry that lives inside your PC. Everything inside your PC attaches to the motherboard, including the video card. (See Color Plates 8 and 9 in the color insert pages in this book for labeled photos of motherboards.)

The rest of this section explains the types of video you find in PCs today and how to figure out exactly which one lives inside your PC.

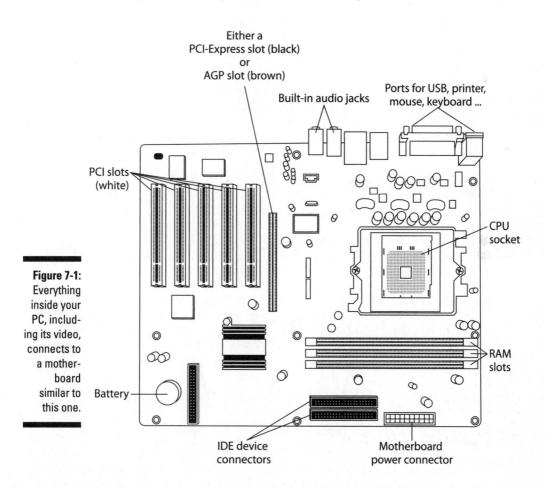

Figure 7-1: Everything inside your PC, including its video, connects to a motherboard similar to this one.

Onboard video

Older, cheaper, and less powerful computers come with *onboard video*. That term means the video circuits live directly on your PC's *motherboard*, the large flat platter inside your PC that all the computer's other parts connect to. The video has been reduced to a few low-power chips and tossed onto the motherboard.

Look where your monitor's cable plugs into your PC, as shown in Figure 7-2. If the cable plugs in near where your mouse and keyboard plug in, your PC is cursed with onboard video.

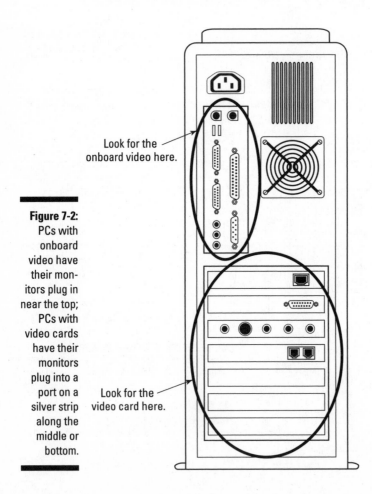

Look for the onboard video here.

Figure 7-2:
PCs with onboard video have their monitors plug in near the top; PCs with video cards have their monitors plug into a port on a silver strip along the middle or bottom.

Look for the video card here.

Onboard video can be upgraded by slipping a video card into the PC's unused video slot. The next section explains how to see which type of video slot lives inside your PC so you can slip the right type of video card into it.

Almost all laptops come with onboard video. Unfortunately, none of them have a video slot. That means you can't upgrade their video, nor can most laptops access Vista's most graphics-intensive features. Contact your laptop's manufacturer to see if they support video upgrades for your model, but don't be surprised when they say no.

Video cards

More powerful (and more expensive) PCs don't bother with the slow onboard video described in the previous section. Instead, they rely on a *video card* — a circuit-filled card that slides into a matching slot inside your PC.

To see whether your computer has a video card, look where the monitor's cable plugs into your PC. If the cable plugs into a port on a long strip that's relatively far away from where your mouse and keyboard plug in, as shown in Figure 7-2, your PC has a video card.

The hard part is narrowing down which type of slot your video card fits into. All PCs come with at least one of these three types of slots that accept video cards: PCI, AGP, or PCI-Express. Upgrading the PC is as simple as sliding the right card into the right slot.

The rest of this section explains these three types of slots and cards and how to figure out which type of card you need for your PC.

PCI (Peripheral Component Interconnect)

The slowest and oldest of the three types of slots that accept video, PCI slots sit in a row on your PC's motherboard. Most PCs come with three to five PCI slots, shown earlier in Figure 7-1. (Figure 7-3 shows a close-up of a PCI card slipping into a PCI slot.) Most PCs sold before the late 1990s came with a video card in one of their PCI slots.

Quick identifier: PCI slots sit together in an evenly spaced row of three or more. They're almost always white, and every PC has several PCI slots. PCI slots accept many breeds of cards, including modems, TV tuners, network adapters, and more, so don't be surprised to see a few other cards plugged in nearby. For easy identification of a PCI card, turn to Color Plate 14 in this book's color insert. The photo shows a PCI card and its dimensions. You can see several white PCI slots in Color Plates 17 and 18.

Upgrade options: Vista's arrival has spawned a new flow of PCI video cards to capture the older-PC market. You should find a Vista-compatible replacement fairly easily. But if your PC has an AGP or PCI-Express slot, both described next, upgrade to one of those type of cards, instead: They're *much* faster.

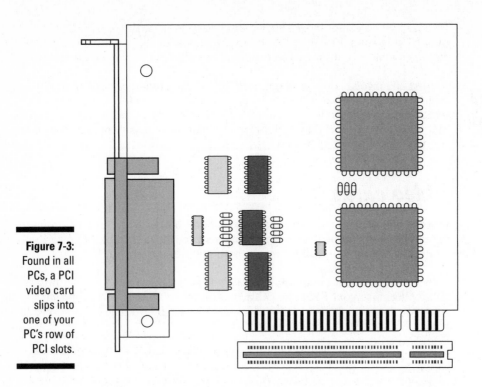

Figure 7-3:
Found in all PCs, a PCI video card slips into one of your PC's row of PCI slots.

AGP (Accelerated Graphics Port)

As graphics became more powerful and detailed, the old PCI slots couldn't keep up. The engineers solved the problem by adding a single AGP slot next to the row of PCI cards. Built specifically for video cards, the speedy AGP cards appeared on PCs sold mostly in the late 1990s through 2005.

Quick identifier: Shown in Figure 7-4, an AGP slot is usually chocolate brown and offset a bit from the row of PCI slots. The bottom of the AGP card in Figure 7-4 has one notch; some AGP cards add a second notch. For easy identification of an AGP card, turn to Color Plate 15 in this book's color insert. The photo shows an AGP card and its dimensions. You can see a chocolate brown AGP slot in Color Plate 17.

Upgrade options: AGP video cards and slots have moved through several revisions, called 1X, 2X, 4X, and 8X. However, most PCs sold since the late 1990s accept either 4X or 8X AGP cards — the type sold in stores today. AGP slots accept only AGP cards.

PCI-Express (Peripheral Component Interconnect-Express)

Once again, as computer graphics became more powerful, the aging AGP standard couldn't keep up. The solution came with a PCI-Express slot, which replaced the AGP slot. PCI-Express slots appear on most PCs sold since 2005. PCI-Express slots come in different sizes.

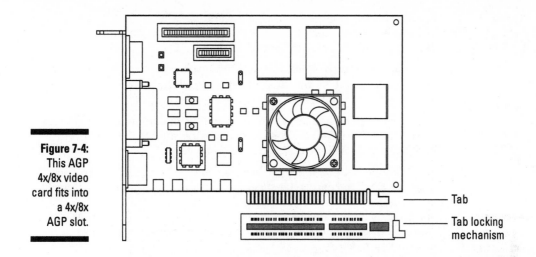

Figure 7-4:
This AGP
4x/8x video
card fits into
a 4x/8x
AGP slot.

Tab

Tab locking
mechanism

Quick identifier: PCI-Express slots are usually black and are set off a bit from the row of PCI cards. Note how the card's bottom, shown in Figure 7-5, has one tiny tab and one long one. The tabs on AGP cards, by contrast, are more evenly spaced. Although PCI-Express slots come in several sizes, the vast majority of video cards come in the largest size, called 16x. For easy identification of a PCI-Express card, turn to Color Plate 16 in this book's color insert. The photo shows a PCI-Express card and its dimensions. You can see a black 16x PCI-Express slot in Color Plate 18, as well as two 1x PCI-Express slots.

Upgrade options: PCI-Express 16x video cards are widely available.

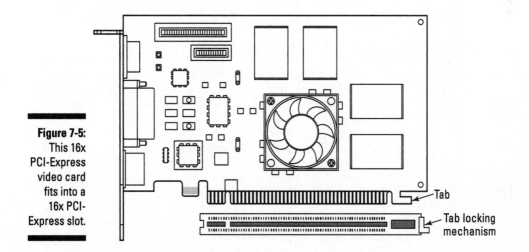

Figure 7-5:
This 16x
PCI-Express
video card
fits into a
16x PCI-
Express slot.

Tab

Tab locking
mechanism

✔ For most video upgraders, the big question is whether to buy an AGP or PCI-Express video card. The answer depends simply on which type of video slot your PC has: AGP or PCI-Express.

✔ When in doubt as to which slot your PC has, look at the tiny white letters printed on the motherboard next to the slots. You'll spot the letters *AGP* next to AGP slots, for example.

✔ Each type of slot works only with its own type of card. An AGP card won't work in a PCI or PCI-Express slot, for instance, nor will a PCI-Express card work in an AGP or PCI slot.

✔ Slots sit together in a long row, like rake marks left in dirt. When you plug in a card, the card's flat *silver* end rests against the back of your PC, allowing its ports to protrude from the back of the PC's case. Don't be confused by other slots you may spot on your motherboard — the smaller, thinner slots you may see are reserved for memory (see Chapter 8 for more about memory).

✔ Computer gurus refer to the row of slots as your computer's *expansion bus*.

✔ When in doubt as to your computer's type of video port, check your PC's manual or download SiSoftware Sandra Standard (www.sisoftware.co.uk), a popular free utility that reveals lots of boring information about your computer's innards — including its video card and slot.

Installing a new video card

Difficulty level: Easy

Tools you need: One hand and a screwdriver

Cost: Anywhere from $50 to $200 or more

Stuff to watch out for: Cards are particularly susceptible to static electricity. Tap your computer's case to ground yourself before touching the card. If you live in a particularly dry, static-prone area, wear latex gloves — the kind that doctors and dentists wear.

Cards are delicate, so don't bend them. Handle them only by their edges, as the oil from your fingers can damage their circuitry. Finally, those little silver dots on one side of the card are sharp metal pokers that leave ugly scratches on your skin.

When shopping for a new video card, make sure it's the same type that fits in your PC's video slot, either PCI, AGP, or PCI-Express. Make sure it also has a TV-Out port if you plan on connecting your PC to your TV.

To install a video card — or any other type of card, for that matter — follow these steps:

1. **Turn off your computer, unplug it, and remove the cover.**

   Don't know how that cover comes off? Flip to the Cheat Sheet at the front of this book for the answers.

2. **Locate the right slot for your card.**

   Line up Figure 7-1 with what you see on your own PC's motherboard to identify your computer's expansion slots and locate the right one for your card. Check Color Plate 17 in the color insert pages in this book to see a motherboard in full, glorious color. Don't confuse your computer's row of expansion slots with its memory slots.

   If you have a lot of room, keep your cards spaced as far apart as possible. That helps keep them cooler.

3. **Remove the slot's cover if necessary.**

   If you're replacing a card, skip this step.

   Unused slots often have a little cover next to them to keep dust from flying in through the back of your computer. With a small screwdriver, remove the screw that holds that cover in place, as shown in Figure 7-6. (Turn to the color insert pages in this book and take a look at Color Plates 19 and 20 to see this step in color.) Don't lose that screw! You need it to secure the card in place.

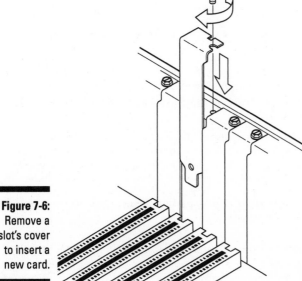

Figure 7-6:
Remove a slot's cover to insert a new card.

Dropped the screw in there somewhere? Keep poking at it with a screwdriver or chopstick until you get it out. If you lose the screw inside the computer, your computer could electrocute itself.

If the screw's still lost inside your PC, pick up your computer and shake it upside down until the screw falls out. Keep the screw handy, and keep the little cover bracket, too.

4. **Push the card into its slot.**

   When you've identified the card's appropriate slot, hold the card by its edges and position it over the correct slot. (See Color Plates 22 and 23 in the color insert pages.) The edge with the shiny metal bracket should face toward the *back* of your computer. (That shiny bracket replaces the cover you removed in Step 3.)

   Line up the tabs and notches on the card's bottom with the notches in the slot. Push the card slowly into the slot. You may need to rock the card back and forth gently. When the card pops in, you can feel it come to rest. Don't force it!

   Don't let any card come into contact with any other card. That can cause electrical problems, and neither the card nor the computer will work.

   Some but not all AGP and PCI-Express video slots have a little retaining clip that fits over a tab on the end of the video card. Slide the clip so it holds down the card tightly.

5. **Secure the card in the slot with the screw.**

   Yep, your expensive new video card is held in place by one screw.

6. **Plug the computer back in, turn it on, and see whether Windows recognizes and installs the card.**

   Windows usually recognizes newly installed cards and sets them up to work correctly. If something goes wrong, head for Chapter 19 for quick-fix tips about installing drivers. If everything's working, however, put your PC's cover back on.

   Whenever you install a new video card or any other card, be sure to visit the manufacturer's Web site to download and install the latest drivers. Card manufacturers, especially video card manufacturers, constantly update their drivers to fix bugs.

   If the card doesn't work after you've installed the latest drivers, head for the next section: Troubleshooting.

Troubleshooting a Card That Doesn't Work

When you turn your PC back on, Windows usually greets the card with excitement and either kick starts it into action or asks for drivers. That's when it's time to run any installation programs that came with the card, usually tucked away on a CD. Visit the manufacturer's Web site to download and install the latest drivers.

General troubleshooting tips

Still doesn't work? Then try the following:

- You often need to restart your PC before a card will work correctly.

- Make sure that the card is seated securely in its slot and screwed in tightly.

- Nine times out of ten, the problem lies with the software. Although the card is sitting in the slot correctly, the software conflicts with some other card or driver. A new driver often cures it, a fix described in Chapter 19.

- Sometimes newer computers don't get along with older cards. I had an older video capture card that disabled my USB ports for years. Eventually, I replaced the capture card with a USB capture box, and everything works fine.

If one of your older cards stops working, turn off your computer, unplug it, remove the cover, and remove the card. Then take a plain old pencil eraser and rub it over the contacts on the part of the card that fits into the slot. (Be slow and gentle.) This can remove any corrosion or buildup of crud. Also, try pushing the card more firmly into its slot. Sometimes, the cards creep up and out with age.

Dealing with a card that just doesn't seem to fit

Unlike other computer organs, expansion cards have remained remarkably uncomplicated over the years: You push it into the right slot, and it works. If the card's tabs don't fit into the slot, you're pushing them into the wrong type of slot.

Sometimes the tabs aren't the problem, but the card's length and girth are, as those vary wildly depending on the card's designer. Some cards are stubby, others stretch several inches past their neighbors. Some come packed with cooling fans and other circuitry that makes them very thick.

When a card bumps into its neighbors, it's time to rearrange them. Move the cards to different slots, trying different positions until they all fit. It's like packing bags in the car trunk in the grocery store parking lot. You have to try different combinations before the trunk lid will close.

If your cards refuse to pack themselves into your PC, though, single out the wide one that's causing the most trouble and look into buying a USB replacement.

Chapter 8

Adding More Memory

· ·

In This Chapter

▶ Understanding types of memory

▶ Buying the right type and amount of memory

▶ Installing additional memory

▶ Fixing memory problems

· ·

Adding memory is one of the most popular upgrades today, especially for people upgrading to Windows Vista. It's also one of the easiest and cheapest upgrades around. Years ago, memory actually cost more per ounce than gold; computer stores doled it out to the highest bidder. Today, cheap memory chips are sold at your local discount warehouse store, often near the bulk-pack blank CDs.

What exactly *is* memory? When your computer's CPU (Central Processing Unit) tells your computer what to do, it needs a scratch pad for taking notes. Memory works as that scratch pad. The more memory your PC has, the larger the scratchpad, and the more complicated stuff your PC can do. You can run more programs, and more quickly.

This chapter explains the many types of memory, their unfortunate acronyms, how to buy the specific type of memory your PC needs, and how to snap the new memory into the right spot inside your PC.

Understanding Memory Buzzwords

This entire section's tossed in only for those curious about all the awful buzzwords surrounding memory, as well as the different types of memory you'll see for sale. You don't need to know any of this stuff. If you're only looking for a quick way to upgrade your PC's memory, jump to the later section, "Deciding What Memory to Buy."

Still here? Then here's the primer: No matter what type of memory your computer uses, it comes on *chips* — flat black things. (Your CPU comes on a chip, too.) Just as CPUs are rated by their power and speed, memory chips are rated by their storage capacity and speed.

Although all the memory serves the same purpose, it comes in several different packages. How do you know which type you need? The answer lies with your PC's motherboard — the flat panel inside your PC where all your PC's parts connect. Different types of motherboards use different types, speeds, and sizes of memory. If you buy the wrong type of memory, your PC won't be able to use it.

The main types of memory

Although manufacturers have created many types of memory over the years, all of the memory looks pretty much the same: A fiberglass strip about four inches long and an inch tall, with little notches in its sides and edges.

Different types of memory fit into different types of *sockets* — little slots that hold the strip's bottom and sides. The notches on the memory module must mesh with the dividers and holders on their sockets. If they don't line up, you're inserting the wrong type of memory into the socket.

To see what type of memory you have, compare its notches with the ones pictured in this chapter.

A memory module's *pins* refer to the little metallic stripes along the bottom edge that push down into the motherboard's memory socket. Pins aren't little pokey things.

SIMM (Single In-line Memory Module)

SIMMs come in two main sizes, as shown in Figure 8-1, so both sizes require a different-size socket. Ancient, pre-Pentium computers use the smaller size (3½ inches long), which has 30 pins and usually holds less than 20MB of memory.

Early Pentium computers used a larger size (4¼ inches long), which has 72 pins and usually holds no more than 64MB of memory. Both types simply push into a socket, held in place by friction.

Verdict: SIMMs are yesterday's technology from early '90s computers. Don't buy SIMMs for modern PCs.

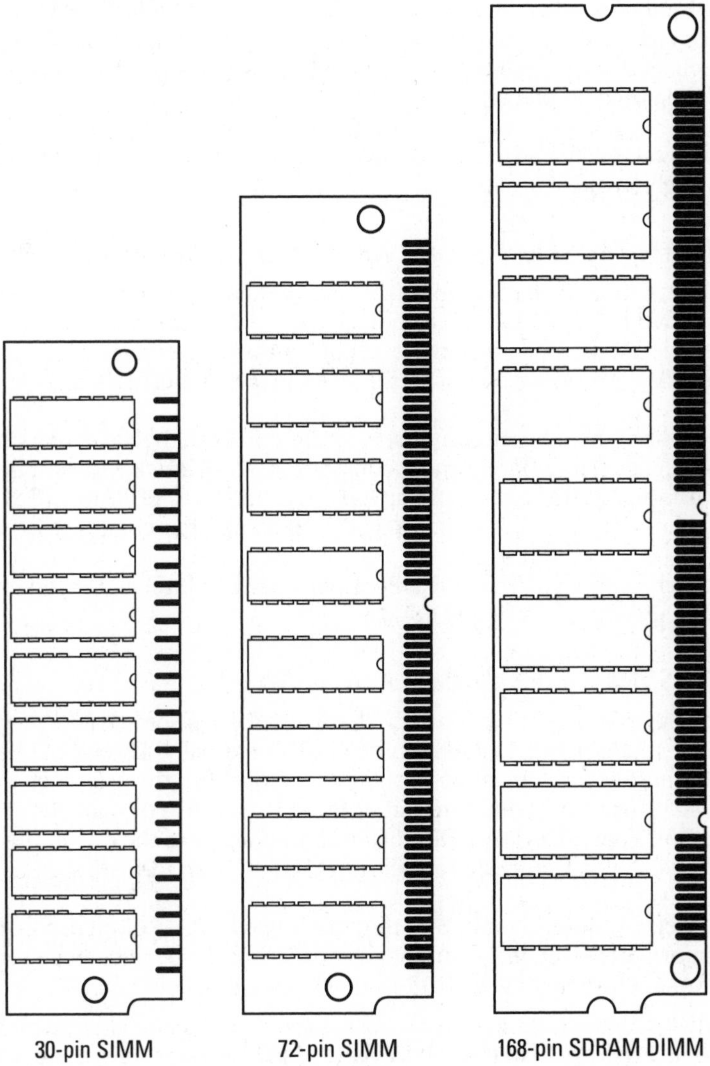

Figure 8-1:
From left to right: a 30-pin SIMM found in 486 PCs, a 72-pin SIMM from the early 90s, and a 168-pin SDRAM DIMM from the mid-to-late-90s.

30-pin SIMM   72-pin SIMM   168-pin SDRAM DIMM

SDRAM DIMM (Synchronous Dynamic Random Access Memory Dual In-line Memory Modules)

To meet the increased memory demands of newer and more powerful Pentium and AMD CPUs, designers created the speedier SDRAM DIMMs. With 168 pins, the 5¼-inch DIMMs (shown on the right in Figure 8-1) look much like longer SIMMs. They slide into newly designed slots with little clips holding them in place.

Verdict: Usually called simply *SDRAM,* DIMMs ruled the computer world through most of the '90s.

RDRAM (Rambus Dynamic Random Access Memory) or RIMM

Rambus, Inc., created a super-fast, super-expensive memory in the late 1990s and covered the chips with a cool-looking heat shield. The speedy 5¼-inch-long memory modules, shown in the left of Figure 8-2, enchanted Intel so much that the CPU maker designed its Pentium 4 CPUs and motherboards around them.

The rest of the computer industry ignored RDRAM because of its high price and licensing fees. Intel's main competitor, AMD, stuck with standard motherboards and SDRAM, the existing industry standard. RDRAM and SDRAM use different slots, so stick with the type of memory your computer is built around.

Verdict: Unless you're using a Pentium 4 with an Intel motherboard, you probably won't be using RDRAM.

DDR SDRAM (Double Data Rate SDRAM)

The biggest competitor to RDRAM, this stuff does some tricky piggybacking on the memory bus to speed things up dramatically. The catch? Because your motherboard must be designed to support it, these 5¼-inch memory modules use slots with different notches than those designed for traditional SDRAM. That means that DDR SDRAM modules, like the one in the middle of Figure 8-2, don't fit into a *regular* SDRAM slot or an RDRAM slot.

Verdict: Pentium 4 computers that don't use RDRAM often use DDR SDRAM memory. However, make sure your motherboard specifically supports DDR SDRAM before buying it. (DDR is also known as *Dual Channel.*)

DDR2 SDRAM (Double Data Rate 2 SDRAM)

DDR2 SDRAM (shown on the right in Figure 8-2) is simply a newer, faster version of DDR SDRAM. Yet again, your motherboard must be designed to support it, as these modules use yet another system of slots and notches.

Verdict: The latest PCs use DDR2 SDRAM, but like all other memory decisions, make sure your motherboard supports it before buying it.

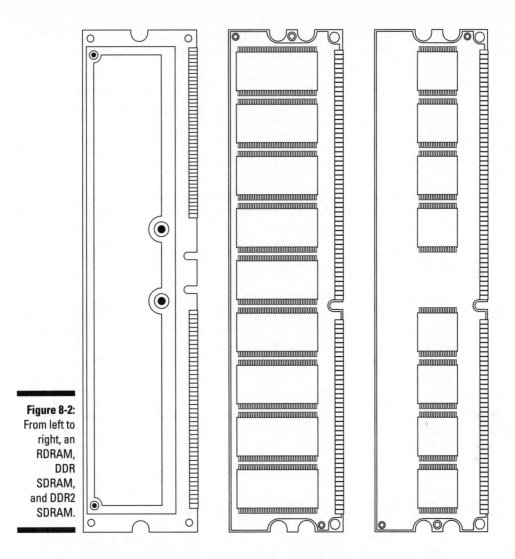

Deciphering memory advertisements and packaging

Your computer probably uses one of the five types of memory described in the previous section. You'll probably encounter most of the following few words when shopping for those types of memory or browsing the ads:

Bankings: This describes the number of memory slots (also called *banks* or *sockets*) in your PC. Most PCs' motherboards come with at least three or four memory slots.

Matched pairs: Some PCs require you to install memory in *matched pairs*. That means you need to buy and install *two identical* sticks of memory at a time. Also, those two memory sticks must be placed in *matched pairs* of memory sockets inside your PC. Not all PCs are this picky. But if your PC requires memory to be installed in matched pairs, be sure to buy *two identical* sticks.

Free slots: If all your memory sockets are full, you don't have any free slots. That also means you don't have room to insert any more memory sticks. So, how do you upgrade your memory? Unfortunately, you need to remove some low-capacity memory — a 256MB stick, for example — and replace it with a higher-capacity memory. Unfortunately, that tactic leaves you with a leftover-and-useless 256MB stick.

DDR400, DDR533, DDR2-4200, DDR2-6400: Numbers after an acronym describe the speed of a particular DDR SDRAM or DDR2 SDRAM module. The larger the number, the faster the memory — if your motherboard's equipped to handle it. You can usually install faster memory in slower motherboards without problem, but putting slower memory in faster motherboards will slow down your PC.

 Laptop memory: Laptop computers use smaller parts for everything, and that includes memory. Regular sticks of memory won't fit into a notebook, and vice versa. Buy memory designed specifically for your brand *and* model of laptop.

Deciding What Memory to Buy

When faced with the unpleasant task of buying the right type, speed, and size of memory for a PC, most people give up and take it to the shop. Do-it-yourselfers often turn to online memory vendors because they've made the process so easy. Follow these steps for the quickest and easiest way to figure out how much memory is already inside your PC and the best type of memory to add to your particular model.

1. **Visit Crucial (`www.crucial.com`) or another online memory vendor.**

   Most online memory vendors, including Crucial, offer special programs to scan your PC's memory requirements and offer recommendations.

2. **Tell the Web site to find out what memory's inside your PC and to recommend compatible upgrades.**

On Crucial, for instance, click Scan My PC. The Web site sends a small program to your PC to scan its memory and then present the results, as shown in Figure 8-3.

The Web site revealed these three things about my PC:

- *Current memory setup:* The PC currently has four banks of memory; two are filled with 512MB memory modules, and two are empty.

- *Possible upgrades:* Depending on the width of my wallet, I can upgrade my PC to 2GB, 3GB, or 4GB.

- *Memory type:* The details area shows that my PC can hold no more than 4096MB (4GB) of DDR2 memory running at a speed no faster than 3391. The memory must be installed in matched pairs.

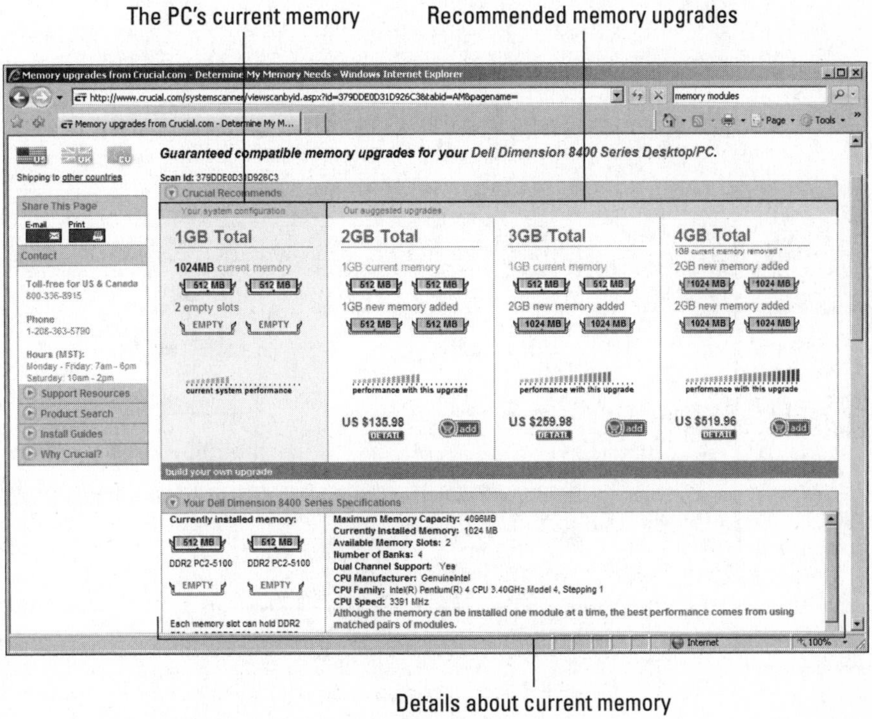

The PC's current memory · · · · · · · Recommended memory upgrades

Figure 8-3:
Crucial's online scanner shows this PC has 1GB of memory, which can be upgraded to 2GB, 4GB, or 8GB.

Details about current memory

3. Decide how to upgrade.

My best bet is to fill the two empty slots with either 512MB (upping the PC's total to 2GB) or 1024MB memory modules (upgrading the PC's RAM to 3GB). To upgrade to 4GB, I need to discard the two existing 512MB modules and place a 1GB module in each slot — an expensive proposition.

My laptop fares worse, as shown in Figure 8-4.

Its two slots are filled with 256MB of memory each. My only choice is to discard them both and fill their two slots with two 512MB memory modules. That upgrades the laptop to 1GB of memory — the most memory the laptop can handle.

4. Buy the memory that meets your needs.

When you've identified the type and amount of memory you need, you're ready to make your purchase. Feel free to make a printout of what you've learned about your PC and memory-buying strategy at Crucial, and compare prices at other sites (or local stores) before buying. Or simply buy it from Crucial.

The PC's current memory   Recommended memory upgrades

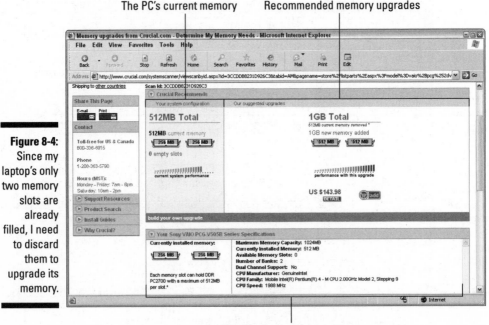

Figure 8-4: Since my laptop's only two memory slots are already filled, I need to discard them to upgrade its memory.

Details about current memory

If you can't figure out what kind of memory your computer has, write down its make and model number, along with its number of memory slots. Carefully pluck out your computer's existing memory chips, put them in a plastic sandwich baggie, and bring them to the local computer store. The salesperson can then sell you the right type and amount. (Some memory chip stores may even accept trade-ins on memory modules you need to discard.)

Installing memory chips

Difficulty level: Medium

Tools you need: None

Cost: About 25 cents per megabyte, although the price constantly changes

Stuff to watch out for: Memory has more rules than Mrs. Jackson during her shift on lunch duty:

- ✔ First, be sure to buy memory that fits the same *size* as your motherboard's sockets. Not all memory fits every socket.

- ✔ Second, buy memory that's the right *speed* so that your computer can use it without tripping.

- ✔ Third, buy memory that's the right *capacity*. Different motherboards have different limits on how much memory they can handle.

- ✔ Finally, some computers require their memory to be installed in matched pairs. If yours does, you must buy and install two sticks of memory, not just one.

These four details are covered more fully in the "Deciding What Memory to Buy" section, earlier in this chapter. Choosing the right memory requires *much* more time than installing the darn stuff, which is why I recommend using the online programs supplied by memory vendors.

To install your new memory modules, follow these steps:

1. **Turn off the computer, unplug it, and remove the case.**

   These steps get the full treatment on the Cheat Sheet in the front of this book. I also show how to remove a PC's case in the color insert pages in Color Plates 1 through 3.

If you live in a static electricity–prone environment, buy a grounding strap that wraps around your wrist and attaches to the computer. Even if you don't have static electricity problems in your area, you should still ground yourself by touching a metal part of your computer's case before touching its innards.

2. **Locate the memory sockets on your motherboard and install the new memory chips.**

See the Color Plates 10 through 13 in the color insert pages.

If you're working in a dry area with lots of static, take off your shoes and socks. Working barefoot can help prevent static buildup.

Need to remove an existing memory module to make room for the newcomer? Pull the socket clasps away from the existing memory module's sides and then pull the module up and out. (It's the reverse of the steps described later.) Place the extracted memory in a plastic baggie for safekeeping.

Check your motherboard's manual, if possible, to make sure that you're filling up the correct sockets and rows.

Look for the notched sides and bottom of the memory module. Align the notches with the socket's dividers and clasps, as shown in Figure 8-5 and in Color Plate 13. Push the memory stick straight down into its socket and then push its little locking clips toward its edges to hold it in place.

Figure 8-5:
Line up the notches on your memory module with the socket's dividers and clasps and push it into the socket.

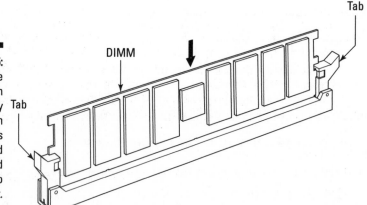

To fit memory into a laptop or notebook computer, remove the panel from the bottom of the laptop. (Check your notebook's manual to see exactly where its memory modules live.) Although different models and brands often use slightly different modules, most install somewhat like Figure 8-6.

Figure 8-6:
A laptop's tiny memory module pushes into a small socket beneath a special cover on the bottom of the laptop.

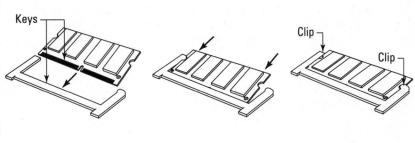

3. **Double-check your work.**

   Are all the memory modules firmly in position? Wiggle them a little bit and make sure their clips hold them firmly. Are any of their pins showing? The pins should be deeply embedded in the socket.

4. **Plug in the computer and turn it on.**

   Your computer might greet you with an error message about memory mismatch or something weird. The message sounds scary, but it's good news! Your computer found the new memory chips and was startled to find more than the last time you turned it on.

   If your computer doesn't recognize your new memory chips, turn it off and push those chips into their sockets a little more firmly. That may do the trick.

5. **Put the case back on.**

   Windows should run faster, more smoothly, and be able to juggle more programs at once.

Dealing with failing memory

Some computers are pickier about memory than others. Some, for instance, don't like you to replace their slower memory with faster memory. If you have a problem with your memory modules (your computer usually tosses up an error message bearing the keywords *parity error*), try isolating the problem: Remove all but one module of memory, turn on your computer, and see if the trouble remains.

If the computer runs fine, try reinserting the other memory modules, one by one, and turning on your computer each time. Eventually, you'll discover the module that's causing the problems and that needs replacement.

Chapter 9

Adding Storage with a Hard Drive

*P*eople pile their junk into closets, garages, and kitchen drawers. Computers stuff it all onto a humming hard drive. Unfortunately, hard drives suffer from the same problem as their household counterparts. They're rarely large enough to hold everything, especially after you've been computing for a few years.

Every new Windows version consumes more hard drive space than the previous version, and new programs always grow larger, too. The Internet keeps dishing up stuff that's fun to store. E-mail keeps piling up.

To deal with the constant information flow, some people upgrade to a larger hard drive. Others add a second hard drive, either inside the PC or by plugging an external hard drive into one of their PC's USB or FireWire ports.

This chapter shows you how to replace an existing drive, add a second internal drive, or add an external drive — a great way to make easy backups.

Understanding Hard Drive Buzzwords

People began stuffing hard drives inside their personal computers in the late '70s. Each year or so afterward, technicians found new ways to store more data on those little spinning disks trapped inside metal boxes. Today, several incompatible hard drive standards rule the computer store shelves. Each new release brings a new handful of abbreviations and numbers to sort out.

This section serves as a translation guide to the words, letters, and numbers you're bound to encounter when hard drive shopping. Support your back with a pillow and get comfortable; hard drives use plenty of buzzwords.

Vista technologies

Vista takes advantage of two new technologies being built into hard drives, and both of them help laptops most of all:

Hybrid drives: For best performance, look for a hard drive that's labeled as "Windows ReadyDrive." Inside these hybrid drives lives some *flash memory* — the same type of memory found on keychain drives. Your hard drive dumps frequently needed items into the speedy memory, letting Windows Vista grab that information quickly without waiting for the slower, mechanical part of the hard drive to grab it.

Hybrid hard drives work best in laptop PCs, because they prolong battery life. Instead of draining the batteries by turning on the mechanical hard drive, Vista grabs the information from the flash drive, keeping your PC quieter and cooler.

BitLocker Drive Encryption: If somebody steals your PC or laptop, they also steal something even harder to replace: All the information on your hard drive. Most hard drives contain passwords, credit card numbers, and other sensitive information, making a bad situation even worse. Hard drives with a special chip can take advantage of Vista's new BitLocker technology that locks your information up on your hard drive. Thieves won't be able to access the data on your hard drive, keeping your information safe.

Drive types

Hard drives constantly move to new technologies to pack more information into successively smaller spaces. These words describe the storage technology built into the drives found today:

IDE/ATA/PATA (Integrated Drive Electronics or Intelligent Drive Electronics): This fast and cheap standard quickly chased its decrepit precursors out of the barroom a long time ago. Today, most hard drives still use some form of IDE technology, often referred to as ATA (AT Attachment). Because these drives use technology called *parallel,* they've picked up the acronym PATA to describe all drives from this old school.

UDMA, UIDE, AT-6, Fast ATA, Ultra ATA, UDMA, and more: These subsequent flavors of IDE/ATA technology each add new technologies and longer acronyms. The result? More speed and more storage capacity.

SATA (Serial ATA): The newest incarnation of the IDE/ATA drives, these offer still greater performance. Older drives moved information to your computer through awkward, stubby ribbon cables. SATA drives transfer their information faster through sleek, thin cables that route through your computer's innards more easily.

External SATA: You guessed it, external SATA drives live outside your PC and plug into special eSATA ports you can add to your PC.

SCSI (Small Computer Systems Interface), Fast Wide SCSI, Ultra SCSI, Wide Ultra2 SCSI, and more: Pronounced "scuzzy," this popular drive variety worked its way into the hearts of power users and network administrators. Today, SATA is slowly pushing SCSI away from even those folks.

Speed and space

The following terms appear on nearly every hard drive's box to help you find the drive with the size and speed you need:

Capacity: The amount of data the hard drive can store; the larger, the better. When buying a new drive, look for something with 50 gigabytes (GB) or more. Always buy the biggest drive you can possibly afford.

Access or seek time: The time your drive takes to locate stored files, measured in milliseconds (ms). The smaller the number, the better.

DTR (Data Transfer Rate): How fast your computer can grab information from files after it finds them. Larger numbers are better. Data transfer rates are broken down into burst and sustained, each described next.

Burst/sustained: These figures show how quickly your computer grabs and delivers information from your hard drive. The burst rate determines the speed at which your computer can fetch one small piece of information from your hard drive. The sustained rate, by contrast, refers to how fast it constantly streams data — fetches a large file, for example. Naturally, burst rates are much faster than sustained rates.

5000/7200/10000 RPM: The speed at which your hard drive's internal disks spin, measured in revolutions per minute (RPM). Bigger numbers mean faster and more expensive drives. (For some reason, techies leave out commas when discussing RPM.)

When you're purchasing a drive for everyday work or sound/video editing, buy a very *fast* one. If you're looking to simply store large amounts of data, such as MP3s, videos, text, or similar items, save money by buying a slower drive.

Hard drive hardware, mechanics, and connections

These terms describe your drive's physical characteristics — an important thing to know when you're installing the drive inside your PC.

Master/slave/Cable Select: Some hard drive cables come with two connectors, and this system lets you tell the PC which drive is attached to which connector. The drive containing the operating system (Windows) is known as the *master;* the other drive is a *slave.* By placing a little jumper across certain rows of pins on each drive, you tell it whether it's a master or slave.

The two connectors on a special Cable Select cable come with Master/Slave labels. Connect the drive you want as master to the cable's Master connector; put the other on the cable's Slave connector. Then choose the Cable Select jumper on both of the drives to let the PC know of your handiwork.

To designate their jumpers as master, slave, or Cable Select, some drives use abbreviations like MA, SL, and CS, or something even more obscure. The first letter of the abbreviation is the give-away.

Unlike IDE/ATA drives, SATA drives don't bother with master/slave/Cable Select relationships. Each SATA cable connects to its own drive, sparing you from fiddling with jumpers.

Cache: Memory chips included on a hard drive. Because memory chips work much faster than hard drives, they temporarily store, or *cache,* recently acquired pieces of information. If the computer needs the information again, it grabs it straight from the cache, saving time by not mechanically rooting for it on the disk. The more megabytes in the cache, the faster the drive.

Partition: A division of space inside a hard drive. When you take a hard drive out of the box, it's like a large warehouse. Before you can use it, you must *partition* it. Partitioning tells the hard drive what boundaries to use for storing data. In Windows XP and Vista, most people create one partition — often called a *volume* — that fills their entire hard drive.

Format: The structure a partition uses to store data. After you create a partition on a hard drive, the partition needs to be set up with virtual shelves so that the computer may stack data onto it. *Formatting* prepares the partition to accept data. All new partitions must be formatted before use. (Windows XP and Vista work most securely with the NTFS file system, so choose that when you're formatting your hard drive.)

Dual boot: A system that enables two operating systems to work on your PC. Some people want to run more than one operating system on their computers. They want to use Windows Vista part of the time, for instance, and Windows XP part of the time. Computers running with a dual-boot system present a menu when first turned on, enabling you to choose which operating system to use.

Internal/external: An internal drive installs inside your computer, hiding out of sight in the case. An external drive (sometimes called a portable drive) plugs into one of your computer's fastest ports and sits on your desk. An iPod can work as an external drive.

FireWire (also known as IEEE 1394): An optional port allowing for speedy data transfers. Many external hard drives plug into a computer's FireWire port, allowing them to work as quickly as their internal cousins. (No FireWire port? Slip a FireWire card into one of your PC's PCI slots, the same way as adding a graphics card, covered in Chapter 7.)

USB: A standard port used by most PCs. Early-to-mid '90s computers come with a USB 1.1 port, which transfers information too slowly for external hard drives. The newer USB 2.0 ports are 40 times faster.

PC card: Frequently found on laptops, these cards (which are about the size of a credit card) sometimes contain itty-bitty hard drives to be inserted into a PC slot for grabbing data while you're on the go. (Some people still call PC Cards by their earlier name, PCMCIA cards.)

Microdrive: IBM's miniscule hard drive that stores information on a Compact Flash card. Microdrives are used by some MP3 players and digital cameras.

Knowing Your Hard Drive Upgrade Options

You always know when it's time for a new hard drive. Windows constantly whines about needing more room, for instance. Programs refuse to install, complaining of not enough available space. Or perhaps your C drive suddenly grinds to a silent halt.

If your C drive dies and you can no longer boot your computer from it, try desperately to rejoice! Physically, this is the *easiest* hard drive upgrade of all. Because you're starting from scratch, you needn't make any complicated installation decisions. You simply replace your dead drive with a bigger, faster new one, covered in the later section, "Replacing a Dead Internal Hard Drive."

Converting SATA to IDE/ATA and vice versa

Some thoughtful manufacturers sell PCs that come with both SATA and ATA connectors on their motherboards. That lets you install either or both types of drives. But many motherboards come with only SATA or ATA connectors, and that's a problem when you're holding the wrong type of drive.

How do you connect a PC's ATA connector to a SATA drive? Or a SATA connector to an ATA drive?

The solution is a SATA/ATA converter. They cost around 20 bucks online, and many computer stores carry them. The converter slips onto the end of your hard drive's cable, converting its connector to the type that matches your PC's connector.

Emotionally, of course, replacing a dead hard drive is the most draining upgrade of all because you may have lost all your data (unless you backed it all up faithfully; see "Backing Up Your Hard Drive," later in this chapter).

If you simply need more storage space, you must make some difficult decisions. Here are your options:

- ✔ Add an external hard drive.
- ✔ Add a second internal drive.
- ✔ Add a second internal drive and install Windows on it; then use your old drive for storage.

Choosing either of the first two options leaves you with two nagging problems, though. First, your C drive, where Windows lives, will still be full. How do you clear up some free space? Windows doesn't do that automatically. If your C drive contains plenty of data files (MP3 files, text documents, spreadsheets, videos, and other files), move those files to your new second drive. You can also uninstall your C drive's largest programs and reinstall them onto your new, second drive. (Unfortunately, both choices still leave you with the next problem.)

The second problem lies here: Your newer drive is undoubtedly bigger and faster than your older drive. If Windows lived on your new drive, your computer would run faster. That's why many people choose the third option in the preceding bulleted list: Install Windows on the new internal hard drive and use the old one for storage.

The next three sections explore all the options and show you how to complete each upgrade.

If you have any doubts about installing a new hard drive and feel you might inadvertently lose some important information, please buy a backup system in addition to your new hard drive. Then back up all your important information before proceeding with any of these steps. Even if you're not installing a new hard drive, a working backup system makes good sense.

Replacing a Dead Internal Hard Drive

Difficulty level: Medium

Tools you need: One hand and a screwdriver

Cost: Roughly $150 to $500

Upgrading a laptop's hard drive

You can upgrade your laptop's hard drive just like you can upgrade your PC's hard drive. The biggest problem is copying the contents of your old laptop's hard drive onto your new drive. You need an *exact image* of your current hard drive; you can't just copy the contents over, or Windows won't run.

The easiest solution comes from Apricorn (www.apricorn.com) and its EZ Upgrade Universal Hard Drive Upgrade Kit. The kit comes with software and an empty box with a cable that plugs into your USB port. The kit works like this:

1. You buy a replacement hard drive, put your new drive in the box, and plug the box into your laptop's USB drive.

2. Run the kit's bundled software.

   The software takes a snapshot of your laptop's current drive and duplicates the drive's image onto your newer, larger drive.

3. When the software's finished, turn off your laptop, remove its battery, and pop off the laptop's bottom cover (it's usually held on by a few screws).

4. Remove your laptop's old drive, put in your new drive, and replace the laptop's cover.

5. Put your laptop's battery back in, and when you turn on your laptop, it starts up with your new drive, complete with all your old drive's contents.

It's quick, it's easy, and it leaves you with a perk: Put your laptop's old drive into the leftover USB box, reformat it from within Windows, and you've created an external hard drive — great for backing up a PC or storing large files. For only $50, it's the easiest way yet to upgrade a laptop's hard drive.

Stuff to watch out for: Severe emotional stress. Losing your hard drive can be devastating unless you have your original Windows disc, the discs for all your programs, and a backup of all your data.

The key point with this upgrade is making sure your replacement drive uses the same settings and cable as your old one.

Follow these steps to replace a dead hard drive:

1. **Identify your old drive and buy a replacement of the same type.**

   Examine your old drive's cable. If the cable's flat like a ribbon (usually light blue or beige), it's a traditional IDE/ATA drive. No flat ribbon cable? Then you have a SATA drive. Replace your old drive with the same type as the old one, either IDE/ATA or SATA.

   Buy a fast, large, and dependable hard drive. Don't skimp on quality; you've already experienced the pain felt when one doesn't last.

   You can buy new hard drives at office supply stores, computer stores, or online at places like Amazon (www.amazon.com) or Newegg (www.newegg.com).

2. **Turn off your PC, unplug it, remove your computer's case, and examine your drive's connections.**

   Removing the case is covered on the Cheat Sheet in the front of this book. Examine where the cables currently plug into your dead hard drive; those cables will plug into the same spot on your new one.

3. **Remove the old drive and then slide in the new one in the old one's place.**

   Use your screwdriver for this task; save the screws.

4. **If you're installing an IDE/ATA drive, set the new drive's master/slave jumper to match the jumper on the old hard drive.**

   Master/slave jumpers are explained in the "Hard drive hardware, mechanics, and connections" section, earlier in this chapter. If your dead drive is set to master, for instance, set the replacement drive to master.

5. **Plug in the data cable and the power cable.**

   The cables from the old drive fit into their new drive's connectors only one way — the right way — on both ATA/IDE and SATA drives. (See Color Plates 24 and 26 in the color insert pages in this book.)

6. **Screw down the drive (see Color Plates 26 and 17 in the color insert pages) and reinstall your data.**

Partition and format the new drive as described in this chapter's "Partitioning and Formatting a Drive in Windows" section. Install Windows Vista onto the new drive as covered in Chapter 20, install your programs from their original discs, and run your backup software, if you have any, to retrieve your old data.

I cover backup systems in the "Backing Up Your Hard Drive" section, later in this chapter.

Although these are the basic steps, you'll find more detailed information for hard drive installation in this chapter's upcoming sections.

If your old hard drive had some extraordinarily valuable information on it, call a computer repair shop and ask for its Computer Forensics department. Many shops can grab information from a damaged hard drive — for a price.

Installing an External Hard Drive

Difficulty level: Easy

Tools you need: One hand

Cost: Roughly $150 to $500

Stuff to watch out for: External hard drives are by far the easiest way to add extra storage space to your computer. Most PCs come with a USB 2.0 port, so shop for a USB 2.0 external drive. (USB is the same port most iPods plug into.) Don't choose a FireWire or eSATA external drive unless you know your PC has one of those ports.

External hard drives can easily be moved from one PC to another. Just plug it in, and the drive's icon shows up next to your existing drive in Windows. They make excellent backup drives, and they're handy for moving large files from one PC to another.

To install an external hard drive, follow these steps:

1. **Plug the external hard drive into its power adapter, and plug the adapter into the wall.**

   Some external hard drives use rechargeable batteries, but if the AC adapter is handy, use that when plugging the external hard drive into your computer.

   Most hard drives require external power for reliability. Geeks call their little black power adapters *wall warts*.

2. **Install any software required by the hard drive and plug the cable into the hard drive's enclosure.**

   A few external hard drives come with a program that formally introduces the new hard drive to the computer, making the first bits of conversation less awkward.

   Some external drives also require partitioning and formatting when they're first purchased, a process described later in this chapter in the "Partitioning and Formatting a Drive in Windows" section.

   External hard drives come with a cable that fits into a port on the hard drive's enclosure. (The cable only fits into the port one way — the right way.)

3. **Plug the other end of the hard drive's cable into your USB, FireWire, or eSATA port and turn on the drive.**

   All three of these ports are usually found on the back of your PC:

   - A *USB port* looks like the one shown in the margin. If your drive is USB 2.0, make sure to plug it into a USB 2.0 port, as well. (I describe USB ports in this book's appendix.)

   - A *FireWire port,* shown in the margin, is sometimes called an IEEE 1394 port.

   - An *eSATA port,* shown in the margin, is still relatively uncommon on today's PCs.

   No matter how you plug your drive into your PC, Windows greets the newcomer and places a little icon for it next to your clock, as shown in Figure 9-1.

Figure 9-1:
When plugged in, the external hard drive's icon appears in Windows Vista, top, and Windows XP, bottom.

4. **Wait for the new drive's icon to appear in your Computer or My Computer window.**

   In Vista, choose Computer from the Start menu to see your drive's icon (shown in the margin). In Windows XP, choose My Computer from the Start menu.

   Most external drives work as soon as you plug them in. An occasional few need to be formatted, which I cover in the "Partitioning and Formatting a Drive in Windows" section, later in this chapter.

5. **Double-click the new drive's icon to see the drive's contents.**

   That's it. Double-click the icon to open it and start moving files to and fro just as with any other drive.

6. **Always tell Windows before you disconnect your drive.**

   You can sometimes damage your data or your external hard drive by not telling Windows before you disconnect it. To tell Windows, right-click the drive's icon in your Taskbar and choose Safely Remove from the menu, as shown in Figure 9-1.

   External drives hate to be dropped. Make sure that both your shoelaces are tied before carrying one across the room.

Adding a Second Internal Hard Drive

If you've decided that you would like to buy a second internal hard drive instead of replacing the one you already have, you need to make another key decision: How should you set up that drive within your computer?

The main reason to install a second hard drive inside your PC is to increase your storage capacity. That gives you two options as to how the new hard drive will work with the existing drive:

- ✔ **Use the new drive for additional storage.** Install the new hard drive, keeping your existing drive set up the same way. Windows gives the new drive the next available drive letter, usually D. Then, you can start moving your large data files from your C drive to your D drive. (Windows isn't smart enough to move the files over automatically, even though that empty new drive is sitting there.)

- ✔ **Replace your existing hard drive with your new drive and begin using your older drive for storage.** By installing Windows on your new drive, you can take advantage of its faster speed and capacity. This option also allows you to upgrade to Windows Vista during your installation.

To assign an IDE/ATA drive as either master or slave, check the drive's manual or simply eyeball the label affixed to the drive. In either case, you find an illustration, like the one in Figure 9-2, showing two rows of dots or pins. Movable jumpers slide on or off the pins in different combinations to assign the drive as master, slave, or Cable Select.

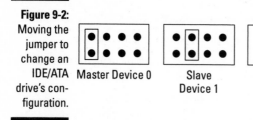

Figure 9-2: Moving the jumper to change an IDE/ATA drive's configuration.

Master Device 0   Slave Device 1   Cable Select

 SATA drives don't require any jumpers to be moved. Just plug the drive's SATA cable onto the motherboard's next available SATA connector (shown in the margin).

The following section covers the first, easiest option: How to add a second hard drive to your computer and use it for storage. Your current Windows drive stays the same; your computer just has a big new hard drive for you to begin filling with files.

Adding extra storage to your computer with a second hard drive

Difficulty level: Easy

Tools you need: One hand, a screwdriver, and tweezers (or a paper clip)

Cost: Roughly $150 to $500

Stuff to watch out for: You may need special rails or an adapter to mount your hard drive inside your computer. Some drives come with mounting rails and/or an adapter, like the drive in the color insert's Color Plate 26. Others screw directly to the case, like the drive in the color insert's Color Plate 27. If your hard drive doesn't slide snugly into your computer, you may need to head back to the store. (Rails and adapters are pretty inexpensive.)

Follow these steps to add a second hard drive inside your PC:

1. **Turn off and unplug your computer and remove the case.**

   If you live in a static electricity–prone environment, buy a grounding strap that wraps around your wrist and attaches to the computer. Even if you don't have much static electricity in your area, remember to touch your computer's case to ground yourself before touching its innards.

2. **If you're installing an IDE/ATA drive, move the new drive's jumpers to set it as slave.**

   Drives come with two rows of pins, as shown previously in Figure 9-2. Using a pair of tweezers or an emergency bent paperclip tool, remove the jumper and push it onto the pins that designate the drive as slave. Check the drive's manual or labeling. (The drive in the color insert's Color Plate 24 is set as slave.)

   Because your existing drive is already set up as master, you don't need to mess with it.

   If you're installing a SATA drive, don't worry about setting master/slave jumpers; those drives don't need them.

3. **Slide the new drive in a mounting bay next to the existing drive.**

   Drives usually sit in a *mounting bay:* a collection of compartments inside your computer. Your CD-ROM or DVD drives usually take up some of the compartments, as does your existing hard drive. Find an empty bay — you can often find a spot right next to your existing hard drive — and slide the new drive in place.

   When you're handling a hard drive, be careful not to damage its exposed circuitry by bumping it into other parts of your computer.

4. **Attach the cables to the new hard drive.**

   Look for the hard drive's cable connections carefully, as SATA drives and IDE/ATA drives use different cables. If you find yourself trying to connect an IDE/ATA cable to a SATA drive or vice versa, head back to the store with the drive and ask for a converter.

   Here's how to connect both types of drives:

   IDE/ATA drives:

   • *Data cable:* One end of a flat ribbon cable already connects to your motherboard; the other end has two connectors, one for each of your PC's two drives.

   The flat ribbon cable should have a second, empty connector a few inches away from where it connects to your existing drive. Push that empty connector into your new drive's data cable connector (labeled in Figure 9-3). The cable's connector has a little tab that aligns with the notch where it plugs in. (See the color insert's Color Plate 24 for close-ups of the notch in the data cable and its connector.)

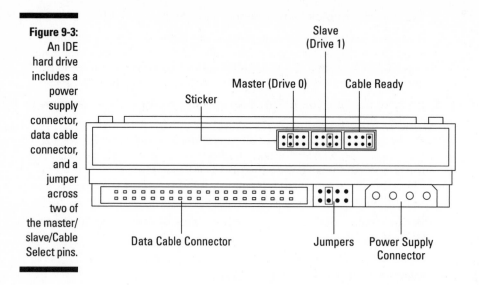

Figure 9-3:
An IDE hard drive includes a power supply connector, data cable connector, and a jumper across two of the master/ slave/Cable Select pins.

Slave (Drive 1)

Master (Drive 0)   Cable Ready

Sticker

Data Cable Connector   Jumpers   Power Supply Connector

• *Power supply:* See that bundle of power supply cables dangling from your computer's power supply? Find an unused cable and insert its connector into your drive's power supply connector (labeled in Figure 9-3). The plug fits into the drive's socket only one way, as shown in the color insert's Color Plate 24. (Power supplies are covered in Chapter 10.)

SATA drives:

• *Data cable:* Follow the cable of your first drive to see where it plugs into a motherboard connector marked SATA 0. Plug your second SATA drive into the motherboard's SATA 1 connector, adjacent to where the first drive plugs in. (Or, if the SATA 0 connector isn't used, plug your new SATA drive's cable into that connector instead.)

Plug the other end of this thin cable leading from your PC's motherboard connector into the smaller of your SATA drive's two connectors, as shown in Figure 9-4 and in the margin. The color insert's Color Plate 25 shows the cables inserted into a SATA drive.

• *Power cable:* This thin cable leading from your PC's power supply (Chapter 10) pushes onto the larger of the drive's two connectors, as shown in Figure 9-4 and in the margin.

Some SATA cables come with the data and power connectors melded together as one connector. They're aligned properly so they both push onto the drive's two adjacent connectors fairly easily.

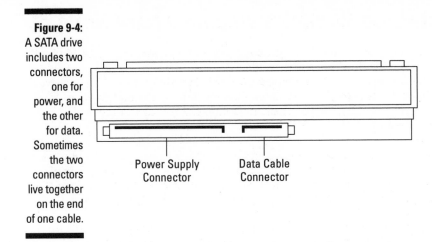

Figure 9-4:
A SATA drive includes two connectors, one for power, and the other for data. Sometimes the two connectors live together on the end of one cable.

Power Supply Connector

Data Cable Connector

5. **Screw the drive in place, if necessary.**

   Cables attached? Master/slave jumper set, if necessary? If the drive didn't come with mounting rails, fasten the drive in place with its little screws. The drive didn't come with its own screws? Then head back to the computer store, look in the hardware aisle, and buy screws for mounting hard drives. The screws should be short enough to keep from going in too far and possibly damaging the hard drive.

   If your two hard drives are in the same large bay, sometimes loosening the existing drive's screws helps you slide the new drive into place. If you loosened the other drive's screws to make room for the second drive, retighten them after the new drive is in place.

   Awkward position? Sometimes it's easier to attach the cables *after* the drive is in place. Use your own judgment.

   Technically, each drive is held in place with *four* screws. If only two screws are within reach of your screwdriver, skip the other two screws; the hard drive won't walk away. Just don't over-tighten any of the screws.

6. **Replace the PC's cover, plug in your computer, and turn it on.**

   Chances are, your computer recognizes the drive right off the bat, and you see the drive's name appear on the screen as the computer first wakes up. If the name doesn't appear, and Windows can't find the drive, head to the "Windows doesn't recognize my hard drive's full size" section, later in this chapter.

7. **Partition and format your new hard drive.**

   You find this information in the "Partitioning and Formatting a Drive in Windows" section, later in this chapter.

Installing Windows on a new hard drive

Because your new hard drive is probably bigger and faster than your old hard drive, where Windows currently resides, it makes sense to install Windows onto the new drive. You may then use your older drive as your storage drive. Yes, this process is more complicated than just adding the new drive as your second drive and keeping your existing Windows drive as is. But it's also worth the effort.

If you're already running Windows on your existing drive, save a *lot* of work and time by buying a Windows XP– or Windows Vista–compatible copy of Norton Ghost by Symantec. Install your new drive as the slave drive, and tell Norton Ghost to copy an image of the entire C drive to the D drive.

When it finishes, reverse the two drives' positions so your new drive is on the C drive. (Or, if you're installing a SATA drive, plug that one into the motherboard's SATA 0 connector.)

After booting from Windows on your new drive, reformat your old drive, as explained the next section, and begin using the old drive for storage.

Partitioning and Formatting a Drive in Windows

Before Windows will store information on a new hard drive, the drive must be partitioned and formatted. Luckily, Windows makes this chore fairly easy. Windows usually chooses the correct settings for you, so you often just click the Next button to proceed through all the menus.

If you don't have Windows XP or Windows Vista, rummage through your new hard drive's packaging for a CD supplied by the manufacturer. That CD's setup software can partition and format the drive. No setup software? Download it from the drive manufacturer's Web site.

When using Windows, make sure you're logged on with an Administrator's account. Other accounts aren't able to partition or format drives.

Planning to install Windows onto your newly connected hard drive? Then don't bother with this section. Both Windows Vista and Windows XP partition and format a newly installed drive as part of their installation process. Check out Chapter 20 for the scoop.

To partition and format a hard drive in Windows Vista or Windows XP, follow these steps:

1. **Open the Start menu, right-click Computer (Windows Vista) or My Computer (Windows XP), and choose Manage from the pop-up menu.**

   The Computer Management window appears, as shown in Figure 9-5.

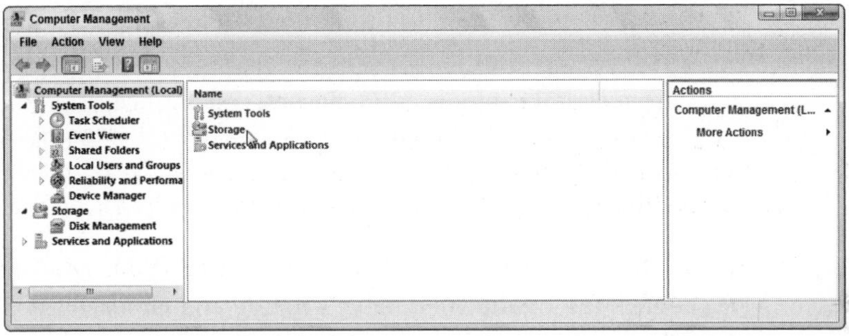

Figure 9-5:
The Windows Vista Computer Management area contains many ways to control your computer.

2. **Double-click Storage to reveal its contents, if necessary, and then click Disk Management to see your drives.**

   Windows lists all your recognized drives, including your CD drives and memory card readers, as shown in Figure 9-6.

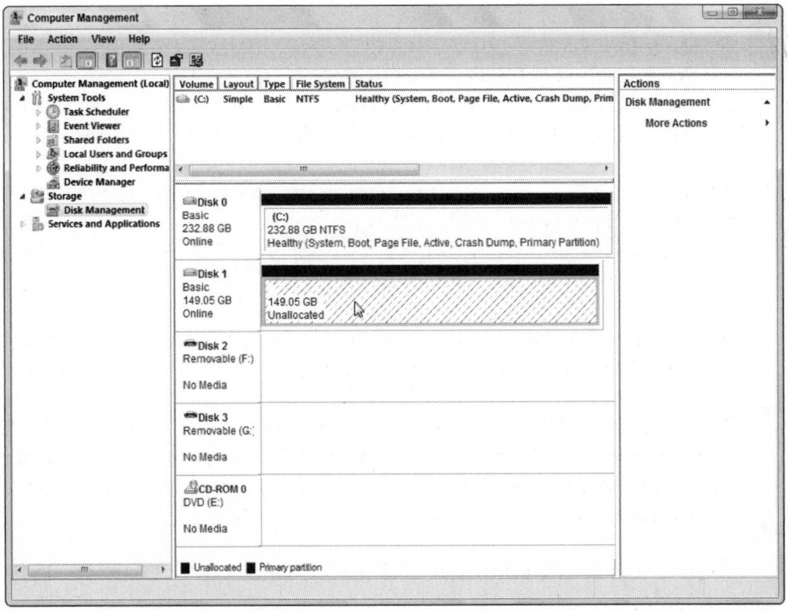

Figure 9-6:
Windows displays information about your drives and enables you to prepare a newly installed hard drive.

Windows Vista lists five drives in Figure 9-6 (this window looks nearly identical in Windows XP):

- *Disk 0:* This is the current C drive, the one Windows Vista lives on.

- *Disk 1:* This is the newly installed drive. It's listed as being *unallocated*, meaning it has been neither partitioned nor formatted. When you partition and format the drive, Windows converts the unallocated space into usable space and assigns a letter to it.

- *Disks 2 and 3:* These are memory card readers, which read cards from digital cameras, MP3 players, cell phones, and other toys. (There are currently no cards plugged into the card readers shown in Figure 9-6.)

- *CD-ROM 0:* This is the computer's CD or DVD drive.

You may see other drives listed here on your own PC.

3. **Right-click the unallocated drive's listing and choose New Simple Volume (Windows Vista) or New Partition (Windows XP), as shown in Figure 9-7.**

Windows Vista uses the term *volume* to describe what Windows XP calls a *partition*: a managed space for Windows to begin filling with information.

The New Simple Volume Wizard (Windows Vista) or the New Partition Wizard (Windows XP) appears. Both wizards do the same thing.

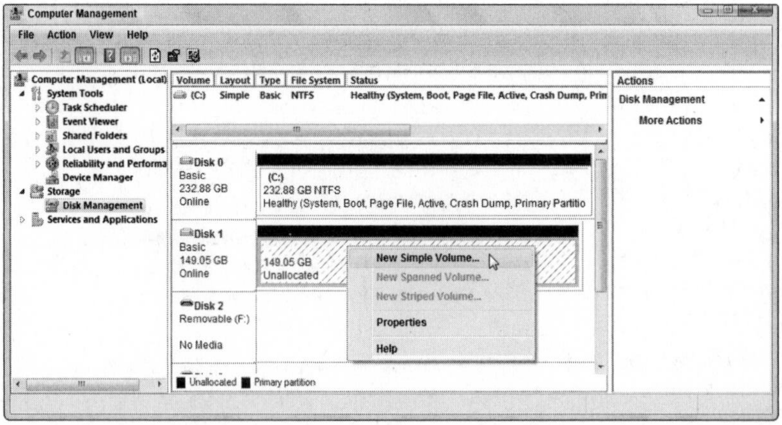

Figure 9-7:
Right-click the new drive and choose New Simple Volume (Windows Vista) or New Partition (Windows XP) to summon the wizard that walks you through the process.

4. **When the wizard's opening window appears, click Next.**

   At this point, Windows XP opens another window for you to choose Primary Partition; Windows Vista skips that step.

5. **Choose your partition size and click Next.**

   Windows Vista and XP can both handle huge partitions, so choose the biggest one offered. (Windows usually chooses that size automatically, as shown in Figure 9-8.)

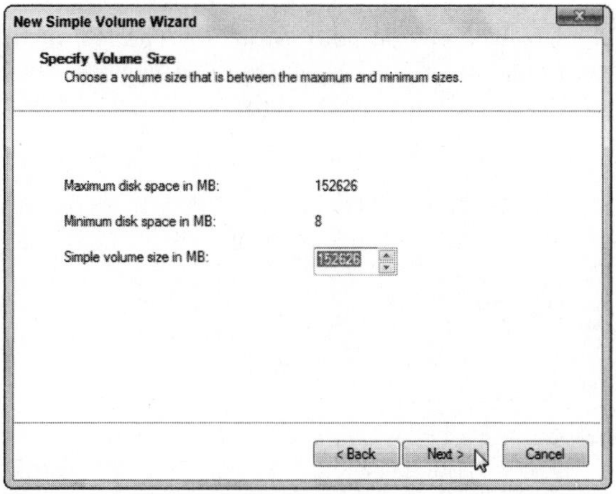

Figure 9-8: Choose the largest partition size offered and click Next.

6. **Select the Assign the Following Drive Letter option button and click Next.**

   As shown in Figure 9-9, Windows looks for the first available drive letter and assigns that to the incoming drive. Feel free to choose that letter, as Windows allows you to change the letter anytime you want.

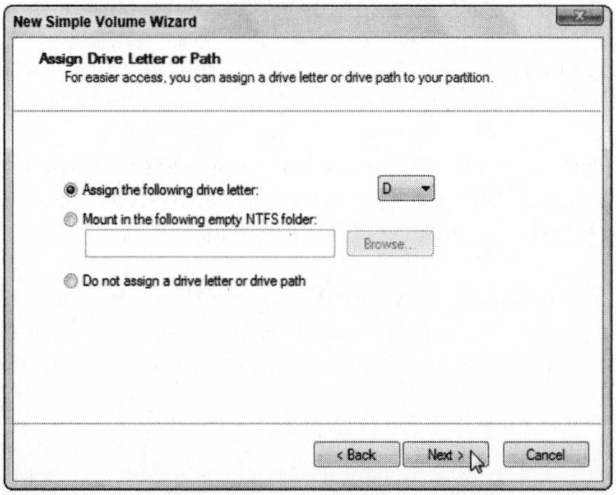

Figure 9-9: Choose the drive letter offered by Windows — you can always change it later.

7. Choose how to format the newly created partition and click Next.

Now that you've created the partition and assigned your new hard drive a letter, it's time to format the drive. Windows automatically offers the best option. As shown in Figure 9-10, Windows offers to format the drive using NTFS and using its standard allocation size.

Windows automatically names a newly installed drive New Volume, but feel free to choose something more imaginative. (The name simply appears as a label by the drive's icon in Windows.)

8. Click Finish.

The meticulous wizard sums up your choices on its last page. If you don't like something, click Back to change it. Otherwise, click Finish, and the wizard begins formatting your hard drive.

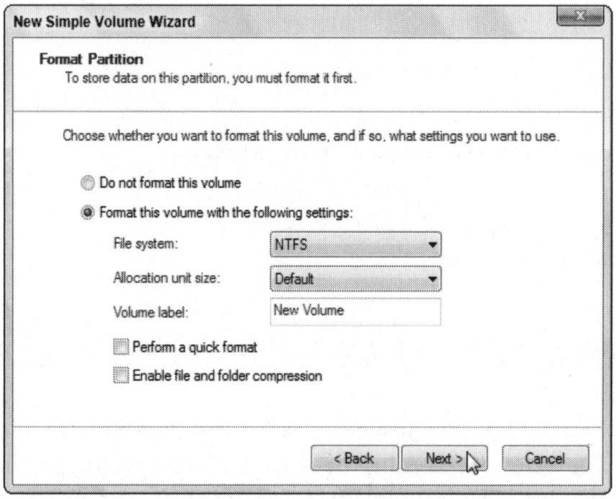

Figure 9-10: Choose NTFS for the most secure system in Windows Vista and Windows XP, leave the second option at Default, and give the drive an optional name.

You can't use the new drive until it's through formatting, but you may continue working with your other drive during the formatting process.

When Windows (or your drive manufacturer's software) finishes partitioning and formatting your new hard drive, the Computer Management window's Disk Management area looks similar to Figure 9-11.

✔ When you're formatting a drive for Windows XP or Windows Vista, be sure to choose NTFS in Step 7. If you choose any other format, your user accounts won't be secure, and users can access files from other user accounts.

✔ Want to change a drive's letter, perhaps to bump your CD drive up to E and give your newly installed second hard drive the letter D? Right-click the drive's name in your Computer Management's Disk Management window (refer to Figure 9-6) and choose Change Drive Letter and Paths. Windows lets you select any available drive letter.

It's usually safe to change drive letters on CD and DVD drives as well as USB drives. But be very careful when changing letters on drives that contain installed programs; the programs may not work afterward.

If Windows ever complains that it can't find something on a drive with a newly changed letter, a Browse dialog box pops up. Click the Browse button and select the drive's new letter.

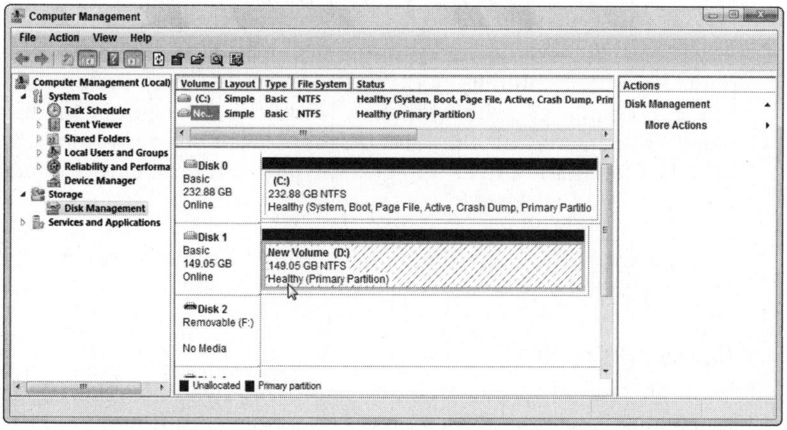

Figure 9-11:
Windows
pronounces
the newly
partitioned
and
formatted
drive
healthy.

Dealing with a Broken Hard Drive

The difficulty of hard drive installation often corresponds to the age of a computer. The problems increase drastically with age. If your computer is only a few years old, you probably won't have much trouble installing a new hard drive. But as you move past three years, well, the problems increase. This section explores some typical hard drive problems, from installation to everyday use.

First, though, here are a few things to check right off the bat:

✔ **Check your connections to make sure that gremlins didn't loosen any cables.** Is the ribbon cable plugged in all the way on both the drive and the motherboard? Is the power cable plugged in all the way? Are your master/slave/Cable Select jumpers set correctly?

✔ **Make sure that you're using an 80-pin ribbon cable.** A ribbon cable is made of dozens of little wires pushed together into a flat ribbon. Older hard drives used a 40-wire ribbon cable; the newer ones use 80 wires. When in doubt, start counting.

✔ **Are you trying to start your computer off a newly formatted master hard drive?** The computer can't start properly because the drive doesn't yet contain an operating system. Turn the computer on with your Windows CD or DVD in the disc drive and install Windows.

Windows doesn't recognize my hard drive's full size

When you first turn on your computer, words dash onto the screen. Those come from your computer's BIOS (Basic Input/Output System) as it scopes out your computer's vital statistics. Notice how the computer discovers and displays the names of your hard drives — even before Windows loads? Your BIOS has found the drives and dutifully noted their names so that it can pass them along to Windows.

The work your BIOS does in the background occasionally causes problems, each described as follows, along with the solution.

Improperly set BIOS

Your BIOS recognizes hard drives in either of two ways. You can either type in the hard drive's settings yourself — a laborious process — or you can set your BIOS to Auto so that it recognizes the new hard drive automatically.

The solution? Make sure that your BIOS has its hard drive settings on Auto so that it automatically recognizes your new hard drive. Although breeds of BIOS differ from each other, you can usually find this setting in its IDE Configuration area.

To change that setting, watch your computer's screen carefully when it boots up. It usually says something like `Press F1 to enter Setup`. Press that key to enter your BIOS settings. Make your changes, save your settings, and hope it solves the problems. If it doesn't, you may have an outdated BIOS, covered next.

I'd give you the exact steps, but there aren't any: Different PCs come with different BIOS versions, each with its own particular steps.

Outdated BIOS

Historically, hard drive capacity quickly outpaced other computer technology. The BIOS on pre-1994 computers, for instance, couldn't handle hard drives larger than 504MB. The next generation of BIOS chips could work with hard drives up to 8.4GB. Another revision moved the limit up to 32GB.

The solution? Ask your computer manufacturer or head to its Web page to see your computer's current hard drive size limitations. If your computer's BIOS can't handle your hard drive's full capacity, your BIOS might need upgrading.

When your computer boots up, quickly write down the BIOS version displayed on-screen. Then compare that version with the latest update listed on your manufacturer's Web site. If your BIOS version is older, try downloading and installing the update.

The drive isn't formatting correctly

Today's large hard drives have outgrown older formatting methods. The method Windows XP and Vista prefer, NTFS, handles the largest drive you can find on store shelves. But Windows XP offers an older method, FAT32, for compatibility purposes. FAT32 can only recognize partitions of up to 32GB. The solution? Reformat your partition, but use the NTFS system.

Defragmenting the hard drive

When your computer first copies a bunch of files on the hard drive, it pours them onto the hard drive's internal spinning disks in one long strip. When you delete some of those files, the computer runs over and clears off the spots where the files lived.

That leaves holes in what used to be a long strip. When you start adding new files, the computer starts filling up the holes. If a file is too big to fit in one hole, the computer breaks up the file, sticking bits and pieces wherever it can find room.

After a while, a single file can have its parts spread out all over your hard drive. Although your computer remembers where to find everything, it takes more time because the hard drive has to move around much more to grab all the parts.

To stop this *fragmentation,* a concerned computer nerd released a defragmentation program. The program picks up the information on your hard drive and pours it back down in (approximately) one long strip, putting all the files' parts next to each other.

Windows Vista defragments your hard drive automatically on a regular schedule, but Windows XP doesn't. But if you want to defragment your drive immediately in either Windows version, follow these steps:

1. **Right-click your hard drive's icon in Windows and choose Properties.**

   Right-click the drive from either Computer (Vista) or My Computer (Windows XP). Windows displays the drive's Properties dialog box, which tells you its capacity and how much space it has left.

2. **Click the Tools tab and then click the Defragment Now button.**

   Windows brings the Disk Defragmenter dialog box to the screen.

3. **In Windows Vista, click Defragment Now to start the process. In Windows XP, click the Analyze button, and then, if Windows recommends defragmenting the drive, click the Defragment button.**

   Clicking the Analyze button in Windows XP tells Windows XP to analyze your hard drive to see if it needs defragmented, as shown in Figure 9-12.

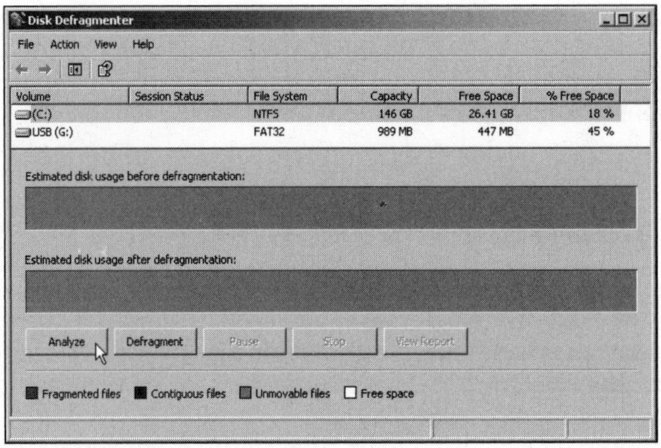

Figure 9-12: The Windows XP Disk Defragmenter.

Windows XP examines your drive, displays a colored, graphical analysis of your drive's condition, and makes a recommendation as to whether you need to defragment the drive or not. Let it go to work if it thinks your hard drive needs defragmentation.

✔ If at least 15 percent of your hard drive's volume doesn't consist of free space, defragmentation will take a *long* time. Better consider buying a larger hard drive, or a second one that can hold some of the information packed onto your current drive.

✔ When Windows is through defragmenting, it issues a report on its results. Some files can't be defragmented, so don't worry if you see that message. If a file is being used at the time, Windows can't defragment it. Some files will always be in use, as Windows needs them to keep running.

✔ Compact discs don't have a defragmentation problem because computers only *read* information from them. Even CD-RW drives aren't constantly erasing and adding new information to the discs, so the information on the discs is never broken into many pieces.

> ✔ Defragmenting a drive can take several minutes, especially if you haven't done it for a while. In fact, on some slow drives, the process may take up to an hour. The more often you defragment a drive, however, the less time it takes.

Checking for disk errors

Ever lost your train of thought after somebody snuck up and tapped you on the shoulder? The same thing can happen to your computer.

If the power goes out or a program crashes while a computer is working, the computer loses its train of thought and forgets to write down where it put stuff on the hard drive. (That's why you should always close your programs before turning off your computer.)

These lost trains of thought result in *disk errors,* and Windows fixes them pretty easily when you follow these instructions. In fact, Windows can often sense when it has crashed and can automatically fix any resulting errors. If your computer is running strangely, checking for disk errors is often the first step toward a quick fix:

1. **Right-click your hard drive's icon and choose Properties.**

   Open Computer in Vista or My Computer in Windows XP and right-click the hard drive's icon.

2. **Click the Tools tab from the top of the Properties dialog box.**

3. **Click the Check Now button.**

   A new dialog box pops up, offering several options.

4. **Choose all the options.**

   Different Windows versions offer different options, but clicking them all results in the most thorough check.

5. **Click the Start button.**

   Windows examines your drive, looking for suspicious areas and fixing the ones it can. The process can take a *long* time; feel free to let it run overnight.

   When Windows finishes the process, the proud little program leaves a dialog box on the screen summing up the number of errors it found and fixed.

Depending on the way your hard drive's error-patching program is set up, your computer may gather any unused file scraps and store them in files like `FILE000.CHK`, `FILE001.CHK`, `FILE002.CHK` — you get the point. Feel free to delete those files. They contain nothing worthwhile, as you quickly discover if you try to open them with your word processor.

Backing Up Your Hard Drive

Nothing lasts forever, not even that trusty old hard drive. That's why it's important to keep a copy — a *backup version* — of your hard drive for safekeeping. Table 9-1 shows some of the most popular backup methods and their pros and cons.

Table 9-1	Ways to Back Up a Hard Drive	
Method	*Pros*	*Cons*
Backup program and discs	Cheap; comes with Windows.	Windows Vista can back up to CDs or DVDs, but Windows XP can only back up to CDs. But the catch to both versions is you must sit in front of your PC, slowly feeding it new discs.
Backup program and tape drive	Relatively inexpensive. The program can back up your hard drive automatically while you're sleeping — meaning that you do it more often.	Although tape drives are easy to install and boast a large capacity, they're slow. If you're choosing tape, choose the more expensive, high-quality systems. They're more reliable.
External hard drives and Window's built-in backup software	Fairly inexpensive, easy to install and use, fast, and versatile.	None.

Other things to consider about choosing your backup method are as follows:

✔ Windows Vista and Windows XP Professional come with backup software that automatically searches for backup systems to use. Both versions can also back up your hard drive to an external hard drive.

✔ Although the best backup method changes over the years according to capacity, cost, and the size of the hard drive, external hard drives are the best choice for home and small business users.

✔ Don't skimp on your backup system. If it's not accurate, it's a waste of time. And if it's not convenient, you'll never use it.

Chapter 10

Replacing the Power Supply or Laptop Battery

In This Chapter

▶ Understanding power supply terms

▶ Replacing your power supply

▶ Replacing your laptop's battery

▶ Quieting your power supply

*Y*ou can't see it, but you can sure hear it: Your computer's power supply sits in a corner of your computer's case with its cooling fan whirring away. Some fans add a pleasant, running-water ambience to the room. Others whine like a weed whacker.

Power supplies suck in the voltage from the wall outlet and reduce it to the 5 or 12 volts preferred by your computer's dainty innards. This simple task heats up the power supply, however, so it needs a noisy, whirling fan to keep it cooled off.

The power supply's fan sucks hot air out of your computer's case and blows it out the hole in the back. In fact, if you keep your computer too close to the wall and don't move it for awhile, the fan leaves a black dust mark on the wall.

Power supplies retire faster than many other computer parts. This chapter shows how to interview potential replacements and place the newly hired power supply into its proper cubicle.

Understanding Power Supply Buzzwords

A power supply is simply a metal box with lots of wires dangling from it. The box screws to the back of your PC, and the wires connect to various spots inside your PC. You'll encounter these words most often when shopping for or replacing power supplies:

Internal power supply: The cable running from your wall outlet to the back of your computer plugs directly into your computer's power supply. From there, the power supply distributes the proper voltage to all of your PC's parts.

AT: A computer's parts sit on a *motherboard*, a large flat piece of circuitry that moves information throughout your computer. A large number of older computers use an AT-style motherboard. AT motherboards require a different type of internal power supply than their newer cousins, ATX motherboards. Why talk about motherboards in a chapter about power supplies? Because one of the power supply's many cables plugs into a connector on the motherboard, and different motherboards use different-sized connectors. Older motherboards use what's called an "AT-sized" connector (shown in Figure 10-1) that feeds electricity from the power supply to the motherboard.

Figure 10-1:
The newer, ATX power supplies sport a single plug and socket; the older AT power supplies sport two plugs that nestle together into a single socket.

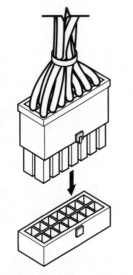

ATX socket and connector

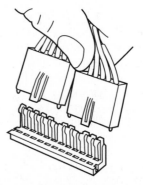

AT socket and connectors

ATX: These newer motherboards require different types of power supplies than AT-style motherboards. They come with a single plug (see Figure 10-1) that connects to the motherboard.

Proprietary: Here's where things get ugly. Some manufacturers don't always use standard power supplies. Instead, they design their own proprietary models with plugs that don't work on most motherboards. Some Dell PCs have this problem, for example. When shopping for a power supply for a Dell PC, make *sure* the power supply specifically says it's for your year and model of Dell PC.

Surge protectors: If you live in an area where the power fluctuates a lot, buy a *surge protector.* Glorified power strips, surge protectors plug into the wall; you plug the computer into the surge protector. When a power surge occurs, the protector sacrifices itself to save your computer. The power still flows, but the now-dead surge protector no longer monitors it.

Always buy a surge protector with an indicator light that lets you know when it's worn out. Otherwise, you have no way of knowing whether it's still protecting your computer.

The best (and most expensive) surge protectors also contain *line conditioners,* which level out the power's subtle ebbs and flows, ensuring best performance.

Uninterruptible Power Supply (UPS): Although they're much more expensive than surge protectors, these goodies do much more. You plug your computer into the UPS and plug the UPS into the wall. A UPS, like the one in Figure 10-2, conditions the power but also keeps your PC running during a power outage: When the power dies suddenly, the batteries in the UPS immediately kick in, keeping your computer up and running. Most uninterruptible power supplies last for only 5 to 15 minutes, but that's usually plenty of time to save your work, shut down your computer, grab a soda, and feel good about your foresight while you wait for the lights to come back on.

A UPS works only for a few minutes during a power failure. Then it, too, runs out of power, cutting off your PC's electricity. That's why it's important to always save your work before leaving your PC.

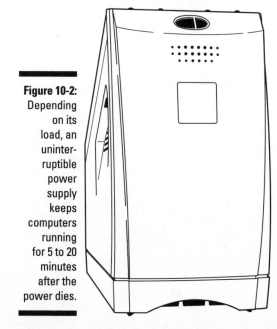

Figure 10-2:
Depending on its load, an uninterruptible power supply keeps computers running for 5 to 20 minutes after the power dies.

Deciding which power supply to buy

If you expand your living room by knocking down a wall, you need more than a single 100-watt bulb to light everything up. Similarly, the more gizmos you've plugged into your computer, the more watts you need to feed them.

To ensure enough power for everything inside your PC, make sure that your replacement power supply is rated for at least 400 watts. Feel free to grab an even higher-rated one, if you like; you won't be wasting electricity. A power supply's wattage rating explains how many watts it's *able* to send when your PC needs it. The 400-watt rating doesn't mean your PC will suddenly start sucking up wattage like an electric sponge. If your PC needs only 100 watts for a task, the power supply sends only 100 watts.

If you've been upgrading lots of computer parts lately — a second hard drive, a powerful Windows Vista–capable video card, or lots of USB or FireWire peripherals — a more powerful power supply is a wise choice for your next upgrade.

I buy power supplies from PC Power and Cooling at www.pcpowercooling.com. The site offers an online form where you answer questions about your computer's setup. As you begin listing your PC's number of disk drives and other parts, the Web site narrows down your options, eventually listing several power supplies that meet your needs. PC Power and Cooling sells top-notch (and quiet) power supplies that should keep your computer's parts happy.

Installing a New Power Supply

Difficulty level: Medium

Tools you need: One hand and a screwdriver

Cost: Approximately $50 to $100

Stuff to watch out for: Power supplies can't be repaired, just replaced. Throw away or recycle your old power supply.

Don't *ever* open your power supply or try to fix it yourself. The power supply stores powerful jolts of electricity, even when the computer is turned off and unplugged. Power supplies are safe until you start poking around inside them.

If you're confused about which power supply to buy, bring your old one with you to the computer store and match its connectors and screw holes with a new one, making sure the wattage is the same or higher. Or buy a new one online from Power PC and Cooling. Check out the company's Web site at www.pcpowercooling.com and answer a few questions about your computer. Power PC and Cooling recommends the right replacement.

To install a new power supply, perform the following steps:

1. **Turn off your PC, unplug it, and remove its cover.**

   If you've never gone fishing inside your computer, the Cheat Sheet in the front of this book details how to remove your computer's cover.

2. **Unplug the power supply cables from the motherboard, the drives, and the power switch.**

   Your power supply is that big boxy thing in your computer's corner. Bunches of cables run out of a hole in the power supply's side.

   Each cable has one of several types of plugs on its end. The plugs have several different shapes to keep them from plugging into the wrong place. Even so, put a strip of masking tape on the end of each plug and write down its destination. You and your computer will feel better that way.

   Here's a rundown of the plugs, their shapes, and their destinations:

   - *Motherboard:* Power supplies come with either one or two rectangular-shaped plugs that fit into a single socket on the motherboard. They're most likely either AT- or ATX-style connectors (refer to Figure 10-1).

   - *Drives:* Disk drives, tape backup units, and other internal goodies get their power from three different sizes of plugs, as shown in Figure 10-3.

   - *Power switch:* Small wires lead straight from the motherboard to the power switch on the computer's case.

   Unless your computer is packed to the brim with goodies, a few cables on your power supply won't connect to anything. (Those cables are thoughtfully supplied to power any future additions.)

Figure 10-3:
From right to left, drives receive power from either the smaller "Berg" plugs, the larger "Molex" plugs, or the svelte SATA power plugs.

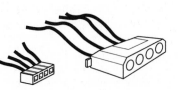

3. Remove the screws holding the power supply to the back of the computer's case.

Look on the back of your computer near the fan hole, and you see several screws. Some of these screws hold your power supply in place, as shown in the color insert's Color Plate 5, but other screws may hold your fan inside your power supply.

With the computer's case off, you can usually tell which screws hold the power supply in place. Try loosening the screws slightly; that sometimes makes it easier to tell which screws are which.

The screws that hold the power supply in place are generally closer to the outside edge of the computer's rear. The screws that hold the fan are generally closer to the fan's edge. Don't loosen the fan's screws if you can help it.

You may need to remove extra plastic vents from the power supply; they help route air around your CPU to keep it cool and refreshed.

4. Lift out the power supply.

Does the power supply come out easily? If the power supply is cramped, you may need to loosen the screws holding some drives in place and pull them forward a bit.

If the power supply still won't come out, make sure that you've removed all the screws. Some power supplies have extra screws around the base to hold them down.

5. Buy a replacement power supply.

If you don't want to purchase a replacement power supply online, take the old one to the store and look for an exact replacement. If you're planning on adding more computer toys — CD or DVD drives, a powerful graphics card, sound cards, USB gadgetry — or filling up your slots with more gadgets, buy a power supply with a higher wattage.

If you can't find a replacement power supply, you're probably stuck with a proprietary model. Head to your computer manufacturer's Web site and look for the replacement for your particular computer model.

Some crafty people plug in their new power supply before installing it, just to listen for the fan. If the fan doesn't work, return the power supply for one that works.

6. Make sure that the voltage is set correctly.

Look on the back of the power supply, which is near the fan. A red switch toggles the power to either 120 volts or 220 volts. If you're in the United States, make sure that the switch is set to 120 volts. If your country uses 220 volts, flip the switch to the 220-volt setting.

7. **Place the new power supply where the old one sat and tighten the screws.**

8. **Reconnect all the cables to the motherboard, the drives, and the power switch.**

   Grab any little pictures you drew and look at any masking tape labels you put on the old power supply's cables. (Forgot to label them? Well, it doesn't really matter which disk drive gets which plug, but labels offer a sense of assurance.)

   The two black wires on the two AT-style plugs almost *always* face each other when pushing them into their motherboard sockets (refer to Figure 10-1). Make sure that they snap into place. Make sure that you hook up the power switch connectors according to your notes.

   You rarely connect all of a power supply's available cables to your computer; just leave the rest tucked away some place so they won't touch the motherboard. If you install a new toy later, use one of those extra cables to give it power.

   If you didn't find a SATA power cable attached to your new drive, buy an AT-to-SATA converter power cable. The converter plugs into an unused AT plug on the power supply to transform it into a SATA plug.

   Be sure that you tighten down any disk drives you may have loosened.

   Also, check to make sure that you haven't knocked any other cables loose while moving around inside your computer.

9. **Reconnect the power cord.**

   Plug your computer back in; its power cord should push into the socket near the fan.

10. **Turn on the power and see whether it works.**

    Do you hear the fan whirring? Does the computer leap to life? If so, then all is well. If the fan is not spinning, though, something is wrong with the new power supply or your power outlet.

    Try plugging a lamp into the power outlet to make *sure* that the outlet works. If the outlet works, take the power supply back. The computer store sold you a bad power supply. (That's why some people follow the tip in Step 5 and plug in the power supply to test it before they install it.)

11. **Turn off the computer and put the case back on.**

    Is everything working right? If it is, turn off the computer, put its case back on, and put a cool glass of iced tea in your hands. Congratulations!

Replacing Your Laptop's Battery

Even if they don't explode in a ball of flames, laptop batteries eventually die of old age. Most batteries last between 18 and 24 months, depending on how often they're used and recharged. Toward the end, you'll notice that it doesn't hold a charge nearly as long, and you're constantly prowling for power outlets.

Difficulty level: Medium

Tools you need: One hand and a new battery

Cost: Approximately $50 to $150

Stuff to watch out for: Laptops only accept batteries made specifically for their make and model. Others either won't fit or may not put out the right voltage. Visit your laptop manufacturer's Web site to see if they sell replacement batteries. If you're shopping online for a third-party replacement, make sure the part number printed on your battery matches the part number of the battery you're purchasing. (Don't shop by the battery's photo on the Web site, as some Web sites use generic photos.)

When it's time to replace your old battery with a new one, follow these steps:

1. **Save all your open files, close your programs, and turn off your laptop.**

   You want to turn it off — completely off. Don't just choose hibernate or sleep modes.

2. **Release the latch on the battery compartment and remove the old battery.**

   A sliding lever on the laptop's side or bottom usually reveals a trap door that opens, letting you slide out the old battery.

3. **Slide in the new battery, replace the cover, and slide the latch closed.**

   The battery only fits one way — the right way. After it's inside, replace the cover and slide the latch to lock the cover back in place.

4. **Charge the new battery inside your laptop.**

   Although replacement batteries often come with enough charge to give them a quick test, your laptop may need to charge the new battery before running on battery power alone. Leave the laptop turned off but plugged in overnight to ensure a good charge.

Quieting Your Power Supply

Power supply problems usually announce themselves in obvious ways. A strong signal that you've got a problem is that, suddenly, your computer stops turning on; another big one is that the fan never blows. In these situations, your only hope is to replace the power supply.

Unfortunately, there's not much you can do about the annoying whining noise that many power supplies make.

Whining power supplies: Replace 'em

Some power supplies wail like a mid-'60s Volkswagen heading up a steep hill. Others purr quietly like an idling BMW.

The noise comes from the fan inside the power supply that blows air across the power supply's innards. The fan cools off the inside of your computer at the same time.

As for the racket? Well, many power supplies are just noisy little beasts. There's just no getting around the racket without buying a new one that's designed to run less noisily.

✔ If your power supply is much too noisy, consider replacing it. Today's power supplies are much quieter than the rumblers released five or more years ago.

✔ If your power supply doesn't make any noise, you're in even *worse* rouble. Hold your hand near the fan hole in the back. If you don't feel any air blowing out, the fan has died, and your computer is getting hotter by the second. Save your work quickly and immediately turn off your computer. Buy a new power supply before turning on your computer again. Without a power supply's cooling fan, a computer can overheat like a car in the desert with an empty radiator.

Don't try taking apart your power supply to quiet down the fan or make repairs. Power supplies soak up electricity and can zap you, even when they're unplugged. Never mess around inside a power supply.

Diagnosing the source of a whining noise

Sometimes it's hard to differentiate between a noisy power supply fan and a noisy hard drive. Each has a constantly spinning motor, so both are susceptible to the burned-out bearing syndrome.

To tell whether the noise is coming from your power supply or your hard drive, turn off your computer, unplug it, and open the case. Then pull the power supply's cable out from the back of your hard drive. (It's one of the two connectors toward the right side of Figure 10-3.) Plug your computer back in and turn it on. Because the hard drive isn't getting power, it doesn't turn on with the rest of your computer. If you hear a noise, it's your power supply.

If you don't hear a noise, it's your hard drive. Unfortunately, hard drives cost much more to replace. For more information about hard drives, see Chapter 9.

Part III
Teaching an Old PC New Tricks

The 5th Wave   By Rich Tennant

"So I guess you forgot to tell me to strip out the components before drilling for blowholes."

In this part . . .

Finally, it's time for the fun stuff! Your PC's been a glorified typewriter for too long. This part of the book explains how to turn it into an entertainment center.

It explains how to hook up your PC to your stereo, so you can hear cannonballs fired in front of you and splashing in the water behind you.

Several versions of Windows Vista come with a digital video recorder, and Chapter 12 explains how to put it to work by installing a TV tuner in your PC. That not only lets you watch TV, but automatically record TV shows and movies, as well. Plus, you can watch your PC on your big television screen — perfect for gaming.

If you prefer making your *own* movies, Chapter 13 walks you through upgrading your PC for heavy-duty video editing. (That lets you take advantage of Windows Vista's new Movie Maker program and new DVD Maker program.)

No DVD burner yet? Chapter 15 walks you through the confusing acronyms and explains which one to buy. Scanners find their due, as well, in Chapter 14.

Chapter 11

Fine-Tuning Your PC's Sound

In This Chapter

▶ Understanding sound card terminology and connectors

▶ Installing a sound card

▶ Hooking up a PC's sound to a stereo

▶ Adjusting sound on a PC

*Y*ears ago, computers simply beeped when you turned them on. A few early games managed to strangle the computer's little speaker into making squawking noises, but that was no fun. After a few years of awkward sputters, engineers created *sound cards:* circuit-filled gadgets that plug inside your PC to add music and explosions to computer games.

Gamers still cherish computerized sound, but sound appeals to many other people, as well. Musicians turn their home PCs into full-fledged recording studios, for example, and movie lovers connect them to their home theater systems to hear seven-channel sound tracks. And anybody who's created a digital-photo slideshow or home movie knows how well a soundtrack can liven up boring vacation shots and disguise muffled dialogue.

This chapter explains how to upgrade the sound on your PC or laptop, adjust it properly, and connect it to speakers or your home stereo.

Understanding Sound Card Buzzwords

Almost every PC and laptop sold today comes with at least two sound jacks. The pink or magenta jack's for plugging in a microphone; plug your speakers or headphones into the other jack (often green).

High-end PCs, however, come stuffed with enough ports to satisfy the needs of musicians, movie fans, *and* gamers. Here's a rundown on the terms surrounding computerized sound and an explanation of the ports found on a typical sound card, like the one shown in Figure 11-1. Most PCs come with at least the first four jacks on this list; the other jacks appear on high-end cards bound for the homes of gamers, musicians, or home theater enthusiasts.

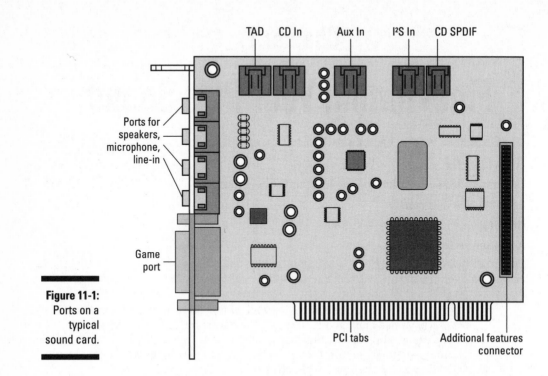

Figure 11-1:
Ports on a
typical
sound card.

Microphone: Used exclusively for recording through a small microphone, this ⅛-inch stereo port works fine for podcasts. Professional microphones sound much better but come with a ¼-inch plug. To plug a ¼-inch plug into an ⅛-inch jack, you need an inexpensive adapter sold at RadioShack and similar stores. (Sometimes ⅛-inch jacks are called "mini-jacks" or "stereo mini-jacks.")

Speakers: The ⅛-inch stereo speaker jack found on all PCs and laptops works with either headphones or small desktop speakers.

Line Out: To hear the best sound your PC has to offer, connect a stereo cable between this ⅛-inch stereo jack and the Line In jack of a home stereo or amplifier.

Line In: Built to accept amplified sounds, this ⅛-inch stereo jack lets your PC record music that comes from a small radio, tape recorder, mixing board, or an amplifier's Line Out jack.

 Game port: Sized midway between a parallel port and a serial port, this accepts a joystick for games. Plug in a Y-adapter to plug in *two* joysticks.

Sound boxes and accessory cards: Sound cards try to pack as many ports into as little space as possible: Everything needs to fit onto that little metal strip accessible from the back of your PC. That's enough space to add jacks for a microphone, speakers, game port, and the handy Line In/Out. But how do you cram in extra ports for MIDI (Musical Instrument Digital Interface), digital, optical, front speakers, rear speakers, middle speakers, and a subwoofer?

Some sound cards solve the lack-of-space problem by hogging an adjacent slot. A second card, shown in Figure 11-2, replaces a slot cover but doesn't actually plug into the motherboard. A ribbon cable then connects the main card to the second card, providing the extra connectors. (Some call this small accessory gadget a *daughterboard*.)

Figure 11-2:
High-end sound cards often take up two slots by using a second card to add more connectors.

Other manufacturers skip the daughterboard, instead providing a small box that plugs into the sound card and sits on your desk or adds ports along your PC's front end. Some manufacturers don't bother with the sound card at all. They stuff all the circuitry into a port-filled sound box that simply plugs into one of your PC's USB ports.

 TAD (Telephone Answering Device): A few computers come with built-in answering machines. The Audio Out cable from the answering machine plugs into the Universal Audio Connector port (shown in the margin) that sits inside a sound card. Most people ignore it.

 AUX In (Auxiliary In): You might wind up with an extra sound-producing gadget inside your computer that doesn't have a designated plug-in spot on your sound card. To accommodate any unexpected, usually obsolete toys, some sound cards have an AUX In connector. It's rarely used today.

I_S In (Inter IC Sound bus): Digital sound information plugs in here, although different cards use the port in different ways. For example, a DVD drive's hardware decoder cable might plug in here. Chances are yours will go unused.

 CD S/PDIF (Sony/Philips Digital Interface): Some older CD drives came with a digital output that plugs in here. (The connector has two pins.) This is rarely used today, as most CD drives just send their audio directly to the PC through their data cable. This connector can be safely ignored.

 CD In: This is for the CD drive's analog sound output. (It usually has four pins.) Like the CD S/PDIF connector, this is rarely used. Today's CD drives send their audio digitally to the PC through their data cable. Don't bother hooking this up unless you're specifically told that it's necessary.

 MIDI In: MIDI stands for Musical Instrument Digital Interface. Plug a MIDI cable from your music synthesizer's MIDI Out port into this port. If you're not a musician with a MIDI instrument, ignore this and the MIDI Out port described next.

MIDI Out: The cable from the MIDI synthesizer's MIDI In port plugs in here so it can send your PC instructions on what sounds to play.

If your PC lacks MIDI ports, some sound cards let you plug a special Y converter cable, available at music stores, into your sound card's game (joystick) port. The cable then provides both a MIDI In and MIDI Out port.

AC-3 (Audio Code 3): Although Dolby Laboratory calls its audio series *AC-3*, it actually uses *six* separate sound channels. Because AC-3 uses five speakers plus a subwoofer, AC-3 is often called a *Dolby 5.1* system.

Subwoofer: The coolest sound cards come with a way to send sound to a *subwoofer* — a big box with a large speaker that plays the bass rumbles of explosions and drums.

Surround sound: Sometimes referred to as 4.1, surround sound uses a pair of speakers by the monitor, a pair of speakers behind the listener, and a subwoofer wedged in a corner to shake the walls.

5.1, 7.1: These numbers refer to the number of speakers. The .1 part always refers to the subwoofer, so a 5.1 system has six speakers: one atop the monitor for the center channel, one on each side of the monitor, a pair behind the listener, and a subwoofer in the room's corner. A 7.1 system works like 5.1, but adds an extra pair of speakers, one on each side of the listener.

Amplified speakers: Most sound cards don't crank out enough power to drive a traditional set of bookshelf speakers. To increase the volume, most computer speakers come with a tiny amplifier hidden inside their box. If your speakers require batteries or an AC adapter for power, they're amplified speakers.

Converter cables: All of a sound card's jacks must fit onto the card's narrow slot. To pack them all in, you're stuck with stereo mini-jacks — small ⅛-inch jacks similar to the headphone jack on an MP3 player. If you want to plug in cables with larger jacks, like those found on musical instruments and professional microphones — buy some adapters. (RadioShack sells them, as do most consumer electronics and office supply stores.)

For the best sound, connect your sound card's speaker output through one of your home stereo's input jacks, described in this chapter's "Connecting Your PC's Sound to a Stereo" section. An amplifier and decent speakers can make a cheapie sound card sound like the best on the market.

RadioShack carries many converter cables and adapters. When faced with a confusing situation, draw or snap a photo of your sound card's connectors, as well as the connectors on what you're trying to plug in. Bring the pictures to the store and buy a cable or adapter that converts one connector to the other.

When you're not sure what plugs in where, glance at Table 11-1. Some forward-thinking computer manufacturers now color-code their jacks the same way.

Table 11-1	Deciphering a Sound Jack's Color-Coding
The Jack's Color	*What Plugs into It*
Pink	Microphone (unamplified sound)
Light blue	Line Input (iPod, VCR, tape deck, or other amplified source)
Lime green	Stereo speakers (two front speakers or headphones)
Black	Stereo speakers (two rear speakers)
Silver	Stereo speakers (two side speakers)
Orange	This jack sends out digital audio signals meant mostly for home theater amplifiers that accept 5.1 sound.

Creating a podcast

A *podcast* is a fancy word for an audio recording shaped around a particular interest. Some are spoken-word documentaries, others take a talk radio format, and others play music. But they're all served up on the Internet as *MP3 files,* a format playable by any computer, iPod, or portable digital music player.

You can make your own podcast with your PC's bundled microphone and the free recording software that came with your sound card. But your podcasts will sound *much* better if you invest about $100 in a small mixing board, a better microphone, and a sound editing program. (Audacity (`http://audacity.sourceforge.net`) costs nothing, but requires a bit of fiddling to figure out.)

After you've recorded your podcast in an MP3 format, you face your biggest hurdle: Finding people who want to listen.

To learn more about creating, marketing, and even making money on podcasts, pick up a copy of *Podcasting For Dummies,* by Tee Morris and Evo Terra (Wiley Publishing). Feel free to drop by the author's site at `www.podiobooks.com`. You can download podcasts there, as well as at podCast411 (`www.podcast411.com`), or even from iTunes itself: Click the word *Podcasts* in iTunes' left column.

Upgrading Your PC's or Laptop's Sound

The next two sections explain how to upgrade your PC's sound. The best sound quality comes by opening your PC's case and installing a sound card. If you own a laptop or don't want to remove your PC's case, a sound box is the next best thing: The box simply plugs into a USB port on your PC or laptop.

But no matter which route you choose, be sure to read the following section, "Connecting Your PC's Sound to a Home Stereo." That's the only way to hear the best sound your PC has to offer.

Installing a new sound card

Difficulty level: Easy

Tools you need: One hand and a screwdriver

Cost: Prices range from $30 for cheap game cards to $500 for mid-level recording studios, with quality cards averaging between $100 and $200.

Stuff to watch out for: Before removing your PC's old sound card, look at the existing wires plugging into the card's connectors. Then find those same connectors on your new card so you know where to plug back in those same wires. Sometimes adding tape labels to each wire and its connector lets you find the right places after you install the card.

Some PCs don't come with a sound card. Instead, the PC's manufacturer places a small sound chip directly on the motherboard. If you hear sound from your PC but don't find a sound card inside, your sound comes straight from the motherboard. You can still upgrade those PCs by installing a new sound card, just as described here.

To install a sound card, follow these steps:

1. **Turn off your computer, unplug it, and remove the cover.**

   Don't know how your PC's cover comes off? Flip to the Cheat Sheet at the front of this book for the answers.

2. **Locate a vacant PCI slot.**

   See that row of metal strips on the back of your PC's case? Inside your PC, you'll spot a row of slots lined up with those metal strips. (They're usually white.) Those are your PCI slots, and you need to push your new sound card into one of them. The sound card's ports then extend out that vertical slot in your PC's case, making them accessible.

3. **Remove the slot's metal backplate cover if necessary.**

   If you're replacing your PC's current card, skip this step. If you're adding a new card, though, keep reading.

   Unused slots often have a thin metal backplate cover over them to keep dust from flying in through the back of your computer. Remove the screw that holds that cover in place, (refer to Figure 7-6 in Chapter 7 and to Color Plates 19, 20, and 21 in the color insert pages in this book), and then lift out the cover. (Save the screw, as you need it to secure the new sound card in place.)

   If the screw accidentally drops into your PC, pick up your computer and shake it until the screw falls out.

4. **Push the card into any vacant PCI slot.**

   Hold the card by its edges and position it over any empty PCI slot. The edge with the shiny metal bracket faces toward the *back* of your computer. (That lets your card's ports extend out the back of your PC.)

   Line up the tabs and notches on the card's bottom edge with the notches in the slot. Push the card slowly into the slot. You might need to rock the card back and forth gently. When the card pops in, you can feel it come to rest. Don't force it!

If your card's so thick that it bumps into a neighboring card, move it to a different slot so they don't touch. You might need to juggle several cards to find the right fit.

5. Secure the card in the slot with the screw you removed in Step 3.

6. Install any accessories, if necessary.

Some sound cards come with a port-filled plate that's accessible from the *front* of your PC. It usually sits in an unused *drive bay* — the area where a disc drive normally lives. Be sure to connect the wires from the plate back to its connector on your sound card.

On the rare chance that one of your PC's internal parts — old CD or DVD drives, modems with built-in answering machines, or other sound-producing gizmos — need to connect to your sound card, connect their wires to the sound card's specialized jacks discussed earlier in this chapter.

7. Plug the computer's power cord back into the wall and PC, turn on your PC, and see whether Windows recognizes and installs the card.

Windows usually recognizes newly installed cards and sets them up to work correctly. If something goes wrong, head for Chapter 19 for quick-fix tips about installing drivers. If everything's working, however, put your PC's cover back on.

8. Install the latest version of the card's drivers and software.

Whenever you install a new sound card or any other card, visit the manufacturer's Web site. Find the site's Support or Customer Service section, and then download and install the latest drivers for that particular model and your version of Windows, be it Vista or XP. Card manufacturers constantly update their drivers and software to fix bugs.

If the card doesn't work after you've installed the latest drivers, head for this chapter's last section: "Diagnosing and fixing hardware problems."

Installing a sound box

Difficulty level: Very Easy

Tools you need: One hand

Cost: Prices range from $30 for a USB flash drive-sized model to $500 for home theater models. Plan on spending between $100 and $200 for a good one.

Stuff to watch out for: Most sound boxes use the ubiquitous USB port, but before buying, check the fine print to make sure it uses a USB *2.0* port. Some older models use the much less powerful USB *1.1* port found on PCs built more than five years ago.

Follow these steps to install a sound box to a PC or laptop.

1. **Plug the sound box's USB plug into the USB port of your computer or laptop.**

   Although a few small portable sound boxes draw their power right from your PC's or laptop's USB port, larger ones plug into a wall outlet. If the outlets by your desk are crowded, you might need a power strip. Because some adapters are large enough to cover up an adjacent outlet, look for a power strip with lots of extra space between outlets.

2. **Install the sound box's software.**

   Sound boxes are notorious for dumping huge amounts of borderline-useful software onto your hard drive — trial versions of software with rapid expiration dates, for example. Be prepared for that bit of rudeness with a post-installation trip to the Control Panel to remove any unwanted software.

3. **Choose the new sound box for your PC's Default sound.**

   If you're leaving your old sound card in place — a must with laptops, as the sound circuitry is permanently installed — then the sound box installs itself as second sound device in Windows. That leaves your old sound card's settings intact and lets you switch to whichever one you want to play the sounds.

   To switch to your newly installed sound box, choose Control Panel from Windows' Start menu. Then, open Windows Vista's Hardware and Sound category and open the Sound icon. (In Windows XP, choose Sound, Speech and Audio Devices category, choose Sounds and Audio devices, and click the Audio tab.)

   Finally, choose the sound box as your new default device, as shown in Figure 11-3.

   Some sound cards and boxes ignore Windows' Control Panel icons and add their *own* icon to the Control Panel. If you spot a Control Panel icon named after either your card or its manufacturer, open it with a double-click. It usually offers many more options than Windows' standard settings area.

4. **Connect your gadgets to the sound box.**

   Now's the time to make a trip to RadioShack or an office supply store. Many sound boxes come with only one cable: a USB cable for plugging into your PC. That means you'll have to buy cables for everything else you want to connect to the sound box: speaker cables, a microphone, optical cables for hooking up to a surround sound system, and similar items.

Figure 11-3: The Control Panel lets you choose the Default device (your PC's chief sound-making gadget) in both Windows Vista (left) and Windows XP (right).

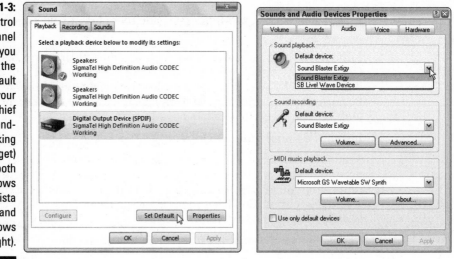

Like anything else, sound boxes have their pros and cons:

✔ Sound boxes finally bring fantastic sound to laptops. Musicians record concerts and jam sessions with their laptops and a sound box.

✔ A sound box lets you hear true, 5.1 surround sound while watching a DVD on your laptop. But to *hear* that sound, you must also tote along five speakers and a subwoofer. For true portability, check out the inexpensive 5.1 surround sound headphones that sell for less than $50 at computer stores and online. (They plug into a standard laptop headphone jack.)

✔ When you install a sound box or different type of sound device to a laptop, be sure to set the new device as Default in Step 3. Otherwise, your laptop will keep using its own built-in speakers.

✔ Like sound cards, sound boxes work best when hooked up to a home stereo and *real* speakers — not the plastic amplified desktop speakers commonly sold with computers today.

✔ Before buying, make sure the sound box contains all the ports you need. Some leave off a game port (shown in the margin), for example, to fit all the other stuff onto the front of the box. That limits your joystick to a USB model.

Installing a headphone/microphone set

The most popular online computer games call for players to interact both verbally as well as through the keyboard. To make sure your exclamations, insults, and praises are heard by all the game players, pick up a headphone/microphone headset. Although it makes you look like a telemarketer, the headset places the microphone right where you need it: in front of your mouth.

The best headsets plug into your USB port or are wireless, using Bluetooth technology. If your PC doesn't support Bluetooth, pick up a tiny USB Bluetooth adapter for less than $25. The Bluetooth adapter plugs into your USB port and lets your PC connect with *all* your nearby

Bluetooth devices: headsets, cell phones, mice, and other Bluetooth-equipped gadgets.

For convenience, look for a headset that has a volume control either on the cord itself or an easily accessible part of the headphone. Comfort is the number one problem with most headsets, so be sure to try on the headphone before laying down your cash.

Finally, after installing the headset, run through Windows' sound settings described in the "Fixing Windows sound settings" section to make sure the microphone and headphone levels are to your liking.

Connecting Your PC's Sound to a Home Stereo

The only way to hear your PC or laptop at its best is to hook it up to a home stereo. There's just no comparison in sound. To hear how good your PC's sound can be, invest a few dollars in cables and try it yourself.

If you're connecting your sound to a home theater system and want surround sound through five speakers and a subwoofer, flip ahead to Chapter 12, where I explain how to hook up a surround sound system.

But if you're connecting your PC through an amplifier to a pair of speakers, follow these steps:

1. **Plug a converter jack into your PC's Line Out jack.**

   Most Line In ports on home stereos accept connections through RCA jacks. To connect your PC to those jacks, pick up RadioShack part number 274-369, officially known as a *Y-Adapter, Phono Jacks to Stereo ⅛-inch Plug*. The handy adapter, shown in the margin, plugs into your sound card's ⅛-inch jack and offers two handy RCA ports on its other end, one for each stereo channel.

This same handy RadioShack converter lets you plug your iPod and most other portable music players into your home stereo, as well. Just unplug it from the back of your PC and plug it into your iPod or music player. Plug it back into your PC when you're through.

Plugging the jack into your sound card's *speaker jack* might work, but the sound might be too loud for your home stereo, leading to distortion.

2. **Connect a stereo audio cable from the converter jack's two RCA ports to your stereo's two Line In ports.**

   Pick up a stereo RCA cable long enough to reach between your PC and your home stereo. Found at any electronics stores, office supply stores, or even most drugstores, the stereo cable has two RCA jacks on each end, ready to plug into the two RCA ports on both your PC's adapter and your stereo.

   If your stereo lacks a free pair of Line In jacks, connect the cable to any other jacks designed to accept sound: a tape deck, for instance, or VCR.

   The *red* jack connects to the stereo's *right* channel. The other jack (usually white) connects to the left channel.

3. **Set your stereo's front sound input to Line In.**

   Most stereos let you hear sound from a variety of gadgets: tape players, radios, VCRs, or record players. To hear your PC, turn the stereo's input to Line In — or the name of the jack you've plugged the cable into in Step 2.

4. **Adjust the volume.**

   Play music through your PC at a low volume, and then slowly turn up the volume on your stereo. You'll probably want to control the volume at your PC because that's within reach. So turn the volume up on your stereo, and leave your PC set fairly low. Then, as you turn up the volume on your PC, your stereo will grow louder, as well.

   ✔ Tweak the volume settings until you find the right mix. If the PC's too loud and the stereo's too low, you'll hear distortion. If the PC's too low and the stereo's too loud, you'll blast your ears when you turn up your PC's sound.

   ✔ Don't bother spending the extra cash for super-expensive "high-fidelity" audio cables. They won't make your PC sound any better.

Healing a Sick Sound Card

When trying to fix a problematic sound card, leave off the computer's case until the sound works correctly. You'll find yourself constantly checking connections or peering at the card's innards for its part number when checking for the latest drivers or support on the Internet.

The next section covers Windows settings that control your computer's sound. Run through each one until you solve the problem. If you're still scratching your head, continue to the last section. Something might be wrong with the sound card itself or some of its cables.

Fixing Windows sound settings

Windows offers oodles of ways to craft your computer's sound, tweak your sound settings, and fix things that stopped working. You can troubleshoot the way the card's drivers work with the computer, and you can adjust the sound quality through software settings. Because Chapter 19 covers drivers in detail, this section covers how to tweak Windows' built-in software settings.

Windows packs all the important settings into several areas, so these steps run you down the line, enabling you to adjust everything until it's just right in both Windows Vista and Windows XP.

Changing Windows Vista sound settings

Follow these steps to run through all of Windows Vista's sound settings, calibrating your volume level, speaker placement, and microphone recording level.

Note: The sound programs included with some laptops and desktops overwrite Vista's sound setting windows with their own versions. Depending on your PC's sound circuitry, your windows may differ slightly from the ones described here.

1. **See if you've muted any programs by right-clicking the taskbar's speaker icon near the clock and choosing Open Volume Mixer.**

   Windows Vista's new Volume Mixer window, shown in Figure 11-4, differs from the one found in Windows XP. Windows XP lets you change only your PC's *entire* volume or mute *everything;* Windows Vista, by contrast, lets you change the volume of each program *individually*. That means you can turn down or mute Vista's error message sounds, for instance, but keep your music playing loudly.

   Make sure you haven't inadvertently muted or turned down the volume of one of your programs. Close the Volume Mixer window when you're through.

2. **Right-click the taskbar's speaker icon near the clock and choose Playback Devices to see the Sound window.**

   As shown earlier in Figure 11-3, the Sound window lists all the gadgets connected to your PC that can play sounds: Your speakers, for instance, as well as a digital connection to your home stereo that provides 5.1 or 7.1 sound.

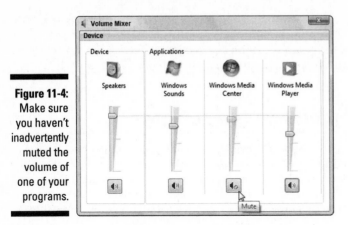

Figure 11-4:
Make sure
you haven't
inadvertently
muted the
volume of
one of your
programs.

3. **Click a listed sound device, check its settings, and then move to the next listed device until you've tested them all.**

   Click the device marked as default (look for a green check mark by the name) and click the Configure button. For example, clicking Speakers and clicking the Configure button lets you test your PC's speaker setup, as shown in Figure 11-5.

   Click any speaker shown in Figure 11-5 to hear Vista play a sound through it. It's a very simple test, but it's also a lifesaver when trying to figure out whether you've set your eight speakers in the right locations for a 7.1 surround setup. Even if you're using a simple pair of speakers, you can make sure you haven't switched their left and right positions.

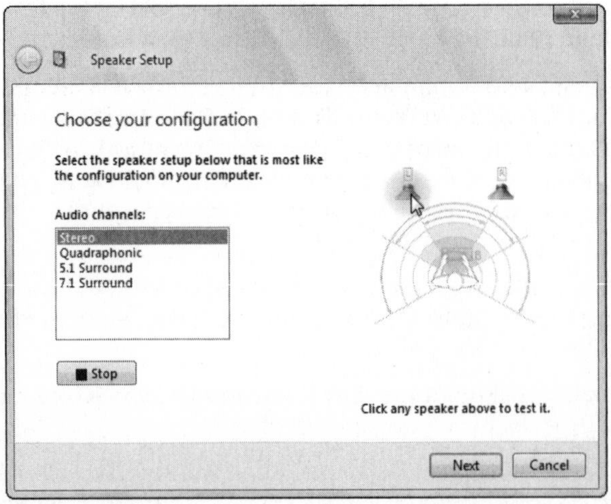

Figure 11-5:
Windows
Vista lets
you test
each
speaker
individually
to make
sure its
working and
correctly
placed.

> Speaker Setup
>
> Choose your configuration
>
> Select the speaker setup below that is most like the configuration on your computer.
>
> Audio channels:
> Stereo
> Quadraphonic
> 5.1 Surround
> 7.1 Surround
>
> ■ Stop
>
> Click any speaker above to test it.
>
> Next   Cancel

4. **Click the Sound window's Recording tab, click your microphone, and check its Properties settings.**

   On the Recording tab, shown in Figure 11-6, Vista lists everything able to record on your PC. On most PCs, you see at least the microphone and the Line In jack.

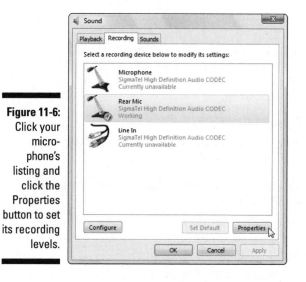

Figure 11-6:
Click your micro-phone's listing and click the Properties button to set its recording levels.

Click your microphone and click the Properties button. (The micro-phone's Configure button lets you set up Vista's speech recognition system, *not* adjust your sound levels.) When the Microphone Properties window appears, click the Levels tab.

Although the sliding control on the Levels tab lets you change the recording volume, there's no way to gauge its effect. For a visual indica-tor of what you're doing, open Vista's new Sound Recorder program from the Start menu (Start⇨All Programs⇨Accessories⇨Sound Recorder) and begin speaking into the microphone.

As you speak, a little green bar in Sound Recorder moves according to your microphone's recording level. Slide the levels in the Levels tab area until the microphone records at a middle level — not moving all the way to the right or left. You'll have to play back a few recordings until the recording levels sound right.

Close the Microphone Properties window when you're through.

Vista's Sound Recorder saves files in only WAV or WMA format. Neither are suitable for iPods and many other music players, so don't bother using that program to make any podcasts. Instead, try Audacity (http://audacity.sourceforge.net), a free program for recording and editing sound.

5. Click the Sound window's Sounds tab to assign different sounds to Windows events.

Bored with the same old opening music when Windows loads? Tired of your New Mail sound? Replace them by selecting your favorite sounds from computer games or other areas. Unfortunately, the menu allows only WAV files, so you can't assign the vastly more popular MP3s or MIDI files.

If you're not hearing any sounds when Windows loads, fix the problem by assigning a sound.

Windows Vista keeps its sounds on your C drive in the Media folder within the Windows folder. In other words, look in `C:\windows\media` for the sounds. They're named after their events. Windows' opening sound is called Windows Startup, for instance.

Changing Windows XP's sound settings

Windows XP owners can run through these steps to fine-tune their PC's sound settings.

1. From the Start menu, choose Control Panel and double-click the Sounds, Speech, and Audio Devices icon.

If you've switched to Windows XP's Classic View, where the Control Panel shows dozens of icons, double-click the Sounds and Audio Devices icon. Then jump ahead to Step 3.

2. Double-click the Sounds and Audio Devices icon.

The Sounds and Audio Devices Properties window appears. A huge switchbox of controls, it includes settings that change nearly every aspect of your sound.

3. Click the Volume tab and look for muted items.

The biggest problem by far with sound cards comes from their mixing software. A sound card controls everything in your computer that makes sound. And because you don't necessarily want to hear everything at once, some devices are usually muted. To make sure you haven't muted what you're trying to hear or record, click the Advanced button in the Device volume area, examine the Play Control window, and look for anything marked as Muted.

4. Add missing devices to the mixer and remove any unused ones.

Sound cards control so many devices that the mixer leaves some off so that the panel fits on the screen. To see *all* your sound card's available sound components, choose Properties from the Play Control's Options menu. Make sure that the devices you're using are checked, and the ones that aren't connected stay unchecked.

Click OK to close the window.

5. **While still on the Volume tab, choose your number of speakers.**

   In the Speakers settings area, the Advanced button tailors the sound for your particular speaker setup. Choose the one that's applicable for your setup.

6. **Click the Sounds tab to assign different sounds to Windows events.**

   Bored with the same old opening music when Windows loads? Tired of your New Mail sound? Replace them by selecting your favorite sounds from computer games or other areas. Unfortunately, the menu allows only WAV files, so you can't assign your favorite MP3s or MIDI files.

7. **Click the Voice tab to test your sound card's capabilities.**

   Almost all cards play and record sounds. A few old ones, however, can't do both at the *same time*. This makes them terrible for holding conversations over the Internet, editing sound and video, and using other areas where you need to hear and record simultaneously.

   To test your sound card's ability to play and record simultaneously, click the Test Hardware button to start the Sound Hardware Test Wizard.

Diagnosing and fixing hardware problems

Today's sound cards come with zillions of jacks, so check to make sure that everything is plugged into its correct spot. Check them all systematically so that you can rule out bad connections and move to other areas. Are the left and right speakers placed on the correct sides? Are the front and rear speakers plugged into the correct jacks?

Check out these things when your computer doesn't sound as good as it should:

- ✔ If you're using *digital* speakers, often required for surround sound, make sure you've connected your digital cable into your PC, not an *analog* cable. The digital cable usually resembles a mono RCA cable that connects a port on your sound card with a port on your speakers. Sometimes the digital cable plugs into the subwoofer, which sends the sound to the other speakers. If that cable's not connected, you won't hear anything when in digital mode.

- ✔ If you're using *analog* speakers, make sure you've connected your analog cables. You need a stereo cable for each pair of speakers. (The subwoofer gets a mono cable.)

✔ If none of your speakers plug into the wall, they probably use batteries. Try a new set of batteries. (And try to remember to turn those speakers off when you're away from your computer.)

✔ When you're stumped, turn to the Internet for help. Thousands of frustrated computer users have posted questions — and received answers — on the Internet's Newsgroups area. Those messages and their answers still linger on the Internet, waiting for you to read their solutions. Chapter 22 shows how to search the Newsgroups for the answers you need.

Chapter 12

Turning Your TV into a Home Theater with Vista's Media Center

....

In This Chapter

▶ Identifying audio and video cables and connectors

▶ Installing a TV tuner

▶ Connecting the TV signal to the PC

▶ Connecting the PC's video to the TV

▶ Connecting the PC's sound to the TV

....

*D*etermined to pry TiVo off the nation's TV sets, Microsoft tossed its *own* digital video recorder into Windows Vista: Windows Media Center. Formerly sold separately, Windows Media Center comes with two versions of Windows Vista, and it lets you schedule movie and TV show recordings automatically with your PC. The catch? Your PC needs three things to record television:

✔ A TV signal, which usually enters your home through a cable in the wall

✔ A TV tuner, which is usually a card that drops into a slot inside your PC

✔ Vista's Home Premium or Ultimate version, as Windows Media Center isn't included with Vista's other versions

This chapter explains how to install the TV tuner for recording and watching TV on your PC. It also explains how to connect your PC to your TV and home stereo, turning your PC into the backbone of a home theater.

The problem with recording digital cable and satellite channels

If you subscribe to digital cable channels or satellite TV, I've got some bad news: Those providers encode their TV signals to thwart thievery. Unscrambling the signal requires a special decoder box that connects to your TV. The box then feeds your TV one unscrambled channel at a time. Because that evil decoder box controls both the channel changing *and* the decoding, your PC's TV tuner won't work: It can't unscramble the channels, nor can it switch channels to record your scheduled shows.

Digital cable subscribers can still record the *non*-digital channels entering their home, which are channels 2 through 99 — those aren't scrambled. But your digital channels, usually channels 100 and above, must go through the cable box before entering your TV or TV tuner.

One solution comes in the form of an Infrared (IR) control cable — a little Infrared transmitter on a cable. You tape the IR transmitter over your box's IR receiver and plug the transmitter's other end into your PC's TV tuner. Then, when it's time to change channels and begin recording, Media Center tells the IR transmitter to tell the box to switch channels. As the channel pours in, your PC's tuner starts recording the unscrambled channel straight from the decoder box.

Not all TV tuners come with the Infrared control cable, however, and if yours doesn't, you're stuck with channels 2-99.

Identifying the Cables and Connectors on Your TV Tuner and TV

Your TV tuner comes with plenty of ports to grab video and send it to your TV screen in a variety of ways. Table 12-1 helps you identify the cables, their connectors, and their purpose in life.

Table 3-1:		A Cadre of Connectors	
The Cable and Its Connectors	**Its Name**	**Its Location**	**Its Purpose**
	Coaxial (RF) cable	Almost all TV tuners and TV sets	Most TV tuners and TV sets come use this port to transport TV channels.
	RCA (composite)	Some TV tuners andsome TVs	These carry sound, video, or both from the currently tuned channel. Yellow cables always carry *video*. Red (right) and white (left) cables carry stereo sound.

The Cable and Its Connectors	Its Name	Its Location	Its Purpose
	S-Video	Some TV tuners and some TVs	This cable, usually black, carries high-quality video but no sound.
	Optical/ Toslink	Some sound cards and home stereos	This carries Dolby AC-3 sound (sometimes called _multichannel, surround sound,_ or _5.1_) but no video.
	USB	TV tuner	Here's where you plug an external TV tuner into your PC or laptop.
	Infrared	Some TV tuners	Bundled with some TV tuners, this lets you change channels on your TV tuner (not your TV set or its decoder box) with a remote control.

Installing a TV Tuner

Difficulty level: Medium

Tools you need: One hand and a screwdriver

Cost: Cards average between $50 and $200.

Stuff to watch out for: When shopping for a TV tuner, make _sure_ it comes with Vista-compatible drivers. Many older and inexpensive TV tuners don't include Vista drivers and never will.

TV tuners that come with handheld remotes receive bonus points. You'll be watching the screen from a distance and need a handy way to control the action.

Some TV tuners plug into a USB port, providing a great way to turn laptops into portable TV sets.

To install a TV tuner, follow these steps. (If you're installing an *external* TV tuner, plug it into your USB port, shown in the margin, and jump ahead to the following section, "Connecting Your TV Signal to Your PC.")

1. **Turn off your computer, unplug it, and remove the cover.**

   Don't know how your PC's cover comes off? Flip to the Cheat Sheet at the front of this book for the answers.

2. **Locate a vacant PCI slot.**

   See that row of metal strips along on the back of your PC? Inside your PC, you'll spot a row of slots lined up with those metal strips. (They're usually white.) Those are your PCI slots, and you need to push your new TV tuner card into one of them.

3. **Remove the slot's back plate cover if necessary.**

   If you're replacing a card, skip this step, as the cover has already been removed.

   Unused slots often have a little cover over to them to keep dust from flying in through the back of your computer. With a small screwdriver, remove the screw that holds that cover in place. (Refer to Figure 7-6 in Chapter 7 and to Color Plates 19, 20, and 21 in the color insert pages in this book.) Don't lose that screw, as it will hold your new tuner card in place.

   If the screw accidentally drops into your PC, pick up your computer and shake it until the screw falls out. Keep the screw handy, and save the little cover, too; if you remove the card, you need the bracket to cover up that slot again.

4. **Push the card into any vacant PCI slot.**

   Hold the card by its edges and position it over any empty PCI slot. The edge with the shiny metal bracket should face toward the *back* of your computer. (That shiny bracket replaces the cover you removed in Step 3.)

   Line up the tabs and notches on the card's bottom edge with the notches in the slot. Push the card slowly into the slot. You might need to rock the card back and forth gently. When the card pops in, you can feel it come to rest. Don't force it!

    Don't let any card come into contact with any other card. That can cause electrical problems, and neither the card nor the computer will work.

5. **Secure the card in the slot with the screw you removed in Step 3.**

6. **Plug the computer back into the wall outlet, turn it on, and see whether Windows recognizes and installs the card.**

   Windows usually recognizes newly installed cards and sets them up to work correctly.

If something goes wrong, head for Chapter 19 for quick-fix tips about installing drivers. If everything's working, however, put your PC's cover back on.

7. **Install the latest version of the card's drivers and software.**

Whenever you install a new tuner card or any other card, visit the manufacturer's Web site. Find the site's Support or Customer Service section, and then download and install the latest drivers for that particular model and your version of Windows, be it Vista or XP. Card manufacturers constantly update their drivers and software to fix bugs.

8. **Install the IR receiver for the remote control, if needed.**

TV tuner cards that include handheld remote controls sometimes come with an IR receiver that gives you something to aim at. The IR receiver is a thin cable with a jack on one end and little plastic receiver on the other end. Plug the cable's jack into the card's IR port, and then place the receiver within sight of where you'll point the remote.

TV tuners that plug into a USB port usually have the receiver built into their box. Aim the remote control at the little box's built-in receiver when changing channels. (The built-in receiver is usually hidden by dark translucent plastic.)

After you've installed the TV tuner, it's time to connect it to your TV signal, described in the next section.

Connecting Your TV Signal to Your PC

This part's easy, as the vast majority of TV tuners grab a TV signal only one way: through the coaxial port shown in the margin.

Knowing that, here's the easy way to connect it to your PC: Unplug the coaxial cable from the back of your TV and plug it into the coaxial port on your PC's new TV tuner. Then jump to the "Connecting Your PC's Video to a TV" section to finish the job.

A better alternative, however, is to buy an inexpensive splitter that turns that single cable into *two* cables: One stays plugged into your TV, and the other plugs into your PC's TV tuner. This has two big advantages:

✓ You can watch a show on your TV while your PC's TV tuner records a second show on a different channel.

✓ Your TV still functions normally, even when the PC is turned off.

Follow these steps to connect your TV signal to your PC (and your TV, if desired):

1. **Unplug the coaxial cable from your TV's RF In port.**

   Found on the back of every TV, this accepts the signal from a cable that runs from either the wall or an antenna. The cable's connector pushes or screws onto the port on the back of your TV.

   Although a few coaxial cables push onto their connectors, most screw onto them. You might need a pair of pliers to loosen the connector; your fingers can handle the rest.

2. **Plug the cable into a splitter, if desired. (The cable goes into the side of the splitter with only one port.)**

   If you don't have a splitter, skip to Step 5 and plug the cable directly into your TV tuner's TV In port.

   The splitters cost a few dollars at any consumer electronics shop. The splitter has one coax port on one end and two coax ports on the other. While buying the splitter, buy two coaxial cables — one for your PC and the other to plug back into your TV.

   Coaxial cables always screw onto a splitter; the push-on connectors tend to fall off.

3. **Plug a coaxial cable onto each of the two ports on the splitter's other side.**

4. **Plug one of those two cables back into your TV where you unplugged the first.**

5. **Plug the other cable into your TV tuner's TV In port.**

   That's it. The splitter then lets your TV keep its same connection, so it still receives the same channels. Plus, your PC receives all the channels, as well.

Connecting Your PC's Video to a TV

TV tuners let you watch TV on your PC without problem. But you can also route the TV shows back onto your TV screen, letting you enjoy them on the big screen. You can do this either of two ways:

- ✔ **TV tuner:** Some TV tuners can connect directly to a television set.
- ✔ **Video cards:** Some video cards (see Chapter 7) offer a television connection, as well.

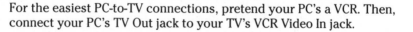

The secret is to find a TV Out jack on your PC's TV tuner or video card that matches a Video In jack on your TV. After you find those two jacks, you simply connect the appropriate cable between the two matching jacks.

For the easiest PC-to-TV connections, pretend your PC's a VCR. Then, connect your PC's TV Out jack to your TV's VCR Video In jack.

Look for any of these four jacks on both your PC and TV:

- ✔ **S-Video:** If your TV and PC's tuner both offer this port, connect the two with an S-Video cable for the best picture. Found on high-quality TV sets, S-Video not only carries a good picture, it lets you keep your PC's monitor plugged in (unlike the last two jacks on this list).

- ✔ **RCA:** Found on most TV sets and some TV tuners, this yellow port sends medium-quality video to the TV. If your PC doesn't have S-Video, connect an RCA cable between the RCA port on both the PC and the TV.

- ✔ **DVI:** Many HDTV (High Definition Television) sets come with a DVI port — the same one found on most LCD monitors and PCs. That makes the TV connection as easy as unplugging your PC's monitor and plugging the cable into your HDTV set. Unfortunately, you lose the convenience of seeing the picture simultaneously on both your TV and your PC's monitor.

- ✔ **VGA:** Some HDTV sets also come with a VGA port. Although it doesn't provide nearly as good a picture as the DVI port, this port also lets you turn your HDTV into a replacement monitor.

After you've chosen the highest quality port on both your PC and TV, follow these steps to connect your PC to your TV:

1. **Set your PC and your TV within a few feet of each other.**

   Most video cables are less than six feet long, which doesn't give you much working room.

2. **Connect a cable between the matching TV ports on both your PC and your TV.**

   Connect the appropriate cable between your PC's TV Out port and your TV's Line In, Video In, or VCR Video port. RCA and S-Video cables line the shelves of most consumer electronics stores.

   If your TV has more than one Line In or Video In port, remember which port you're plugging it into. You'll need to switch your TV's Video Input, usually located through a button on the TV's front or its remote, to that port.

3. **Adjust your PC's video settings so the picture fits on the TV's screen.**

   Unless you're connecting your PC's DVI port directly to an HDTV's DVI port, this could be the most difficult part of all: A PC's high-resolution image is too large to fit on a TV's low-resolution screen. These tweaks make it look the best, though:

   a. *First, set your PC's video to display a low-resolution of 640 x 480:*

   Windows Vista: Right-click the desktop, choose Personalize, and choose Display Settings. Then slide the Resolution slider on the Display Settings window toward the left until the resolution shows 640 x 480. Click OK to make the switch.

   Windows XP: Right-click the desktop, choose Properties, and click the Settings tab. Then slide the Screen Resolution slider to the left until the PC switches to 640 x 480. Click OK to make the switch.

   b. *Finally, adjust your TV's vertical and horizontal settings to squish the picture onto the screen as best as you can.*

   You can usually access these settings through knobs on a fold-down panel along the TV set's front.

After following those steps, your Windows desktop should appear on your TV. If you're still having trouble, try these tips:

✔ When connecting your PC to an HDTV, set your PC's video resolution to 1280 x 720 with a refresh rate of 60 Hz. (Step 3 describes how to change the resolution.) If that works, try bumping up the resolution to 1920 x 1080 to take full advantage of the TV's highest quality. Not all video cards offer these resolutions, however, so experiment with your PC's resolution to see what looks best on the big screen.

✔ These steps connect your PC's *video* to your TV, but not its sound. If your PC's own sound isn't good enough, connect your PC's sound to your home stereo, explained in this chapter's next section.

✔ If you can't find matching connectors on your PC and TV, you have two choices: Install a new video card with a TV Out port inside your PC (Chapter 7), or buy a PC-to-TV converter box from Amazon (www.amazon.com) or a computer store. The box plugs into your USB port, giving your PC an RCA or S-Video port to connect to your TV.

✔ If you still can't see anything on your TV, reconnect your monitor, head to your video card's settings in Step 3, and tell your video card to turn on its TV Out port. Different video cards offer this option through their own manufacturer's software, unfortunately, so I can't give you exact instructions.

Connecting Your PC's Surround Sound to a Multispeaker Home Stereo

Most home stereos cost several hundred dollars more than the cheap desktop speakers sold with many PCs today. If you watch a lot of DVDs on your PC and want surround sound — or you simply want higher-quality sound when listening to MP3s — this section explains how to connect your PC's sound to a stereo or home theater with surround sound: five speakers and a subwoofer.

Most of today's home stereos accept sound from at least three types of connectors: digital, optical, or RCA jacks. As with connecting video, the key to success is finding the best sound source your sound card dishes up, and connecting it to the best sound source accepted by your home stereo.

Follow these steps to connect your PC's sound to your home stereo.

1. **Count the speakers connected to your home theater or stereo.**

   If your stereo sends sound through a single pair of speakers, usually one speaker on each side of the TV, it's probably using *analog* sound. If it's piping walls of sound through five or more speakers, however, it's probably using *digital* sound. Those two types of sound use different connections, as I explain in the next few steps.

   There's little point in setting up digital sound if you're only listening through two speakers on your stereo.

2. **Discover the type of sound offered by your PC's sound card.**

   All sound cards can send analog sound; the better sound cards send digital sound, as well.

   Examine your sound card's jacks on the back of your PC. Most sound cards offer at least two of these three connectors.

   - **Optical/Toslink (digital):** A Toslink digital connector, shown in the margin, resembles a square hole. Sometimes it's called an *optical* connector. When not in use, the hole's usually plugged with a small plastic cover that pulls off with a little effort.

   - **Coaxial/RCA (digital):** Sometimes called a S/PDIF or digital coaxial connector, this single RCA jack is sometimes orange.

   - **⅛-inch (analog):** When your sound card offers only a single ⅛-inch headphone or Line Out jack, you're limited to stereo sound.

3. **Find your stereo's matching Audio In jack.**

   Examine the bundle of jacks along the back of your stereo.

   If you have only two speakers connected to your home stereo, you'll probably spot a pair of RCA Audio In jacks.

   If you have more than two speakers, you'll probably find either a Toslink or a single RCA connector.

4. **Connect the matching cable between the matching ports on your PC's sound card and your stereo.**

   The instructions differ depending on whether you're connecting with analog or digital cables.

   Analog: To connect your PC's sound card to a pair of RCA jacks on your stereo, pick up Radio Shack part number 274-369. Shown in the margin, it's officially known as a *Y-Adapter, Phono Jacks to Stereo ⅛-inch Plug.* Plug the adapter into your sound card's ⅛-inch Line Out jack. Plug a stereo RCA cable into the adapter's other two jacks and connect the cable's other end to your stereo's two RCA Audio In ports. (The *red* jack connects to the stereo's *right* channel. The other jack [white] connects to the left channel.)

   This same handy adapter lets you plug your iPod and most other portable music players into your home stereo, as well. In fact, if you can't find the adapter, buy an iPod-to-stereo connection cable, as it does the same thing.

   Digital: Buy whichever digital cable matches the digital ports on both your PC and home stereo, Toslink or RCA. Connect the cable between the two ports, and jump to Step 6.

   Stuck with a Toslink connector on your PC's sound card and a RCA connector on your home stereo or vice versa? Pick up a Toslink/RCA converter from Ram Electronics (`www.ramelectronics.net`) or a stereo store. For less than $30, the converter lets the two connect.

5. **Switch your stereo's Audio In knob to either Line In or the jack with your PC's sound.**

   Most stereos let you hear sound from a variety of gadgets: tape players, radios, VCRs, or even record players. To switch to your PC, turn the stereo's input selector knob to Line In — or the name of the jack where you plugged in your PC's sound cable.

   If you've plugged in a digital connection, you might need to flip a switch on your stereo to switch it to digital mode or the one used for DVD players.

6. Adjust the volume.

Play music through your PC at a low volume, and then slowly turn up the volume on your stereo. You'll probably want to control the volume at your PC because that's within reach. So turn the volume up on your stereo, and leave your PC set fairly low. Then, as you turn up the volume on your PC, your stereo will grow louder, as well.

- ✔ Play around with the volume settings for awhile until you find the right mix. If the PC's too loud and the stereo's too low, you'll hear distortion. If the stereo's too loud and the PC's too low, you'll blast your ears when you turn up the sound on your PC.

- ✔ Don't bother spending the extra cash for expensive "high-fidelity" audio cables. They don't make your PC any sound better.

Connecting Your PC's Sound to a TV

Earlier in this chapter, I explain how to connect your PC's video to your TV set, letting you watch shows on the TV's larger screen. For the best sound, most people then connect their PC's sound to their home stereo, which I describe in the previous section.

But if you'd prefer to hear the sound coming from your TV set's built-in speakers, you want this section.

Here's the secret to viewing and hearing your PC's TV shows through your TV: Pretend that your PC is a VCR. By thinking that way, the job's as easy as plugging your PC's sound cable into the TV's jacks that are meant for a VCR's sound.

1. Buy a cable with a ⅛-inch stereo plug on one end and two RCA jacks on the other.

Commonly sold as an iPod accessory, this cable also lets you plug your iPod into a stereo.

If you can't find the right cable, buy Radio Shack part number 274-369, shown in the margin and described in the previous sections. The handy adapter plugs into your sound card's 1/8-inch jack and offers two RCA ports on its other end. Then buy a two RCA cables and plug them into the adapter's two RCA ports.

2. Plug the cable's ⅛-inch plug into your PC's Line Out jack.

That leaves you with a pair of RCA jacks that contain your PC's stereo sound.

3. **Connect the two RCA cables into your TV's VCR Audio In jacks.**

   Only one RCA port on your TV? Connect the red jack to the red port, and leave the other dangling. You'll hear only mono sound rather than stereo.

4. **Set your TV's Input to VCR.**

   This brings in the video from your PC's TV Out jack, which you hooked up in this chapter's "Connecting Your PC's Video to a TV" section. And it brings in the sound that you've just connected.

5. **Adjust the volume.**

   Play music through your PC at a low volume, and then slowly turn up the volume on your TV. You'll probably want to control the volume at your PC because that's within reach. So turn the volume up on your TV and leave your PC set fairly low. Then, as you turn up the volume on your PC, your TV will grow louder, as well.

Chapter 13

Making Movies

In This Chapter

▶ Translating digital camcorder technobabble

▶ Downloading movies from a digital camcorder

▶ Upgrading a computer for video editing

*F*or years, computers merely replaced typewriters. Today, they're replacing reels of family movies and old tapes. More and more people have ditched their bulky old camcorders for the convenience and accuracy of digital camcorders. Digital videos are easier to edit and easier to pour into your PC for editing and copying to a DVD.

This chapter explains some of the concepts behind digital videography and shows you how to prepare your computer for the oncoming onslaught of embarrassing video memorabilia.

Understanding Camcorder Buzzwords

In digital moviemaking, your camcorder stores each movie inside one huge file. The first obstacle is pouring that huge file into your computer. Engineers have created several differently sized funnels for you to choose from, which I explain in this chapter.

The second stumbling block comes from the language that's sprouted up around digital video. Before you can set up a digital editing room that meets your needs, you must understand some of the most frequently encountered buzzwords.

This section explains the terminology surrounding the world of digital video. Grab your philosopher's cap and march forward to tread the waters of analog and digital.

Analog camcorders: Analog camcorders — the bulky old ones used before digital camcorders hit the shelves — save your video onto tape as magnetic waves, not numbers. Because analog camcorders can't dish up numbers, they don't work with Windows Movie Maker or other video editing programs. To edit those movies on your PC, you must first import the video with a video capture card, covered in the sidebar, "Capturing sound and video from analog camcorders."

DV (Digital Video) camcorders: Working like high-speed digital cameras, DV camcorders measure the light and sound hitting their sensors and store the measurements as numbers on special digital videotape. Because the video already lives as a string of numbers, it's easy to copy to your PC as one big file, ready for editing.

Optical/digital zoom: Digital cameras and camcorders can use two different methods when zooming in for close-ups of distant images. An *optical* zoom works like a telescope to magnify the image. When the optical zoom finds its best image, the camcorder takes the picture.

With *digital* zoom, by contrast, the camcorder examines the best image its optical lens could gather. Then it mathematically exaggerates the image, guessing at how an even closer view would appear. Unfortunately, the camcorder's mathematical guesswork usually adds jagged edges, which destroys the natural beauty of an image.

Optical zooms provide much more realistic images than digital zooms, so when shopping, give optical zoom rates much more credence than digital zoom rates.

Webcam: Webcams usually plug into a USB port to send a snapshot to your PC at regular intervals, usually for uploading to a Web site. (You can check out my webcam at `www.andyrathbone.com`.) Digital camcorders and some digital cameras can double as webcams.

FireWire (IEEE 1394 or Sony i.LINK): Digital video files are *huge,* requiring a speedy method of transportation from your camcorder to your computer. FireWire ports move information rapidly, and their early lead quickly captured the digital camcorder market.

USB: As the digital camcorder market matures, more of them now support the popular USB ports used by most digital cameras. The digital video standard remains FireWire, though, so you might have trouble finding a USB-compatible digital camcorder.

Capturing sound and video from analog camcorders

Older camcorders are *analog,* not *digital.* Unlike digital camcorders, they're not converting their video into numbers as they record. That makes it harder to move the camcorder's video onto your number-lovin' PC. The solution is a *video capture device* — a gadget that comes in two forms: a card plugged inside your PC or a box plugged into your PC's USB port.

To dump an analog camcorder's video into your PC, connect the camcorder's Video Out cable to your video capture device's Video In port. Then connect its audio cables to your sound card's Line In jacks. When you begin playing back the

camcorder's video, the video capture card's software combines the incoming video with the sound and saves the movie as a large digital video file.

When the video's on your PC, you can edit it just as easily as if it came from one of today's digital video camcorders.

Bought a new digital camcorder? Check its manual. Some digital camcorders will connect to an analog camcorder and convert that old analog video into digital footage.

Capturing Sound and Video from Digital Camcorders

Digital camcorders cooperate with your computer quite easily. As you shoot your footage, the digital camcorder packs both the video and sound into a single file.

That leaves the problem of moving the file from the camcorder to the computer. (When recording a TV show with a TV tuner card, covered in Chapter 12, the card dumps the file straight onto your hard drive, sparing you any transportation troubles.)

To move the video from your camcorder to your PC, you need one cable that's plugged into one of the jacks discussed in this section.

FireWire cable: Several years ago, Apple placed FireWire ports onto their computers as standard equipment. Some PC folks refer to a FireWire port as an *IEEE 1394* port, but they're both the same thing. Some PCs don't come with a preinstalled IEEE 1394 port, unfortunately. If yours lacks that port, you need to buy a FireWire card and install it inside your computer. (See Chapter 7 for more about installing video cards and other cards into your computer.)

USB cable: Although most digital camcorders still use FireWire, a few have switched to USB, instead. Check your camcorder's manual to see which type of port it uses.

Although it's called digital *video,* the signal coming from a DV camcorder's port contains both video *and* sound. The clever video-editing software figures out which part of the file contains the guitar solo and which contains the close-up of fingers racing across the fret board.

The few digital camcorders that use USB ports require USB 2.0 ports, not the USB 1.1 ports found on some older PCs. If your camcorder takes forever to dump a file onto your PC, make sure your PC has a USB 2.0 port.

Upgrading a PC for Video Editing

If your PC's able to run Windows Vista and its 3D graphics, transparent windows, and built-in video recorder, your PC can probably stand up to the rigors of video editing.

Still, different PCs work better than others. The next three sections describe what things in a PC make for the best video editing: a fast PC, two fast hard drives, and video editing software.

A fast computer

Any PC with a FireWire port can grab incoming video fairly quickly. After all, you're simply copying a file from one place (your camcorder) to another (your PC). Editing the video — cutting away the boring parts and stringing together the good ones — doesn't require much processing power, either. The entire editing process is just telling the PC when to start and stop playing your video. Even when you add transitions between shots — fades, for instance — you're only giving the PC instructions on what to do later, when you've finished editing.

A fast PC proves its mettle when you're through editing the movie and want to apply all your editing work to the video. At that point, your PC examines all your edits, extracts the good parts, discards the bad, and weaves them back together into a cohesive whole, complete with transitions between the scenes. The process can take hours, even on a relatively fast PC.

When your PC's too slow for the jobs you're throwing at it, it's time to buy a new one. If you plan on making lots of videos, buy as fast a PC as you can afford. Look for the words *Intel Core Duo* or *AMD Athlon 64 X2* on the PC's spec sheet.

If you can't afford something that powerful, you can still edit videos on a slower PC. But transforming your edited work into a finished creation will take a lot longer. Be prepared to let it sit and work all night.

Showing off your digital photos on TV

Most PCs sold in the last five years work fine for connecting to digital cameras and then grabbing and storing their images. The problems begin when the photos are *inside* your PC. How can you show them off to family and friends without crowding everybody around your PC?

Connecting your PC to a TV, covered in Chapter 12, solves that problem. Vista's Windows Media Center, the software bundled with Windows Vista Premium and Ultimate editions, does a nice job of displaying your photos in a slideshow, complete with a soundtrack. And *every* Vista version comes with Windows Photo Gallery, which also creates a slideshow. (Fire up Media Player in the background to add music to the show.)

But Vista offers another alternative if you're not keen on connecting your PC to your TV. Windows Vista's DVD Maker, bundled with Windows Vista's Premium and Ultimate Editions, also creates a smooth slideshow from your digital photos, complete with a soundtrack of your choice. Then it copies the show onto a blank DVD for easy playback on any DVD player.

I explain how to put DVD Maker to work in *Windows Vista For Dummies* (Wiley Publishing).

Bonus: Outfitting a PC for video editing also turns it into a fantastic game machine, letting it run all the latest games at their finest.

Two fast hard drives

Digital video consumes about 3.6MB for each second of footage, or about 13GB of space per hour. For many PCs, that's a *lot* of space. But I'm just getting started. After you've edited the video, you need additional space to store your finished movie.

To capture an hour's worth of vacation video from your camcorder, edit out half, and create a new, half-hour video, you need at least 20GB of empty hard drive space.

Also, video-editing software writes files to the disk in one smooth stream. That means that best results happen when you use two *separate* hard drives. You heard me right. You're best served by using one hard drive to capture the incoming video and the other drive to collect the edited video as the software writes it to the disk.

In short, if you're considering editing digital video, take a look at the amount of space left on your hard drive.

Vista makes it easy to see your PC's hard drives and the amount of space left on them. Open Computer from the Start menu, and Vista lists the hard drive's size and amount of free space, as shown in Figure 13-1.

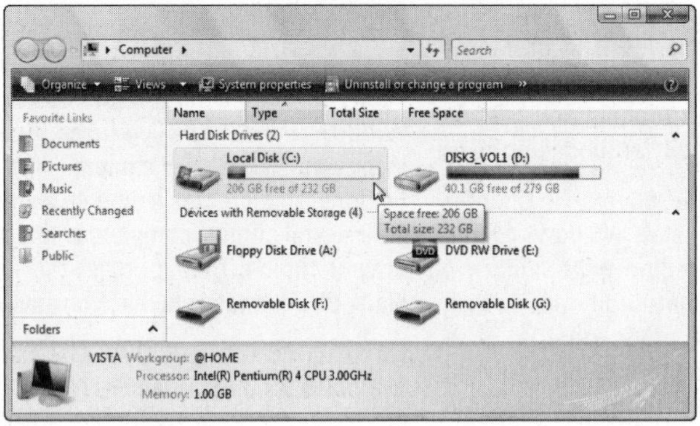

Figure 13-1:
Open
Computer
from the
Start menu
to see your
hard drive's
size and
free space.

For example, my PC in Figure 13-1 contains two hard drives. Hard drive C is 232GB in size and has 206GB of free space. The second hard drive, D, is 279GB in size and has 40GB of space. That's plenty of room for editing video.

To see your hard drives and their free space in Windows XP, open My Computer from the Start menu and click one of your drive's icons. The hard drive's amount of free space appears in the window's bottom left corner. In Figure 13-2, for example, my PC's C drive is 145GB in size, with 44.1GB of free space.

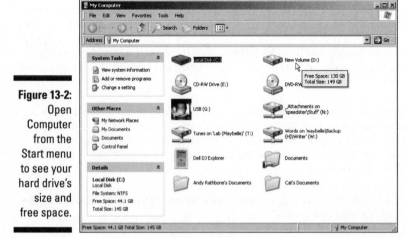

Figure 13-2:
Open
Computer
from the
Start menu
to see your
hard drive's
size and
free space.

To see a hard drive's size and amount of free space in either Windows Vista or Windows XP, hover your mouse pointer over the drive. A pop-up appears, shown in Figures 13-1 and 13-2, listing the drive's total size and amount of free space.

Consider these tips when preparing a PC's hard drives for video editing:

✔ When buying a new hard drive, make sure your hard drives are fast. Look for the code words *7200 RPM* or *10,000 RPM* on the drive's box, as they indicate speed. Bigger numbers mean faster drives. (I cover hard drives in Chapter 9.)

✔ Before transferring digital video from your camcorder to your Windows XP computer, defragment your hard drive. Right-click the drive's icon in My Computer and choose Properties from the pop-up menu. In the dialog box that appears, click the Tools tab, and then click the Defragment Now button. That liberates a large continuous area of free space that your hard drive can use to quickly write incoming video information.

Windows Vista automatically keeps your hard drive defragmented, sparing you the trouble.

✔ Be sure your Windows XP hard drive is formatted in NTFS format rather than FAT32 or FAT16, or you'll run into file size problems. FAT32 limits a file's size to only 4GB, and FAT16 limits it to 2GB. (Windows Vista automatically formats hard drives in NTFS.)

Video-editing software

Windows Vista's Premium and Ultimate versions and Windows XP all include free video-editing software called Windows Movie Maker. Although the pros might turn up their noses, Windows Movie Maker (shown in Figure 13-3) does a great job of importing your digital camcorder footage, letting you hack out the ugly bits, save the good, weave in a soundtrack, and patch together the results in a single file.

It's fine for splicing together vacation videos, editing out commercials from recorded TV shows, and creating other small video projects. Combined with the DVD Maker program bundled with Vista's Premium and Ultimate versions, you can turn your videos into finished DVDs, complete with opening screen menus.

Even if you plan to move into the big leagues by purchasing a third-party video-editing program, try editing your first videos in Windows Movie Maker to get a feel for how video-editing packages work. (The all work in a very similar fashion.)

Figure 13-3:
Windows
Movie
Maker
works fine
for editing
videos to
play back
on your
computer,
television
set, e-mail
to friends, or
save as
DVDs.

Note how your computer handles Movie Maker's demands. Teamed with your current computer, Movie Maker might be all you need to edit out the embarrassing portions of your vacation videos.

Always store a copy of your original videotapes *and* your finished DVDs in a safe place. You or your ancestors will want to see them in the future.

Chapter 14

Adding a Scanner

*S*canners work like a tiny, flat copy machine. But instead of printing paper copies of what you place onto the scanner's bed, a scanner stores a copy of your item as a computer file.

In the process of taking this detailed digital picture, scanners magnify *everything*. That means that any extraneous item on the original — a piece of dirt, a lint speck, a cat hair, a grain of sand, or a fingerprint — shows up in full detail in the scanned version stored on your computer. Be sure to clean the scanner's glass before putting it to work.

This chapter leads you through scanning, from installation to pushing the Scan button.

Understanding Scanner Buzzwords

You might notice some of the same words appearing on the boxes of both scanners and digital cameras. That's because scanners work much like digital cameras, except they're limited to close-ups of large, flat items. Because of this specialized purpose, scanners come with their own specialized words, making you wade through awkward acronyms like dpi and TWAIN.

When you find yourself sinking into your scanner's vocabulary, use this rope to help pull you out.

dpi (dots per inch): Choosing a higher dpi setting tells the scanner to collect more detailed information about your image. That translates to a larger image on your monitor, a larger-sized file, and a higher-resolution image with higher quality when printed.

Dots per inch also means *pixels per inch,* and monitors display everything by lighting up pixels on the screen. Using a higher-resolution setting on your monitor lets you view a higher-resolution image more comfortably. (Chapter 3 explains pixels, as well as how to change your monitor's resolution settings.)

You'll scan the majority of your photos and documents at between 75 and 300 dpi.

OCR (Optical Character Recognition): Scanners take high-quality, up-close pictures, usually of flat surfaces. The key word is *pictures*. You can't scan a letter and expect to read it in a word processor. But wouldn't it be nice if you *could* do just that? Well, some brainiac invented OCR software that analyzes images for recognizable characters. Then it dumps the characters into a text file as words. That lets you scan a document, run OCR software on the image, and save the text into a file for importing into a word processor.

Neither Vista nor Windows XP includes OCR software, although some scanners toss it in for free. Check your scanner's bundled software.

When using OCR software, be sure to align the document or book onto the scanner in the correct position, usually with the top sheet against the top edge of the scanner's glass plate. Then scan at 300 dpi. Finally, most OCR software understands neither grammar, spelling, nor etiquette. That's up to you and your word processor to fix.

Optical/enhanced: Many scanners list an optical dpi rating and another rating for enhanced. The difference? The enhanced mode is a computerized exaggeration of the optical mode. For a true look at what your scanner can handle, rely on the optical figures. (Digital cameras and camcorders, discussed in Chapter 13, use similar computerized exaggerations with their digital zooms.)

TWAIN: A not-for-profit group decided to liberate scanners from their complicated bundle of software. So the group created a set of standards for manufacturers to incorporate into their scanners. Thanks to TWAIN, many programs — including some versions of Windows Vista and Windows XP — can easily bypass your scanner's bundled software and access your scanner directly.

The initials TWAIN don't stand for anything. The TWAIN organization says it lifted the name from Rudyard Kipling's poem, "The Ballad of East and West," which contains the line, "and never the twain shall meet." However, one of TWAIN's founders said he coined the term from *Toolkit Without An Interesting Name* after frustration at finding a name for a rather dry topic.

TWAIN is a *device-specific* driver. You need to install the specific version of TWAIN that comes with your device. The TWAIN driver that comes with one scanner, for instance, won't necessarily work with other scanner models.

WIA (Windows Imaging Architecture): Incorporated in Windows Me and carried through to Windows XP, WIA builds upon TWAIN to enable users to run their TWAIN-compatible devices directly from Windows. With WIA, for instance, you may access many scanners from Vista's Paint program, shown in Figure 14-1, or most other graphics programs, using the same commands for every brand or model of scanner.

Some graphics software — Adobe Photoshop, Jasc Paint Shop Pro, and others — can also control your scanner directly. Turn on your scanner, insert the material to be scanned, and load your graphics program. Choose Acquire or Import from the program's File menu. The program tells your scanner to grab the image and dump it directly into your graphics program, conveniently bypassing your scanner's bundled software. (The Acquire/Import trick works through the scanner's TWAIN driver, so it only works with TWAIN-compatible scanners.)

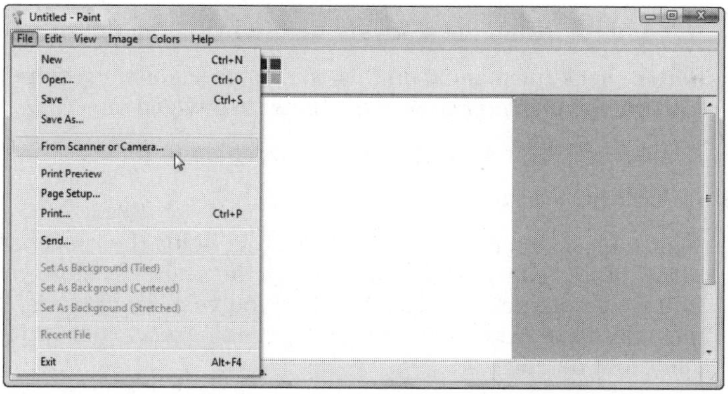

Figure 14-1:
To avoid a scanner's complicated bundled software, open Paint's File menu and choose From Scanner or Camera to control the scanner directly with Vista's built-in software.

24-bit color and 48-bit color: Computers use *bits* — a state of being turned on or off — to process information. Any item boasting 24-bit color means it can handle 16,777,216 colors, a standard known as True Color or photo quality. It's fine for most needs. (Some design and printing professionals scan at 48-bit color mode.)

USB: Almost all scanners support USB 2.0 ports. The speedy USB 2.0 standard enables them to dump high-quality images onto your computer much faster than allowed by the older USB standard. If your old computer lacks a 2.0 USB port (you'll know because color scans take so long), pick up a USB 2.0 card and install it into your computer. (See Chapter 7 for more about installing cards; USB 2.0 cards plug into a PCI slot.)

Installing a Scanner

Installing a scanner works much like installing a printer (see Chapter 4), except that you needn't worry about ink nor toner cartridges. Installing the scanner's fairly easy. (The hard part comes when trying to figure out all the confusing options offered by the scanner's bundled software.)

Follow these steps to install a scanner:

1. **Remove the scanner and its accessories from the box.**

   Be sure to search the scanner's box for a cable — probably USB — the software, the manual, and any weird-looking plastic holders for negatives or slides. Some scanners come with their lids detached, so you might need to rummage around for that.

2. **If required, install the software before installing the scanner.**

   Better check the manual on this one. Some scanners require their software to be installed *before* the scanner is plugged in.

3. **Remove any tape securing the scanner's lid in place.**

4. **Unlock the scanner.**

   Almost all scanners come with a lock that holds their mechanism in place during transport. Be sure to lock the scanner before you move it. And always unlock the scanner when you've put it in place. Although most new scanners have safeguards, running a scanner while it's locked can cause damage.

   Look for a round plastic area with a notch along the scanner's side. Rotating that round piece of plastic usually unlocks the scanner. (Sometimes there's a little slot to insert in the lock; a coin often works in the slot as a makeshift screwdriver.)

5. **Put on the scanner's lid and fasten its connecting cable, if necessary.**

   Most lids don't have a firm hinge. Some have two prongs that slide in and out of holes, and others have spring mechanisms.

6. **Plug your scanner into the power outlet and plug its connector into your computer.**

Some use FireWire ports, others USB. (Some older ones connect to their own expansion card or, heaven forbid, your PC's antiquated parallel port.)

7. **Press the power button.**

After a second or two, Windows recognizes your new scanner. If it doesn't, try fiddling with your bundled software to see if it recognizes your new software.

If your computer doesn't seem to notice all your work, it's time to head to the next section.

Dealing with a Scanner That Doesn't Work

The biggest problem with scanners comes from their bundled software. It's often stuffed with options you don't need, making it harder to find the ones you want. To solve the problem, try skipping the software completely. Both Windows Vista and Windows XP include simple scanning software, described in the following section.

Another problem comes from plugging a USB 2.0 scanner into an older USB 1.1 port. USB 2.0 scanners want to throw information around quickly, and a computer's older, USB 1.1 port can't grab it that quickly. If your scanner takes forever to dump its image into your PC, you probably need to upgrade to a USB 2.0 port.

If you're still having troubles, try some of these solutions:

- Scanners often go to sleep when you haven't used them for a while. Try pushing the power button off and then on again to wake the scanner back up.

- If you're using a USB hub, try plugging the scanner directly into the computer's USB port. Some finicky devices don't care for hubs.

- If low-resolution scans work but your computer freezes or sends odd error messages during high-resolution scans, your computer might need more memory. Computers use memory to store information as they scan, and high-resolution scans contain a *lot* of information.

- Close down all other programs and try running the scanner by itself.

- Sometimes it's difficult to tell if the scanner itself is causing problems, or if complicated software is making the scanner act up. If your scanner doesn't seem to be working properly, bypass its software and try scanning it directly from Windows, as described in the next section.

Scanning with Windows' Built-in Software

If you find your scanner's bundled software cumbersome and downright difficult, you have an alternative. Windows Vista and Windows XP come with their own simple software for scanning images. Using Windows' menus also lets you diagnose trouble, as it lets you know if the problem lies with your scanner's software or within the scanner itself.

Follow these steps to hand the scanning reins to Windows Vista; the steps in Windows XP are almost identical. Although it's good for a quick scanner test, it's so simple you might find yourself using it for quick tasks: scanning an item for a fax, e-mail, or party flyer.

Before scanning anything, always clean it and the scanner's glass thoroughly with a lint-free cloth. Any dirt or residue will show up on the scan.

1. **Lift your scanner's cover, place the item to be scanned on the glass, and close the cover.**

   Most scanners seem to prefer that you nestle the scanned item in the top-right corner. Yours might be different. Very few, however, like you to place the image haphazardly on the middle of the glass, as the resulting images will tilt when viewed on your screen.

   Like cooking grills and tennis rackets, some inexpensive scanners have sweet spots where the picture looks its best upon scanning. If you're having trouble with poor optics, light leaks, or uneven light along the scanner's edges, search the Web site to see if your particular model of scanner has a sweet spot. (Chapter 22 covers Web searches.) You might need to experiment by moving your item to different spots on the bed.

2. **Open Paint, click the File menu, and choose From Scanner or Camera.**

   Paint comes with every version of Windows, so I'm using that as an example here. But almost every graphics software offers a similar option under the File menu. If you prefer a different graphics program, click its File menu and choose Acquire, Import, or something similar to start scanning.

   Windows' built-in scanning software jumps in, shown in Figure 14-2, with your scanner's name listed along the window's top edge.

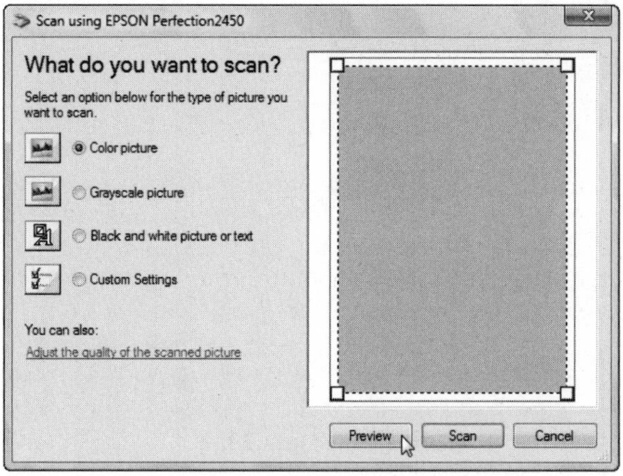

Figure 14-2:
Windows
offers much
simpler
menus than
the software
bundled
with most
scanners.

If the scanner's name doesn't appear, it isn't WIA and TWAIN compatible (see the "Understanding Scanner Buzzwords" section earlier in the chapter for an explanation of those terms), and you're stuck with its bundled software.

If you own more than one scanner, choose your model from the pop-up menu.

3. Choose your scan type and click Preview.

Windows offers four choices:

- *Color Picture:* This is the obvious choice for anything with color or being sent to a color printer.

- *Grayscale Picture:* Choose this for black-and-white photos where you want lots of shading. Try it to see how your color photo would look when printed by a non-color printer.

- *Black and White Picture or Text:* This is *literal,* as it separates everything into either black or white. It's mainly used for scanning text and line art, *not* old black-and-white photos.

- *Custom Settings:* Choose the resolution here, discussed in this chapter's "Choosing the right scanning resolution" section, or fiddle with the brightness/contrast settings.

When you click the Preview button, Windows scans the picture and places it on the screen. The crop marks surrounding the image, shown in Figure 14-3, show the exact area being scanned.

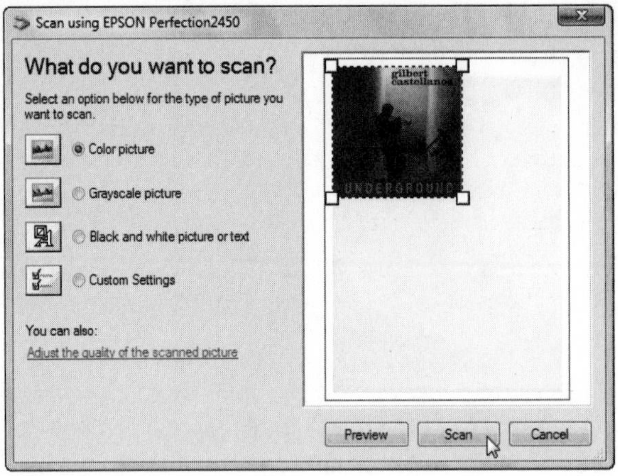

Figure 14-3:
Click the
Preview
button and
Windows
scans the
picture; drag
the little
boxes to
surround the
image so the
scan crops
its edges.

No crop marks around your image? Drag the corners of the little boxes to surround the image so the scanned file includes the image only — not the entire scanner area. Spend a little time adjusting them so you don't accidentally lose part of the image.

4. Click the Scan button and save the image in Paint.

When you click the Scan button, Paint scans your image and brings it into the program, as shown in Figure 14-4. From there, you can save the image as either a JPG or TIF file:

Figure 14-4:
The scanner
drops your
scanned
image into
your graph-
ics program,
ready for
touchup,
resizing or
printing.

- **JPG:** Choose JPG format if you're saving a photo. The JPG compresses images to save disk space, removing details that you'd never notice or miss. Almost all Internet-posted photos use the JPG format.

- **TIF:** Choose TIF for something you'll print, like a party flyer. Unlike JPG, TIF doesn't compress the image. That results in a larger file but saves the highest-quality image possible. (You can always convert the image to JPG later.)

I save all my images in Windows Vista's Pictures folder or Windows XP's My Pictures folder. Each of those folders live directly on Windows' Start menu.

✔ Windows' built-in scanning tool works great when you need a simple, no-frills way to grab your scanned images. Because the wizard works at such a simple level, it's a good way to test your scanner, making sure it's getting along with Windows.

✔ If your scanner worked fine until you unplugged it and plugged it back in again, repeat the process, but more slowly. Windows needs a few seconds to figure out when a USB or FireWire cable has been unplugged from the computer. Then it needs a few more seconds to recognize that one's been plugged in. Plug and unplug slowly.

✔ Unlike printers and modems, scanners aren't designed for sharing on a network. That's why USB scanners are preferable in multicomputer environments. If a friend down the hall really needs to scan a few photos, he can pick up your scanner, take it to his computer, plug it in, and start scanning. (He probably needs to install its drivers first, though.)

✔ Always remember to lock a scanner into place before moving it. This usually involves turning a knob along its side. Locking the scanner prevents damage to its sensitive scanning mechanism.

Choosing the right scanning resolution

Remember when you bought that 2400 dpi scanner because it sounded so much better than those 1200 or 300 dpi scanners? Well, when you're scanning at 2400 dpi, that's 2,400 dots per inch. Your monitor uses a pixel to display every dot. And very few monitors can display more than 2,000 pixels across their entire screen.

The point? If you scan something at 2400 dpi, you're going to see an extreme close-up of a tiny piece of your image. The rest extends off the edges of your monitor. Instead of automatically choosing the highest resolution your scanner offers, check out Table 14-1 for some common dpi settings.

Table 14-1	General Guidelines for dpi Settings		
To Scan This . . .	*For This . . .*	*Use This dpi Setting . . .*	*And Save As This.*
Photo	E-mail	75	JPG
Photo	Web	75	JPG
Anything	Printing	Printer setting	TIF
Letter	Faxing	200	TIF
Letter	OCR	300	TIF
Anything	Archive	2400	TIF

Don't take Table 14-1 as a mandate; it's a general guideline and a good starting point. Try several scans at varying dots per inch to see which works best for you.

You can always resize or resample an image to a smaller size using graphics software. But you can't make an image larger without making it look blurry.

Turning a scanner into a copy machine

Although scanners look and work much like copy machines, they differ in one frustrating way: They have trouble reproducing your image at the same size on the same-size sheet of paper. The software with some scanners lets you turn it into a copy machine, but if your scanner's software is giving you trouble, try this trick to make a printed copy of something:

1. **Place your item face-down in the top-right corner of the scanner bed.**

2. **Place a sheet of 8.5-x-11-inch office paper on top of it, in the same corner.**

   (Feel free to make a large X on the sheet of paper before setting it on top of your scanned item.)

3. **Preview your image on the scanner, being careful to crop the scan to the *same size* as the 8.5-x-11-inch paper, and then make your scan.**

   (The large X you drew on the sheet of paper makes it easier to see in the scanned preview.)

4. **Open your scanned image in a graphics program and print it on an entire sheet of paper.**

   You can use any graphics program for the last step, but choose Page Setup from the program's File menu and tell the program to print your scan on a single sheet of 8.5-by-11-inch paper. Because that's also the size of your scan, you'll end up with an actual-size printed reproduction of your scan.

If you're scanning something that you want to archive for later use, use 2400 dpi or higher resolution and burn the gargantuan image on a blank CD or DVD. A high-resolution image always leaves you the option of taking it to a professional print shop for making a high-quality print.

Dealing with scans that look awful

A glance at all those menu options on a scanning program should make anyone realize that scanning is a fine art. (If that's not enough, look at the menus on Adobe Photoshop — or just look at the software's price tag.) Like any other art, scanning takes lots of practice before things look exactly the way you want.

Luckily, scans are free, just like digital photos. Take several using different settings and delete the ones you don't like. You're not wasting any paper — just temporarily filling space on your hard drive.

Here are a few basic tips to get the most out of your scanner:

✔ When in doubt, visit the scanner manufacturer's Web site and download the latest versions of the software and drivers. Most manufacturers update them on a regular basis to repair problems discovered by other annoyed users. The warehouse workers stuffed the scanner's box several months before it arrived on store shelves, and its software and drivers are usually out of date.

✔ Always clean your scanner's glass surface with a lint-free rag (never paper towels, which can scratch) and some glass cleaner. Spray the cleaner on the rag, not the glass, or the glass cleaner could seep between the glass and the scanner's sides. Any dust on the glass or your photo (or whatever you're scanning) shows up when scanned.

✔ Make sure your monitor displays as many (or more) colors as your scanner's current setting. (I explain how to change your monitor's color settings in Chapter 3.)

✔ If you're using an older USB scanner, turn off or unplug your other USB devices before making large scans. That speeds up the rate at which your scanner can send information to your computer.

✔ You can find a wealth of information about scanners on the Internet. If you're serious about scanning, definitely pick up a book devoted entirely to the subject. You can apply lots of tricks to scan successfully.

Chapter 15

Adding a CD or DVD Drive

• •

In This Chapter

▶ Understanding CD and DVD terminology

▶ Identifying varieties of CD and DVD drives

▶ Installing a CD or DVD drive

▶ Fixing problems with CD and DVD drives

▶ Recording onto CDs and DVDs

• •

Ds pushed floppy disks off the stage about a decade ago. Only computing old-timers remember when programs arrived on a small stack of floppies, and software installation was like dropping quarters into a slow parking meter. Very few people miss floppy disks.

Today, most new programs arrive on a single CD, ready to pop into your computer like a breath mint. Adding to the fun, CDs can contain music as well as programs. Everybody in the office thinks you're backing up your work, but you're actually copying a Biosphere CD onto your computer.

Now DVDs are moving in, possibly pushing CDs into the realm of floppies. For example, your PC needs a DVD drive to install Windows Vista — Vista's too large to fit onto a CD. Vista can also write to DVDs, letting you create movies as well as make high-capacity backups.

This chapter makes some sense of CDs, DVDs, and the terminology surrounding them. It explains how to install new CD or DVD drives and fix or replace the old ones.

Understanding CD and DVD Buzzwords

CD and DVD drive terminology can be more confusing than the fine print on a credit card bill. Here's a look at the drives you're likely to run across, either in your own PC or those at work.

If you don't feel like putting on your wading boots, jump ahead to the "Just tell me what drive to buy!" sidebar and skip over the large pool of acronyms lying ahead.

CD drives will soon disappear from PCs. Any DVD drive can read both CDs and DVDs. Writable DVD drives can read and write to both CDs and DVDs.

Flavors of CDs and CD drives

CDs and CD drives come in the following flavors:

CD drive (Compact Disc): Still found in older computers, these drives do just one thing: read compact discs (CDs). They can't write (or *burn*) new information onto a blank CD. Many CD drives manufactured before 1998 can't even read audio CDs digitally, considerably reducing their sound quality.

Some evil music publishers sell awful copy-protected CDs that don't play in computers at all. Before buying a music CD, read the label carefully and make sure that you can return the CD if it won't play on your computer.

CD-RW drive (Compact Disc Read/Write): Almost all CD drives read *and* write information to blank CDs. Also known as *recordable drives* or *CD burners,* their prowess is judged by their speed at reading and writing information. (Look for a read/write speed of at least 48x.) The front plate of most CD-RW drives contains a red light labeled Writing that lights up as the CD writes information to the disc.

CD-R (CD-Recordable) disc: Readable in any CD drive, these cheap, blank CDs can be written to only *once* by CD-RW drives. They're meant for storing files you want to keep indefinitely: music CDs, archive copies, and digital photos.

CD-RW (CD ReWritable) disc: More expensive than CD-Rs, these CDs can be written to, erased, and written to again by CD-RW drives. Buy these to store things that change often, like your daily backups. Although most drives can read CD-RW discs, they're most dependably read by the drives that wrote the information onto them.

You can write to only those CDs that are designed specifically for recordable CD drives. You can't reuse those freebie AOL discs given away at the grocery store.

Kodak Picture CD: When you have your film developed, for an extra charge some developers and photo kiosks can stick your pictures on a CD as well as make prints. One example, the Kodak Picture CD, includes a built-in slideshow program for your PC and DVD player, as well as editing tools.

Color Plate 1: Some computer cases open up like a box when you squeeze the top and bottom latches.

Color Plate 2: On other cases, you need to unscrew two thumbscrews.

Color Plate 3: After removing the thumbscrews, slide the cover off by pulling it to the rear.

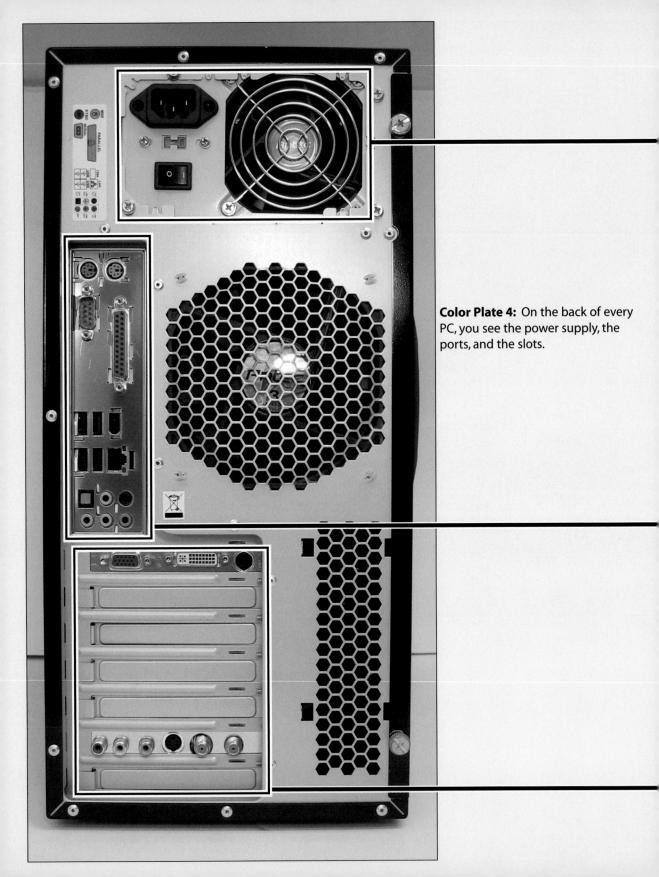

Color Plate 4: On the back of every PC, you see the power supply, the ports, and the slots.

Color Plate 5: The power supply is held in place by four screws (circled).

Color Plate 6: These ports live on your PC's motherboard but poke out the back of the case so you can reach them. See the Cheat Sheet and the Appendix if you need help identifying these ports.

Color Plate 7: The back side of your PC's cards poke out the back of slots cut into the rear of the PC's case. (The bottom card is a TV tuner card; the top is a video card.)

PCI slots for most
types of cards.

AGP slot for AGP
video cards. (Note
the brown color.)

Power supply. The wires
plug into the motherboard
and the disk drives (not
shown).

Ports attached to
motherboard and
poking out the back of
the case.

One memory chip
and two empty
memory sockets.

Color Plate 8: An older motherboard and its components.

These ports are attached
to the motherboard but are
accessible through a cutout
in the back of the case.

Power supply

Three empty PCI
slots

Four SATA connectors for
SATA hard drives.

Ribbon cables for
two CD or DVD drives.

PCI Express slot for PCI
Express video card. Note the
black color; AGP slots are
usually brown.

Four memory slots, with
two of them filled.

Color Plate 9: A modern motherboard and its components.

Color Plate 10:
Line up the memory module's notches with the notches in the slot. If they don't line up, the memory won't fit. (Don't force it.)

Color Plate 11:
Tilt the slot's white clips to the side, and then push the memory module down into the slot.

Color Plate 12:
As you push the memory into the slot, the two clips start to move inward. Push gently, but firmly.

Color Plate 13:
When the memory module snaps into place, the clips automatically move into the memory module's side notches to keep the module from slipping out.

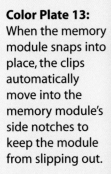

Color Plate 14: A PCI card. A PCI card's tabs are about 1⁵/₈ inches from the card's end.

Color Plate 15: An AGP card. An AGP card's tabs are about 2⁵/₈ inches from the card's end. Note the notched hook on the card's end, which locks into the plastic holder on the end of most AGP slots.

Color Plate 16: A PCI Express card. A PCI Express card's tabs are about 1³/₄ from the card's end. Like AGP cards, most PCI Express cards have a little notched hook on the end that locks into the slot's plastic holder.

AGP slot

PCI slots

Color Plate 17: One AGP slot and several PCI slots. Most PCs have either one AGP slot (usually brown) or one PCI Express slot (below) devoted to the video card. The white slots are PCI slots, which accept almost all cards except for video cards. (The long black slot on the bottom is an ISA slot, now obsolete.)

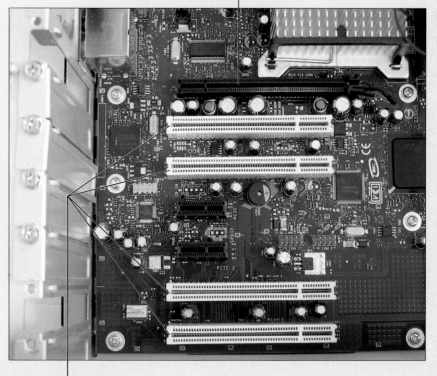

PCI Express slot

PCI slots

Color Plate 18: A PCI Express slot and PCI slots. Most modern PCs come with one PCI Express slot (usually black, although some brightly colored ones are now the rage) for a video card and several PCI slots for the other cards.

Color Plate 19: Remove the screw to add or replace a card. The screw holds either a slot cover or a card in place.

Color Plate 20: After removing the screw, remove the slot cover.

Color Plate 21: If you're replacing a card, pull the old card up and out of its slot.

Color Plate 22: Position the new card over the slot to make sure its tabs line up with the notches in the slot. Some cards, like this one, have an extra notch.

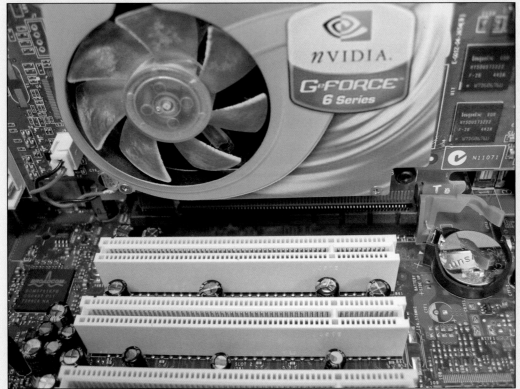

Color Plate 23: Push the card firmly into its slot. If you're installing a video card with a little fin, make sure the fin is held in place by the plastic holder. (The holder is green in this photo.)

Color Plate 24: Plug two cables into an IDE drive, whether it's a hard drive or CD/DVD burner. The other end of the data cable (left) plugs into the motherboard. The power cable (right) extends from your power supply.

Color Plate 25: Plug two cables into the SATA hard drive. The data cable (right) plugs into the motherboard. The power cable (left) extends from your power supply.

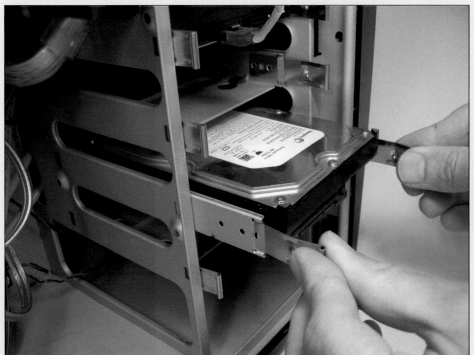

Color Plate 26: Some cases come with rails to screw onto the drives, making them easy to slide in and out of their drive bays.

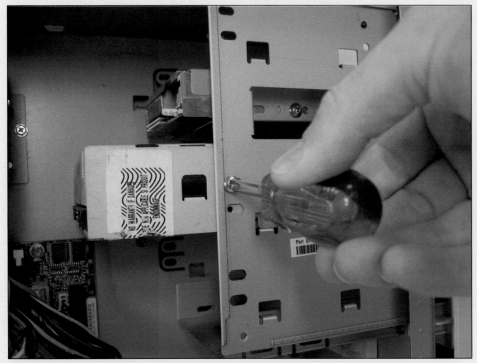

Color Plate 27: When cases don't include drive rails, you screw the drive directly to the case itself. (The screws are a slightly smaller size than the ones that hold cards in their slots, shown in Color Plate 19.)

Color Plate 28: Connect the round cable to your cable modem. Connect an Ethernet cable between your cable modem and the port on your router that's labeled "WAN." Then plug your PC's Ethernet cables into your router's numbered ports.

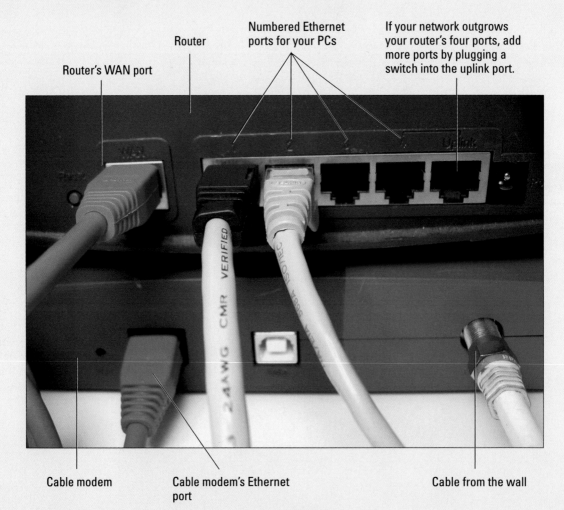

Router

Numbered Ethernet ports for your PCs

If your network outgrows your router's four ports, add more ports by plugging a switch into the uplink port.

Router's WAN port

Cable modem

Cable modem's Ethernet port

Cable from the wall

Color Plate 29: Close-up of the router and cable modem.

Color Plate 30: The largest plug extending from the power supply plugs into the motherboard. Most of the rest plug into your disk drives. (Shown in Color Plates 24 and 25.)

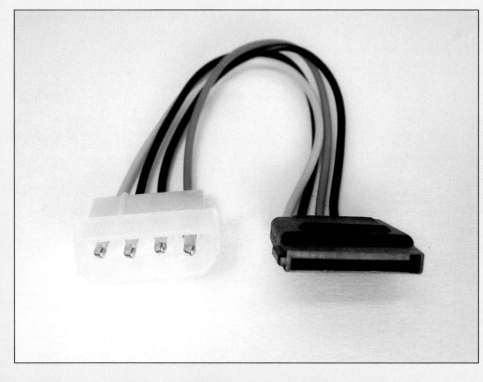

Color Plate 31: If your power supply didn't come with a plug for a SATA drive, buy an IDE to SATA power adapter.

Color Plate 32: Never open your power supply. It can store dangerous amounts of electricity, even when unplugged.

Color Plate 33: Don't let dust collect inside your PC. And when blowing off the dust with compressed air, do it outdoors, so the dust doesn't fill your lungs and get all over the room.

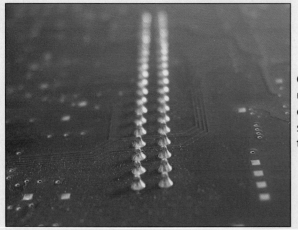

Color Plate 34: The undersides of cards and other circuit boards have sharp spikes. Handle them carefully.

Color Plate 35: The insides of most computer cases have sharp, rusting edges. Be careful not to rub against them.

Flavors of DVDs and DVD drives

DVDs and drives come in the following flavors:

DVD drive: Short for Digital Versatile Disc or Digital Video Disc, these drives read the DVDs you buy or rent at video stores, as well as play music CDs and program CDs. Unlike writable CD drives, writable DVD drives use different formats to write to blank DVDs. Unfortunately, the different formats aren't always compatible with each other.

Windows Vista can *finally* write information directly to a blank DVD, as shown in Figure 15-1. There's no need to buy a third-party program for writing files to a DVD or creating a movie destined for the DVD player.

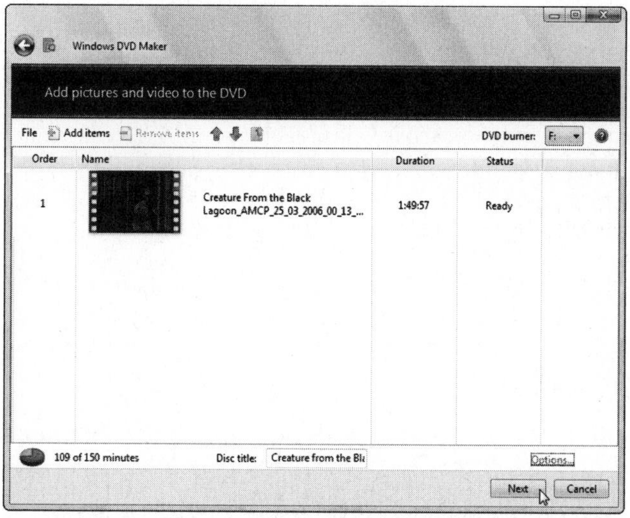

Figure 15-1:
Unlike previous Windows versions, Windows Vista can write files, including video, directly to a blank DVD.

DVD-R, DVD-RW drives: Created by Pioneer and Sony, this first school of recordable DVD standards keeps drives compatible with most (but not all) DVD drives and players. (Note the minus sign between the DVD and the letters R and RW.)

With recordable DVD discs as well as CDs, the term *R (Recordable)* means the blank disc can be written to once; the term *RW (Read/Write or ReWritable)* means the blank disc can be written to, erased, and written to again many times.

DVD+R, DVD+RW drives: Supported by Microsoft and a wide variety of hardware manufacturers, this newer class of DVD standards allows more features, versatility, and compatibility with existing drives and players.

Just tell me what drive to buy!

Don't bother buying a CD drive anymore. Instead, buy a DVD burner — a drive that reads and writes to both DVDs and CDs. When you're shopping for a new DVD burner, buy one that supports *all* the main formats: DVD-R, DVD+R, DVD-RW, and DVD+RW. Some drives abbreviate that entire string of acronyms to one: DVD ± R/RW. When you see that string of acronyms on a DVD drive's box, that drive plays and writes to *all* the DVD formats you're likely to come across.

Most CD drives come labeled with several speed ratings: 48x/24x/16x, for example. That refers to the speed at which a drive can *read, write,* and *rewrite* information, in that order, to or from the disc. The larger the number, the faster the speed, and the less time you spend waiting for the drive to finish its work.

DVD drives, by contrast, ignore those speed rating rules. You must read the fine print to find out which speed applies to which action: reading, writing, or rewriting. Plus, some DVD drives also list their speeds for reading, writing, and rewriting CDs, too. That makes for a *lot* of fine print, unfortunately.

DVD-RAM drives: An oddball format created by Matsushita mostly for computer data storage, these drives use blank DVDs enclosed in little caddies. Like all other DVD drives, they can still play movies and CDs.

DVD-R, DVD+R, DVD-RW, DVD+RW discs: Although most DVD drives sold today can read and write to *all* of these formats, some older drives can't. If you're stuck with an older drive, buy the correct type of blank disc for the format used by your particular DVD drive.

Dual-layer discs: These discs add a second layer of data beneath the first one that's accessible from the same side of the disc. That lets you pack twice as much information onto the DVD, typically 8.5GB or about 4 hours of video. (Normal, single-layer DVDs hold about 4.7GB or 2 hours of video.)

Buzzwords in advertising

These terms pertain to both CDs and DVDs and usually appear listed on the drive or disc's packaging.

Cache (buffer size): To speed things up, drives contain some speedy memory chips to hold information recently grabbed from a disc. If the information is needed again, the drive dishes it up out of the speedy memory *cache*, sparing the delay of rereading the disc. Bigger caches result in faster drives.

700MB/80 minutes: The most commonly found blank CDs today, these hold 700MB of information or 80 minutes of digital audio. Most modern drives handle them fine.

4.7GB/120 minutes: The most commonly found blank DVDs today, these hold 4.7GB of information or 120 minutes of video. Most DVD drives and players handle them without problem.

8.5GB/240 minutes/dual layer: Some newer DVD drives and discs are *dual layer,* meaning they can stuff two layers of information on the same side of the disc for a total of 8.5GB of information or about four hours of video. All DVD players and drives can read dual-layer discs, but only *dual-layer* DVD burners can write to them. Only DVDs specifically labeled as *dual-layer* are dual-layer discs.

Internal/external: Internal drives mount inside your computer. External drives come in their own little box and plug into your computer's USB or FireWire port. External drives can be shared between different computers, making them great for backups and taking to friends' houses.

 USB: The USB 1.0 and 1.1 ports found on older computers limit an external drive's writing speed to about 4x. Most externals require the faster USB 2.0 standard. If you're stuck with an older USB port and a USB 2.0 drive, pick up a USB 2.0 add-on card and install it in one of your PC's PCI slots, a simple and inexpensive procedure described in Chapter 7.

FireWire: These speedy ports support fast external drives just as well as USB 2.0. (They're also well supported by desktop video applications.)

Optical drive: Because CD/DVD drives read information with little lasers, they're sometimes called *optical* drives.

 The most up-to-date compact disc information resides online at Andy McFadden's gargantuan CD-Recordable FAQ Web site (www.cdrfaq.org). A matching smorgasbord of up-to-date online information about DVDs lives at Jim Taylor's www.dvddemystified.com.

Installing an External CD or DVD Drive

Difficulty level: Easy

Tools you need: One hand

Cost: Anywhere from $100 to $200

Stuff to watch out for: Actually, there's not much to look out for. Installing an external CD and/or DVD drive is as simple as plugging in a mouse or keyboard.

1. **Remove the new drive from the box and find all the goodies in the packaging.**

   The drive and its USB or FireWire cable are included in the box. (Older drives sometimes use a parallel or PC card.) Many external drives come with power supplies, as well.

   If you're bored, take a peek at the instruction booklet for specific installation instructions: Some come with software that usually should be installed *before* you plug in the drive — if you can wait that long.

2. **Plug the drive's power cable into the wall, if necessary, and turn it on.**

   Some drives grab their power straight from your computer's USB port.

3. **Install the drive's software, if necessary.**

4. **Plug the drive's cable into the computer.**

   Plug the drive's cable into its port and your computer's appropriate port: USB, FireWire, or parallel. (And with some older drives, a laptop's PC card slot.)

   Windows automatically recognizes your drive when it's plugged into the USB or FireWire port.

   If Windows asks for drivers the first time it's plugged in, insert the drive's installation disc into one of your *computer's* drives — not the drive you're trying to install.

Installing an Internal CD or DVD Drive

Difficulty level: Medium

Tools you need: One hand, a screwdriver, and tweezers

Cost: Anywhere from $25 to $150

Stuff to watch out for: Internal CD/DVD drives install the same way as installing a hard drive, discussed in Chapter 9: Just slide in the drive, screw it in place, and plug in the same two cables (power and data). Check out Figure 15-2 to identify where the cables plug in; the following steps offer more precise instructions.

1. **Turn off your computer, unplug it, and remove its case.**

   You can find complete instructions on the Cheat Sheet at the front of this book.

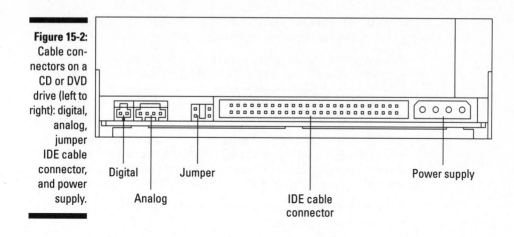

Figure 15-2:
Cable connectors on a CD or DVD drive (left to right): digital, analog, jumper IDE cable connector, and power supply.

Digital   Jumper   Power supply

Analog   IDE cable connector

2. **Decide if the new drive will be master, slave, or Cable Select, and then set its jumper accordingly.**

   Most computers have room for more than one CD or DVD drive these days. Because the drive's ribbon cable usually has two connectors that accept a drive, the computer needs to know which drive is attached to which cable connector.

   You do that by moving a little *jumper* over different pairs of pins on the back of the drive, as shown in Figure 15-3. Use a pair of tweezers to pull the jumper off the existing jumpers and push it onto the appropriate ones. (A bent paperclip pries off a stubborn jumper, if tweezers aren't handy.)

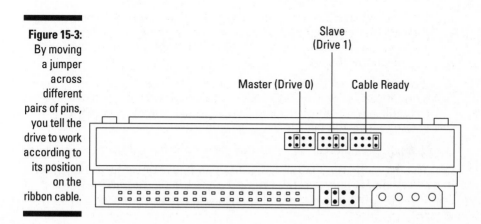

Figure 15-3:
By moving a jumper across different pairs of pins, you tell the drive to work according to its position on the ribbon cable.

Slave (Drive 1)

Master (Drive 0)   Cable Ready

Check the drive's manual to see which pins it prefers in your particular configuration. Here are some suggestions:

- If you're replacing an existing drive, look at the current drive's jumper settings. Then set the new drive's jumpers the same way. If the current drive is set at master, for instance, set the new drive to master, as well. (Different drives use different pin settings, so don't simply duplicate the pin's location; use the labeling, instead.)

- If you're installing a second drive onto the same cable as your current drive and the current drive is set to master, set the second drive's jumpers to slave. (There's one exception: If the current drive is set to Cable Select, use Cable Select for the second drive, as well.)

- If you're installing a new drive onto a cable by itself, set the new drive's jumpers to master.

- If you're installing any drive onto a ribbon cable with connectors labeled master and slave, you'll probably set its jumpers to Cable Select.

If you need more information about master, slave, and Cable Select settings, check out their coverage in Chapter 9.

3. **Slide the new CD or DVD drive into the front of your computer.**

You need a vacant *drive bay,* which is an opening where your disk drives normally live. The drive should slide in the front. You usually need to pry out a rectangular plastic cover from the front of your computer before the drive slides in. (Sometimes you must pry out a thin foil protector from behind the plastic cover, too.)

4. **Connect the flat ribbon cable between the drive and your motherboard.**

The ribbon cable has a plug on each end and a third plug a few inches from another connector. The two plugs that are closest together plug into your drives; the connector that's farthest apart from the pair plugs into the motherboard.

Ribbon cables have a red stripe along one side. One of the pins on the motherboard's (or card's) IDE connector is labeled Pin 1. When plugging the cable into the motherboard or card, make sure the edge with the red stripe is closest to Pin 1. (The drive won't work if the cable is reversed.)

Here are the different scenarios for connecting the cable:

- If you're replacing an older drive, simply remove the ribbon cable's connector from the old drive and plug it into the new drive. (The connector only pushes in one way, so don't force it.)

The other end of the connector is already plugged into the proper spot on the motherboard.

- If you're adding a second drive, find the ribbon cable connecting to your first CD/DVD drive. The ribbon cable should have a second connector a few inches from the first drive. Plug that second connection into your new drive. The ribbon cable's other end is already plugged into the proper spot on the motherboard.

- If you're adding a completely new drive, locate where your hard drive's ribbon cable currently plugs into the motherboard; you'll see an unused connector next to it. (It's usually labeled Secondary IDE.) Plug the CD/DVD drive's ribbon cable into that empty connector. Plug one of the other connectors into your drive.

Don't plug a CD/DVD drive and hard drive onto the same ribbon cable. Hard drives work much faster than CD/DVD drives, and you don't want to slow it down.

5. **Connect the power cable.**

   Rummage around the tentacles of wires leading from your power supply until you find a spare power connector. They come in two sizes; plug one of the larger ones into your CD or DVD drive. (The plug fits only one way, so don't force it.)

6. **Screw the drive in place.**

   Although some drives screw in from the sides, others fasten with two screws along the front.

7. **Replace your computer's cover, plug the computer in, and turn it on.**

   When Windows boots up, it should recognize the new drive and automatically install it for you.

8. **Run the drive's software, if necessary.**

   Unlike most things you push or screw into your PC, CD and DVD drives don't require drivers in Windows XP and Windows Vista. Some drivers come with free disc burning software that's more powerful — but more complicated — than the disc burning tools built into Windows Vista and Windows XP.

Although CD and DVD drives don't require drivers, they might need updates to their *firmware* — built-in software that helps them write to discs. Visit your drive manufacturer's site, download the latest firmware for your drive, and run the installation program to bring your drive up-to-date.

Dealing with a CD or DVD Drive That Doesn't Work

When that newly installed drive doesn't work, it's time to retrace your steps. Sometimes the master/slave jumpers are in the wrong place. Other times a cable isn't plugged in to the right connector. Run through the steps in the preceding section, making sure everything connects the way it should.

If you're having trouble hearing theater-quality sound from your DVD player, Chapter 11 covers computer sound issues.

Dealing with a burner that doesn't burn discs

If your computer is having trouble writing information to a CD or DVD, several things could be the problem. Here's a list to check:

- ✔ Your hard drive needs up to 1GB of free space when your drive burns data to a blank CD; it needs up to 8GB of space when burning to a blank DVD. If Windows says it needs more hard drive space, use the Disk Cleanup program, covered in Chapter 21. If you burn a lot of DVDs, you might need a larger hard drive, covered in Chapter 9.

- ✔ Always burn information that's currently on your *own* PC. If the information lives on a *networked* PC, copy the information to your own PC, and then burn it. Your PC needs to write to the disc in an uninterrupted stream, and your network might not send the information quickly enough.

- ✔ Disc burning programs usually burn at the fastest speed possible. That might be more than your particular CD or DVD drive can handle, leading to botched burns. Look at the blank disc's label for its rated burning speed, and then reduce Windows' burn speed accordingly.

- ✔ Drives must write information to the disc in a continuous flow. If your computer is interrupted during the process and doesn't feed information to the drive quickly enough, the disc might suffer, leading to skips or gaps in the data. To be extra safe, don't run other programs when you're burning CDs or DVDs.

- ✔ Buy blank discs in bulk, as some damaged discs inevitably turn into coasters. You'll feel less guilty about throwing a damaged one into the trash if you still have 49 more on your stack.

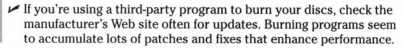

✔ Third-party disc burning programs often disable Window's own method of burning to CDs and DVDs. Use one program or the other, but don't try to use both.

✔ If you're using a third-party program to burn your discs, check the manufacturer's Web site often for updates. Burning programs seem to accumulate lots of patches and fixes that enhance performance.

Understanding MP3 and DVD decoders (MPEG)

As described in Chapter 9, digital sound and video consume *lots* of disc space when stored in files. To shrink the file's sizes, Windows uses special *codec* software. (*Codecs* contain mathematical algorithms for compressing and decompressing digital sound and video.) Similarly, a *decoder* decompresses the files so that you may hear or view them.

The problem? Not all versions of Windows contain those decoders, and you can't create an MP3 or watch a DVD without them.

Here's the scoop:

Windows Vista and Windows XP both include a free MP3 codec that lets you listen to and create MP3 files in Media Player. (If your version of Windows XP *can't* create MP3 files, fix the problem by installing Service Pack 2 from Windows Update.)

It's another story with DVDs, though. By themselves, only two Windows Vista versions can play DVDs: Vista Home Premium and Vista Ultimate. If you own any other version, you need to buy third-party software to watch DVDs on your PC.

Windows XP treats DVDs even worse. No Windows XP versions let you watch a DVD on your PC. To fix the problem, you must install a Windows XP-compatible DVD codec.

Some DVD drives and most new PCs come packaged with free DVD software made by a third party. The software installs the codec that enables Windows to decode and play the videos. If you reinstall Windows XP from scratch, be sure to install your DVD drive's software in order to watch DVDs.

How do I know my disc drive's model and speed?

Unfortunately, Windows doesn't tell you your drive's speed rating nor the type of discs it requires. That leaves the sleuth work up to you, by following these guidelines:

✔ Look at your PC's documentation, if it came with any.

✔ Check out your PC's sales receipt. Some of them list every part inside your PC, including your drive's type and speeds. At the least, it should list the drive's model number and manufacturer.

✔ Visit the drive manufacturer's Web site, look up the drive's model number, and download its information sheet.

✔ When all else fails, open the case on your computer, remove the drive, and look at the stickers on its case. They'll list the manufacturer and model number. From there, you can visit the drive manufacturer's Web site to see the drive's ratings.

Buying the right blank discs for your CD or DVD drive

When you're creating something you want to keep around for awhile — backups of your digital photos, a duplicated music CD, and similar permanent items — buy blank CD-R discs.

When you want to write information repeatedly to the same disc — a daily backup, for example — buy blank CD-RW discs.

The same rules apply to blank DVDs, but it's a little more complicated, as DVDs come in two flavors: DVD-R and DVD+R. Early DVD drives could write to only one of those two formats. Newer players can write to both.

As you've noticed, the cost for blank CDs and DVDs ranges wildly. How do you know which one to buy? That question's not answered easily, however, because you never know what you're getting. Most vendors buy their blanks from third parties, and then put their own name on them.

Because there's no way of knowing who *really* made the discs, there's no way of sticking with a particular brand.

To increase your odds of success, try several brands, and then stick with the ones that work the best with your particular drive. Borrow a disc or two from your friends and see how it works for you. You'll run across a few duds, but that's the way the blank disc business works.

Part IV
Communications

The 5th Wave   By Rich Tennant

I hate this
stupid
dial-up modem.

In this part . . .

Windows Vista loves to chat. As soon as you install or upgrade to Windows Vista, it tries to connect with the Internet and announce its presence.

Windows Vista is ready to talk to any other computers sitting in your home or office, as well. Don't want to string networking cables around the house? Windows Vista is content to chatter through the airwaves — it includes built-in support for wireless networking.

This part of the book shows you how to install or upgrade your modem for dialup Internet access as well as send and receive faxes. You find out how to set up your own home network, as well as add wireless access so that you can check your e-mail while you're gardening.

And if you're ready to sooth your paranoia level a notch, Chapter 18 shows you how to set up Windows Vista's built-in firewall and poke holes in it, if necessary, for those programs that need to chat in special ways.

Chapter 16

Replacing a Modem

● ●

In This Chapter

▶ Figuring out dial-up, DSL, cable, and other fast modem technologies

▶ Upgrading to a better modem

▶ Installing an external modem

▶ Configuring Internet Explorer for a dialup modem

▶ Buying a cable modem to replace a rental unit

▶ Stopping call waiting disconnects

● ●

*W*indows keeps a constant finger on the Internet's pulse, turning the Internet from a luxury into a necessity. Vista even drops by Microsoft's Web site occasionally to make sure you've paid for your copy of Windows. Because Windows loves the Internet so dearly, it's understandable that nearly every computer sold in the past few years comes with a built-in dialup modem and a network card for high-speed Internet connections.

So, what's left to explain in a chapter on modems? Well, how to understand their language, for one. What's *broadband* service, for example, and how do you use it to speed up an Internet connection? Where do you prod your computer when it suddenly stops talking to the Internet? How do you replace a modem that no longer works?

This chapter tackles those questions and more, including how to replace your rented cable modem with your own inexpensive model, which stops the cable company from charging you rental fees.

Understanding the Various Types of Internet Services

Internet services — the companies you pay for the privilege of connecting to the Internet — come rated largely by how fast they spew information back and forth to other places. Here's a rundown of the three most common types of Internet connections available today: dialup, cable, and DSL.

Although you're probably tempted to eyeball the fastest type of Internet connection and say, "Gimme that one there, mate," it's not always that easy. Your Internet options depend largely on where you live. Most companies offer their services to certain areas only, and your options decrease the farther you live from larger cities. Choose the fastest one you can afford that's available in your area.

The speeds listed for each type of service constantly vary. Though your car's engine can move the car at 100 mph, you can't always drive that quickly because of stoplights, narrow streets, and traffic. The Internet has traffic problems as well, which slow down things for everybody. In fact, when a Web site loads slowly on your PC, the problem could very well lie with the Web site itself, not your connection.

Dialup or POTS (Plain Old Telephone Service)

The slowest by far, dialup modems still provide the Internet's gateway for many people, especially those in rural areas. An ordinary phone cord connects the computer's modem to an ordinary phone jack. To log on, the Internet browser dials a number provided by the Internet Service Provider (ISP) and waits for a connection. Most dialups work at speeds between 28,800 bps (bits per second) and 56,000 bps (also known as 56K).

The higher the bps number, the more information the modem is able to move in and out of your computer. Faster modems enable you to connect to the Internet more quickly, making Web sites splash onto your screen faster.

People with dialup connections hog the phone line when connected — nobody else in the house can use it. Also, even though modems can connect at 56K, they rarely connect at that high a speed; the speeds average in the high 40s.

For many people, this is the only type of Internet service offered in their area. Be patient. Broadband — the faster service provided by cable and DSL modems — will come to you one of these days.

Cable modems

The speediest of all, cable modems grab Internet data at anywhere from 1,500 to 10,000K and send data at speeds from 256 to 1,500K. (My cable modem downloads at 7,000K and uploads at 512K.) That's pretty darn fast.

The Internet rushes into your home through the same coaxial cable that your TV shows flow through, making your cable TV company your Internet Service Provider.

To set things up, a cable techie drops by your house or office to do this: Install a network card in your computer (if it needs one), split your cable TV signal, and hook the cable to a special cable modem, which you rent for a monthly fee. After the cable modem's connected to your PC's network card, your cable modem lets you connect to the Internet at blistering speeds.

Yes, the family can still watch cable TV or listen to cable radio at the same time you're blazing around the Internet.

Many cable providers and other broadband ISPs claim to offer "unlimited Internet access." *Unlimited* is a marketing term, of course. They all get upset if you start downloading too much information — lots of movies, for instance — and they'll slow down or cut off your access.

People with Internet connections like cable and DSL (described in the next section) should read Chapter 18 on setting up a firewall. Because they're always on and constantly receptive to Internet commands, broadband modems make irresistible targets for evil computer hackers.

DSL (Digital Subscriber Line)

DSL offers yet another broadband modem that attempts to squeeze the most information through your home's tiny copper phone lines. Phone companies use digital signal processing techniques to beef up the copper wire's bandwidth. DSL enables you to download from 640K to 3,000K and send data at up to 768 Kbps.

The downside? You must live near a phone-switching station for DSL to work, and the closer you live to the station, the faster your connection. Some people ask a realtor if a house is near good schools. Others ask if it's close to a phone-switching station.

Asymmetric DSL, or *ADSL*, shuttles data at different speeds, depending on whether you're uploading or downloading. It's fine for home users, who rarely upload many files. *Symmetric DSL* moves data at a constant speed in either direction. *SDSL* works better for businesses that must transmit large amounts of information.

Baud, bps, Kbps, Mbps, and other tidbits

Modem speed is measured in *bps* (bits per second). Some people measure modem speed in baud rate, a term that only engineers really understand.

If you see the term *Kbps*, it's the metric system way of saying, thousands (Kilo) of bits per second.

That means that 56K (pronounced *fifty-six KAY)* is *56,000 bits per second.*

With the advent of broadband technologies like the cable modem, a new unit of measure arose: 1 Mbps means roughly 1,000 kilobits, or roughly a million bits per second.

Installing or Replacing a Modem

Difficulty level: Easy

Tools you need: One hand and, for internal modems, a screwdriver

Cost: Anywhere from $25 to $150

Stuff to watch out for: These three sections explain how to replace the three most common types of modems: internal dialup, external dialup, and cable modems.

PC card modems for laptops don't warrant a section because they're so easy to install: Slide the PC card into your laptop's PC card slot, usually found on the laptop's side. Install the PC card's bundled software, and you're done.

Replacing your internal dialup modem

Replacing an internal modem consists of pulling out the old modem card from a slot inside your PC, pushing the new one into that newly vacated slot, and plugging the phone cord into the modem's Line jack. If you're not keen on opening your PC's case, plug in an external modem, instead, described in the next section.

Internal dialup modems cost the least, followed by external dialup modems, followed by cable modems.

Cards are particularly susceptible to static electricity. Tap your computer's case to ground yourself before touching the card. If you live in a particularly dry, static-prone area, wear latex gloves — the kind that doctors and dentists wear.

To install a card, follow these steps:

1. **Turn off your computer, unplug it, and remove the cover.**

   Don't know how that cover comes off? Flip to the Cheat Sheet at the front of this book for the answers.

   If you're adding a new internal modem — not replacing your old one — jump to Step 4.

2. **Locate your existing internal modem.**

   See that row of slots toward the back of your PC? Those slots line up with the slots on the back of your PC — the part where you plug in most of your cables. Look to see where you plug in your phone cable — that's the back end of your internal modem card. The bottom of the card rests inside a slot.

3. **Remove your old modem card.**

   With a small screwdriver, remove the single screw that holds that card in place. Save that screw, as you need it to secure the new card in place.

   After you remove the screw, only friction holds the card in its slot. Pull up on the card until it pops out of the slot.

   If you drop the screw inside your PC, poke it out with a screwdriver or chopstick. If that fails, shake your PC upside-down until the screw falls out.

   If you're adding a new card to an empty slot, remove the screw holding the cover in place. Then remove the cover and proceed to Step 4.

4. **Push the new card into its slot.**

   Line up the tabs and notches on the card's bottom with the notches in the slot. Push the card slowly into the slot. You might need to rock the card back and forth gently. When the card pops in, you can feel it come to rest. Don't force it!

5. **Secure the card in the slot with the screw.**

   Yep, your precious modem is held in place by one screw.

6. **Plug the computer back in, turn it on, and see whether Windows recognizes and installs the new internal modem.**

   Windows usually recognizes newly installed cards and sets them up to work correctly. If your modem came with a CD, be sure to insert it when Vista begins clamoring for *drivers* — translation software that helps Vista talk to new parts.

   If something goes wrong, head for this chapter's "Troubleshooting Modem Problems" section. If everything's working, however, put your PC's cover back on.

7. **Connect a phone cable from the modem's Line jack to the phone jack in the wall.**

   If you need a place to plug in your telephone, plug it into the modem's second phone jack — the one with the icon of the phone next to it. Not sure which jack is which? Jump to Step 3 in the next section, "Installing an external dialup modem," for more detailed instructions.

Installing an external dialup modem

External USB dialup modems — the most common external modems — are the easiest type of modem to install. Check the box at the store to see if it includes a USB or serial cable. No cable? Pick one up at the store.

To install an external modem, follow these steps:

1. **Locate where to plug in your new modem.**

   Examine the back of your computer, and then match up its ports with the pictures in this book's Appendix. External modems plug into an unused serial or USB port. (Most plug into the USB port.)

2. **Connect the cable between your modem's port and the port on your PC.**

   Almost all modems plug into your PC's USB port, that rectangular slot shown in the margin. If the plug doesn't push easily into the port, turn the plug upside down and try again. (Only friction holds it in place.) The cable should fit perfectly at both ends; the plugs fit only one way.

   If your modem cable's plug *isn't* rectangular, it probably plugs into a serial port, shown in the margin.

3. **Plug the phone line into the back of the modem.**

   If your modem has a single phone jack in the back, plug one end of the phone cord into that jack and plug the cord's other end into the phone's wall jack. However, if your modem has *two* phone jacks, the procedure is a little harder: One phone jack is for the phone line cord, and the other is for a telephone. If you plug the cables into the wrong jacks, neither the modem nor the phone will work.

   If you're lucky, the two phone jacks are labeled. The one that says *Phone* (or shows a picture of a phone) is where you plug in your telephone. The one that's labeled *Line* is for the cord that runs to the phone jack in your wall.

   If the two jacks *aren't* labeled, just guess at which line plugs into which jack. If the modem or your phone doesn't work, swap the two plugs. (Having them wrong at first doesn't harm anything.)

4. **Plug the modem's AC adapter into the wall and plug the other end into the modem. Then turn the modem's power switch on.**

   Almost all external modems need an AC adapter. Then they need you to turn them on. (These are two things that can go wrong.)

5. **Tell Windows to search for your modem, if necessary.**

   As soon as you turn on your newly plugged in modem, Windows should recognize it and set it up for use. If Vista starts asking for drivers, now's the time to insert the CD that came with your external modem.

   If something goes wrong, head for this chapter's "Troubleshooting Modem Problems" section. If everything's working, however, put your PC's cover back on.

6. **Adjust any settings, if necessary.**

   If this is your first modem, there's one thing to set up: Internet Explorer. If Internet Explorer doesn't find your modem, drop by this chapter's last section, "Troubleshooting Modem Problems."

Replacing a cable modem

Sooner or later, you're going to grow tired of paying a monthly rental fee to your cable company for its cable modem. And as you note the rapidly decreasing prices of cable modems, you might want to buy your own. Or at least, that's what I did. Here's how.

1. **Visit your cable provider's Web site and note what modems it accepts.**

   Not all cable modems work with every provider. To see which modem brands and models your ISP supports, visit the Support area of your cable company's Web site. Some cable providers support more than a dozen different models from different manufacturers.

2. **Buy one of the supported cable modems.**

   You can find many cable modems available online at Amazon (www. amazon.com). If your city has offered cable service for a year or so, you might also find them available at computer stores and even home stereo stores.

3. **Choose a time to install the modem.**

   Find out the hours your cable company offers technical support and install the modem while the technical support lines are open. *You will need to talk to them after installing the modem or the modem won't work.*

If your company offers 24-hour technical support, replace your modem in the late evenings or weekends, so you don't have to wait on hold so long.

4. **Turn off your computer.**

5. **Turn off and unplug the old cable modem's power cord.**

   Remove the old modem's AC adapter from the wall.

6. **Plug your new cable modem's AC adapter into the wall.**

   Plug the adapter's other end into your new modem.

7. **Unplug the cables from your old modem and plug them into the new modem.**

   You find two cables:

   Remove the network cable (it looks like a big phone line) from the old modem and plug it into the new one. The jack fits only one way.

   Remove the cable connection from your old modem and plug it into the new one. This looks like the same cable that plugs into your TV or cable box.

8. **Turn on your new cable modem and turn on your computer.**

   Don't panic when your new modem doesn't work. It's not supposed to work yet. Every modem has a *MAC address* (Media Access Control) — a special code number that enables the cable company to find it over the Internet.

   You often find your modem's MAC address on a sticker placed on its side or bottom. If it's not there, check the modem's box. *You need that number!*

9. **Call the cable company's technical support line and give them your new MAC address.**

   The technical support people diligently type your new MAC address into their computers, replacing the old modem's MAC address.

10. **Make arrangements to return the old cable modem and its AC adapter.**

    At first, my cable company wanted me to drive 50 miles to its drop-off station. I complained and asked to talk to a supervisor. The supervisor agreed that was too far away and sent a truck out to pick it up the next day — for free.

11. **Play FreeCell until your new modem starts working.**

    It takes your cable company's network anywhere from a few minutes to several hours to locate your new modem and start sending information.

    During this time, the new modem's lights will flash, frantically trying to find someone to talk to. When the cable network finally connects, Internet Explorer and your e-mail program start working again. You're done!

Your new cable modem won't connect any faster than the old one because your ISP determines your connection speed. But it sure is nice to remove that monthly rental fee from your cable bill.

Troubleshooting Modem Problems

Installing modems is pretty easy, actually. The more difficult part is making sure your software knows how to talk to it. Here's how to complete the process by configuring Internet Explorer to work with a new Internet Service Provider, turn on a dialup modem's fax capabilities, and tweak a modem's settings.

Windows Vista can't find my dialup modem!

Sometimes all your modem installation work goes unnoticed: Vista looks the same when you turn on your PC and complains that it can't find a modem. Should this humiliating experience happen to you — a frequent occurrence with modems connecting through a PC's serial port — follow these steps to point Vista's gaze toward your newly installed modem.

If your dialup modem came with software or an installation program, run it now to save yourself lots of time and trouble.

1. **Click Start, choose Control Panel, and choose Phone and Modem Options from the Hardware and Sound category.**

   Depending on your PC's setup, Vista's Location Information window might appear, as shown in Figure 16-1. If it doesn't appear, jump to Step 3.

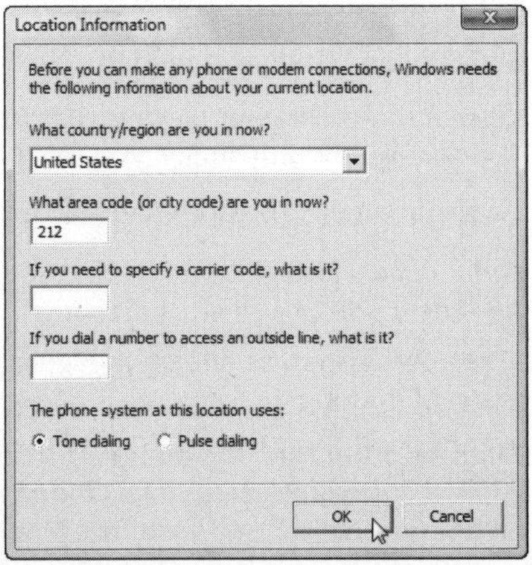

Figure 16-1: Enter your area code, as well as any other dialing or location information.

Location Information dialog box:

Before you can make any phone or modem connections, Windows needs the following information about your current location.

What country/region are you in now?
United States

What area code (or city code) are you in now?
212

If you need to specify a carrier code, what is it?

If you dial a number to access an outside line, what is it?

The phone system at this location uses:
• Tone dialing   ○ Pulse dialing

[OK]   [Cancel]

2. Fill out Vista's Location Information window, should it appear, and click OK.

For most people, this means entering your area code in the text box below What Area Code (or City Code) Are You in Now?

Feel free to fill out the other boxes if you're not in the United States, you need to dial a number to access an outside line, you're using a rotary (not tone) dialing system, or you need to enter a long distance carrier code.

When you click OK, Vista leaves you at the Phone and Modem Options dialog box.

3. Click the Modems tab of the Phone and Modem Options dialog box, and click the Add button.

That magic sequence of clicks fetches the Add Hardware Wizard's Install New Modem dialog box, as shown in Figure 16-2. That *finally* lets you tell Vista about your new dialup modem.

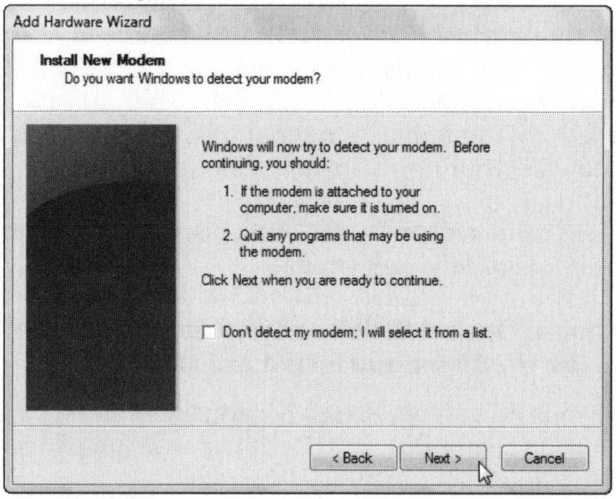

Figure 16-2:
Click Next
to let Vista
automat-
ically find
your new
modem.

4. Click Next, and then if Vista still can't find your modem, click Next again.

The Add Hardware Wizard tries to detect your modem. If it found it — a rare occurrence, indeed — you're not only lucky, you're through.

Chances are, though, the wizard comes up empty-handed, forcing you to click Next and move to the next step.

5. Select your modem from a list.

Vista lists all the modems it knows about, as shown in Figure 16-3, and leaves you with three courses of action:

• If Vista lists a manufacturer other than the Standard Modem Types shown in Figure 16-3, click it: Chances are, Vista's found your modem. Then select your modem's model from the Models column.

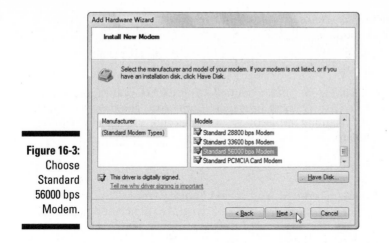

Figure 16-3:
Choose
Standard
56000 bps
Modem.

- If Vista *doesn't* list your modem's manufacturer, though, choose Standard 56000 bps Modem from the Models column. That usually works for most dialup modems. Click Next, choose All Ports, and click Next to finish the process.

- If your new modem came with software, insert the disc now — even if you've already run the software previously. Vista will scrutinize the disc's contents for any files it recognizes or knows how to use.

Chances are, one of these three things will successfully introduce Vista to your modem. If it still doesn't work, however, you need to find a driver written specifically for your modem, a chore tackled in Chapter 19.

Setting up your Internet account with Internet Explorer

Windows Vista constantly prowls your PC in search of a working Internet connection. If it finds a connection, through a cable modem, a network, or a wireless hotspot, you're set: Vista passes the news along to Internet Explorer, letting your PC connect to the Internet automatically and smoothly. If Vista can't find the Internet, however — a frequent occurrence with dialup modems — the job's up to you.

Vista helps Internet travelers through connection problems by sending them a questionnaire that quizzes you about the details. After your short interrogation, Vista connects to your ISP and lets you start surfing the Web.

If you're setting up a wired or wireless network, a job I describe in Chapter 17, Vista should automatically find the network's Internet connection and share it with every PC on your network. If Vista still has trouble, flip to Chapter 17 for network and wireless troubleshooting tips.

To transfer your existing Internet account settings between computers, fire up Windows Vista's Easy Transfer program (Chapter 5). The program copies one PC's settings (including ISP settings) into the other PC, sparing you the bother of following these steps.

Here's what you need to get started:

✔ **Your username, password, and access phone number.** If you don't have an ISP yet, Vista's wizard finds you one, so grab a pencil and paper. (The wizard's ISP suggestions are a tad pricey, however. You're often better served by calling local carriers listed in your phone book under Internet Access.)

✔ **A plugged-in, turned-on modem.** Follow the steps in the "Installing or Replacing a Modem" section to make sure your modem's both plugged in and turned on.

Whenever your Internet connection gives you log-on problems, return here and run through the following steps. Vista walks you through your current settings, letting you make changes. Summon the wizard by following these steps:

1. **Click the Start button and choose Connect To.**

   The Connect To button fetches a list of every way your PC currently knows how to connect with the Internet. But when Vista can't find a way for your PC to connect, it comes up with an empty list.

   Instead, Vista immediately complains that it can't find any networks connected to your PC. Ignore its whines and move to Step 2.

   If Vista found a *wireless* network, by chance, you're in luck. You can hop aboard the signal by double-clicking the network's name. (I cover networks in Chapter 17.)

2. **Choose Set Up a Connection or Network.**

   Scour the window's fine print for this option. When clicked, depending on your PC's model and setup, Vista might display any or all of these options:

   • *Connect to the Internet:* Vista makes yet another valiant effort to sniff out an Internet signal. Broadband users should click here, for example, to let Vista find and automatically set up their Internet connection.

   • *Set Up a Wireless Router or Access Point:* Head here to set up a wireless Internet connection you've set up in your home or office, a task I cover in Chapter 17.

- *Manually Connect to a Wireless Network:* You click here mostly when connecting to paid wireless networks at airports or coffee shops. It lets you enter a wireless network's name and password, should Internet Explorer suddenly demand them.

- *Set Up a Wireless Ad Hoc (Computer-to-Computer) Network:* Very rarely used, this option lets you connect two or more PCs for exchanging files and other information.

- *Set Up a Dialup Connection:* Dialup users want this one, as it lets you tell Vista what to do with that phone line you've plugged into your modem's phone jack.

- *Connect to a Workplace:* This setting lets you connect securely to your office — *if* your office network supports this sophisticated type of connection. If so, ask your office's computer department for your *Virtual Private Network (VPN)* settings and instructions.

- *Connect to a Bluetooth Personal Area Network (PAN):* If your PC has *Bluetooth* — a short-range form of wireless that replaces cables — click here to set up the connection. You head here to connect with Bluetooth cell phones, for example.

3. Choose Set Up a Dialup Connection and click Next.

Because you're not choosing wireless or broadband, dialup is your only Internet connection option. To speed things along, Vista passes you a questionnaire, shown in Figure 16-4, ready for you to enter your dialup ISP's information.

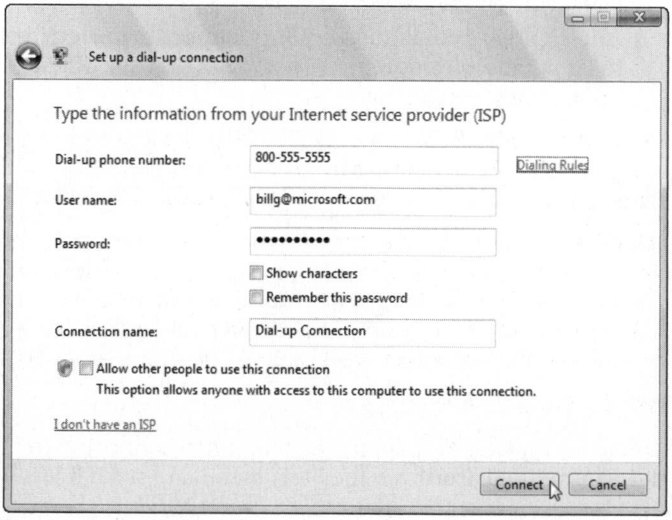

Figure 16-4:
Enter your
ISP's dialup
phone
number,
your
username,
and your
password.

Set up a dial-up connection	

Type the information from your Internet service provider (ISP)

Dial-up phone number:	800-555-5555 — Dialing Rules
User name:	billg@microsoft.com
Password:	••••••••••
	☐ Show characters
	☐ Remember this password
Connection name:	Dial-up Connection

☐ Allow other people to use this connection
This option allows anyone with access to this computer to use this connection.

I don't have an ISP

Connect   Cancel

If Vista complains that it "could not detect a dialup modem," your modem is too old for Vista to find it automatically. Instead, you need to offer the type of handholding found through Vista's Add Hardware Wizard, covered in the preceding section.

4. **Enter your dialup ISP's information.**

   Here's where you enter your three all-important pieces of information: Your ISP's dialup number, your username, and your password, as described in the following list.

   - *Dialup phone number:* Enter the phone number your ISP gave you, complete with the area code.

   - *Username:* This isn't necessarily your name, but the *username* your ISP assigned to you when giving you the account. (Your username is often the first part of your e-mail address.)

   - *Password:* Type your password here. To make sure that you're entering your password correctly, select the Show Characters check box. Then deselect the check box when you've entered the password without typos.

   Be sure to select the Remember This Password check box. That keeps you from reentering your name and password each time you want to dial the Internet. (*Don't* select that check box if you don't want your roommate or others to be able to dial your connection.)

   - **Connection Name:** Vista simply names your connection Dialup Connection. Change it to something more descriptive if you're juggling several dialup accounts from different ISPs.

   - **Allow Other People to Use This Connection:** Select this option to let people with other user accounts on your PC log on with this same dialup connection.

   Clicking the words I Don't Have an ISP brings up a window where you can sign up for Internet access from Microsoft's own ISP or with one of Microsoft's partners. (No, they're not giving away Internet access for free.)

   Click the words Dialing Rules, next to the phone number. There, you can enter key details, such as your country code and whether you need to dial a number to reach an outside line. Windows remembers this information, making sure that it dials a 1 if you're dialing outside your area code, for example. Laptoppers should visit Dialing Rules for every city they visit.

5. **Click the Connect button.**

   If you're lucky, your PC announces that it has connected to the Internet. Load Internet Explorer from the Start menu and see if it lets you visit Web sites.

   If Internet Explorer still can't visit the Internet, move to Step 6.

6. **Click the Start menu and choose Connect To.**

   Your newly created dialup connection will be waiting, as shown in Figure 16-5.

7. **Click Dialup Connection and click Connect.**

   Vista tosses one more screen in your face, as shown in Figure 16-6. This gives you a chance to type in your password, for example, if you didn't select the Remember This Password check box in Step 4. It's also where you can tweak your connection settings, handy for temporarily changing the phone number, for example.

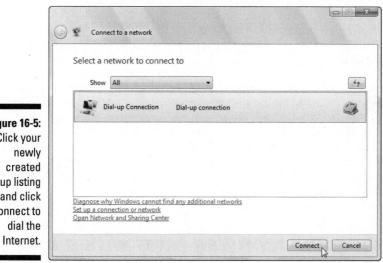

Figure 16-5: Click your newly created dialup listing and click Connect to dial the Internet.

Figure 16-6: Change the phone number, if necessary, and then click Dial to dial the Internet.

8. Click Dial to dial the Internet and connect to your ISP.

> You're done. Windows Vista automatically leaps into action, uses your settings to call your Internet provider, and lets you know when it's connected.

Then it's time to load Internet Explorer from the Start menu and start browsing. In the future, though, just load Internet Explorer when you want to browse. Your PC automatically dials the Internet using the connections you've created here.

Always plugging its own products, Microsoft drops you off at one of its own Web pages (Windows Live), and you're ready to browse. Need a place to go for a quick test? Log on to www.andyrathbone.com and see what happens.

Don't be afraid to bug your ISP for help. The best ISPs come with technical support lines. A member of the support staff can talk you through the installation process.

Internet Explorer doesn't automatically hang up when you're done browsing. To make your PC hang up the phone when you close Internet Explorer, choose Internet Options from the program's Tools menu and click the Connections tab. Click the Settings button and then the Advanced button. Finally, select the Disconnect When Connection May No Longer Be Needed check box and click OK. (You can also hang up by right-clicking your dial-up connection icon from the bottom right corner of the taskbar and choosing Disconnect from the pop-up menu.)

Sending and receiving faxes with a modem

Almost all dialup modems can send and receive faxes, but you probably don't have software that can take advantage of it. That's because Windows Vista removed the fax software from its Home Basic and Home Premium versions — the two versions preinstalled on most home PCs. (Microsoft left its fax software only in Vista's Business, Enterprise, and Ultimate versions.)

If you want to send or receive faxes with your dialup modem in Vista Home or Premium versions, you need to drop by your local office supply store and buy fax software. (WinFax is a popular program.)

Only *dialup* modems can send and receive faxes; cable and DSL modems don't know how to fax. Most PCs come with a built-in dialup modem preinstalled, however, so this might not be a problem for you.

Dealing with a modem that inappropriately disconnects

Some exceptionally popular people have call waiting installed on their phone lines. When these people talk on the phone and another call comes in, the phone makes a little beep sound. That's the signal for the person to interrupt the conversation and say, "Can you hold on a second? I have another call."

Your modem behaves more rudely than that. If somebody calls your house while your modem is talking to another modem, the beep makes your modem hang up, cutting off your Internet session in the process.

The solution? Dial the four characters ***70,** (that's an asterisk, the number seven, the number zero, and a comma) before dialing the other modem's number. For example, rather than tell your computer to dial **555-1212,** tell it to dial ***70,555-1212** to turn off your call waiting. That funky little code tells the phone company to turn off call waiting during that call. (Incoming callers hear busy signals.) When you finish that call, your call waiting is automatically turned back on.

To make your modem automatically disable call waiting before connecting to the Internet, follow these instructions:

1. **Double-click the Hardware and Sound icon in the Control Panel.**

2. **Click the Phone and Modem Options icon.**

3. **On the Dialing Rules tab, choose your current location and click the Edit button.**

4. **Click the box to disable call waiting and choose the appropriate code.**

   Select the check box marked, To Disable Call Waiting, Dial:, as shown in Figure 16-7.

   Click the adjacent pull-down menu and select your appropriate code.

   The ***70,** command works only with the newer tone (push-button) phones. If you're one of the few holdouts with the older, rotary phones, dial **1170,** (the numbers 1170 followed by a comma).

5. **Click the OK button to save your settings and exit.**

   Click OK on the next dialog box, as well.

Following these instructions disables call waiting whenever your computer makes a phone call.

The following is a figure of the "Edit Location" dialog box:

Edit Location

Tabs: General | Area Code Rules | Calling Card

Location name: My Location

Specify the location from which you will be dialing.

Country/region: United States   Area code: 212

Dialing rules

When dialing from this location, use the following rules:

To access an outside line for local calls, dial:

To access an outside line for long-distance calls, dial:

Use this carrier code to make long-distance calls:

Use this carrier code to make international calls:

☑ To disable call waiting, dial: 70

Dial using: ● Tone   ○ Pulse

[OK] [Cancel] [Apply]

Chapter 17

Linking PCs with a Network

· ·

In This Chapter

▶ Understanding network buzzwords

▶ Choosing between a wired or wireless network

▶ Installing and configuring a wired and wireless network

▶ Sharing files and printers in Windows Vista

▶ Troubleshooting a network

· ·

*A*few years ago, if you wanted a computer network in your home, you were automatically considered a nerd who built robots in the garage.

Now, networks are for average, everyday folk. Many families today are on their second computer, having outgrown the first a few years ago. Some families are on their third PC, if you count the laptop.

Just tell me what to buy!

For the greatest speed, reliability, and the least expense, buy these things to create a home network:

✔ **Fast Ethernet PCI cards:** Slip one of these cards into slots inside each of your PCs.

✔ **Wireless router:** In the approximate center of your group of PCs, place a wireless router with a port for each PC. (Most wireless routers support up to four PCs.) Connect your cable or DSL modem to the router's WAN port.

✔ **Fast Ethernet cables:** Connect a cable between a port on your router and a port on each of your PCs.

✔ **Wi-Fi network adapters (optional):** If one of your PCs lives farther than a cable's length from your router, buy that PC a Wi-Fi network adapter. (Many wireless network adapters plug into a USB port for easy installation.)

If none of your PCs need wireless, save money by buying a router *without* built-in wireless — if you can find one. Most routers today come with built-in wireless because wireless is so handy for laptoppers.

And that's where a network comes in. Connecting your PCs with a network lets them easily and cheaply share a single Internet connection. A home network also lets families share a printer or dip into the MP3 stash on other PCs.

Whatever your networking needs might be, this chapter explains how to set up a simple home network between Windows Vista PCs. If your Windows XP PCs are already networked — a job I explain in *Windows XP For Dummies* (Wiley Publishing) — these instructions let the Windows Vista PC join their fold. (As a bonus, I explain how to add wireless access for surfing the Web while laptopping beside the pool.)

Understanding Network Buzzwords

No matter what type of network you use, you're likely to stumble into some very odd terminology when shopping or reading packaging. Here are translations for the most common stumbling blocks:

Network adapter: A gadget that attaches to your PC to send and receive network signals. Wired network adapters transport the signals through cables; wireless network adapters come with a small antenna for sending and receiving network signals.

Router: An intelligent box that links your PCs into a network, letting each PC access both the Internet and your other PCs. Most routers today let you plug in at least four PCs, as well as send and receive wireless network signals to dozens of other PCs.

Routers make great firewalls, as explained in Chapter 18. Because the router sits between your PCs and the Internet, the bad guys can't get in nearly as easily.

Network cables: Wires that connect your PC's network adapters to your router. The network adapter, router, and cables are the three main parts of any network. If your PCs are too far away for cables to be practical, you can use wireless, described next.

WAP (Wireless Access Point): A device that transmits wireless networking signals between the wireless network adapters on other PCs. Most routers now come with a built-in wireless access point to send information through the air to distant PCs.

Local Area Network (LAN): A relatively small group of connected computers, modems, and printers.

Internet Connection Sharing (ICS): A way that Windows lets several PCs share one PC's Internet connection. All those piggybacking PCs slow down the original PC, however, so most people prefer buying a router to send the Internet connection among PCs.

Gateway: A connection between any smaller network and a larger one. A router, for example, works as a gateway that lets all the PCs on your home network connect to the biggest network of all: the Internet.

Switch: A box that keeps track of which computer asked for which piece of information and manages the flow of information accordingly. Most routers include a built-in switch that handles at least four PCs.

Encryption: A coding method for keeping information private. Each computer on an encrypted network uses a password system to scramble and descramble information sent between them. Wireless networks use encryption to keep miscreants from eavesdropping.

WEP (Wired Equivalent Privacy), WPA (Wi-Fi Protected Access): These two different security methods use encryption to keep eavesdroppers out of your wireless network. Although Vista supports both types of encryption, choose WPA — if your equipment allows it — as it's *much* more secure than WEP.

IP (Internet Protocol) Address: Each computer on a network has an *IP address* — a unique identifying number. By routing information to and from IP addresses, the network enables everything to communicate.

Choosing Between a Wired or Wireless Network

Today's home network consists of a small box called a *router* that links your PCs, letting them exchange information. Your biggest decision is how to link the PCs to the router: with wires or wirelessly. The answer is easy: look at the distance between your PCs.

If your PCs sit relatively close together, created a *wired* network. It's the easiest to set up, most reliable, secure, and best of all, the cheapest way to go.

If your PCs live too far apart to connect them comfortably with wires, choose *wireless.* Wireless networks cost more and require *much* more setup time, but they let you hop onto the Internet with your laptop from any room in the house — or even in the yard.

If some PCs are close, but a few are far away, mix the two: The most versatile networks combine both wired and wireless, letting your closest PCs connect with wires and saving the wireless for the laptop or the game console near your TV.

The hardest part of setting up a network comes when looking at the dizzying number of wired and wireless equipment available, so the next two sections explain your options.

Understanding wireless (Wi-Fi) home networks

Wireless is all the rage today. People don't want to string wires across the hallways and under the carpet anymore. They just want their computers to start talking to each other. But because wireless networks come in *three* main flavors, which wireless network is best? The next few sections look at the major players, but keep these things in mind before coming home with a bag full of wireless gear:

✔ Wireless networks work best in open spaces, such as outdoors or inside a big room. Wireless signals lose speed and strength as they travel through walls, ceilings, and floors. Consider the location of each computer before choosing between a wireless or wired network. The best solution often lets some PCs connect with wires and others wirelessly.

✔ Wi-Fi devices communicate at a range of several hundred feet, depending on how many barriers the signal must pass through. Many airports and restaurants offer them for visitors who compute while having coffee. To cater to the laptop crowd, small adapters like the Linksys Wireless USB network adapter, shown in Figure 17-1, stash easily into a laptop bag.

Wireless comes in three basic flavors, shown in Table 17-1, all with a variation on the number 802.11. From slowest to fastest, they're known as 802.11*b*, 802.11*g*, and 802.11*n*, each described below. Because all three are compatible, your wallet's width usually determines the one you take home: The cheapest of the three wireless types is the slowest, and the fastest costs the most.

Table 17-1:	The Three Types of Wireless Networks at a Glance		
Standard	*Speed*	*Range*	*Cost*
802.11b	Slowest	100 feet	Lowest
802.11g	Medium	100 feet	Medium
802.11n (Due in early 2008)	Fastest	150 feet	Highest

Figure 17-1:
By plugging into a USB port, the Linksys Wireless USB network adapter allows a computer to connect to a Wi-Fi network.

802.11b

Although it's the slowest wireless network speed today, 802.11b provides enough oomph for moderate networking and Internet needs. The 802.11b standard sends and receives signals at 11 Mbps. (The lower the Mbps number, the slower the connection.)

Compatibility: 802.11b devices can also talk with the faster 802.11g and 802.11n speeds described next. But those faster devices must slow their chatter to 802.11b speed when communicating.

An extension to the 802.11 wireless standard, 802.11b allows up to 11 Mbps communication in the 2.4 GHz band with fallback rates to 5.5, 2, and 1 Mbps during signal drops.

802.11g

This newer, faster wireless standard tweaks the Wi-Fi (802.11b) standard to add five times the speed and a slightly wider range. The speed drops dramatically the further it travels.

Compatibility: Fortunately, 802.11g devices work fine with Wi-Fi (802.11b) devices on your network. They simply lower their speed to match the slower Wi-Fi speeds.

Yet another extension to the 802.11g standard provides speeds up to 54 Mbps in the 2.4 GHz band with fallback rates of 48, 36, 24, 18, 12, 9, and 6 Mbps.

802.11n

The standards for the even faster 802.11n wireless standard are still being hammered out, but that hasn't stopped manufacturers from releasing *Pre-N* wireless equipment that guesses at the final standard. If you buy Pre-N equipment — network adapters and wireless transmitters — buy it all from the *same* manufacturer to ensure it all works well together.

Compatibility: The 802.11n wireless networks will remain compatible with the two earlier wireless networks by simply slowing down when talking with them.

The fastest wireless standard yet, 802.11n will provide speeds up to 540 Mbps in the 2.4 GHz and 5 GHz bands with fallback rates to remain compatible with earlier standards.

Understanding wired home networks

The fastest networks use cables. And because cabled systems have been around long enough to work out most bugs, wired networks are relatively inexpensive, fast, reliable, and compatible with each other.

Ethernet, a relatively old, wired networking standard, shuffles information through cables and connectors resembling phone lines, but with larger connectors.

Although the term *Ethernet* refers to several types of networks, only two are widely used in today's home networks: *Fast Ethernet* and its older and slower cousin, which I refer to as simply *Ethernet*.

The newer Fast Ethernet standard shuffles information ten times more quickly than the older Ethernet standard. Fast Ethernet is heavily favored by people who move around large files: sound, video, or graphics.

Both types of Ethernet work in a spider-like layout, as shown in Figure 17-2: A box called a *router* sits at the center, moving information to other computers through their individual cables, arranged like legs on a spider.

Unplugging cables with Bluetooth

Unlike wireless networks, which link groups of PCs, Bluetooth works to replace a different type of wiring: the single cable that traditionally connects two devices. Bluetooth's short-range, low-speed technology lets a cell phone pair up securely with a headset, for example, or lets a mouse talk wirelessly with a PC.

Bluetooth devices also communicate in *pairs,* not groups. A digital camera with Bluetooth connects to a single computer with Bluetooth, for instance, to dump its photos onto the computer.

Stuck with a Bluetooth gadget and a PC or laptop that doesn't support Bluetooth? Pick up a Bluetooth USB adapter — a little stick that plugs into an unused USB port. They usually cost less than 30 bucks.

Bluetooth works at short ranges — less than 30 feet — and it's not compatible with Wi-Fi or other networks. Don't expect your Bluetooth camera to dump photos into your Wi-Fi enabled-PC down the hallway.

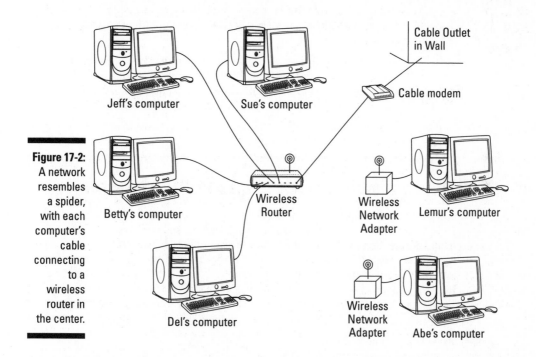

Figure 17-2: A network resembles a spider, with each computer's cable connecting to a wireless router in the center.

Jeff's computer
Sue's computer
Cable Outlet in Wall
Cable modem
Betty's computer
Wireless Router
Wireless Network Adapter
Lemur's computer
Del's computer
Wireless Network Adapter
Abe's computer

The biggest compatibility problem between Ethernet (10Base-T) and Fast Ethernet (100Base-T) comes with their cables. Although the cables look identical, Fast Ethernet won't run reliably over Ethernet cable. Always buy Fast

Ethernet cables to stay as compatible as possible. (The words Category 5 or CAT-5 are usually printed on Fast Ethernet cable.)

You can mix Ethernet and Fast Ethernet equipment because they contain auto-sensing equipment that translates the speed differences. The auto-sensing router at the center sends information to each computer at its appropriate speed level.

These terms might help you decipher the code words on the packages of networking equipment at the store:

✔ Based on the IEEE 802.3 standard, 10Base-T moves data at 10 Mbps through Category 3 (CAT-3) cables with RJ-45 connectors and a length of no more than 994 feet.

✔ Officially based on the IEEE 802.3u standard, Fast Ethernet moves data at the rapid rate of 100 Mbps through Category 5 (CAT-5) 100Base-T cables with RJ-45 connectors and a length of no more than 325 feet. It's also called *UTP* (Unshielded Twisted Pair) wiring. CAT-5 cables also work with Ethernet 10Base-T, so CAT-5 is the logical cabling choice these days.

✔ Some networking equipment offers a newer, faster type of Ethernet, 1000BASE-T. It moves data at 1000 Mbps through Category 5 (CAT-5e) cable, but Category 6 (CAT-6) cables are more reliable. It's used mostly in offices for PCs that constantly move large amounts of information. It's overkill for most home networks.

Turning electric outlets into network ports

Very few rooms come with a network port in the wall, but *every* room comes with a power outlet, a fact exploited by the HomePlug network system. Plugging a HomePlug adapter into a power outlet turns the outlet into a network jack. Buy a HomePlug adapter for each PC, and all your computers can talk to each other.

The HomePlug standard encrypts the data as it moves between devices; that keeps neighbors from plugging into your porch light's outlet to swipe your MP3 files.

HomePlug still has several problems, though: It's relatively high-priced, slower than Ethernet, hard to find in stores, and you still need a router to inject the Internet into your outlets so your PCs can Web surf. But for some people, it lets them finally add a network port to an out-of-the-way place: The basement, for example, the wine cellar, or other places that wired and wireless systems can't reach well.

Creating a Wired and Wireless Computer Network

Networks can be *very* scary stuff. But if you're just trying to set up a handful of computers in your home or home office, this section might be all you need.

Start by drawing a picture of your network. Find your closest grouping of computers and draw their relative locations onto a piece of paper. Draw a dot near the closest group of computers — you want to place your router there.

Using your drawing for reference, measure the physical distance between each of your computers and the router, adding enough feet to snake the cable around desks or along the walls. When in doubt, give yourself ten extra feet for each computer. Write down the length of cable required to connect each computer to the router.

Some homes come with networking jacks built into the walls. If you're that lucky, write down the length of cable necessary for reaching from each computer to its network jack.

Are some computers too far apart for cables? Buy them wireless network adapters, and make sure your router has built-in wireless (most do).

The easiest way to connect two computers

Sometimes you simply need to link two computers, quickly and easily, to move information from one to another (from an old computer to a new one, for example, as I describe in Chapter 5).

The easiest way is to buy a network adapter for each PC (new PCs usually come with one pre-installed) and a *crossover cable,* which is a special breed of Ethernet cable. Be sure to emphasize *crossover* or *crossed* cable when shopping at the computer store; a regular Ethernet cable won't work. Connect the crossed cable between the two computers' network adapters, and Vista creates a quick network between the two computers. If one computer has a way to connect to the Internet, the second computer should be able to share that Internet connection.

Or, connect an Easy Transfer Cable between the USB ports of two computers, as I describe in Chapter 5. Created especially for Windows Vista, the cable creates a makeshift network between the two PCs.

Finally, connect to the Internet with one PC, and then turn on Vista's Internet Connection Sharing to let the second PC piggyback on the first PC's connection.

Don't worry about printers. If one PC has a printer, every PC on the network can access it, printing to it as if it were their own.

The following sections explain how to buy the three parts of a network, how to install the network hardware, and how to make Windows Vista create a network out of your handiwork.

Buying parts for your network

Here's your shopping list. Drop this onto the copy machine at the office and take it to the computer store.

- ✔ **Fast Ethernet cable:** Buy one Fast Ethernet cable for each PC that won't be using wireless. Fast Ethernet cable is known by a wide variety of names, including 100Base-T and CAT-5. But if you're hunting for it at the computer store, just look for the network cable that looks like telephone cable and says *CAT-5* or *Category 5* on the label.

  For any computer placed too far away for a cable, buy a wireless network adapter, described next.

- ✔ **Network adapters:** Each PC needs its own network adapter, either wired or wireless. For wired PCs, buy one 100Base-T Ethernet PCI card for each PC. Don't want to open your PC's case to install a PCI card? Then buy a USB network adapter, instead. Make sure the adapters are Windows Vista compatible.

- ✔ Many new computers (and almost all laptops) come with a wired network adapter preinstalled, so look at the back of the computer for the giveaway: something that looks like a large phone jack.

  If the computer is too far away to connect with wires, buy it a wireless network adapter. (They plug into USB ports, too.)

- ✔ **Wireless router:** Every computer's network cable must plug into a single *router*, as shown in Figure 17-3. Most routers today come with built-in wireless to connect any PCs farther than a cable stretch away. Buy a wireless router with enough ports (jacks) to plug in each computer's cable — plus a few extra ports for computers you might want to add later.

Installing wired or wireless network adapters

Difficulty level: Medium

Tools you need: One hand and, for installing internal network adapters, a screwdriver

Cost: Anywhere from $25 to $150

Stuff to watch out for: If you're using a USB network adapter, just plug the adapter into your PC's USB port. (Bought a PC Card network adapter for the laptop? Slide it into your laptop's PC Card slot, that credit-card sized slot in the laptop's side.) Install the adapter's software, if it came with one, and you're through.

Figure 17-3:
The router sends information directly to the computer that asks for it, keeping up the network's speed.

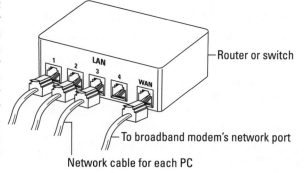

Router or switch

To broadband modem's network port

Network cable for each PC

Some wired and wireless adapters, however, come on cards. To install a network card, either wired or wireless, follow these steps:

1. **Turn off your computer, unplug it, and remove the cover.**

   Don't know how that cover comes off? Flip to the Cheat Sheet at the front of this book for the answers.

2. **Find an empty slot.**

   See that row of slots toward the back of your PC? Those slots line up with the slots on the back of your PC — the part where you plug in most of your cables. Find an empty one for your new network card.

3. **Remove the slot's cover.**

   With a small screwdriver, remove the single screw that holds that card in place. Save that screw, as you need it to secure the new card in place.

   If you drop the screw inside your PC, poke it out with a screwdriver or chopstick. If that fails, shake your PC upside-down until the screw falls out.

4. Push the new card into the empty slot.

Cards are particularly susceptible to static electricity. Tap your computer's case to ground yourself before touching the card. If you live in a particularly dry, static-prone area, wear latex gloves — the kind that doctors and dentists wear.

Line up the tabs and notches on the card's bottom with the notches in the slot. Push the card slowly into the slot. You might need to rock the card back and forth gently. When the card pops in, you can feel it come to rest. Don't force it!

5. Secure the card in the slot with the screw.

Yep, your precious card is held in place by one screw.

6. Connect the cables between the network cards and the router.

The cables all snake around until they plug into a numbered port on the router. You might need to route cables under carpets, around doorways, or through a hole in the floor or ceiling to move between floors. (Don't forget to plug the router's power cord into the wall.)

Don't plug any PCs into the router's WAN port. That's for plugging in your cable or DSL modem to connect with the Internet.

7. Turn on the computers and their peripherals.

Turn on the computers and their monitors, printers, modems, and whatever else happens to be connected to them.

Windows usually recognizes newly installed equipment and sets everything up to work correctly. If your network adapter card came with a CD, be sure to insert it when Vista begins clamoring for *drivers* — translation software that helps Vista talk to new parts.

If something goes wrong, head for this chapter's "Dealing with a Network That Isn't Networking" section. If everything's working, however, put your PC's cover back on.

8. Select a location for your network.

When Windows Vista wakes up and notices the newly attached network equipment, it asks you for your network's *location:* Home, Work, or Public Location. Choose whether you're working at home or work (safe) or in public (less safe), and Vista automatically adds the proper security level to protect you.

Vista does a reasonably good job of casting its networking spells on your computers. If the computers are all connected correctly and restarted, chances are they wake up in bondage with each other. If they don't, try restarting them all again.

Bothersome workgroup names

Like anything else in life, networks need names. A network's name is called a *workgroup,* and for some reason, Microsoft used different workgroup names in different versions of Windows, and that causes problems if you have Windows XP PCs on your network.

Here's the problem: Windows XP Home PCs automatically use MSHOME as their workgroup name. Windows XP Professional and Windows Vista PCs, by contrast, use WORKGROUP as their workgroup name. The result? Put a Vista PC and a Windows XP Home PC on the same network, and they can't find or talk with each other: One PC searches in vain for other MSHOME PCs, and the other looks for only WORKGROUP PCs.

The solution is to give them both the *same* workgroup name, a fairly easy task with these steps:

1. **On your Vista PC, click the Start menu, right-click Computer, and choose Properties.**

   The System screen appears, revealing basic techie information about your PC.

2. **Choose Change Settings.**

   That task lives in the section called Computer Name, Domain, and Workgroup Settings. Clicking it fetches a questionnaire.

3. **Click the Change button.**

   The Computer Name/Domain Changes dialog box appears.

4. **In the bottom box, change the Workgroup name to MSHOME.**

   That puts Vista on the same workgroup as your Windows XP PC.

   Alternatively, you can change your Windows XP PC's workgroup name to WORKGROUP by following these same five steps but clicking the Computer Name tag in Step 2. But no matter what you call your network's workgroup, make sure that every networked PC bears the *same* workgroup name.

   Tip: Be careful in this step to change each PC's *workgroup* name, not its *computer* name, as they're different things.

5. **Click OK to close the open windows and when asked, click the Restart Now button to restart your PC.**

   Repeat these steps for your other networked PCs, making sure that the same name appears in each Workgroup box.

Keep these things in mind when setting up your network:

- ✔ Although Windows Vista usually sits up and takes notice as soon as you plug in a network cable, wireless networks require more tweaks before they catch Vista's attention. To make your wireless network adapters start working, head for the next section, "Connecting Wirelessly."

- ✔ Windows Vista automatically shares one folder on every networked PC — the Public folder — as well as any folders inside it. Any files you place inside that folder are available to everybody on your PC as well as anybody connected to the network. (I explain more about sharing files, folders, printers, and other items later in this chapter's "Connecting to and Sharing Files with Other PCs on Your Network" section.)

Windows XP names its shared folder Shared Documents. Vista names that same folder Public, instead. But both do the same thing: Provide a place to share files with other people on your network.

✔ Click your Start menu and choose Network to see your other computers on your network.

✔ If your PC connects to the Internet through a dialup connection, run the Internet Connection Wizard, as described in Chapter 16. (That wizard then lets all your networked computers share that computer's Internet connection.) After that computer is set up, run the wizard on the other networked computers.

✔ If your PCs can't see each other, make sure that each PC uses the same Workgroup name, covered in this chapter's "Bothersome Workgroup Names" sidebar.

Connecting Wirelessly

Setting up your own wireless home network takes two steps:

1. Set up the wireless router or wireless access point to start broadcasting and receiving information to and from your PCs.

2. Set up Windows Vista on each PC to receive the signal and send information back, as well.

This section covers both of those daunting tasks.

Still haven't installed your wireless network adapter? Head for the previous section, "Installing wired or wireless network adapters."

Setting up a wireless router

Wireless connections bring convenience, as every cell phone owner knows. But they're also more complicated to set up than wired connections. You're basically setting up a radio transmitter that broadcasts to little receivers attached to your PCs. You need to worry about signal strength, finding the right signal, and even entering passwords to keep outsiders from listening in.

Wireless transmitters, known as *Wireless Access Points* (WAPs), come either built into your router or plugged into one of your router's ports. Unfortunately, different brands and models of wireless equipment come with different setup software, so there's no way I can provide step-by-step instructions for setting up your particular router.

However, the setup software on every wireless router requires you to set up these three basic things:

- **Network name (SSID):** Enter a short, easy-to-remember name here to identify your particular wireless network. Later, when you tell Vista to connect to your wireless network, you'll select this same name to avoid accidentally connecting to your neighbor's wireless network.

- **Infrastructure:** Choose *Infrastructure* instead of the alternative, *Ad Hoc.*

- **Security:** This option encrypts your data as it flies through the air. Turn it on using the recommended settings.

Some routers include an installation program for changing these settings; other routers contain built-in software that you access with Internet Explorer or any other Web browser.

As you enter settings for each of the three things, write them on a piece of paper: You need to enter these same three settings when setting up your PC's wireless connection, a job tackled in the next section.

Setting up Windows Vista to connect to a wireless network

After you've set up your router or wireless access point to broadcast your network's information, you must tell Windows Vista to receive it.

To connect to a wireless network, either your own or one in a public place, follow these steps:

1. **Turn on your wireless adapter, if necessary.**

   Many laptops turn off their wireless adapters to save power. To turn it on, open the Control Panel from the Start menu, choose Mobile PC, open the Mobility Center, and click the Turn Wireless On button. Not listed? Then you need to pull out your laptop's manual, unfortunately, because it doesn't fully support Vista's wireless networking.

2. **Choose Connect To from the Start menu.**

   Windows lists all the wireless networks it finds within range, as shown in Figure 17-4. Don't be surprised to see several networks listed — they're probably your neighbors'.

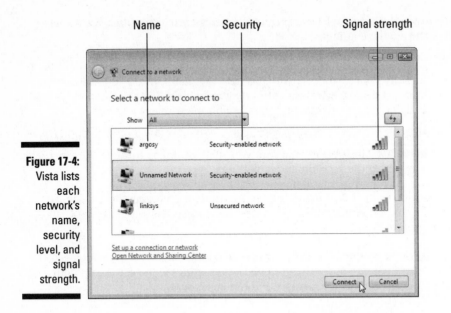

Name   Security   Signal strength

Figure 17-4:
Vista lists
each
network's
name,
security
level, and
signal
strength.

Vista sums up each available connection three ways, all shown in
Figure 17-4:

- **Name:** This is the network's name, also known as its *SSID* (Service
  Set IDentifier). Wireless networks frequently overlap, so network
  names let you connect to the specific network you want. Choose
  the SSID name you gave your wireless router when you set it up,
  for example, or select the name of the wireless network at the
  coffee shop or hotel.

- **Security:** Networks listed as *Unsecured Network* don't require a
  password: You can hop aboard and start surfing the Internet for
  free. Unsecured, however, means they aren't encrypted: technical-
  minded snoops can eavesdrop. Unsecured networks work fine for
  quick Internet access but aren't safe for online shopping. A network listed as a *Security-Enabled Network,* by contrast, is safer,
  as the network's password filters out all but the most dedicated
  snoops.

- **Signal Strength:** These little vertical bars work much like a cell
  phone's signal strength meter: The more bars you see, the stronger
  the signal. Connecting to networks with two bars or less will be
  frustratingly sporadic. You might want to reposition your laptop or
  PC, if possible, or try moving the antennas on the router or wireless adapter.

If you need to revisit a previous step, click the little blue Back arrow in the window's top-left corner.

3. **Connect to the desired network by clicking its name and clicking Connect.**

   If you spot your network's name, click it and then click the Connect button.

   If you *don't* spot your network's name, head to Step 6.

4. **Choose whether you're connecting from Home, Work, or a Public Location.**

   When you connect, Vista asks whether you're connecting from Home, Work, or a Public Location so that it can add the right layer of security. Choose Home or Work only when connecting to a wireless connection within your home or office. Choose Public Location for all others to add extra security.

   If you're connecting to an Unsecured Network — a network that doesn't require a password — you're done. Vista warns you about connecting to an unsecured network, and clicking the Connect Anyway button lets you connect.

   If you're connecting to a Security-Enabled Network, however, Vista asks for a password, described in the next step.

5. **Enter a password, if needed, and click Connect.**

   When you try to connect to a security-enabled wireless connection, Vista sends you the window shown in Figure 17-5, asking for a password.

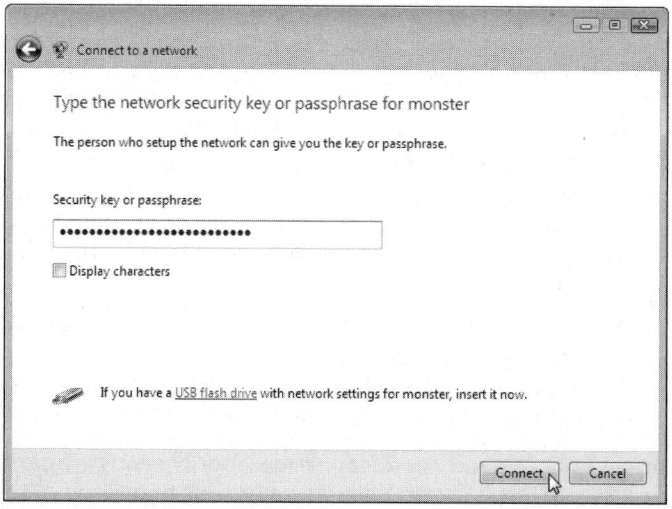

Figure 17-5:
Enter the wireless network's password and click Connect.

> Connect to a network
>
> Type the network security key or passphrase for monster
>
> The person who setup the network can give you the key or passphrase.
>
> Security key or passphrase:
>
> `••••••••••••••••••••••••`
>
> ☐ Display characters
>
> If you have a USB flash drive with network settings for monster, insert it now.
>
> [Connect] [Cancel]

Here's where you type the password you entered into your router when setting up your wireless network.

If you're connecting to somebody else's password-protected wireless network, pull out your credit card. You need to buy some connection time from the people behind the counter.

Don't see your wireless network's name? Then move to Step 6.

6. **Connect to an unlisted network.**

   If Vista doesn't list your wireless network's name, two culprits might be involved:

   - *Low signal strength:* Like any radio signal, wireless networks are cursed with a limited range. Walls, floors, and ceilings sap their strength. Keep moving your computer closer to the wireless router or access point, continually clicking the Refresh button (shown in the margin) until your network appears.

   - *It's hiding:* For security reasons, some wireless networks list their names as Unnamed Network. That means you must know the network's *real* name and type in that name before connecting. If you think that's your problem, move to the next step.

7. **Click a wireless network listed as Unnamed Network and click Connect.**

   When asked, enter the network's name (SSID) and if required, its password, described in Step 5. (You need to get the SSID and password from the wireless network's owner.) When Vista knows the network's real name and password, your PC will connect.

If you're still having problems connecting, try the following tips:

✔ When Vista says that it can't connect to your wireless network, it offers two choices: Diagnose This Connection or Connect to a Different Network. Both messages almost always mean this: Move Your PC Closer to the Wireless Transmitter.

✔ If you can't connect to the network you want, try connecting to one of the unsecured networks, instead. Be sure not to enter any passwords, credit card numbers, or other sensitive information, however, and just stick to Web browsing.

✔ Unless you specifically tell it not to, Vista remembers the name and password of networks you've successfully connected with before, sparing you the chore of reentering all the information. Your PC will connect automatically whenever you're within range.

✔ Cordless phones and microwave ovens, oddly enough, interfere with wireless networks. Try to keep your cordless phone out of the same room as your wireless PC, and don't heat up that sandwich when browsing the Internet.

Connecting to and Sharing Files with Other PCs on Your Network

Even after you've set up your network, Vista *still* might not let you see your connected PCs or their files. That's right: Yet *another* security measure prevents PCs from seeing each other or sharing files on your private network. Here's how to knock some sense into Vista's security:

1. **Click the Start menu and choose Network.**

   When it's working right, you should see icons for all your connected PCs here. To connect to a PC and see its shared files, just double-click its name.

   But the first time you set up a network, Vista's Network window comes up blank. A banner across the window's top warns, "Network discovery and file sharing are turned off. Network computers and devices are not visible. Click to change."

2. **Click the window's warning banner or click the Network and Sharing Center button.**

   Clicking either one fetches the Network and Sharing Center, as shown in Figure 17-6.

Figure 17-6: Open the Network and Sharing Center to change settings that let you find other PCs on your network.

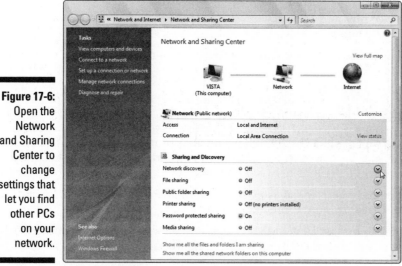

3. **Change the following areas in the Network and Sharing Center.**

   To turn an area on or off, click the little downward-pointing arrow, shown with the mouse pointer pointing at it in Figure 17-6. When the panel drops down, click to turn the feature on or off.

   - *Network Discovery:* Turn this on. This allows people on other PCs to see your PC on the network.

   - *File Sharing:* Turn this on. This lets people access files or printers you've chosen to share with them.

   - *Public Folder Sharing:* Turn this on. You want to share your Public folder, as it's the common place where everybody places files they want to share with others. Choose Turn on Sharing so Anyone with Network Access Can Open, Change, and Create Files.

     To let other people open your Public folder's files but *not* change them or place their own files there, choose Turn on Sharing so Anyone with Network Access Can Open Files instead.

   - *Printer Sharing:* Turn this on if you've attached a printer to your PC. That lets other PCs print to it.

   - *Password Protected Sharing:* Turn this off. If it's turned on, only people with user accounts on your *own* PC can access your Public folder and other shared items.

   - *Media Sharing:* Turn this on. That makes your songs, photos, and videos accessible to anybody else on your network.

4. **Place files and folders you want to share with others into your PC's Public folder.**

   The Public folder lives one click away in every Vista folder: It's listed in the folder's left column.

If your PC still can't see other PCs, or those PCs can't see your PC or its files, check out the following tips:

- ✔ Turn off all the PCs, the router, and your broadband modem. Then turn on your broadband modem, your router, and your PCs — in that order, waiting 30 seconds between each one.

- ✔ Retrace your steps, making sure to turn on Public Folder Sharing and turn off Password Protected Sharing.

- ✔ Make sure that all your PCs have the same workgroup name, described in this chapter's sidebar, "Bothersome workgroup names."

WARNING!

Deleting files from a networked PC

Normally, anything you delete on your PC ends up in your Recycle Bin, giving you a last chance at retrieval. That's not true when you're working on a file in a *networked* PC's Public folder. When you delete a folder on another PC's Public folder, it's gone for good — it doesn't hop into the Recycle Bin of your PC *or* the networked PC. Beware.

Sharing a Printer on the Network

Many households or offices have several computers but only one printer. To let everybody on the network print on that printer, share it by following these steps on the Vista computer connected to the printer:

1. **Click the Start menu, choose Network, and click the Network and Sharing Center button along the top.**

   The Network and Sharing Center window appears, as shown earlier in Figure 17-6.

2. **Turn on Printer Sharing and click Apply.**

   Look in the Printer Sharing category and click the Off button to reveal the menu. When the menu drops down, choose Turn on Printer Sharing and click Apply to share that printer with the network.

Now, tell your other networked PC (or PCs) about your newly shared printer by following these steps:

1. **Click the Start menu, choose Control Panel, and select Printer from the Hardware and Sound category.**

   The Printers window lists icons for any installed printers. (Ignore the Microsoft XPS Document Writer, as it's not a real printer.)

2. **Click the Add a Printer button.**

   The Add Printer window appears.

3. **Choose Add a Network, Wireless, or Bluetooth Printer and click Next.**

   Your PC glances around the network for the other PCs' shared printer. When it finds it, click its name and click Next to install it. If it doesn't find it, move to Step 4.

4. **Choose The Printer That I Want Isn't Listed, and then click Browse to go to the shared printer.**

   Clicking the Browse button fetches a list of your networked PCs. Double-click the PC with the attached printer, and Vista lists the printer's name.

5. **Double-click the shared printer's icon and click Next.**

   Vista finally connects to your networked printer. You might also need to install the printer's software on your PC before it can print to the networked printer.

Dealing with a Network That Isn't Networking

Sometimes networks communicate as gleefully as birds on a sunny spring morning. Other times, they stand still and refuse to talk, like strangers in an elevator. Wireless and wired computers each come with their own special types of problems. I tackle both of them in their own sections.

Fixing problems with wired networks

Books on troubleshooting and setting up networks easily run into the 1,000-page range. Before cracking the spine on one of those books, though, many network gurus start with these tricks:

- If some computers don't recognize the network, turn off all the computers and networking equipment. Then turn on the cable modem, wait a few moments, and then turn on the router.

  Then turn on the other computers one by one to isolate the problem computer. Before moving on to another computer, make sure that the one you're working with connects to the Internet and to the other computers.

- After you've isolated the problem computer, check the wiring. Make sure you're using CAT-5 cable and that the cable's no longer than 300 feet. Make sure that the cable is plugged firmly into both the router and the network adapter. (It's not plugged into your modem's phone jack by mistake, is it?)

- Call up the Windows Device Manager, described in Chapter 19, and make sure that Windows doesn't list any codes or errors next to your network adapter. Make sure you're using the adapter's newest drivers.

✔ Make sure that the Windows Vista firewall, covered in Chapter 18, is turned off while you're troubleshooting the network. If everything works when the firewall's turned off, you've found the culprit: Check the firewall's settings.

✔ Choose Help and Support from the Start menu, run through the three help sections listed in the networking section. Windows Vista leads you through setting up the network, step by step, to make sure you haven't forgotten anything.

Fixing problems with wireless networks

Wireless networks have many more potential problems than wired networks, primarily because of their security issues. Wireless networks use passwords and setup codes to keep out the bad folks. That extra layer of protection sometimes keeps things from working correctly.

✔ Keep an eye on your signal strength by checking the properties of your wireless network adapter. Without a strong enough signal, wireless computers can't speak to each other. Try relocating the wireless access point for optimal signal strength.

✔ While you watch your adapter's signal strength meter, slowly point its antenna in different directions. If you're using a USB adapter with a cable, move the adapter to different spots on your desk. If necessary, stick it to a wall with Velcro. Antenna position is often key; have somebody watch your computer's signal strength meter while you slowly move the antenna on your router.

✔ Many companies sell antennas specifically designed to increase your signal by pointing it in specified directions. They don't work with all models of routers, but try Googling your router's model and the term *wireless antenna*.

✔ Try temporarily disabling your encryption. If the wireless connections work with the encryption disabled, concentrate on setting up the same encryption on each computer so that they all match.

✔ Run through all the suggestions listed for wired networks and see if any of them work.

✔ The Internet holds a wealth of information about networking, as well as friendly, informative people. Chapter 22 shows you how to discover them and their advice for your particular computing problems. (The Troubleshooting & Tutorials section of `www.practicallynetworked.com` can be especially helpful.)

Chapter 18

Filtering Out Evil with Firewalls

*E*ven if you're not using a traditional network in your home or office, you're probably using a network every day. The Internet is a vast network connecting computers around the world. And with those connections come dangers.

See, your computer opens a door to the Internet whenever it asks for information. And naturally, because your computer needs to receive information — a Web page, for example — the computer holds the door open.

Unfortunately, some people make a habit of looking for open doors and trying to sneak in when nobody's looking. Why? For some people, the childish thrill of seeing if they can sneak into Jeff's locker and snoop around without getting caught is just too tempting to resist.

Others sneak in like burglars, looking for things they can steal: credit card numbers, e-mail addresses, or other private files. Some work like vandals, sneaking in and destroying whatever they get their hands on.

Simply put, your computer needs somebody to stand guard at the door, opening and shutting the door at the right times to filter out the bad folks.

A *firewall* is that security guard. A firewall can be either software or hardware, and this chapter explains how it works, how to find one, and how to make sure it does its work without constant supervision.

Understanding Firewall Buzzwords

The Internet is a computer network, and anybody who's looked at a network's settings menu knows how complicated it is. Because firewalls work at your computer's Internet connection point, they, too, come with some pretty complicated setups. Here are some of the words that you might encounter when choosing and setting up a firewall:

Firewall: A piece of hardware or software that watches the information going in and out of your PC. Depending on its settings, the firewall either permits or blocks the information.

Hardware firewall: A router or other specialized box that connects directly to the modem and inspects the information as it passes to or from the modem. Because the hardware firewall — the router, in most cases — sits between your PC and the Internet, potential attackers can't attack the PC directly. That limits their attacks to the router itself, which is more difficult to exploit than a PC.

Software firewall: A program that polices the information flow between computers, letting you decide what programs can exchange information with other computers. A software firewall helps keep worms from spreading between PCs linked in a home or office network.

Windows firewall: The firewall software built into both Windows Vista and Windows XP. (Before Service Pack 2 arrived, Windows XP's firewall went by the name *Internet Connection Firewall,* and Microsoft left it turned off by default.)

Rules: Settings on a firewall that describe its behavior. Your router looks at its rules to decide who can communicate with your PC. Rules can dictate which programs may talk to the Internet, for instance, and which may not. Other rules can allow some computers to talk to your PC, but not others. If you don't set any rules, the firewall follows the ones Microsoft initially set up, which are reasonably safe.

Shared: Drives and folders that have been given permission for others to access. Windows Vista automatically shares everything inside its Public folder with other users on a local computer network, like the one I describe how to set up in Chapter 17. The Public folder's contents can't normally be reached from the Internet.

IP Address: A specific number assigned to a computer by your Internet Service Provider that lets it connect to the Internet. Working like a house's street address, the IP address enables the Internet to route information directly to and from your computer.

Why cable and DSL modems need firewalls

Cable and DSL modems can be more dangerous than dial-up Internet connections, and here's why:

Whenever your computer connects to the Internet, your Internet Service Provider (ISP) assigns it a number known as an *IP address*. Because a dialup user's computer's IP address changes each time she dials the Internet, a hacker might have more trouble finding and relocating that particular computer. That keeps the computer safer from unauthorized connections. Even if a hacker breaks in once, the computer will have a different address the next time it connects to the Internet, making it more difficult for the hacker to relocate.

Most cable and DSL modems, by contrast, remain constantly connected to the Internet, which means that the computer's IP address doesn't change nearly as often — if ever. After a hacker locates a susceptible computer's address on the Internet, he or she can break into it repeatedly. Firewalls help weed out hackers trying to break into your PC.

Hacker: A person who enjoys fiddling with computers and exploring their limits. Good hackers (sometimes called "white hat" hackers) enjoy challenges like creating robots that bring them drinks. Evil hackers (sometimes called "black hat" hackers) enjoy exploring other people's computers — regardless of whether or not they've asked for permission.

Turning On (or Off) Windows Vista's Firewall

Windows Vista comes with a built-in firewall, just like Windows XP. Actually, the two firewalls are very similar. Both Windows XP (with Service Pack 2) and Windows Vista turn on the firewall automatically when you set up a network or connect with the Internet.

In both Windows XP and Windows Vista, you must be logged on with an Administrator's account to access Windows' firewall.

It's easy to see if Windows Vista's firewall is turned on: Vista constantly nags you if the firewall's ever turned *off*. But to see for yourself that Vista's firewall is running — and turn it on if it's turned off — follow these steps:

1. **Choose Control Panel from the Start menu.**

2. **Click the Security icon and choose Windows Firewall.**

The Windows Firewall window appears, as shown in Figure 18-1, showing whether the firewall's turned on or off.

If the Windows Firewall screen says "Your computer is not protected: turn on Windows Firewall," as shown in Figure 18-1, Vista's firewall is turned off. Turn it back on by following the next step.

3. **Click Update Settings Now.**

The little hand mouse pointer points to those words in Figure 18-1. When you click the words, Windows Vista immediately turns on your firewall.

Figure 18-1:
The
Windows
Firewall
window tells
you whether
your firewall
is turned
on or off.

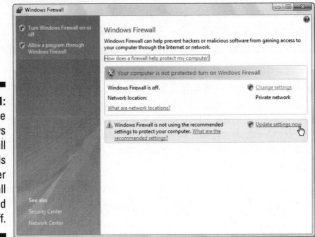

You might not always want the firewall turned on, as described in the next two tips:

- ✔ If you're using a firewall from a third party company, keep Windows firewall turned off. Unlike anti-spyware programs, firewalls interfere with each other, so you should run only one. To turn off Windows firewall, click Change Settings, click Off (Not Recommended), and click OK.

- ✔ Windows firewall sometimes nags you when it's turned off. But if you *want* the firewall turned off, turn off the nag screens, as well: Choose Start⇨Control Panel⇨Security⇨Security Center. Then, from the Windows Security Center window's left column, choose Change the Way Security Center Alerts Me. Finally, choose Don't Notify Me and Don't Display the Icon (Not Recommended).

Turning on Windows XP's firewall

Windows Vista and Windows XP turn on their firewalls in slightly different ways. If you're still using Windows XP, follow these steps to see your PC's network connections, see which ones are firewalled, and turn on the connections you want protected.

1. **Choose the Control Panel from the Start menu, click the Network and Internet Connections icon, and click the Network Connections icon.**

   Windows XP lists all your computer's network connections, including dialup, broadband Internet gateways (a network's Internet connection), and network bridges (a connection of two networks, like FireWire and an Ethernet network).

2. **Right-click the Internet connection you want to protect and choose Properties.**

3. **Click the Advanced tab.**

4. **Click in the little box in the Internet Connection Firewall section.**

   Clicking in the little box turns on the firewall.

5. **Click the OK button.**

   Depending on whether you left a little check mark in Step 4's little check box, you've turned the firewall on or off.

Enable Windows XP's firewall only on connections to the *Internet*. (You needn't turn on the firewall for your Bluetooth connection, for example, even though Windows XP lists Bluetooth as a network connection.)

Using America Online to connect to the Internet in Windows XP? Then these instructions won't help at all. America Online uses its own, special dialup connection that doesn't allow members to tinker so easily with their network settings. That includes turning on the firewall.

Letting a Program Poke through Windows Vista's Firewall

Although firewalls offer protection, they can be as annoying as an airport security scan. In their zest for security, firewalls sometimes go overboard, stopping programs from working the way they should.

You might try to run a new program, for example, only to be greeted with the window in Figure 18-2. If you spot that window and you *haven't* tried to run a program, click the Keep Blocking button: You've effectively stopped what could be a rogue program from connecting with the Internet.

But if you want the program to run, click the Unblock button instead. The firewall adds that program to its Exceptions list and no longer bugs you about it.

Figure 18-2:
Windows
firewall lets
you know
when it's
stopped a
program
from
connecting
with the
Internet.

On a few conditions, however, you'll need to delve deeper into the firewall's settings:

✔ Manually add a program to the Exceptions list.

✔ Change how the firewall blocks a particular program.

✔ Unblock a program you've blocked by mistake.

To do any of those three things, follow these steps:

1. **Choose Control Panel from the Start menu.**

   The Control Panel appears, listing its categories.

2. **In the Security category, choose Allow a Program Through Windows Firewall.**

   The Windows Firewall Settings window opens to its Exceptions tab, as shown in Figure 18-3. Here, Windows Firewall lists the programs it recognizes. Programs with a checked box are able to accept incoming connections through the firewall. No check mark in a program's box? Then that program is blocked.

   From this window, you can take any of the following actions:

   • **Add a program to the Exceptions list.** Don't see your program on the Exceptions list? Click the Add Program button, and the Add a Program window lists all your known programs. Click the program's name and click OK to put it on the Exceptions list.

   • **Unblock a program.** Unblock any mistakenly blocked program by putting a check mark in its adjacent box and clicking Apply.

- **Block a program.** Block any suspicious program from accepting Internet connections by removing the check mark from its box and clicking Apply.

- **Delete a program's name.** If you've uninstalled a program but it still appears on the list, click its name and click Delete to remove its entry.

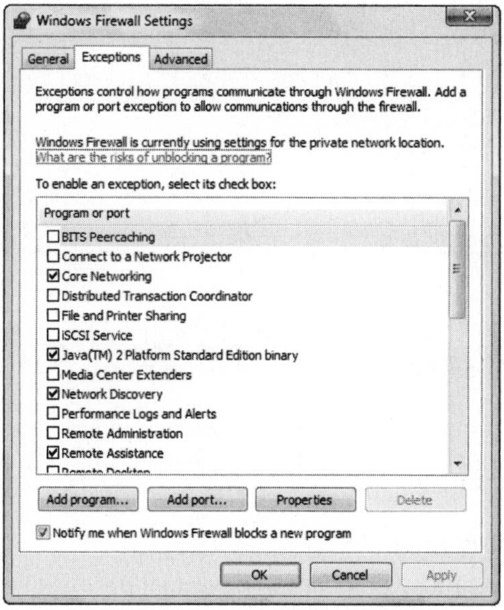

Figure 18-3:
Programs
with a
check mark
may accept
incoming
Internet
connections;
programs
without a
check mark
have those
connections
blocked by
Windows
firewall.

> **Windows Firewall Settings**
>
> General | Exceptions | Advanced
>
> Exceptions control how programs communicate through Windows Firewall. Add a program or port exception to allow communications through the firewall.
>
> Windows Firewall is currently using settings for the private network location.
> What are the risks of unblocking a program?
>
> To enable an exception, select its check box:
>
> | Program or port |
> |---|
> | ☐ BITS Peercaching |
> | ☐ Connect to a Network Projector |
> | ☑ Core Networking |
> | ☐ Distributed Transaction Coordinator |
> | ☐ File and Printer Sharing |
> | ☐ iSCSI Service |
> | ☑ Java(TM) 2 Platform Standard Edition binary |
> | ☐ Media Center Extenders |
> | ☑ Network Discovery |
> | ☐ Performance Logs and Alerts |
> | ☐ Remote Administration |
> | ☑ Remote Assistance |
> | ☐ Remote Desktop |
>
> [Add program...] [Add port...] [Properties] [Delete]
>
> ☑ Notify me when Windows Firewall blocks a new program
>
> [OK] [Cancel] [Apply]

3. **Click OK to save your changes.**

   The firewall saves your work and closes the window.

These tips help you wring the most work out of your firewall:

✔ Want more information about a program listed in the firewall? Click that program's name and click the Properties button. (Refer to Figure 18-3.) A window appears, explaining the program's purpose.

✔ Think you've messed up your firewall settings? Click the Advanced tab and click Restore Defaults. That removes any changes you've made to the firewall, leaving it set up the way it was when first installed. (Clicking Restore Defaults might also keep some programs from working until you add them to the Exceptions list again.)

✔ Don't want the firewall to monitor one of your network connections — your FireWire or Bluetooth connection, for example? Click the Advanced tab and remove the check mark from that particular connection's name.

The difference between hardware and software firewalls

Like antivirus programs, firewalls usually butt heads: You don't want to install two firewalls on the same PC. The exception comes with hardware firewalls. Most routers come with a built-in hardware firewall that manages the traffic flow between the Internet and your network or PC. Hardware firewalls don't conflict with software firewalls, like the ones built into Vista and Windows XP. Feel free to run them both, and they'll both get along fine.

In fact, the software firewall does something extra that the hardware firewall can't: It manages traffic between the PCs on your network. If an evil program infects a PC on your network, the software firewall can help stop that PC from infecting the other PCs on your network.

Manually Configuring a Firewall's Ports

Sometimes adding a program to the firewall's Exceptions list, described in the preceding section, isn't enough. Specifically, some programs want you to open specific channels so they can chatter through them. These places are called *ports*.

You might come across a finicky program with special port requirements. For example, the *World of Warcraft* online game needs TCP protocol on port 3724 to be open for outbound TCP connections.

Here's how to tell Windows Vista's firewall to accommodate that pesky program:

1. **Choose Control Panel from the Start menu.**

   The Control Panel appears, listing its categories.

2. **In the Security category, choose Allow a Program Through Windows Firewall.**

   The Exceptions tab appears on the Windows Firewall Settings window, as shown earlier in Figure 18-3.

3. **Click the Add Port button.**

   The Add a Port window appears, as shown in Figure 18-4, ready for you to poke the required holes in your firewall.

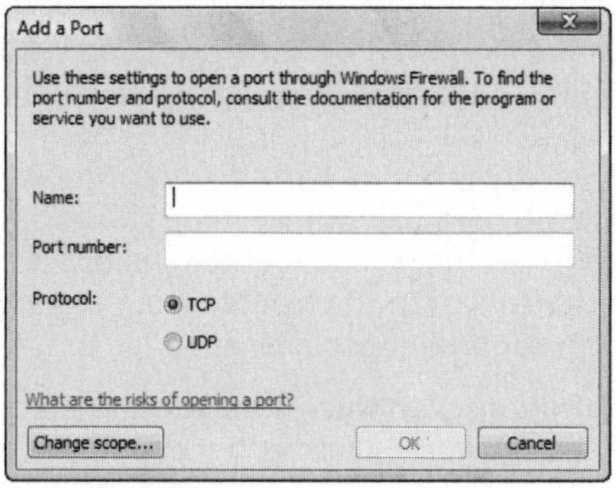

Figure 18-4:
The Add
a Port
window lets
you open a
port on your
PC for
programs
to com-
municate
through.

4. **Describe what you're doing in the Name box.**

   This is for your own use so you can remember later why you're doing this. For instance, type **Enabling Port 3724 for World of Warcraft**.

5. **Type the required port number in the Port Number box.**

   Here's where you tell the firewall which ports to open; in the case of *World of Warcraft,* you want it to open 3724.

   Need to open several ports, or a range of ports? Enter every port number, separated by commas, like this: **3724,3725,3726,3728**.

6. **Click either the TCP or UDP radio button, and then click OK.**

   World of Warcraft wants the *TCP* port changed, so click that radio button. The Add a Port dialog box now looks like Figure 18-5.

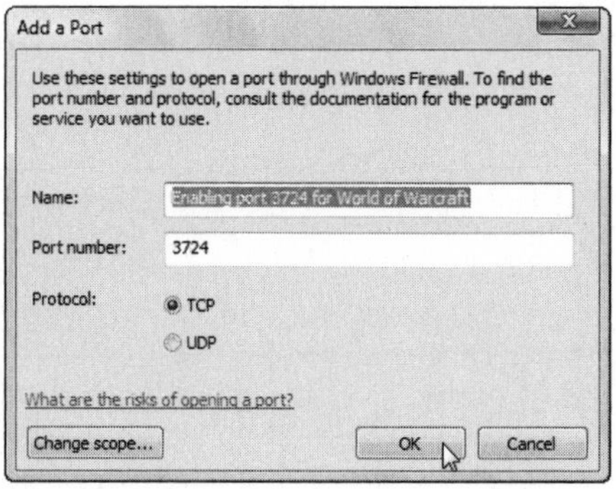

Figure 18-5:
When filled
out properly
to open TCP
port 3724,
the Add a
Port box
looks like
this.

7. **Repeat these steps for any other ports that need to be opened.**

    After you've opened the port required by your program, Windows Vista should allow the program to hold its conversations through the firewall.

    ✔ *World of Warcraft* isn't the only program with these special needs. You might find yourself changing ports for other online games and chat programs where it's important that the computer can accept communications that it didn't initiate. (Search the troublesome program's manual or help area for *firewall* to see which ports to open.)

    ✔ Internet file-swapping programs also want certain ports open so they may communicate and share files. It's a drag, but check the program's fine print to see what ports it craves. Then add those ports to the firewall by following the steps in this section.

Part V
Introducing Parts to Windows

The 5th Wave   By Rich Tennant

"We should cast a circle, invoke the elements, and direct the energy. If that doesn't work, we'll read the manual."

In this part . . .

This part of the book aims directly at Windows Vista owners. Today, most upgraders pick up their screwdrivers because they want their PCs to be strong enough to handle Windows Vista. Or if they've already upgraded, they want to fix or replace the parts and software that Windows Vista snubs.

When you're ready to upgrade to Windows Vista — or you're not sure you've done it correctly — this part of the book details exactly how to install Microsoft's latest Windows version. You can upgrade from Windows XP or install Windows Vista onto a newly installed, gargantuan hard drive.

Also, be sure to turn here if somebody or some error message says that you need a new driver. You discover how to find the right one, replace the old one, and tweak the settings on the new one if it's still not driving diligently along the dotted yellow lines.

Finally, if something leaves you completely in the lurch, read Chapter 22 to find out how to consult the ultimate Free Tech Support System: the Internet's Web sites and newsgroups.

Chapter 19

Hiring the Right Driver for Windows

- -

In This Chapter

▶ Understanding drivers

▶ Installing a driver for a new computer part

▶ Finding a driver for a computer part

▶ Locating a driver's version number

▶ Updating a problem driver with a newer driver

▶ Rolling back a driver to the earlier one

- -

Sometimes upgrading a computer goes as smoothly as throwing a well-catered party. You install the new part, and Windows instantly recognizes it, announcing its name in a merry pop-up window for everybody to see. Windows embraces the latest arrival, hands it a drink, and immediately introduces it to all parts of your computer.

Other times, well, it's a party disaster. Windows snubs the part when you plug it in, and the computer turns a cold shoulder, as well. Or when you turn your computer back on, your computer responds with an antisocial error message that ruins the fun for everybody.

Often, installation problems lie not with the part itself, but with its driver — the software that lets Windows put the part to work. Although Windows Vista comes with nearly 20,000 drivers on its DVD, some of your PC's parts will probably go unrecognized. This chapter shows you how to go about finding and installing decent drivers. If a driver doesn't seem to be doing the job, you discover how to replace it politely, with a minimum of hard feelings on anybody's account.

And if the new driver does an even worse job than the old one, heaven forbid, this chapter reveals the button hidden in Windows Vista's Secret Panel: At one click of a button, Windows fires the new driver and puts the older driver back in place until you can find a better replacement.

This is a meaty chapter, and you troubleshooters will spend a lot of time here because many of Windows' hardware problems start and end with drivers.

Understanding Driver Buzzwords

Whenever anything goes wrong in Windows, nearby computer gurus often exclaim, "Sounds like a driver problem! You'd better get an update." Of course, it's an easy conversation stopper, freeing the guru from fixing your computer.

But what exactly does that mean? What's a driver? Where do you find an updated one? How do you know which driver works the best? This section probes the background behind Windows' continuing problem with its drivers.

But, first thing's first. A *driver* is piece of software that enables Windows to communicate with a specific computer part — an interpreter, if you will. Some drivers use several files to carry out their duties; others use just one. Their names vary widely. But almost every piece of hardware in your computer needs its own, specific driver, or Windows doesn't know how to communicate with it.

Because outside companies — your printer's manufacturer, for instance — write drivers for their own printers, tech support people like to pass the buck: If you have a problem with your printer, your printer's tech support people might say you have a *Windows* problem and should contact Microsoft. Microsoft's tech support people are likely to tell you that you have a *driver* problem and that you should contact your printer's manufacturer.

Here's a list of the buzzwords to remember when you're installing new hardware, troubleshooting a PC problem, or tracking down an updated driver for a bothersome computer part.

Version: Manufacturers continually update their drivers and release new replacement versions. Sometimes new versions add new features. Often, they fix problems with the previous driver versions. And sometimes, if a version is so new that it hasn't been tested under a wide variety of conditions, the new driver doesn't work as well as the *old* driver.

Version Number: Manufacturers assign the number 1.0 to a driver when it's first released to the public. Whenever they release a new version of the driver, they change its number, often giving a hint as to the extent of the driver's changes. A driver moving up an entire digit, from 1.0 to 2.0, for instance, probably offers substantial new features. A driver with a smaller number change, version 1.1, for instance, probably just fixes small problems or adds minor features to version 1.0. Version 1.11 usually fixes tiny problems with the version 1.1 update. (Version 1.11a fixes miniscule problems with Version 1.11.)

The driver bearing the *highest* version number is the most current release. It's usually (but not always) the most reliable. The Windows Device Manager, described later in this chapter, enables you to view a driver's version number. (Jump ahead to Figure 19-13 to see an example.)

Version History: The best companies stock their Web sites with a detailed description of every driver's version number, its date of release, and the features that each version repairs or adds. By examining a driver's version history, you can easily spot the newest driver and discover whether it repairs the problems that you've been experiencing.

Device Manager: Windows collects more information about drivers than your local DMV. The Windows Device Manager, the archive of driver details, lists the drivers used by every part of your computer. The Device Manager serves as the starting point for anything to do with drivers, including their installation, update, or removal. (The Device Manager gets its own arena in this chapter's "Using the Device Manager to fix driver problems" section.)

Device Provider: Listed in the Device Manager, the device provider is the company that created the driver. Most manufacturers write their own drivers for their products. They then hand the drivers to Microsoft; Microsoft then bundles those drivers with each new release of Windows. When you install Windows, it can then recognize and begin using a computer's parts.

Many manufacturers balk at creating drivers for their older parts, unfortunately, because the companies are too busy pushing their newer parts. Not wishing to strand the millions of people still using older computers, Microsoft picks up the stick and writes its *own* drivers. Drivers listing Microsoft as the Device Provider usually came bundled with Windows.

Microsoft's drivers are often generic, though. Microsoft writes a driver that recognizes *all* game controllers, for instance, allowing any game controller to move things around on the screen. However, manufacturers often write separate drivers for specific models of a game controller. When you update to the manufacturer's driver, Windows suddenly realizes that your game controller has *seven* programmable buttons, for instance, and finally enables you to use them.

Add Hardware Wizard: Hidden away in the Control Panel's Classic view, this program tells Windows to look for newly installed hardware that *isn't* Plug-and-Play. It's handy for installing older hardware that worked on older PCs, but that Windows Vista doesn't automatically recognize and install. See the "Running the Add Hardware Wizard" section later in this chapter.

Driver signing: Desperate to keep drivers from growing long sideburns, Microsoft prefers to inspect each newly released driver and if it meets approval, stamp it with the Windows logo. If you install a driver that hasn't been through Microsoft's approval process, Windows flashes a warning message, as shown in Figure 19-1.

Figure 19-1:
Windows
complains if
you try to
install a
driver that
hasn't been
through
Microsoft's
approval
process.

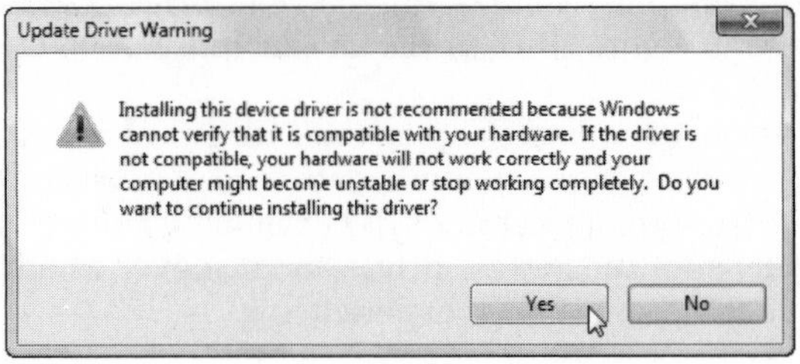

Update Driver Warning

Installing this device driver is not recommended because Windows cannot verify that it is compatible with your hardware. If the driver is not compatible, your hardware will not work correctly and your computer might become unstable or stop working completely. Do you want to continue installing this driver?

Yes   No

Despite its fear-inspiring message, the warning shown in Figure 19-1 appears often when you're installing very new drivers or parts manufactured by smaller companies. Companies often don't have enough time or money to wait for Microsoft to approve their drivers. If the new driver doesn't work, you can always remove it, as described in this chapter's last section, "Using the Device Manager to fix driver problems."

Installing (or Reinstalling) a Driver

Sometimes installing a driver is an automatic, one-time-only process — especially when you plug a Plug and Play device into a USB or FireWire port. It works like this:

1. **Plug in the new part.**

   For instance, I plugged a digital camera into my computer's USB port, and I turned on the camera.

2. **Watch Windows greet your new part.**

   Windows beeps in excitement, spouting the pop-up message shown in Figure 19-2. In less than a minute, Windows spun out a second message, shown in Figure 19-3, saying that my camera was ready to use.

   ✔ After you've installed a Plug and Play item and Windows successfully recognizes it, Windows skips the greeting messages the next time you plug in that same item. Instead, Windows simply recognizes your device. (It also places the device's name in your Device Manager, enabling you to probe it for driver details.)

   ✔ When you unplug or turn off a Plug and Play device, Windows beeps, a way of telling you it knows you've unplugged your gadget. (The sound comes in handy when frantic game-controller movements yank the cord out of your computer.)

REMEMBER

✔ Windows almost always beeps in excitement when you plug something into a USB or FireWire port. If it doesn't beep, unplug the device, wait a moment, and then plug it back in. Never, *ever* unplug and plug in a device quickly. Give Windows a chance to beep in recognition.

Figure 19-2:
As I plug in the camera, Windows begins searching for the right driver.

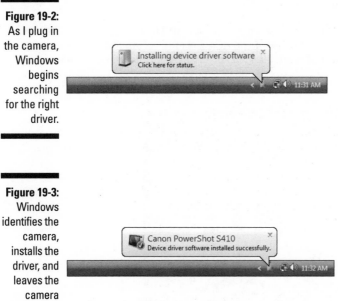

Figure 19-3:
Windows identifies the camera, installs the driver, and leaves the camera ready to use.

Dealing with a Driver That Won't Drive

Sometimes you plug in a new part, and Windows stays mum: No welcome sign. Or you install a part inside your computer, push your computer's power button, and Windows completely ignores your laboriously installed part.

Occasionally, Windows does recognize *something*. It might even recognize the part's name — an Epson printer, for example. But it refuses to put it to work, instead asking you to insert the CD that came with your device. If this happens, you have three options, discussed in the following three sections:

✔ Run the software that came with the device, if any.

✔ Run the Add Hardware Wizard.

✔ Find a driver and install it yourself.

Running a part's bundled software

Windows doesn't always recognize every newly installed part. That's why many products come with their own setup software. Running the setup software automatically installs the drivers and adds any programs that help you use the new part.

To install the software, simply insert its CD into your computer's CD drive. Windows usually takes notice of the new CD and automatically runs the setup software, as shown in Figure 19-4. (It often asks permission before running the setup software.)

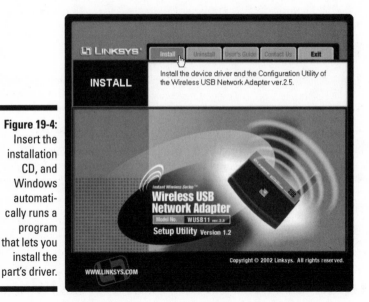

Figure 19-4:
Insert the installation CD, and Windows automatically runs a program that lets you install the part's driver.

Windows often ends the setup process by asking you to restart your computer. When the computer wakes up, Windows takes notice of the new part and begins its welcome messages as shown earlier in Figures 19-2 and 19-3.

✔ If Windows doesn't notice any setup software on the CD, don't worry — the driver is probably on there, but the manufacturer didn't write any software that automatically installs it. In that case, move on to the next section, "Running the Add Hardware Wizard." That section explains how to make the Windows wizard locate the driver on the CD and install it for you.

✔ Still won't install? Then visit the part manufacturer's Web site and look for the latest driver, a process covered in the "Finding a new driver" section later in this chapter. Download the newest available driver, install it, and keep it handy for the next crisis.

✔ Sometimes you want to view a CD's contents, but Vista's darn AutoPlay window keeps jumping up whenever you insert the CD. To bypass the AutoPlay software, hold down the Shift key while inserting a CD. Then right-click the Computer icon, choose Explore, and examine the CD's contents without being bothered.

Running the Add Hardware Wizard

If you install a new part and Windows Vista doesn't recognize it, the first thing to try is to fire up the CD that came with the part. Most CDs usually install the part for you, but a few leave you stranded. When that happens, call in the mysteriously hidden Add Hardware Wizard. Here are the steps for summoning the wizard from its lair in Windows Vista:

1. **Open the Control Panel from the Start menu.**

   The Control Panel appears. If you're like most people, the Control Panel displays its Category view: Ten or so categories appear, each with tasks listed beneath them.

2. **Choose Classic View from the Control Panel's upper-left corner.**

   The Control Panel's upper-left corner lists Control Panel Home, which summons the Control Panel's normal, Category view. Instead of clicking there, click the words *Classic View,* just beneath it, and the Control Panel suddenly shows a swarm of formerly hidden icons.

3. **Double-click the Add Hardware icon, shown in the margin, and click Next at the opening screen.**

   The Add Hardware Wizard leaps into action, as shown in Figure 19-5, offering two options:

   • Search for and Install the Hardware Automatically (Recommended)

   • Install the Hardware That I Manually Select from a List (Advanced)

4. **Choose Search For and Install the Hardware Automatically, and click Next.**

   Vista takes another look for your new part. If you're lucky, it finds and installs it, leaving you with a happy glow as you go about your business.

   Chances are, though, it comes up blank, leaving you with the only option: Click the Next button.

5. **Choose the category of part that you've installed and click Next to install your part, or click Back to return to the previous list.**

   When Vista lists different categories of computer parts, shown in Figure 19-6, click the one pertaining to your newly installed part. For instance, if you've installed a scanner, choose Imaging Devices.

Figure 19-5:
The Add
Hardware
Wizard helps
install older
hardware
that Vista
doesn't
recognize
automati-
cally or that
didn't come
with a
working
installation
CD.

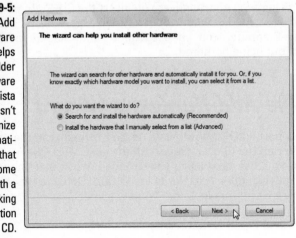

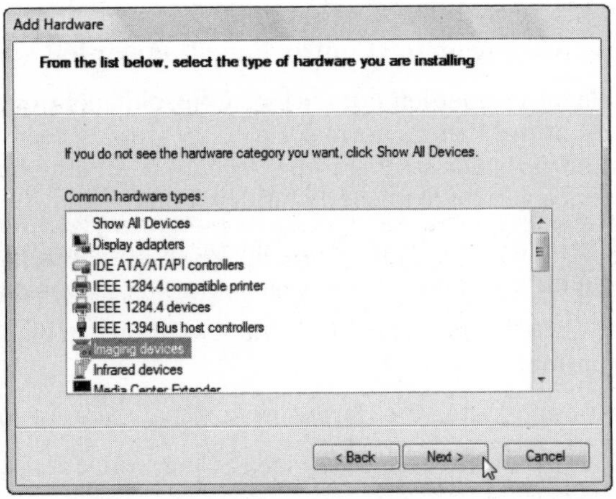

Figure 19-6:
Choose the
category of
your new
device and
click Next.

If you choose Imaging Devices, for example, Windows displays a list of scanner and camera manufacturers, as shown in Figure 19-7.

Click the manufacturer of your part from the list on the left, and then click its model number from the list on the right. The wizard installs your device, and you're through.

If your device came with a CD but no driver installation program, click the Have Disk button in Figure 19-7 and insert the CD. Windows finds the CD's driver, compares it with any other drivers it has, installs the newest or most reliable one.

Don't spot the right category for your part? Not sure of its model name? Vista *still* hasn't installed your part? If any of these three ugly events occur, select the Show All Devices option from the top of the list in the wizard screen shown in Figure 19-6, and click Next.

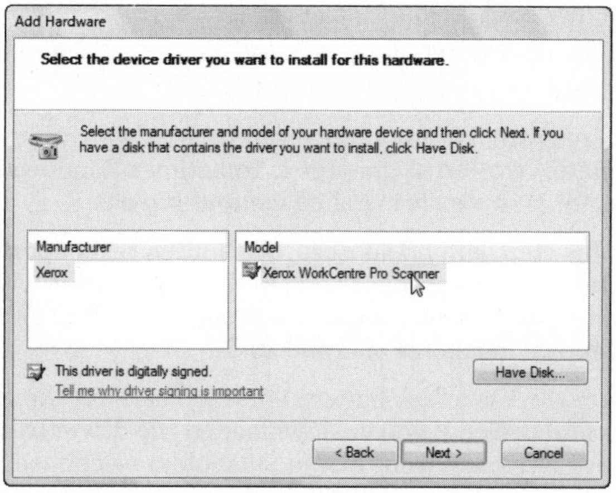

Figure 19-7: Click your part's manufacturer name and model number, if shown.

Add Hardware

Select the device driver you want to install for this hardware.

Select the manufacturer and model of your hardware device and then click Next. If you have a disk that contains the driver you want to install, click Have Disk.

Manufacturer	Model
Xerox	Xerox WorkCentre Pro Scanner

This driver is digitally signed.
Tell me why driver signing is important

[Have Disk...]

[< Back] [Next >] [Cancel]

6. **Choose the device you've installed by selecting the manufacturer or connection device.**

   Windows Vista makes a last-ditch effort to help. Instead of making you choose between categories and model numbers, it lists *all* the part manufacturers and models it can recognize, as shown in Figure 19-8. If you spot your device here, click it; Windows Vista can still install a driver for it, finishing your work.

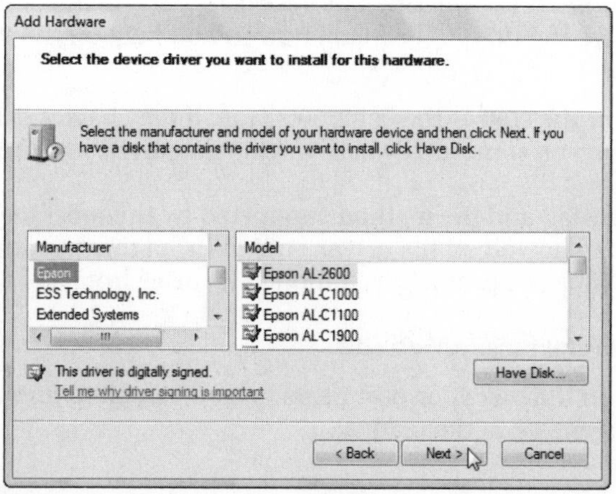

Figure 19-8: Choose your part's manufacturer and model or click Have Disk to install a driver from a CD, USB drive, or a folder on your hard drive.

Add Hardware

Select the device driver you want to install for this hardware.

Select the manufacturer and model of your hardware device and then click Next. If you have a disk that contains the driver you want to install, click Have Disk.

Manufacturer	Model
Epson	Epson AL-2600
ESS Technology, Inc.	Epson AL-C1000
Extended Systems	Epson AL-C1100
	Epson AL-C1900

This driver is digitally signed.
Tell me why driver signing is important

[Have Disk...]

[< Back] [Next >] [Cancel]

If Vista *still* leaves you with an uninstalled part, though, try any of these things before giving up:

✔ Did your part come with a disk or CD but no installation program? Now is your chance: Insert the disk or CD and click the Have Disk button, as shown earlier in Figure 19-8. When the Install from Disk dialog box appears, click the Browse button and tell Windows the letter of the disk drive containing the CD. Windows should scour the CD, find the elusive driver, and install it.

✔ If an installed part still goes unrecognized by Windows, try using Windows Update, covered in Chapter 1. Sometimes Windows Update offers drivers for your newly installed computer parts.

✔ If you reach this step with no success, the burden rests upon you to track down the right driver (described in the next section). When you've grabbed it, return to this section, follow Steps 1–5, and click the Have Disk button, shown in Figures 19-7 and 19-8.

✔ When you click the Have Disk button, Windows asks for the *location* of your newly found driver. If you've downloaded the driver to a folder on your hard drive — usually your Downloads folder — choose that location after clicking the Browse button. Windows finds the driver, installs it, and you're through. *Finally.*

Finding a new driver

Occasionally, Windows forces *you* into the role of grunt worker, and you have to ferret out a driver for a computer part. You can find drivers in four basic ways:

✔ Search the Internet for the manufacturer's Web site and hopefully, the part's driver. (I explain this in the rest of this section.)

✔ Search the Internet for *any* site, not necessarily the manufacturer's Web site, that offers the driver. (I explain how to find help on the Web in Chapter 22.)

✔ Ask a friend or the staff at the computer store if they have a driver. This is doubtful; however, some kindly nerd might take pity, if you can find one.

The easiest way by far, and the method supported by the most manufacturers these days, is to download the driver straight from the manufacturer's Web site. Here's the basic procedure, although it varies from site to site.

1. **Find the manufacturer's Web site.**

   Try looking on the box your part came in; you can often find the site's name listed there or in the manual.

Don't know the manufacturer's name? Look on the part itself. Sometimes the manufacturer's name appears in fine print etched on the part's circuits. After you've found the manufacturer's name, head for `www.google.com` with your Internet browser, type the manufacturer's name into the search box, and click the Google Search button, as shown in Figure 19-9.

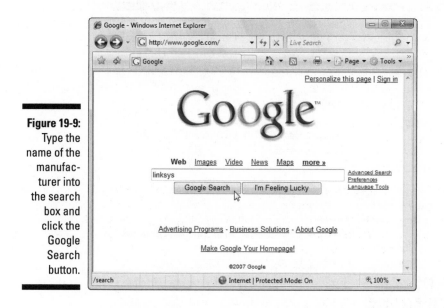

Figure 19-9:
Type the name of the manufacturer into the search box and click the Google Search button.

Google quickly glances at the Web and then displays a surprisingly accurate list of potential Web sites.

2. Go to the manufacturer's Web site.

Google sorts its list by probability, with the most likely candidates at the top. Click the manufacturer's site name to visit the Web site.

3. Find the Web site's page containing the downloadable driver.

Some sites list a menu for *Downloads* or *Drivers* on the opening page. With others, look for *Customer Support* or *Technical Support*. Try clicking a *Site Map*, if you spot one, and search for downloadable drivers from there.

Linksys simplifies the process, as it lists *Downloads* in the top-right corner of its first page. Click the Downloads button, as shown in Figure 19-10.

4. Locate the correct driver for your part *and* Windows version.

Linksys lets you choose both the part's name, as well as your version of Windows. Then it presents a download page, as shown in Figure 19-11.

No Windows Vista driver available? You might still have luck with a Windows XP driver. Don't bother with drivers for Windows versions earlier than that, though, because they probably won't work.

Figure 19-10:
Locate the
Web page
containing
driver
downloads.

Figure 19-11:
Click the
download
button, and
then
download
the proper
driver both
for your part
and your
operating
system.

5. Save the driver into a folder on your computer.

Vista usually saves downloaded files in your Downloads folder. You can find those downloaded files by clicking the Start menu, clicking your username, and opening the Downloads folder.

I created a folder in my computer's Public folder called Drivers Archive. In the Drivers Archive folder, I created a separate folder for each downloaded driver. Because the drivers are stored within the Public folder, they're available to every user on my computer and to every computer on my network.

6. **Log off the Internet and examine the downloaded driver.**

Most drivers come compressed in a *zipped* file to save download time. Double-click the zipped file to see its contents. If you spot a Setup file, click it. The Setup program automatically installs your newly downloaded driver.

No Setup program? Then here's what to do:

- **If you've never installed a driver for your device,** use the Add Hardware Wizard, described in the preceding section. When you arrive at Step 5, click the Have Disk button, click the Browse button, and tell Windows where you've downloaded your new driver. Windows finds the new driver, installs it, and passes around the drinks.

- **If you want to update your existing driver,** head to the "Using the Device Manager to fix driver problems" section coming up next and follow the instructions for updating an old driver.

Using the Device Manager to fix driver problems

When your computer acts up and Windows can't communicate with a computer part or peripheral, a driver's often the culprit. Display adapters (commonly called *video cards*) frequently cause problems like displaying odd colors or borders, or windows that behave in strange ways. Printers, too, rely heavily on their drivers.

Use the Device Manager whenever you have problems with a piece of hardware. There, you can find the version number of the part's current driver and a way to update or repair the driver.

To view your computer's collection of drivers, fire up the Device Manager, as described in the following steps:

1. **Open the Start menu, choose Control Panel, and open the System and Maintenance category.**

The System and Maintenance category spills nearly a dozen icons across the screen. (If Control Panel is already set in Classic View — the view where it *doesn't* show categories — jump to the next step.

2. **Double-click the Device Manager icon.**

The Device Manager window hops to the screen, as shown in Figure 19-12. The Device Manager lists all the parts Windows recognizes inside your computer, as well as whether they're working correctly.

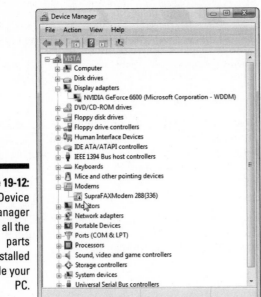

Figure 19-12:
The Device
Manager
lists all the
parts
installed
inside your
PC.

If the Device Manager notices a computer part that's not working correctly, it tells you by placing a symbol on that part's icon. An icon bearing a downward-pointing arrow has been disabled for some reason,
offering a clue that it needs attention. (The Modem icon shown in Figure
19-12, for example, has a downward-pointing arrow.)

Sometimes the Device Manager displays a problem code, number, and
suggested solution next to a problematic part. Searching for these words
and codes on the Internet (see Chapter 22) often can help you solve
problems.

 3. **Click the plus sign next to the category you want to view.**

    Clicking the plus sign next to Display adapters, for example, shows that
    my computer uses an NVIDIA GeForce 6600 video card.

 4. **Double-click the brand name to view details about the part's driver.**

    Double-clicking NVIDIA GeForce 6600 reveals the Properties dialog box
    (shown in Figure 19-13) for that model of video card. There, different
    buttons give you every detail of the driver's private life.

 5. **Click the Properties dialog box's Driver tab, and then click the Driver
    Details button.**

    This reveals all the drivers working to help Windows communicate with
    your part, as shown in Figure 19-14.

Each time that you click one of those driver files, Windows reveals the driver's version number — an essential detail when you're hunting for newer, updated drivers. (Drivers are numbered sequentially, so higher numbers mean newer drivers.)

The other main buttons in Figure 19-13 — Update Driver, Roll Back Driver, and Uninstall — get their own sections, described next.

Figure 19-13:
Click the
Driver
Details
button in the
Properties
dialog box
to view
information
about a
part's
drivers.

Figure 19-14:
The Driver
File Details
dialog box
reveals the
version
number for
every driver
file.

Updating an old driver

Even after installing a brand new part and installing its bundled driver, sometimes the thing *still* doesn't work correctly. In that case, it's time to try updating its driver. Follow these steps to make sure your computer uses the most up-to-date drivers for its parts.

1. **Locate the version number of your current driver.**

   Run through Steps 1–5 in the preceding section, "Using the Device Manager to fix driver problems." In Step 5, click the Driver Details button on the Driver tab, and click each of the driver's files. Write down the file version number for each file. (The files sometimes all use the same number.)

2. **Find an updated driver.**

   You can find complete instructions earlier in this chapter in the "Finding a new driver" section. Be sure to remember where you've saved the new, updated driver.

3. **Repeat Steps 1–5 from the previous section, "Using the Device Manager to fix driver problems." In Step 5, click the Driver tab, click the Update Driver button, and click Next.**

   The Hardware Update Wizard asks where it should search for your new driver, as shown in Figure 19-15.

4. **Choose Browse My Computer For Driver Software, point Windows to the folder containing your new driver, and click Next.**

   Windows offers two options here, as shown in Figure 19-16:

Figure 19-15:
Tell Windows to browse your computer for driver software, and then locate the folder containing your updated driver.

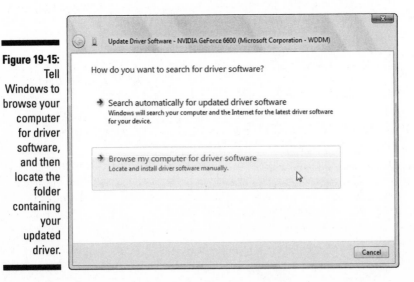

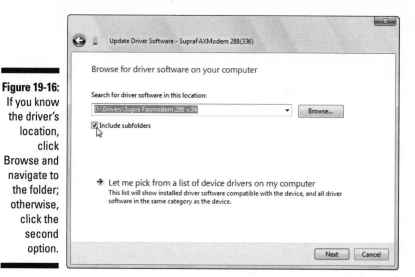

Figure 19-16:
If you know
the driver's
location,
click
Browse and
navigate to
the folder;
otherwise,
click the
second
option.

- If you *know* the driver's location — you downloaded it to a folder, for example, or it's on a CD — click Browse, choose the driver's location, and click Next. Windows searches that location and installs your drivers. Mission accomplished.

  If you downloaded the driver yourself, click Include Subfolders, shown in Figure 19-16, before clicking the Browse button. (That lets Windows know where to search.)

- If you *don't* know the drive's location, however, choose Let Me Pick From a List of Device Drivers on My Computer and move to the next step.

5. **Choose the driver for your new part and click Next.**

   Windows shows you the list of compatible drivers that it found for your part, as shown in Figure 19-17. If you spot your new driver on the list, click it, click Next, and Windows installs it. Whoopee!

   If your driver *isn't* on the list, click the Have Disk button. Tell Windows exactly where your new driver is located and try again. This time, Windows should find it.

   If Windows still balks and says it can't find a better driver than your current driver, stop. The driver you've downloaded isn't a newer version. Head back to the "Finding a new driver" section, try to find a newer driver, and run through this section again.

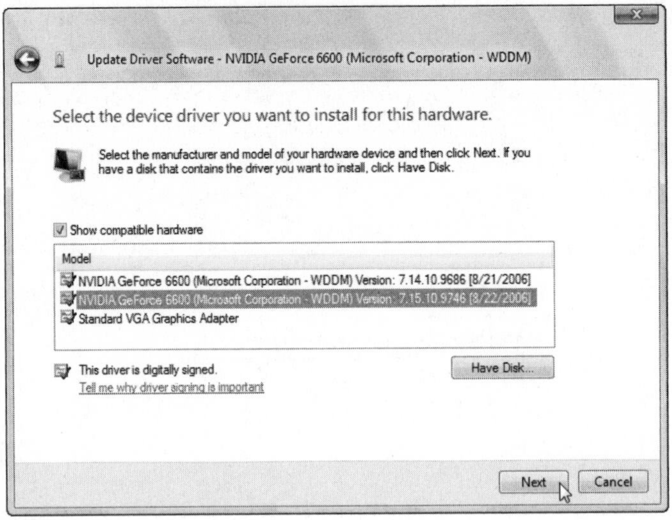

Figure 19-17:
Click the
name of
your new
driver and
click Next.

Here's a last resort if Windows doesn't list your new driver: Click the box to remove the check mark next to the Show Compatible Hardware option, shown in Figure 19-17, and select a driver from that list. (This might install a driver that gives Windows limited use of the part. Although it rarely makes the part work perfectly, it's worth a try because you can always roll back to the old driver, described in the following section.)

✔ Sometimes Windows balks at installing *unsigned drivers,* as described earlier in this chapter in the "Understanding Driver Buzzwords" section. (Figure 19-1 shows the Windows caution message.) Don't worry about the unsigned stuff. Install the driver anyway.

✔ If your new driver makes things even *worse,* feel free to roll back to the original driver using the Roll Back feature, described in the next section.

Rolling back to the original driver

Sometimes the new driver isn't the panacea you'd hoped it would be. Your computer doesn't work any better at all. In fact, sometimes you've not only wasted your time searching for a new driver, but you've made things much, much *worse.*

Fortunately, Windows keeps your previous driver in its back pocket for times like this. Tell Windows to *roll back* — reach into its back pocket and put the original driver back in place. It works like this:

1. **Call up the Device Manager by performing Steps 1–5 in the earlier section, "Using the Device Manager to fix driver problems."**

2. **When you click the Driver tab in Step 5, click the Roll Back Driver button.**

   You see a picture of this dialog box and the Roll Back Driver button in Figure 19-13. When Windows asks if you're *sure* you'd like to roll back to the previous driver, shown in Figure 19-18, click the Yes button.

Driver Package rollback

Are you sure you would like to roll back to the previously installed driver software?

Rolling back to older driver software may reduce the functionality or security of your device. If this doesn't resolve the issues you're having with your device, visit the manufacturer's web site to determine if updated driver software is available.

Yes   No

Windows dutifully removes the naughty driver you just installed and replaces it with the previous driver.

✔ This trick works wonders because Windows always keeps the old drivers in its back pocket for safekeeping.

✔ Changed your mind and decided that the new driver really *was* working better? Feel free to install it again. And then roll back again if you change your mind. You can spend hours doing this.

✔ Yes, indeed, you can spend a lot of time with this entire *chapter*. Finding a driver that works perfectly makes it all worthwhile, though. If a device gives you constant trouble, keep checking the manufacturer's Web site for a newer driver.

Chapter 20

Installing or Upgrading to Windows Vista

*A*lthough Windows Vista might be the latest step in Microsoft's long, climbing staircase of Windows versions, it has a long way to go before reaching a comfortable plateau. Many people still stumble over its perplexing mix of product versions, product keys, activation codes, and zillion-page licensing agreements.

This chapter covers those obstacles and explains how to install the darn thing onto your current computer, either by upgrading Windows XP or installing Vista onto an empty hard drive.

Understanding Windows Vista Buzzwords

One of the most perplexing problems you might face when you're ready to make the Windows Vista upgrade begins at the computer store. Which version should you buy? Or, for people who bought new computers with Windows Vista preinstalled, which version came on its bundled DVD? Here's a quick taste of the Windows Vista flavors. I discuss them all in more detail throughout this chapter.

Upgrade version: The upgrade versions of Windows Vista are cheaper than the full versions (usually about 50 bucks less), but there's a catch: They upgrade only certain versions of Windows XP, as described in Table 20-1. If you don't have a working copy of one of those Windows XP versions on your PC, the upgrade version won't install.

Unlike Windows Vista's upgrade version, Windows XP allowed its upgrade version to be installed onto an empty hard drive. To prove you owned a qualifying previous Windows version, you simply needed to *insert your old Windows CD* during the installation process. Windows Vista's upgrade edition, by contrast, doesn't allow that. It installs itself onto only a *working, activated copy of Windows XP with Service Pack 2 installed.*

Full version: If you're not upgrading a working copy of Windows XP on your PC, you need the *full* version to install Windows Vista. You pay extra for the privilege, of course. Most people buy the full version if they want to do a clean install, described next.

Clean install: When you do a clean install, you're installing Windows Vista onto an empty hard drive. Although more difficult and more expensive, it's the best way to ensure Vista works well on your PC.

OEM (Original Equipment Manufacturing) version: Microsoft sells stripped-down versions of Windows to manufacturers to preinstall on the PCs they sell. The OEM version is locked to that specific computer.

Microsoft doesn't support OEM versions, as the manufacturer custom-configures them to work with your computer's preinstalled parts. Questions about these versions should be aimed at your computer's manufacturer. (Visual ID: The disc usually bears the letters OEM.)

Recovery or Reinstallation disc version: New computers that come with Windows Vista preinstalled sometimes don't include an OEM version *or* a real Windows Vista DVD. Instead, they include a Recovery disc that restores your hard drive to the state it was in when you bought it. That recovery technique usually wipes out all your files in the process, unfortunately. (Visual ID: Look for the words Recovery, Recover, or Reinstallation on the disc. Always check with your computer's manufacturer before using this version; it'll tell you how it affects your computer.)

Activation: Windows Vista's Activation feature takes a snapshot of your computer's parts and links it with Windows Vista's serial number, which prevents you from installing that same copy onto another computer — even your laptop. Unfortunately, the Activation feature might also hassle you if you change a lot of parts in your computer. Vista's official Hassle Window gives you a phone number to call and convince Microsoft that you're not a thief.

Product key: This is a 25-character code that comes with each Vista version as a form of copy protection. You must type in that 25-character code when installing Vista, or the program refuses to install.

Partition: This is a sectioned-off storage area on a hard drive. Usually, a hard drive contains one large partition bearing the letter C as its name. But some meticulous folks want to divvy up their hard drives into several smaller partitions to keep their information orderly. The computer then assigns those partitions different letters. In Windows, a hard drive with two partitions looks like two smaller hard drives bearing the letters C and D.

Preparing to Install Windows Vista

Installing Windows Vista takes more thought than simply popping the DVD into the drive and following the instructions. You need to choose a version of Windows Vista that meets your needs. Plus, you must decide whether to upgrade your Windows XP PC or start from scratch by installing Windows Vista onto an empty hard drive.

Here's a rundown on how to start planning your upgrade to Microsoft's latest operating system. Make up your mind about these things before buying any version.

Choosing the right version of Windows Vista

Windows Vista comes in four main versions, and that makes upgrading Windows XP to Windows Vista a tad complicated. Not all versions of XP will upgrade to every version of Vista. Table 20-1 shows which XP versions can be upgraded to which Vista versions.

Table 20-1:	These Windows XP Versions Can Upgrade to Windows Vista			
	Windows Vista Home Basic	*Windows Vista Home Premium*	*Windows Vista Ultimate*	*Windows Vista Business*
Windows XP Professional	No	No	Yes	Yes
Windows XP Home	Yes	Yes	Yes	Yes
Windows XP Media Center Edition	No	Yes	Yes	No
Windows XP Tablet PC	No	No	Yes	Yes

Surprisingly, the inexpensive Windows XP Home wins the versatility award here, as you can upgrade it to Vista Home Basic, Vista Home Premium, Vista Ultimate, or even Vista Business version.

Windows XP Professional, sold mostly to power users and business owners, can be upgraded to only Vista's Ultimate or Business versions.

So, which version do you choose? Here's the rundown:

Windows Vista Home Basic: Windows Vista Home works fine for home or small office users who want cut-rate basics such as e-mail and Web browsing. It leaves out most of the fun stuff, though, such as making automatic, unattended backups, creating fancy digital photo slideshows, recording TV shows, and copying movies and slideshows to DVDs.

Windows Vista Home Premium: The most popular version for consumers, this contains features Vista Home left out. Vista Home Premium makes automatic backups and photo slide shows, for example, and — if you install the right hardware (covered in Chapter 12) — records TV shows, edits movies and recorded shows, and writes them to DVDs. It also contains what used to be known as Windows Media Center Edition, designed to let you connect your PC to a TV set.

Windows Business: Meant for businesses, this leaves out all the fun multimedia stuff from Vista Home Premium: No DVD maker, photo editor, movie maker, or fancy games. But it adds in a more robust backup program for automatic, unattended backups.

Windows Ultimate: This full-sized cruise vessel contains *all* of Windows Vista. It's Windows Vista Home, Home Premium, and the Business edition rolled into one mega-package. It's for computer enthusiasts who want it all.

The following list might help you decide which version is best for your needs:

✔ No version of Windows Vista is any easier to install onto your computer than any other.

✔ If you're planning on connecting to a large network at work, ask the network manager whether your corporate network insists that you open the wallet for either the Windows Vista Ultimate or Business version. (Remember to write it off as a business expense.)

✔ Always place the CD from your *old* version of Windows XP into the same box as your Vista upgrade DVD. You'll need that Windows XP CD if you ever need to reinstall the upgrade version of Windows Vista. If that's too much for you to remember, buy Vista's full version.

✔ The Microsoft Windows Vista Web site explains the differences between the different Vista versions in more detail, if you haven't made up your mind. Head to www.microsoft.com/windowsvista.

Choosing between a clean install or an upgrade

When you perform an *upgrade* you're installing Windows Vista over a previously existing operating system. It's a fairly simple process. A *clean install* means that you're completely erasing the computer's hard drive and installing Windows Vista onto the empty drive. Naturally, the clean install is more complicated.

Nevertheless, many people choose the more complicated route for these reasons:

- ✔ **Upgrading is quicker and easier to install but leaves room for more problems down the road.** Upgrading to Windows Vista is like painting a house without removing the old layer of paint first. Because the old operating system's cracks and peeling edges still lurk beneath the surface, an upgrade leaves some potential problems. Windows Vista must work harder to untangle your computer's unsolved mysteries and problem areas and apply its own languages and designs on top of them.

- ✔ **Windows Vista usually runs more reliably when it's written onto a clean slate.** A clean install strips the house down to the drywall. Windows Vista then pours itself into place, filling the cracks and providing a solid layer of protection with no chance of initial confusion. Clean installs require more upfront work, but it means that when something goes wrong, you know it's Windows Vista's fault — not the result of some earlier problem that keeps cropping up.

When choosing between an upgrade or clean install, keep the following in mind:

- ✔ If your computer's been running fairly smoothly or if you don't want to bother with the extra work required by a clean install, upgrade your existing operating system. Although you're increasing your chance for problems, Windows Vista is usually fairly good about sorting out what's what.

- ✔ If your computer's been giving you problems, you're simultaneously installing a new hard drive, or you just like the feeling of moving into a newly built house, choose the clean install. It takes much more preparation and time, but your computer will probably run more smoothly. However, be prepared to flex a little more computer techie know-how.

- ✔ Only Vista's full versions can perform a clean install of Windows Vista; the upgrade versions can't. For more details, check out the definitions of upgrade and full versions in the "Understanding Windows Vista Buzzwords" section and read this chapter's last section.

Doing this legwork *before* you install Windows Vista is essential, as you might experience problems getting online immediately after installing the program. The better prepared you are, the smoother your installation will be.

Installing Windows Vista

Whether you're doing a clean install or an upgrade, you still must make the same basic preparations before you put Windows Vista on your computer. Grab your pencil and check these off as you go.

✔ **Compatibility:** Before upgrading or installing, run the *Upgrade Advisor,* the Windows Vista compatibility checker that I discuss in Chapter 6. The program analyzes your computer's hardware and existing software and points out potential problem areas. After you've solved all the problem areas by finding new versions, patches, and drivers, move to the next step.

✔ **Research:** If the Upgrade Advisor shows you might have problems, visit Chapter 22. It explains how to search Web sites to see how other people have handled their Windows Vista compatibility problems.

✔ **Security:** The Upgrade Advisor usually points out these computer bodyguards: antivirus software, security programs, system utilities, and other programs designed to protect you. You don't want them to protect you from Windows Vista's installation process, however, so turn them all off, disable them, or even better, uninstall them: Most security programs won't work with Vista until you buy their upgraded Vista-compatible version.

✔ **Clean up and defragment your PC:** Uninstall the programs you've collected over the years but never used much, if ever. Run Disk Cleanup (see Chapter 9) to clean up as much trash as possible. Finally, defragment your C drive (covered in Chapter 9) to give Vista as much space as possible to settle in for the long haul.

✔ **Back up:** Back up all your important data. If you don't have an external hard drive, covered in Chapter 9, now's the time to buy one of these little critters. Dump all your important data onto it. (Don't worry so much about backing up your programs, as they can always be reinstalled from their original discs.)

Upgrading to Windows Vista

After you've followed the preparations outlined in this chapter's previous two sections, it's time to upgrade to Windows Vista. The better your preparations, the better your chances are for a successful upgrade.

Follow these steps to upgrade your existing Windows operating system to Windows Vista. (The next section shows you how to perform a clean install.)

You can't return to Windows XP after upgrading to Windows Vista. When you move past Step 5 in the following list, there's no going back.

Follow these steps to upgrade your copy of Windows XP to Windows Vista:

1. **Insert the Windows Vista DVD into your DVD drive and choose Install Now, as shown in Figure 20-1.**

   Vista churns away, preparing to install itself. If Vista doesn't appear on the screen, make sure you haven't inserted the DVD into a *CD* drive.

   If it still doesn't appear, open My Computer from Windows XP's Start menu and double-click your DVD drive's icon.

   You must upgrade while running Windows XP. Don't try to upgrade by starting or restarting your PC with your Windows DVD in the DVD drive.

   Choosing the Check Compatibility Online option takes you online to download Vista's Upgrade Advisor, which I cover in Chapter 6.

Figure 20-1: Choose Install Now from the Windows Vista installation screen.

2. **Choose Go Online to Get the Latest Updates for Installation (Recommended), as shown in Figure 20-2.**

   This step tells Vista to visit Microsoft's Web site and download the latest updates — drivers, patches, and assorted fixes — that help make your installation run as smoothly as possible.

   If Vista skips this step, it can't find your PC's Internet connection. Make sure your PC can connect to the Internet, and then try again.

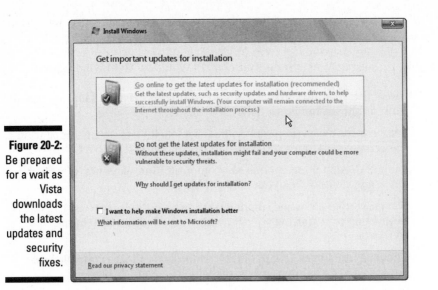

Figure 20-2:
Be prepared
for a wait as
Vista
downloads
the latest
updates and
security
fixes.

3. **Type your product key and click Next, as shown in Figure 20-3.**

   The *product key* usually lives on a little sticker affixed to the DVD's packaging. No product key? You're stuck. You can't install Windows Vista without a product key, or Vista will stop working after 30 days. (If you're reinstalling a version of Vista that came preinstalled on your PC, look for the product key printed on a sticker affixed to the side or back of your PC.)

   While at this screen, do these two things, as well:

   • **Product key:** Write your product key on top of your Windows Vista DVD with a felt-tip pen. (Write on the side of the DVD that's *printed.*) That way, you'll always have your valid product key with your DVD.

   • **Activation:** *Don't* select the Automatically Activate Windows When I'm Online check box. You can do that later, when you know Vista works on your PC.

4. **Read the License Agreement, select the I Accept the License Terms check box, and click Next.**

   Take an hour or so to read Microsoft's 47-page License Agreement carefully. You need to select the I Accept the License Terms check box option before Microsoft allows you to install the software.

5. **Choose Upgrade and click Next.**

   Upgrading preserves your old files, settings, and programs. If this option's unavailable, either of two things could be wrong:

- You're trying to upgrade an incompatible version of Windows XP. You can't install Windows Vista Home version on Windows XP Professional, for example. See Table 20-1 for the lowdown. Take your copy of Vista back to the store and plead for mercy.

- Your copy of Windows XP doesn't have Service Pack 2 installed. To fix this, visit Windows Update (www.windowsupdate.com) and download Service Pack 2. If the site refuses, you probably don't have a genuine copy of Windows XP installed, a problem you should take up with your PC's vendor.

- Your hard drive isn't big enough. Your hard drive needs up to 15GB of free space to install Vista.

When you click Next, Vista copies files onto your PC's hard drive, and then installs itself. It usually restarts your PC a few times during the process.

6. **Choose your country, time and currency, and keyboard layout and click Next.**

   Vista looks at how your Windows XP PC is set up and guesses at your location, language, time and currency. If it guesses correctly, just click Next. If it guesses wrong, however, set it straight on your country, local time, currency, and language used with your keyboard.

7. **Choose Use Recommended Settings.**

   Vista's recommended security settings keep Vista automatically patched and up to date.

Figure 20-3: Type the product key and click Next.

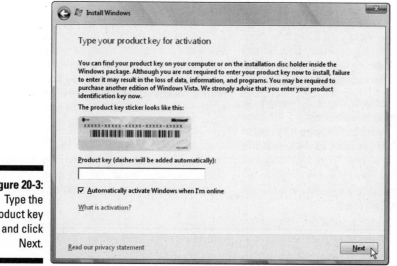

8. **If you're connected to a network, choose your PC's location.**

   Vista gives you two options: Home, Work, or a Public Location.

   Choose Home or Work, and Vista eases up on the security a bit, letting the PCs on the network see each other. If you're in a public setting, though, choose Public Location. Vista keeps your PC more secure by not letting other PCs share any of its files.

   After rummaging around inside your PC for a few more minutes, Windows Vista appears on the screen, leaving you at the logon screen. But don't rest yet. Run through the following steps to complete the process:

   - **Use Windows Update.** Visit Windows Update, described in Chapter 1, and download any security patches and updated drivers issued by Microsoft.

   - **Make sure that Vista recognizes your software.** Run all your old programs to make sure that they still work. You might need to replace them with newer versions or drop by the manufacturer's Web site to see whether they offer free updates.

   - **Check the user accounts.** Make sure that your PC's user accounts all work correctly.

   Welcome to Windows Vista!

Copying your old hard drive's files and settings to your new Vista drive

If you're installing Vista onto a big new hard drive, you face one big question: How do you transfer your *old* drive's information onto your new hard drive after installing Vista?

The answer comes with Vista's Windows Easy Transfer Program, covered in Chapter 5. Although the program is meant for copying information between two PCs, it can also tuck away your PC's information in a safe place. Then, after you install Vista on your new hard drive, the program can grab that tucked-away information and place it on your new drive with Vista.

Before installing your new drive, turn to Chapter 5 and find the section about transferring information between two PCs with Windows Easy Transfer. When running the Easy Transfer program on Windows XP, tell Vista to stash your old PC's information on CDs, DVDs, an external hard drive, or even a place on a network.

Then, after installing your new hard drive and installing Vista on it, run Windows Easy Transfer again. This time, though, tell it to grab your old drive's information from where you've stashed it.

Doing a Clean Install of Windows Vista

The best way to install Windows Vista is to buy a large new hard drive, install it as described in Chapter 9, and install Vista on the new drive. Installing Vista on an empty drive — known as a *clean install* — has several advantages:

✔ The new drive is likely larger and faster than your old one. That means Windows Vista runs faster, significantly speeding up your computer. Your new drive's larger size gives Windows Vista ample room to run at top performance.

✔ Windows Easy Transfer can stash away your old hard drive's information onto CDs, DVDs, an external hard drive, a network location, or if there's enough room, as a file on your old drive itself. By stashing away your old drive's information in advance, you can use Windows Easy Transfer to copy it onto your new Vista drive. (See the sidebar, "Copying your old hard drive's files and settings to your new Vista drive.")

✔ You still have access to your old operating system — your entire old computer, if you will — for emergencies. If you still need to access your old operating system, exit Windows Vista and turn off your computer. Swap your old drive with your new one and restart your PC with your old drive installed, bringing your old operating system and its programs to the screen.

When you're confident that Windows Vista is installed and running well, reformat your old hard drive and use it for storage.

Windows Vista carefully sets up its installation menus so that the most likely option rests at the top. You can usually install Windows Vista simply by pressing Enter at each menu.

To perform a clean install of Windows Vista onto a new hard drive — or to perform a clean install of Windows Vista on your old drive (erasing its contents in the process) — follow these steps:

1. **Turn off your computer, insert the Windows Vista DVD into your DVD drive, and restart your PC.**

   If you see a message asking you to press a key to boot from the CD or DVD, press any key. Vista will begin loading itself from the DVD.

2. **Confirm your language, time and currency format, and language for your keyboard and click Next.**

   Vista has woken up in a strange place and doesn't know where it is. If you're in the United States and you speak English, just click Next. Otherwise, choose your appropriate regional options.

3. **Choose Install Now.**

   Vista churns away for a few moments.

4. **Type in your 25-character product key, shown earlier in Figure 20-3, and click Next.**

   The *product key* usually lives on a little sticker affixed to the DVD's packaging. No product key? You're stuck. You can't install Windows Vista without a product key, or Vista will stop working after 30 days. (If you're reinstalling a version of Vista that came preinstalled on your PC, look for the product key printed on a sticker affixed to the side or back of your PC.)

   While at this screen, do these two things, as well:

   - *Product key:* Write your product key on top of your Windows Vista DVD with a felt-tip pen. (Write on the side of the DVD that's *printed*.) That way, you'll always have your valid product key with your DVD.

   - *Activation: Don't* select the Automatically Activate Windows When I'm Online check box. You can do that later, when you know Vista works on your PC.

5. **Read the License Agreement, select the I Accept the License Terms check box, and click Next.**

   You need to select the I Accept the License Terms check box option before Microsoft allows you to install the software.

6. **Choose Custom.**

   The Upgrade option will be grayed out because you started Windows from the DVD.

7. **Choose where you want to install Windows; partition the drive, if necessary, and click Next.**

   A window appears listing all the hard drives in your PC.

   If you're installing Vista onto a single empty hard drive, choose Disk 0 Unallocated Space and click New, and then Apply. Vista adds a partition to the drive, making it ready for Vista to bed down.

   If you're installing Vista onto a single drive that's already empty and partitioned, choose Disk 0 Partition 1.

   If you're installing Vista onto a single drive that's partitioned and has some information on it — perhaps your old Windows XP drive — choose Disk 0 Partition 1, choose Drive Options (Advanced), and choose Format to permanently delete the disk's contents. (You should back up any information you want to save *before* you get to this step.)

8. **Wait for Vista to install itself.**

   Vista takes its time here, with nothing for you to do but twiddle your thumbs for at least 15 minutes.

9. **Choose your User Name and picture and click Next.**

   Type in a name for yourself — your real name or your cat's name, Vista doesn't care. Make up a password and type one in, as well. It's not required, but it makes your PC much safer.

   Then either click one of the suggested pictures to represent your account, or just click Next to have Vista assign one to you. (You can always change it later through the Control Panel's User Accounts area.)

10. **Type a name for your PC and click Next.**

    Or just click Next to use your User Name with the letters -PC after it: Andy-PC, for example.

11. **Choose Use Recommended Settings and click Next.**

    Vista's recommended security settings keep Vista automatically patched and up to date.

12. **Confirm the time and your time zone, click Next, and click Start.**

    Vista jumps to the screen on your new hard drive, ready to be put to work.

When Vista won't boot from your DVD drive

When you turn on or restart your PC with your Vista DVD in your DVD drive, your PC usually asks you to press a key to start from the DVD or CD. When you press any key, Vista loads from the DVD.

But if that doesn't happen, you need to do some fiddling. Specifically, you need to tell your computer to use its DVD or CD drive as the first startup device. And to do that, you need to visit your PC's BIOS (Basic Input/Output System). Here's what to do:

1. **Restart your PC with your Windows DVD in the DVD drive.**

2. **Press the key that enters your PC's BIOS area.**

   Watch your PC as it starts up. You'll see a message like, "Press F1 for BIOS" or something similar. (Different PCs use a slightly different message.) When you see that message, press F1 or whatever key your PC

says to press. Your BIOS screen should appear on the screen.

Note: Updating the BIOS is a technical adventure for nerds. If you change the wrong setting, your PC might stop working properly. If you think you've made a mistake, don't save your changes. Just restart your PC and start over.

3. **Look for a setting in the BIOS called Boot Order or something similar.**

4. **Select your DVD drive as the first startup device.**

5. **Save your changes, exit the BIOS, and restart your PC.**

Vista should start from your DVD drive. If this still doesn't work, check to make sure your DVD drive is set as Master on its cable (covered in Chapter 15) and try again.

Chapter 21

Troubleshooting and Fixing Windows

*L*ike its little brother Windows XP, Windows Vista includes a large sack of troubleshooting tools. This chapter shows you where to find the tools and offers tips as to which ones to reach for during certain awkward moments.

It explains how to nuke those unwanted programs that you find loading themselves as soon as Vista appears, for example. It explains how to diagnose your PC's performance to find its weakest links. Hard drive full? Check out the "Clean Out Your Hard Drive with Disk Cleanup" section to do some digital housekeeping.

Should a problem seem too much for you to deal with, read the "Using Remote Assistance" section. It explains how to invite a friend to see your PC's screen on their *own* monitor, letting them push the magic button sequence that fixes its problems.

Don't be afraid to browse through these tools, even when things are running fine. Grow familiar with them and how things should look. Choose your favorite tools. Later, when you need the information, you'll know exactly which tool to reach for. Dig in.

Handling Windows Vista's Incompatibilities

Windows Vista is a snob. It only likes Windows Vista–approved parts and software. If Vista comes across something that's not written especially for it to use, it sometimes refuses to acknowledge the part or program's presence. Usually Vista tells you of this incompatibility problem; other times, it leaves you guessing what's wrong.

Windows Vista upgraders often experience this problem immediately. Their computer is stuffed with older parts and software written for earlier versions of Windows. As Windows Vista takes over, it sniffs your computer, finds any incompatible software or parts, and then disables them to avoid problems.

Bought a computer with Vista preinstalled? You're still not safe. If you try to install software or parts that don't specifically claim to be Windows Vista–compatible, they might not work. Others may work with reduced features.

This chapter shows you how to discover potential incompatibilities *before* installing or upgrading to Windows Vista. It also shows how to use Windows Vista's Program Compatibility Wizard to cure software problems that may pop up down the road.

Understanding incompatibility buzzwords

Some parts of your computer stop working when you upgrade to Windows Vista. Chances are, the parts still function, but they lack *drivers* that enable Windows Vista to understand them. The solution? Find and install new, Windows Vista–compatible drivers for those parts, a process I cover in Chapter 19.

To make incompatible software work, visit the software manufacturer's Web site and look for *upgrades* or *patches* that allow the software to run with Windows Vista.

Here are some common compatibility epithets you find flying through the air as Windows Vista examines your computer's parts and software.

Program Compatibility Wizard: A Windows Vista program that enchants older programs into thinking they're still running under their favorite version of Windows. When the wizard tricks a Windows Me–era program into thinking it's still running under Windows Me, for instance, the program runs without problem.

Nonstandard: Hardware or software that deviates slightly from established guidelines, usually to add or remove features. Some keyboards, for example, come with extra keys: You can push an E-mail button to load your e-mail program. Because that keyboard's software might not be compatible with Windows Vista, the keyboard's custom buttons may stop working when you upgrade. The solution? Head for the keyboard manufacturer's Web site and download that keyboard's Windows Vista drivers.

Windows 9x: A phrase used to identify Windows versions 95, 98, and Millennium (Me). Windows Vista and Windows XP run with a different type of *engine* than the one used by those three earlier Windows versions. Those different engines account for most incompatibilities.

Windows 2000 (W2K): A version of Windows that shares similar features to Windows XP and, potentially, Vista. If you can't find a driver written specifically for Vista or Windows XP, try one written for Windows 2000. (Drivers written for Windows 9x versions, described previously, rarely work in Vista.)

DVD Decoder: Only Windows Vista Home Premium and Ultimate editions can play DVD movies. That's because a DVD's video files come in a compressed format. Microsoft left out the decompresser or *decoder* from all Vista versions but Home Premium and Ultimate. If you own another Vista version, you must buy either the decoder or a DVD-playing program from another company. (If you buy Vista preinstalled on a PC, the manufacturer usually tosses in a free DVD decoder so you don't have to hunt one down.)

iPod: Windows Vista refuses to acknowledge that an iPod exists. To use an iPod in Windows Vista, you must download and install Apple's free iTunes program at `www.apple.com/iTunes`.

Finding out what's compatible

Windows Vista tries to keep compatibility surprises to a minimum. Before you install it, Windows Vista can analyze your computer and alert you as to which parts and programs in your computer will have compatibility problems.

I explain how to run Vista's Upgrade Advisor program in Chapter 6.

✔ By downloading and running Windows Vista's Upgrade Advisor before you actually install the software, you can get a good idea about what needs attention. Some things may need to be replaced, but the program explains possible solutions to those problems, as well.

✔ Be sure to print out the program's results and findings. That list comes in handy when you're heading to the computer store to find new parts.

Fixing problem programs with Vista's Program Compatibility Wizard

You need to replace *everything* that Windows Vista says is incompatible. Many of the parts work after you find and install the correct drivers, as described in Chapter 19. And some of your software will work after you run the Program Compatibility Wizard.

Some programs written for earlier versions of Windows — Windows Me, for example — might become confused when running in an operating system that offers so many new security settings, like Windows Vista. To fix this problem, the Windows Vista Program Compatibility Wizard can place a soothing Windows Me blanket of settings over the confused program, tricking it into thinking it's still running in Windows Me. The program still runs, Windows Vista still has control, and you still get your work done.

Best yet, Windows Vista remembers which blanket settings the program finds most cozy. Then, whenever you run the program in question, Windows Vista automatically fetches those blanket settings so that you don't have to keep bothering with the wizard. Although the wizard can't make up for problem drivers, it's great with Windows-version trickery.

Don't try to use the wizard for anti-virus, backup, or most utility programs. It won't work. You need to buy new Vista-compatible versions of those types of programs.

Here's a look at how to use the Program Compatibility Wizard to keep your older programs running strong:

1. **Choose Start, choose Control Panel, and click the Programs category.**

   The Programs category appears, listing all the Control Panel settings that cover programs.

2. **In the Programs and Features category, choose Use an Older Program with This Version of Windows and click Next.**

   The Program Compatibility Wizard leaps to the screen, as shown in Figure 21-1, ready for you to bypass its opening screen with a click of the Next button.

3. **Choose a method to locate the program and click Next.**

   The wizard offers three options, as shown in Figure 21-2.

   Here's when you want to choose which option:

   - *I Want to Choose from a List of Programs:* Choose this option most often for programs installed on your hard drive. The wizard searches all your programs, lists them all on the screen, and enables you to select the problem program.

• *I Want to Use the Program in the CD-ROM Drive:* This option works well for programs that won't install or that play directly from the CD.

• *I Want to Locate the Program Manually:* Select this option if the first one doesn't work. Click the Browse button to locate the program that you want the wizard to fix.

4. **Select your program and click Next.**

As the wizard lists the programs on the screen — whether they're all the ones it found on your hard drive, on your CD, or in the directory you chose — click the one that's causing the problem.

The file is usually the name of the program, as shown in Figure 21-3, but you might have to experiment. Choose Setup or Install, for instance, if you're trying to install a program from a disc.

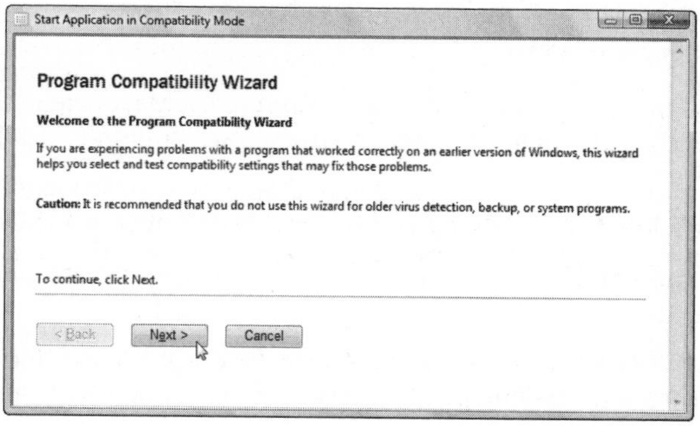

Figure 21-1:
The Program Compatibility Wizard offers to trick older programs into thinking they're running under their favorite older version of Windows.

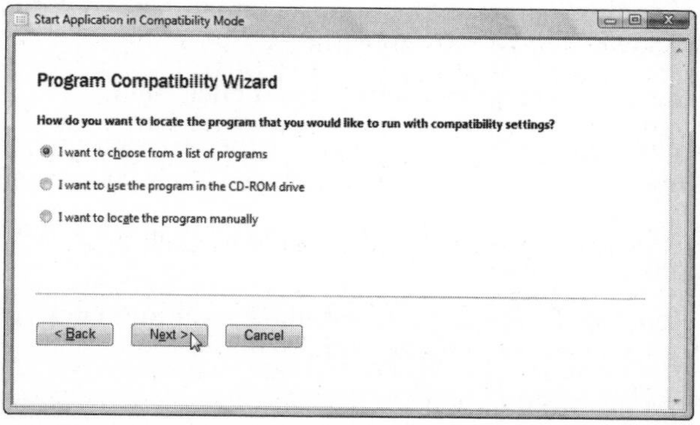

Figure 21-2:
Choose the first option unless your program is on a CD. If the first option doesn't work, try the third option.

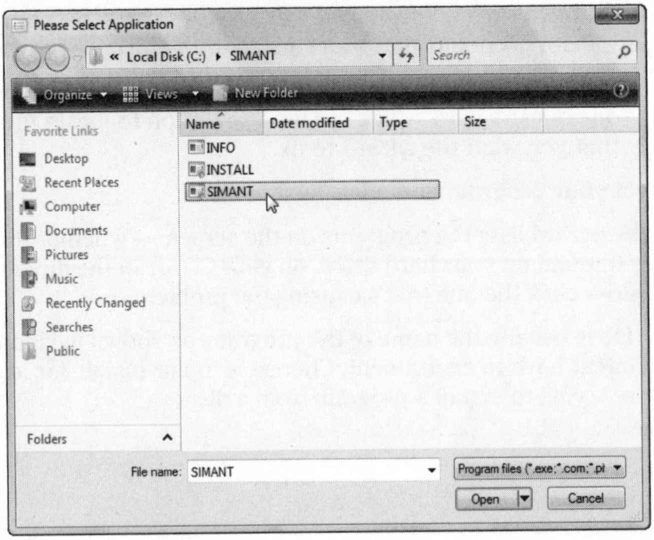

Figure 21-3:
Click the
name of the
program for
the wizard
to trick.

I manually selected the SIMANT file (*SimAnt* is a Maxis game that came out in 1991) from its folder because the wizard couldn't find it.

If you manually locate the program in Step 3, the wizard lists that program's location, enabling you to change it, if needed. Click Next.

5. **Choose the version of Windows that the program prefers, and then click Next.**

   Look at the program's box (you kept the box, right?) and find the System Requirements in the fine print. You need to enter much of that information in the next few steps.

   Start by choosing the version of Windows the program was designed for, as shown in Figure 21-4.

   I chose Windows 95 because SimAnt ran under DOS. (But it didn't work under Windows Vista — the game froze.)

6. **Choose the game's required settings and click Next.**

   As shown in Figure 21-5, you may choose the program's required colors and resolution, as well as turn off Windows Vista's visual themes.

   Because SimAnt is very old, I clicked them all to make Windows Vista seem as old as possible.

7. **Choose Run This Program as an Administrator and click Next.**

   Choosing this option tells Vista not to butt in and say you're not authorized to run the program.

Start Application in Compatibility Mode

Program Compatibility Wizard

Select a compatibility mode for the program

Choose the operating system that is recommended for this program, or that previously supported the program correctly:

- Microsoft Windows 95
- Microsoft Windows NT 4.0 (Service Pack 5)
- Microsoft Windows 98 / Windows Me
- Microsoft Windows 2000
- Microsoft Windows XP (Service Pack 2)
- Do not apply a compatibility mode

[< Back] [Next >] [Cancel]

Figure 21-4: Choose the version of Windows the program likes.

Start Application in Compatibility Mode

Program Compatibility Wizard

Select display settings for the program

Choose the settings that are recommended for this program, or that previously supported the program correctly:

- ☑ 256 colors
- ☑ 640 x 480 screen resolution
- ☑ Disable visual themes
  Try this option if you are experiencing problems with menus or buttons on the title bar of the program.
- ☑ Disable desktop composition
  Try this option if you are experiencing problems with the display when running the program.
- ☑ Disable display scaling on high DPI settings
  Try this option if you are experiencing problems with the program display on high DPI settings.

[< Back] [Next >] [Cancel]

Figure 21-5: Choose the program's require-ments.

8. Click Next to test the game's new settings.

✔ If the program freezes, press Ctrl+Alt+Del simultaneously and then choose Start Task Manager from the list. Click the problem program's name and choose End Task from the menu.

✔ If it runs, you're set. Choose the Yes, Set this Program to Always Use These Compatibility Settings option. Click Next, and Windows Vista remembers to use those settings whenever you run the program.

✔ If it doesn't work correctly, choose the No, Try Different Compatibility Settings option and try again.

✔ Or give up by clicking the No, I Am Finished Trying Compatibility Settings option. Then look for help on the Internet, as described in Chapter 22.

When the wizard finishes, you're asked whether you'd like to tell Microsoft what you found out. If the wizard solved your program's problems, Microsoft updates its database so that it knows how to solve those problems in the future. (Click No if you don't want to share your results with Microsoft.)

Don't like wizards? Do-it-yourselfers can right-click the program's icon and choose Properties. The Compatibility tab offers all the wizard's settings, and the Memory tab offers even more settings that you can tweak.

Don't forget to visit Windows Update if a program or part doesn't work. Microsoft often stockpiles fixes and patches for problem programs there; Windows Update, covered in Chapter 1, can automatically install them for you.

Vista has trouble running old DOS programs in full-screen mode. If your DOS program won't run in a window, you may have trouble running it in Vista.

Stopping Unwanted Programs from Running When Windows Starts

Spyware and other nuisance programs often slipped themselves into cracks in earlier versions of Windows and then ran automatically when you turned on your PC. They hid themselves so well that finding them turned into a Herculean task.

With Windows Defender, it's easier to see which programs are running automatically behind your back. When you spot any that are giving you trouble, you can snip them off your PC so they stop running.

Windows Defender comes built-into Windows Vista; Windows XP owners can download the free program here: www.microsoft.com/athome/security/spyware/software/default.mspx.

Follow these steps to stop programs from running when Vista loads:

1. **Open Windows Defender by clicking Start, choosing All Programs, and then clicking Windows Defender.**

   The program rises to the screen, as shown in Figure 21-6.

2. **Click the Tools menu and choose Software Explorer.**

   Clicking the Tools menu shows Windows Defender's Settings and Tools areas, each ripe with options. Choosing Software Explorer brings up the Startup Programs page, as shown in Figure 21-7. It lists every program that runs automatically when Vista is loaded, as well as technical details: filenames, authors, versions, and installation dates.

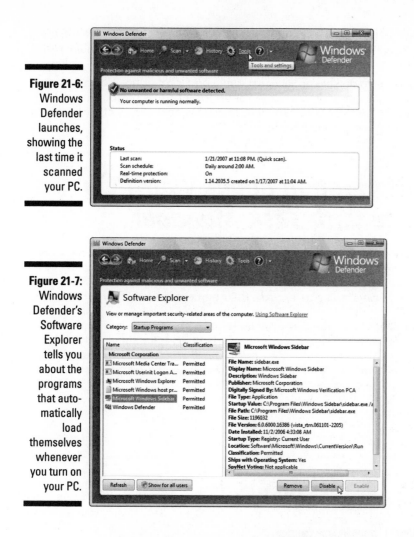

Figure 21-6: Windows Defender launches, showing the last time it scanned your PC.

Figure 21-7: Windows Defender's Software Explorer tells you about the programs that automatically load themselves whenever you turn on your PC.

3. Click an unwanted program's name and choose Disable.

The big question comes down to this: How do you know what programs to disable? Sometimes the answer's obvious. You find a program with an installation date and time that matches when you mistakenly installed a rogue program from a Web site.

Sometimes the program's Publisher name rings a bell, particularly if you've found that company's name bad-mouthed on Google a few times.

Clicking the program and clicking Disable doesn't delete the program, but it keeps it from running automatically.

✔ Disabled the wrong program? Follow these steps again but click the program's name and choose Enable in Step 3 to start running that program again.

✔ You can also disable programs running under other people's accounts. To see those programs, click the Show for All Users button, shown in Figure 21-7. That lets you clean up rogue programs from other accounts without having to log into them.

Finding Information about Your PC's Performance with Task Manager

Early Windows versions offered a boring performance monitor. Clicking the Control Panel's System icon showed `System Resources: 75% free` or a similar percentage. It certainly wasn't much, but many people watched it constantly, always trying to increase their percentage.

Windows Vista makes the task even more fun with moving graphs, resizable columns, and adjustable options. Press Ctrl+Alt+Del simultaneously and choose Start Task Manager to view the updated Windows Vista Task Manager. The chart in Figure 21-8, for instance, shows how much energy my CPU consumed while I was playing Vista's 3-D chess game.

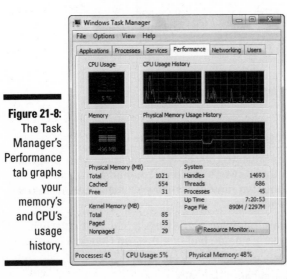

Figure 21-8: The Task Manager's Performance tab graphs your memory's and CPU's usage history.

Clicking a different Task Manager tab reveals monitors for a different activity, as described in the following paragraphs:

Applications: Click this tab to see exactly what programs you're currently running on your PC. If a program is frozen, click its name and click the End Task button to close it down without affecting your other programs. (Or right-click the program's name and choose Go To Process to see its filename and how it affects your computer, described in the next paragraph.)

Processes: This tab lists each currently running program by name, the User Account that's using it, and the amount of CPU activity and memory it consumes. If something consistently consumes CPU activity, even when the computer is idle, scan your system with a virus checker.

Services: Here, you see all the background operations Windows Vista runs to support itself. They're listed mostly for techies to start and stop services manually. (Vista usually handles them all automatically.)

Performance: This tab shows you how much power your CPU uses. You may be surprised at how little of your CPU's power you actually use. If it's fluctuating drastically, you might need more memory or a bigger hard drive.

Networking: The Network tab enables network users to monitor the percentage of bandwidth your computer consumes. You see spikes as your computers swap data.

Users: This tab lets you see at a glance the number of people currently using your computer. (When they log off their User Account, they fall from the list.)

Using System Restore

The Windows System Restore feature provides an excellent first assault against computer troubles. It enables you to tell your computer to use settings saved when everything worked correctly. Follow these steps to fire up System Restore in Windows Vista:

1. **Click Start⇨All Programs⇨Accessories⇨System Tools⇨System Restore.**

   Alternatively, click Start and type **System Restore** in the Search box to see the program's name and launch it with a click.

2. **Click Next to apply the recommended Restore Point.**

   This undoes the most recent major change to your PC, be it a recent update, driver, or piece of software that may have messed things up.

3. **Click Finish to confirm and return to the Restore Point.**

Windows Vista applies the Restore Point and restarts your PC. When Vista wakes up, it behaves like it did when the Restore Point was first made. If Windows works better, you're through. If it behaves even worse, or System Restore didn't fix the problem, head to Step 4.

4. **Select Choose a Different Restore Point and click Next.**

Vista lists all the available Restore Points and their dates. Choose a Restore Point from a different date and click Next to try that one, instead. This brings you back to Step 3, a cycle you repeat until a Restore Point fixes the problem.

Hopefully, one of the Restore Points applies the right elixir to make Windows behave correctly. But if you want to return to the way things were *before* you began messing with System Restore, choose the Restore Point called "Undo: Restore Operation." That brings you back to square one, so you can try some of this chapter's other fixes.

Using Remote Assistance

Ever described your computer problem to a friendly computer guru over the phone, only to hear, "Gosh, I could fix that in a second if I was sitting in front of your computer"? The Remote Assistance tool solves that logistical problem. Remote Assistance enables a computer guru to connect to your computer, view your screen on his monitor, and use his mouse and keyboard as if they were your own. By remotely controlling your computer on-screen, a guru can fix problems and demonstrate solutions.

Send out a Remote Assistance invitation *only* to somebody you trust *completely* because he or she will have access to your PC and your files. Whoever controls your Remote Assistance session can see your desktop, any open documents, and anything you have visible on your screen.

Here's how to invite and receive help from a friendly expert over the Internet or company network:

1. **Click Start, choose Help and Support, and click Use Windows Remote Assistance to Get Help from a Friend or Offer Help.**

That option lurks atop the Help and Support page's "Ask Someone" section.

2. **When the Remote Assistance page appears, click the Invite Someone You Trust to Help You option and choose your invitation method.**

As shown in Figure 21-9, clicking the Invite Someone to Help You option starts the Remote Assistance program.

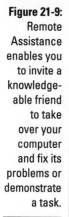

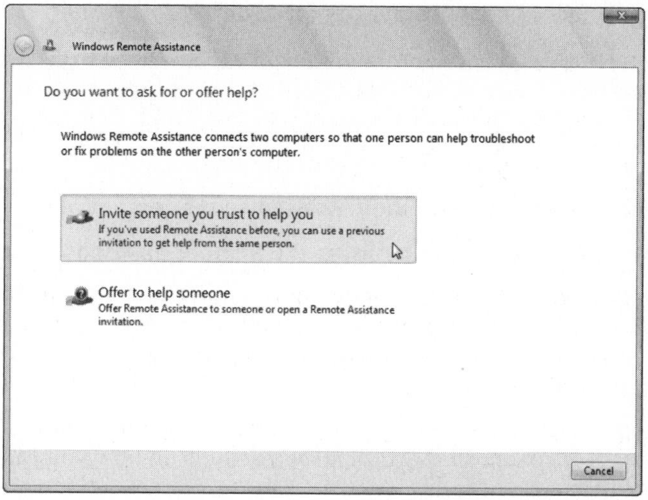

Figure 21-9:
Remote
Assistance
enables you
to invite a
knowledge-
able friend
to take
over your
computer
and fix its
problems or
demonstrate
a task.

Vista offers two ways to connect to your friendly expert:

- *Send an invitation through e-mail.* You can e-mail an invitation to your friend. This sends the invitation as an attachment to your message. However, it only works with Windows Mail or similar e-mail programs. If you read your mail on the Internet, choose the next option.

- *Save an invitation as a file.* Instead of e-mailing the invite as an attachment, this simply saves it as a file called `Invitation.msrcincident` and places the file on your desktop. Then you can attach it through a Web-based e-mail program like Yahoo! Mail, for example, or send it through an instant messaging program.

3. Create a password for your invitation.

To keep unwanted folks from breaking into your PC, you must create a password that locks the invitation. Call your friend and tell him the password. (Or tell him in person.)

Then, kick back and wait for your guru to receive your invitation and start the connection. (For some reason, a phone call begging for assistance often helps speed up the process.)

To keep unauthorized folks from connecting to and controlling your computer, always use a password that only you and your guru know. You should also be able to talk to the guru on the phone as he or she works on your computer.

4. **Wait for the recipient to connect to your PC.**

Upon receiving your invitation, the guru types in your password on his or her PC.

A notice appears on your screen, like the one shown in Figure 21-10, saying that the guru wants to start the session now.

5. **Click Yes to start the Remote Assistance session.**

6. **Carry out your session by using the Remote Assistance window.**

The Remote Assistance window, shown in Figure 21-11, quickly appears on-screen for both you and your friendly connected guru. Throughout the session, your screen appears on your guru's screen, and your guru sees everything you type, as well.

You may both type messages back and forth. At this point, the guru works as a coach, simply typing instructions on how you can fix your computer.

It helps if you and your friend can talk on the phone during the session. That's faster and easier than typing at each other.

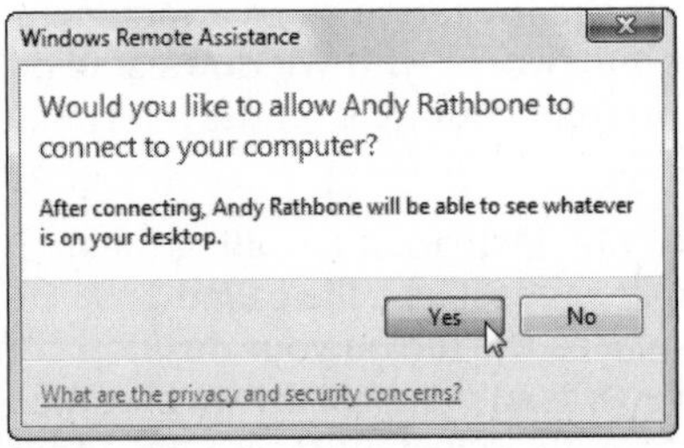

Figure 21-10:
Click Yes to
allow the
guru to
see your
computer
screen.

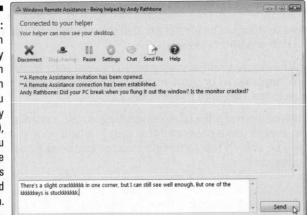

Figure 21-11:
Your screen
immediately
appears on
the screen
of your guru
(Andy
Rathbone),
and you
may type
messages
back and
forth.

7. **Allow the guru to take control of your computer, if asked.**

   The guru may tire of simply typing messages to you and watching you fumble around on your screen. Eventually, your guru may press the Take Control button on his or her own computer, requesting to share control of your computer.

   Click Yes when the request comes through, as shown in Figure 21-12. Be sure to click the box that lets your friend respond to User Account Control prompts, or else you'll have to keep clicking them yourself as your friend works.

   At this point, the guru controls your mouse and keyboard, opening menus where needed, and changing settings on your computer.

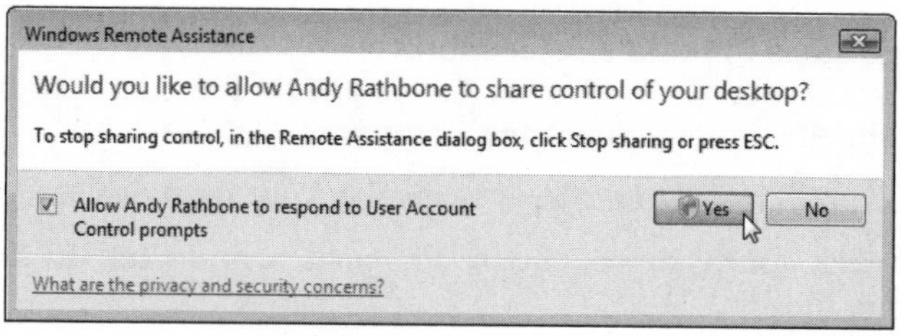

Figure 21-12:
Click Yes to
allow the
guru to
watch *and*
to share
control
over your
computer's
mouse and
keyboard.

8. **Click the Stop Control button to disconnect the session when you're through.**

   When you're done communicating, and the guru solves your problem, click the Stop Control button to stop the session. (Pressing Esc does the same thing, as does holding down Ctrl and pressing the C key.)

   ✔ When the guru takes control, you and the guru *both* share the mouse and keyboard. Just kick back and watch the guru control your computer. If you both fiddle with the mouse and keyboard, the computer freaks out, annoying everybody.

   ✔ If you're connected to the Internet through a dialup connection and the phone hangs up, quit the program and send out a new invitation. (The old one works only once.)

   ✔ Windows Remote Assistance comes with several restrictions: It only works with Windows XP and Windows Vista computers, you may only send invitations through a compatible e-mail program or as an attached file, and the two computers must be connected through the Internet or a network. Also, users must both have administrator accounts for best results.

✔ Problems? Right-click Computer on the Start menu, choose Properties, and click Remote Settings from the left column. Make sure you've checked the Allow Remote Assistance Connections to This Computer option. Click the Advanced button for more options, which is handy when you want to change an invitation's default life of only 6 hours.

Cleaning Out Your Hard Drive with Disk Cleanup

When Vista sends threatening messages about your hard drive running out of space, send in the Disk Cleanup program to clean out some of the trash. The program examines your hard drive for virtual flotsam and offers to delete it for you with a single click of the OK button.

Follow these steps to run Disk Cleanup:

1. **Click the Start menu and open Computer.**

   The Computer program opens to display your hard drives.

2. **Right-click your C drive, choose Properties, and click the Disk Cleanup button.**

3. **Choose whether to clean up your own account's files or those of everybody on the PC.**

   Normally, you choose Files from All Users on This Computer. It won't delete anything valuable. The biggest threat is that it empties everybody's Recycle Bin, making a final dump of items they've already deleted.

4. **Click the areas to be deleted and click OK.**

   As shown in Figure 21-13, the Disk Cleanup tool displays the amount of trash sitting in Internet Explorer's cache, your Recycle Bin, Temporary files area, and other disk clogging areas.

   Normally, Disk Cleanup just deletes the two biggest hogs: the Recycle Bin and the trash leftover from Internet Explorer as you surf the Web. But if those deletions *still* don't create enough room for your new computer game, put a check mark next to each item. (If you're curious about what you're deleting, click an item's name; Vista explains that item's purpose in the lower part of the window.)

   When you click the OK button, Disk Cleanup deletes everything you selected from your hard drive.

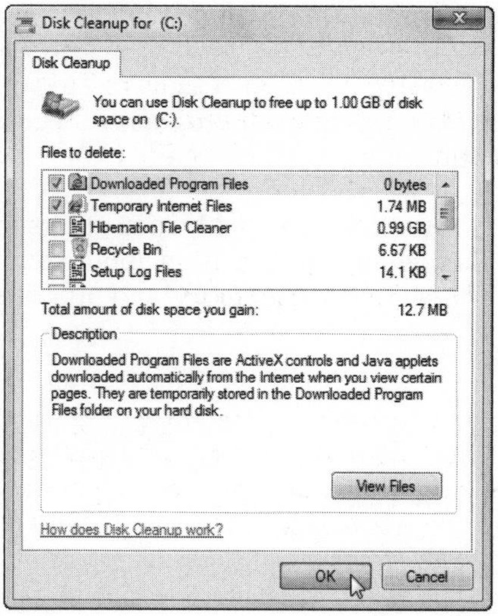

Figure 21-13: Disk Cleanup examines your computer's trash accumulation areas and offers to clear them.

Tidying Up Your Hard Drive with Disk Defragmenter

As your computer moves data around on your hard drive, it frequently breaks files into pieces, stuffing them wherever they fit. That makes the drive work harder when retrieving files because it must search in different locations to collect all the pieces.

Disk Defragmenter searches your hard drive for broken files and places all the pieces next to each other for quicker access. For more about defragmenting your hard drive, see Chapter 9.

Viewing Advanced System Information

When you really want to see what's under the hood, fire up Vista's System Information program. It exposes every technical detail about your computer and its parts.

Most important of all, its entire haystack of data is searchable as a whole, enabling you to extract specific data needles when needed. Using System

Information is a great way to search for information about mystery objects that appear in other listings.

To fire up System Information, choose Start⇨All Programs⇨Accessories⇨ System Tools⇨System Information.

The System Information tool, shown in Figure 21-14, opens to its System Summary page. There, you'll find detailed information about your edition of Windows Vista, your PC's CPU, amount of memory, and other technical information.

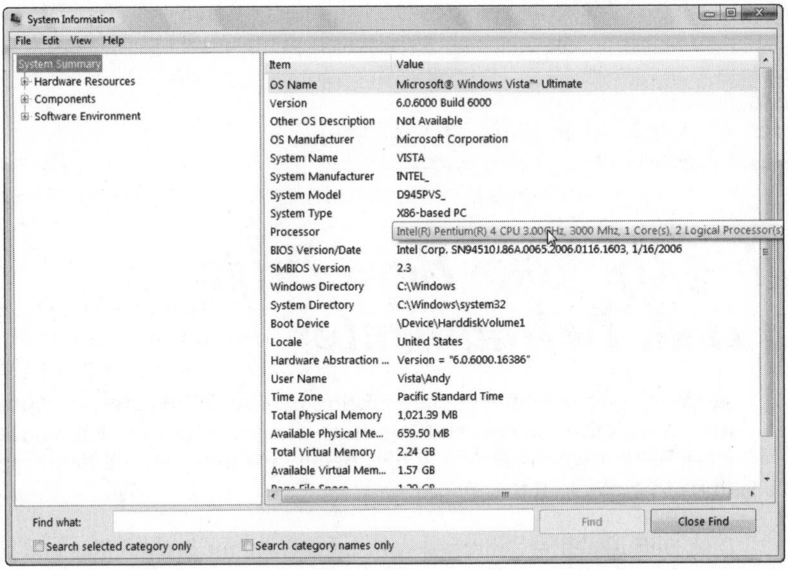

Figure 21-14: The System Information tool packs detailed, searchable information about your computer onto one page.

Clicking the categories on the left — Hardware Resources, Components, and Software Environment — reveals even more details about your PC's parts and the way Vista interacts with them. As you click the plus signs in the boxes along the window's left side, the entries expand along the right to show detailed information about that item.

In short, the tool wrings every piece of data out of your computer's hardware resources: components like networks, codecs, drivers, printers, USB devices, and modems; software, including drivers; running tasks; and Internet settings.

You'll probably never need it, but it's good to know it's there for emergencies.

Avoiding Virus and Worm Attacks

The best way to stop a virus from damaging your computer is to keep it from infecting your computer in the first place. Follow the tips in the following sections to reduce your risk of infection.

Use Windows Update often

Most viruses take advantage of weak spots within Windows. For instance, one virus programmer figured out a way to launch a virus when the user simply opened an e-mail. Users didn't have to open the e-mail's attachment to become infected by that virus because it launched itself automatically.

Microsoft released a patch to repair the problem, but it was too late: The virus had infected thousands of computers. However, long after Microsoft released the update, that particular type of virus continues to infect computers. Why? Because many people haven't used Windows Update to install the patch that fixes the problem.

To make sure you've installed all the security updates available for your Microsoft software, use Windows Update — a Web site that scans your computer and recommends what patches to install. Installing any patches marked *Critical* helps you avoid potential security problems.

You can access Windows Update in several ways in both Windows Vista and Windows XP:

- ✔ Using Internet Explorer, visit Microsoft's Windows Update Web site at www.windowsupdate.com.
- ✔ Open Internet Explorer and choose Windows Update from the Tools menu.
- ✔ Click the Start menu, click All Programs, and choose Windows Update.

You can also tell Windows Update to automatically check the Microsoft Web site, download any new critical updates, and let you know when they're ready to install. When you receive the notice about the new patch, you may examine it before allowing it to install.

 Windows Vista comes set up to check Windows Update automatically. To make sure Windows Update is working as it should, click the Start menu, choose Control Panel, and choose Check This Computer's Security Status in the Security category.

In Windows XP, right-click the Start menu's My Computer icon, choose Properties, click the Automatic Updates tab, and tell Windows XP to download updates automatically and let you know they're ready to install.

Install and use antivirus software

Antivirus programs constantly patrol your computer, seeking out signs of a possible virus and destroying or deactivating the virus before it has a chance to infect or damage your computer. Windows doesn't include antivirus software, so unless your computer came with preinstalled antivirus software, you must purchase it from a third party.

Antivirus software wears out very quickly. In order for it to remain effective, you must continually download new updates or definitions from the software manufacturer's Web site. Without those updates, your antivirus software can only protect you against old viruses. It can't protect you from any *new* viruses that appear.

Some antivirus software enables you to turn on an automatic update feature. That enables the antivirus program to automatically link to the manufacturer's Web site and download new virus definitions as they become available. Look for that feature in your software and make sure that it's turned on.

Also look for a feature that performs automatic scans on your computer on a timed basis or every time you connect to the Internet.

Table 21-1 lists popular antivirus software, its manufacturer, and its Web site.

Table 21-1	Popular Antivirus Software	
Manufacturer	*Product*	*Web site*
Symantec Corporation	Norton Antivirus	www.symantec.com
McAfee.com Corporation	VirusScanOnline	www.mcafee.com
F-Secure	F-Secure Anti-Virus	www.f-secure.com/
Trend Micro, Inc.	PC-cillin	www.trendmicro.com
Norman	Norman Virus Control	www.norman.com

Never open e-mail with unexpected attachments

An *attachment* is a program or file sent along with a piece of e-mail. Friends may send you digital photos, for instance. Others may forward a piece of e-mail or a chain letter. Some people send programs they've found helpful.

Whenever you see *any* attachment on an e-mail message, be suspicious immediately — even if you know who sent it to you. Viruses can place anybody's name in the From: box, making the message look like it came from a friend instead of a stranger.

If a friend sends you a message with an attachment that you didn't specifically ask for, *don't open it.* Don't respond to it, either. Instead, send a separate e-mail to your friend, asking whether he or she has sent you an e-mail with an attachment. Then wait for his or her response before opening the e-mail.

- ✔ Today, most viruses spread when people open attachments apparently sent to them by a friend.

- ✔ When a virus mails itself out to other people, it does it secretly. The owner of the computer rarely knows what's going on. That keeps the virus from being detected for as long as possible, allowing the virus to send a copy of itself to the contacts listed in the person's address book.

- ✔ The most suspicious e-mail attachments end in the letters EXE, VBS, and COM. However, they can use dozens of other types of files to do their dirty work.

- ✔ If somebody sends you e-mail saying that you've sent him or her a virus, immediately unplug your computer's phone line from the wall or turn off its modem. If you're sending e-mail through a network, unplug the network cable from the network card. That keeps your computer from sending the virus to even more people. Then run your antivirus software to disinfect your computer.

Scan downloaded software for viruses before using it

Some hackers create programs, infect them with a virus, and post them onto the Internet for unsuspecting people to download. When people run these infected programs, they infect their own computers.

To avoid this, don't download programs from suspicious places: newsgroups, pirate software sites, or sites that don't scan their programs for viruses before posting them. Scan any downloaded programs with antivirus software before running them on your computer.

Flushing Windows' System Restore cache

System Restore is normally a lifesaver when it comes to computer problems. The program takes automatic snapshots of your computer's settings while it's up and running. Then, if your computer crashes, a visit to System Restore can roll back your computer to one of those snapshots, which are called *Restore Points*. When your computer restarts with its new settings, everything usually works fine.

Unfortunately, System Restore doesn't work well to repair virus damage. In fact, System Restore can inadvertently save your computer's settings while it was still infected. If you use an infected Restore Point after you've disinfected your computer, you could reinfect your computer with the virus.

To keep this from happening, be sure to delete your System Restore points or cache after you disinfect your computer. Follow these steps to delete Restore Points in Windows Vista:

1. **Right-click Computer from the Start menu and choose Properties.**

2. **Click the System Protection tab and remove the check mark from any drive listed in the** Automatic Restore Points section. (It's usually just your C drive.)

3. **Click the Apply button, click OK, and restart your computer.**

   Restarting your computer with System Restore turned off makes it delete all your existing Restore Points.

4. **Download the latest virus definitions and updates for your antivirus software.**

5. **Scan your entire computer and its memory for any viruses.**

6. **Repeat Steps 1 and 2 to add check marks to your C drive (and any others that had check marks) and then click Apply.**

This turns System Restore back on and tells Windows to begin taking its automatic snapshots and making new Restore Points. Feel free to create your own Restore Point and label it something like, "Created after disinfecting from the virus."

Use a firewall

A firewall places a guard at your computer's connection to the Internet. Windows Vista and XP come with a firewall that helps keep malicious people from connecting to your computer through an unsecured Internet connection and planting viruses or backdoors.

Chapter 18 explains how to turn on the firewall built into Windows Vista.

Don't forward hoaxes

Just about everybody has received a message saying that a new virus is spreading rapidly and isn't detected by virus programs. The message usually says to search for a certain file on your computer and immediately delete it. The message ends by asking you to pass along the message to all your friends.

Almost all of these messages are *hoaxes* — the computer equivalent of April Fools' Day pranks.

Don't pass along these types of messages to your friends because they only cause more paranoia and uncertainty about viruses.

To check the truth of an e-mail like this, visit any of the sites listed in Table 21-2.

Table 21-2	Web Sites That Identify Hoaxes
The Site	*The Address*
Symantec's hoax site	`www.symantec.com/avcenter/hoax.html`
TruthOrFiction	`www.truthorfiction.com`
CIAC's HoaxBusters	`http://hoaxbusters.ciac.org`

Repairing virus damage

Although antivirus software programs work well at detecting viruses and disinfecting your computer, disinfection only removes the virus from your computer; it doesn't reverse the damage done by the virus. If your computer is infected, follow these steps to repair as much of the damage as possible:

1. **Write down or print out the name of the virus.**

   Your antivirus program tells you which particular virus strain attacked your computer.

2. **Locate the damaged programs and files.**

   Many antivirus programs provide you with a list of your damaged files. A few list your damaged programs, as well, if they can figure out what's been damaged. Print out the list, as you may need it for reference.

3. **Visit your antivirus program's Web site.**

   The nice antivirus companies write special programs that automatically repair damage done by major viruses. If you get lucky and find one for your particular strain of virus, download the program, run it, and let it repair the damage.

4. **Figure out what programs contained the damaged files.**

   This is the most difficult part and requires some major sleuthing on your part. If the antivirus software doesn't list the programs that contained your damaged files, and it doesn't offer a free repair tool, you have to figure out what programs are damaged on your own. By carefully researching your list of damaged files, you can often tell which programs contained them.

   I've had the best luck using the Google search engine (www.google. com) described in Chapter 22. Carefully type in the exact name of the damaged file into the Search box and search Google's Web and Groups areas to see what programs those files are associated with.

   Chances are, you'll spot the file's name listed somewhere in a context that makes it possible for you to identify it.

5. **Reinstall the program that contained the damaged files.**

   If you have a backup, great! Use that to reinstall your damaged programs. If not, reinstall your program from its original installation CDs. Then visit the program manufacturer's Web site; you may need to download updates or patches released since you bought the program.

Chapter 22

Finding Help Online

- -

In This Chapter

▶ Figuring out Internet buzzwords

▶ Finding answered questions on newsgroups

▶ Tips and tricks for successful searches

▶ Using manufacturers' support Web sites

▶ Using community support sites

- -

Some problems can't be fixed by reading a book. That's because many problems pop up only when a certain version of software tries to run on a specific model of computer containing a specific combination of hardware. Only a small handful of people ever experience that particular problem.

No one person can explain the solution to every possible problem that might occur. However, I can show you the best way to find somebody else who has experienced the same problem as you, stumbled upon a solution, and posted the solution on the Internet.

This chapter explains how to arm yourself with the tools you need to extract those solutions from the bazillions of sites that make up the Internet.

Understanding Internet Buzzwords

Although you can find zillions of unknown words relating to the Internet, here are a few you may encounter when you use the Internet as a troubleshooting detective:

Search engine: An online resource that helps you find what you're looking for. The Internet resembles an unbound book with its pages thrown into the air and scattered randomly on the ground. A search engine provides an index to those haphazard pages. Search engines use software robots that race through the pages they find, cataloging their contents to create an index of all their words. Type a word into a search engine, and it lists all the sites that it knows that mention the word or subject.

Newsgroups: Online areas where people exchange messages about their particular interest. Newsgroups started in the Internet's early years; today, more than 50,000 newsgroups exist. Because people posting to newsgroups use computers, many newsgroups deal with specific areas of computing. Some people refer to newsgroups as *Usenet*.

Microsoft Knowledge Base: Microsoft's gigantic online collection of information about its products (`http://support.microsoft.com`). The Knowledge Base Web site not only lists documented problems, but it gives solutions for fixing them.

Workaround: A solution that helps bypass or minimize a problem's effects. Sometimes a specific computing problem can't be fixed. However, by taking some extra steps, you can learn to live with the problem. Microsoft's Knowledge Base frequently lists workarounds for problems.

FAQs (Frequently Asked Questions): A well-indexed list of commonly asked questions and their answers. Most people ask the same common questions the first time they encounter something new. Tired of repeating the same answers, knowledgeable people started creating lists of Frequently Asked Questions. Now FAQs are standard elements of most well-designed Web sites, newsgroups, and other online resources.

Acronym: A word that's derived from the first letters of other words. Because the phrase "Frequently Asked Questions" is rather awkward, people often substitute the acronym FAQ. The complex world of computing leads to an overabundance of acronyms, such as WWW (World Wide Web), CPU (Central Processing Unit), RAM (Random Access Memory), and many more.

Finding Help through Search Engines

Without a doubt, the first stop when you're searching for solutions to computing problems should be Google, the best search engine on the Internet. As I write this, Google's search robots are scouring umpteen pages on the Internet, indexing them word by word, and letting you search the results for free.

Google lets you search for information in many different ways, but searching Web sites and newsgroups brings the best results for troubleshooters. I describe how to search both in the following sections.

Searching Google for specific information

When I'm troubleshooting a computer problem, I *always* begin my search on Google (`www.google.com`), as shown in Figure 22-1. Google provides a quick and easy way to find just about any company's Web site, as well as Web sites dealing with particular types of computing problems.

Google has indexed newsgroup conversations going back more than 20 years — a treasure trove for problem solvers.

Although it doesn't always reveal the exact solution, a Google search usually points in the direction to look. Google, like some other search engines, enables you to search by keywords, phrases, or a combination of the two. The key to using Google is to know when to search by *words* and when to search for *phrases*.

- ✔ **Words:** Search for specific words when you don't care where those words appear on a page. For instance, if you're having password problems when you connect to the Internet, you could type this:

  ```
  password problem internet connect
  ```

- ✔ **Phrases:** Search for phrases, by placing the phrase inside quotation marks, when you *only* want to see pages containing two or more words sitting next to each other. If your password problem always brings up an error message that says *Error 623,* type this into the search box:

  ```
  password internet "error 623"
  ```

By choosing the right combination of words and phrases in your search, you can make sure that Google knows exactly what pages to bring to your attention.

Figure 22-1:
Click the
Google
Search
button to
see Internet
sites
containing
the words
password,
internet, and
"error 623".

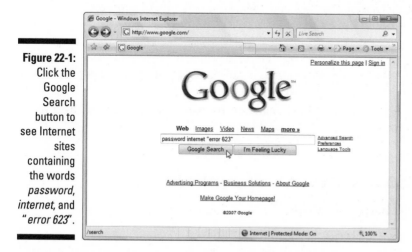

Now that you know how to properly question Google, here's how to use Google's different buttons and tabs:

- ✔ Google offers two buttons: Google Search, and I'm Feeling Lucky. Clicking the Google Search button tells Google to display a list of Web sites that contain your search words or phrases. Clicking the I'm Feeling Lucky button immediately displays the Web site that most closely matches your search.

- ✔ Use the Google Search button most of the time and check out the Web sites that it lists. By contrast, use the I'm Feeling Lucky button as a time-saver when you're confident that Google knows exactly what page you're looking for. Typing in **Andy Rathbone** and clicking the I'm Feeling Lucky button, for instance, immediately brings up my Web site: www.andyrathbone.com.

- ✔ As shown in Figure 22-1, Google offers searches in five different online areas: Web, Images, Video, News, Maps, and More. (More lets you search through even *more* online areas, including mail-order catalogs, scholarly papers, and blogs.) It always searches for Web pages unless you click on one of those other areas. Google then lists many Web sites containing your words, using a patented ranking method to place the most likely choices at the top of the list.

- ✔ Clicking the Images link before clicking the Google Search button tells Google to search for pictures. It's great for finding pictures of computer parts. For instance, a Google Images Search for **nvidia "GeForce 7600"** immediately displays several photos of that video card, its circuits, and its packaging. That lets you confirm the identity of a mysterious card inside your PC, for example.

- ✔ To search through newsgroup postings, click the More link and click Groups before clicking the Google Search button. Because many people post their computer problems in newsgroups, and many other people post solutions, Google spits up a quick list of potential answers to your query.

- ✔ Don't bother searching through video, news, or maps. Those don't bring up answers to computer problems.

Mastering the art of pinpoint Google searching

Although Pinpoint Google Searching would make a great band name, successful Google searching is also an art in its own right. Google is so good that it often brings thousands of pages to your attention. The trick is to find *only* the pages that solve your problem. Here are my favorite tips:

✔ **Search for specific error messages by placing the message in quotes.** Error messages confuse *everybody*. Because messages look identical on every Windows computer, other frustrated people have probably already discussed that error message online. Hopefully, one of them also posted a solution.

✔ **Start your search in the newsgroups.** Many people use newsgroups to discuss particular aspects of computer technology — including beginning computing. Beginners often post their troubles here. Experts seeking to hone their troubleshooting skills try to solve as many problems as possible. It's a great place to start.

✔ **Expand your search to include the Web.** Many people run support sites that answer lots of questions.

✔ **Make your first search as specific as possible, and then expand your search from there.** For instance, type an error message exactly as you see it and put the message in quotation marks, like this: **"Faulting application netdde.exe"**. If you get too many results, add some context, such as the name of the problematic program. Not enough results? Remove the quotes from the phrase or search for the most confusing words in the error message.

✔ **Don't use quotes unless absolutely necessary.** Many people misspell when they post messages to newsgroups. Although Google's built-in spell checker kicks in if it can't find any answers to your query, it may not catch everything. Use quotes only on short phrases or specific error messages.

✔ **Add your Windows version to your search.** Just typing **Vista**, for instance, usually limits your search to Windows Vista issues. Similarly, add the letters **XP** after a search to limit your search to Windows XP problems.

✔ **Search for the letters *FAQ*.** FAQ stands for Frequently Asked Questions. Toss in this acronym along with the name of your problematic subject/product/part. You just might stumble upon a site that contains a FAQ dealing with your particular problem.

✔ **Sort your results by date.** When Google displays results from a newsgroup search, it sorts the results by relevance, with the best result at the top. If you choose Sort by Date, however, Google re-sorts its results, placing the newest results at the top. Some of the Internet's computer information is already obsolete; sorting by date ensures you're finding the newest information.

Think somebody e-mailed you the latest virus? Before opening the suspect e-mail, search Google for the exact words used in the e-mail's subject line. Then sort the results by date to see if people are already talking about it.

✔ **Don't give up too early.** Keep rephrasing your search slightly, adding or subtracting a few words and changing your phrases. Give it five or ten minutes before giving up. Remember, you'll be spending much longer than ten minutes waiting for tech support staff to answer your phone call.

Checking the Manufacturer's Support Web Site

Manufacturers spend big bucks for people to staff the technical support lines. Unfortunately, these employees often don't know any more about computers than you do. Instead, the tech support departments work like telemarketing departments. A person listens to your description of the problem, types the symptoms into his PC, and reads back the scripted responses.

Sometimes this tactic helps, but it's very expensive, both for your phone bill and for the company. And sometimes your questions still go unanswered. That's why an increasing number of companies pack as much technical support information as possible onto their Web sites, helping users find answers as easily as possible.

When you visit a manufacturer's Web site, look for hyperlinks like FAQ, Technical Support, or Driver Downloads. The sites mentioned in the following sections offer much more in-depth help.

Microsoft Knowledge Base

As shown in Figure 22-2, the Microsoft Knowledge Base Web site (`http://support.microsoft.com/search`) contains a continually updated, indexed list of more than 250,000 articles created by Microsoft's support staff.

See the words *Windows Vista Home Premium* in the Search Product box of Figure 22-2? That drop-down menu contains nearly every Microsoft product ever released, making it easy to isolate searches for specific products.

Choose your product in the drop-down menu and type your search words in the box below it. Figure 22-2, for instance, shows the Knowledge Base responding to questions about using Windows Easy Transfer in Windows Vista Home Premium. Browse through the answers supplied by the Knowledge Base to find specific solutions to dealing with your particular problem.

See the number 928634 near the mouse pointer in Figure 22-2? Microsoft assigns every answer its own number. When you're searching the Internet, you often spot a savvy techie respond to a user's question with a terse, "Check out KB 887410." When somebody on the Internet mentions a Knowledge Base number that applies to your problem, immediately write it down and head to the Knowledge Base. Entering the number in the text box immediately displays that solution.

✔ The Knowledge Base has proven to be quite versatile. It offers to fine-tune your search by asking you questions or letting you search within its displayed results. Some pages supply a general overview of the problem and include links to other Knowledge Base numbers that provide specific solutions for specific problems.

✔ If somebody gives you a Knowledge Base number for a solution, you can jump directly there by including it in the URL you type into your browser. To jump to article number 887410, for example, type this into your browser's address bar: `http://support.microsoft.com/kb/887410`.

✔ Although the Knowledge Base sticks to Microsoft products, it also contains information on how Microsoft's products interact with hardware and software from other manufacturers, as well as up-to-date information about viruses and other potential problem causers.

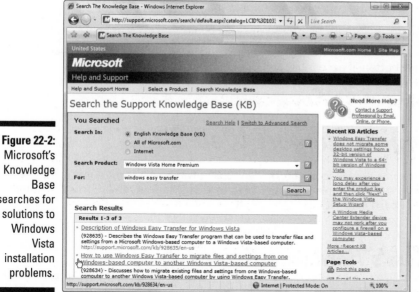

Figure 22-2: Microsoft's Knowledge Base searches for solutions to Windows Vista installation problems.

Serial number and service tag Web sites

Some manufacturers stamp a serial number or service tag on the invoice of every computer they sell. (Many place a sticker with the number onto the computer's case.) Then they create a custom-built Web page based around that particular computer: its motherboard chipset, expansion cards, CPU, and other hardware, as well as its bundled software.

Long after you've lost your computer's invoice and manuals, a quick trip to the manufacturer's Web site enables you to view everything that came with your computer, including part models and numbers, specific support information, warranty expiration information, driver downloads, and in some instances, upgrade information.

Dell and Gateway, among other computer makers, offer this service on their Web sites. If you're unlucky enough to have lost everything *and* scraped off your computer's serial number sticker, visit Dell or Gateway's site anyway. Both sites have technology that can peek inside your computer, grab its long-lost serial number, and fetch the customized Web site for you.

Manufacturer's Web sites in other countries

Most manufacturers sell their computers worldwide. And for some reason, some countries offer better support than others.

If a foreign site appears while you're searching, don't be afraid to give it a visit. If it turns up while you're searching in Google, use the Translate This Page button, if necessary, and Google offers to translate the site's language into one you can (mostly) understand.

Community Support Web Sites

For some people, computers aren't just a way to get work done — they're a passion. I've compiled a list of sites to visit for thorough information about their particular niche.

Tom's Hardware Guide

`www.tomshardware.com`

Although this site leans toward the technical, it's the best site for up-to-date information on computer hardware. You can find the latest performance rankings on CPUs, motherboards, memory chips, video cards, hard drives, and other peripherals — even joysticks. Tom's site is chock-full of reviews, how-to articles, community forums, and techie news. Even though it's written mainly for techies, Tom keeps the site surprisingly easy to understand.

When you're ready to buy something the site raves about, check out the page's adjacent Shop For section to search for the lowest-priced retailer.

Acronym Finder

`www.acronymfinder.com`

No one understands *everything* about computers, so don't be depressed if you spot YACA (Yet Another Computer Acronym) that you don't understand. Instead, head to the Acronym Finder site, type in the mystifying initials, and see the definition.

Although the site works well for technology-oriented items, it provides definitions for acronyms from many other areas, as well. GL2U.

Wikipedia

`www.wikipedia.org`

An editable online encyclopedia created by visitors, Wikipedia offers a wealth of information on all subjects, including technology. It doesn't offer help for specific questions, but the site gives you general background on computer parts and technologies, making for more informed shopping.

Since Wikipedia can be edited by anyone who visits, don't take it as an authoritarian source. Instead, use it as a branching-off point for finding further information.

Legacy, relic, and cult Web sites

Some great products hit the market only to die off in a few years. Some disappear when the company folds; other times a company may discontinue its older products in favor of new ones. Yet the owners of these older products find that they're still working fine and see no reason to upgrade.

To their credit, some manufacturers still offer drivers to support products released many years ago. Thanks to the Diamond Multimedia Web site, for instance, my 15-year-old Supra FaxModem still dials the Internet and sends and receives my faxes. Many other manufacturers still offer drivers for long-discontinued parts.

The key word is *legacy*. Toss in that word when searching on Google, and you may be surprised at how many drivers still exist for that outdated computer part. Few, if any, manufacturers still offer assistance, support, or guarantees that old parts, software, and drivers still work. But all the same, you may just need one old Windows XP driver to get parts to work with Windows Vista.

✔ Many older products develop almost a cult following with a core group of people who provide grassroots support to each other. Some write their own drivers or software for the products, allowing them to take advantage of new features or keep them up to date with newer versions of Windows.

✔ When searching for support for your older product, try searching the newsgroups through Google's Groups search. When the list appears, choose Sort by Date so that the most recent discussions appear at the top. That gives you a quick idea of how much buzz still surrounds your faithful gadget, and it increases your chances of finding a Web site that still offers support.

✔ Stuck with an old MP3 player? RioWorld (www.rioworld.org) supplies working drivers, firmware, and software for more than a dozen Rio MP3 players. (It still offers drivers for the world's first mass-market MP3 player, the Rio 300.)

Part VI
The Part of Tens

The 5th Wave   By Rich Tennant

"Why am I modding my PC? I pimped my Xbox, my
fish tank, and my Water Pik. This was next."

In this part . . .

Those of you with sharp eyes will realize something scandalous about this part right away: The chapters in it don't always contain ten items. Most have a wee bit more information or a wee bit less.

But by the time most people get to this part of the book, they're tired of counting numbers anyway. That's why these lists aren't numbered. They're just a bunch of facts tossed into a basket.

So when you read these chapters, remember that it's quality, not quantity, that matters. Besides, would you want to read a fake tip about 8255 PPI (U20) messages just because one of the chapters in this part needed a tenth tip?

Chapter 23

Ten Cheap Fixes to Try First

*B*efore you spend any money at the shop, try these cheap fixes on your computer. You might get lucky. If you're not lucky, give yourself a good stretch and flip back to Chapter 21 for some deeper system-sleuthing tips.

Plug It In

Sure, it sounds silly, but industry experts get paid big bucks to say that unplugged equipment is the leading cause of "electrical component malfunction." Sometimes a yawning leg stretch can inadvertently loosen the cord from the wall. Rearranging a computer on the desk almost always loosens cables that aren't pushed tightly into the back of the computer.

Check your power cord in *two* places: It can creep out of not only the wall outlet but also the back of your computer or whatever you've plugged into one of your PC's ports.

If you use a UPS or a surge protector, check *three* places: Check the back of your computer, check that your PC's power cord is plugged firmly into the UPS or surge protector, and check that the UPS or surge protector is plugged into the wall outlet.

And, uh, the machine *is* turned on, isn't it? (That's the leading cause of printer malfunction, by the way.) Some surge protectors have an on/off switch, so make sure the switch is in the On position. (Anytime you spot a light that's on, the part is plugged in.)

Turn Off the Computer, Wait 30 Seconds, and Turn It On

Before going any further, try closing the troublesome program and restarting it. Doesn't cure the problem? Then log off from Windows, and log on again.

If that doesn't fix it, shut down Windows and your computer and then turn it back on after about 30 seconds.

Sometimes the computer just gets confused for no apparent reason. If your computer drifts off into oblivion with no return in sight, try tapping the spacebar a few times. Try pressing Esc or holding down Ctrl while pressing Esc. One of my laptops woke up only when I prodded an arrow key.

Still no return? Then it's time to get ugly. The next few steps may cause you to lose any unsaved work. Sorry!

- ✔ Try rebooting the computer: Press the Ctrl, Alt, and Del keys simultaneously. Sometimes that's enough to wake up Windows and bring the Task Manager to life. (In Vista, it brings up a menu where you can choose Start Task Manager.) If one of your programs is the culprit, click the Task Manager's Applications tab for a chance to snuff out the troublemaking program with a click of the End Task button.

- ✔ If the computer still acts like an ice cube, head for the next level of attention grabbing: Press your PC's reset button. No reset button, or no results? Move to the next step.

- ✔ If the computer's *still* counting marbles on some virtual playground, turn off the computer, unplug the darn thing, or in the case of some laptops, remove its battery. (Windows often makes you hold the power button down for ten seconds or so to turn it off.) Then wait 30 seconds after it's been turned off, giving it a chance to really settle down. Finally, turn the computer back on and see whether it returns in a better mood.

You'd be surprised how much good a little 30-second vacation can accomplish.

Install a New Driver

When you suspect some part is involved — not always an easy call with Windows — your best chance at fixing the problem comes by finding a better driver. Drivers serve as translators between Windows' language and the language spoken by a manufacturer's particular part.

The better the translator, the smoother the conversations. Installing an updated video driver, for example, can fix irregularities in the display you'd been blaming on your monitor. An updated sound driver might rid your soundtracks of that awful static.

I describe how to track down and install drivers in Chapter 19.

Google the Error Message

When your PC gives you an annoying error message, write it down on a scrap of paper. Then type that error message into the search box on Google (www.google.com). Be sure to type in the *exact* error message and put it in quotes.

Thousands of people have seen that same error message. Dozens of them have already asked about it on Google. And if you're lucky, it won't take long before you find the few people who've posted solutions that could be as easy as clicking the right check box.

I describe how to search on Google in Chapter 22.

Find and Remove Spyware

Spyware programs sneak into Windows, often through Internet Explorer, as you visit Web sites. Some spyware hops onto your PC surreptitiously, other spyware piggybacks on programs offered by sneaky Web sites.

Spyware tracks your Web activity, sending your browsing patterns back to the spyware program's publisher. The publisher then sneaks targeted advertisements onto your PC's screen, either through pop-up ads, banners, or changing your browser's Home page.

Most spyware programs freely admit to being spies — usually on the 43rd page of the 44-page agreement you're supposed to read before installing the supposedly helpful program.

The biggest problem with spyware comes when you try to pry it off: They rarely include an uninstall program. That's where spyware removing programs come in.

Microsoft's Windows Defender spyware removal program, for example, comes preinstalled in Vista, and Windows XP owners can download it from Microsoft's Web site (www.microsoft.com/downloads). Windows Defender prevents some spyware from installing itself, and it removes any spyware it finds inside your PC. To help Windows Defender recognize the latest strains of spyware, Windows Update keeps Windows Defender up to date.

To make Windows Defender scan your PC immediately, a potential solution when your PC's acting strange, click the Start menu, choose All Programs, and launch Windows Defender. Click the Scan button, if the program hasn't already begun scanning your PC, and wait for it to finish.

But don't be afraid to run more than one spyware scanner on your PC. Unlike firewalls and anti-virus programs, spyware scanners don't conflict with each other: Each program does its own scan, killing off any spyware it finds. Two other popular programs are Ad-Aware (www.lavasoftusa.com) and Spybot Search & Destroy (www.safer-networking.org). Both programs are free, hoping to entice you into buying their more full-featured versions.

Avoid Viruses by Not Opening Unexpected Attachments

This isn't really a quick-fix tip, but it's certainly a way to avoid having to do a lot of fixing when a virus infects your PC. Most viruses can be avoided by following this simple rule: Don't open *any* e-mailed file unless you're expecting to receive it.

That rule works because most viruses spread by e-mailing a copy of themselves to *everybody* in the address book of an infected PC. That means most viruses arrive in e-mail sent from your friends' e-mail accounts.

Before opening any suspicious file, e-mail the sender and ask him if he meant to send you the file. That little bit of effort not only keeps your PC safer, it keeps you from having to clean up problems left over by rogue programs.

Run System Restore

Windows Vista and Windows XP include a wonderful tool for setting things right again. Called System Restore, this tool remembers the good times — when your computer worked fine and all the parts got along.

When your computer becomes a problem child, System Restore sends it back to that time when everything worked fine. I explain this miracle worker in Chapter 21.

Check for Overheating

Nobody likes to work when it's too hot, and your computer is no exception. Your computer normally works naked, but after a few months, it wears a thick, hot coat of dust.

Your first step is to look at the fan's round grill on the back of the computer. See all the dust flecks clinging to the grill, swapping barbecue stories? (See an example in Color Plate 33, in the color insert pages in this book.) Remove them with a rag or vacuum cleaner, being careful to keep the worst grunge from falling inside.

Second, check the vents on the front and sides of your computer case. Although the fan in the power supply is creating the airflow, the air is actually being sucked in these little holes and crevices. If these vents are clogged with crud, very little air moves across the components to cool them.

Don't just *blow* on the dust, either. The microscopic flecks of spittle in your breath can cause problems with the computer's moisture-sensitive internal components.

For best results, buy a cheap can of compressed air from a local computer store, remove your computer's case, and blast the dust off its innards every few months, paying special attention to crevices and grills. (Unplug it and carry it outside first. Angry dislodged dust particles float everywhere.)

REMEMBER

The more parts and peripherals you add to your computer, the hotter it runs. Be sure to keep the vents clean.

TIP

Don't tape cards or cheat sheets (including the one from this book) across the front of your PC's case. That can block your PC's air vents, which are often disguised as ridges across the front of the case. When air can't circulate inside your PC, your computer heats up in a hurry. Also, don't keep your computer pushed up directly against the wall. It needs some breathing room so that its fan can blow out all the hot air from inside the case.

Install a New Power Supply

When computers simply refuse to turn on and do *anything,* and you know that the power cord isn't loose, it's probably because the power supply died.

Power supplies have become increasingly reliable over the past few years. Still, be sure to replace the power supply if the computer doesn't even make a noise when you push its power button.

Chapter 10 provides power supply replacement instructions.

Run Check Disk

Windows comes with several programs designed to keep it running trouble-free. Every few months — and immediately if Windows starts giving you some vague, unidentifiable trouble — follow these steps to find and run some of the troubleshooters:

1. **Open the Start menu and click Computer (in Vista) or My Computer (in Windows XP).**

   Windows lists your PC's disk drives and other storage areas.

2. **Right-click your hard drive's icon and choose Properties from the pop-up menu.**

   You want to right-click the Local Disk (C:) drive because that's the drive where Windows sets up camp.

3. **Click the Tools tab to get to the goodies.**

   The Tools tab reveals three buttons that check the drive for errors, defragment the drive, or backup the drive.

4. **Click the Check Now button and then click the Start button.**

   When the Check Disk dialog box appears, automate the disk checking process by checking the two boxes, Automatically Fix File System Errors and Scan For and Attempt Recovery of Bad Sectors.

   Because you're checking the drive Windows lives on, the program will ask permission to run the disk check the next time you restart your PC. (That gives the program access to areas it can't reach while Windows is running.)

5. Repeat the process on your other hard drive icons.

If your PC has other hard drives, repeat the process on them, as well. If your PC has a card reader, this trick also works on memory cards, like the ones used in most digital cameras. (It also works on USB thumb drives.) It won't work on CD or DVD drives, however.

To defragment your hard drive — a way to speed it up by reorganizing its information — repeat the first three steps above, but click the Defragment Now button in Step 4. (I explain how to defragment a hard drive in Chapter 9.)

Chapter 24

Ten Handy Upgrade Tools

*T*he next time you're at the computer shop, pick up a computer toolkit. You get most of the tools mentioned in this section and a snazzy, zip-up black case to keep them in. Most kits cost less than $20.

If you don't want to spend money, you can probably salvage most of this chapter's handy items from a garage, junk drawer, kitchen, or laundry room.

But no matter whether you buy a toolkit or assemble your own, make sure that you keep it within reach when you're ready to open your computer's case.

Using the Manual and Online Sources

You *did* save all the documentation that came with your computer, didn't you? Unfortunately, those manuals and papers often come in handy when you're upgrading your PC. The documents describe the parts and model numbers of your PC's innards and how to fix certain things. Keep the manuals in a safe place, preferably sealed in a large Ziploc freezer baggie. Even a receipt helps: It usually contains the model number and brands of your PC's components.

Can't find anything? Then head to your PC manufacturer's Web site to see its vital statics. Did you buy a Dell or Gateway computer? Find the PC's serial number on the sticker affixed to your PC's case; then head to www.dell.com or www.gateway.com for a list of your computer's parts and drivers. (You can sometimes find out whether your PC is still under warranty, too.)

Save the manuals for every part or piece of software you buy for your computer. They're your first defense when something goes wrong.

A working knowledge of the Internet helps you keep your PC running smoothly, no doubt about it. The Internet contains information posted by millions of PC users, and some of them have gone through the same problems you have. When you can't figure out what's wrong, head for the Internet's newsgroups. (They're searchable from Google.) People post messages on the newsgroups about their computer problems and how they solved them.

Diagnosing and fixing your computer through the Internet gets its due in Chapter 22.

The Internet does you no good after you've installed a part and your computer stops working. Doing a little research *before* you start your fix-it job can save a lot of time.

The First Tools to Grab

Phillips screwdrivers: Phillips screwdrivers have a little square cross on their tip, not a flat blade. The pointed tip fits directly into the crossed lines on the screw's top, shown in the margin. Regular screwdrivers don't work.

The Phillips screwdriver doesn't need to be a tiny thing; most computer screws have fairly deep holes. Sometimes an over-eager computer nerd over-tightens the screws that hold on your computer's case. If this is your problem, a nut driver does a better job of removing it.

Tighten screws just enough so they won't come out by themselves. Don't overtighten them. In fact, overtightening the screws that hold in a hard drive can damage the drive.

Nut drivers: By far my favorite tool, the nut driver looks like a common screwdriver but with a socket wrench on the end. It's useful because most computer screws not only work with a Phillips screwdriver, but also a ¼-inch socket wrench. Notice how the Phillips screw in the margin also has six sides?

When you push the screw's six-sided head into the nut driver, it usually stays put. From there, you can often guide the end of the screw to its target deep inside your computer, push it into the hole, and start turning. The socket end grips the screw the entire time, so the screw doesn't fall out. You can't do that with a Phillips screwdriver — even the ones with magnetized tips don't grip as well as a nut driver.

A nut driver also works well when unscrewing things. Again, the screw stays lodged inside the socket better than it would with a screwdriver, enabling you to lift it out of the computer's case without dropping it.

Almost all the screws lurking inside your computer — including the frequently accessed screws holding in the extension cards — work well with a quarter-inch nut driver.

Turning Household Items into Tools

Paper clips: They don't look like much, but you'd be surprised what they can do when they're partially straightened. Then they come in handy for several things:

- ✔ **Making stuck CD drives spit out their trays.** You find a tiny hole on the front of many CD-ROM drives — a hole much smaller than the headphone jack. If the disc gets stuck, try pushing the end of your straightened paperclip into the hole. The hole serves as an Emergency Eject System that extracts stubborn compact discs.

- ✔ **Prying jumpers off pins.** Although needle-nose pliers work better for this, a paper clip is often handier, and it doesn't damage the pins. (You may come across unruly jumpers when installing hard drives and CD/DVD drives.)

- ✔ **Flipping DIP switches.** Short for Dual Inline Package, these little rows of switches appear on some motherboards and hard drives. How do you flip those tiny things, shown in Figure 24-1? Grab the paper clip.

Figure 24-1:
Use a straightened paper clip to flip tiny switches.

Empty egg cartons: An egg carton works great for holding a computer's removed screws. Drop screws from different parts into different depressions. Forgetful people label each depression with a pen so that they remember which part uses them.

A small flashlight: Most of the stuff inside your computer's case is jammed in pretty close together. When everything's so dark inside, a flashlight helps you locate the right expansion card, find the model number of a sound card, or locate missing screws.

Small keychain flashlights work well to illuminate your PC's crevices, as do pen lights. Look for freebie keychain flashlights the next time you stay at a fancy hotel or visit a trade show. Flashlights are handy tools to add to your computer repair arsenal.

Keep a pad of paper and a pencil handy for writing down part numbers.

Magnetized Screwdrivers and Dust Blowers

The following items aren't crucial, but oh, they certainly are handy at the right times. If you spot one while shopping, think about buying it for an upcoming repair.

A magnetized screwdriver: The magnet makes it easier to grab a fallen screw you've just spotted with the flashlight. Just touch the screw with the end of the screwdriver and gently lift it out when it sticks to the end of the screwdriver.

Anything with a magnet can wipe out information on your floppy disks. To avoid problems, don't keep your magnetized screwdriver near your work area. Just grab it when you need to fetch a dropped screw and then put it back on the other side of the room. (Compact discs don't have this problem, by the way.)

Compressed air canisters: Commonly found at PC repair shops and art supply shops, *canned air,* as it's also known, lets you blow all the gross things out of the inside of your PC. Pranksters can also squirt coworkers in the back of the head when they're not looking.

Be sure to take the PC *outside* before you blow the dust off it, or it can make a mess on the floor. Plus, the smaller dust particles float through the air — you don't want to breathe that junk in, or to have it get sucked back into your PC through the fan.

Don't blow with your own breath on your PC's innards to remove dust. Although you're blowing air, you're also blowing moisture, which can be even worse for your PC than dust.

Every few months, vacuum off the dust balls that clog the air vent on the back of your PC. The cooler you can keep your PC, the longer it lasts.

Your Windows Vista DVD or Windows XP CD

Even when your computer's hard drive fails, it will still boot from its original Windows Vista DVD or Windows XP CD. Pop it into your disc drive, turn on your computer, and Windows appears on your screen. However, you still need to install Windows onto a working hard drive, described in Chapter 20, before you can run any of its programs.

Chapter 25

(Nearly) Ten Upgrade
Do's and Donuts

Over the years, as hungry computer repair technicians swapped tales of occupational stress, they gradually created a list known as *The Upgrade Do's and Donuts*. The following tips have all been salvaged from lunch rooms across the nation and placed here for quick retrieval.

Do Upgrade One Thing at a Time

Even if you've just returned from the computer store with more memory, a wireless network card, a hard drive, and a monitor, don't try to install them all at once. Install one part and make sure that it works before going on to the next part. If you can stand it, wait a day to make sure no problems turn up.

If you install more than one part at the same time and your computer doesn't work when you turn it on, you may have trouble figuring out which particular part is gagging your computer.

Do Make a Restore Point before Every Upgrade

The Windows System Restore feature does a great job of reinstating your computer's settings that made it run smoothly and cleanly. However, System Restore only works if you've created a Restore Point for it to return to.

If you're installing anything that involves software, drivers, or setup programs, head to System Restore, covered in Chapter 1, and make a Restore Point that describes what you're about to do. Before installing that wireless network adapter, for instance, make a Restore Point with the name, "Before installing the new wireless network adapter."

Then, if the wireless network adapter bulldozes your finely tuned network settings, System Restore can return to those peaceful days when your network buzzed happily, giving you time to troubleshoot the problem.

Do Watch Out for Static Electricity

Static electricity can destroy computer parts. That's why many computer parts, especially things on circuit cards, come packaged in weird, silvery bags that reflect light like the visor on an astronaut's helmet. That high-tech plastic stuff absorbs any stray static before it can zap the part inside.

To make sure that you don't zap a computer part with static electricity, you should discharge yourself — no matter how gross that sounds — before starting to work on your computer. Touch a piece of bare metal, like the edge of a metal desk or chair, to ground yourself. You also must ground yourself each time you move your feet, especially when standing on carpet, wearing slippers, or after moving the cat back out of the way.

If you're living in a particularly static-prone environment, pick up a wrist-grounding strap at the computer store. (They usually sell them near the packages of memory.)

Do Hang On to Your Old Boxes, Manuals, Warranties, and Receipts

When you need to pack up your computer for a move, nothing works better than its old boxes. I keep mine on the top shelf in the garage, just in case I move. Don't bother hanging on to the smaller boxes, though, like the ones that come with a video card or mouse.

Hang on to *all* your old manuals, even if you don't understand a word they say. Sometimes a newer part starts arguing with an older part, and the manuals often have hints on which switch to flip to break up the fight.

Just push some dust mice aside from under the bed and slide all the manuals under there.

Don't Force Parts Together

Everything in your PC is designed to fit into place smoothly and without too much of a fight. If something doesn't fit right, stop, scratch your head, and try again using a slightly different tactic.

When trying to plug a cord into the back of your computer, for example, look closely at the end of the cord and then scrutinize the plug where it's supposed to fit. See how the pins are lined up a certain way? See how the plug's shape differs on one side? Turn the plug until it lines up with its socket and push slowly but firmly. Sometimes it helps if you jiggle it back and forth slightly. Ask your spouse to tickle you gently.

How to fish out dropped screws

When a screw falls into the inner reaches of your PC, it usually lands in a spot inaccessible to human fingers. The following should call it back home:

✔ Is it in plain sight? Try grabbing it with some long tweezers. If that doesn't work, wrap some tape, sticky-side out, around the end of a pencil or chopstick. With a few deft pokes, you may be able to snag it. A magnetized screwdriver can come in handy here as well. (Don't leave the magnetized screwdriver near your floppy disks, though; magnets can wipe out the information on the disks.)

✔ If you don't see the runaway screw, gently tilt the computer to one side and then the other. Hopefully, the screw will roll out in plain sight. If you can hear it roll, you can often discover what it's hiding behind.

✔ Still can't find it? Pick up the computer's case with both hands, gently turn it upside down, and tilt it from side to side. The screw should fall out.

✔ If you still can't find the screw and it's not making any noise, check the floor beneath the computer. Sometimes screws hide in the carpet, where only bare feet can find them.

Do not power up your computer until you can account for every screw, or you'll find yourself with an even worse problem: a shorted-out motherboard.

Things that plug directly onto your motherboard seem to need the most force. Things that plug onto the outside of your PC, by contrast, slip on pretty easily. They also slip off pretty easily, so some of the cables have little thumb screws to hold everything in place firmly.

Don't Bend Cards

Many of your computer's internal organs are mounted on fiberglass boards. That's the reason there's a warning coming up right now.

Don't bend these boards, no matter how tempting. Bending the board can break the circuits subtly enough to damage the card. Worse yet, the cracks can be too small to see, so you may not know what went wrong.

If you hear little crackling sounds while you're doing something with a board — plugging it into a socket or plugging something into it — you're pushing the wrong way. Stop, regroup, and try again. Check out Chapter 7 and make sure you're pushing the right type of card into the right slot: PCI, PCI-Express, or AGP. Also check the color insert pages in this book — Color Plates 17 through 23 show full-color photos to help you see where and how to insert cards.

Don't Rush Yourself

Give yourself plenty of time to install a new part. If you rush yourself or get nervous, you're much more likely to break something, which can cause even more nervousness.

And never, ever, start a new project on a Friday evening. Many tech support lines are closed during the weekend, leaving you with no help and no way to play *The Sims 2* or *Microsoft Flight Simulator*.

Don't Open Up Monitors or Power Supplies

You can't repair anything inside monitors or power supplies. Also, both the power supply and monitor store voltage, even when they're not plugged in.

To avoid an electric shock, don't ever try to open your power supply or monitor.

Appendix

The Rathbone Reference of Fine Ports

● ●

In This Appendix

▶ Identifying the plugs and ports on your computer

▶ Understanding what devices use what plugs and ports

▶ Finding out what ports can be added, expanded, or converted

● ●

Computers come full of holes (ports) where you insert a cable's end (plug). Unfortunately, computer ports rarely get better with age. Unlike a fine wine, a computer's ports grow obsolete with age, and engineers create new types of ports to replace them.

Chances are, many of your computer's existing ports will go unused. And in the coming years, you might have to buy port upgrades before you can plug in the latest devices.

Because it's increasingly difficult to keep track of what plugs in where — or what used to go here but now goes there — I've created the Rathbone Reference of Fine Ports.

The reference, spread throughout the following sections, shows pictures of all the plugs and ports you're likely to encounter on your computer and the gear that plugs into it. Next to the pictures, you see the symbol commonly placed next to a port by computer manufacturers to identify its function.

Feel free to peek at this section whenever you plug something new into your computer during repairs and upgrades.

Throughout this book, you find a drawing of the appropriate plug and port next to the spot where it's used. Use that drawing as a memory jogger and return here if you need more information.

USB (Universal Serial Bus)

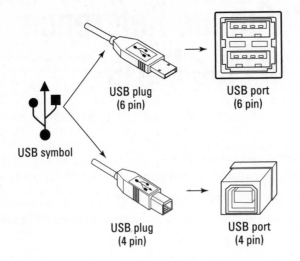

USB plug
(6 pin)

USB port
(6 pin)

USB symbol

USB plug
(4 pin)

USB port
(4 pin)

The Dirt: For the past ten years, manufacturers have shipped their computers with *USB ports* — small, rectangular-shaped holes ready to accept small, rectangular-shaped plugs. At first, everybody ignored them. But slowly, companies began creating items to plug into those holes.

USB plugs and ports now come in two sizes: The large rectangular ones (often called *six-pin*) come on most computers. The smaller, more squarish ones (sometimes called *four-pin*) appear on smaller items like MP3 players. The small, four-pin models lack the two pins supplying power, so gadgets with those ports usually come with batteries or an AC adapter.

You can buy a cord with a big, six-pin plug on one end that fits into your computer and a small, four-pin plug on the other end that fits into your small gadget (such as a digital camera).

USB 1.1 ports and plugs look identical to those using USB 2.0, a much faster standard designed about five years ago. Those old USB 1.1 devices still work in a USB 2.0 port, but USB 2.0 devices work reliably only in USB 2.0 ports.

What's Connected: Today, store shelves brim with USB keyboards, mice, sound modules, digital cameras, hard drives, CD-ROM drives, and just about every other computer peripheral.

Background: Why the fuss about USB ports? Because manufacturers finally realized that most people don't *enjoy* removing their computer's cases to install things. People don't *want* to figure out which specialized hole their new gadget plugs into. And nobody enjoys explaining to a confused computer what's been plugged in.

USB solves all three problems. People plug any new USB gadget into any available USB port, and the computer almost always recognizes the new device and begins feeding it power through the cable. Simple. (A few power-hungry USB gadgets also plug into the wall or require batteries.)

USB's popularity created a problem, though. Older computers come with only two USB ports, and now everybody wants more than two USB devices. The solution is to buy an inexpensive USB hub. Shown in Figure A-1, a *USB hub* plugs into one of your existing USB ports and provides four or more USB ports. It works like a power strip, enabling bunches of USB gadgets to plug into a single port. Many hubs must be plugged into the wall to provide enough power for all the devices attached to it. A few finicky USB gadgets don't like hubs, however, and insist on plugging into the computer's original USB port.

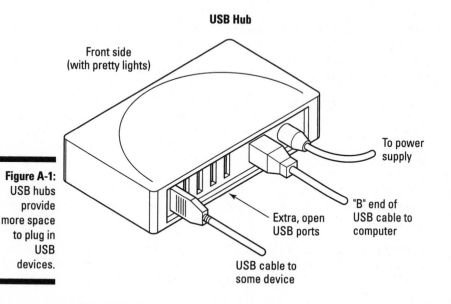

Figure A-1: USB hubs provide more space to plug in USB devices.

The Verdict: Windows Vista automatically recognizes almost anything plugged into a USB port, including mice, webcams, joysticks, printers, hard drives, video capture devices, external CD/DVD burners, and scanners.

Standard talk about IEEE

For more than 100 years, the Institute of Electrical and Electronics Engineers (IEEE) has assigned numbers to things. (IEEE is pronounced *EYE-trip-ul-ee*, by the way, in case you want to earn points at geek gatherings.)

For instance, Apple Computers named its speedy information transfer system *FireWire*. Not to be outdone, IEEE named it *IEEE Standard 1394*.

Computer networks, commonly called *Ethernet*, are actually called *IEEE Standard 802.3*. When printers communicate with computers, they use *IEEE Standard 1284*. IEEE's dictionary, where they keep track of all the numbers, is called *IEEE 100*. (Seriously.)

Don't be surprised by all the IEEE numbers that pop up in this book. For riveting late-night reading, visit the group's Web site at www.ieee.org. Unfortunately, the popular IEEE 100 dictionary is not available online.

IEEE 1394 (Also Known as FireWire or Sony i.LINK)

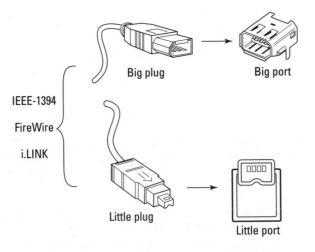

Big plug → Big port

IEEE-1394
FireWire
i.LINK

Little plug → Little port

The Dirt: *IEEE 1394* officially stands for the Institute of Electrical and Electronics Engineers Standard Number 1394. Apple, the hip engineers who created Macintosh computers, mercifully named it *FireWire*. And Sony calls it *i.LINK*. (I use the term *FireWire* in this book.)

Most new PCs come with built-in FireWire ports. If you own an older computer, you might need to upgrade with a FireWire port on a card, as described in Chapter 7. (When you're shopping, look for a combination FireWire/USB 2.0 card so you can plug in *lots* of goodies.)

What's Connected: IEEE 1394, er, FireWire is a way to transfer lots of information *very* quickly, so it's gathered a large following with digital camcorder owners who want to copy video into their PCs for editing.

The Verdict: Make sure that your computer has a FireWire port if you plan to edit video from a digital camcorder that requires one. (Some digital camcorders have switched to USB 2.0.)

The first and most popular version of FireWire, known as FireWire 400, can transfer information up to 400 Mbps (megabits per second) through a cable length of up to 15 feet. FireWire's latest version, FireWire 800, transfers information up to 800 Mbps. FireWire 800 is still new, and few devices yet support it. Unlike Windows XP, Windows Vista no longer recognizes FireWire for networking two PCs.

Standard VGA Video Port

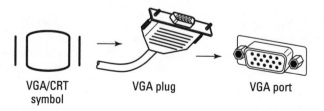

VGA/CRT   VGA plug   VGA port
symbol

The Dirt: Everybody needs a video port (also called *VGA port)* to plug in their monitor, and some Windows Vista and Windows XP Professional users can install a second video port to add a second monitor to their desktops. (Windows XP Home doesn't support two monitors.)

What's Connected: Video ports have been around for years to support standard CRT (Cathode Ray Tube) monitors — the kind that look like old TV sets. The first variety of LCD monitors required special digital ports (described next), but now many LCD monitors also plug into normal video ports.

The Verdict: Almost every video card still supports standard, cathode-ray monitors. Most also support the cool, flat-panel LCD monitors. If you want to upgrade to an LCD monitor, make sure your PC's video card can handle it. (Chapter 7 explains this in more detail.)

Flat-Panel LCD Video Port (DVI)

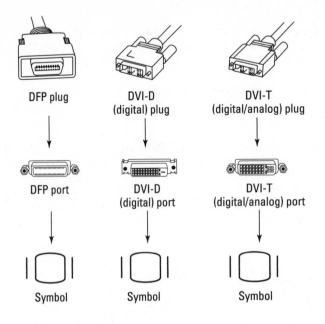

DFP plug	DVI-D (digital) plug	DVI-T (digital/analog) plug
DFP port	DVI-D (digital) port	DVI-T (digital/analog) port
Symbol	Symbol	Symbol

The Dirt: If your new computer came with a traditional monitor, it probably plugs into a standard VGA port, which I describe in the previous section. If you're upgrading to a flat-panel monitor, you might need a new video card for it to plug into. You find much, *much* more about this complicated stuff in Chapter 7.

When "flat-screen" LCD monitors arrived in the late '90s, they brought two different connectors with them: Some used the 20-pin DFP (Digital Flat Panel) connector, and others had the 24-pin DVI (Digital Visual Interface) connector. DVI won the battle, so those old DFP monitors don't work with most of today's video cards. You'll find DFP-to-DVI adaptors on the Internet (try www.dvigear.com), but DVI cards still won't work on all DFP monitors.

The Verdict: If you're buying a flat-panel LCD monitor, your video card needs the correct type of port for it to plug into. "Digital" LCD monitors require a DVI port. "Analog/Digital" LCD monitors can use either. To be on the safe side, many video cards today come with a VGA *and* a DVI port. To be *really* safe, consider buying your monitor and card as a matched set. Chapter 7 offers the scoop.

Analog Video

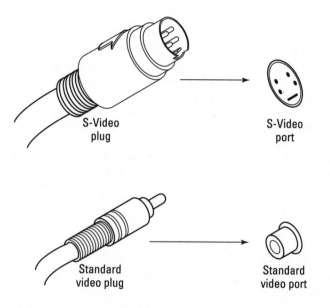

S-Video
plug

S-Video
port

Standard
video plug

Standard
video port

The Dirt: These connectors enable computers to exchange video signals with a variety of sources, usually your VCR, analog camcorder, or television. To capture video, the cards convert incoming video signals into a digital format by measuring the video signals and storing the measurements as numbers.

When you're sending video — displaying a laptop's screen on a television, for example — the converters do just the opposite, converting the computer's digital signals to analog.

The Verdict: Look for these jacks to transfer video signals to and from your computer. The lower-quality RCA connectors are almost always yellow. The much higher-quality S-Video connectors are almost always black. (Being more expensive, S-Video connectors aren't found on all computers or video sources.) Chapter 7 covers digital video.

Ethernet (RJ-45)

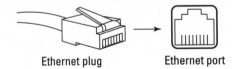

Ethernet plug → Ethernet port

The Dirt: When you accumulate too many household appliances, you hold a garage sale. When you accumulate too many computers, you connect them with a network so that they can share resources (such as printers, for example) and information. IEEE Standard 802.3, nicknamed *Ethernet,* is the most popular cabling used for small networks, so your computer might already have an Ethernet jack (also known as an *RJ-45 jack)* built in.

The Verdict: Ethernet jacks look almost identical to standard telephone jacks, but they're slightly larger. You can't fit an Ethernet jack into a phone jack, but you can accidentally push a phone cord into an Ethernet jack. (The phone won't work, though.)

Telephone (RJ-11)

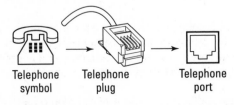

Telephone symbol → Telephone plug → Telephone port

The Dirt: If you're using a dialup modem to connect to the Internet, you'll probably see two of these jacks on the back of your computer.

The Verdict: Examine the two jacks closely. One jack usually says Line; the other says Phone. (The Phone jack often bears a telephone symbol.) You must run a cord from the Line jack to the telephone jack in the wall. The Phone jack enables you to plug in a telephone handset for convenience's sake.

Stereo Sound

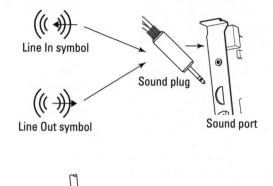

Line In symbol

Line Out symbol

Sound plug

Sound port

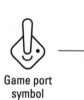

Game port
symbol

Game port
plug

Game port

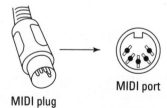

MIDI plug

MIDI port

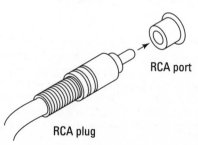

RCA plug

RCA port

The Dirt: Sound cards come with bunches of jacks, so they get their own special figure. Line In is where you plug in stuff you want to record or have the computer play through its speakers. Line Out is where you plug in your speakers or headphones. (You can also connect that port to your home stereo's Line In port to hear your PC through your stereo.) The joystick or game controller plugs into the game port; most people use inexpensive Y-adapters to fit two joysticks into one port.

Some MIDI adapters plug into the sound card's game port, providing MIDI plugs for musicians to plug into a musical instrument's MIDI ports, such as those on a synthesizer keyboard. Finally, five-speaker sound cards often use an RCA port to power the subwoofer. High-end cards often use external RCA ports for S/PDIF digital audio transfers, described in Chapter 11.

The Verdict: Sound cards vary widely according to their expense. Some offer digital sound options, others offer surround sound and home theater plug-ins. Chapter 11 covers it all.

Coaxial Cable

Coaxial cable   Coaxial port

The dirt: Found on almost all TV tuners and TV sets, this carries TV channels. The cable usually pokes out of the wall and plugs into your cable box or TV set. The cable usually screws onto its connector by hand, although some simply push on.

The Verdict: You must plug your TV's cable directly from the wall into your PC's TV tuner *without* plugging into a cable box first. If you plug it into the cable box first, you'll be able to record only one channel: The channel your cable box is tuned to. I explain TV tuners in Chapter 12.

RCA (Composite)

The Dirt: These carry either sound (on a pair of cables) or video. To tell which jack carries what, look at its color: Red (right) and white (left) jacks each carry one channel of stereo sound; a yellow jack carries video. Because most PCs pipe out sound through a tiny ⅛-inch jack, this jack usually pipes out video on a PC.

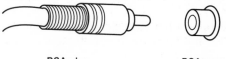

RCA plug   RCA port

The Verdict: Connect a cable from this jack to the same jack on your TV set to bring your PC's screen to your TV set. (To connect the sound to your TV set, run a cable from your sound card's Line Out jack to the red and white RCA ports on your TV.)

S-Video

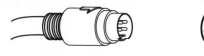

S-Video plug   S-Video port

The Dirt: This cable, usually black, carries high-quality video but no sound.

The Verdict: These appear on both TV tuners and high-quality video cards. Both let you use your TV set as a monitor. If your TV accepts both RCA or S-Video jacks, use S-Video, as it's higher quality. (To hear TV soundtracks, you must still connect your PC's sound to your stereo or TV.)

Optical/Toslink

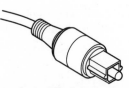

Optical/Toslink plug   Optical/Toslink port

The Dirt: Found on some high-quality sound cards, this carries Dolby AC-3 sound (sometimes called *multichannel*, *surround sound*, or *5.1)* but no video. Some sound boxes and cards offer an optical jack, others offer a Toslink jack, but they both carry the same thing: high-quality, six-speaker sound.

The Verdict: If your PC has optical but your stereo has Toslink — or vice versa — you can't connect your PC to your home stereo until you buy an adapter, a chore I cover in Chapter 11.

The Legacy Devices

A *legacy* device is simply an older piece of hardware, usually designed to be used with Windows Millennium (Windows Me) and earlier Windows versions. Legacy devices usually aren't *Plug and Play*–compatible, meaning that your computer doesn't automatically recognize and install them for you when you plug them in.

Although new computers often include these legacy ports, they usually go unused. These connectors are here in case you find a device that still requires one.

PS/2 mouse and keyboard

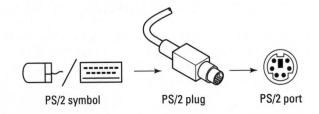

PS/2 symbol   PS/2 plug   PS/2 port

The Dirt: Older keyboards and mice often plug into a slim, round goodie called a PS/2 port. Most current models plug into a USB port, instead.

The Verdict: PS/2 keyboards work better for troubleshooting, as they work as soon as your computer boots up — before Windows begins running. Feel free to buy a USB mouse and keyboard, though.

Serial connectors

Serial symbol   Serial plug   Serial port

The Dirt: Today, serial ports usually remain empty. Modems, their prime users, usually live inside the computer. A handful of other gadgets cling to them, mostly older PocketPCs, Palm Pilots, label printers, and similar nerdy gadgets. Most high-end PCs still include a serial port, but the budget models leave them off.

The Verdict: Ignore them.

Parallel (printer) connectors

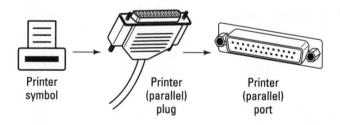

Printer symbol   Printer (parallel) plug   Printer (parallel) port

The Dirt: Hunkered down next to a computer's two serial ports sits a parallel or printer port. (Nerds call it a *DB25 port.*) It's always been there for connecting to the printer.

The Verdict: Like serial ports, parallel ports are being replaced by USB ports. A few printers still use them, though, so they haven't yet dropped off high-end PCs. You probably won't find one on a budget PC.

Index

BUSINESS, CAREERS & PERSONAL FINANCE

0-7645-9847-3

0-7645-2431-3

Also available:
- Business Plans Kit For Dummies
  0-7645-9794-9
- Economics For Dummies
  0-7645-5726-2
- Grant Writing For Dummies
  0-7645-8416-2
- Home Buying For Dummies
  0-7645-5331-3
- Managing For Dummies
  0-7645-1771-6
- Marketing For Dummies
  0-7645-5600-2

- Personal Finance For Dummies
  0-7645-2590-5*
- Resumes For Dummies
  0-7645-5471-9
- Selling For Dummies
  0-7645-5363-1
- Six Sigma For Dummies
  0-7645-6798-5
- Small Business Kit For Dummies
  0-7645-5984-2
- Starting an eBay Business For Dummies
  0-7645-6924-4
- Your Dream Career For Dummies
  0-7645-9795-7

HOME & BUSINESS COMPUTER BASICS

0-470-05432-8

0-471-75421-8

Also available:
- Cleaning Windows Vista For Dummies
  0-471-78293-9
- Excel 2007 For Dummies
  0-470-03737-7
- Mac OS X Tiger For Dummies
  0-7645-7675-5
- MacBook For Dummies
  0-470-04859-X
- Macs For Dummies
  0-470-04849-2
- Office 2007 For Dummies
  0-470-00923-3

- Outlook 2007 For Dummies
  0-470-03830-6
- PCs For Dummies
  0-7645-8958-X
- Salesforce.com For Dummies
  0-470-04893-X
- Upgrading & Fixing Laptops For Dummies
  0-7645-8959-8
- Word 2007 For Dummies
  0-470-03658-3
- Quicken 2007 For Dummies
  0-470-04600-7

FOOD, HOME, GARDEN, HOBBIES, MUSIC & PETS

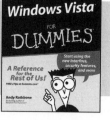

0-7645-8404-9

0-7645-9904-6

Also available:
- Candy Making For Dummies
  0-7645-9734-5
- Card Games For Dummies
  0-7645-9910-0
- Crocheting For Dummies
  0-7645-4151-X
- Dog Training For Dummies
  0-7645-8418-9
- Healthy Carb Cookbook For Dummies
  0-7645-8476-6
- Home Maintenance For Dummies
  0-7645-5215-5

- Horses For Dummies
  0-7645-9797-3
- Jewelry Making & Beading For Dummies
  0-7645-2571-9
- Orchids For Dummies
  0-7645-6759-4
- Puppies For Dummies
  0-7645-5255-4
- Rock Guitar For Dummies
  0-7645-5356-9
- Sewing For Dummies
  0-7645-6847-7
- Singing For Dummies
  0-7645-2475-5

INTERNET & DIGITAL MEDIA

0-470-04529-9

0-470-04894-8

Also available:
- Blogging For Dummies
  0-471-77084-1
- Digital Photography For Dummies
  0-7645-9802-3
- Digital Photography All-in-One Desk Reference For Dummies
  0-470-03743-1
- Digital SLR Cameras and Photography For Dummies
  0-7645-9803-1
- eBay Business All-in-One Desk Reference For Dummies
  0-7645-8438-3
- HDTV For Dummies
  0-470-09673-X

- Home Entertainment PCs For Dummies
  0-470-05523-5
- MySpace For Dummies
  0-470-09529-6
- Search Engine Optimization For Dummies
  0-471-97998-8
- Skype For Dummies
  0-470-04891-3
- The Internet For Dummies
  0-7645-8996-2
- Wiring Your Digital Home For Dummies
  0-471-91830-X

* Separate Canadian edition also available
† Separate U.K. edition also available

Available wherever books are sold. For more information or to order direct: U.S. customers visit www.dummies.com or call 1-877-762-2974.
U.K. customers visit www.wileyeurope.com or call 0800 243407. Canadian customers visit www.wiley.ca or call 1-800-567-4797.

SPORTS, FITNESS, PARENTING, RELIGION & SPIRITUALITY

0-471-76871-5

0-7645-7841-3

Also available:

- Catholicism For Dummies
0-7645-5391-7
- Exercise Balls For Dummies
0-7645-5623-1
- Fitness For Dummies
0-7645-7851-0
- Football For Dummies
0-7645-3936-1
- Judaism For Dummies
0-7645-5299-6
- Potty Training For Dummies
0-7645-5417-4
- Buddhism For Dummies
0-7645-5359-3

- Pregnancy For Dummies
0-7645-4483-7 †
- Ten Minute Tone-Ups For Dummies
0-7645-7207-5
- NASCAR For Dummies
0-7645-7681-X
- Religion For Dummies
0-7645-5264-3
- Soccer For Dummies
0-7645-5229-5
- Women in the Bible For Dummies
0-7645-8475-8

TRAVEL

0-7645-7749-2

0-7645-6945-7

Also available:

- Alaska For Dummies
0-7645-7746-8
- Cruise Vacations For Dummies
0-7645-6941-4
- England For Dummies
0-7645-4276-1
- Europe For Dummies
0-7645-7529-5
- Germany For Dummies
0-7645-7823-5
- Hawaii For Dummies
0-7645-7402-7

- Italy For Dummies
0-7645-7386-1
- Las Vegas For Dummies
0-7645-7382-9
- London For Dummies
0-7645-4277-X
- Paris For Dummies
0-7645-7630-5
- RV Vacations For Dummies
0-7645-4442-X
- Walt Disney World & Orlando For Dummies
0-7645-9660-8

GRAPHICS, DESIGN & WEB DEVELOPMENT

0-7645-8815-X

0-7645-9571-7

Also available:

- 3D Game Animation For Dummies
0-7645-8789-7
- AutoCAD 2006 For Dummies
0-7645-8925-3
- Building a Web Site For Dummies
0-7645-7144-3
- Creating Web Pages For Dummies
0-470-08030-2
- Creating Web Pages All-in-One Desk Reference For Dummies
0-7645-4345-8
- Dreamweaver 8 For Dummies
0-7645-9649-7

- InDesign CS2 For Dummies
0-7645-9572-5
- Macromedia Flash 8 For Dummies
0-7645-9691-8
- Photoshop CS2 and Digital Photography For Dummies
0-7645-9580-6
- Photoshop Elements 4 For Dummies
0-471-77483-9
- Syndicating Web Sites with RSS Feeds For Dummies
0-7645-8848-6
- Yahoo! SiteBuilder For Dummies
0-7645-9800-7

NETWORKING, SECURITY, PROGRAMMING & DATABASES

0-7645-7728-X

0-471-74940-0

Also available:

- Access 2007 For Dummies
0-470-04612-0
- ASP.NET 2 For Dummies
0-7645-7907-X
- C# 2005 For Dummies
0-7645-9704-3
- Hacking For Dummies
0-470-05235-X
- Hacking Wireless Networks For Dummies
0-7645-9730-2
- Java For Dummies
0-470-08716-1

- Microsoft SQL Server 2005 For Dummies
0-7645-7755-7
- Networking All-in-One Desk Reference For Dummies
0-7645-9939-9
- Preventing Identity Theft For Dummies
0-7645-7336-5
- Telecom For Dummies
0-471-77085-X
- Visual Studio 2005 All-in-One Desk Reference For Dummies
0-7645-9775-2
- XML For Dummies
0-7645-8845-1

HEALTH & SELF-HELP

0-7645-8450-2   0-7645-4149-8

Also available:

- Bipolar Disorder For Dummies
  0-7645-8451-0
- Chemotherapy and Radiation
  For Dummies
  0-7645-7832-4
- Controlling Cholesterol For Dummies
  0-7645-5440-9
- Diabetes For Dummies
  0-7645-6820-5* †
- Divorce For Dummies
  0-7645-8417-0 †

- Fibromyalgia For Dummies
  0-7645-5441-7
- Low-Calorie Dieting For Dummies
  0-7645-9905-4
- Meditation For Dummies
  0-471-77774-9
- Osteoporosis For Dummies
  0-7645-7621-6
- Overcoming Anxiety For Dummies
  0-7645-5447-6
- Reiki For Dummies
  0-7645-9907-0
- Stress Management For Dummies
  0-7645-5144-2

EDUCATION, HISTORY, REFERENCE & TEST PREPARATION

0-7645-8381-6   0-7645-9554-7

Also available:

- The ACT For Dummies
  0-7645-9652-7
- Algebra For Dummies
  0-7645-5325-9
- Algebra Workbook For Dummies
  0-7645-8467-7
- Astronomy For Dummies
  0-7645-8465-0
- Calculus For Dummies
  0-7645-2498-4
- Chemistry For Dummies
  0-7645-5430-1
- Forensics For Dummies
  0-7645-5580-4

- Freemasons For Dummies
  0-7645-9796-5
- French For Dummies
  0-7645-5193-0
- Geometry For Dummies
  0-7645-5324-0
- Organic Chemistry I For Dummies
  0-7645-6902-3
- The SAT I For Dummies
  0-7645-7193-1
- Spanish For Dummies
  0-7645-5194-9
- Statistics For Dummies
  0-7645-5423-9

Get smart @ dummies.com®

- **Find a full list of Dummies titles**
- **Look into loads of FREE on-site articles**
- **Sign up for FREE eTips e-mailed to you weekly**
- **See what other products carry the Dummies name**
- **Shop directly from the Dummies bookstore**
- **Enter to win new prizes every month!**

* Separate Canadian edition also available

† Separate U.K. edition also available

Available wherever books are sold. For more information or to order direct: U.S. customers visit www.dummies.com or call 1-877-762-2974.
U.K. customers visit www.wileyeurope.com or call 0800 243407. Canadian customers visit www.wiley.ca or call 1-800-567-4797.

What Readers Are Saying About
Balance Your Body, Balance Your Life

"*Balance Your Body, Balance Your Life* is one of the most amazing books I've ever read. It has really changed my life. I will never think of food in the same way again. Thank you for such wonderful insight. This book is a must-read for everyone."

—Sheila, Nashville, Tennessee

"*Balance Your Body, Balance Your Life* is simply the most honest and best researched book on permanent weight loss that has ever been written! I believe that just reading it will inspire people to lose weight forever . . . and it could change their lives."

—Joan, Registered Physical Therapist, Laguna Beach, CA

"I am so happy to have found your book, *Balance Your Body, Balance Your Life*. I declared it my health bible. I've read it, I think, three times. I cannot tell you how thankful I am to have found you!"

—Gertrude, Texas

"A true healer . . . where were you when I was 20 and foolish? *Balance Your Body, Balance Your Life* is well grounded and very much an idea that can be implemented as a way of life for me. Dr. Taub's book is more like me and the way I am naturally."

—Susan, Chicago

"I love your book, diary—and especially the Wellness Retreat Plan."

—Lynn, Pennsylvania

"I just finished reading your book, *Balance Your Body, Balance Your Life*. I have dramatically increased my intake of fresh fruits and vegetables. Eating fruits and whole grains before noon is perfect, and does leave me with more energy during the day."

—Maria, New Hampshire

"I have your book, *Balance Your Body, Balance Your Life*, and I think it's wonderful."

—Rosemary, South Dakota

"I have read your book, *Balance Your Body, Balance Your Life*, and learned *so* much. Thank you for taking the time to cut through all the misinformation we are bombarded with, and teaching us how we can take responsibility for our health, by following your guidelines."

—Lisa, California

"I am writing to tell you of the wonderful change in my life, and it all started with your book *Balance Your Body, Balance Your Life*. I have lost 12 pounds in all, one pound each week, which I know is the safest way to lose. After reading your book fresh fruits and vegetables actually started tasting much better to me than they ever had. I'm eagerly searching for vegan recipes everywhere and have enjoyed many of the recipes you included in the book. We also take your vitamins and wish to thank you for caring enough to give us the true secret to losing weight . . . thank you, thank you, Dr. Taub!"

—Marcia, Colorado

BALANCE YOUR BODY

BALANCE YOUR LIFE

Total Health Rejuvenation

EDWARD A. TAUB, M.D.

POCKET BOOKS

New York   London   Toronto   Sydney   Singapore

The ideas, procedures, and suggestions in this book are not intended as a substitute for the medical advice of your trained health professional. All matters regarding your health require medical supervision. Consult your physician before adopting the suggestions in this book, as well as about any condition that may require diagnosis or medical attention. The author and publisher disclaim any liability arising directly or indirectly from the use of the book.

 POCKET BOOKS, a division of Simon & Schuster, Inc.
1230 Avenue of the Americas, New York, NY 10020

ISBN: 0-7434-1259-1

First Pocket Books trade paperback printing December 2000

10 9 8 7 6 5 4 3 2 1

POCKET and colophon are registered trademarks of
Simon & Schuster, Inc.

Cover design by Carolyn Lechter; front cover photo by James Holb

Printed in the U.S.A.

To David and Debbie Oliphant

L'Chaim, To Life!

ACKNOWLEDGMENTS

———————————◆———————————

David Oliphant, my friend and partner, first envisioned this book and then wove the vision into reality by encouraging me to believe that I could discover a new theory of nature. He nurtured and strengthened my work with an enormous personal effort that challenged me to new heights.

Debbie Oliphant, my friend and partner, contributed hard work, loving skills, unwavering patience, and artistic ingenuity to this book. Along the way, her courage and personal healing power provided inspiration to everyone in this project.

I'm grateful to Claire Oliphant and Alieta Kalman Fresenius for giving David and Debbie such keen intelligence and imagination.

Lora E. Taub, Ph.D., my daughter and editor, helped me to shape and inspire this book from conception to completion. Her devotion, skills, and sage guidance continue to define my career as an author; every page of this book lives up to her high ideals. Mostly, I hope that my work reflects her best hopes for me. *Namaste*.

Anneli Taub, my wife and cookbook writer, cares for me every day with friendship, unending patience, and wholesome food. How she manages to make green bean soup taste better than boeuf bourguignon is a tribute to my mother-in-law, too.

At Kensington Books, I owe a great debt of gratitude to Walter Zacharius, Steve Zacharius, Lynn Brown, Paul Dinas, Laura Shatzkin, Diane Wright, and Richard Ember, for their grasp, understanding, and belief in my work. My heartfelt thanks also go to Senior Editor Allan Graubard, who critically evaluated each of my ideas and applied his keen intelligence to bring this book to fruition.

I am deeply grateful to all friends and colleagues at QVC for making a Wellness Medical Doctor's dreams come true. Douglas Briggs, Darlene Daggett, Robert Ayd, Judy Grishaver, Jeanine Gendrachi, Jackie Mack, Kim Sheller, Paula Piercy, Scott Sentell, Kevin Else, Marty Rusnak, Lena Hoover, John Link, Robb Cadigan, Babette Burns, and Betty Broder helped me refocus my career into one continuing house call to over 65-million homes.

I want to express my sincere appreciation to Gale Bensussen, Scott Rexinger, Peter Cosgrove, Craig Angell and the rest of the team at Leiner Health Products.

Kathryn Koether contributed a long labor of love by typing the manuscript, providing sound grammatical advice, and keeping us all on deadline. Denise Lerner rose to an urgent task with energy and grace. Publicist Anita Halton, assisted me with dignity and skill. Michelle Di Vincenzo, a former student of the Culinary Institute of America, gave sensitive help with preparing, testing, and tasting recipes.

Justine Amadeo helped me to organize my thoughts and provided me with invaluable insight and editorial assistance for this revision. Artist Mark Hannon depicted the Food Energy Ladder beautifully. Marcus Laux N.D. was very kind to allow me to use his strength training drawings by artist Barbara Mindell. Clint Thompson, C.P.T. inspired the strength training aspect of this revision by keeping me motivated and helping my body feel better at 60 than at 50.

I am grateful to Doug Batezel, Bob Myers, Fred Stern and Julie Schneider of the Bergen Brunswig Company for their support.

I am especially thankful for my friends at Media Productions International, Inc. The trust and skills of Bob Marty, Bill Marty, Jim

Scalem, JoAnn Young and Sven Nebelung are responsible for making this revision for the PBS Special into a reality.

Lanny Taub, M.D., served me with brotherly kindness and advice. Marc Taub, M.D., provided me with much food for thought, and the joy of my first grandchild, Lucas. My parents, Daniel and Roslyn, continuously demonstrated that, after all, love is really all there is.

CONTENTS

◆

◆

Part Three

TRUTH IS ON THE MARCH AND NOTHING WILL STOP IT

Part Four

ENERGY NUTRITION AND THE CYCLE OF LIFE

Part Five

BUILDING A NEW PATH OF LEAST RESISTANCE

Part Six

FOOD IS ENERGY:
A New Mindset and Plan for Permanent Weight Loss and Balanced Energy Throughout the Cycle of Life . . . The Blueprint

Part Ten

NUTRITIONAL SUPPLEMENTS . . .
BEYOND DEFICIENCY 387

Part Eleven

PREVENTIVE THEOLOGY 409

FOREWORD

By Harvey Diamond

———————————————◆———————————————

My colleague and friend, Dr. Edward Taub, is a man fulfilling his life's purpose. He teaches patients how to assume responsibility for their personal health destiny, and shows physicians how to be gentler and more noble. Ever since he first glimpsed the paradigm of wellness, not illness, he has been spreading the word that health is primarily determined by personal responsibility, self-value, and reverence for life. At the same time, he has diagnosed the illness that is undermining Western medicine: *It is based almost entirely on repairing the human body rather than stimulating the will to be well.*

Fifteen years ago, Dr. Taub's powerful foreword for my book, *Fit For Life*, conferred upon it the scientific credibility that helped it become a success. I was grateful for his generous words designating the book a "giant step forward in extending life's span and life's quality." Amazingly, ever since writing that foreword, Dr. Taub has devotedly conveyed its nutritional principles to thousands of patients around the world. Now, on the basis of his extensive clinical experience, he has created *the next step forward in extending life's span and life's quality.*

Readers should cherish this work and take it seriously; Dr. Taub has written a practical guide to the link between nutrition and wellness. His message is essential: Food is nourishment for body, mind, and spirit.

Here is a book from a physician who sees the presence of God in all life, and defines wellness as the graceful dance of energy in balance. I can think of no words that more accurately describe Dr. Taub's contribution to wellness than those in which Albert Einstein described himself and his work: *"The ideals which have lighted me on my way and time and time again given me new courage to face life cheerfully, have been truth, goodness, and beauty."*

These ideals grace the principles that Dr. Taub shares with you in this book, the first modern scientific update of *Fit For Life*. When I was first asked to write this foreword, I unhesitatingly and enthusiastically agreed to do so. As we make our way through this life, on occasion we are fortunate enough to cross paths with others whose integrity and desire to improve the human experience is exceeded only by their love and genuine caring. Just such a man is Dr. Edward Taub, who exemplifies these high-minded ideals. I wholeheartedly support his healing and educational work, for I know his intent is for personal, community, and planetary transformation. I feel honored to have been asked to write this foreword.

—Harvey Diamond,
co-author, *Fit For Life*

INTRODUCTION

◆

What a wonderful opportunity to update my book to help you live life to the fullest! When I originally wrote this book, my intent was to help as many readers as possible by setting the record straight on some disturbing misinformation about nutrition. I created a scientifically sound plan for a healthy way to eat foods you love and still lose weight. But since this book was first published just one year ago, stress, obesity and degenerative diseases have soared to record levels in America. Now even people of other nations who are following our example are becoming as stressed, obese and ill as we are. The truth about good food and nutrition has been hidden from us until now, and we are almost helpless to fight back against the so-called experts who keep assuring us they know what's best. *This is why I have updated and revised this book. It is even more important now than ever before for you to read the pages that follow—to absorb it and live it.*

As a Wellness Medical Doctor, I have always sought to help my patients and readers stay healthy and live healthy, especially women and children—*because they are our future.* In order to do this, I have developed a psychotherapeutic treatment plan to help you *prevent* and *reverse* disease, as well as lose weight permanently through *"Total Health Rejuvenation."* This requires stimulating your own natural healing force, which is equivalent to the presence of God in every one of your trillions of cells. Medical science defines the "healing force" as "merely an array of polypeptide chemicals such as endorphins and enkephalins," so no wonder your healing force beguiles physicians who search in all the wrong places and ask the wrong questions! If you will allow me to be your Wellness Medical Doctor, I promise to help create a healthier understanding and environment in which your body, mind and soul can thrive. *Please . . . just trust me to touch your life in a positive manner.*

"Total Health Rejuvenation"—stimulating your healing force—begins deep inside you, at the level of your soul, and radiates outward. This is why my plan is based on "Integrative Medicine"—combining the best of modern science with traditional spirituality. I believe your health is mostly determined by your own personal responsibility, self-value and reverence for life. Therefore, I have now introduced the concept of "Preventive Theology." Basically, you will be asked to expand your words and beliefs into action by behaving ethically and being a loving person. "Preventive Theology" entails having faith, that if you take one step towards God, God will take a thousand steps towards you. You see, your natural healing force is like an eternal flame, perhaps neglected but still burning deeply within you. *Now you can rekindle your healing force from a tiny flicker to a brilliant flame . . . you **can** do it . . . you can live life to the fullest!*

I also promise you that just *reading* this book will change the way you look at food forever, and cause you to lose excess weight permanently, healthfully and naturally. In modern terminology, this phenomenon is known as *cognitive restructuring* and *conscious re-programming.* In other words, enough seeds will be planted in your mind so that one day, very soon, they will sprout. You may try to ignore what you are about to read in *Balance Your Body, Balance Your Life,* but you will always remember what you have read . . . *that's why it is so important to read on.*

The truth about good food and proper nutrition cannot be conveyed to you in mere words, because you have much too much mental baggage blocking the way and you are limited to looking at the world through rose-colored glasses placed before your eyes by the so-called nutrition experts. However, *just by reading this book,* you will begin to peel away the layers of misinformation about food that now befog your mind. Once you glimpse the truth, and then realize the full extent of the following truth, you will begin to live life to the fullest: Americans are being fed, fattened and sickened for profits; you and your loved ones, *especially women and children,* have simply become a commodity for the giant food industry, which controls our food supply as well as our minds. *Please . . . just observe the changes that will occur in you as you read on.*

I wish to bring the following news items to your attention. They were published in 1999, after the first edition of *Balance Your Body, Balance Your Life* was published.

▶ An article in the *Journal of the American Medical Association* announced that the long-term intake of *cereal fiber* decreased the risk of coronary heart disease among women by as much as 34 percent. This article provided further reason to replace refined, processed junk food with whole grain products, especially since the *already proven* benefits of fiber include preventing diverticulitis, hypertension, non-insulin dependent diabetes mellitus and cancer of the mouth, pharynx, larynx, esophagus and stomach.

▶ Yet despite the benefits of fiber—*especially cereal fiber*—an article in the *Los Angeles Times* announced that a major cereal company would probably drop its new line of healthy, grain-based, cholesterol-lowering foods by year's end because it had not achieved its "sales and distribution" goals. The products, which contained natural fibers, will be dropped because "the company stands to make a higher profit on new convenience foods and extensions of its breakfast snacks *(popular sugar-laden cereals)*, rather than spend a lot of time and money trying to interest consumers in the healthier products."

▶ A 1999 article in *Pediatrics*—the professional journal of America's pediatricians—reported the stunning news that the results of a 1996 article about fruit juice in *Pediatrics* were false! The earlier article had concluded that "Excessive fruit juice intake was associated with short stature and obesity in pre-school children." However, while the results of the earlier false study were quickly sensationalized throughout the major news media, the *updated* 1999 report was virtually ignored! Unfortunately, for the last three years, America's pediatricians have not been recommending that preschool children drink much fresh fruit juice . . . *and even worse, the myth has spread to millions of parents and growing children.*

▶ Finally, the United States Department of Agriculture (USDA) announced the "Children's Food Pyramid," which actually *recommends* and features pictures of ice cream and hamburgers for kids! The National Food Processors Association, the voice of the $430 billion food processing industry, immediately sent out a press re-lease: "We are pleased that the new 'Children's Food Pyramid' in-cludes depictions of various processed foods. These graphics will be useful in helping children and their parents to understand that canned and frozen fruits and vegetables—as well as other pro-cessed foods—should be just as much a part of a healthful diet as fresh foods." Thankfully, the prestigious and non-profit "Center for Science In The Public Interest" headlined *its* press release this way: "The USDA's 'Children's Food Pyramid' reinforces kids' *worst* eating habits and may *increase* heart disease in the next generation. It shows once again that the USDA's mission to promote the meat and dairy industries is incompatible with its responsibility to promote good nutrition." *Wow! Wake up, Americans! Can you believe what is being recommended to our children—our future?*

Let's try a test so that you can prove to yourself what you already intuitively know. Go to your local market and buy some fresh or-anges, fresh strawberries, fresh peaches and fresh tomatoes. Then buy some orange juice from concentrate, frozen strawberries, a can of peaches and a can of tomatoes. Now squeeze the oranges to make a glass of juice and place it next to a glass of juice from con-centrate. Defrost the strawberries and put them next to the fresh ones. Finally, after pouring out the canned peaches and tomatoes, place them next to the freshly sliced produce. Close your eyes and do a taste test. *Which would you rather be eating or drinking?* I know this isn't exactly "rocket science," but it's time for you to stop believ-ing all the so-called experts who insist that "freshness" doesn't mat-ter as long as the same "scientifically measurable nutrients" are present . . . *Sure!*

It's also clearly time for the Food Energy Ladder (see Part Six) to replace the harmful and obsolete food pyramid myths. Foods that are among the top steps of the Food Energy Ladder are infused with energy and vitality transferred from the sun through photo-synthesis. When you eat these foods, they transfer the sun's energy and vitality to you, igniting the healing force within you, which is the only natural and proper way to lose weight permanently. It's so very simple: *Foods at the top of the Food Energy Ladder are natural fat burners and foods at the bottom are natural fat accumulators!* Yet there are no forbidden foods and there is no sense of deprivation.

♦

The Food Energy Ladder motto is "Everything in moderation, including moderation." *How about actually eating more and weighing less?*

For this updated and revised edition of *Balance Your Body, Balance Your Life*, I have rearranged the Food Energy Ladder based on further science and research (especially to help men and women in the second half of their natural human lifecycle (see Part Four). For instance, if you are approaching fifty years old, you will need to lessen your intake of pasta and white rice, and increase your daily intake of water. You see, *Balance Your Body, Balance Your Life* is all about learning to pinpoint where you are in your own personal human lifecycle in order to take appropriate steps for "Total Health Rejuvenation" and permanent weight loss. You will find that the Food Energy Ladder is truly a picture that is worth a thousand words . . . *and a concept that is user-friendly and easy to understand.*

Unfortunately, we have become the most overweight, hypertensive, atherosclerotic, diabetic, ulcer-ridden, cancer-, stroke- and coronary-prone people in the world. Fifty-five percent of Americans are overweight with dire consequences for health—*especially women and children.* The rate of obesity in children has doubled in the last 25 years so that we may soon be facing a major crisis in the incidence of type II Diabetes Mellitus. *In 1999, researchers at a major hospital reported a quadrupling of the disease among children and teenagers in the last few years!* Our minds have been programmed into actually expecting illness—especially diseases related to the way we eat. Media messages have led us to believe we have no choice but to accept illness and enjoy eating food that is lacking in energy and vitality. *But you do have a choice . . . and you don't have to be overweight!*

SOLUTIONS TO THE CRUEL DIET HOAX

A multibillion-dollar-a-year diet industry has grown into a cruel hoax that is threatening your health because yo-yo diets don't work *and they can harm you.* The biological makeup of men and women has not changed in thousands of years. So why are there thousands of diet books in the marketplace? Because diets don't work and we are always looking for a quick fix! The current fad diets based on

◆

eating high amounts of animal protein and avoiding fresh fruits are especially harmful. The way high protein diets work is by first causing the body to turn acidic, and then as a result, become sick. Sick bodies tend to lose weight—just as those that are afflicted with cancer. But people ought not to be tampering with their God-given metabolism in order to lose weight, especially with diets that discourage fruits—*God's food.*

The current fad diets based on eating according to your blood type are so completely ridiculous that there is little to say about them other than you might as well believe that the moon is made out of cheese! Also, reading *Balance Your Body, Balance Your Life* will be far more beneficial to you *(and a whole lot safer)* than any over-the-counter or prescription diet pills. *Please use your common sense. There is nothing new under the sun.* Food is energy that nature provides to sustain you in good health during your entire personal human lifecycle, from birth to death. So, if you are trying to lose weight, stop yo-yo dieting now! Trying to diet your excess weight off is like trying to bail water out of a rowboat without first plugging the leak. Now you have a choice—with the new Food Energy Ladder, you don't have to be overweight and you can still eat the foods you love!

All my proven clinical solutions for *"Total Health Rejuvenation"* are in this book because it's important to realize that losing excess weight is much more than just a cosmetic issue. Are you short of breath, suffering with high blood pressure, experiencing backaches or afflicted with adult-onset diabetes? *Losing weight will help you solve these problems.* Losing weight will also help you prevent, or even reverse: fibromyalgia, chronic fatigue syndrome, arthritis, varicose veins, gallbladder disease, colitis, irritable bowel syndrome, strokes, heart attacks and even cancer! By taking control of your own health destiny, you can lose weight permanently and naturally, and live longer and more lovingly. *This is not a diet book . . . it's about "Total Health Rejuvenation" . . . and I promise you that just reading this book will begin triggering your own natural healing force.*

Yes, there are no quick fixes and just a cursory reading will not cause a miracle to happen. But being overweight begins and persists in your mind, and I have written this book to instigate *change* in your mind. You will realize that food is your "energy, not your enemy." Just reading this book . . . *very carefully and very thoughtfully* . . . will cause you to lose weight permanently and naturally because it will help you to rediscover love for yourself, love for others, and love for God. This goal is crucial because being overweight means your body is ill. And in this time of incredible stress, I.L.L. has become largely equivalent to *"I Lack Love."* Just reading this book empowers you to regain love . . . *the most powerful healer of all!*

You can lose as much as 10% of your excess body weight each year and keep it off until you approach your natural weight. Also, women will understand why they should weigh more than they imagine (weight standards are created by males with visions of beauty that are culturally driven by the widespread images of fashion models). I have also added a very simple strength training section to the book, especially to help men and women over fifty to strengthen and tone their bodies so that they can live life to the fullest.

I have expanded the scope of the book's journal writing section (Part Six), because again, more new research published in 1999 suggests that keeping a journal is far more therapeutic than even I was aware of. An article in the *Journal of the American Medical Association* showed that asthma and arthritis patients who wrote about their traumatic experiences and stress for just 15–20 minutes a day, for only three or four days, reduced their recurring symptoms of asthma and arthritis by as much as 47 percent. *Remarkably, the improvements lasted for up to four months.* An accompanying editorial praised the study and noted that if a similar outcome had been experienced with a new drug, it would be in widespread use within a short time. I surely agree, and that's why I have updated and revised the book into a psychotherapeutic and spiritual road map for just 28 days to get you going . . . *so that you can learn to live life to the fullest, forever!*

IT'S JUST FOR A DAY!

Finally, I have some more very good news that makes the book's 28-Day Plan for *Total Health Rejuvenation* and permanent weight loss even easier. Because your health is mostly determined by per-

♦

sonal responsibility, self-value and reverence for life, it's obvious that you are required to take at least one small step to prepare for the psychotherapeutic and spiritual benefits of the book. Your Personal Wellness Retreat (described in Part Five) provides you with the powerful *kick-start* necessary to trigger the internal process of *"Total Health Rejuvenation."* However, now further clinical research has allowed me to cut the time of your Personal Wellness Retreat in half. *It's just for a day!* It's a day for setting aside time for healthy food, fresh air, easy exercise, soft music, meditation, journal writing, resting and prayer. It's a day for catharsis (your Day), and for getting rid of old baggage to make room for a leaner, healthier, and more energetic you. It really sounds like a vacation, doesn't it? Please remember that you can take *"your Day"* as many times as you wish in the future—especially when life's challenges seem to be throwing you off balance and you need to get back on track. You're going to be absolutely amazed at how good you will feel when you start living life to the fullest and realize your full potential. That's just the beginning. *I know you can do it . . . please read on . . . and remember, I only have your health and well-being in my heart.*

TO-LIFE!

BALANCE YOUR BODY
BALANCE YOUR LIFE

Part One

FAT IS NOT JUST A PHYSICAL PROBLEM

How to Change Your Inherited Beliefs and Emotions to Solve Your Weight Problems Forever

As Medicine has become more specialized, we have lost sight of the fact that love is the most powerful medicine of all. We forgot how a simple mother's kiss can help take away our hurt, and we also forgot how a concerned doctor's reassurance and guidance can help make us better. My patients have become healthier and lost weight permanently by following this 28 Day Plan for *"Total Health Rejuvenation."* It's based on TLC . . . *tender, loving care that keeps you well.*

Health is your most precious asset, but with all the confusing information about how to be well, and especially how to lose weight, how in the world do you know if you are even close to doing the right thing? This is why my plan for *Total Health Rejuvenation* consists of 28 daily doses of self-administered TLC! Just reading this book will cause you to become a person of strength and conviction who recognizes the truth and power of your choices.

You probably know that the foods you eat affect your health, vitality, and well-being. However, it is also important to know that most of the deadly diseases that afflict Americans are influenced by food—heart disease, cancer, stroke, diabetes, chronic liver disease and atherosclerosis. Small changes in the way you eat today will help you and your family to live a healthier life in the future.

Small changes in diet, though, are not enough. What really matters are your attitudes toward food. Your thoughts, beliefs, and emotions determine which foods you choose to eat. That is why *you eat only as well as you think*. It is the reason why the path to permanent weight loss and healthy nutrition begins with what you think and how you feel about food. When it comes to beliefs about food and eating, we have been raised on a media diet of misinformation and myths. Simply put, some of our basic perceptions about food, learned as early as infancy, are unhealthy misconceptions.

Surprisingly, most of us take better care of our cars than our bodies. You surely can think of many other examples that are more applicable to you in your own life, such as your work, home, boat, garden, or even your pet. Think of one example with which you can identify and apply it to yourself as you read on. When you were born, your body, generally, was like a fine-tuned, upscale car. Just as a car requires proper care and maintenance, so does your body. If you care for your body, maintain its health, and, most of all, provide it with proper fuel, then, like a fine car, it will thrive for a long, long time. But, like an automobile, if you neglect your body, fail to maintain it, and fill it with inferior fuel, it will deteriorate into a junk heap.

Conventional Nutritional Wisdom: Separating Fact from Fiction

Now, I would like you to start giving your body the nutritional tune-up it is starving for by tuning up your attitudes and thoughts about food. Thoughts, after all, are the motor behind every action. Moreover, without a change in attitude, most people cannot make lasting changes in their diet. Your diet may change, but as long as your underlying attitudes about food remain unchanged, you will probably revert back to the eating habits from which you want to free yourself in the first place. Your thoughts are the driving force behind what you choose to eat. So, as you embark on this journey to nutritional well-being, you need to flush out the misperceptions about food that corrode and clog your mental motor. Remember: *what you eat is a response to how you think*.

Why have your thoughts about nutrition been steered in the wrong direction? Almost every month a new nutritional "theory" flashes across the television screen or splashes across the front page of newspapers. Most of these "theories" are fads, developed to market and sell some new diet product—a meal-replacement shake, a miracle herb, a cellulite-busting cream. The claims of some are so outrageous, they are almost laughable; but because we are hungry for better health and weight loss, we do pay attention to them. How can you reliably distinguish between the hype and the hope? *Balance Your Body, Balance Your Life* will teach you how by constantly reminding you of your own innate nutritional wisdom.

Why is there so much confusion? The often contradictory data on nutrition that reach us, sometimes daily, is one answer. It seems that recommendations from the halls of science are always changing: Once we were told to reduce starchy foods, now we are told to eat more starch; then we were advised that all oil is bad, only to find out later that olive oil is healthful. No wonder it's so hard for us to know exactly what we should or should not eat!

Because few of us have the time or inclination to personally track the scientific research, we rely on information filtered to us through the media. Unfortunately, most of this information just fuels the myths and misconceptions about food that dominate our culture. Most of us also acquire our nutritional information from television. But, for the most part, television is an unreliable guide to healthful eating. What can you really learn about food from TV? By today's standards, an "in-depth" television news story lasts two minutes. The average news story is closer to thirty seconds. And the result?

Diluted, oversimplified, often contradictory data that contributes more to our confusion than to our clarity.

Television is in the business of entertainment, which is supported by its advertisers. TV advertisers profit from creating new food fads. New diets and diet gurus are sensationalized on television, because sensationalism attracts audiences and boosts ratings, which in turn draws advertising dollars. The advertisers who pay billions of dollars to promote their products during the news shows, for example, are also among the leading contributors of nutritional misinformation! The food industry, fast-food chains, and diet/exercise industries generate much of the advertising revenues for the television stations.

As public awareness about nutrition and health has grown, so has our dissatisfaction with the information the media makes available to us. A recent poll revealed that people believe the most trustworthy source of nutritional information is our doctors. Yet for most people, correct nutritional advice/information has become harder and harder to come by—and it isn't free! Access to doctors is limited by HMOs and managed care. If you do get in to see your doctor and want to talk about nutrition, you may discover that he or she is among the 60 percent of physicians who are themselves overweight! In many cases, even your doctor's nutritional advice may be outdated and misleading.

Balance Your Body, Balance Your Life will help guide you out of this maze of myths that influences how you think and feel about food. Then and only then can you get back on the road to eating properly.

There is one myth in particular that you should toss from your mental baggage right away. It is the prevailing belief that, if you have been overweight for a long time, once you reach a certain age you will always be overweight. *No one is predestined to be overweight all of their life.* There is no "magic age" at which losing weight becomes improbable or impossible. And although it is commonly believed that it is easier to lose weight when you are young, recent findings suggest just the opposite. Older people trying to lose weight may actually have an advantage because they turn their past experiences with failed diets into knowledge that will help them lose weight now. In other words, people between the ages of thirty and fifty who have spent years trying to lose weight can draw from that experience in effective ways. They have greater knowledge and experience of what does *not* work, are less likely to be drawn to fads, and have great determination to succeed at last.

So, readers upwards of thirty who want to lose weight—a lot or a little—let go of the idea that you will always be overweight. *No one is born to be fat, and no one is predestined to be fat forever.* Heredity influences body shape and size, but fatness is not a biologically inherited trait. A genetic disposition toward obesity may exist, but *it is the culture of eating that you live in* that will turn a disposition into reality. The fact that you have overweight relatives does not mean that you are destined to live *your* life overweight. Even if you have dieted unsuccessfully in the past, now you can turn those experiences around—you can use them to help you.

There is a second powerful myth that discourages many people from trying to lose weight: the only way to lose weight is to eat less. Although many studies have shown that reductions in food intake will not lead to healthful, lasting weight loss, this myth refuses to die. *Eating less does not guarantee success.* You can, in fact, eat *more* of some foods and still lose weight. It is not the *amount* of food you eat, but the *kinds* of food you eat. Foods low in fat and high in fiber—like vegetables, fruits, and grains—contain fewer calories than high fat foods, so you can enjoy them in plentiful amounts without gaining weight.

As you get ready to make changes in your diet, let's get rid of the thought that *you must eat less to lose weight.* Erase the notion from your mental blackboard that deprivation is the key to dieting. Eating to *balance your body* and *balance your life* encourages you to eat less of some foods, but invites you to enjoy plenty of delicious, healthful, natural foods.

Because the lessons you have learned about food are so deeply ingrained, even going back to your childhood, they are difficult lessons to unlearn. Each one of us has in our memory a child who recalls the lessons of the four food groups. The knowledge you received as a young child was just the start of a long, misleading education about food and your relationship to food. Much of that education now hurts your health more than it helps. It is time to graduate from the school of thought you've been swimming in since childhood. It is time to change the way you think about food altogether, and forever.

Balance Your Body, Balance Your Life is not a diet. Diets, as everyone who has tried them knows, do not last. This plan doesn't begin by changing what you eat. The more important change occurs in what you know, how you think, and how you feel. *Short-term weight loss results from dietary changes, but lasting, successful weight loss results from changes in your attitudes, habits, emotions, and beliefs toward food.*

You must recognize the myths of nutrition that have contributed to the way you think about food, the majority of which took root in your mind when you were a child. As a child, you were taught to believe certain things about food; as an adult, these beliefs are reinforced on a daily basis by the food, diet, and exercise industries. These multibillion-dollar industries are so powerful and so profitable because they succeed at making people feel weak. Even though most people know from firsthand experience that diets generally do not live up to their promises, billions of dollars are spent on diet products every year. Stop giving these industries your attention and your money. They will not make you thinner, only poorer. And they may make you sick.

To change the way you think about food, you must look at the values, feelings, and thoughts about food that you were raised on, shaped by your family, your teachers, your environment, and your culture. Once you examine these long-standing misperceptions, you can redefine the value and meaning of food in your life and in the lives of your loved ones forever!

Time and time again, I've seen many patients who have struggled for years to lose weight make the final, necessary breakthrough and reach their weight loss goals. Why? Because they stopped wasting time and money on diet gimmicks. They gave up the belief that they had to suffer on starvation diets or use medicinal or surgical shortcuts. After years of unsuccessful, painful, and disappointing attempts to lose weight, they finally found the key to permanent weight loss. It wasn't in a bottle of pills, in a strict calorie-controlled diet, in meal-replacement shakes or in fanatical exercise programs. *The key was in changing their outlook on food.* Instead of feeling denied of foods that were keeping them unhealthy and overweight, they began to focus on foods that naturally promote health, energy, and weight loss.

One patient, a 45-year-old woman named Emily,* who had been on and off diets from the time she was nine, explained the change in perception that led to dramatic changes in her weight: "I used to spend all of my time worrying about the foods that I was *not allowed* to eat. Because they were fattening and forbidden, I wanted them even more, especially rich desserts. Either I was eating them all the time, or I was on a diet and *thinking* about eating them all the time. Finally, I realized that diets and denial were getting me nowhere, and what I really needed to do was get out of the dieter's mindset of deprivation." Like so many other patients with whom I have worked, when Emily redefined the meaning of food in her life, when she stopped obsessing about dead foods and just started eating live foods, she began to lose weight and has kept it off ever since.

The way you think and feel about food, and the value you give to it, is not natural. These attitudes, feelings, and meanings are as much created by the culture you grew up in as by food industries and their marketing allies. Once you understand the origins of your thoughts and emotions about food, however, you can resist the values that marketers especially attach to food. You can then create your own truly natural and healthy relationship with food.

Unfortunately, we have learned to think of food as the enemy, and to see the refrigerator as a battlefield. *But food is not the enemy; it is your energy!* Once you realize this, the refrigerator no longer has to be a battlefield; instead, it becomes a lively garden of health and vital energy.

Because we live in a diet-crazed culture, many of us are battling with our bodies. Diets are our weapons. But most of these weapons are just blunt knives. The only way to end the battle is to surrender to your body's nutritional needs and wisdom. Your body knows exactly what it needs for nourishment, and it knows exactly how to achieve and maintain your personal optimal weight. Your greatest resource in losing weight and keeping it off is not a weapon—it is

*I thank my patients who thoughtfully agreed to share their stories with my readers. To protect their privacy, the names used in this book are fictitious.

the wisdom hidden within you. Now you can learn to use that wisdom despite the roadblocks set in your path.

Since the early 1980s in particular, weight consciousness has turned into a cultural obsession fed by an over $50-billion-per-year diet and exercise industry. Our society is choked with images and messages about appearance and body weight. And with the average person encountering numerous commercial messages each day, they become very hard to resist. In fact, these images and messages create very powerful myths on their own about health, beauty, and strength. They found expectations and standards that, for the majority of us, are simply unattainable, unrealistic, and unhealthy.

Right now, as you are reading this, nearly 60 million Americans are dieting in some manner or another. At the same time, nearly another 60 million people think they need to be on a diet but are not. Diets have become a national obsession that afflicts men, women, and children. On average, males are twenty to thirty pounds heavier than their ideal weight; women are between fifteen and thirty pounds overweight; and even children carry, on average, ten to twenty percent more weight than they should. If so many of us are dieting, and spending billions of dollars to do it, ask yourself: Why are rates of obesity increasing rather than diminishing?

Along with such obesity, a shocking number of people suffer from eating disorders such as anorexia and bulimia—currently about 10 million—another indication of the ineffectiveness of the available methods of dieting. The way we think about food is hurting our health and sabotaging our efforts to lose weight and keep it off. Our nation's collective consciousness about nutrition is extremely out of balance.

How did food become the enemy? What turned the refrigerator into a place of fear rather than a Garden of Eden? Take a look at your children's attitudes or of those children close to you. Children observe and internalize their parents' eating habits—the good and the bad. From their parents, children first learn what foods to crave, to resist, to indulge in, and to avoid. Children initially learn from their parents how to *feel* and *think* about food. Children learn that some foods carry positive emotional associations while others carry just the opposite.

When I was growing up, I learned from my parents that different foods were charged with symbolic meanings. My father associated food with his success as the family provider. For him, success meant the finest beef on the table every night. My mother taught us another lesson. Even when she said she was famished, my mother never finished a meal. Only later did I realize that, for her, leaving food on her plate symbolized her restraint, her ability to resist temptation. The untouched potato and the half-eaten steak were signs that her willpower was stronger than the temptation to clean her plate.

If you don't have children, think about your experiences around the table when you were a child. What meanings did your parents attach to different kinds of food? What foods did they insist you eat? What foods were you forbidden to eat?

When I was a boy, my grandparents always encouraged my brother and I to eat second and third helpings when they were available. Do you remember this? *"Eat, eat, it's good for you."* We were never cautioned about overeating. In fact, a little bit of extra weight was considered ideal—a sign that we were well cared for. Today, the message is different.

What Children Learn About Nutrition May Be Bad for Their Health

Parents worry about their children's weight much more today than they used to. Some of this concern is justified, as the rate of overweight children has increased steadily over the past decades. Approximately one out of every four children between the ages of six and seven is overweight, which is *double* the number from just thirty years ago. This may seem surprising, but keep in mind that children's weights have followed the same patterns as their parents' weight. Statistics vary, but approximately one-half of all adults are overweight.

Parents should be proactive if their children are overweight, but worrying tends more to feed the problem than not. Often, when parents worry excessively about their children's weight, they perpetuate their children's overeating. Children learn from their parents to worry about food, to be obsessed about how much and what they eat, and this worry feeds their anxieties about food. This is where unhealthy attitudes toward food begin. What is the greatest risk for overweight children? It is that they will grow up with the mindset and emotions that will lead them to become overweight adults.

Like so many things, food often becomes a focus for children's rebellion against their parents. Unless your children are excessively overweight, *don't* worry about their weight. *Do* be a good role model and teach your children positive lessons about food. *Don't* put your children on diets or monitor how much they eat at every meal and in between. *Do* encourage physical activity. *Do* prepare healthful meals of wholesome natural foods that are low in animal fat and refined sugar, and have abundant amounts of fresh fruits available when your children want a snack. *Set the example*. This approach will not only help them shed the excess weight they carry around with them but, most importantly, it will help prevent them from becoming overweight adults. *Don't teach your children that food is the enemy. Teach them that food is a wonderful source of energy . . . food is energy!*

There is a big difference between modifying your overweight children's eating habits and putting them on a diet. Most diets are based on cutting calories. Children at any age can sense when something is being taken away from them. When food is withheld from children, they usually don't understand why. It can feel like they are being punished or deprived. Feelings of hurt then undermine the goal of the diet, because they usually lead an overweight person to seek food to heal the hurt of being punished. Remember, your children's peers may be eating the foods that you do not allow or want your children to eat.

Diets don't teach children about nutrition. Diets teach children about deprivation and craving. And every child hungers for what they feel deprived of having, whether it's a new bicycle, a trip to Disneyland, a new pair of tennis shoes, or junk food. Trying to teach children to resist the temptation of cookies, candy bars, hamburgers, pizza, and ice cream only makes those foods more appealing. What is off-limits in the fridge is, inevitably, the food your children most crave! You don't have to be a trained psychologist to understand why—it's common sense!

Growing children need proper nutrition, and diets just don't deliver. In fact, children whose parents or doctor have placed them on low-calorie or low-fat diets are known to experience many health problems: mental and physical fatigue, constipation, muscle loss, dehydration, dry skin, hair loss, and restless sleep. When kids feel this crummy, they are likely to eat poorly. For parents and children alike, the best approach is a comprehensive one, where food is perceived as part of an enjoyable, healthy, active lifestyle. Increase the amount of live, fresh foods in your diet, balance this with healthy amounts of physical activity, and set a vibrant, healthy example.

For adults and children, inactivity is often a greater culprit than eating too much. *Inactivity inspires obesity.* It has been reported that children spend more time in front of the television than they do in the classroom. And while in front of the television, they're often snacking on fat-laden or sugar-filled junk foods. Children who spend several hours watching television each day are much more likely to be overweight than those who do not. Children should take part in hobbies and interactive activities that stimulate their minds while building healthy bodies and self-esteem.

In 1996, the U.S. surgeon general reported that approximately half of the children and young adults between the ages of twelve and twenty-one do not engage in any vigorous activity. Inactivity contributes to unhealthy weight gain. The encouraging fact is that even a small increase in physical activity, coupled with proper eating habits, is the best way to healthy weight loss. Children's opportunities for physical activity are also shrinking: Nearly two-thirds of our schools have cut down on physical education classes, while after-school clubs are losing their appeal because they are too costly for schools and parents and, in some cases, even too competitive for children to enjoy them.

Computers are another issue. Today kids play more on computers than they play outdoors. And while children's computer skills and knowledge are important to develop, at the same time children

are losing other skills that are just as crucial. The strength, endur-
ance, and coordination that comes from physical activity builds
children's self-confidence. Just like adults, when children feel good
about themselves, they will naturally feel more motivated to take
better care of themselves.

Overcoming obesity and promoting health should also be a *family affair*. Both adults and children need more physical activity than
they currently get. When the whole family engages in playful physical activities—hiking, swimming, biking, or walking, to name just
a few—everyone benefits. As a parent, you will also reap the benefits of physical activity for your own health—a great double benefit!
You will set for your children a positive example to ensure their
good health and well-being. Remember, your children will carry
these lessons with them wherever they go and for the rest of their
lives.

How can it be that in a culture so obsessed with dieting, one out
of every four children is overweight? How can parents raise
healthy, nutritionally smart children in a culture so consumed with
dieting? You *can* grow healthy children in a diet-crazed culture. As
I've said before, the positive examples you set are vital to your children now and as they grow up. Parents can make healthful eating
and physical activities fun for their children. You can guide them
on a path to nutritional awareness from the get-go. Once they are
firmly on that path, they will not succumb to false promises. They
will not let the diet culture's mindset about food become their own.
You will build up their defenses against false premises and promises through example and education.

Involve your children in the learning process while you are learning new things about nutrition and health. Make it fun and exciting! The patterns of eating that children develop are based on their
observations of how and what you eat. It's never too early to turn
your children on to natural eating. Let them accompany you when
you shop for food. If you can, spend some time in the produce area
and show them the different fruits and vegetables. Make going to
the supermarket a fun learning adventure!

A Saturday trip to a local farmer's market introduces kids not
only to a dazzling display of the freshest foods, but it gives them a
chance to meet the people who grow these foods with care and love.

The farmers usually will invite you to taste their delicious produce, which is a great way to introduce children to new varieties of fruits and vegetables. Make sure, however, that whatever you or your kids eat is thoroughly washed. Let kids taste for themselves the enormous difference between the flavor of a canned peach and that of a perfectly ripened peach picked fresh from the tree that morning. Explain the difference to them, and point out the additives in the ingredients section of the label on the can. Also point out that one peach is fresh and full of energy while the other is old, canned, and chemically preserved!

Establishing new eating habits can be fun for you and your family, especially when everyone is involved. The entire family can experience together how tasty healthful eating is. Remember, this is *not* about dieting. The changes you are making are for a lifetime of better health and ideal weight for you and your loved ones. Developing healthy eating habits for yourself and your children (or the children you care for) is important. It is a beginning, a beginning that, when taken collectively, can work against what I call our *nutritional crisis.*

This crisis can be overwhelming, especially for young girls. Simply, too many young girls succumb to obsessive dieting and worrying about their weight, even as early as age six. I call this the *sexy fashion doll complex.* Judith, a six-year-old girl, came for an office visit once, carrying with her a daintily dressed doll. As I spoke with her mother and examined the child, Judith chatted away with her doll. She was infatuated with the doll, petting her hair, praising her beauty, admiring her body. I couldn't help asking Judith why she liked the doll so much. She told me with her bright, innocent eyes, "Because she's skinny and beautiful, and I want to be just like her."

Now, it's just a doll, after all, so what's the big deal? I could see the power that the doll had over Judith. I also saw how a doll whose own body did not possess natural human proportions was shaping Judith's body image. Still, the doll enticed Judith, as it entices most young girls, teaching them to admire a physical form both unhealthy and unrealistic. From a very early age, young girls can develop a distorted image of their bodies, including an unreasonable weight for which to strive.

By the age of ten, most girls have already begun a career of dieting. A recent study of fourth-grade girls found that almost 90 percent of the girls were already on a diet. By high school, the numbers soar even higher. By the time young women reach college, this obsession with weight has often escalated to grievous levels. One out of every four young women is bulimic or anorexic.

You can keep your children from falling into the trap of obsessive dieting by helping them, at an early age, to increase their knowledge and change their mindset about food. If children develop healthy attitudes about food early in life, they will have a strong foundation for nutritional health throughout the rest of their life.

I cared for thousands of children in my pediatrics practice and observed that, except for those with metabolic disorders, the children who were overweight had parents who were also overweight. Research is inconclusive on how much obesity is genetically inherited. But while we're unsure about which parents pass on fat genes to their children, we have no doubt that children inherit their parent's attitudes, habits, and beliefs about food.

Low self-esteem and body hatred foster poor eating choices. With eating disorders, the food choices fueled by these self-deprecating thoughts can be disastrous. Why do children and adults fall into traps of obsession and body hatred? How do we become ensnared in dangerous webs of weight obsession? In addition to poor eating habits, many of us—especially females—have poor images of ourselves and our bodies. It's important to keep in mind that *good nutrition begins with body image*. Remember also that *you eat only as well as you think*. It's not just how you think about food, but how you think about *yourself* that influences what you eat.

Each of us has something we would like to change about our body—we crave longer legs, smaller feet, narrower hips. Many of us tend to take this desire to the extreme and develop distorted body images, which can drive poor eating habits. So take a moment to think about the questions in the following chart. Assessing your body image is just as important as assessing your body fat, cholesterol level, and blood pressure. Your thoughts and emotions about your body are the very thoughts that compel you to eat foods that raise your body fat, cholesterol level, and blood pressure. So, review each question below, as if you were having an honest, heart-to-heart talk with yourself.

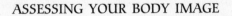

ASSESSING YOUR BODY IMAGE

▶ When you look in the mirror, are you generally happy with what you see?

▶ Do you avoid looking in full-length mirrors?

▶ Looking in the mirror, do you focus on things you'd like to change?

▶ Is there a part of your body that you dislike?

▶ What part of your body do you like best?

▶ How do you think others see you?

▶ What would you like to change about your body?

▶ Can you look in the mirror and smile?

It's okay to want to change things about your body, okay to long for leaner legs, a flatter tummy, a trimmer waist. But too many of us let these longings spin into obsessions. A recent poll by a leading magazine found that among four thousand readers, 56 percent of women and 43 percent of men were unhappy with their overall appearance. Two-thirds of the women and over half of the men were specifically unhappy about their weight. Females between the ages of thirteen and nineteen felt the worst about their weight and appearance.

Even people who are not overweight often think they are in other people's eyes. In fact, thin girls often have the lowest self-esteem and most distorted body image. Sometimes a negative body image drives females to diet incessantly and to such extremes that anorexia or bulimia set in. Other men and women let a poor body image keep them from caring for their bodies by overeating. Becoming sedentary, overeating, and engaging in other self-destructive behaviors are frequent among people with severely negative body images.

If your body image gets in the way of your health and happiness, if it causes you to make poor food choices, then now is the time to take a small step toward improving your self-image. The information in *Balance Your Body, Balance Your Life* will help you do that. It begins with eating more fruits, vegetables, and grains, fresh foods for vivacity and vitality—and which will help generate more positive changes in your behavior and habits.

Aim for self-improvement, but don't let your body become an obsession. Accept who you are and how you are; be realistic about how you want to be. Go for it . . . you can do it! Fixating on your body image will likely fuel unhealthy eating habits, which in turn will reinforce your negative body image. When it comes to body image and food, it is easy to get trapped in an unhealthy cycle, where a negative body image fosters poor food choices that make you feel worse about your body.

It is easy to get off the deceptive merry-go-round. Eating wisely and naturally will generate a more positive body image, which will reinforce your new, healthy eating habits. The way you think and feel about your body will inspire you to eat healthier, and eating healthier will inspire positive thoughts and feelings about your body, building confidence and self-esteem.

Children develop their own body image mostly through the overt and covert values their parents give to them. How you feel about your body reflects outwards, and your children see it. A girl whose mother constantly diets and calls herself fat may very well learn to feel the same way about herself. Unless she learns otherwise, she may grow up to dislike her own body as well.

Food and emotions go hand in hand. In a phrase, food is emotional. Children, of course, learn from their parents what emotions to feel about food. Children can learn positive, healthy food emotions just as easily as they can learn the opposite. If children learn to criticize their bodies, they will develop a love-hate relationship with food. Food will become their enemy. And these feelings and emotions will grow deeper as children grow older.

When I was in college and medical school, I spent my summers as a camp counselor in upstate New York. I remember one summer in particular, when I was in charge of a cabin of eleven-year-old boys. From the very first day of the summer, Joshua isolated himself from the rest of the group. He was a chubby boy—not obese, but very self-conscious about his body. He never wanted to partici-pate in water activities because he was embarrassed to wear a bath-ing suit. When the other boys canoed or played on rafts, he would sit under a tree, eating candy bars from CARE packages sent from his mother back home. For Joshua, food was his comfort and com-panion, but it was also his enemy.

The more Joshua ate, the worse he felt about himself, and the more he withdrew from social activities with fellow campers. Ashamed of his belly, Joshua ate candy bars to feel better. Ulti-mately, it made him feel worse. As he grew more self-conscious about his weight, he felt lonelier and lonelier sitting on the side-lines, as he did, during camp activities. His mother reinforced this cycle by sending him weekly packages stuffed with sweets. Parents, try always to remember: Take care of yourself and set the example!

The Myths of Infant Nutrition

As a family doctor and pediatrician for more than three decades, I've seen how parents' nutritional mindset and body image affects even young infants. It is what I call the *tube syndrome:* a condition among infants whose parents begin to perceive them as tubes that begin at the mouth and end at the anus. These parents worry excessively about what goes into the child at one end, and then worry excessively about what comes out of the child at the other end.

I discovered the infant tube syndrome after noting skyrocketing sales of prescription baby medicines. These baby medicines con-tain atropine, belladonna, hyoscyamine, phenobarbital, and alco-hol, and are most commonly prescribed to treat gastrointestinal problems and colic in infants. In my own practice, it seemed that most of the gassy infants had mothers or fathers—often both parents—who were insecure about parenting, stressed about their new responsibilities, and generally lacking in parenting skills.

These parents were caught in a maze of fear and worry over any sign of discomfort in their infant. To cope, they did what many people do; they turned to food for comfort. They began to feed their babies more and more, and with different kinds of food. They began to fret over what and how much food went into their baby, agonizing over the amount, consistency, flavor, smell, and temperature, as well as over the frequency and timing of feedings. When the feeding was over, they worried about the contents of their baby's diaper. And at that end, there was reason to worry. So many of the new foods introduced to the baby's system generally caused changes in stools: colic, constipation and diarrhea were common.

Parents who worry too much about their infant's diet and diaper content are not bad parents. They are like many people who associate food with love. When their baby was feeling bad, they showered him or her with love in the form of food. The best food, in fact, is served with love, but not in this way, and certainly not with worry, anxiety, insecurity, and fear. As adults, we characteristically turn to food for comfort when we are bored or need love. A pint of ice cream or slice of chocolate cake will do fine, the so-called "comfort foods" that soothe us when we are down. "Eat a little something and you'll feel better." How many of us learned this before we could even walk?

Moms and dads, worry less about what goes in and what comes out of your babies! He or she is not a tube, beginning at one end and ending at another. When you see your infant as a lively, thriving human being, love and nurturing will express themselves naturally, not through excessive feeding. This is the love and nurturing babies truly want. You see, in times of distress, babies swallow air, which causes colic and elicits loving attention from parents. Give your baby all the genuine love and attention he or she hungers for. You will all feel more comfortable and more at ease, and food will not be a problem.

Soon after birth, emotions about food and eating subtly register in a newborn's mind. The first taste of mother's milk establishes eating as one of life's most delightful pleasures. Infants eat for nutrition and nourishment, but also for comfort and pleasure. This emotion is carried with you throughout your lifetime, but as you grow, you can choose the wrong foods for comfort and pleasure. Instead of foods with the natural vitality and energy your body knew from mother's milk, you are guided by the demands of your taste buds.

Your eating experiences as an infant establish an emotional framework toward food that stays with you for the rest of your life. In those first months of life, food and eating can evoke joy, comfort, and nurturance. Or, like the tube syndrome babies I just described, meals can be stressful, even traumatic events. Imprinted in infants' memories, both experiences will influence the way they feel and think about food as they grow up.

Long before a newborn arrives in the world, the mother already thinks about how to nurture her baby. Contributing more to this anxiety than is healthy is the baby food industry. Who thrives most from creating and sustaining the impression that formula from a can or bottle has more nutrients than milk from a mother's breast, and that mashed, processed, refined food from a jar is nutritionally superior to food provided by Mother Nature?

Nothing in a can, bottle, or jar can match the nutritional power and nurturing force of breast milk—nothing. Science may indicate otherwise, but the value of mother's milk to nurture and nourish a baby cannot be seen under a microscope or measured in a test tube. Breast milk is all the baby needs. It is the natural source of infant nutrition and nourishment. If, however, you physically cannot breastfeed, for whatever reason, then an appropriate baby formula is quite acceptable.

The Myths of the Four Food Groups

It may be hard for you to digest the fact that our basic, earliest learned beliefs about food contribute to the weight and health problems we suffer. The good news is that you can change these beliefs and, with a little effort, revolutionize the way you think about food.

In school, one of the first things children learn about food is the story of the **four food groups:**

- meat, fish, and poultry
- grains
- dairy
- fruits and vegetables

On its own, of course, this division is quite benign. But as interpreted for us in 1956 by the U.S. Department of Agriculture (USDA), the four-food-group philosophy emphasized heavy meat and dairy intake. These foods, once the image of optimal nutrition, now embody all of our worst eating habits. Our belief in the need for daily doses of meat and dairy in our diets is literally making us sick.

Keep in mind that the four food groups were also promoted vigorously by the National Dairy Council. We now can understand that the four-food-group campaign was more a strategy to bolster the public's view of the dairy and meat industries than a public health message. As children learned to think of milk, eggs, and meat as pillars of good health at every meal, such eating practices, promoted as they were across elementary schools throughout the United States, were, in fact, advertisements that we taxpayers paid for then with money and now with poor diet. The result is clear: Americans—and American children, in particular—have become the most overfed, undernourished, and overweight people in the world!

Because of the eating habits instilled by the four food groups, Americans eat too many foods that diminish and not enough foods that boost health. Adhering to the four-food-group philosophy, Americans consume excessive amounts of:

- fat
- protein
- salt
- sugar
- calories
- red meat
- dairy products

Because Americans consume so much of these favorites from the four food groups, they eat too little of the foods that promote balanced health and energy, including:

- fruit
- vegetables

- fiber
- grains

For many children now, the four food groups seem to be candy, soda, potato chips, and cookies! A National Cancer Institute study discovered that only one in five children (just 20 percent) eats the recommended daily five or more servings of fruits and vegetables. What's more astonishing is that the leading source of vegetables for children and adolescents is deep-fried, fat-soaked french fries!

Now, you may be asking yourself, "Didn't the USDA recently launch a new food groups campaign, based on a pyramid emphasizing vegetables, fruits, and grains?" Absolutely. In 1991, under pressure to respond to the "New Four Food Groups" guidelines issued by the Physicians Committee for Responsible Medicine, the USDA launched a new campaign based on the Food Pyramid. Although the revised recommendations do emphasize eating more vegetables, fruits, and grains than the original four food groups, the USDA still advocates two or three servings of meat and two or three servings of dairy products daily!

Let's look more closely at the myths of nutrition underlying the four-food-group philosophy, and still influencing the new food pyramid. These myths take us straight to the heart of many health and weight problems suffered by Americans.

Because of the amount of saturated fat they contain, whole milk and cheese are two of the worst foods to drink and eat. (Joining them among the worst foods kids frequently eat is bologna.) Yet these foods are still promoted as staples of children's diets. The excessive amounts of dairy that children eat contribute greatly to the soaring numbers of cases of gastrointestinal illness, allergies, bacterial and viral infections, sore throats, and congestion seen by pediatricians every year.

At the same time, public awareness about the health hazards of consuming too many dairy foods is increasing. The dairy industry has responded with two recent ad campaigns that target adults more than children. The "milk" ads you see on street billboards and TV commercials, featuring celebrities wearing milk mustaches, are designed to restore adults' faith in milk. Here, drinking milk is good for your children and you, not to mention your whole family's image. These ads also acknowledge that concerns about reducing fat in our diets have lowered milk consumption. Does the dairy industry need, once more, to *milk* our nutrition?

Now these ads don't promote the health benefits of milk (for adults, there are actually very few that can't be more heathfully received from other sources). Rather, they project an image of happiness, hipness, beauty, and strength that has *absolutely nothing* to do with the product itself. The milk-mustache campaign, featuring sports heroes, models, and actors, plays on the popularity of the celebrity holding the empty glass. Drinking milk may not make you healthy, but the ads seem to promise that it can make you popular and cool.

The truth behind the promises promoted by celebrity endorsements is that *dairy products are the leading source of saturated fat in our diet*, with red meat a close second. Diets abundant in dairy products are high in fat, and are linked with certain types of cancer, especially of the colon and prostate. But the ads don't mention that.

From my more than three decades of medical experience, I do not believe that cow's milk is good for humans. It is good for baby cows. Only humans believe they should drink the milk of another species. Even adult cows don't drink cow's milk. And despite the dogma from the dairy board, children will develop and grow just fine without four servings of milk a day. Kids can get enough calcium for growth from other sources.

And women, who are now scared into drinking milk to prevent osteoporosis, should know that behind the milk myth is the fact that you can still get sufficient amounts of calcium from nondairy, plant-based sources. Women don't get osteoporosis because they don't drink enough milk. Osteoporosis develops as a result of calcium-robbing eating and lifestyle habits, *including over consumption of dairy products!* It's true: The very substance touted as essential to prevent osteoporosis can contribute to its onset when consumed excessively. The best sources of calcium don't come from dairy, but from green leafy vegetables, peas, beans, nuts, broccoli, and cauliflower.

Like the myth about milk, the national belief that you need meat to be healthy underlies some of the worst health and weight problems we suffer. Everybody needs protein, especially growing children. But, as a general rule, *our problem is not that we consume too little protein; we consume too much protein!* Few people have cause to worry that they are not getting enough protein in their diet. Most of us get much more than we require.

In the United States especially, the majority of protein in diets comes from animal sources. No other country in the world depends on animal protein as much as Americans do. It is a long-standing myth that you need meat for the protein that makes you healthy. A daily variety of plant foods can provide your body with an adequate supply of high-quality protein, as well as the iron and vitamin B_{12} that red meat supplies.

Recently, researchers at the National Academy of Science's Institute of Medicine announced that "there are no known benefits and possibly *some* risks in eating diets with a high meat content." What an understatement! There are numerous very well-known risks associated with a meat-laden diet.

For the good of your health, as well as that of your family, lower the amount of meat in your diet, especially red meat. Despite the National Academy of Science's hedging, evidence shows that meat consumption heightens the risks of developing a variety of diseases. At Harvard Medical School, researchers conducted a study of approximately forty-five thousand male health professionals and found that the men who ate red meat as a main dish five or more times a week had four times the risk of colon cancer compared to the men who ate red meat less than once a month. Men who regularly consume large amounts of red meat also double their chances of getting prostate cancer.

The good news is that simply cutting down on red meat in your diet will have tremendous health benefits. There are endless and delicious healthful alternatives to bring to the table, which you will discover as you read on. Medical research has shown that people whose diets contain little or no meat have notably lower rates of heart disease, hypertension, obesity, lung cancer, coronary artery disease, diabetes, and gallstones. Studies also have shown that a virtually meat-free diet lowers cholesterol significantly and, when combined with exercise and stress reduction, can actually reverse coronary artery damage.

It is not only the high rates of saturated fats in meat that contribute to health problems. Even *lean* red meat increases the risk of colon cancer. "Lean" labels on meat in the supermarket are misleading as well. For example, for foods to meet the USDA's "lean" requirements, they must not contain more than 10 percent fat by weight. The USDA allows the "lean" label on ground beef, however, that is up to 22.5 percent fat. The labels get even more confusing. The USDA allows claims like "85 percent lean" only on foods that are "low fat" (no more than three fat grams per serving). But the same regulations do not apply to ground beef. At some stores, you can find ground round labeled "85 percent lean" even though you learn that, upon closer inspection, one serving contains as much as fourteen fat grams. Ground beef is one of the fattiest meats available, yet it isn't held to the same "lean" standards as other kinds of meat. Ground beef labels are not even required to list "nutritional facts," which are now required on other foods.

If you want to improve your health, lower and stabilize your weight, and feel alive with energy and radiant vitality, then incorporate more and more vegetables and fruits into your diet. The healthiest diet you can eat is one based primarily on plant foods—fresh vegetables, fruits, beans, and grains—as opposed to animal muscles and organs. The evidence is so convincing that the chair of the nutrition department at the Harvard School of Public Health attests that "it's no longer debatable" that "largely vegetarian diets are as healthy as you can get."

Note the term "largely vegetarian." The health benefits are not only for those who eliminate meat entirely from their diets, but are enjoyed by people who just *reduce* their meat intake. Adopting the balance your body, balance your life eating habits will not require that you never eat meat, fish, poultry, or dairy products again. Simply eat less of the unhealthy animal foods and more of the fresh plant foods. It's really that simple!

There are many compelling reasons to eat less meat and more fruits, vegetables, and grains. I have already emphasized how eating foods containing less refined sugar and animal fat will help you lose weight and keep it off. But consider these other factors which favor a diet abundant in plant foods:

- Fruits and vegetables have protective properties against gastrointestinal cancers and even smoking-related cancers, including cancers of the stomach, mouth, larynx, colon, lung, esophagus, and bladder.

- People who eat a largely vegetarian diet have lower incidents of cardiovascular disease, high blood pressure, and noninsulin-dependent diabetes compared to meat-eaters.
- A largely vegetarian diet reduces the risk of osteoporosis, kidney stones, and gallstones.
- Women who eat less red meat have less breast cancer. Men who eat less red meat have less prostate cancer.

Limiting meat intake reduces amounts of saturated fats and cholesterol, but plant foods themselves have properties that protect the heart in other ways:

- The "sticky" soluble fiber in plants such as beans, peas, oats, and barley helps to lower blood cholesterol.
- Fruits and vegetables are excellent sources of folic acid, a B vitamin that can reduce the risk of heart disease.
- The antioxidants in fruits and vegetables can help protect the heart from cholesterol damage.
- Eating more fresh fruits and vegetables and less animal flesh will help protect you and your loved ones from food-borne illnesses. Fresh fruits and vegetables are safer than animal foods. The most common sources of food-borne illnesses are meat, seafood, and poultry. *E.coli* bacteria and salmonella occur in these foods much more frequently than they do in raw fruits and vegetables. In addition, emphasizing fruits and vegetables in your diet is better for the environment. Diets high in animal foods also take a tremendous toll on the environment, including three factors:

  - Stockyards and chicken factories cause catastrophic pollution of our water supplies with their waste, which is several hundred times more concentrated than raw domestic sewage.
  - Raising beef cattle depletes the water supply. It takes almost four hundred gallons of water to produce a pound of beef for consumption.
  - Producing and transporting livestock consumes about ten times more energy than growing and distributing vegetables.

From every angle, the nutritional scales tilt strongly in favor of a largely vegetarian diet. You don't have to give up all animal foods to reap the health benefits. Often, a strictly vegetarian diet is not reasonable, depending on geographic location and local food supplies. Improving your health and weight is as simple as shifting the balance of your eating in the direction of more plant foods and away from fatty animal foods. You will then be steering clear of perhaps the biggest roadblock obscuring your path to a healthy diet and permanent weight loss.

Now let's look at our nutritional evolution. There is very good evidence to suggest that man is not, as is commonly believed, a carnivore by nature. Archaeological studies indicate that the diet of our earliest ancestors was based primarily on plant foods. As hunter-gatherers, our ancestors passed most of their days searching the landscape for plants and only occasionally killed an animal for food. Early man, therefore, ate a very low-fat diet. Although we've evolved in many ways from our early ancestors, when it comes to nutrition, humans have been digressing for centuries!

The good news is that there are hopeful signs that this process of nutritional digression is coming to a halt. As more people move toward a low-fat diet, filled with vegetables, fruits, and grains, we are moving closer to the diet on which our ancestors survived and thrived.

Obviously, we are very different creatures than our ancestors, living in radically different environments, filled with creature comforts our ancestors never knew. When it comes to obtaining food as well, no longer are we hunter-gatherers. Our ancestors spent the majority of their time searching for adequate food; we don't need to. In 1800, 95 percent of Americans ate food fresh from their own or a local farm, or from the sea; today, however, 95 percent of all Americans eat food produced at a distance, then processed, preserved, and mass distributed to supermarket chains across the country.

As we navigate the aisles of the supermarket, we encounter an almost overwhelming range of foods from which to choose. The health claims that their bright packages and slick wrappings project are equally overwhelming. Learning how to sift through this jungle of offerings to find the foods that are best for us and our family does not come by instinct, however. For our ancestors, eating was a simple pleasure. Now, simply by taking a trip to the supermarket we enter a bit of a battleground, as packaging, displays, and brand names fight for our attention and the dollars in our wallets!

Your body naturally craves nourishment and nutrients. *Balance Your Body, Balance Your Life* will help you reawaken your body's wisdom. You can restore the natural cravings suppressed by decades of poor eating habits and the nutritional misinformation that promoted them. Your body has an inherent wisdom that is largely at odds with our food culture. But now is the time to turn the odds back in favor of your health and the health of your loved ones.

Our natural appetite for foods has been profoundly altered by a century of mass food production for mass consumption, by processing, refining, preserving, and packaging. If there are really only four food groups to which you need to adhere for good health, why in the world are there so many new kinds of foods appearing on the shelves of supermarkets every year?

It is the lifeblood of the food industry—the processors, marketers, advertisers, distributors, and retailers—to constantly create new tastes. Combined, they spend billions of dollars to sell us new foods, new flavors, and new categories of foods. In 1994, more than twenty thousand new food products made their appearance on grocery store shelves. Many of the products are not new at all, just dressed up in fancy new packaging. Examine the fine print on the nutritional label—the contents on the inside haven't changed; only the wrapping on the outside is different.

Is this progress? I don't think so. The food choices we are given are really not choices at all. In certain categories, all of the processed foods that line supermarket shelves taste exactly the same. They all have the same artificial flavors, textures, and qualities. Perhaps they taste the same because they have so many chemicals in common.

These foods take you further and further off the road to nutritional health and well-being. The same can be said of foods promoted for your convenience, foods engineered to save you time cooking and eating. These foods may or may not save you a few nickels and a few minutes, but convenience comes with hidden health costs. What these foods save you in preparation time is lost in both short- and long-term health benefits.

Food should make eating a simple pleasure for you to enjoy, not a time-saving convenience. Most people are willing to spend a few extra dollars for high-grade gasoline. Why cut corners when it comes to how you fuel your body? Eating healthy, the natural way, saves you more than time and money—it protects you from illness and disease, it inspires health and happiness, and it makes you feel more energetic and alive. Remember, *food is your energy!*

The wisdom of your body has been overshadowed by your senses, seduced by unhealthy foods. Supermarkets are designed, and the food on their shelves is displayed, to seduce your senses. Bright colors on packaging, attention-grabbing labels, and fancy wrappings capture your interest and tantalize your taste buds. Like everything else in our consumer culture, food has been turned into a fashion, with food styles changing as rapidly as clothing styles.

If you really pay attention to the refined and processed foods, if you eat them with awareness, you will find that they aren't so tasty after all. When the initial rush of fat, salt, and sugar on your taste buds subsides, you will be amazed to find that highly processed foods actually lack flavor. In the process of refining and processing, the natural flavors—the flavors from nutrients your body truly craves—have been stripped away.

Imagine making a salad from canned lettuce! The idea sounds ridiculous. You want your salad to be fresh and crisp, even freshly picked from the garden. Nobody likes wilted lettuce. Wilted lettuce is flavorless, lifeless, and unappetizing. Canned and processed foods are often *worse* than wilted lettuce. Processing, refining, and canning have reduced, even killed the natural energy of these foods. While the label on canned fruit salad, for instance, lists the nutrients it contains, read on—they aren't natural, they're added. Why would the food manufacturer need to *add* nutrients to naturally nutrient-rich fruits? It's because the manufacturing process destroys those nutrients, and then must replace them. But there is no substitute for nature's nutrients. A fresh fruit or vegetable salad satisfies and nourishes your body's natural cravings. You should expect the same from all of the foods you eat.

Processed, canned, dehydrated, and bottled foods have a uniform blandness. It's not really the flavor of the food that seduces your senses and tempts your taste buds. More seductive and appealing than the food is the image attached to it. Food advertisements and packaging work hard to create positive images that link foods to a sensual and beautiful lifestyle. But there is an enormous gap between the image of these foods and the reality of the life they actually help to create.

A romance brews between two thirty something professionals flirting over a cup of freeze-dried coffee. A grandfather and his grandson share touching smiles over a table at a fast-food restaurant and a box of chicken nuggets. A family comes together at breakfast to share a glass of "fresh" orange juice from concentrate, with the sun rising gloriously over the meadow in the background. These are all typical images used to sell processed foods. But how can something claim to be fresh after it has been boiled, dehydrated, crystallized, chemically preserved, and concentrated in a cardboard can? When you look long and hard at these images, they change; they become quite unbelievable. Now, we may not believe the images promoted in the name of foods they are not, but they do effect us emotionally. Supermarket sales tell us so. We continue to purchase such foods as fast as they hit the store shelves.

These foods never taste as good as their advertisements or packaging suggest. The promises of romance, happiness, or success, however, are simply promises—and promises can't be eaten. In a way, these promises are as empty as the nutritional value contained in a can of frozen, concentrated orange juice! Look where eating these foods has lead us: Our annual health care costs surpass the gross national product of every country in the world except for the eight major industrialized nations!

In reality, the general flavorlessness of processed foods found in supermarkets or fast-food restaurants actually contributes to overeating, undernourishment, and obesity. Researchers at Duke University Medical School, for example, found that the blandness characteristic of processed, packaged foods triggers you to eat more because, nutritionally speaking, you are satisfied less. When you learn to listen to the wisdom of your body, you will instinctively hunger for foods that are highly satisfying and you will eat less because you have met the needs of your appetite and your senses.

Our appetites have been cultivated by the multibillion-dollar food, diet, and advertising industries. Nor has the food industry lagged behind in response to our emerging public concern with health and nutrition. It has created whole new categories of foods designed to cash in on the dietary changes we are all desperately trying to make. Let's take a closer look at these so-called healthy foods.

Thousands of food products have been developed and marketed as healthy substitutes for the unhealthy foods we are trying to cut out of our diets. Sugar, fat, and salt are the main targets. Advised to reduce our intake of these substances, new products are chemically engineered to take their place. The seductive idea is that now you can have your cake and eat it, too. Or so it seems! These "healthy," "guilt-free" substitutes are filled with chemicals that may actually have side effects more injurious to your health than the products for which they are supposed to substitute!

Americans spend nearly $10 billion a year on products that claim to promote weight loss. Why do we spend so much money on these products? Why do we fill up our shopping baskets with "lite" salad dressings, "nonfat" frozen desserts, and "diet" shakes? There is good reason to be suspicious of claims that something is low fat or lite. In fact, some "lite" salad dressings contain 80 percent of their calories from fat. "Lite" may actually refer to the product's color!

How can you be sure anything is good for you? Forget all the fine print on the labels of these new products. The rule of thumb to follow is this: *It's generally best to stay away from foods that appear to be something they are not.* "Fake" foods have little or no nutritional value, and whatever flavor they provide is unnatural. Frozen orange juice from concentrate isn't fresh. "Fruit drinks" without fruit juice are not fruit—they aren't even juice!

Fake fats, fake meats, fake cheese, fake ice cream: These are foods produced in laboratories, not in nature. Even foods labeled "natural" are not necessarily natural at all, but filled with additives. "Food engineers" in white lab coats may say there is no nutritional harm in a chemical substance concocted to resemble butter. But just because a food does no *nutritional harm*—a claim you should always take with a grain of salt—does not mean it has any *nutritional value*. If it's fake, it's not fresh, and it does not nourish. *Fake is fake!* Ask yourself, "Would I rather feed myself and my loved ones food produced by a farmer or food developed by a 'food engineer'?"

It is vital that you learn to listen to your body's innate nutritional wisdom—because even science is not always a safe source of nutritional information. Some myths of nutrition come from the halls of our country's most respected and prestigious scientific institutes. Recently, a health newsletter produced by the esteemed Mayo Clinic asserted that *genetically engineered food is superior to what Mother Nature herself creates.* Wow!

High-tech tomatoes, *low-fat* french fries, *super* strawberries: Genetic engineering has produced fruits and vegetables that defy nature's seasons. How can tomatoes, a summer produce, be produced year-round? Can these tomatoes, engineered in laboratories, really be as fresh as vine-ripened tomatoes? Can molecular biology really produce foods that are healthier than those grown under natural farming conditions? Is food genetically engineered to have a longer shelf life really more fresh? (You might ask yourself this question: If it lasts that long on the shelf, how long is it going to linger in my body?)

These are the benefits touted by genetic engineering. But some things cannot be seen under a microscope. Tampering with the purity of food destroys its natural energy. New technology can add nutrients like vitamins C and E, as well as beta carotene, to fruits and vegetables. But if you eat a diet abundant in fresh fruits and vegetables, you will get these nutrients—in a form that ensures absorption and usefulness to your body—*naturally.*

The benefits of genetic engineering are often overstated, and it is downright misleading to claim that science is superior to Mother Nature! Good nutritional science has many lessons to learn from Mother Nature, and scientists are quite presumptuous to suggest it is the other way around.

When the wisdom of your body is in harmony with the wisdom of nature, that wisdom will be your guide and you will not be confused or misled by science gone astray. The ultimate nutritional science comes from the laboratory of your own body, which knows exactly what nutrients you need and where to get them. You can be your own expert on eating if you just learn to be guided by your natural hungers and not the seductions of your senses.

If I sound redundant, there is good reason. **Unhealthy ideas about food are so firmly ingrained within us, it requires repetition to break through those mental barriers**. Some points cannot be emphasized enough, since changing your mindset about the foods you eat, along with understanding what you have been exposed to, is absolutely essential to your successful journey to achieving your optimal weight and permanent weight loss.

Break the Mental Chains That Bind You to Poor Eating Habits Forever: Simple Mental Exercises

As you make your way through this book, you will learn how your thoughts and beliefs influence your health, weight, and energy. You will learn how, since the moment you were born, you have experienced myth after myth about food and eating. Years and years of exposure to such myths have created a mindset that is at odds with the good health, weight loss, and energy you are now striving for.

You will begin to build a new mindset about nutrition and weight loss, based on a clearer understanding of how and why your thoughts and feelings influence the food choices you make. Now that I have begun to help you separate the nutritional facts from the fictions still current in our society, you will understand why you must break the mental chains that keep your body's natural nutritional wisdom locked tightly away. The information you are now gaining will help you break these chains, one link at a time.

Are you ready to free yourself from these chains forever? Sound nutritional information is the first key. Since you have read this far, you already possess that first key. You are now prepared for the second, a simple method of mental relaxation that will help you obtain the discipline and determination to break free, once and for all, from the mindset that has kept healthy nutrition and perma-

◆

nent weight loss locked away from you. These simple mental exercises will speed your journey down the proper path and steer you safely on the road to abundant health, energy, and lasting weight loss.

Your mind is like a radio. Your thoughts, beliefs, and emotions about food and eating have created static. Radio static, for instance, distorts the sound of lovely music. Your impulse to reach for the dial and fine tune your radio so that you can hear the music as it's played is a sound one. Your mind works the same way. Unless you retune your mind, and *tune out* the static of misinformation and negative thoughts, the static will smother the feeling of good health you wish to be yours. Over time as well, that static in your mind will tend to make you ill and overweight.

You have read about some of the myths that cloud your understanding of good nutritional health. Depending on your own background, your own childhood, where you grew up, and so forth, you probably have other myths to add to this list. You have your own stories about the value and meaning of food told to you by your parents, your teachers, and your friends. Those stories are there, playing in the radio of your mind, shaping your attitudes and feelings toward food.

Now that you have a better idea about where these myths come from, and how they have influenced your health and weight throughout your life, here is your the next step: to reinforce this knowledge so that misinformation about food and eating will never again steer you off the road to well-being and weight loss. As you continue to read on, you will gain a tremendous amount of useful and accurate information that will help ensure your successful journey toward permanent weight loss. One of the most effective ways to develop new, healthy attitudes and feelings about food is through simple mental exercises. There is a method of mental relaxation that literally clears away the static of negative thoughts and emotions and retunes your mindset for well-being.

You may already be familiar with techniques of stress management, deep relaxation, or meditation. There are many, many varieties of meditation. When it comes to mental exercise, I promote the same approach I take to nutrition and physical exercise: *keep it simple*. In each of these arenas of activity—eating, exercising, relaxing—a simple approach is usually best. Of course, the tendency in these areas is to *overdo*. Among my patients, the simple method of mental relaxation I teach has been enormously effective. There are no fancy techniques to bog you down. You don't have to buy anything to do it, and it takes as little as ten minutes a day. Meditation is a simple and effective method for re-tuning your mindset and stimulating your body's internal pharmacy and healing forces to restore *homeostasis*—the medical term for internal balance. Restoring homeostasis, or your internal balance, is the key to achieving *Total Health Rejuvenation* and permanent weight loss naturally.

What happens when you practice these mental exercises? You help clear away the roadblocks. All of the confusion, anxiety, guilt, and fear about food that has created mental cobwebs in your mind are swept away. All of the thoughts and emotions about food that are keeping you off the road to weight loss disappear. You can build a healthy new mental outlook on food and your body. This retuned mindset will spark your self-esteem and guide you in making health-promoting food choices, in developing eating habits that ignite your energy and vitality, and increasing your physical activity.

On a deeper level, these exercises will allow you to quiet your thoughts so that you can listen to the voice of your own inner wisdom. Remember, the wisdom of your body is a perfect compass, always pointing in the direction of health, energy, and vitality. To follow that compass, you have to clear away the mental cobwebs, tune out the static of myths and misperceptions, and learn how to respond to your natural hungers.

MENTAL RELAXATION EXERCISES

These exercises should be done every day, even after you feel secure in your new eating habits. Use them more frequently from time to time to reinforce your new mindset, especially when old habits seem hard to resist.

► *To begin, choose a comfortable, quiet place in your home. You will need at least five to ten minutes of privacy and silence, so take the phone off the hook, and if others are at home, just ask them to leave you undisturbed.*

► *Sit up with good posture, but do not be uncomfortable or stiff. Uncross your legs and ankles, and let your hands rest gently in your lap. After you know these exercises from memory, you may gently close your eyes and keep them closed until the end of your meditation. Until then, just relax, and be very calm, and read each step of the meditation.*

► *Begin to relax even more now and get ready to take several deep, full and long breaths. Every breath will relax you more and more, particularly as you exhale.*

► *While taking your first deep, long and even breath, relax all of the muscles in your face. As you exhale, let go of all traces of tension in your forehead and in the muscles around your eyes.*

► *Take a second long and deep and even breath now, and as you exhale, consciously relax all the muscles of your neck, your shoulders, your arms and forearms and hands.*

► *Take a third deep breath, and as you exhale, relax all the muscles of your chest, your abdomen and your back. Just relax.*

► *Take a fourth deep breath, and as you exhale, feel all the muscles in your buttocks, your thighs and your calves relax . . . all the way down to your feet and toes . . . relax.*

► *Take a fifth deep, full breath now and as you breathe in, scan your body for any tension. As you breathe out, let go of any tension and just relax. Breathe in, locate the tension; breathe out, let the tension go.*

▶ *Now just breathe normally, but slowly and calmly. Feel your entire body becoming even more and more relaxed. Be still and silent . . . just relaxing and breathing.*

▶ *Begin to imagine a warm healing golden light shining from your heart. Imagine this warm healing golden light filling your heart and radiating outward to fill your entire body with warmth . . . and healing . . . and relaxation.*

▶ *Imagine the warm healing golden light filling your lungs, your stomach, and your pelvis. Imagine the golden light flowing through your legs, feet and toes. Imagine the light flowing through your neck and your shoulders, and then down your arms, forearms, to the very tips of your fingers. Feel your fingers tingle with warm golden light.*

Imagine the warm golden light flowing upward, filling your mouth, your nose, your eyes, your ears. Imagine the warm golden light flowing through every cell of your brain. Imagine your entire body, from head to toe, radiating with warm . . . healing . . . golden light.

▶ *Now that your body is filled with warm and radiant light, silently and slowly say these words to yourself over and over and over again . . .*

I Have Strength . . . I Have Strength . . . I Have Strength

▶ *Repeat this empowering message to yourself at least a dozen times. Make sure to take plenty of time to pause and feel the strength flowing through your entire body. (If you wish, you may also say the following words too . . . over and over and over again . . .)*

God Loves Me . . . God Loves Me . . . God Loves Me

▶ *When you are ready, take a nice, slow, deep breath. Feel happiness and energy flowing through your body as you exhale. Now, slowly open your eyes and come back to your waking consciousness. Gently wiggle your fingers and toes. Just sit for a quiet moment, enjoying the stillness of your thoughts and the refreshed feeling throughout your body.*

How do you feel? What are your thoughts? Do they seem more quiet than usual? Do you feel less restless? Do you feel more energetic? How is your mood? You should feel relaxed but not tired, calm but energized. And you should feel a sense of mental clarity and satisfaction. Practicing these mental exercises daily will help to develop your new outlook on food and eating. You'll find that when you allow yourself to relax and your thoughts to quiet down and stop moving, a wonderful thing happens within you: *Your own natural healing mechanisms are ignited*. That is when the wisdom of your body can point your inner compass in the right direction. When you quiet your mind using these exercises, your inner compass will guide you to do exactly what is right to achieve *Total Health Rejuvenation* and a balanced, healthy weight forever.

Part Two

YOUR HEALTH PROFILE:

Profile Questionnaires to Help You Evaluate Your State of Wellness and Chart a Personalized Course to Lasting Weight Loss and Expanding Energy

Before continuing, I want you to understand that your health and weight are affected more by what you are willing to do for yourself than by what any doctor is capable of doing for you. The sophisticated tools of Western scientific medicine can tell you many things about your body. But you are the expert when it comes to assessing the habits of thought, belief, attitude, and action that underlie your current state of health. So now, let's do some personal evaluating and assessing to help prepare you for the tremendous knowledge that lies ahead.

The following sets of questionnaires are designed to help you assess your current health and weight profile. Please note that it is important for you to answer the profile questionnaires *at this point*, before you read any further parts of the book. Don't skip ahead and come back to the questionnaires later. The questions are geared primarily toward your *attitudes, thoughts, and emotions* about food, exercise, body image, and stress. Factors such as cholesterol level, blood pressure, body fat percentage, and body frame are very important. Your doctor or health professional can also help determine your physical health profile. But if you really want to understand your current health profile and, more importantly, *the reasons why you are where you are*, then your honest, insightful responses to the following questions are essential.

The questions are divided into four groups, dealing with four areas that contribute to your level of wellness and weight: body image, nutrition, exercise, and stress. Answer every question in each section and calculate your total points for each section. When you have completed the entire set of questionnaires, calculate the total points for all sections combined. At the end of the question-naires you will be given a formula for interpreting your score and diagnosing your current level of wellness and weight. Determining this information will help you understand your needs and achieve your goals. Don't be nervous; there are no wrong answers. Just try to be as accurate as you can.

BODY IMAGE QUESTIONS

In Part One you read a brief survey about your body image. The following questions delve more deeply into this important area— for many people, it is the motor that drives poor eating habits. An-swer all the questions. Be perfectly honest and direct with yourself. The more truthful you are in answering, the more accurate your assessment of your Health Profile will be. Keep in mind that your body image underlies many, if not most, of your eating habits and food choices. Before you restore balance to your diet, you need to restore balance to your self-image. Total your score at the end of the questionnaire.

1. When I look in the mirror I feel
   (a) discouraged and disappointed   4
   (b) critical of everything I see   3
   (c) critical of some things, but accepting of others   2
   (d) generally pleased with who I see   1

2. I compare my physical appearance to others
   (a) constantly   4
   (b) often   3
   (c) sometimes   2
   (d) never   1

3. My perception of my body is probably
   (a) very distorted 4
   (b) somewhat skewed 3
   (c) mostly realistic 2
   (d) right on target 1

4. When I see a model in a magazine or on television I
   (a) criticize myself for not looking like her or him 3
   (b) compare myself to her or him 2
   (c) don't give it any thought 1

5. What sets the standard of ideal weight, fitness, and beauty I aspire to?
   (a) fashion magazines 4
   (b) television and film 3
   (c) friends and family 2
   (d) my standard comes from within 1

6. My image of ideal weight, fitness, and beauty is
   (a) unattainable and probably unhealthy for me 3
   (b) possibly too ambitious 2
   (c) well within my reach 1

7. My thoughts about my body are
   (a) generally negative 4
   (b) sometimes negative 3
   (c) basically neutral 2
   (d) mostly positive 1

8. Does the way I feel about my body keep me from doing certain things (such as going to the beach, dressing up for a night of dancing, etc.)?
   (a) yes, I feel limited by my body 4
   (b) only sometimes 3
   (c) I do these things but feel shy or self-conscious 2
   (d) no, I do not feel limited by my body 1

9. When people comment on my looks, I feel
   (a) they must be lying 4
   (b) very embarrassed 3
   (c) slightly uncomfortable 2
   (d) appreciative and special 1

10. When the topic of conversation is weight, I
    - (a) disappear — 4
    - (b) feel like all eyes are on me — 3
    - (c) feel self-conscious — 2
    - (d) am comfortable and secure — 1

11. When someone gives me a compliment
    - (a) I completely dismiss it — 4
    - (b) I generally feel undeserving — 3
    - (c) I accept it but with embarrassment — 2
    - (d) I accept it graciously and appreciatively — 1

12. I haven't been happy with my body
    - (a) ever — 4
    - (b) since I was a child — 3
    - (c) in the last year — 2
    - (d) I'm okay with my body now — 1

Body Image Total: _____

NUTRITIONAL WELLNESS QUESTIONS

As you respond to the following questions, choose the answer that most closely fits you. You are not judging or criticizing yourself here, but identifying the eating habits and choices that you may take for granted. Now that you have decided to be proactive about bringing your nutritional energy back into balance, you need to know what food choices are disrupting that balance. When you complete the questionnaire, total your score.

1. I eat in my car
   - (a) most days — 4
   - (b) when I'm running late — 3
   - (c) almost never — 2
   - (d) never — 1

2. When I eat dinner, I am usually
   - (a) in front of the TV — 4
   - (b) still at work — 3
   - (c) in a restaurant — 2
   - (d) at home, at the table — 1

3. I usually eat my meals
   (a) alone   2
   (b) with family or friends   1

4. Meal times are
   (a) something I am usually too busy for   3
   (b) a necessary interruption from work   2
   (c) a pleasurable experience I look forward to   1

5. I eat while doing other activities
   (a) always   3
   (b) sometimes   2
   (c) never   1

6. In the grocery store, I spend most time
   (a) in the cookies and sweets aisle   4
   (b) in the butcher's section   3
   (c) in the canned or frozen foods aisle   2
   (d) in the fresh produce section   1

7. The following best describes my eating habits:
   (a) I am a meat-and-potatoes person   4
   (b) I eat whatever is convenient or around   3
   (c) I usually try to eat well   2
   (d) I am nearly a vegetarian   1

8. I eat fried or high-fat, greasy foods
   (a) at most meals   4
   (b) once a day   3
   (c) twice a week   2
   (d) I do my best to avoid fried and high-fat, greasy foods   1

9. I experience indigestion, heartburn, or other intestinal problems
   (a) regularly   4
   (b) a few times a week   3
   (c) once in a while   2
   (d) never   1

10. I am overweight by about
   (a) 50 or more pounds   4
   (b) between 25 and 50 pounds   3
   (c) 10 pounds or less   2
   (d) I am not overweight   1

11. I eat junk foods
    - (a) daily   4
    - (b) often   3
    - (c) sometimes   2
    - (d) rarely   1

12. In a restaurant, I'm most likely to order
    - (a) a juicy steak   4
    - (b) deep-fried chicken   3
    - (c) pasta with chicken or fish   2
    - (d) something vegetarian   1

13. I need to make some changes in my diet
    - (a) but I'd rather enjoy what I eat than suffer   4
    - (b) but my food habits are so ingrained   3
    - (c) and I am moving in that direction   2
    - (d) and I am ready now   1

14. The amount of water I drink each day is
    - (a) less than a glass   4
    - (b) one or two glasses   3
    - (c) three or four glasses   2
    - (d) at least six glasses   1

15. I eat _____ serving(s) of fresh fruit each day. (One serving equals one piece of fruit, one cup juice, or one cup fruit salad.)
    - (a) zero   4
    - (b) one   3
    - (c) two or three   2
    - (d) at least four   1

16. I eat _____ serving(s) of fresh vegetables each day. (One serving equals a half cup raw or cooked vegetables.)
    - (a) zero   4
    - (b) one   3
    - (c) two or three   2
    - (d) at least four   1

17. I eat _____ serving(s) of whole grains each day. (One serving equals a slice of bread, a half cup cereal, pasta, or rice.)
    (a) zero   4
    (b) one to two   3
    (c) three to four   2
    (d) at least five   1

18. I eat _____ serving(s) of dairy foods each day. (One serving equals one glass of milk, one cup of yogurt, two cheese slices, one scoop of ice cream.)
    (a) five   4
    (b) four   3
    (c) three   2
    (d) one or two   1

19. When I eat dairy foods
    (a) I eat regular, whole milk, full-fat products   4
    (b) I eat some low-fat varieties   3
    (c) I eat mostly low-fat varieties   2
    (d) I eat nonfat whenever possible   1

20. I eat vegetarian meals (without meat)
    (a) virtually never   4
    (b) once a week   3
    (c) two or three times a week   2
    (d) regularly   1

21. I eat fried foods
    (a) as much as possible   4
    (b) often   3
    (c) rarely   2
    (d) almost never   1

22. The amount of coffee (caffeinated and decaffeinated) I drink each day is
    (a) more than six cups   4
    (b) three or four cups   3
    (c) one or two cups   2
    (d) none   1

23. I drink alcoholic beverages
  (a)   three drinks a day   4
  (b)   two drinks a day   3
  (c)   a few drinks a week   2
  (d)   occasionally   I

Nutritional Wellness Total: _____

PHYSICAL WELLNESS QUESTIONS

Do you think that improving your level of exercise at the same time you are improving your nutrition is demanding too much? Now is the time to think again. Even moderate exercise helps prevent you from overeating or eating poorly. Determining your current state of physical wellness and your attitudes toward exercise will help prepare you for the information you will be reading later in this book. Total your score after completing this section.

I. In general, I lead a _____ life.
  (a)   sedentary   3
  (b)   moderately active   2
  (c)   very active   I

2. When I think of exercise
  (a)   I grimace at the thought   3
  (b)   I feel guilty for not doing it   2
  (c)   I look forward to doing it   I

3. My ideal weekend involves activities such as
  (a)   sleeping and watching lots of TV   4
  (b)   drinking and late-night partying   3
  (c)   some outdoor activity   2
  (d)   vigorous activities such as gardening, walking, hiking, cycling, etc.   I

4. The amount of physical activity I do at work is
  (a)   none   4
  (b)   minimal   3
  (c)   moderate   2
  (d)   vigorous   I

5. My health and ideal weight are strongly influenced by physical activity.
   (a) I don't believe this—genetics is everything 4
   (b) I believe this but don't care 3
   (c) I believe this but lack motivation 2
   (d) I believe this and am motivated to improve 1

6. What keeps me from engaging in physical activity?
   (a) Low self-esteem 4
   (b) Too busy, and other things are more important 3
   (c) It costs too much or the weather is bad 2
   (d) Nothing keeps me from exercising 1

7. When I exercise
   (a) I curse the bike I'm riding (weights I'm lifting, etc.) 4
   (b) I'd really rather be doing something else 3
   (c) I struggle but stick with it 2
   (d) I enjoy myself and feel good 1

8. My confidence in my ability to stick with an exercise program is
   (a) nonexistent 4
   (b) low 3
   (c) wavering 2
   (d) I don't know if I can put my mind to it and stay with it 1

9. My motivation for exercise is best described as
   (a) nonexistent 4
   (b) low 3
   (c) changes from day to day 2
   (d) good to high 1

10. To raise my motivation to exercise, I am willing to enlist an exercise partner.
    (a) no 3
    (b) yes 2
    (c) I'm already motivated on my own 1

11. How many times in the last month have I taken a walk?
    (a) not at all 4
    (b) once or twice 3
    (c) once a week 2
    (d) regularly; more than once a week 1

12. When was the last time an activity made me a little huffy and puffy and break into a slight sweat?
    (a) it's been so long, I can't remember   4
    (b) over a month ago   3
    (c) in the last month   2
    (d) in the last week   1

13. Does my present weight keep me from doing certain physical activities in which my body would be exposed (such as swimming, aerobics, joining a gym)?
    (a) yes   2
    (b) no   1

14. Sitting on the floor with my legs outstretched, I can bend forward and touch
    (a) my thighs   4
    (b) my knees   3
    (c) my shins   2
    (d) my feet   1

15. I engage in some aerobic activity (something that gets my heart beating faster and makes me a little sweaty)
    (a) hardly ever   4
    (b) a few times a month   3
    (c) a few times a week   2
    (d) almost every day   1

16. If I have a choice between the elevator or stairs, I usually
    (a) wait for the elevator   2
    (b) climb the stairs   1

17. If I have a choice between walking or driving, I
    (a) usually drive my car   2
    (b) usually walk the distance   1

18. In a parking lot
    (a) I circle the lot looking for the spot nearest my destination   2
    (b) I don't mind parking a distance away   1

19. When I climb a flight of stairs, I feel
    (a) I avoid stairs   4
    (b) exhausted   3
    (c) huffy and puffy   2
    (d) a little tired but energetic   1

20. My back
    (a) aches chronically and causes me to miss work   4
    (b) aches sometimes and limits my range of motion   3
    (c) rarely aches   2
    (d) is strong and flexible   1

21. When I look at myself in the mirror I think I look
    (a) unfamiliar to myself   4
    (b) tired and old   3
    (c) somewhat tired   2
    (d) healthy   1

22. My digestive health seems
    (a) poor, with frequent indigestion and constipation   4
    (b) fair, with occasional upset or discomfort   3
    (c) mostly fine   2
    (d) fine and regular   1

23. Overall, I consider myself to be in
    (a) poor shape   4
    (b) decent shape   3
    (c) fairly good shape   2
    (d) excellent shape   1

24. When it comes to getting into better shape
    (a) what's the use?   4
    (b) I don't think I can do it   3
    (c) it will be hard work   2
    (d) I can make the commitment because my health is worth it 1

25. It's too late to start exercising because
    (a) I'm too old   4
    (b) exercise is for other people, not me   3
    (c) I've tried but failed   2
    (d) it's never too late to start exercising   1

26. Smoking is the number-one detriment to good health.
   (a) I don't care, I smoke anyway   10
   (b) I know, but it's too hard to quit   9
   (c) I smoke only occasionally   8
   (d) I don't smoke   1

27. I smoke
   (a) a pack or more a day   10
   (b) less than a pack a day   9
   (c) a few cigarettes a day   8
   (d) never   1

28. In the last year, after having several drinks, I have driven a car
   (a) several times   10
   (b) more than once   9
   (c) once   8
   (d) never   1

29. In the last year, drinking has interfered with a relationship or with my work
   (a) several times   10
   (b) more than once   9
   (c) once   8
   (d) never   1

Physical Wellness Total: _____

MEASURE YOUR STRESS

Review the following list of stressful situations and events and circle all that apply to your life now or within the past twelve months. Remember, stressors in and of themselves do not do the health damage; it is your harmful responses to stressors that eat away at your energy and well-being. After identifying the stressful situations in your life, proceed to the next set of questions, which will help you assess your current ability to respond to stress in positive, healthful ways.

Stressors

- death in the family
- job loss
- financial burdens
- conflict with a neighbor

- marital difficulty
- severe illness or health challenge
- sexual difficulty
- end of a relationship
- anxiety about a new relationship
- increased responsibilities at work
- new child
- going back to school

- buying a home
- mounting debt
- changes in workplace or job responsibilities
- moving or relocating to a new town or state
- problems with children
- irregular sleep patterns
- visit from family members
- deadlines at work

Total number of stressors circled: _____

How Many Stressors Do You Have in Your Life?

The more stressors you are dealing with, the greater the likelihood you will not be able to deal with them constructively and in a healthy way. *Stress is the leading cause of poor eating and overeating,* and the more stress in your life the greater the tendency to eat unhealthily. Use the following chart to determine your personal evaluation from the total number of circled stressors in your life.

(**Please Note:** Do *not* include the number of stressors you've circled when you calculate your total scores from the *Body Image, Nutritional Wellness, Physical Wellness,* and *Stress Resilience* questions.)

Number of Stressors	Evaluation
1–5	Your stress level is relatively low.
6–10	Your stress level, if not managed well, may easily spiral out of control.
11–15	You have a dangerously high level of stressors in your life and must become proactive in reducing your stress and managing your response to stressful situations.
16–20	The high number of stressors in your life could drain your energy to risky levels. This much stress, unmanaged, almost surely leads to illness.

STRESS RESILIENCE QUESTIONS

Don't worry if the previous exercise revealed that you have many stressors in your life. Worry will only compound the stress. The most important factor is how well equipped you are to deal with these stressors. Answer the following questions to determine your strength in coping with stress. Once you have evaluated your present coping abilities, you will be ready to learn new strategies to improve your resilience against stress and stress-related illness. Total your score at the end.

1. In general, I think the amount of stress in my life is
   - (a) out of my control — 4
   - (b) moderate but usually present — 3
   - (c) minor but sometimes a problem — 2
   - (d) inconsequential — 1

2. Compared to those around me, my life seems
   - (a) like a nightmare — 4
   - (b) fairly chaotic — 3
   - (c) relatively calm — 2
   - (d) fairly stress-free — 1

3. I feel like other people seem happier than I am
   - (a) almost always — 4
   - (b) sometimes — 3
   - (c) once in a while — 2
   - (d) never — 1

4. The last time I felt truly happy was
   - (a) so long ago I can't remember — 4
   - (b) within the last year — 3
   - (c) within the last six months — 2
   - (d) I'm happy right now — 1

5. I would characterize my attitude toward life as basically
   - (a) pessimistic — 4
   - (b) resigned — 3
   - (c) hopeful — 2
   - (d) optimistic — 1

6. When I wake up in the morning, I feel
   (a) like I'd rather stay in bed   4
   (b) nothing until I have my first cup of coffee   3
   (c) on autopilot   2
   (d) ready to face the challenges of the day   1

7. My relations with people at work are
   (a) strained because I don't like my coworkers   4
   (b) sometimes tense, but I mind my own business   3
   (c) generally okay   2
   (d) productive and positive   1

8. When things feel really stressful
   (a) I fall apart   4
   (b) I ignore them   3
   (c) I sometimes face them   2
   (d) I take it one step at a time and do the best I can   1

9. Under pressure at work, I
   (a) get agitated and take it out on others   4
   (b) panic but get the job done   3
   (c) sometimes panic but manage to just get by   2
   (d) ask for help when needed and do my best   1

10. My temper is best characterized as
    (a) a short fuse   4
    (b) occasionally volatile and unpredictable   3
    (c) usually under control   2
    (d) calm and reasonable   1

11. I feel my friends and family
    (a) are a burden   4
    (b) mean well but don't know how to relate to me   3
    (c) are sometimes supportive   2
    (d) support me and want the best for me   1

12. My philosophy of life goes something like this:
    (a) life's difficult and then you die   4
    (b) sink or swim   3
    (c) we're all in this together   2
    (d) everything will be okay because there's a purpose
        behind everything   1

13. How often do I laugh?
     (a) I don't have anything to laugh about   4
     (b) rarely; I'm too busy   3
     (c) sometimes   2
     (d) I laugh frequently and heartily   1

14. Resentment and hostility are feelings
     (a) that eat away at me constantly   4
     (b) that sometimes get the best of me   3
     (c) that I experience on rare occasions   2
     (d) that are not part of my life   1

Stress Resilience Total: _____

INTERPRETING YOUR SCORE

Now that you have completed the questionnaires concerning your *body image, nutritional wellness, physical wellness,* and *stress resilience,* totaling all of your combined scores will enable you to evaluate your overall Health Profile. Add up your totals for each of the four questionnaires and mark your overall score below. Remember, DO NOT include in your total the number of stressors in your life that you have circled.

TOTAL SCORE: _____

Use the following guide to interpret your overall score:

Score	Evaluation
220–320	Your current health profile is extremely poor. Your energy is drastically out of balance and your beliefs are supporting poor nutritional habits. You are not getting the energy your body requires to burn fat, fight illness, and resist stress. But don't be discouraged. Help is on the way! The 28-Day Plan, presented later in the book, can help turn all of this around.
140–219	Your current health profile indicates that it is time to make changes. You are on the borderline of bad health and need to be proactive about taking steps that will increase your energy and bring it back into balance. High-energy nutrition, physical activity, and a strategy for coping with stress are essential to improving your health and weight.
78–139	Your current health profile indicates that you are on the path to wellness by taking personal responsibility for your health. It is important to continue caring for yourself, and this book will help you.

Part Three

TRUTH IS ON THE MARCH AND NOTHING WILL STOP IT

Are you stressed-out, out of shape and lacking energy? Do you suffer with headaches, neck aches, backaches, fibromyositis, or other pain syndromes? Are you short of breath or do you have high blood pressure, diabetes or heart problems? What about constipation, diarrhea, hemorrhoids, irritable bowel syndrome or colitis? Do you take antacids regularly? Does it take a long time for you to fall asleep or do you worry about things a lot of the time? If you answered yes to any of these questions, you have probably been accepting an invitation to illness. But as a person of strength and conviction who recognizes the power of your choices, you can just as easily turn down the invitation through *Total Health Rejuvenation*.

"Truth is on the march and nothing will stop it," was Emil Zola's battle cry a hundred years ago. "I accuse," he wrote in a public letter to the president of France. "Our nation has a stain upon its cheek and history will record that a social crime has been committed."

France's leading literary figure shocked the nation by standing up to the powerful forces leading the government and society. He had dared to denounce the widespread corruption and falsehood of his time. Captain Alfred Dreyfus, a Jewish military officer, had been convicted of treason for selling secrets to Germany and sent to prison on Devil's Island for the rest of his life. His trial had led to a vicious wave of anti-Semitism throughout France. But Emil Zola discovered that Dreyfus had been framed. The true facts were being covered up by the government, the generals, and the wealthy individuals who controlled society. Emil Zola was convicted of libel and exiled, then died in a mysterious manner. But in the meantime, Captain Alfred Dreyfus was exonerated and set free.

In ancient Greece, Socrates also dared to challenge the wisdom of the powerful leaders of society. He simply said they had no idea how much they didn't know. Socrates was proclaimed guilty of treason and forced to drink poison hemlock. Fortunately, Plato and Aristotle carried on his challenge by introducing the Socratic method of questioning so-called wisdom to the entire world. Many have since lived and died so that the truth could make others free.

How does all this relate to weight loss? In a nutshell, if you want to lose weight and be less sick and tired, then start questioning and stop listening to the so-called authorities who have led us to the perilous state in which we now find ourselves. Over half of all Americans are overweight, the incidence of childhood obesity has doubled in the last twenty-five years, and our country spends over $1 trillion a year on disease repair. That's $3,759 per person—substantially more than most people in the rest of the world earn in an entire year of hard work. So, if you really want to lose weight permanently and experience wellness, why would you listen to the same authorities? Why continue bothering with nonsense? As a wellness medical doctor, my challenge to the government, the food industry, and the media is this: *"I accuse you of committing the social crime of fattening and sickening the people."*

Physicians, Heal Thyselves

For what seemed like the thousandth time in my medical career, I was lecturing about weight loss to an audience of medical doctors, trying to teach them that what they learned in medical school about diet and nutrition was now largely irrelevant and doing their patients more harm than good. At the end of the lecture, I stressed again that deprivation and dieting were not effective means of permanent weight loss, that the only sure way to help patients lose excess weight was to encourage them to eat more foods that are full of life-energy and to engage in regular exercise. This combination, I explained, stokes the body's furnace and supplies it with the fuel it requires to burn off excess fat.

What did I mean by life-energy? Foods that are full of life-energy, I said, are provided by nature, *not* made in factories. Potato chips are not found under the soil. There are no fields flowing with *white* bread. Fruit does not appear floating in sugary syrups. Streams are not filled with soft drinks. Fruits, vegetables, nuts, and whole grains capture the energy of the sun to sustain the human lifecycle. They are steeped in starlight, infused with the elements.

I explained to the group of physicians that stress was the major virus of our time, affecting virtually every infant, child, and adult, causing obesity and many other illnesses. I also reminded my colleagues about something we had first learned in medical school: We had spent years studying the ways nature provides nourishment to sustain the lifecycles of every animal and plant species on earth. We had all graduated medical school believing that our task as physicians was to assist nature in her work. But sometime later we fell under the spell of technology, allowing high tech to replace the personal touch, care, and compassion that needs equal time for true healing to work its wonders.

I had hoped this group would be especially receptive to new ideas about permanent weight loss because they were the types of physicians that patients rely on for sound nutritional information. These were pediatricians, general practitioners, internists, and obstetricians—the primary care doctors who work in the trenches of everyday patient care. Each doctor who came up to me afterwards, however, could only share his or her unsuccessful experiences in trying to help patients lose weight. More disturbing still, most of the doctors were overweight themselves!

What stunned me even more, though, was hearing the doctors admit they no longer had the time or energy to consult with overweight patients who wanted help. They complained that all they could do was tell patients to eat less food, particularly less fat, and exercise more, suggestions already obvious to patients trying to lose weight. Or they could prescribe the latest diet pill and cross their fingers that no irreparable side effects would result.

Finally, I asked Dr. Frank Thomas, an old friend who started a practice next door to me over thirty years ago, why he and the other doctors weren't more interested in what I had just said regarding food as energy. After all, I thought, they must realize that healthy food contains a life-force patients need to sustain, and possibly extend, their natural human lifecycle. Moving closer, he looked me in the eye and replied, "Of course I'm interested. But I'm also a physician and I can't let my personal beliefs or intuition cloud my scientific judgment." Then he added that there was a more practical issue to be considered. "How can you expect practicing doctors to take the huge amount of time that's necessary to convince our patients to take better care of themselves, much less teach them that what they think they know about nutrition is totally irrelevant?"

On a sadder note, he continued: "For those of us who are still in medical practice, everything has changed. Under managed care and HMOs, we can't prescribe what we want to prescribe. We can't order the tests we think our patients need. We can't even send our patients for consultations we believe are necessary. But the worst thing is that we have to see forty to fifty patients a day just to survive. That's just a few minutes per patient! And that doesn't count all the paperwork and phone calls for prior authorization for just about everything I do except go to the bathroom! It's a jungle out there. It's not about patients anymore. It's about profits. So maybe you'd be better off teaching 'energy nutrition' directly to all the people out there who want to lose weight, because we doctors have too much else to worry about right now."

Dr. Thomas's response was absolutely typical of most Western medical doctors. They tend to maintain a very rigid scientific division between their work as physicians and their lives as ordinary people who realize food is basically life-energy that nature provides to sustain our human lifecycle. In my lecture, I had informed my colleagues that the health of our patients is primarily determined by personal responsibility, self-value, and reverence for life. I then reminded them that the deepest purpose of our profession is to empower our patients to unleash their own internal, pharmacy-powerful healing forces that are capable of reducing weight and reversing disease.

My own belief is one thing; convincing other medical doctors to put such beliefs into their own practices is entirely different. That is why I address and dedicate this book to patients themselves—to everyone who finds him or herself stuck on the path to permanent weight loss and good health. It is my genuine attempt to help heal my noble profession and patients across the United States (and perhaps the world). This book is for everyone who is sick and tired of being sick and tired. It also is for everyone who is well and wishes to stay that way. It is a carefully-thought-out scientific plan for *Total Health Rejuvenation* and permanent weight loss.

The Expert Conspiracy

Do you remember the story of the emperor's new clothes? All the subjects in the kingdom pretended that the emperor was wearing beautiful garments but, in fact, he was naked. Just like the emperor, the nutrition establishment in the United States has no clothes on. You are being fattened without questioning its wisdom. Entire industries depend on you to be sick and overweight. Did you know that more money in the United States is spent on repairing illness and reducing weight than on our military and defense budget? In fact, about 15 percent of this country's gross national product is spent on disease repair. Actually, in the United States we spend more money repairing bodies than all of the countries in the entire world produce in an entire year, combined, except for the eight major industrialized nations.

Wake up! Misinformation has caused you to lose sight of the fact that nature provides you with food that contains the life-force you require to nourish your body. You have been brainwashed. Your taste buds have become enslaved and your appetite has been inflamed. Your mind is being managed by powerful people and institutions making enormous profits by fattening you, as well as by causing you to become ill. So-called orthodox nutritional science has become a sham, and your food information is coming from the very companies and people who prosper most by your becoming overweight. You are being inundated with so much refined, processed, fake, factory-made food that it is often difficult to find food that still has some of nature's life-force left in it.

Being chronically overweight is a disease, but you can determine your own health destiny and lose weight far more effectively than you have been taught to believe. But to do so, you must stop giving yourself to the same people and industries that caused your problems in the first place. Approximately half of all Americans are overweight and the major reason is clear: the industries and people we depend upon for nutrition and weight loss information are the very ones that prosper most by our unhealthy eating habits. That's why it's time to stop putting the foxes in charge of the chicken coops!

The people and institutions of great wealth and influence can't afford to speak the truth about health or weight loss. Neither can the politicians and industry-funded scientists, nor the food, tobacco, and alcohol industries; ditto for the drug, for-profit hospital, and managed care industries. They, along with the advertising, radio, television, and newspaper industries, are all singing in unison, from the same sheet of unhealthful music, while living off the fat of the land—yours!

Just look around at all the overweight adults and children who are joining what I call the legions of the worried well and walking wounded. There are tens of millions of people who are stressed out, tired, and easily fatigued. These are the people who don't have the symptoms that indicate a specific disease, but who nonetheless lack vitality and don't feel well.

Americans are the most atherosclerotic, hypertensive, hemorrhoidal, diabetic, ulcer-ridden, arthritic, cancer-, stroke- and coronary-prone people on the planet. We also are the most overmedicated, overtested, overradiated, and oversurgerized people since the very beginning of recorded history. Yet we are still getting sicker and sicker. We are also getting fatter than ever before, and we should be asking ourselves the following question: *Why do we continue to rely on the same old information, from the same politicians, scientists, industries, and media that have been responsible for fattening us in the first place?*

If so many are overweight, why should you believe that the guidelines of the so-called nutritional experts are applicable in the real world, when it has been reported that only one percent of our children ages two to nineteen follow the governmental guidelines for nutrition? If virtually everybody who goes on a diet gains back their lost weight (and usually more), why should you continue looking to "diet experts" for help?

Telling the Truth

In George Orwell's classic novel *1984*, powerful leaders of society programmed people's minds to believe "war is peace." Orwell wrote the novel to demonstrate the horrors of a society in which mental habits were so programmed into people that all other modes of thinking were made impossible. New words and phrases were invented to replace unacceptable ones, which were outlawed. "War is peace" replaced the term "Love thy neighbor."

In America, we have been programmed to believe that refined, processed, irradiated, genetically engineered, fake food is real. Recall the advertising slogan for a cola—is chemically flavored, syrupy sugar water really the "real" thing?

The truth is that the food industry has committed a travesty against the natural food chain—and against our health—by inundating us with refined, fake, or dead foods to enhance its profits.

The first scientific paper on coronary artery disease and myocardial infarction was not even published until 1912. The first description of a heart attack due to a blocked artery was published in the *Journal of the American Medical Association* during this century. Since then, coronary vascular disease has become a major killer, and autopsy studies of even young adults reveal that their coronaries are typically slathered with fat! We are being killed by what we eat.

A recent study, *Chronic Care in America: A 21st-Century Challenge*, reported that there is a vast army of people, nearly 100 million, who suffer from chronic ailments such as heart disease, cancer, and diabetes—all diet-related diseases. For the sufferers and their families, the hardships associated with these diseases are all too real. Add to that army the legions of the worried well and walking wounded, those who lack energy and zest for life, and you begin to discern the enormity of the problem we face.

My professional and ethical commitment to my patients is to tell them the truth, blunt and undisguised. I find this necessary because they, as you, have been so thoroughly deceived that I must, so to speak, flatten your old ideas—so that new ideas can rise up and take their place. Consider the once vibrant houseplant whose leaves suddenly begin to droop and decay. You can give it plant food or cut it back. Or you can place it in a new pot with fresh soil, move it to a new spot where it receives more sunlight, and give it water. Under better conditions, it will more than likely sprout new buds and return to good health. Just like the plant, if you change the way you eat and live, your body can restore itself to optimal health—and that is the miracle of homeostasis.

The Broken Contract

Staying healthy is a matter of keeping your energy in balance. This is the wisdom of Hippocrates, the Greek physician known as the father of Medicine. He believed that medicine should work to build the patient's strength through appropriate diet before taking more drastic steps. He also recognized the link between environment and disease. Unfortunately, Western medicine is based almost exclusively on repairing the human body with drugs and surgery, instead of stimulating the will to be well. Since the average doctor's office visit is only twelve minutes long (and declining rapidly!), how can physicians devote even five minutes to helping overweight patients lose weight if there are only seven minutes left over to deal with other issues of infection, pain, and degenerative diseases?

As flawed as Western medicine may be, however, there has always been an unspoken contract for the public to rely upon. Two shining attributes have never failed patients. First, for patients in need of medical care or surgical repair, there is no more advanced technology available anywhere in the world than that which we possess in the United States. Second, there is the medical profession's underlying ethic: *primum non nocere*—first do no harm. We have, indeed, been fortunate to depend upon such an unspoken contract—until now.

Our present misfortune is this: The huge for-profit managed care industry has broken the first part of the contract. It has locked out approximately 50 million people, mostly middle-class citizens who are not eligible for insurance through their place of employment and cannot afford to pay for it themselves but are not poor enough to qualify for aid. Even if those patients were able to access the system, what good is advanced technology such as MRI machines when doctors are denied authorization to use them because stock prices rise on the basis of how little, rather than how much, can be done for patients? That's called the bottom line . . . *profits!*

Furthermore, it is extremely troubling to observe that the managed care industry does not support traditional charitable care for patients without insurance or money; nor does it support the efforts of non-profit teaching hospitals, which are our primary means of advancing medical research. Profits, not quality of care, come first now.

Corporate profit-seekers have also broken the second part of the unspoken contract with physicians, their pledge to practice ethically. The best and most outspoken doctors have their hands tied when profit, not care, is the new priority.

A Call to Action

The following example of the broken contract with the American public was published in the December 3, 1997, issue of the *Journal of the American Medical Association*. This call to action was signed by 2,300 medical doctors and nurses who were protesting being bribed and punished by corporate profit-seekers.

> We are Massachusetts physicians and nurses from across the spectrum of our professions. We serve patients rich and poor, in hospitals and clinics, private offices and HMOs, public agencies and academia. . . .
>
> Mounting shadows darken our calling and threaten to transform healing from a covenant into a business contract. Canons of commerce are displacing dictates of healing and trampling our professions' most sacred values. Market medicine treats patients as profit centers. . . .
>
> The time we are allowed to spend with the sick shrinks under the pressure to increase production, as though we were dealing with industrial commodities rather than afflicted human beings in need of compassion and caring. . . .
>
> Doctors and nurses are being prodded by threats and bribes to abdicate allegiance to patients, and to shun the sickest, who may be unprofitable. Some of us risk being fired or "delisted" for giving, or even discussing, expensive services, and many are offered bonuses for minimizing care. . . .
>
> Listening, learning and caring give way to deal-making, managing and marketing. The primacy of the patient yields to a perverse accountability—to investors, to bureaucrats, to insurers and to employers. And patients worry that their doctors' and nurses' judgment and advice are guided by the corporate bottom line. . . .
>
> Public resources of enormous worth—non-profit hospitals, visiting

nurse agencies, even hospices—are being taken over by companies responsive to Wall Street and indifferent to Main Street. . . .

Communities find vital services closed by remote executives; savings are committed not to pressing health needs, but to shareholders' profits. Not-for-profit institutions, forced to compete, must also curtail research, teaching and charity, or face bankruptcy . . . A single HMO president nets $990 million in a takeover deal; and insurers' overhead consumes $46 billion annually. . . .

At the same time, the ranks of the uninsured continue to grow, while safety-net public hospitals and clinics shrink and public health programs erode. Even many with insurance find coverage deficient when they need it most; care or payment is too often denied for emergencies or expensive illnesses. . . .

The sick are denied skilled nursing care, rushed out of hospital beds and hurried through office visits. Increasingly, the special needs of the elderly, infirm or disabled are ignored if they conflict with the calculus of profit. . . .

The shift to profit-driven care is at a gallop. For doctors and nurses, the space for good work in a bad system rapidly narrows. For the public, who are mostly healthy and use little care, awareness of the degradation of medicine builds slowly; it is mainly those who are expensively ill who encounter the dark side of market-driven health care. . . .

We criticize market medicine not to obscure or excuse the failings of the past, but to warn that the changes afoot push medicine further from caring, fairness and efficiency . . .

The headlong rush to profit-driven care has occurred . . . through a process largely hidden from public scrutiny and above citizen participation. This must be replaced by an open and inclusive process that is not dominated by the loudest voices—those amplified by money and political influence.

Integrative Medicine

Perhaps the best thing that can be said about the whole HMO and managed health care mess is that it may have done us a great favor by pointing out how important it is for us to take more responsibility for our own health and well-being. Wise physicians already know that the spiritual, physiological, and mental resources of their patients are a crucial part of any total treatment strategy, along with the best that modern medicine has to offer.

We are not overweight because we aren't receiving enough medical care. We are overweight because our homeostasis is suppressed and our energy is out of balance. Until we move away from a medical system based on disease repair to a system based on stimulating our body's natural will to be well, we will continue to suffer with the highest levels of stress-related illness in the world.

Throughout world history, except for Western medical science, almost all other healing traditions are based on the concept of life-energy. They share a common understanding that this vital force is responsible for life. Chinese medicine calls it *ch'i*. Indian medicine calls it *prana*. Plato envisioned it as the Ideal Good, breathed into us at the very moment of conception. Aristotle understood it as simply the Breath of God.

We seem to have forgotten the three-thousand-year-old wisdom of Hippocrates, who taught us that health is a matter of balancing our physical, mental, and spiritual energies. Western medicine is based on repairing disease, instead of stimulating the will to be well. The understanding of illness and excess weight as energy imbalance has evolved for nearly three millennia. In each century, however, the essential idea that health is a matter of energy balance has been refined and filtered through the beliefs of a given culture at a given historical moment. In our own medical culture, governed by a profit-driven health industry and the mechanical logic of disease repair, this belief has become so diluted as to almost be forgotten. But just because medicine has forgotten about the healing power within us does not mean it no longer exists.

Be very alert because even Integrative Medicine is now being diluted by marketing hype for all sorts of "holistic" treatments for diseases from arthritis to cancer. I developed and first presented Integrative Medicine to the Institute of Medicine in Washington, D.C., in 1982, in a paper entitled: "A Scientific and Spiritual Approach to Health." *Anything less is not Integrative Medicine.*

Living Downstream

The following fable illustrates why I believe Integrative Medicine is so important for the twenty-first century.

The town of Downstream is located just where a stream of sparkling waters enter into a river. It used to be rather idyllic, with townspeople peacefully raising their families and making a decent living, mostly as farmers, shop owners, and workers at the town's button factory. One day, much to everyone's amazement, a few weakened and ill people, clearly not from this town, were found floating in the stream. Exhausted and in need of assistance, they were rescued by kindly townspeople, who nurtured them back to health.

Soon, hundreds and then thousands of similarly sick people, desperately in need of care, were found floating in the stream every day. New ambulance companies, paramedic companies, laboratory companies, medical supply companies, and insurance companies (housed in skyscrapers) were formed to service new nursing homes and hospitals employing respiratory therapists, occupational therapists, physical therapists, dietitians, social workers, X-ray technicians, and nurses, all of whom were under the command of an army of physicians led by very important surgeons and specialists who were overseeing legions of family doctors.

The people of Downstream have become so very busy, and gainfully employed, that to this day, no one has the time, or perhaps the insight, to stop and wonder for a moment: What in the world is going on upstream?

We are finally stopping and wondering. There is a moral imperative for offering better health care, particularly to children, families, and senior citizens. Furthermore, to save Medicare from bankruptcy, as well as to help balance the federal budget, Congress wants the elderly to enroll in managed health care plans. This will be a decade of destiny for the health care industry. The political

power structure has created an unprecedented opportunity for preventive medicine and wellness services. Managed health care is
supposed to reduce overall costs via a prepaid scheme in which
consumers pay a set monthly bill, whether or not they need care,
and providers are paid, whether or not they deliver care.

Although health maintenance is the basis of this scheme, its reality is somewhat different: the established medical system has no
traditional means of maintaining health. Prevention is not merely
the early detection of disease after it has started. Pap smears and
mammograms, for instance, are for early detection, not prevention,
of disease. Because nearly 80 percent of diseases, including cancer,
are related to lifestyle, and therefore need to be addressed *before
they occur,* the current situation is no longer economically tenable.
Integrative Medicine helps turn patients into partners with their
physicians. It is dedicated to helping people control their own
health destiny.

Twenty-first Century Health Care

Wise patients can become partners in their health care
by combining the best that modern medicine has to offer with other
means of care that seek to strengthen and balance the energies of
the body, mind, and spirit. Your health is much too important to
leave up to science, but it's also much too important to be unscien-
tific about.

Your body is a complex, self-repairing energy system comprised
of ever-replicating DNA, an exquisite healing force and a biological
clock. Unfortunately, in the prevailing medical system with its
focus on drugs, surgery, and radiation, such concepts are very difficult to deal with. To do so requires a shift in consciousness—from
a sickness paradigm to a wellness paradigm.

The Integrative Medicine approach to permanent weight loss is based on the following simple and easy-to-understand precepts:

- *Homeostasis* is the medical term for energy balance. Hippocrates called it the *"Vix Mediatrix."*
- If you are well, your energy is in balance.
- If you are ill or overweight, your energy is out of balance.
- Your natural healing force remembers wellness; thus, it strives always to balance your energy. However, it requires life-energy to do its work.
- There are basically two types of food: food filled with life-energy and food that is relatively dead.
- Your body requires clean and efficient fuel to nourish and sustain it through its cycle of life.
- Food filled with life-energy provides efficient fuel for the body's metabolic requirements.
- Your body uses any life-energy in excess of daily metabolic needs to burn off excess fat and attain a healthful balance.
- Food comprised mostly of dead energy fuels the body's metabolism like cheap, low-grade gasoline runs in a high-powered car—with knocks, pings, poor starts, and dirty emissions.
- Leftover dead energy is converted to fat, which first drenches the blood and organs, then is stored in the larger blood vessels, abdomen, thighs, and buttocks.

Wellness Genetics

DNA is the substance of human genes. It contains billions of bits of ancestral information, including the templates of disease that we have been inheriting from our family since time immemorial. The information encoded in our DNA appears to date back over 60 million years. Your own gene pool is as vast as the stars. It carries your mental characteristics, including your temperament; your physical characteristics, such as hair color; and an inborn biological clock to signal adolescence, adulthood, menopause, even the time for hair to grow in your ears!

In the first half of life, your genes strive to keep you healthy and to enable you to pass on your DNA to preserve our species. During the second half of life, your genes strive to keep you alive for as long as possible to enable you to pass on your intellect, love, skills, and devotion, to protect our species. Nobel laureate physicist David Bohm pointed out that even the very atoms of a human being are invested with meaning and purpose. Although most people believe it is difficult to establish a sense of higher purpose or mission in life, it's much easier than one would think. We are all part of the very fabric of life. What touches others touches us.

The major function of your genes is to transmit health and the inborn resolve to remember wellness. In the sickness paradigm, we are taught that disease-carrying genes determine our destiny. This is a false and life-threatening view. If we were truly destined to live by such genes, we would suffer from the thousands of diseases experienced by our ancestors for as long as we lived, which would not be very long at all. Fortunately, our ancestral templates, or blueprints of disease, are influenced by factors well within our control. Disease-carrying genes are not our destiny because they must answer to our inner compass, our healing force, which remembers wellness and keeps templates of diseases safely stored away in vaults within our cells. Even if the vaults containing the templates have already been unlocked, it is still possible to summon our healing forces to fight for wellness. Our physical, mental, and spiritual vitality stimulates our natural internal pharmacy of biochemical healers.

Everything in Moderation—Including Moderation

How do you get motivated to lose weight permanently? Others cannot or will not do it for you. Motivation requires setting realistic goals, like a 5 to 10 percent (of your total weight) weight loss for the first year. Motivation also requires understanding life-energy versus dead energy. Finally, motivation requires developing a reverence for life through understanding the beauty and power of the human lifecycle.

It is truly remarkable that the decline in coronary vascular disease and stroke in the United States during the past twenty-five years has not been accompanied by a decrease in obesity. Actually, the prevalence of excess weight has doubled during that time period. Although the majority of medical and nutritional scientists believe that the incidence of coronary vascular disease and stroke has declined because we have become more cholesterol-conscious, this may not actually be the case because of two other phenomena: in the past twenty-five years 60 million Americans quit smoking and the diagnosis and treatment of hypertension improved dramatically.

Despite all the complicated theories about why we gain weight and all the scientific terms that describe what we eat—calories, saturated fats, trans-fats, polyunsaturated fats, monounsaturated fats—we are still getting fatter. New weight-loss drugs won't help; you can't tinker with your metabolism and expect to be all right. Fad diets won't work, because they disobey natural laws (which we will discuss later on) and ignore the fact that obesity is largely a symptom of inaccurate information, stress, and inner dis-ease. Your inner works—the mind and soul—need fixing before your body can look good and feel better. It would be impossible to underestimate the magnitude behind this shift in vision. Nor does such a discovery diminish present nutritional science. Instead, it shapes it into a clinically effective field that allows people to lose weight permanently. Remember: The triumph of one scenario over another does not necessarily mean the loser must be discarded. In fact, good nutritional science means using past nutritional science in a more accurate manner.

Attitude and weight are inseparable. Your body and your mind are a complete ensemble. From this viewpoint, it is obvious that fat begins and persists in the mind. It is no wonder, then, that the idea of changing the mind's appetite for food has been the impetus behind thousands of diet books. After all, it seems so obvious: Eat well, exercise, and just kick the habit! The problem is that this simple idea never works in practice for very long. Why? When we are stressed, we forget or ignore our resolve. This is the *stress disinhibition effect*, which I will revisit throughout this book. Practically, it means that our food urges and cravings are so strong that, once we get stressed, we obey them.

What does it mean if you make a resolution to eat more appropriately and then don't do it? Is it a matter of copping out, giving up too easily, not having the courage of your convictions, being weak-willed or looking for the easy way out? Absolutely not. If you are stressed, you can actually forget or ignore your resolve. If the desires of your taste buds are unfulfilled, you become further stressed. It's a vicious cycle that causes dieters to always lose—their hope, that is, but unfortunately not their weight.

While sitting at my computer for seemingly endless days and nights writing this book, a personal problem began looming larger and larger for me. I was developing a powerful for craving chocolate. And I also gave into it, big time! I tried to stop my chocolate cravings mentally but couldn't. My mind said to me, "Eat the chocolate," and I did. I began to pay more attention to my craving for chocolate and tried to ascertain the feelings behind them. I remembered my early childhood, and Grandma showering me with incredible love by letting me lick the warm chocolate pudding right out of the pot. This was exactly the type of comforting feeling I was now getting from eating chocolate when I overworked.

How could I block out that warm memory, along with the quivering feeling it caused in my stomach? Certainly not by using my very same chocolate pudding–drenched desires to make a resolution to break my habit. Chocolate pudding goes a long way toward soothing the savage beast called stress!

We can combine good science and effective stress management to forge a brand-new frontier for lifelong healthy weight. But the journey there can only be accomplished by building a *new path of least resistance*. This is a matter of human nature and good common sense. Unhealthy eating habits begin in the mind, where stress and misinformation create "mental malnutrition." The overweight person's mind is deficient in mental nutrients such as love, serenity, and self-esteem. Once we repair such deficiencies, the mind naturally hungers for food with life-energy. Then, and only then, the process of natural weight loss begins.

Imagine the mind as a mental pantry whose shelves we must clear out. First we take inventory, then we clear out the thoughts and feelings that cause weight gain. Finally we restock the pantry by filling the shelves with essential ingredients for permanent weight loss: self-respect, stress management, enjoyable exercise, and food filled with life-energy.

My chocolate habit? There was one basic fact that was so obvious that even my chocolate-drenched thoughts could not obscure it: Everyday joys of youth, especially candy, may have little effect on a body that is mostly intent on passing on its DNA to the future. Those same youthful pleasures, however, become the potbellies of middle and older age. More regular meditation and exercise helped me overcome my urges and cravings. It was amazing how some simple steps enabled my brain to search for different meanings and make new connections to bypass my inflamed appetite, building a *new path of least resistance** to a much healthier frontier.

My chocolate habit is still there, but it's safely tucked away in the vaults of my memory. Fortunately, *"Moderation in all things— including moderation"* is an unspoken tenet of Integrative Medicine. I only remove my craving from its safety-deposit box when I go to the movies, where I enjoy chocolate-covered raisins. It's not a

---

*Robert Fritz addresses this general concept very well. See bibliography.

problem I can readily solve, because my pleasurable memory is always there, perhaps a part of my very being. Instead of solving the problem, I created a new result.

Looking for Help in All the Wrong Places

The troubling paradox of modern medical science is that doctors, with so many years of schooling, find it hard to accept that the natural healing abilities of the body are more intelligent than medical science. But don't let your mind become prey to the tempting notion of medicating away the results of your misguided eating habits. The most inspiring resource we have to overcome obesity is within ourselves. Our own natural healing force is equivalent to an inner pharmacy. It is like a biological compass within our cells that always remembers wellness.

Only in the past century have our natural healing forces been so neglected by technology and diminished by stress. Yet they still struggle to maintain our energy balance and health against all odds. My 28-Day Plan will help get you on track. It is a strategy for *Total Health Rejuvenation*—unleashing the power of your healing forces so that the spirit of wellness reigns throughout your body and mind.

Your healing force is like a sacred song echoing through the chambers of your heart and the deep spaces of your soul. It is the music that drenches your spirit, calms your mind, and gives your body the strength to shed its excess fat. Your healing force is like an eternal flame, still burning even in those people who have forgotten its soothing light. It is your inner biological compass that stimulates your body's will to be well. Let us embark upon a healing journey to lose weight comfortably and permanently.

A Special Note From Me To You

Now that you have completed Parts One, Two, and Three of this book, it is very important for you to understand what I have been trying to help you accomplish. I consider this book a "gift of life" from me to you.

Now you will be so much more knowledgeable and discriminating about what you put in your body. For the rest of your life, every time you watch a television commercial about food, you will be able to think, *What audacity! Does anyone have the right to suggest to me (or my children) that I eat something that is not good for me?* You will be able to look at food advertisements with a skeptical eye and say to yourself, *No way!* And, with an inner laugh, you can add, *Don't insult my intelligence.*

When you are in the supermarket, don't be fooled. You know the advertising game, so ignore all the fancy packaging. Now that you are beginning to understand the myths and advertising images created to sell food to you, be alert and discriminating. Be sensible . . . be healthy . . . and you will achieve your optimal weight. Whenever you are in doubt, think about what you have learned in Parts One, Two, and Three. Just feel good about yourself and read on! Remember, *you have strength!*

Part Four

ENERGY NUTRITION
AND THE CYCLE
OF LIFE

How do you feel about what you have read so far? I wish we were face-to-face so we could discuss weight loss one-on-one. For the moment, at least, that's not possible, but books are a helpful medium; they allow physician-authors to talk to so many people in a thorough and complete manner.

Isn't it amazing that we can go through life with our eyes open, yet miss so much of what's around us, especially when our environment so totally influences our health and life? Unfortunately, with our busy lifestyles, heavy workloads, and two-income families, we don't take the time to take care of ourselves. Yet it is so easy and possible to do. Once you have a new mindset about the food you eat, you will develop new healthful eating habits, along with many other wonderful and healthful benefits. It requires no more time or work to eat and live the *healthy balanced way*, as opposed to the *out-of-balance way*.

Did you know that you are one of trillions of components of nature? Your own personal human lifecycle regulates and guides the sequence of events occurring in your body from the moment of your conception until the time of your death. Beyond that, who knows? Perhaps we humans are just like animated star dust, hurtling through time and space until we return to the heart of God. What the caterpillar calls the end of the world, nature calls the butterfly.

The cycle of life is represented by the following stages:

- Prenatal
- Infancy
- Childhood
- Adolescence
- Young Adulthood
- Middle Adulthood
- Maturity

Throughout your entire lifecycle, you require proper fuel to nourish and sustain each stage of the cycle. Your body derives the necessary fuel by extracting energy from the earth, air, water, and sun. Your human lifecycle is clearly an endangered entity. Most of us drink more soft drinks than water, and most of our food is refined or artificial, stripped of its life-energy. The air is so polluted with dirt and particulate matter that millions of us develop asthma with each passing month. The sun's rays cause cancer because much of the ozone in the atmosphere has been depleted.

What can you do to better sustain your own lifecycle? You must truly glimpse the truth for yourself. Only in that way can the information in this book give birth to wisdom. It is essential that you read about each stage of the human lifecycle. I am going to teach you about certain aspects of human biology, psychology, and natural laws in a deeper, more profound manner than even physicians learn in medical school. Please do not skip over the parts of the book that you believe are not relevant for you. Even if you are over fifty years old, it is essential that you understand the prenatal, childhood, and adolescence stages of your human lifecycle. And even if you are twenty-five years old, it is essential that you understand the maturity stage of the human lifecycle. Each stage of the lifecycle is part of nature's entire cycle of life, and it is essential for you to understand the truth. You are a component of nature.

In the Beginning

Let me take a moment to give you a brief definition of DNA. Simply put, DNA is the basic building block of life. The scientific chemical name for DNA is deoxyribonucleic acid. Now here's a more in-depth definition:

> Each of our trillions of cells contain genes that are made up of our DNA molecules. These molecules consist of two long strands that are twisted together to form a double helix. DNA molecules contain the intelligence, information, and instructions that are required for our cells to function well and stay alive.

Your personal human lifecycle encompasses more than just the length of time between your conception and death. Your DNA is comprised of your parents' DNA, and their parents', and their parents', and so on. It is said that there is a species of bamboo tree in China which, in twelve months, grows more than one hundred feet from its initial sprout. But its seed, buried deep in the soil, requires weekly watering for thirty years before sprouting to the surface. Does this tree grow one hundred feet in one year, or did it take thirty-one years? Did the prenatal stage of your personal human lifecycle take nine months, nine generations, or nine millennia?

Every human lifecycle is rooted in one common ground—an inexhaustible universal storehouse of energy that initially breathes life into every living thing. Therefore, let us begin by considering your own personal human lifecycle. The initial breath of energy that ignited the spark of your own human lifecycle occurred as the sperm of your father united with the egg of your mother. Your human lifecycle began at the moment of fusion between their DNA, ancestral genetic matter that had been accumulating for millions of years. Then, in the moment it took for your mother's fertilized egg to divide into two cells, you were transformed into a microscopic pre-embryo.

What an incredible chain of events had to occur before your human lifecycle could actually begin! Did you know that your mother had all the eggs she would ever have in her life already present in her ovaries at the moment of her own birth? As many as a quarter of a million eggs lay quietly in her ovaries, awaiting the adolescence stage of her human lifecycle so that she could start yet another human lifecycle: yours!

Examining the various stages of the human lifecycle will allow you to understand the normal changes you should expect during the seasons of your time on earth. More importantly, it cannot help but cause you to be in awe of your body. From the time of fertilization right up to the present moment, your human lifecycle has been persistent and resolute, conquering almost any obstacles that you may have raised along the way. Your body is like a bird that flies. If you allow it to, it will flourish.

Your own human lifecycle began when one particular egg in one of your mother's ovaries, responding to some dim message, perhaps in phase with the moon, began a migration for which it had been preparing for a lifetime, or even longer. This solitary egg began moving slowly toward the thick, fibrous coating of her ovary. Finally, the egg burst through the ovarian wall in a splash of blood. Free-floating in your mother's pelvis, a wave of energy propelled the egg through a space which, in terms of the egg's tiny size, was equivalent to jumping across the Grand Canyon.

Arriving safely at its destination at the opening to one of your mother's fallopian tubes, the egg began to roll down almost one-third the length of this tube. It did this slowly, through forty-eight hours, to await the arrival of one particular sperm from your father's ejaculate of over 50 million sperm. That's how you were born. Now that's energy!

Until recently, we believed that tens of millions of your father's sperm engaged in furious battle with each other to conquer your mother's egg, enter it, and close it off to all competitors. Alas, the warrior's tale is no longer told! Yes, it is true that millions of sperm in your father's ejaculate were propelled toward your mother's uterus with an explosion of energy that allowed them to burrow

through the thick plug of mucous in her cervix, then climb vertically upward along her inner uterus wall, find the tiny opening to
the correct fallopian tube and climb further upward to meet her
waiting egg, into which only one sperm would penetrate and enter.

However, it now appears that your mother's egg chose that particular sperm that made you. In a sense, your mother's egg invited
this one special sperm to fuse its DNA with hers in order to give
birth to you. This one special sperm had to race at top speed, over
a distance that, for its tiny size, was equivalent to running a race
nonstop from Los Angeles to New York City, before entering into
your mother's waiting egg, then rolling down her fallopian tube
while dividing into a sixteen-celled pre-embryo that had to be embedded in the wall of her uterus within seventy-two hours in order
to prepare you to be nourished by your mother's life-energy for the
first nine months of your human lifecycle. Now that's energy, too!

How, Why, and When Obesity Begins

A serious mistake has been made that continues to
harm us later in life. The most basic nutritional standards for keeping infants and children in energy balance are wrong! A growing
body of evidence shows that the food requirements of the infancy
and childhood stages are a good deal lower than previously estimated, up to 20 percent lower for infants and 25 percent lower for
children from one to ten years of age. We have been mistakenly
encouraged to overfeed our babies and children from the very
beginning.

What happened? It's really very simple. The old testing methods
used to measure food intake data were inaccurate. Weighing foods,
keeping records of food intakes, then submitting personal diet his-
tories to researchers do not produce objective data. In fact, we now

realize that such subjective methods produce grossly inaccurate data. When questioned, adults generally misrepresent their own food intake patterns because less makes them feel better. On the other hand, adults tend to overestimate the food intake of their infants and children because more makes them feel like they are better parents.

New testing methods with nuclear isotopes can now measure the actual energy requirements of infants and children directly. These tests demonstrate that the food energy requirements of infants and young children are significantly lower than scientists once thought. That's too bad, because human fat-storing cells (adipocytes) develop to handle excess energy during infancy and childhood, and then tend to hang around for life.

Another reason why current recommendations for food energy are too high is that food intake data collected during the 1970s are not very relevant to the 1990s. The reason? Today children exercise less and less often. Physical activity burns up about a third of a child's food energy intake, yet current food intake standards fail to account for the huge decline in exercise in children. If children continue to consume the same amount of calories suggested since the 1970s, while continuing to watch more TV and exercise less, then childhood obesity will continue to skyrocket. So will the incidence of diseases associated with being overweight, including cardiovascular disease, diabetes, and many types of cancer.

If you really look fat, then you probably are fat. This is a fairly workable measure of excess weight during the adolescent and adult stages of the human lifecycle. The same is definitely not true, however, during infancy and early childhood, because most chubby babies and kids are fine. If they are truly overweight, then adjusting their food intake or exercise patterns will help them. During the early stages of the human lifecycle, the only real obstacle to predictable weight loss may be overweight parents who are unable to recognize the need to make healthful changes.

Time is a friend for chubby infants and young children. Six- to twelve-month-old babies normally accumulate more body fat than at any other time in their human lifecycle, until puberty ensues. This is why the "little Buddha" appearance is so common during the early months. As the human lifecycle progresses, plumpness diminishes because children start growing two to three inches in height every year, while their body fat remains stable.

Most children appear rather lean by the time they reach their fifth or sixth year. After that time, however, muscle mass as well as body fat begin to increase dramatically until the growth spurt at puberty. As a result, many boys and girls appear a bit chubby or husky just before they enter adolescence.

It is important to understand these earlier stages of the human lifecycle. Remember: The number of overweight children has doubled in the past twenty-five years. Nearly 40 percent of overweight seven-year-olds and 70 percent of overweight adolescents will turn into overweight adults. Although heredity is a powerful factor, it's important to realize that heaviness in the adulthood stages of the human lifecycle is not related to birth weight. If one or both parents are heavy, however, there is greater likelihood that an overweight infant or child will grow into an overweight adult. When it comes to heaviness, the type of adult we become is largely determined by our childhood habits.

What can parents do to prevent their children from becoming overweight? What is the best help parents can provide for children who are already overweight? It's relatively simple during the early stages of the human lifecycle. Breast-feed infants for at least six to twelve months. Avoid giving solid foods until six months. Never use a baby bottle as a pacifier. During the childhood stage of the human lifecycle, a more holistic approach is very helpful. It involves the entire family's eating habits, assuring regular exercise, building self-esteem, and controlling the amount of time that children watch television.

The Prenatal Stage of the Human Lifecycle

Your mother's fertilized egg divided into two identical cells within twenty-four hours of your conception. In the next twenty-four hours, the two cells divided into four cells, which also began to divide. By seventy-two hours, a sphere consisting of your first twelve cells began to form. It rolled down your mother's fallopian tube to enter her uterus and then implanted itself in the wall, where it would grow, over the next 265 days, into what would ultimately become you.

Do you ever wonder whether you were really meant to be alive? Albert Einstein answered the question by saying, "God does not play dice with the universe." Here are the approximate odds and the obstacles you had to surmount in order for you to come into this world: One special sperm out of 50 million had to reach one special egg from out of a quarter of a million that had been awaiting its arrival since the very day of your own mother's birth. Now, consider the fact that less than 20 percent of fertilized eggs ever reach the uterus, and that less than half successfully implant themselves within the uterus wall. What odds you overcame! What obstacles you transcended! But that was not the end of your early journey.

Once you were implanted in your mother's uterus as a microscopically small pre-embryo, a massive organization began to occur among your dividing cells. They became thousands, then millions, then tens and hundreds of millions of dividing cells. Within six weeks, your dividing cells formed islands of cells to create a primitive brain and spinal cord, then a rudimentary heart and circulatory system, and then an early type of skeleton. It is estimated that just 10 percent of all embryos are able to survive this very complex growth period.

After six weeks within your mother's uterus, your body developed very rapidly and became an embryo. Tiny outgrowths of cells became the beginnings of your arms and legs. Other groups of cells coalesced to start forming your esophagus, stomach, and intestines. Islands of other cells began growing into your eyes and ears. Miraculously, by the tenth week, your sex was evident and you were transformed into a tiny humanlike fetus, about one inch in length. By eighteen weeks, your brain had most of its cells, your mother felt your first movements, and you were well on your way to becoming a viable baby with a life expectancy, as a girl, of almost eighty years, and, as a boy, of seventy-five years.

In the womb, through a placenta and an umbilical cord, you received from your mother sufficient life-energy to sustain your human lifecycle. About ten days after implantation into her uterine wall, your mother's fertilized egg began developing into the marvelous structure called a placenta, to which you were attached via your umbilical cord. The placenta has two components—one from your mother and one from yourself. The maternal component was rich in blood vessels that delivered nourishment to you. Yours also was rich in vessels that carried blood to your organs and heart. These two circulatory systems do not normally mix with each other. They are separated by a thin layer of cells through which nutrients pass from mother to baby. Can you imagine how much life-energy your mother had to supply for you to sustain the first stage of your human lifecycle, driving your growth from a one-inch fetus at twenty-eight days to a twenty-inch infant at 270 days?

During the prenatal stage, it is impossible to overestimate the importance of good nutrition. Pregnant women need abundant amounts of fresh fruit, fresh juice, fresh vegetables, nuts, beans, lentils, and complex carbohydrates. They also require large amounts of water. How much? At least five servings of fresh fruit, five servings of fresh vegetables, and six to eight eight-ounce glasses of water a day. It is wise either to boil tap water or use bottled water if the chemical content of the local water supply is reported to be high.

Additionally, even if a pregnant woman eats well, it is crucial for her to take a daily multivitamin-mineral supplement. Recent studies indicate that the incidence of premature births is lower among women who take a daily supplement. Moreover, taking four hundred micrograms of folic acid daily helps to prevent up to 80 percent of the congenital spinal cord malformations called spina bifida.

By a true miracle of nature, even mothers suffering with malnutrition can produce healthy full-term babies. Certain hormones released within them cause their bodies to supply sufficient nourishment to the growing fetus, even when it detracts from their own survival.

It is the mother who can also help to resolve the major problems facing the prenatal stage of the human lifecycle, including infection, diabetes, alcohol, drug, and tobacco use. Exposure to secondhand smoke is dangerous, too. Even if only the father smokes during pregnancy, nicotine can be found in his newborn's hair. Radiation and exposure to environmental toxins also can be disastrous to the growing fetus. Consider what small doses of X-rays or toxins might do to a tiny bundle of cells undergoing rapid growth.

The current trend of using ultrasound to determine the sex of a fetus is also cause for concern. Routine ultrasound for an unborn baby is unnecessary. Why should a new growth industry influence prenatal care while we still don't know conclusively the effect of high frequency sound waves on the fetus? We may one day look back on such casual use of ultrasound with the same concern that we physicians experience when we look back just forty years ago, when it was common to use X-rays in shoe stores to fit shoes.

The amount of sunshine, fresh air and exercise that an expectant mother gets is important. So is her attitude. A fetus who shares his or her mother's body also shares her feelings and emotions. In fact, there is a new science called, Psycho-neuro-immunology, which actually demonstrates the ways that feelings and emotions affect all the cells of the body. What is on your mind and in your heart can help keep you well or make you sick. The intricate network of mind-body connections in pregnant women affects their babies, too. Growing humans in the prenatal stage experience their mother's stress as well as her gladness and joy.

Let's review some of what you have learned about the prenatal stage of the human lifecycle. First there was the cross-country race of sperm while the egg was jumping the Grand Canyon. Then there was the tumultuous six-week growth period, during which 90 percent of human lifecycles fail to survive. Thereafter, very many more human lifecycles could also come to an end during the remaining months of pregnancy. Surely you were meant to be!

You are already a winner. Despite all the obstacles, the mighty healing force within you has sustained your human lifecycle. Knowing this empowers you to take charge of the present stage of your life, no matter how old you are, including losing excess fat. You control your own health destiny to a far greater extent than you have ever been led to believe.

Total health rejuvenation ignites the healing force present in all your cells, which remembers wellness. What Hippocrates called *vix mediatrix*, the French call *le mileu interieur* and the English call homeostasis. It doesn't really matter what we call the force; perhaps it is just God's presence in each of your cells. What matters is that your body is a marvelous, self-repairing, complex energy system. Yes, you may have been overweight for a very long time, but your inner healing force has infinite patience. It is merely awaiting your resolution to *take charge of your own health destiny*.

The Infancy Stage of the Human Lifecycle

Babies require breast milk for optimal health. There's nothing like it. Unfortunately, generations of medical doctors, mostly men, have been trained not to urge mothers to breast-feed too much for fear of making them feel guilty if they don't breast-feed. Additionally, billions of dollars have been spent by the baby formula industry to offer subtle enticements to women not to breast-feed. There is a loud and clear message attached to the sample bottles and cans of baby formula given out freely by the most prestigious hospitals, even to contented breast-feeding mothers. "This is good. This is convenient. This is scientific. This is best."

The truth is that the benefits of breast-feeding for your baby's health go far beyond that which scientists can measure. We know that breast milk passes a mother's antibodies on to her baby, as well as nutrients that cannot be reproduced in formula. Through her breast milk, a mother helps protect her baby against infections during infancy. But how can scientists measure the vital emotional, psychological, and physical bonds that emerge between mother and baby during breast-feeding? How can science measure the positive, comforting feelings toward food and eating that are communicated to a breast-fed baby?

Breast milk is easier to digest than formula, and babies fed on breast milk are less likely to experience the gastrointestinal problems so common among "tube syndrome" babies. In a study of twenty thousand babies, those who were bottle fed experienced twice as many infections as their breast-fed counterparts. Some bottle-fed babies tend to sleep longer, because formula takes longer to digest. But the benefits of a baby who rests more are not as important as the health benefits a baby derives from breast milk. Breast-fed babies grow up to have lower cholesterol levels and lower rates of heart disease as adults; iron deficiency is less frequent in breast-fed babies; certain enzymes in breast milk have the power to lower the incidence of allergies, diarrhea, upper respiratory infections, otitis media, sinusitis, pneumonia, blood poisoning, meningitis, botulism, urinary tract infections, enterocolitis, and sudden death syndrome in both infants and children.

Overall, breast-fed babies become ill nearly half as frequently as bottle-fed babies. And finally, recent surveys indicate that breast-fed babies are less prone to becoming overweight adults. There is also strong evidence that breast-feeding decreases the incidence of diabetes, Crohn's disease, ulcerative colitis, and lymphoma during adulthood.

The energy in breast milk is live and pure, compared to the so-called high energy of artificial baby formulas. Along with added minerals and vitamins, baby formulas contain whey, nonfat milk, lactose, palm olein oil, soy oil, coconut oil, high oleic sunflower oil, carrageenan, monoglycerides, diglycerides, sodium chloride, potassium hydroxide, adenosine 5-monophosphate, cytidine 5-monophosphate, disodium guanosine 5-monophosphate, and disodium uridine 5-monophosphate. Not a single one of these ingredients possesses life-energy. Not even a mixture of one hundred times more of all of them could direct an ant's leg to move or a butterfly's wing to flutter. That requires life-energy.

Each stage of the human lifecycle benefits from the life-energy in breast milk. Breast-feeding definitely protects the mother by reducing her blood loss after birth and by improving her bone mineralization so that risk of hip fractures during menopause decreases. It also appears that the mother's risk of ovarian and breast cancer is lessened. When it comes to nutrition and nourishment—for babies as well as adults—nothing manufactured in a laboratory can ever match, let alone surpass, the goodness and vitality of food made by nature. This same principle applies to what we eat throughout our lives.

I am not suggesting that bottle feeding is wrong, or that mothers who bottle feed are bad, or that their children are doomed to a lifetime disadvantage. Many women are unable to breast-feed, and in these cases, commercially available formula is an adequate substitute for breast milk. But the healthiest nutritional beginnings come from breast milk. Like fast and convenience foods for adults, the makers of formulas promote their product not only as a way for a mother to save time, but as an anxiety-free way to keep track of how much a baby eats. It is an anxiety that they, the formula makers, have helped to create! It is simply not necessary to monitor exactly how much your baby eats. The breast-feeding mother and her baby develop a natural code of understanding as to when the baby is hungry and when the baby has had enough. Nothing is more assuring and comforting to a mother caring for her newborn than the knowledge that her baby is thriving and growing naturally.

Every physician should take a strong position on behalf of breast-feeding and work toward eliminating the standard hospital practice that discourages breast-feeding by giving away free infant formula packs at discharge. Dr. Oliver Wendell Holmes (1809–94) aptly noted: "A pair of substantial mammary glands has the advantage over two hemispheres of the most learned professor's brain in the art of compounding a nutritious fluid for infants."

The natural rate of growth during the infancy stage of the human lifecycle is about six ounces a week for the first six months. Birth weight then doubles at about four months of age and triples by about a year. Cow's milk should be particularly avoided during infancy. Soy milk, fresh juices, and even nut milk are good alternatives when the breast-feeding days are over. Solid foods do not need to be a part of a baby's menu until six months or later.

When it comes to solid foods, just remember that the later the better, the fresher the better, and the least amount of variety the better. Nutritionally, it's impossible to match the energy of foods prepared in your kitchen to that of the factory. Preparing fresh baby food is easy and convenient, and it saves money. Be sure to wait at least seven days before introducing another new food. Steaming food helps to preserve its vitamins and minerals. Parents can even feed their baby some of the food they are serving for their own meal if it's free of added salt, sugar, other spices, and fat.

Babies don't have an inborn preference for spices or fat. Nor should you encourage them to develop an early taste for salt, sugar, and other additives. Try a single grain cereal such as home-prepared rice cereal, or mash up some potato, squash, string beans, sweet potato, pumpkin, green peas, pear, apple, or banana, then serve it to your baby knowing that the food is free of the additives, spices, chemicals, and fillers found in factory-made baby foods. Making your own baby food, full of life-energy, doesn't require a lot of equipment: a clean pot to steam, boil, heat, simmer, or sauté food; a fork for mashing food to a soft, easy-to-swallow consistency, and a simple strainer to remove seeds and lumps is all you need.

The Childhood Stage of the Human Lifecycle

Toddlers want to eat more and more like Mom and Dad. This is the perfect time for parents to involve children in food preparation, from helping to mash a banana or a baked apple to shopping together to pick out the reddest tomato. Now is the time to educate children as to what is good for them and what is not, before television does the job for you. Teach them the difference between good and not-so-good bread by having them squeeze the soft white kind and saying "Yuck!" and the firm dark variety while saying "Yum!" Teach them how good it is to drink water instead of soft drinks, tell them about the goodness of fresh fruit juice. Mostly, don't instill in them the idea that if they eat more, you will love them more. Don't bring junk food into the house. Your children are what they eat, and they will emulate their parents' eating preferences—what to eat as well as how to eat.

Good childhood nutrition is a holistic adventure comprised of equal parts nurture, nourishment, and nutrition. Besides good food, it's about sunshine, love, family, fresh air, cleanliness, prayer, and self-discovery. Parents can teach children as young as two or three years old that food is energy that makes them happy, healthy, and strong. You can show them colorful apples, bananas, carrots, or tomatoes, then explain that they all give us strength because they grow on trees or underneath the soil, outside in the sunshine, and in nature. You can show them a potato that comes from the soil and a potato chip that comes from the factory, then explain that one contains life-energy and the other does not. You can show them a glass of water and a glass of cola, explaining how one flows healthily in rivers and streams, while the other does not. You can compare the feel and texture of a slice of grainy whole wheat bread with that of a slice of white bread containing dead energy.

Everyone talks about the need for five servings of fruit and five servings of vegetables a day. How realistic is that? As it turns out, not very! According to recent surveys, only 20 percent of our children and teenagers have five servings of fruit and vegetables per day. Moreover, only one percent follow the general governmental guidelines for nutrition. It is realistic, though, not to buy junk food, and to continually reinforce how wonderful fresh fruit and vegetables are. Serve lots of carrots, sweet potatoes, and green peas. Have fun with spaghetti squash. Make a meal out of a baked potato. But keep in mind: french fries should not be counted as a vegetable serving!

Fish and poultry can be introduced after the first year. Red meat is just not necessary and should be eaten sparingly, if at all. Buy good food that is full of life-energy, insist on family meals, complete with conversation, and don't serve food while watching television. Everyone should be sitting while they eat, taking care not to gobble down their food. Make eating healthy and fun; your children will remember this throughout all the later stages of their human life-cycles.

Celebrate summer with watermelons. Don't forget to introduce special foods such as pumpkins when autumn approaches. Make sure to call attention to ordinary foods when they are at the height of their season, so that your children can understand the taste of a really special tomato in summer as compared to the bland, genetically engineered variety. Always point out to growing children how much they are helping themselves to become healthy and strong by eating foods from nature as close as possible to the way nature first offered them.

Encourage your children to eat what you serve, but never coerce them to eat by pleading or showing anxiety or annoyance. Never, ever broadcast the subtle notion that you would love your children more if only they would eat more. The childhood stage of the human lifecycle is initially associated with a decrease in appetite, as the natural growth rate slows to about one and one-half ounces weight gain per week during the second year of life—just about 30 percent of the growth rate during the infancy stage of the human lifecycle. As iron deficiency commonly occurs about this time, consider iron supplementation as a solution.

The nutritional needs of babies and children change as they develop through the human lifecycle. Foods containing life-energy support the ability to develop clear vision and fine movement, so that a growing baby can begin to use its fingers, then its hands, to grasp objects, and soon will be able to pass a toy block from one hand to the other. The baby will start to lift its head, sit up unsupported, roll over from front to back and back to front, crawl and, finally, walk. Hearing and speech develop as the baby babbles away, imitates sounds, says a few words like "ma-ma, da-da," and even links words together to form a simple sentence: "I love you." Social awareness develops as the baby smiles or cries, behaves in uneasy or friendly ways with strangers, makes eye contact, gurgles, laughs, and grows more alert.

The concept, *we are what we eat*, along with my recommendations for proper nutrition during the early stages of the human lifecycle, are also crucial to understanding weight loss, no matter how old you are.

Older babies and toddlers need a wholesome, single grain (not mixed) cereal, a few fresh fruits and some vegetables, not milk from a cow, food from a jar, or complicated main courses. Why spend a dollar on a jar of organic mashed carrots when you can mash less expensive, fresh carrots yourself? Toddlers thrive on a variety of whole grains, including breads, cereals, rice, and pasta, along with many kinds of fresh fruits and lots of vegetables. Older children thrive (and stay lean) by eating plenty of fresh fruits, vegetables, whole grains, and complex carbohydrates like good breads, pasta, rice, and potatoes.

By all means, it is important for parents to avoid turning mealtime into a battleground. Forcing children to be "clean-platers" only backfires later in the human lifecycle. Many children are picky eaters but still grow well despite that fact. During the early stages of the human lifecycle, nutrition doesn't really get a whole lot more complicated than this.

The natural growth rate of the human lifecycle slows down during the childhood stage, until puberty begins. During this time, children build strong food preferences as they increasingly develop more control over what they will or will not eat. Because the eating patterns established in childhood will last forever, a holistic approach here is vital. Believe it or not, osteoporosis, irritable bowel syndrome, diabetes, and atherosclerosis are pediatric diseases; this is when they begin.

For a growing child to achieve increasing degrees of independence for the next stages of the human lifecycle, he or she will experience tremendous physical and emotional changes. Obviously, it is important for these changes to occur in an environment of love and security. Quality time between children and parents is essential, particularly talking, eating, playing, and reading. The basic holistic approach to raising healthy children who are not overweight, and preparing them for the next phase of the human lifecycle, requires good sense. It's all about instilling healthy habits. Get children outside to play when it's daylight and the weather permits. Hats, scarves, boots, and mittens help to stretch the limits of "permissible."

Don't use the television as a baby-sitter. Limit watching TV to an hour or two at most on any day, and make sure that the show is not violent or sexual in content. Better still, get rid of the TV. Children who spend a lot of time sitting on the couch watching television are more than likely to be overweight. Actually, in the last three decades, TV has been the leading factor in weight gain among children. Kids and teenagers now spend on average more time sitting in front of the television than they do in school. Being sedentary most of the day, instead of running around and burning off excess energy takes its toll. *Energy that is not burned is converted to fat.*

A landmark study published by Dr. Steven L. Gortmaker and his colleagues at the Harvard School of Public Health examined the relationship between the amount of time spent watching television and the prevalence of obesity among ten- to fifteen-year-olds. The results were startling. There was more than a 500 percent increase in the rate of obesity among youths watching more than five hours of television per day, compared with those who watched for two hours or less per day. The study found that the average child watched television 4.8 hours per day, or thirty-four hours per week. Only 11 percent of the youths watched television for less than two hours per day.

This Harvard study was conducted in 1990. Now, a decade later, the numbers are considerably higher. Each hour spent sitting in front of the television means one less hour of hopping, skipping, jumping, running, playing tag, baseball, or just hide-and-seek. The lack of vigorous physical activity in kids is as alarming as their generally poor nutrition. To add insult to injury, while they are sitting in front of the TV, kids are bombarded with thousands of commercials that seduce them into making poor food choices, forever.

Believe it or not, the most important thing that parents can do to prevent obesity in children is to *turn off the television!* The Harvard study also showed that if your child or teenager is already overweight, each hour he or she spends watching television increases the odds of remaining overweight by 130 percent. Although the American Academy of Pediatrics recommends that television be limited to no more than two hours per day, I believe even less would be good. And none is best.

Spending half an hour at bedtime or an hour during the day reading to a young child is rewarding for child and parent alike. Children fondly remember reading time, and time spent playing games with parents, throughout their entire life. Reading should be fun, not a task; make it interactive by letting your child read to you, too. These are the times that become ingrained memories that enhance self-esteem and begin to pay big dividends as young people enter adolescence. Here's a fun poem to share, especially at bedtime:

> *The more you read,*
> *the more you know;*
> *the more you know,*
> *the further you go.*

Whatever happened to playing cards, chess, or checkers during quiet times? What about hobbies—collecting stamps, baseball cards, or coins? What about jigsaw puzzles? Jumping rope? What about reading a book? If your kids are not in school, then they should be outside playing and running around as long as there is daylight. If it's too cold out, visit the local library or be active indoors.

Make no mistake about it, obesity is the most significant childhood disease of our time. More than a third of children and teens are overweight, and the numbers are rising. While genetics may predispose some kids to plumpness, most are getting fat because they don't exercise and eat too much of the wrong kinds of foods. Fifty years ago, most plump kids would have outgrown their weight problem because they would be outside playing tag or climbing trees, but that is not happening today.

Another major reason children become overweight is because of malnutrition. I'm not talking about the malnutrition that comes from starvation or famine but its modern form that comes from overeating, eating too much dead food, or both. Being overweight is a terrible disease for kids. Besides the fact that it sets them up for many adult diseases, it detracts from the very joy of childhood. Many overweight kids are called lazy, but it is really their excess fat that limits them. In other words, they easily lose their breath and suffer from all sorts of discomfort.

Also, there is the emotional trauma of being ridiculed and called names. As a result, kids withdraw, become depressed, and fall behind in school. Losing weight, however, can have a dramatic effect. Not only do children feel better and become more physically agile, they gain self-esteem, improve in school, and develop more friendships. Diets can help kids lose weight, but they are rarely successful in keeping the fat off later on.

Cow's Milk Is for Baby Cows

I am sure the following paragraphs will surprise you, since you have been taught to believe that cow's milk is essential for your good health. One of the major causes of malnutrition, however, is cow's milk. Don't get me wrong: Cow's milk is wonderful food; that is, if you are a baby cow. Facing this issue during the early stages of the human lifecycle is the key to preventing a terrible disease that occurs in the last stage of the human lifecycle: osteoporosis. In fact, osteoporosis is a pediatric disease, because it is during childhood that we are trained to believe in the necessity of cow's milk.

Cow's milk should be kept to an absolute minimum, especially after the first year of life. Many prominent medical doctors have tried to inform the public that dairy consumption contributes to acne, allergy, anemia, asthma, bronchitis, dental cavities, diarrhea, ear infections, eczema, sinusitis, osteoporosis, and atherosclerosis. Flip through the pages of many major medical journals and you will find research linking cow's milk to sudden infant death syndrome, childhood cancer, and diabetes mellitus. Contrary to what the commercials tell you, cow's milk is not good for your health.

Doctors have been all to slow to recognize and accept the truth about milk. Frank Oski, M.D., the late director of the Department of Pediatrics at the John Hopkins University School of Medicine, devoted a major part of his career to trying to inform physicians that the consumption of large amounts of cow's milk is unhealthy. Dr. Oski had his hand in over twenty medical textbooks, including several that are still the standard at most U.S. medical schools. Yet, at the time of his death, in 1996, too many medical doctors still ignored his concern about cow's milk. The story is similar to the experience of Dr. Ignaz Semmelweiss, who pleaded with physicians to wash their hands before delivering babies or conducting surgery . . . a plea that was widely ignored until the turn of the 20th century!

We have been taught to believe that children need cow's milk for health and strength. Adults believe they need cow's mild to prevent bone weakness. The marketing here is so successful that one dollar of every seven spent for food in the United States goes for milk and dairy products. Indeed, we now regard milk ads almost as public service announcements. These ads don't tell us that the milk of humans, cows, elephants, camels, wolves, walruses, and yaks are different. The milk of each mammalian species differs a great deal in its content because nature designed each type of milk to provide optimum nutrition for the young of that species. This is why in many parts of the world, particularly in East Asia, Africa, and South America, people regard cow's milk as unfit for human consumption.

Before we can absorb lactose into the bloodstream, the primary sugar in cow's milk, it must be broken down by the lactase enzyme. Far more people are unable to digest lactose than are able to digest it because most children gradually lose the lactase in their intestines by the time they are four years old. This is a normal process that accompanies the progression of the human lifecycle. As many as 75 percent of people at every age with low levels of lactase will experience cramping pain, gas, or diarrhea after drinking just one glass of milk. The worldwide prevalence of lactase deficiency according to Dr. Oski, may surprise you:

- Japanese 85 percent
- Chinese 85 percent
- Arabs 78 percent
- Ashkenazic Jews 78 percent

- African-Americans 70 percent
- Peruvians (as representative of South Americans) 70 percent
- American Indians 50 percent
- American Caucasians 15 percent

It is no wonder that Dr. Oski wrote, "Being against cow's milk is equated with being un-American. Yet, the milk of each species appears to have been specifically designed to protect the young of that species. Cross-feeding does not work."

He continues: "Since the human infant was never supposed to drink cow's milk in the first place, it is not surprising that they are most vulnerable. And since no other animal drinks milk after it has tripled its birth weight or has been weaned (except perhaps domesticated house cats), it is not surprising that the drinking of cow's milk after one to two years of age will produce disease. What is surprising is how frequently cow's milk does produce disturbances and how long it has taken for the medical profession to recognize this factor."

Preventing children from becoming unhealthy and overweight during the early stages of the human lifecycle requires a comprehensive, holistic approach—changing the ways kids think, move, and eat, not just for a few months but for life. Parents can make a tremendous investment in their children's health by reducing the role of dairy products in their life.

The Adolescent Stage of the Human Lifecycle

The onset of puberty in American children is occurring earlier than ever. Adolescence now begins in girls between the ages of eight and ten, and in boys between nine and eleven. Times are changing!

Developing breasts and a dramatic growth spurt are most often the first signs of puberty in girls. Pubic hair tends to appear about a year later as the uterus, ovaries, and vagina grow progressively larger. Menarche, the time of the first menses, usually occurs between 11 and 13 years of age. For boys, the first sign of puberty is an increase in the size of their testicles, which double, even quadruple, in size. At the same time that their testicles are growing, the skin of their scrotum reddens and wrinkles. Pubic hair appears soon thereafter. About a year later, the penis enlarges and, during the next year or two, facial hair starts to grow and the voice deepens.

Until this century, the menstrual cycle was thought to relate to the twenty-eight-day lunar cycle. Women in most other parts of the world still believe this to be true. Scientists now know that hormones regulate the menstrual cycle. Interestingly, groups of women living or working together often synchronize their periods. Scientists say this is because the primitive part of the female brain unconsciously detects almost imperceptible changes in the body odor of surrounding females and adopts accordingly.

A girl's growth spurt usually occurs at the very beginning of puberty, peaks at around twelve years old, then continues until about sixteen. A boy's growth spurt generally begins about two years after the onset of puberty, when his penis is already well developed and his testicles are producing sperm. Male growth peaks at about fourteen years old, then continues until about seventeen years old.

During no other time in the human lifecycle, other than the infancy stage, is growth so rapid. Visible growth usually begins with the hands and feet. Then there is rapid growth of the legs and spine. Energy requirements increase dramatically. This explains why teenage boys are seen so often with their heads in the refrigerator, trying to eat everything in sight.

At this stage, girls are gaining fat, as they are supposed to. It is also at this time that girls are bombarded with social messages to closely monitor their weight and fear fat. At the beginning of the human lifecycle, boys and girls are born with the same amount of body fat. But by six weeks, girls normally develop more body fat than boys, so that by one year girls have about 10 to 12 percent more body fat than boys. This normal body fat difference is fairly constant until early adolescence, when girls' normal body fat percentages begin to rise to 30 percent to 35 percent more than boys', and then stay at that level during the height of their reproductive stage. Female body fat does not normally lessen until about the age of thirty, when it levels off to about 20 to 25 percent more than men.

Junk food and adolescence have become synonymous. The best thing parents can do is to take control over what is served at meals and what is available at home for snacks. They should also do whatever they can to encourage physical exertion. It's important to have already prepared the groundwork for healthful eating *before* adolescense sets in. Otherwise, hot dogs, hamburgers, colas, french fries, and pepperoni pizza may be as good as it gets. In any case, this is the ideal time to strengthen the amount of healthy fiber in the diet by having plenty of fresh fruits and vegetables around the house.

Dramatic changes in body shape and composition are primarily controlled by male and female sex hormones, androgens in boys and estrogens in girls. The most obvious changes in boys are the increase in muscle mass, the widening of the shoulders, the growth of the heart and lungs, and the decrease in body fat, allowing boys to better adapt to more strenuous work. Indeed, by the end of adolescence, boys are about 50 percent stronger physically than girls. In girls, the hips widen, body fat increases, and breasts develop, as preparations for renewal of the cycle of life through yet another generation.

Infants sleep about sixteen to eighteen hours a day. Children younger than five years old sleep about twelve to fourteen hours a day, and then about ten to twelve hours until puberty. At puberty, both boys and girls experience a marked decrease in their sleep requirements, to about only eight hours a day. Additionally, boys begin ejaculating sperm while they sleep, as if they, too, are preparing to do their part in the renewal of the human cycle of life.

Nature's Code

Before continuing on with the adult stages of the human lifecycle, it is important for you to gain a deeper perspective on how the human body functions—especially the ways that it uses and stores energy. This is the key to achieving permanent weight loss. Examining the natural human lifecycle allows you to understand the normal changes you should expect during the stages of your time on earth. More importantly, it cannot help but cause you to be in awe of your own body.

Your mother's and father's fused genetic material, DNA, has controlled the phases and rhythms of your body from your conception up until now, no matter how old you are. From the time of your conception to the present moment, your inner healing force has been so resolute that it has conquered untold numbers of obstacles you may have encountered along the way. This is because your personal human lifecycle is an integral component of nature's code, which controls everything under the sun . . . and under other suns!

Nature's code is so vast and incomprehensible that we cannot even begin to conceive of where it all begins and where it ends. Apparently, our galaxy alone contains over 400 billion suns, and the entire universe contains at least 600 billion galaxies, with that many more suns. We have no idea how big infinity might be. The entire universe that is familiar to us might be equivalent to just one mere atom, with planets orbiting around suns much as electrons of atoms orbit around their nucleus. Nor do we know how small the smallest object might be. The infinitesimally tiny quarks present in atoms may themselves contain a universe of even smaller objects.

The infinitesimal and the infinite elude us. But however big or small the universe is, nature's code regulates all of its components.

Science has actually measured some of these components, which are called natural laws. If you are overweight, then you have thwarted certain natural laws. The information contained in this book will help you work with nature's code rather than against it. The fact that there are so many thousands of failed diet strategies is a testimony to the power of what we call the *Natural Laws of Thermodynamics*.

Everything Is Energy

The First Law of Thermodynamics is based on the conservation of energy. This law states that energy can neither be created nor destroyed. Albert Einstein discovered that energy constantly transforms into mass while mass constantly transforms into energy. In a phrase, everything is energy, or can be converted into energy. The energy in food is converted into the actual substance of your body. Thus, according to this natural law, *you really are what you eat*.

Any food you eat in excess of your body's energy needs is stored—and mostly as fat. It is an exercise in futility to try to avoid this law; energy cannot be created or destroyed. If you consume too much food energy, or too much of the wrong type of food energy, your body must either (1) burn off the excess energy with exercise; (2) eliminate the excess energy through its lungs, skin, kidneys, or intestines; or (3) store the excess energy as fat.

You are a complex energy system. Did you know that once your body stores excess energy as fat, it then attempts to conserve the fat for some future time of famine or starvation? Is this a defense mechanism that came into play during evolution, when famine and starvation for our cave-dwelling ancestors were common dangers? At the moment we do not know for sure. But we do know that the body tends to burn away its healthy muscle before it burns away its stored-up fat.

The purest type of fuel, that which contains life-energy, can bypass your body's natural defenses to conserve its fat. This is why deprivation and dieting are not effective means of permanent weight loss. The most effective way to lose your stored-up fat permanently is to consume foods bursting with life-energy and to engage in regular exercise. This is the combination that stokes your body's internal furnace and gives it the fuel it needs to burn excess fat.

Life-energy is highest in foods that are grown in the soil, that are fresh, and are as close to their natural state as possible. Processed, refined, irradiated, microwaved, and fake foods are stripped of fat-burning life-energy. The Food Energy Ladder, described in Part Six, will help you understand which foods are dead energy.

Everything Falls Apart

The Second Law of Thermodynamics is based on entropy. Simply stated, the law of entropy means that everything eventually falls apart. Entropy is the force that makes all energy systems fall apart. This is why everything in nature, including the human body, breaks down with age.

Everyone who has reached the middle adulthood stage of the human lifecycle, especially those over age fifty, will know what entropy means. Entropy causes the human body to experience its natural decline in concert with all of nature, so that nature, can replenish itself. Just as leaves fall from the trees in autumn so that new leaves can come back in spring, entropy causes the physical substance of your body to eventually return to the vast storehouse of universal energy from which it came.

The plant kingdom captures the life-force of the sun to help human bodies slow down entropy. Nature sustains the human cycle of life with plant-based foods that are steeped in sunlight and infused with the energy of the soil and rain—pure life-energy. We know that plants utilize the energy of sunlight in a process called photosynthesis to create the oxygen that is crucial to the very survival of the human species. It is not surprising that nature also sustains the human lifecycle by offering it the very essence of its life-energy through vegetables, fruits, nuts, lentils, beans, and grains.

Animal-based and artificially created foods contain little sunlight. They have poor life-energy and tend to hasten entropy. Of course, flesh food and animal products are essential for humans living in less temperate climates, such as extremely hot or cold places, where the availability of plant-based food is limited.

We can slow down entropy by eating foods that are full of life-energy. How and when we eat is also critically important. The added ingredient to every meal must be patience and care in its preparation, as well as in its consumption. Believe it or not, when we eat with calm and appreciation, it helps our body change food into healthful energy that can then be used to burn up excess fat. Slowing down and being aware of what we are eating also helps us eat less, because we realize when we have eaten enough, instead of rushing to stuff as much food as we can into our stomachs.

Just think of the fact that your food enables you to see, hear, touch, breathe, grow, and love. Surely eating deserves a moment of wonder! I first realized this while wandering through the farmers' markets near Bellagio, Italy. There, local farmers and gardeners rent booths to sell their fresh foods daily. The fruits and vegetables are so fresh, in fact, that the ripe soil still clings to the tomato vines. In these markets, the colors are overwhelming; neon green apples still attached to their stems, tomatoes a brilliant orange-red, onions purple and sweet enough to eat like fruit, peaches dripping with juice. Combining these foods together in a bowl is like serving up rainbows.

Body Time

We have been discussing *what* to eat and *how* to eat, but learning *when* to eat is equally important. The human body processes its food in certain ways to best extract and utilize its energy. This means that it naturally gathers, assimilates, and eliminates its energy in rhythm with the rising and setting of the sun. All three of these bodily functions mix together to some degree, but they are most natural and most intense during three distinct phases of the day.

After all, the human lifecycle is part of nature, in which such rhythms occur in all living things. Your body thrives by ingesting the food it requires for energy from about noon until 8:00 P.M. Your body functions best by assimilating its food and extracting its energy from about 8:00 P.M. until 4:00 A.M. From about 4:00 A.M. until noontime, your body's natural inclination is to eliminate yesterday's waste products and food debris as well as take in high-energy fuel to start the day. Let's look at these phases more closely.

REJUVENATING AND REPLENISHING
(Noon–8:00 P.M.)

You can slow down entropy with foods that are full of life-energy. The best time to supply your body with the fuel needed to sustain the human lifecycle is between noon and 8:00 P.M. These are the healthiest hours of the day in which to eat substantial meals. It is best to have at least one meal consisting almost entirely of life-energy during this time; for instance, a lunch of vegetables in a salad or a soup, or both, perhaps with some good bread. If you are still hungry, it would be good to have a heartier meal of life-energy by combining complex carbohydrates like rice, pasta, or potatoes, with vegetables. Americans usually prefer to eat their heartier meal at dinner. Europeans prefer it at lunch.

Remember, dead foods actually deplete your body of its own life-energy. This occurs because your body must use its life-energy to get rid of and excrete dead food. Unfortunately, this energy is no longer available to your body to help bring itself into healthier balance and to burn off excess fat. If you are overweight, your body needs all the life-energy it can get to retain its balance and burn off its fat.

RESTING AND REBALANCING
(8:00 P.M.–4:00 A.M.)

During the later part of the evening, from about 8:00 P.M. to about 4:00 A.M., your body assimilates what you have eaten by absorbing it into its cells and fluids to sustain your metabolic needs. Depending on the type and amount that you eat, food can remain in your stomach for about four hours, so it is important to finish eating by 8:00 P.M. to give your body the chance to do its work. For proper absorption, food needs to leave your stomach and enter your intestines.

During the night, as the body goes into its natural fasting pattern, people can go without eating for almost twelve hours without feeling hunger. Bodily rest is important during this phase of the day. If you feel you must have something to eat after 8:00 P.M., it is best to limit your choice to fresh fruit or vegetables. If your work schedule necessitates it, eat at least two hours before bedtime.

Finally, if you have an occasional evening out for fine dining (or even some not-so-fine dining), it's okay! Remember, *everything in moderation—including moderation*. You will find, however, that as you age and the force of entropy builds in your body, the pleasures of the past become the pains of the present. Haven't you noticed that the later you eat and the more you eat, the more lethargic and muddle-headed you feel in the morning? In any case, just following the natural daily cycles of your body is a wonderful strategy for becoming healthier, happier, more energetic, and leaner.

REAWAKENING AND ELIMINATING
(4:00 A.M.–Noon)

Eat mostly fresh fruit and drink mostly fresh fruit juice from the time you wake up until noon. You may eat as much fresh fruit and drink as much fresh juice as you wish. If you remain hungry, some foods are more suitable than others, as discussed later.

Having only fresh fruit and fresh juice from the time you wake in the morning until about noontime is the single most important way to kick-start yourself to a healthier, happier, more energized, and leaner future. Fresh fruit and fresh juice demand the least amount of energy for digestion because they are filled with so much life-energy. While the typical American breakfast leaves you stuffed and ready for a nap, fresh fruit will give you a lasting surge of energy to help your body eliminate its wastes and burn its excess fat.

From about 4:00 A.M. until noon, your body processes the wastes and debris of the food you consumed the day before by eliminating them. Digestion, of course, takes more energy than any other bodily function. Most foods that people eat during their natural morning elimination cycle also tend to deplete their energy; for example, bacon, eggs, and toast slathered in butter. These foods seriously interfere with the orderly process of your body's elimination cycle. Couple this with the slow production of digestive fluids such as saliva, stomach acid, pancreatic secretions, and bile—our fasting nighttime metabolism—and you will see why you can interfere with your body's waste removal mechanisms—if you continually eat outside of the general guidelines that are best for your body's natural functioning.

We are consuming more food that nourishes us less and leaves behind much more residue and debris in our intestines. People who eat food full of life-energy tend to be healthier and leaner. People who don't are, among other things, constipated! It seems as if having regular bowel movements is an old-fashioned concept, but it's isn't. A major function of our intestines is to process our food into a firm, well-formed, mildly odorous stool and then expel it from the body daily. Constipation is one of the most prevalent conditions that contributes to lethargy, moodiness, and disease.

The body eliminates waste products in a variety of ways, including breathing through your lungs, perspiring through your skin, urinating via your kidneys, and discharging leftover food debris in your stools. One of the very best things you can do to move the waste process along is to limit your intake of flesh foods to no more than once every three days. Why? It takes the body about seventy-two hours for the debris from the last consumption of flesh to pass through your intestines.

Constipation contributes to obesity, lethargy, moodiness, sexual dysfunction, backache, irritable bowel syndrome, colitis, and other diseases. Dairy also causes constipation, especially after age and entropy set in. Substitute sugars, particularly in diet soft drinks, cause constipation. Excess animal protein causes constipation. Plant food is steeped in sunlight; it's as if you're eating and absorbing the very rays of the sun. Flesh food captures very little sunlight, which is why it quickly rots, outside as well as inside your body. George Bernard Shaw quipped: "Think of the force concentrated in an acorn. You bury it in the ground and it explodes into a great oak. Bury a sheep and nothing happens but decay."

All sorts of refined, processed, irradiated, factory-made, and genetically engineered foods cause constipation. If you feel like napping after you eat, it's probably because your meal actually drained your body's available energy to digest food that is so poorly digestible. It also depletes the energy the body needs to discharge its wastes. The human body, which has survived countless generations of evolution, is apparently stymied by products such as diet colas.

Our grandparents were right when they said it was important to stay regular. The body is a complex and integrated energy system; what affects one part of the body affects its other parts. It is ludicrous to think that years of constipation—the buildup of residue and waste in the intestines—is of no serious health consequence. Regularly accumulating several pounds of solid waste that stagnates in the colon is not compatible with performing daily activities with a great deal of zest!

The best ways to avoid or overcome constipation while supporting your body's elimination cycle are simple:

- Get regular exercise
- Ingest more fiber-containing food or take a fiber supplement

- Drink at least six to eight glasses of liquids a day, preferably water, juices, and herbal teas
- Eat mostly fruit until noon

Hippocrates Would Agree

Health, as Hippocrates knew, and as modern medical scientists must know again, is a matter of energy, of energy in balance. Being overweight in this regard, is an illness, a sign that energy is out of balance. Your body is a complex energy system that seeks to maintain its healthy equilibrium at all times by staying in energy balance. *Your body remembers wellness.*

Your body requires food for energy. If you consume more food energy than your body needs, it must either burn it, eliminate it, or store it. It naturally burns foods that contain pure life-energy. It stores up the impure energy of other foods in its attempt to maintain energy balance. *Your body tries to stay well.* When you store up too much fat there comes a time when you begin to look and feel overweight. Eventually, your body is no longer able to maintain its energy balance and dynamic equilibrium. *Your body becomes ill.*

But how many extra pounds does it take before your body becomes unhealthily overweight? Unfortunately, current weight standards are notoriously inaccurate and overly restrictive. They don't take into account perfectly normal, sex-related, and age-related weight gain!

Considerably lower weight standards have arbitrarily been proscribed to women, without any evidence proving that women stay healthier or live longer by weighing so much less than men of the same height and stature. Men's current visions of female attractiveness, rather than true science, have decreed that women should be so much slimmer than men. Furthermore, normal fat accumulation during the later stages of the human lifecycle in both men and women has been roundly ignored by the accountants and actuaries who helped to develop the standard height and weight tables—standards based on life insurance company statistics that measure longevity rather than health and quality of life values.

Traditionally, obesity was defined this way: as 20 percent or more above the optimal weight for height derived from life insurance company tables that correlate with the lowest death rates. New numbers that account for some normal weight gain with aging are partially replacing those statistics. Currently, it is also believed that where your extra fat is located is more important than the actual total amount of extra fat in your body. Hip and thigh fat is thought to be healthier than abdominal fat, because the former travels through the general blood circulation to take care of your metabolic needs, while the fat in a potbelly goes straight to the liver and interferes with its ability to clear insulin from your bloodstream. Higher levels of blood insulin can then cause cells to become insulin-resistant, which results in elevated blood sugar level. Supposedly, in response to the elevated blood sugar, your pancreas secretes more insulin, which prompts your autonomic nervous system to produce adrenalinelike chemicals, which then sets the stage for you to develop diabetes, hypertension, and heart disease.

Sound like gobbledygook? All or some of the above theory may or may not be true. I try to be skeptical about such scientific statements. I began studying the history of science at a very young age and was taught early on to maintain a state of permanent doubt. All we truly know is this: when our body's energy is in balance, we are generally healthy and well. Conversely, when our energy is out of balance, we are generally sick and tired or overweight.

Because each of your fat cells can balloon up to more than ten times its original size and then divide, when necessary, to make new fat cells, your body has an immense capacity to store extra fat. That is why the human body can get bigger and bigger, as well as heavier and heavier. Perhaps it's an evolutionary holdover from the days when our ancestors huddled together in cold caves, ready at all times to use stored-up energy in order to outrun saber-toothed tigers.

Furthermore, *obesity* and *overweight* are arbitrary terms. There is no absolutely standard definition for either, and there probably never will be. It's all relative because every added pound of body fat is not a threat to health. Actually, in otherwise healthy individuals, there is a relatively healthy "safe zone" of about ten to fifteen pounds above their "best common sense weight when looking in the mirror." Fat cells also become less metabolically active as the levels of our sex hormones change, particularly in women. This means that excess fat becomes a lot more difficult to burn off, even with exercise. Fortunately, the human body adjusts and allows us to gain weight with age and still be healthy. Carrying around some extra pounds as we age is perfectly normal!

The definition of obesity should expand to meet two important new criteria. Healthy weight standards should increase steadily throughout the stages of the human lifecycle. In the real world, gaining one-half to three-quarters of a pound a year (five to seven-and-a-half pounds a decade), from age twenty-five years to sixty-five years, is usually within healthy limits (unless, at twenty-five, you are already overweight). So if, as a woman, your "youthful weight" was 120 pounds at age twenty-five, you might healthfully weigh as much as 150 pounds by the time you turn sixty-five. A man who weighed 160 pounds at age twenty-five could healthfully weigh as much as 190 pounds at age sixty-five.

Furthermore, there should be an approximate 20 percent increase in the healthy weight standards for women throughout adulthood when compared to men of the same height. In other words, most of the current height and weight tables should be adjusted, so that if a woman's ideal weight is listed as 130 pounds compared to 160 pounds for a male of the same height, then the thirty-pound difference should be increased by six pounds, to make 136 pounds the more ideal weight for the woman.

The National Institutes of Health recently announced a new set of numbers defining healthy and unhealthy body weights. According to the federal government, 55% of Americans or about 97 million American adults are overweight. The numbers are calculated by using a formula known as the body mass index (BMI), which measures weight in relation to height. The announcement also noted that obesity leads to more preventable deaths than all other causes, except smoking.

The new governmental guidelines are a mixed blessing. On the one hand, the numbers remind us how serious the epidemic of excess weight is in the United States. In response to the announcement, re-searcher James O. Hill at the University of Colorado, blamed the American environment: too much food available, too many people who eat too much of the available food, and too much technology making it too easy to avoid exercise. The negative side of the new guidelines is that they do a clear disservice to women in general, and to individuals who are in the later stages of the human lifecycle. The BMI is a single number that represents height and weight without regard to gender or age. Clearly, we are not all young male athletes!

Being overweight, then, is related to heredity, environment, atti-tude, how much we eat, what we eat, and our age, gender and level of physical activity. Heredity is an exceptionally important determi-nant of how much we weigh as well. Some people are simply more prone to weight gain than others, even when their food intake and levels of physical activity are the same. In the last decade, I have watched my wife eat more than I do and exercise less, yet maintain her weight exactly as it was ten years ago, while I have gained about seven pounds during that time. Many other people are even less fortunate, those who seem to gain weight simply by looking at food. Here, genetic factors, apart from diet or lifestyle, strongly influence how much a person weighs. How much does the genetic factor con-tribute to being overweight? Approximately 25 percent.

Because nutritional science teaches that all calories are created equal, it is crucial for you to understand the heredity factor as well as some simple arithmatic. For instance we have believed that ap-proximately four thousand excess calories will convert into one pound of fat, and that's that! We are taught that the human body has certain basal metabolic needs that require a certain amount of calo-ries for fuel. Beyond such metabolic needs, we commonly believe that the body requires extra calories to fuel any unusual physical activities. However, every four thousand extra calories consumed is supposed to result in a one-pound weight gain. Conversely, every four thousand fewer calories consumed is supposed to result in a one-pound weight loss. The standard thinking is as follows:

- Assume that an individual requires about two thousand calo-ries a day to maintain his or her healthy weight, with neither weight gain nor weight loss, during a day of routine physical activity.

- Therefore, if the individual eats an extra four hundred calories a day, without an increase in physical activity, he or she will gain an extra pound of fat in ten days (400 calories × 10 days = 4,000 calories = 1 pound of fat).
- Conversely, if the person eats just 1,600 calories a day, in ten days he or she will lose one pound of fat.

This simple notion and arithmetic is the basis for most standard nutritional teachings, diet books, and medical treatment plans to lose weight. Over the years, this formula has misled me into counseling thousands of dieting patients (mostly women) that if they weren't losing three pounds a month by eating 400 fewer calories than the daily requirements, they were just not telling the truth about how much they were really eating. I'm embarrassed by how bad I must have made my patients feel before I knew better. The whole theory is wrong!

The theory is wrong because heredity plays an influential role and all calories are *not* created equal in terms of their effect on your body. Identical twins have the exact same genetic makeup, whereas fraternal twins do not. Studies of fraternal twins eating large amounts of food show that in three months, some will gain ten pounds, while others will gain more than twenty pounds. On the other hand, the weight of identical twins, even when raised apart from each other, varies hardly at all. There may even be a recessive obesity gene. This means that a strong tendency to gain weight could occur if a child gets the same gene from each parent.

Furthermore, calorie counting, doesn't work—not all calories are the same once they enter your body. Three hundred calories from a piece of fresh fruit is *not* equivalent to three hundred calories from a slice of factory-prepared dead bologna. Restricting food intake to 800 or 1,200, or 1,500 calories a day in order to lose weight doesn't work either, because your body will do just what it is "programmed" to do. As a marvelous, self-adjusting energy system, once its food intake is limited, the body will just lessen its metabolic rate to burn fuel more slowly. Once your body begins losing weight, it begins to protect its stored fat by producing certain chemical substances that actually promote more fat deposition in the very fat cells that have already shrunken through dieting.

Apparently the more weight you lose, the more your body fights to regain it. That is why people trying to lose weight by calorie counting fall into a yo-yo pattern of weight loss and weight gain. Your body is able to defend itself very well from the danger of starvation, but it is not evolutionarily equipped to handle the eating opportunities of modern civilization.

Consider the fact that 60 to 80 million Americans are dieting right now. Most of them are women, and only a few will ever achieve, at risk to their health, the image of slimness projected by the advertising industry. Adding to this injustice is the fact that fat cells in a woman's thighs and buttocks are used for long-term energy storage, while fat cells in the abdominal area of men release their contents more easily for quick energy needs.

According to current medical science, being overweight is associated with diabetes, gallstones, gout, hypertension, heart disease, varicose veins and osteoarthritis, as well as colon, rectal, prostate, breast, uterine, and ovarian cancer. But being overweight is so much more than that. It is an illness itself, and a signal that the excess fat in and on your body may have gone beyond the limits of good balance and good health. Despite this, it has recently become more fashionable, and even politically correct, to believe that being overweight is just a normal and acceptable part of modern life. This is truly an amazing public relations feat accomplished by the economic interests that thrive on fattening us.

An editorial published in the prestigious *New England Journal of Medicine* in December of 1997 provides a perfect example of how nutritional nonsense can become widespread belief, even among physicians. The editorial informed medical doctors in no uncertain terms that their ongoing efforts to encourage their patients to change their behavior and lose excess weight were probably misguided. The editorial claimed that such efforts may be causing more harm than good because they were making patients feel bad. As predicted, the article received widespread publicity, with front-page headlines in major newspapers and lead features in syndicated television news programs.

A few years ago, the same journal accepted no drug advertisements whatsoever. The edition of the journal containing the "forget about encouraging weight loss" editorial comprised eighty-two pages of scientific articles and ninety-four pages of drug advertisements, many of which are directly or indirectly associated with diseases related to obesity. Most stunning of all was the fact that the April 2, 1998, edition of the *New England Journal of Medicine* contained a full-color, eight-page advertisement for Meridia, the latest weight-loss drug! Advertising money taints editorial choices.

Permanent Weight Loss Anyone Can Achieve

The ultimate goal for virtually all of you who are overweight should be a weight loss of 5 to 10 percent of your total weight, over a period of between eight and twelve months. It's crucial to be realistic about your weight loss goals. The *vast majority* of overweight people need to lose only five to twenty-five pounds in the first year to look good and feel great, as well as to counter the most serious effects of being overweight. Trying to lose more weight at a faster rate, through dieting, only creates temporary illusions of success. Dieting causes most people to ignore their natural biological signals of hunger and satiety. Then, once people stop dieting, they don't know when to naturally stop eating. That is why various studies indicate that approximately 90 percent of dieters who lose weight gain it all back, and often even more.

In this book, I will show you how to *safely* lose up to 10 percent of your excess body weight in eight to twelve months, and keep it off *permanently*. For those who want to lose much more weight, this is attainable by allowing more time. The secret is simple: eat more food containing the life-energy that allows your body to regain its balance and burn its excess fat.

You will lose excess fat *steadily and permanently* by climbing the

Food Energy Ladder presented in this book and staying on its upper rungs. This means eating less flesh, fewer eggs, less dairy, less refined sugar, and less junk food. But more importantly, it means eating more fruits, more vegetables, more whole grain breads and cereals, more beans, more lentils and legumes, more rice, pasta, and potatoes.

Your excess fat is directly linked to the proportion of animal fat and sugar in your diet. Many studies show that limiting total fat intake to 10 to 20 percent of total calorie intake helps people lose weight, even though they have failed to do so on a variety of calorie-reducing programs. But why bother? By staying on the top five steps of the Food Energy Ladder, you will not feel deprived and you will not have to bother with counting calories or multiplying, then dividing, to determine the percentage of fat calories. Just restrict your use of oils to olive oil and canola oil, and make sure to use them in moderation. You don't have to be a rocket scientist either to know how to eliminate 95 percent of the fat in your diet: *Eat less animal flesh and animal products!*

Perhaps you were surprised to learn that scientists consider all calories equal. In a laboratory, a calorie is the amount of heat that it takes to raise the temperature of one kilogram of water by exactly one degree centigrade. Thus, science doesn't differentiate between calories that come from fat, carbohydrates, or protein. In a laboratory, one hundred calories produced by burning carrots is the same as one hundred calories produced by burning chocolate!

This calorie measurement has led us, scientists and public alike, to accept a major delusion. What happens in a test tube does not happen in the same way in a human body. Carbohydrates, fat, and protein are burned differently in the human body than they are in a test tube. They are also used differently by the body. Furthermore, different bodies use the same calories differently because of heredity. It's as if there were some absurd "Dieter's Law of Thermodynamics" which states that, calorie for calorie, pork chops and milkshakes are no more responsible for weight gain than carrots and peas, as long as the amount of calories they contain are the same.

It gets even sillier. A gram of fat produces nine calories when it's burned in a test tube or a calorimeter in the laboratory. But a gram of carbohydrate or a gram of protein produces only four calories. Therefore, it is assumed that for the same number of calories an individual can choose to eat more than twice as much protein or carbohydrates than fat. Also, if the fat in a gram of avocado contains the same amount of calories as the fat in a gram of bacon, why not have the bacon? The reality is that the energy of an avocado is different than the fat from a pig's belly. One contains life-energy, while the other is dead!

Potato Chips Don't Grow Under the Soil

There are no easy gimmicks to make you lose weight. Fat-blocking pills, fat-burning pills, whole meals in a glass—in the long term, they just don't work. It's also absurd to spend money on commercial weight-loss programs that eliminate normal food choices by offering prepackaged meals. Almost all these dieters slide back into their old eating habits when they go back to the real world of eating. Additionally, it is dangerous to depend on drugs for losing weight. Amphetamines and their derivatives, as well as new drugs that affect your serotonin levels, have serious side effects.

So-called diet drugs make billions of dollars for drug companies, but their effects are short-lived once the drug is withdrawn. Both patients as well as doctors should stop deluding themselves into thinking that diet pills are an answer to permanent weight loss. It is an ethical travesty for scientific medical journals to accept millions of dollars from drug companies to feature eight-page, colorful advertisements that lull physicians into prescribing diet drugs without reading the small print.

It's disingenuous to claim and naive to believe that advertising dollars do not taint the editorial content of the scientific journals that physicians rely upon for their up-to-date information. These journals are currently publishing more articles about diet drugs, based on even skimpier information, and highlighting positive rather than negative results. Diet drugs are dreadful science because we just cannot tinker with the human metabolism and not expect serious side effects. There really is no such thing as a free lunch!

Another spectacular full-color advertisement for Meridia, the latest diet drug, appeared in the February 14, 1998, *Journal of the American Medical Association*. The following are some of the adverse reactions that were listed in very small print at the very end of the ad:

ADVERSE REACTIONS OF MERIDA

Headache	30%	Tachycardia	2.6%
Dry mouth	17.2%	Sweating	2.5%
Anorexia	13%	Vasodilation	2.4%
Constipation	11.5%	Taste	
Runny nose	10.2%	perversion	2.2%
Insomnia	10%	Hypertension	2.1%
Increased		Palpitation	2%
appetite	8.7%	Nervous system	
Back pain	8.2%	stimulation	1.5%
Flu syndrome	8.2%	Emotional	
Dizziness	7%	lability	1.3%
Nausea	5.7%	Rectal	
Nervousness	5.2%	disorder	1.2%
Sinusitis	5%	Joint	
Dyspepsia	5%	disorder	1.25%
Depression	4.3%	Vaginal	
Painful		moniliasis	1.2%
menses	3.5%		

This small print goes on to report additional adverse events occurring in patients using Meridia in less well-controlled studies: flatulence, gastroenteritis, tooth disorder, peripheral edema, arthritis, leg cramps, abnormal thinking, bronchitis. Finally, again in small print, the following warning appears: *"The safety and effectiveness of Meridia, as demonstrated in double-blind placebo-controlled trials, have not been determined beyond one year at this time."*

Shockingly, Meridia has been introduced to the public less than six months after one of the largest drug disasters in history. Tens of millions of patients may have been put at risk for heart valve disease because of the popular diet drug Redux, which was recently removed from the market. Even though Wall Street analysts are hailing the introduction of Meridia as a well orchestrated 500 million dollar national marketing campaign, I call it a glaring example of irresponsibility and undisguised greed in the weight-loss marketplace. *Are you awake yet?*

It should be obvious to you that advertising money taints so-called scientific editorial choices. Medical journals are also printing second-rate articles while accepting research support or advertising dollars, in glaring conflicts of interest. For instance, the *Journal of the American Medical Association* (January 1998) published an outrageously poor lead article about fat-free, fried potato chips. The article was based on research funded by the manufacturer of this so-called miracle fake fat!

A few hundred people of unstated age, attending a movie of an unstated nature, were given free potato chips and some soda to wash them down. Half of the people received potato chips made with fake fat, while the other half received "normal" potato chips, and no one knew which was which. The participants were called a week later to ascertain whether there was any difference in gassiness, indigestion, or anal leaking between the fake-fat potato chip eaters and the real-fat potato chip eaters. The article concluded that there were no reported significant differences. This conclusion was then widely reported in most of the major news media as a green light for dieters to enjoy their fake-fat potato chips. *Is this any way to conduct science?*

The study itself was supported through a grant from the manufacturer. Ironically, an April 1, 1998, editorial in the *Journal of the*

American Medical Association concludes that one-third of grant donors request prepublication reports of any articles and that grant
recipients frequently believe grant donors place restrictions on
their work and expect certain returns. Clearly, if researchers hope
to tap into more funds in the future, it makes sense that their natural bias would lead to positive results for the company that funded
their research.

The real bottom line is this: Potato chips made with fake fat are
not the answer to permanent weight loss. Potatoes are found under
the soil, not potato chips of any kind. There is no free lunch—only
lots of not-so-free advertising money!

The Seasons of Our Lives

Imagine the human lifecycle as a slowly spinning wheel.
Scientific concoctions like diet pills and faddish meals in a can—
these are like sticks poked through the spokes of that wheel. They
disrupt the natural flow and balance of energy in the body. We've
now looked extensively at the first four stages of the human lifecycle: prenatal, infancy, childhood, and adolescence. These are
foundational stages in the development of your nutritional habits
for life. *For life!* That is why it is so important, before going on to
the adulthood stages of the human lifecycle and a permanent solution to weight loss, to revisit some basic concepts.

We have seen how nature functions according to predictable cycles with beginnings and endings. Thus, the human lifecycle and
your own natural body cycles are in tune with the daily rising and
setting of the sun, the monthly phases of the moon, and the seasonal cycles of the earth's tilt on its axis. To everything there is a
season. Spring and summer—growth and reproduction—define the
early stages of the human lifecycle. Autumn and winter—maturity

and aging—comprise the times for nurturing ourselves and others, then letting go. This wisdom allows you to move through your cycle of life as normally and effortlessly as leaves drop from trees.

A major focus of this book centers around the biological differences during the stages of the human lifecycle. To understand why we gain excess weight and how we can lose such weight, however, it is important also to understand the psychological aspects involved. It is particularly important to consider the influence of social and family roles during the various phases of our life. Modern studies, by such esteemed scholars as Erik Erikson and D. J. Levinson, indicate how each stage of the human lifecycle is organized around specific mental and social issues.

What are the psychological and emotional characteristics of the early stages of the human lifecycle? During these foundational years, the feelings and thoughts that enter our hearts and minds are just as vital as the foods that enter our stomachs. During the prenatal stage, a mother's feelings of gladness, sadness, fear, or happiness effect her infant in as yet unmeasured ways. It is also important to realize that in good science, absence of measurable or quantitative evidence does not mean evidence of absence.

The infancy stage lasts until the time a baby is able to walk and be naturally independent of mother's milk. Infancy is a time for babies to receive nurturing and develop trust or mistrust of themselves as well as others. Babies who are comforted by loving and nurturing parents grow up to be more trusting than those whose parents do not behave that way.

The childhood stage lasts until boys and girls can pass on their DNA to the future. Childhood is a time for gaining autonomy and acquiring values. Thus, the "terrible twos" are marked by stubbornness and a child's exclamation of an emphatic *no*! This is why school-age children explore and experiment. Parents who encourage and support appropriate behaviors teach children to become autonomous. Parents who are critical and punishing teach children to feel shame and guilt.

During late childhood, just before puberty, humans develop a sense of being either industrious or inadequate. This sense tends to develop according to how productive children are in school, how well they get along with other children, and how much quality time their parents spend with them. These are the crucial years for parents to be actively listening to their children, helping them to understand their experiences at school, reading to and with them, and helping them with their homework.

Adolescence is a time of psychological turmoil, during which the growing child decides which mental and emotional "clothing" he or she wishes to wear as an adult. Social approval from friends is often more important than pursuing good physical or mental health. Developing a well-balanced adult identity, including the inclination to serve others, doesn't develop automatically, and experimentation is often the painful key to choosing well. Adolescence is marked by the human lifecycle coming of age into a reproducing, autonomous adult. Spring arrives in every sense of the word.

Reviewing the early stages of the human lifecycle is crucial for you to fully appreciate your present and future potential for *Total Health Rejuvenation* and weight loss. In the remainder of this book, I will turn my attention to adulthood, when entropy slowly begins to reign supreme.

To understand why you gain excess weight and how you can lose such weight, it is important to recognize the physical as well as the mental and social aspects of the human lifecycle. It is also crucial to realize how different the male and female human lifecycles are from each other. Men and women are as different internally as they are externally. All the egg cells females need to produce offspring are present at the time of their own birth. They are there until the time is right for them to develop into mature eggs that might be fertilized. Also, even though a woman's reproductive system stops functioning during the middle stage of her life, the woman still remains strong and full of vitality. In contrast, a man's testicles do not begin creating sperm until puberty, but then they keep producing sperm continuously, often into their eightieth or ninetieth year, despite the loss of overall strength and vitality.

Yet women generally live longer than men, because of their physiology as well as their lifestyle. Estrogen gives premenopausal women some built-in protection against heart disease, and men more often engage in high-risk behaviors. On the other hand, men are naturally leaner. The comparison between males and females leads to many intriguing questions. Why is there such a remarkable sex difference in the normal physiology of reproduction across the entire human lifecycle? Does this account for the marked behavioral differences between males and females throughout life? Are men normally leaner than women, regardless of chronological age, because of evolution? Perhaps only the fittest and leanest of our male ancestors survived their testosterone-driven "warrior mentality" to continue to reproduce the species. Is this the reason why, on average, men are 50 percent physically stronger than women as young adults?

I doubt if we will ever answer such questions. Immortality, as well as the keys to staying young forever, are not available to the human lifecycle. And yet we truly are immortal, because our DNA has been passed down to each of us from our ancestors, and lives on in the future. Bearing children is not required for immortality though, because our family's DNA thrusts toward the future through our siblings, cousins, nieces, nephews, and other blood relatives.

Understanding the stages of life is a wonderful way to gain a true perspective on the human condition: how we are conceived, how we grow from an infant into an independent adult, how we reproduce, how we mature and grow older. The deterioration of time takes its toll on the human body, but it is counterbalanced by growth in character and wisdom. This perspective has the power to propel you to change your eating habits in order to keep making progress in your life. Let's continue now with the adulthood stages of the human lifecycle.

The Young Adulthood Stage: Mating, Reproducing, and Testing Values

The young adulthood stage (about eighteen to forty years old) is a time of active human reproduction. High levels of estrogen and progesterone maintain the female shape, with a narrow waist, in spite of the worst eating habits imaginable. Raging testosterone levels in males bulk up their muscles, lower their voices, and cause hair to sprout all over their body, as they don the plumage of much of the animal world in a search of their mates during the summer of their lifecycle. During young adulthood, a need for intimacy develops, which propels both sexes toward marriage, childbearing, and childraising. A healthy, growing sense of intimacy results in the development of enduring relationships that allow us to embrace compromise and sacrifice. Establishing a career is paramount as well, at this time, which is also marked by learning to serve society and testing values.

Often, and amazingly, neither beer nor grease nor sugar nor the worst food excesses imaginable seem to have much of an effect on either sex until after age thirty. Then, young men and woman notice an extra pound or two of fat appearing, and remaining, on their bodies each year until nature, as well as society, begins ushering in the autumn of the human lifecycle.

A difference in the normal amount of body fat between men and women becomes very evident during this stage of the human lifecycle. During adolescence, the average amount of fat in growing boys is 18.5 percent, compared to 21 percent in growing girls— about a 12 percent difference. During young adulthood, between the ages of eighteen and thirty, the average male body is 16 percent fat and the average female body is 22.5 percent fat, almost a 30 percent difference!

Before the age of thirty, women tend to experience more urinary infections and vaginal discharges. Both sexes contract sexually transmitted diseases. Asthma, hay fever, and allergies begin to occur or worsen. Men experience more strains and sprains and are involved in more accidents. During these years, when accidents are the main threat to life, seven out of each thousand men will die, compared to just three out of each thousand women.

Aging happens. We begin to age the moment we are conceived. Then a complex combination of genetic, biological, cultural, and environmental factors come together to determine how many years we will live and how well we will live. The force of entropy increases throughout the entire human cycle of life and, with the force of life, we are in a state of constant balance and interplay.

The force of entropy begins overtaking the force of life toward the latter half of young adulthood, between ages thirty and forty. Hypertension, lung infections, stomach ulcers, enteritis, ulcers, and neuropsychiatric disorders, such as schizophrenia, begin occurring more frequently. Fourteen out of every thousand men will die during these years, compared to ten out of every thousand women, with cancer, heart disease, and accidents as the main culprits here.

Today's adults in their mid-thirties are likely to notice that their eyesight starts to worsen, hearing begins to deteriorate, gum disease becomes common, and facial wrinkles appear where before there were none. Women experience the effects of gravity and fat deposition as their breasts and buttocks sag. Men suffer with new sore spots in their ligaments and joints. Staying out late at night takes more of a toll and hangovers take on a new meaning for both men and women.

More excess fat begins accumulating now, which becomes more difficult to burn off. Both men and women have to work harder to stay in shape. They notice that their bodies don't seem to be able to take the same punishment. Those who are more likely to be leaner start to realize, as they age, that their bodies require a little more respect.

Perhaps you are somewhere in this stage of the human lifecycle, between eighteen and forty years old. This is the ideal time for you to take more personal responsibility for your overall health and weight loss. By now, you have lived long enough to know the direct consequences of your actions. Also, your raging sex hormones may finally be waning, while your ability to make adult decisions is rising. If you don't do it now, it will be more difficult to do it later. Health and weight during the next stages are very much a reflection of the habits you have acquired during the earlier years of young adulthood, while your biological clock was still ticking slowly toward autumn.

Right now, you have a great opportunity to launch a preemptive strike against the major enemy of your later years. Atherosclerosis is most likely building up in your body right now—fatty deposits building up in your blood vessels that could trigger heart attacks and strokes down the road. But why would a magnificent self-regulating and self-protecting energy system such as the human body persist in slathering the inner lining of its crucial blood vessels with fat?

It makes no sense whatsoever, yet the current scientific understanding of atherosclerosis is based on the simplistic notion that the cholesterol we ingest is somehow deposited on the walls of our heart and brain arteries, causing eventual obstruction and possible heart attack or stroke. But there is a better explanation. First, the inner linings (endothelium) of our blood vessels suffer injury from stress. Then the fatty deposits that lead to heart attacks and strokes begin to occur.

It wasn't too long ago that scientists also believed that maggots were the major cause of rotten meat. It was only when enough people observed that meat having become rotten allowed maggots to flourish, that scientist changed their tune. Now scientists believe that a bacterial infection, rather than stress, is the major cause of duodenal ulcers. Wrong again! It is more likely that the bacteria found growing in duodenal ulcers only begins flourishing after the stress-induced ulcers start to develop.

How do such examples relate to atherosclerotic heart disease and stroke? It's simple. The health of our heart and brain vessels is first compromised, then plaque builds up and creates obstructions. Keep in mind that the human body isn't so poorly constructed that it would just deposit excess fat on the inner linings of the very blood vessels that support life by nourishing the brain and heart. Indeed, mounting scientific evidence supports the notion that the fatal buildup of atherosclerosis occurs *after* the inner linings of our arteries have become thickened and damaged. Moreover, I believe that the deposition of fatty material upon these injured cells represents our body's ill-fated attempt to protect the injury and halt the damage. I call this the *inadequate Band-Aid effect*. I will discuss this later on in the book insofar as it relates to elevated homocysteine levels, and the importance of taking a well-balanced nutritional supplement each day.

The Middle Adulthood Stage: Applying Values and Facing Entropy

Middle adulthood (about forty to sixty-five years old) marks the beginning of many not so subtle emotional and physical changes. Individuals face the challenge of being creative and productive so they don't become stagnant and complacent. The so-called midlife crisis commonly arises, and many people begin to ask themselves, *What does it all matter?* The common thread in finding the answer to such a question rests on *how well you have made the successful passage from each stage of the human lifecycle to the point you are at now.*

In our forties, the growing force of entropy begins taking over; by fifty, it is in full swing. As we age our muscles atrophy while our body fat rises. Thus, both men and women find themselves developing larger bellies but smaller arm and leg muscles. With each new year it becomes easier to gain a few excess pounds of fat, and much more difficult to lose them.

Before menopause, estrogen and progesterone maintain the female shape, with narrow waist and rounded hips. In middle age, women find their waists thickening and their curves lessening, while deposits of fat settle around their abdomen, buttocks, and thighs. Women then also begin to catch up to men in the incidence of cardiovascular disease.

Men begin losing considerable amounts of hair on their scalps while growing more and more hair in the ears and nose. By age fifty, half the hairs on an average person's head, male and female, will be turning gray. The nails, especially the toenails, thicken and develop ridges. Wrinkles in the skin begin to form. The lenses of the eyes lose elasticity and cause difficulty in focusing on objects close up. Ligaments become less flexible and joints become stiffer, causing new aches and pains.

Weight gain as well as a variety of stress-related disorders begin to occur with greater frequency: migraine, hypertension, backache, indigestion, irritable bowel syndrome, depression, and chronic fatigue syndrome. The incidence of breast and lung cancer increases sharply, too.

Remember that encoded in your DNA are the templates of most of the diseases of your ancestors. Diabetes has two forms: insulin-dependent and non-insulin dependent. Insulin-dependent diabetes tends to develop in overweight people during this stage. Very often, the disease can be controlled simply by balancing the diet and losing weight. If diabetes is not well controlled, a decline in kidney function and eyesight loss may occur as the individual ages, along with atherosclerosis, cardiovascular disease, and stroke.

Hiatus hernias are also much more common in overweight people, especially if they smoke, suffer constipation, or are stressed. The opening through which the esophagus goes through the body's diaphragm is called a hiatus. Sometimes the lower part of the esophagus, and even part of the stomach, is pulled up through this hiatus and causes severe pain and discomfort.

Also remember that very few templates of diseases inherited from your ancestors are ever meant to appear during your personal lifecycle. Guarded by the force of homeostasis and your body's will to remember wellness, they will not manifest. On the other hand, when your energy falls out of balance you are at risk. And during middle adulthood, that risk usually relates to diseases caused by stress.

Surely the digestive system shows the effects of aging and the cumulative effect of decades of eating a poor diet. As a result, an estimated 30 percent of Americans suffer from irritable bowel syndrome (IBS). This condition affects mostly women, beginning in their thirties and becomes more bothersome to them in their forties. People with IBS have mild to severe abdominal pain, flatulence, chronic constipation, or sometimes diarrhea. Although IBS is generally thought to involve only the large intestine, it actually affects the esophagus and small intestines, causing nausea, heartburn, and dyspepsia.

Additionally, many patients with IBS have urinary tract complaints that are presumably caused by bladder irritability. Gynecologic symptoms, often including pain with sexual intercourse, are probably related to pelvic irritability. Other associated problems include depression, anxiety, insomnia, chronic fatigue, and migraine. Interestingly, a large proportion of patients with IBS also have symptoms caused by lactose intolerance, particularly abdominal distention, flatulence, and diarrhea.

Stress control, along with dietary adjustment, is the key to treatment of IBS. The overall systemic imbalance is a prime example of how a template of disease affects not only the target organ, which in this case is the gut, *but the entire body and mind*.

The typical human body, formerly able to tolerate myriad lifestyle indulgences and dietary indiscretions, cannot do so any longer. As entropy takes a firm hold during middle adulthood:

- gassiness and flatulence commonly occur after drinking milk and eating dairy products.
- constipation results from too little fiber, too few liquids, and too many diet colas. It leads to crankiness, lethargy, and decreased sexuality.
- heartburn, indigestion, and dyspepsia are caused by eating fried and greasy foods.
- alcohol starts to cause tiredness and irritability.
- coffee leads to headaches, heartburn, jitteriness, and frequent urination.
- refined sugar (pastries and candy) cause mental fuzziness and sleepiness.
- salt becomes a stimulant, leading to mental edginess and water retention.
- cellulite forms on the thighs, hips, and buttocks of women as they gain more weight.
- backache occurs with stress, lack of physical activity, and failure to stretch.
- sleepiness occurs sooner at night, while awakening occurs sooner in the morning.
- hormonal variations of menopause lead to hot flashes, sweats, irregular bleeding, and mood changes.

- an enlarging prostate gland begins causing men to wake at night to urinate.
- depression, panic disorder, anxiety, and despondency become common.
- widespread gum disease loosens the teeth.

Much misunderstanding surrounds middle adulthood. For example, it is common to say that people who cannot tolerate milk are "lactase deficient." This means that they have inadequate amounts of the lactase enzyme required to digest lactose, the sugar in cow's milk. That's nonsense! The vast majority of the world's adult population can't digest lactose very well, especially in the later stages of life. Humans lose their ability to manufacture lactose because nature never intended lactose-containing foods, such as milk, to be consumed after infancy or childhood.

We cannot fool Mother Nature, and perfectly normal people who were able to consume lots of milk and ice cream during their youth begin to experience gassiness, flatulence, constipation and irritable bowel syndrome during middle adulthood.

Osteoporosis is characterized by a serious loss of bone material and predisposes us to softened, easily broken bones. Osteoporosis affects as many as half of all adults, especially women over the age of fifty. The key to preventing osteoporosis is to initiate preventive measures earlier in life. You know, when I was in medical school, just thirty-five years ago, osteoporosis was a relatively uncommon and not very serious condition.

Today, however, nearly 50 percent of women over age sixty experience broken bones from osteoporosis, especially broken vertebrae; approximately 30 percent of men experience broken bones, mostly vertebrae, as well. But will milk consumption help stave off osteoporosis, as we are encouraged to believe? A recent analysis of the diet of nearly eighty thousand nurses tracked by Harvard Medical School certainly challenges this prevalent assumption. In fact, the study found no evidence that women who consume more milk or dairy products reduced their incidence of hip fractures, which is the standard measure of osteoporosis.

Calcium derived from cow's milk is not the key to preventing osteoporosis. A Cornell University study demonstrated that osteoporosis is exceptionally rare in Chinese men and women, although they consume little, if any, dairy products. Instead, the Chinese tend to eat lots of green vegetables and stay physically active.

A study in the *Journal of Clinical Nutrition* (March 1983) also demonstrated that vegetarians have stronger bones than meat-eaters. Indeed, the study showed that by age sixty-five, meat-eaters had five to six times more bone loss than vegetarians. Clearly, calcium is essential to building strong bones and preventing osteoporosis later in life. Supply your body with the calcium it needs, by reducing your consumption of flesh and animal products and increasing your consumption of fresh green vegetables, including a daily calcium and vitamin D supplement. Stopping smoking, drinking less coffee, and staying active, are also important here. Later in this book, I will discuss the importance of exercise in building strong bones.

During middle adulthood, it is particularly crucial to eat more foods filled with life-energy. Other simple steps to smooth out this autumn of your lifelong journey, and prepare the way for the final season of your lifecycle include the following:

- Know what happens to you physically at your age. For example, women are usually healthier after menopause, even if they are about 10 percent heavier than they were in their twenties, and about six to eight pounds heavier than they were just before menopause. In other words, don't worry about maintaining your youthful figure at this stage of the lifecycle; it could be injurious to your health!

- Drink more water. The amount of water stored in the human body dwindles as it ages. When the body is dehydrated, it is more vulnerable to disease. The body normally loses about twelve glasses of water each day through the skin, lungs, kidneys, and feces. Half that amount of water is usually replaced by water in the foods we eat, particularly fruits and vegetables. Carrots are 88 percent water and bananas are 76 percent water. The rest must come from drinking at least six to eight glasses a day.

- Exercise. Just a brisk, twenty-minute walk will substantially change the way you look and feel about yourself before you enter the final season of the human lifecycle.

Keep in mind that even cancer is a preventable illness if you start now! According to the *Harvard Medical School Report on Cancer Prevention*, published in 1997, approximately 50 percent of all cancers are preventable through better diet, increased exercise, decreased alcohol use, smoking cessation, and using common sense with the sun. Nearly two-thirds of cancer deaths in the United States are linked to tobacco, diet, and lack of exercise.

Prevention is clearly the best hope for reducing suffering and death caused by cancer. It can be your hope, as well, but only if you stay informed about what places you at risk. The following measures will help you to reduce your cancer risk:

1. **Exercise at least 20 minutes a day.** The evidence is overwhelming that physical activity helps protect against breast and colon cancer. Physical inactivity is associated with a twofold increase in the rate of colon cancer, which is the second largest cause of death due to cancer in the United States. In a recent study of nearly twenty-five thousand Norwegian women in the *Journal of the American Medical Association*, the rate of breast cancer decreased by 37 percent among those who exercised approximately four hours per week; there was a 52 percent decrease in breast cancer among women engaged in heavy physical labor at work; and women exercising four hours per week who were also lean had 72 percent less breast cancer!

2. **Avoid excess alcohol intake.** It is important to realize that consuming two alcoholic drinks a day increases the risk of breast cancer by about 25 percent.

3. **Be responsible in the sun.** Use sunscreen with a sun protection factor (SPF) of at least 15. Avoid sunburn and exposure to midday sun. Almost all skin cancer, including melanoma, is caused by sun damage.

4. **Don't smoke.** Lung cancer, at least 25 percent of colon cancer, and a significant amount of uterine cervical cancers are attributed to cigarette smoking. Fortunately, within five years of quitting smoking, the ex-smoker's risk of cancer decreases by half. Within ten to fifteen years, the ex-smoker's risk is comparable to people who have never smoked. More than sixty million Americans have already quit smoking.

5. **Eat more fiber, fruits, and vegetables; eat less animal fat; avoid being overweight.** Overweight women have a 50 percent greater chance to develop uterine, breast, colon, and gallbladder cancer. Simply eating more vegetables is associated with a 20 percent reduction in breast cancer. Women living in the same country in Europe who consume or cook with olive oil have less breast cancer than women who use little olive oil. This raises the intriguing possibility that monounsaturated fats, such as olive oil, may actually help protect against cancer.

   Overweight men have a 40 percent greater chance of developing colon and prostate cancer. The risk of prostate cancer, the most common cancer among men in the United States, increases considerably in men who eat more red meat. In both men and women, high consumption of red meat doubles the risk of colon cancer, a type of cancer rarely seen in vegetarians. Evidence suggests that reducing your intake of red meat to less than one serving per week, and increasing your intake of vegetables and fruit, is likely to reduce your risk of colon cancer.

Truly, the major task of the middle adulthood stage of the human lifecycle is simply to make entropy smooth sailing for the final season.

Maturity: Offering Leadership and Becoming Dependent Again

Maturity (ages sixty-five to eighty-five and beyond), the last stage of the human lifecycle, is marked by individuals offering leadership and sharing knowledge and values—at home, at work, and in society. We all want to leave a legacy behind us. In the United States, the average life expectancy is about seventy-two years for men and seventy-nine years for women. With so many people now living to advanced ages, however, the later years can also be marked by a dependence upon others—in a way, similar to our earliest years.

Nature renews and sustains herself on schedule. It is not surprising, then, that our lifecycle also functions on schedule. Nature supplies us with the necessary life-energy to sustain us healthfully for eight or nine decades. Your body extracts its life-energy from the sun's rays, air, water, and food.

With each decade after young adulthood, it is common to lose about seven pounds of muscle and, to double the amount of body fat in proportion to muscle. This rate of muscle loss usually increases during maturity, but it can be reversed. By age sixty-five, the body's ability to use oxygen efficiently decreases by 35 percent, but this, too, can be reversed. So can the steady loss of bone and rise in blood pressure. The Surgeon General has estimated that two-thirds of the illnesses during this stage of life are preventable.

At no time during the human lifecycle is it more important to exercise than during maturity. Before the twentieth century, most people were intensely active and would have scoffed at the idea of exercise. But at that time, human labor accounted for 80 percent of the work needed just to till the soil on a farm. Human labor now accounts for only one percent of the energy needed to work the land. Cars, stores on every corner, and all sorts of labor-saving devices have caused a dramatic decline in physical activity for city dwellers. Regular exercise, proper nutrition, and an enhanced sense of well-being are keys to energy balance and weight loss during maturity. Your body strives to remember wellness.

If we do not care for ourselves properly, entropy overcomes us and can unlock many of the disease templates stored within us. Atherosclerosis and hypertension begin to predominate and lead to heart attack and stroke. Bone and joint disorders, such as osteoporosis and arthritis, occur. Neoplastic diseases develop as colon, prostate, and uterine cancers. Also, about 35 percent of adults over age sixty, mostly women, develop diverticulosis, or small sacs within the walls of the colon. Many will then develop painful inflammations. Diverticulosis is found most often in people who eat too little fiber. Insufficient dietary fiber also contributes to a near 50 percent higher rate of cancer in the gastrointestinal tract.

For most Americans, dietary fiber intake in general is much too low. Fiber, also known as roughage or bulk, is important for preventing as well as reversing unhealthy weight gain. High fiber foods are bulky, take longer to chew, and cause feelings of fullness after eating. Obviously, fiber also keeps the bowels moving because it passes quickly through the digestive system. To increase fiber, eat more vegetables, fruits, whole grain breads, bran muffins, and bran cereals instead of processed baked goods and cereals. Baked beans, kidney beans, and green peas are also very good sources of fiber. You may also wish to take a fiber supplement.

The following list features some of the best high-fiber foods:

- apples
- apricots
- baked potatoes
- bananas
- blueberries
- broccoli
- cabbage
- cantaloupe
- zucchini and zucchini bread or cake
- carrots and carrot cake
- corn
- dates
- dried figs
- nuts and seeds
- oatmeal
- oatmeal cookies
- oranges
- peanut butter
- pears
- popcorn
- prunes
- raisins
- raspberries
- spinach
- strawberries
- sweet potatoes
- turnips
- whole wheat cereals

There are many unhealthy obstacles that are disruptive during maturity. We need life-energy from the sun, but the sun's rays now cause more cancer than ever before due to our depleting ozone layer. Since people spend fewer and fewer hours outside, about half of the people over sixty-five tend to be deficient in vitamin D as well. Recall that our bodies require sunshine to manufacture vitamin D, which is crucial for building strength in our bones and preventing osteoporosis. Moreover, genetic reengineering of foods and leaching the soil of vital nutrients is resulting in widespread B_{12} deficiency and the potential of undiagnosed pernicious anemia.

Pollutants have befouled and depleted the life-energy of our air. Air is so dirty that more than 10 million children a year develop asthma in our smoggiest cities. We are also destroying our rain forests, which supply up to 80 percent of the oxygen in our air. Our water supply is widely contaminated with deadly mercury and other toxic chemicals, which extends to the fish we eat. Our soil is depleted of crucial minerals necessary to produce food filled with life-energy, and most of the food that does manage to grow we refine, process, pulverize, radiate, and genetically reengineer.

A Wakeup Call

What can you do about this? First you can wake up! Just like cows, pigs, and chickens, you are being unnaturally and artificially fattened for profit. Pick up any newspaper and look at the supermarket ads for fake food, artificial food, convenient food, salted food, and seductively packaged food. Where's the *real* food? Our ancestors may have been deprived of supermarkets, with its tens of thousands of items questionably called food. Nevertheless, they were exposed to healthy sunshine, inhaled pure air, thrived on clean water and uncontaminated fish, consumed meat without hormones and antibiotics, and valued fresh vegetables, homemade soups, and whole grain bread. On the other hand, we eat genetically reengineered and microwaved vegetables, our soups come in cans and contain whopping amounts of salt, nitrates, and chemical preservatives, and our bread is white, fluffy, and full of lard.

Do you see why it is time to take more control of your own health destiny? If not for your sake, then for the sake of those you love and care for, especially for children who look to their parents as role models.

We have seen how the human lifecycle encompasses different biological cycles and rhythms that change dramatically with each phase of our human season. The rhythms of our brain waves, the frequencies of our heartbeats, the pressures in our blood vessels, the transit times through our intestines, the cyclic appearances of the human egg, and the ebb and flow of human sperm all create an endless symphony.

Underlying this symphony is the complex living entity called the human lifecycle. Spring blooms with your conception. Summer arrives with your reproductive years and stays until the autumn of middle adulthood. We have to be reminded to take better care of ourselves, so that when winter arrives we have time to savor the fruits of our lifecycle's past as it transforms into the roots of our future. In *Leaves of Grass*, Walt Whitman reminds us of life's healing force and its never-ending quest for energy balance and *Total Health Rejuvenation.*

> *You will hardly know*
> *Who I am or what I mean,*
> *But I shall be good health*
> *To you nevertheless,*
> *And filter and fiber your blood.*
> *Failing to find me at first,*
> *Keep encouraged,*
> *Missing me one place, search another,*
> *I will stop somewhere waiting for you.*

Part Five

BUILDING A NEW PATH
OF LEAST RESISTANCE

After reading Parts One through Four, I hope you have gained a greater understanding about life-energy, permanent weight loss, and your personal "Cycle of Life." This is all part of the process of changing your mindset about the food you eat. When you can successfully achieve that goal, then—and only then—will you attain *Total Health Rejuvenation* and your optimal weight.

As I told you earlier in this book, there are no quick fixes. The healthy way is the *only way*! Can you think of any materialistic thing you own that is more valuable than your health? I can't! And please remember: In addition to bettering your self-image, reaching your optimal weight through *Total Health Rejuvenation* will have *many positive benefits*!

Begin by asking yourself the following questions: Have you ever lost weight and shortly thereafter gained it all back? Do strong urges or uncontrollable cravings cause you to eat too much food, or too much of the wrong type of food, or both? If so, you are not to blame. Urges and cravings have been cunningly programmed into your mind by the advertising industry to create eating habits that help support sales. Profits, not your health, is the priority.

Most overweight people regain their lost weight after dieting because their bad eating habits were merely temporarily overcome, not transformed. Unhealthy habits are continually reinforced—even by the so-called health care industry.

Recall that Americans suffer from the outset simply because we require less food energy than we are taught to believe. Even the nutrition information on food labels misleads us since it depends on an inflated daily energy requirement of two thousand calories for a "typically healthy adult." Potentially, that's a whole lot of dead food.

The 28-Day Plan to Take Advantage of a Perfectly Natural System

My 28-Day Plan takes you step-by-step through the simple processes that allow you to overcome food urges and cravings by establishing a new mindset. The plan literally kick-starts your body into burning its excess fat. Why does the 28-Day Plan work? Because it takes full advantage of a perfectly natural system.

Psychologically, it's called "cognitive restructuring" and "conscious reprogramming." In layman's terms, this means uprooting ideas and thoughts about food, and planting healthful seeds in their place. The bottom line is that once you reconstruct your mindset, you can lose up to 10 percent of your present excess weight in eight to twelve months. And you will keep it off for life without ever feeling deprived. If you have more than 10 percent excess weight, you will simply need more time and more effort, especially exercise, to lose the weight. Your new mindset will enable you to comfortably lose another 5 to 10 percent of your weight during the next year and perhaps another 5 percent during the third year.

This treatment plan is so flexible, it works for the slightly overweight, the very overweight, and for those who are close to their naturally optimal weight and just want to stay healthy. What do *you* want to lose? Your excess weight or your time? If you want to lose weight, then don't waste your time on crash diets and crazy diet pills. The 28-Day Plan uses your time efficiently to lose weight effectively—and for good!

Don't discourage yourself by setting unreasonable expectations. It is realistic to aim for a 10 percent to 15 percent total and permanent weight loss. Here is a letter from a patient who lost 20 percent of her excess weight over four years after attending my Voyage to Wellness program on a transatlantic crossing of the *QE2*. Once she lost the weight, she never gained it back.

> *Dear Dr. Taub,*
>
> *I just finished reading your* Rx For Life *book and I'm so happy that you have not veered from what you taught all of us on the* QE2 *during our memorable voyage to wellness. It's difficult to believe that ten years have already gone by since my half-century struggle to lose weight ended. I had tried so many diets before attending your seminar that I felt like a yo-yo going up and down most of my life. I was depressed, obsessed, and possessed—until you helped me change my mindset about food, exercise, and attitude.*
>
> *I lost fifteen pounds that first year—I went from 160 to 145 pounds—but better yet, I went from a size 12 to a size 10 dress. Then I lost about six pounds a year for the next three years—about a half a pound a month, just like you said I would. So here I am ten years later, now weighing 125 pounds and wearing a size 7 dress. I'm happy as can be with my new habits and my new life—loads of fruit all morning, lots of veggies all day, baked potatoes or pasta whenever I want, and walking at least a half-hour a day, no matter where I am, in virtually any kind of weather. Thanks again for giving me a new life.*
>
> *Sincerely,*
> *Gloria S.*

The psychological changes that occur during the 28-Day Plan refocus the lens through which you view the world. The results are astonishing. You will naturally overcome your previously programmed food cravings and false beliefs. You will overcome your resistance to exercise. It will be natural for you not to want to eat junk. It will be natural that the very thought of red meat and cow's milk will almost nauseate you. You will naturally seek out fresh fruits, veggies, and other foods—with delight!

This plan is not about deprivation, either. Small amounts of butter are perfectly acceptable for cooking delicious recipes. Olive and canola oils are also fine in moderation. Olive oil, more physical activity, and a zest for life are why Mediterranean people are so healthy!

Some say Mediterranean people are healthier because of the red wine that abounds in their diet. This is questionable. We have already seen how nutritional science is severely tainted by economic agendas that have no place in good science. Recently, an article in the *Journal of the American Medical Association* purported that two alcoholic drinks a day increased longevity. Thanks to the wine industry, advertisements as to the benefits of wine suddenly appeared everywhere in the media, literally drenching the public with the "healthy news." I was appalled by this "news" because I have attended many autopsies in which the fatty changes of cirrhosis were present in the livers of individuals who regularly had just two drinks a day. Fortunately, another study in a different AMA journal appeared one month later, showing that two drinks a day were associated with a significant increase in breast cancer among women.

Wine is probably fine in moderation. But too much alcohol is not compatible with *Total Health Rejuvenation* and it makes losing weight virtually impossible because it changes the body's metabolism and ability to burn fat. It's best to limit your alcohol intake to about a drink (a glass of wine, a bottle of beer, or a cocktail) no more than two or three times a week; the less, the better.

Making Progress

No one is born fat. Therefore, no matter how overweight you or your family members are, you still have an inner healing force striving at all times to preserve a healthful energy balance in your body. Being overweight means that your energy is out of balance. It's an illness.

Despite the common misperception, it is common for people to successfully lose weight and keep it off. My patients have terrific rates of personal success. I personally lost 10 percent of my weight fifteen years ago. I went from 200 to 180 pounds. That's twenty pounds I can, *and will*, surely live without.

We simply eat too much dead food and are too sedentary. People sit in front of their computers all day at work and then go home and sit in front of their TVs until bedtime, while they are eating, drinking, and snacking.

The good news is that there is a little bit of hope in everyone, and it seems to be on the rise. A recent study conducted by the National Weight Control Registry and the University of Pittsburgh found nearly two thousand people who refused to stay fat. Instead, they lost an average of sixty pounds and kept if off for an average of six years. Most of the participants in this study were women. About half were between the ages of thirty-four and fifty-five. On average, they dropped from 220 to 154 pounds. Most went from being overweight to what they felt was a normal, healthy weight.

We can learn a great deal from these remarkable people. Remember: The goal promoted in this book is to lose a reasonable 10 percent of your weight. This is about ten to twenty-five pounds for most people. As you lose weight, *how you feel* is most important. Even without a scale, you will know you are losing weight. Your belt/dress size is a fine guide.

You may believe that if you have been overweight since childhood, you will really have to struggle to lose weight and keep it off now. This is a false perception! Almost 50 percent of the successful weight losers in the above study were overweight since they were ten years old, and another 25 percent were overweight from the time they were eighteen.

It is very likely that you also believe that losing weight is especially hard if being overweight runs in your family. Again, this is not so! Seventy percent of the successful weight losers in the above study had at least one obese parent. How did their beat their genes? By refusing to believe that they were destined to be overweight.

Almost all participants in this study reported that they had tried to lose weight before. In this case, 90 percent of them attributed their success to eating less food overall, and eating much less fatty food. They made these changes even while eating out an average of four times per week. They also engaged in very high levels of physical activity, about twice as much as the experts usually recommend. Most participants walked for exercise, while others bicycled, did aerobics, stair climbing, or weight lifting and running.

Surprisingly, 75 percent reported that a specific experience ignited their decision to lose weight. Men were more likely to report a medical event such as back pain, fatigue, high cholesterol, or varicose veins. Women were most likely to report an emotional event: "My husband left me and my lawyer told me it was because I was fat" or "I was going to my tenth reunion and I saw myself in the mirror." For many, the triggering event was someone just commenting on their weight.

Even more surprisingly, although most people believe that it is much harder to maintain weight loss than to lose weight, these successful weight losers said otherwise. About half said that keeping the weight off was actually easier than losing it in the first place. They were not miserable, nor did they spend their time dreaming about food. Ninety-five percent said that the overall quality of their lives improved, and 92 percent said they had greater energy.

Psychologist John Sklare studied thousands of overweight people who sought medical help to lose weight. He discovered that stress was the most common reason that people fail to lose weight permanently. His conclusion? Unless patients address the underlying issues that motivate them to overeat and make poor nutritional choices, they are sure to repeat their old habits and continue to struggle. In Sklare's words, "If you keep doing what you've always done, you'll keep getting what you've always got."

Most people have to try over and over again to overcome unhealthy habits. Overweight people often have to make New Year's resolutions for many years before they keep their promises. Understanding the mental processes that overweight people go through on their way to overcoming their harmful eating habits, however, will help you reach your goals *this year*, not many years from now.

The human psyche goes through a fairly predictable process before it prepares to surrender detrimental habits for better habits.

Psychologists James Prochaska, Carlo DiClemente, and John Norcross identified some of these stages as "precontemplation," "contemplation," "preparation," and "action."

Are you a precontemplator? Precontemplators are people who deny that a problem exists. If this describes you, then you really have no intention of changing your eating habits; you really don't even want to admit that your habits are detrimental to your health. We have all seen troublesome drinkers who deny they have a problem or hacking smokers who say they are just fine. Overweight precontemplators resist change, but all is not yet lost. You can still make progress if you are given the right tools at the right time. A nurturing relationship with a non-nagging spouse, or a friend who is unwilling to give up on you, can help. The 28-Day Plan is a sure strategy to propel you out of the precontemplator's trap.

Contemplators are people who recognize that they have a problem and begin to make plans to change their behavior. But their plans are more or less indefinite. Contemplators will eagerly talk about being overweight, and they will also make promises to change their behavior *someday*. Contemplators are chronic procrastinators. If you're a contemplator, you probably hope for some "magic moment" when you'll know that it's right for you to change your eating habits forever. Or perhaps you're engaged in some wishful thinking, such as hoping that an effective diet pill will be developed. As a contemplator, you may even have taken action prematurely in the past, long before you were really ready to change. Then you could say to yourself, "I just knew I couldn't do it."

Contemplators truly want to change but face a subconscious resistance that causes anxiety and fear and prolongs the procrastination. Contemplators get anxious about sacrificing something comfortable and familiar in their life for something unfamiliar. Additionally, contemplators fear failure once they really do make a commitment to change. If you are a contemplator, your internal fear can be paralyzing. For some people, according to psychologist James Bugental, fear of change is "a fate worse than death."

If you are an overweight contemplator, getting your adrenaline flowing is the best way to ascend from procrastination to preparation to action. In other words, you need some serious emotional and physical arousal to kick-start your final decision to change. The best way for you to get such a boost is to start eating lots of fresh fruit, particularly in the morning. Fruit is particularly full of the life-energy you need to stoke up your mental and physical furnace. It's important to get your endorphins flowing with more physical activity, especially long, brisk walks. Finally, it's necessary to enlist the power of your imagination. Take time to imagine what you might look like and how you might feel if you were happier, healthier, more energetic, and leaner. Just for a moment, imagine how you want look in the future. Imagination is a powerful force, the root of all creativity. We need imagination to plan a meal, build a bridge, write a poem, compose a song, make a friend, build a family. Imagination, along with emotional and physical energy, is your key to move from procrastination to preparation to action for a leaner life.

We have discussed the "thinking, planning, but not accomplishing" phase of weight loss. If that describes you, then it is time for you to cross the bridge to the "proactive and committed" phase of weight loss. Soon you will learn about a *Personal Wellness Retreat* that is designed to help you cross that bridge. Because you are where you are, you probably are familiar with some of the following statements:

"I want to lose weight."
"I know I should lose weight."
"I sure hope I can lose weight."
"I'm not totally sure I can handle the cravings."
"It's going to be very difficult to get some exercise every day."
"I'll never be as thin as the people on TV or in the magazines."
"I wonder whether I can keep the weight off once I lose it."
"How will I manage without hamburgers, french fries, milkshakes, potato chips, and ice cream sundaes?"

As you cross the bridge, you will be saying instead:

"I will lose weight."
"I will be able to handle the cravings."
"I will do some exercise every day that gets me at least a little bit sweaty and breathing faster."
"I'm not supposed to be as lean as the fashion models."

The 28-Day Plan introduced later in this book will help you to establish a lifetime of healthy eating habits, to cross the bridge from procrastination to proactive living once and for all. No matter how old you are, if you want to lose weight permanently, you must create a new frontier in your mind and *build a new path of least resistance* to get you over that bridge. *Balance Your Body, Balance Your Life* is all about creating that new result.

The four crucial elements in creating that new result are the following:

1. **self-respect**
2. **connectedness to others**
3. **accurate nutritional information**
4. **willingness to exercise**

My patient Mary L. provides an outstanding example of the above. She was enrolled in a hospital-sponsored 28-Day Plan I conducted ten years ago:

Dear Dr. Taub:

I saw you on TV last evening and just had to write to let you know how well I am doing. I completed your 28-day stress and weight loss class ten years ago, and I am happy to report to you that because of your teachings on meditation, yoga, exercise, and eating live-energy foods, not dead foods, I am maintaining a very reasonable weight and am very happy with myself.

I just thought of how many of your teachings I do without thinking. I eat low-fat foods, lots of fruit, and exercise regularly. I am sixty years old and have more energy than ever. I can control my stress by using the relaxation techniques I learned in our 28-day class. I have high self-esteem and self-confidence because I am now in control of what gets put into my body. I had dieted all my life, but since completing your 28-day plan ten years ago, I no longer diet, I eat healthy, exercise (even though I do not want to), and practice the relaxation techniques that come out of your classes. I no longer go on yo-yo diets; I simply go back to watching what I put in my mouth.

Most of my friends are overweight and have let themselves go. Of course, as we grow older we slow down and have a tendency to give up on some things. But I refuse to do this. I want to remain young in spirit and healthy enough to keep up with my two-year-old granddaughter. I want her to be proud of her grandmother.

I am so glad that I took your 28-day course because I work eight hours a day, take care of my granddaughter four hours every week-

day, and have an eighty-six-year-old mother who lives with me, so I need to be healthy. I take very few medications and I am never sick. I make sure my eighty-six-year-old mom follows your teachings, too, and she is never sick. She climbs stairs to my apartment every day, walks on a daily basis, does my housework, bakes (healthy foods), crochets, and is super independent. I thank you for this. I thank you for teaching me how to take control of my body and respect what I put into it. Giving myself permission to relax and take time for myself has also helped a lot. Everything I learned from you has benefited my mom as well as myself over the past ten years and we are both thankful for your 28-day plan. We can attest to the fact that eating wise and living well pays off!

I am using your teachings about food with Sara, my granddaughter. If she can learn good habits now, she will be able to control what goes into her mouth and how she acts in years to come. Self-respect, self-discipline, self-esteem, and knowing you are in control can help anyone. Thank you for helping me to gain control of my life.

Sincerely,
Mary L.

Change Is in the Air

Change is in the air and it is time to make your move. A journey of a thousand miles starts with the first step. But to address the fact that, deep down, most people fear making changes when their familiar habits are at stake, let's reconsider science and some more natural laws.

Modern science was launched when Isaac Newton (1642–1727) imagined that the universe was like a giant clock, the motion of its slowly moving external hands caused by the motion of its smaller internal gears. In much the same way, all natural phenomena in the world around us are the result of natural laws working below the surface of what's immediately evident. Newton described the natural laws that apply to motion as follows:

Anything that moves does so in response to the action of one or more forces. This is why blood cells travel through our veins (the heart pumps it), a baseball hurtles through the air (a bat applies a force), and water cascades downward off a cliff (the force of gravity). *Can you see any parallels in human behavior?*

There are two types of motion in nature: uniform motion and changing motion. Uniform motion means that something is either standing still or moving in a straight line at a constant speed. Therefore, both a book that is standing on a book shelf and a rocket that is traveling to the moon at a thousand miles per hour can be said to be in uniform motion. Changing motion means that an object either speeds up, slows down, or changes direction. Thus, a rolling ball that is slowing down or rolling down a hill faster and faster, or veering off in another direction, is said to be in changing motion.

An object at rest will continue to stay at rest unless it is compelled to change by a sufficient force applied to it. Likewise, an object that is moving in a straight line at a constant speed will keep doing so unless it is compelled to change by a force applied to it. When such a force is applied, the object will either slow down, speed up, or change its direction. *Now can you see any parallels in human behavior?*

The tendency of an object to resist a change in motion is called *inertia*. Inertia explains why objects continue doing exactly what they are doing. A book keeps sitting on a table and a rolling ball keeps rolling until a sufficient force is applied. The book moves if it is pushed and the ball eventually slows down because of friction. If the book is pushed far enough, it might also fall from the table, impelled by gravity to follow a new path of least resistance. Likewise, the ball might take a new direction down a steeper slope and also follow a new path of least resistance.

Human behavior is exactly like this! We live by inertia. We resist change. We tend to value what's most comfortable and familiar to us. We follow the most comfortable and familiar path that is available to us. It's all a system of natural laws.

If you habitually eat too much food, or too much junk food, your eating habits, food urges, and cravings naturally direct you toward the comfortable and familiar path of least resistance—appetite and taste bud pleasuring. The curative power of *Balance Your Body, Balance Your Life* is based on creating a **new** path that allows you to neutralize and overcome your food urges and cravings.

Perhaps at this very moment you are still feeling discomfort and apprehension over the very notion of real change. When stressed, people are especially likely to choose the familiar and comfortable path over even temporary psychological discomfort. It's easier to give in to your senses. With detrimental eating habits, the involved senses are always taste, smell, and what we call appetite. Unfortunately, being overweight also inflames your appetite. You mistake your mental appetite for physical hunger and eat more and more food.

This is why you will often eat beyond what is comfortable, even to feeling unpleasantly full. You will also mistake good smells for what people sniff at with delight on television—fat-laden dishes like pepperoni pizza and fried chicken. Finally, you will mistake good taste for lots of sugar, salt, artificial flavors, and fat. Fortunately, taste buds can be reprogrammed to appreciate the taste of fresh fruits and fresh vegetables, especially if you begin subconsciously to reason in a brand-new way: *This carrot is supplying life-energy for my body to stay well, avoid constipation, and burn off its excess fat. It also really does taste good.*

By taking advantage of a system of natural laws, you can begin to consistently override your food urges and cravings. It all depends on creating a new way of living marked by feelings of satisfaction rather than deprivation, and it must lead in the direction of good physical health rather than overweight and fatigue.

Here is a vital new mindset that makes you feel energized and invigorated. It will guide you toward happiness, healthiness, and permanent weight loss. Your food choices will naturally drift toward and travel down this new path.

Picture a woman in a canoe atop a swiftly flowing stream. If she doesn't paddle hard against the current, the canoe just proceeds downstream; it's the natural path of least resistance. Of course, the woman could paddle hard upstream if that is her destination, but when she stops, the canoe will stop and once again float downstream. In much the same way, people who go on a diet discover it's only a temporary fix. When they stop, the river carries them back. *An object in motion will head toward the path of least resistance, and efforts to overcome such a natural system are eventually futile.*

Perhaps there is nothing in life more discouraging than futile and hopeless effort. Sisyphus was a character in Greek mythology. For certain sins, he was condemned by the gods to spend all of his days and nights rolling a huge stone to the top of a mountain. Then, upon reaching the summit, the rock would tumble back down the mountain, and Sisyphus would begin his task once again. Nobel laureate Albert Camus portrayed the torment of Sisyphus straining to push the huge stone up the slope, his face contorted, his cheek against the stone, his shoulder bracing the boulder, his foot wedging it, his arms outstretched and his battered hands covered with earth. Then, at the end of his long effort, Sisyphus watches the stone rushing back down the mountain from whence he will have to push it up again. His face that toiled so close to the stone looks like the stone itself as he goes back down the mountain with heavy steps. But we are left with the feeling that Sisyphus is superior to his fate. He is stronger than his rock. He never gives up. His descent down the mountain is mixed with scorn and joy. Sisyphus believes that all will be well and the struggle toward the heights is enough to fill his heart.

What if Sisyphus found a way to succeed in his task and be reborn? What if he sought a more gentle slope around the mountain? What if he greased the ground in front of the boulder? Or put the boulder on a platform with wheels? Or crushed the boulder into smaller pieces? Sometimes in life you have to travel the path of most resistance to reach the path of least resistance. Perhaps Sisyphus realized that the night is darkest just before the dawn—and so can you. For you can't solve the problem of food cravings and urges that you have accumulated over so many decades just by wanting to. But you can begin there, and you can begin now.

You can build your own new path of least resistance by developing a strong personal vision. Losing weight and growing thinner, however, is not enough. You must develop a personal vision of being healthier, happier, more energetic, more loving, less stressed, and more lean. Then you will break free from the mental inertia that sustains you, yes, but at too great a cost! Your new personal vision will spark a paradigm shift!

By first creating in your mind the person you want to be, as well as the body you want to have, you take advantage of a natural system that Goethe described this way:

> What you can do, or
> Dream you can do, begin it.
> Boldness has genius, power and magic in it.
> Only engage, and then
> The mind grows heartened.
> Begin it, and the work will be completed.

Paradigm Shift

What if the woman paddling her canoe toward the direction of her dreams suddenly determines that she no longer wants to travel in the familiar, comfortable stream driven by currents beyond her control? What if, instead, she determines to reposition her canoe, pointing it in the direction of her greatest dreams, using the natural currents to aid her? With a change in current, a paradigm shift occurs. Her canoe begins to glide effortlessly toward her dreamed-of destination.

A crystal-clear vision and a thorough understanding of your present reality will help you get to where you want to be. No more traveling upstream with fad diets, unused health club memberships, and diet pills. Before we go further, let's look at the paddler's adventure again to ascertain what made the difference. First, she had to realize that the stream was taking her in a direction in which she didn't want to go. Then she had to clarify her desired destination and create a vision to help her determine her destiny.

How open are you to change? Are there some things you won't

budge on: your religion, the hand with which you write, even the side of your head on which you part your hair? Like the canoer, we mostly find ourselves adrift in currents that are too comfortable and familiar to change. There are thousands of books on the subject of personal change, but unless you personally want to change, the books are of no help. Self-help books are only effective if you are motivated to help yourself.

If change seems difficult, what about *improvement*? Nearly everyone says he or she is interested in improving some aspect of his or her life—relationships, appearance, health, job, outlook. Like change, improvement takes people out of their comfort zone and into an arena of uncertainty that has the potential for discomfort or pain.

Why won't people make a persistent effort to even slightly improve their eating habits and lifestyle? Because improvement alone is not a sufficient force to move an object that is quite comfortable at rest. Nor is the force sufficient to change the direction of a life already in motion in another direction. *It's all about a system of natural laws.*

Why do people choose this path in their everyday lives? Often they don't know other paths exist. It's a little like driving a car at night; you can only see the road hit by your headlights. Why do people who have accurate information about other paths and other directions choose to remain where they are? Because it involves moving out of the "comfort zone." Inaccurate information and fear of letting go fuel human inertia. Fear of letting go is why people stay in abusive relationships or unsatisfying jobs. Fear of the unknown is why people resist changing abusive eating habits and lifestyles. It's human inertia!

But imagine this: *Years of inertia can be a powerful springboard for progress!* Progressing toward a healthier lifestyle and attitude about eating doesn't have to be uncomfortable. Rather than saying good-bye to your comfort zone, you simply broaden that comfort zone to embrace new and healthier tastes and habits. The tools I will give you will increase your happiness, comfort, and well-being. I will help you let go of fear and progress toward your vision. Making progress will give you more physical comfort and eating pleasure than you can imagine.

Banish Fear

"The wise man in the storm prays to God,
not for safety from danger, but for deliverance from fear.
It is the storm within that endangers him, not the storm without."
        —RALPH WALDO EMERSON

Previously, we discussed the stage at which you contemplate changing your lifestyle. Contemplators can also procrastinate because they experience a subconscious resistance that causes them too much anxiety and fear. We usually grow anxious about giving up what's comfortable and familiar. It's true that change can seem frightening. If you contemplate only to procrastinate about losing weight permanently, however, your fear may paralyze you!

Remember: a human being is a complex energy system, and energy always moves along the path of least resistance. The reason your body is overweight is because this is the path of least resistance that you have followed. The flow of water from a mountain stream in the Adirondacks to a river in New York City, then to the Atlantic Ocean, follows the path of least resistance. The flow of wind over the Great Lakes and through the widest streets of Chicago follows the path of least resistance. The flow of electricity from a far-off generator to your home, then to your toaster, television, or computer, follows the path of least resistance.

Energy always moves along the path of least resistance, and that's why people tend to move in the direction in which it is easiest for them to go. The reason you are overweight is because, like a river, electricity, and the wind, you have followed the path of least resistance. In our society, the path of least resistance means eating more dead food and becoming increasingly inactive.

Unless you open up a new frontier by building a *new* path of least resistance to get you there, you will always be paddling against the current or pushing the boulder up a never-ending mountain. But you can create an even larger river flowing in the new direction in which you wish to go. Or you can move the boulder sideways around the mountain. Either way, the only thing truly stopping you from creating a *new* path of least resistance is fear of pain and discomfort.

To leave your current path, you must be brave enough to seek a new frontier by finding an alternative path that leads to your desired destination. If you can't direct your canoe to a current leading where you want to go from your present stream, then you may have to pick up your canoe and move it to a different body of water altogether. Instead of searching for a new way around the mountain, you may just have to move to a new mountain. The only thing getting in between you and your progress up that mountain is fear.

Fear is rampant because stress is the raging epidemic of our times. Once you have good nutritional information, fear and stress are the most common obstacles to your quest for permanent weight loss. Your mind tells you that the discomfort or suffering will make life too unpleasant. Your mind also tells you to fear failure and convinces you that success is impossible to attain.

It is important to realize that your fear is only an emotional illusion that has acquired a life of its own because of stress. Unfortunately, though fear exists in your mind, it creates a stranglehold that prevents you from living in peace. President Franklin Delano Roosevelt, himself crippled by polio, inspired the entire free world—faced by the most evil army ever known—with this one moving statement: *The only thing you have to fear is fear itself.*

Unfortunately, you cannot use fearful thoughts to diminish your fear. Just think: Trying to analyze or escape fear with a fearful mind is like fighting fire with fire. But just as your thoughts are able to create fear, they can also create peace. You can learn to replace a restless, worried, or troubled mind with a tranquil, calm, and peaceful mind. The 28-Day Plan described in this book is designed to overcome stress and release you from the bondage of your fear. Freedom from fear requires only that you lift the veil that now obscures your own truth.

Only a quiet mind can dispel fear. You can begin to calmly observe your fear and release it. As you learn to meditate, you will be living more in the here and now instead of mulling over past defeats or worrying about future hopes. If you live in the present, there can be no fear that represents the chains of the past or the pull of the future. The simple relaxation-meditation technique introduced in the first part of this book (see page 34) is powerful. Even the busiest person can set aside five or ten minutes a day to meditate.

Just read this letter I received from Melanie W., a forty-eight-year-old woman, who thought she was in relatively good health:

Dear Dr. Taub:

Just about three years ago, my doctor told me, after a routine checkup, that my cholesterol was mega-high and my EKG was abnormal. Then he warned me that I had better change the way I was eating—completely. I was really sorry that I went to see him in the first place because all I ever suffered with was low energy, headaches off and on, some constipation, and maybe some PMS. And, of course, I was considerably overweight.

I was thrown for a loop, so totally disappointed and upset that I couldn't speak with anyone for a few days. I was literally frightened. No more croissants with bacon and butter for breakfast? No more barbecued steaks with that nice fatty crust? No more ice cream and chocolate creamy cakes? No more mayonnaise slathered on my sandwiches? No more salami and knockwurst? I can never do that! Impossible!

I was totally resistant to change because I love to cook and love to eat. After all, I prided myself on being a gourmet cook, and I loved to create new recipes. How could I just stop all that when I wasn't even that much overweight—maybe twenty pounds or so, just like most of my friends? Actually, to tell you the truth, I was too scared to make a real commitment because it all felt so painful. I thought I'd rather die than change, and that made me scared. Then I thought I'd try but probably fail, and that made me even more scared.

Everything felt like a real catastrophe and I was really in the pits, when my doctor urged me to attend your 28-day weight loss class at the hospital because he had personally benefited so much from it. He told me that he and his wife attended your program, and as a result, never felt better. "Oh sure," I thought, "give me a break!"

I guess what finally convinced me was when my doctor told me he was so impressed by your strategy that he decided to create an entire physician's advisory board just to support your work. I really trust my doctor, after growing up with him caring for me and now having him care for my own kids; so, reluctantly, I tried your plan. Slowly, I began looking at some of your wife Anneli's recipes, while still making a big circle around them; honestly, they didn't make a lot of sense at first. But then, when you actually held a class right smack in the middle of a supermarket aisle, I was stunned to really see, for the first time, that the shelves, the coolers, and virtually all the display cases in there were filled with processed, refined, and fake foods—what you call "dead energy."

And then it finally dawned on me that the contents of my refrigerator were just as appalling! I began shopping and cooking differently and started meditating and wellness walking every day, briskly as you say, "not just loping along." I cooked Anneli's recipes and found them to be even more savory than my old favorites, which just provided a sugar or grease high for my taste buds. For example, when I just had to have some fried potatoes, I got out my Teflon pan and vegetable spray and made them nice and crunchy without the fat. During weekends, when I love to make dishes like spinach, champignons, and cheese sauce, I tried some lot-fat milk instead of heavy cream—I liked it just fine. Same with some low-fat yogurt instead of ice cream, although I still indulge in ice cream now and then, without feeling guilty, because I remember your motto: "Everything in moderation—including moderation."

What was really amazing was the fact that in just four weeks, I lost a bunch of pounds as a bonus, without really thinking about it. What I really just wanted to do was lower my cholesterol rather than take off my excess pounds, which I had given up on long ago. Surprise! It's now five years later and I'm twenty pounds lighter. But the best thing is that I am holding my weight at the present level and it's no problem, because the most wonderful part of my experience is the fact that my taste buds have changed. Everyone else in our class began experiencing the same transformation, too. It seems that our taste buds change after about two weeks and adjust to fewer sweets, less grease, and less fake food. Actually, the previous stuff I used to eat is now much too sweet and greasy. Eating the old way also makes me gassy and upsets my stomach. My taste buds now find concentrated sugar or pure fat disgusting. Steaks, hamburgers, and all the glasses of milk I used to drink revolt me, and I guard against eating them. It's obvious that we don't need a lot of flesh, fat, salt, and sugar to ensure the pleasure of eating. These healthy changes will naturally happen to everybody's common sense as well as to their nose and taste buds. I guarantee it!

From a grateful patient,
Melanie W.

Needless to say, letters of this nature, which I receive all the time, make my heart feel wonderful!

The journey of the human cycle of life is inward as well as upward, striving to attain what Plato called "The Ideal of the Good" and what Aristotle called "the divinity in everything." Every body—every unhealthy, stressed, and overweight body—has the potential to feel better and lose weight permanently.

To realize this potential requires some of the fearlessness of an infant learning to walk for the first time. Fostering this fearlessness requires only a challenge to think differently about your body and your beliefs. The Roman philosopher Seneca said, "It is not because things are difficult that we do not dare; it is because we do not dare that they are difficult."

You are about to move beyond the "contemplating" stage to the "do it" stage. Read on now, so that you will understand your Personal Wellness Retreat and the entire 28-Day Plan that follows it. But before you continue, make sure you have completed the Health Profile in Part Two of this book.

Your Personal Wellness Retreat

I consistently observe that many of my patients become aware of their inner healing strength much quicker than I imagine possible (almost in the space of a heartbeat). The awareness is a function of their heightened self-value and reverence for life. Their experiences led me to create a much simpler, more practical pathway to the wellness and weight loss paradigm. It begins with a One-Day Personal Wellness Retreat.

The key to the therapeutic effectiveness of this one day will be the short but intensive effort you make to set your paradigm shift in motion. Some overweight people may choose to ignore the new paradigm for a while, but it will remain in their consciousness like a seed ready to sprout.

More than ever before, people feel an urgent need for more free time to regain control of their lives. Overweight people are already so enslaved by their senses that it would be ridiculous for them to embark on a lifelong journey to a leaner body without first taking some precious free time for themselves. If you are seriously committed to losing weight, it is time for you to set aside just a day for your Personal Wellness Retreat.

This is a necessary time-out before you begin to regain control of your weight. It can be any day you choose. Even if you have to take some time off from work, it's well worth it. What's more important than your health? You'll be better at work when you return. Your Personal Wellness Retreat will allow you to begin building a new path of least resistance to a healthier and leaner body. You will experience benefits to last a lifetime.

During your Personal Wellness Retreat your main goal is clear: defining your future vision and taking stock of your current situation. After all, you wouldn't rush into redecorating your house or creating an important presentation for your boss without first taking time to clarify what you want to accomplish and how you plan to do it. We are most successful at accomplishing our goals when we have a clear vision.

Make no mistake, this will be a crucial time of reflection for you. The results of the reality check I ask you to take in a moment may disturb you. But don't be discouraged, because your past ended one moment ago and the power of your body to bring itself back into balance is enormous. After all, during the one day of your Personal Wellness Retreat, your heart will beat around 100,000 times and your body will give birth to about 100 billion new red blood cells.

In the same natural way, your mind will ready itself to give birth to a new reality over the twenty-eight days that follow. A healthier and leaner body awaits you, as long as you are ready to embark on a *new* path of least resistance.

The goal of your Personal Wellness Retreat is to create a new vision of a healthier, happier, more energized, and leaner you. During this one day, you will begin focusing in on that vision, making it so intense that it infuses your entire being. Instead of merely problem solving, which is almost always a temporary fix at best, you will be creating a new and permanent result.

Over the twenty-eight days that follow, your mindset and your notion of reality will change—your paradigm will shift. First, you will catch a clear glimpse of who you wish to become. You will be so drawn to the image that you will be able to visualize your future more powerfully than your past. You will experience a physical, emotional, and spiritual epiphany when doing so. Your biochemistry and metabolism will actually shift toward homeostasis, as *your body remembers wellness*. New feelings of self-confidence will cast out fear to allow you to make progress toward your goal. Rediscovering love for yourself, for others, and for nature will make you feel worthy once more of life's blessings.

During the special day of your Personal Wellness Retreat, you will learn simple and reasonable steps to begin determining your own health destiny. Just the smallest effort, when part of a larger and focused vision, can unleash a harvest of health for you. In the space of a day, you will start shattering the physical, mental, and emotional chains that have weakened your own natural healing forces.

The guidelines for your Personal Wellness Retreat are straightforward and allow plenty of room for individual creativity. Commit yourself to following the guidelines, because this day will only be as good as you vow to make it. Your effort begins by taking small steps that stimulate your powerful body-mind connection. It's important for you to realize how much your health depends on your own personal responsibility, self-value, and reverence for life. What is in your heart and on your mind affects your physical well-being, and vice versa.

Quiet time and solitude is essential. If you think there are too many distractions at home, consider asking your spouse or getting a baby-sitter to help with the kids. It would be even better if you could get more in touch with nature by driving or taking a train to somewhere in the countryside. If you have a friend or a mate, you might wish to retreat together. It's wonderful when couples commit to this time together, but it certainly is not necessary. If you are with another person, it is important to be supportive but to still be by yourself. In other words, be together but not too together, because your main goal is to experience peace and quiet.

Have your answering machine take phone messages for the day, or simply unplug the phone. If other members of your family will be around, ask them not to interrupt you unnecessarily. You might want to make an announcement to everyone old enough to understand that their support and understanding will be appreciated. In any case, plan ahead to work together with your family to have everything go as smoothly as possible.

Here are the basic ingredients of *your* special day: healthy food, fresh air, exercise, good reading, soft music, and quiet time for meditation, writing, and prayer. *No* TV, *no* phone calls, *no* movies, *no* newspapers, *no* magazines, *no* radio (except for relaxing music).

Your Personal Wellness Retreat provides you with a good opportunity to relax with an amusing, educational, or inspirational book. It's also a great time to revisit some of your favorite records, CDs, and cassettes. Soft, relaxing music might be nice during, as well as before and after, meals. Dim the lights sometime during the day and light a candle or two for a while, perhaps while eating, bathing, writing, or while just doing nothing. This day is to quiet the mind and focus on *you*.

Make sure to go to bed early the night before, after taking some extra time for personal care: a pedicure or manicure, a bubble bath, facial, or massage. Also, cleansing your inside is as important as cleaning your outside. Many people may benefit from a Fleets enema, a Dulcolax suppository or a mild herbal laxative.

NUTRITION

It's important that you personally shop for your food for this special day. Take your time to carefully select lots of fresh, colorful, ripe fruits, and plenty of fresh vegetables. Pay careful attention to the colors, shapes, and consistencies, and make sure to get what's especially in season. Avoid all types of junk food. Instead, eat fruits and vegetables for snacks. You'll need to drink at least six to eight glasses of fresh water during the day too. Also, begin taking a comprehensive multivitamin and mineral supplement.

The Food Energy Ladder is described in detail in Part Six of this book. Foods at the top of the ladder are high in life-energy and help your body burn its excess fat. Conversely, foods near the bottom steps of the ladder, especially foods that have been processed or refined, are low in life-energy. Foods at the bottom of the ladder cause your body to accumulate fat. The object of this day is to stay as high on the Food Energy Ladder as possible. *It's as simple as that!*

Do not drink any alcoholic beverages or soft drinks during this day, and limit your coffee or non-herbal tea to just a cup. Used excessively, alcohol, refined sugar, and caffeine disrupt the balance of life-energy in your body and lead to harmful effects. Don't smoke! If you must smoke cigarettes though, smoke only outside, and try cutting your usual amount in half.

During the morning, before noontime, consume only fresh fruit and fresh juice. Eat as much and as wide a variety of fruits as you wish, as long as they are fresh. Many people who are not used to so much fruit find that lots of bananas, cantaloupe, and honeydews are best.

Lunch should consist mostly of fresh vegetables, salad and good whole-grain bread. Dinner should consist mostly of rice, pasta, or potatoes, along with vegetables. If you prefer, you can make lunch the heartier meal of the day and have a lighter dinner.

Eliminate flesh food during this day unless you can find some very fresh fish or wish to make some good chicken soup. Drink 6 to 8 glasses of water. Eat only small amounts of eggs and dairy products, essentially, just as needed ingredients for recipes. The recipes in this book will show you that you don't have to give up flavor just because you are cutting back on flesh food, dairy, sugar, and fat. It is best that you not eat anything after 8:00 P.M. If hunger intrudes upon your comfort later in the evening, however, have an apple, a banana, or some other fresh fruit.

PHYSICAL ACTIVITY

One of the major aspects of your Personal Wellness Retreat is reacquainting yourself with nature. If you can arrange it, the benefits of relaxing in a country setting, or near the sea, are tremendous. Wherever you are during this day, get outside as much as you can— just bundle up if it's cold or wet.

Open the windows in your house, weather permitting. Visit a park, walk on the beach, or work in the garden—repotting and transplanting are as healing to our own lives as to plant lives. In the fall, raking leaves is great exercise. In the winter, you might practice such long-forgotten skills as making snow angels and snowmen. Exercise is a major key to permanent weight loss.

Make sure to wake up by 7:00 A.M. on this special morning. Do the simple "wellness yoga" stretches in the exercise part of this book for about ten to twenty minutes, then take a brisk "wellness walk" for at least twenty minutes. Be sure to get at least a little bit sweaty and short of breath. Pick up your legs a little more than usual, swivel your hips, and swing your arms so that you feel like you are dancing or gliding along. The sillier you look, the better you are probably doing it. If you are unable to walk for twenty minutes, then just do what you can. This type of exercise helps to balance your metabolism and burn your excess body fat. It also releases vital endorphins, which heighten your self-confidence and motivation.

My patients unanimously agree that exercise is the turning point on their journey to a leaner life. It is important to take another "wellness walk" in the afternoon, with a few minutes of stretching beforehand. Use your walks to become aware of all the living things around you. This is a time to enjoy nature. Can you imagine God's presence in every living thing? Be sure to listen for sounds of life around you: children's play, birds, pets, etc. Also, pay attention to the colors in your environment. Smell the flowers. Finally, take a leisurely after-dinner stroll to look at the moon and gaze at the stars.

MEDITATION, JOURNAL WRITING, AND PRAYER

Get a notebook to create a journal that is dedicated to your Personal Wellness Retreat and the 28-Day Plan. Twice during the day, take some quiet time for meditation and writing in your journal. Use the simple five- to ten-minute meditation technique described in the first part of this book.

After you meditate, begin writing in your journal as if you are talking to your most trusted friend. Take at least ten to twenty minutes to do this.

Write about your feelings, your purpose, and meaning in this life, and about all sorts of dreams and aspirations. Write steadily without reading over what you are writing until you feel you have finished. Be honest! Admit to your journal what you might not admit to anyone else. Challenge yourself with different modes of expression; you might want to write a poem or write a dialogue between yourself and another person. Always date your journal entries.

Meditate and write in a quiet place where you will not be disturbed. In meditation, you bring your thoughts to stillness. Most people are always thinking, planning, strategizing, worrying, reflecting, or remembering. When you still your thoughts, your body releases endorphins that help overcome stress, stimulate homeostasis, and decrease appetite. Without meditation, your resolve to lose weight may be as superficial as a Band-Aid that covers a wound while the source of the problem continues to fester. An eight-year-old patient once informed me that meditation was the very best way for her to say her bedtime prayers; when she asked God for help, her thoughts were quiet enough so she could hear the answer.

Speaking of prayer, use this special day as an opportunity to renew your soul. Let bedtime be a reminder of your childhood by saying a prayer that was special to you when you were a child. If you wish, kneel down at the side of your bed. This is a wonderful time to think about how your soul touches the souls of others, and how their souls touch yours. However you wish to pray, before you finish, perhaps you might wish to say these words slowly and softly to yourself, over and over: *God Loves Me . . . God Loves Me . . . God Loves Me.*

BEING LOVING

Love is your own inner physician, and its healing energy is more powerful than any medicine. Your Personal Wellness Retreat is meant to balance body, mind, and soul. Balance has many definitions, one of which is "to bring into harmony or proportion." Beneath all physical and emotional imbalance, including being overweight, lies a longing for love. Nothing influences your overall well-being more profoundly than love, not only the love that you receive, but also the love you give. When you feel loved, and when you are being loving, you experience a sense of wholeness that helps heal the feelings of isolation that fuel your detrimental eating habits. Indeed, in this age of incredible stress, I-L-L is equivalent to *"I Lack Love!"*

"Love one another" is a core belief of Judeo-Christianity. Yet most people spend their lives fluctuating somewhere between wholeness and isolation. A sense of wholeness helps to keep your energy in balance. Isolation has the opposite effect. Before you can truly lose weight permanently, you must address the emotional and spiritual aches of "feeling alone." The potential to lose weight is immeasurably increased when you are able to offer your unconditional love to someone.

You may say, "But I have enough love. What I need right now is to lose weight." Maybe you are loved *by* others, but your soul still longs to be more loving *toward* others. When you are more loving, the music of your soul reverberates throughout your body and mind, helping to bring them into healthful balance. When you make a vow to love someone in your life unconditionally, it literally means without conditions. It means that no matter what that person says or does, nothing diminishes your feelings of love. Whether you choose your child, spouse, parent, brother, sister, grandparent, or someone else, nothing the person says or does, no matter how infuriating or insensitive, affects your love for him or her. This type of love overpowers hurt and anger. Unconditional love is offered selflessly, without expectation of receiving anything in return. It is love for love's sake.

In the center of a blank page of your journal, write out the following vow. Make sure to fill in the name of someone special and then sign it and date it:

"I vow to love [   ] unconditionally."

LIVING ETHICALLY

When we are overweight, we often dislike what we see in the mirror, and we dislike ourselves. Trapped in this vicious cycle, even though we know there is a remedy, we usually choose not to take advantage of it. When we dislike ourselves, we don't feel worthy of effort or attention.

You must begin doing whatever it takes to make you feel worthy of having the best in life. Otherwise, a low level of self-respect will eventually wear down even your most intense resolve to lose weight. Your appetite will conjure up a dozen reasons to succumb to your food urges and cravings. Irresistible impulses will become just that!

The single most important factor you must deal with is developing enough self-respect to feel worthy of making progress toward your envisioned goal. You must learn to care for yourself enough to create a vision for the future and to focus on it so intently that you will become that vision.

"God's primary demand of human beings is ethical behavior" is another core belief of Judeo-Christianity. Ethical behavior inspires powerful feelings of self-value and personal confidence. Thus, you must make a personal vow that you will be the very best person you can be. Commit to being a decent, kind, loving, and honest person. This vow will be the framework that makes you feel worthy of progressing toward your goal. Ethics can become a very tangled topic, so you can follow this very elemental principle for your behavior: If you even think that it might be wrong, just don't do it!

In the center of a blank page of your journal, write out the following vow. Make sure to sign it and date it.

"I vow to do nothing that I feel in my heart is wrong."

Personal Wellness Retreat Schedule

Your Personal Wellness Retreat requires only about four hours of your time to accomplish essential and enjoyable tasks.

During the morning:

- Twenty minutes for simple "wellness yoga stretches"
- Twenty minutes for a "wellness walk"
- Twenty minutes for meditation and journal writing
- Sixty minutes for "creating your vision"

During the afternoon:

- Twenty minutes for a "wellness walk"
- Sixty minutes for your "reality check"
- Twenty minutes for meditation and journal writing

During the evening:

- Twenty minutes for meditation and journal writing
- Twenty minutes for an after dinner stroll
- Time for a bedtime prayer

Creating Your Vision

When your mind is exceptionally clear and you are feeling in a peak state (after you've done your wellness yoga stretches, meditation and walk), set aside at least an hour of time to answer the following questions as completely and honestly as possible.

First, take some time to review your answers to the Health Profile in Part Two. This will give you many new insights and ideas. You will be building a new path of least resistance to the vision you are about to create, so be sure to come back to your journal at any time to make any additions. After you read each question below, close your eyes and ponder your answer. This will help keep your thoughts focused. Write down your answers. Make sure no one will disturb your concentration as you identify the following:

"WHERE I WANT TO BE ONE YEAR FROM NOW"

- What will my health be like?
- In one year from now, about how much do I want to weigh?
- After achieving this weight, what three characteristics will best describe my life?

- What will I be doing for fun, and how much fun will I be having?
- What kind of exercise will I be doing?
- What will my body look like?
- How much will I respect myself?
- How much alcohol will I be drinking?
- How many cigarettes will I be smoking?
- How loved will I feel?
- How loving will I be?

Reality Check

The second part of creating a new path of least resistance is to gain a clear idea of where you are right now, and how you will be five years from now if you do not make any progress toward fulfilling a new vision of yourself. In other words, if your plan is to continue living and eating the same way that you do now, then what will you look like five years from now? To avoid the pain that results from resisting progress now, it is crucial to spend some serious time contemplating this type of future.

The reality check may be an emotional jolt, and perhaps somewhat painful, but it is critical in progressing toward becoming leaner. This is meant to be a wake-up call.

After taking an afternoon walk, take some time to once again review your Health Profile from Part Two of the book, then spend at least five minutes standing in front of a mirror with all or most of your clothes off. Treat what you see with honesty but kindness. Look especially at your face, arms, chest, abdomen, hips, thighs, buttocks, and legs. Also look at your skin and hair. Notice your natural curves. After you have observed your body, write down your thoughts in your journal.

Now answer the following questions as thoughtfully and completely as possible (write down your answers):

"WHERE I AM RIGHT NOW"

- What is my health like?
- About how much do I weigh right now?
- What three characteristics most describe my life?
- What am I doing for fun, and how much fun am I having?
- What kind of exercise do I do?
- What kinds of physical pain am I experiencing?
- How sedentary ("couch potato") am I?
- What does my body look like?
- How much do I respect myself?
- How much alcohol do I drink?
- How many cigarettes do I smoke?
- How stressed am I?
- How loved do I feel?
- How loving am I?

Now imagine how you will be five years from now if you continue to live and eat as you currently do. Answer the following questions as honestly and completely as possible as you identify the following (*write down your answers*):

"THIS DESCRIBES ME FIVE YEARS FROM NOW, IF I CONTINUE TO FOLLOW MY PRESENT LIFESTYLE AND EATING HABITS"

- What will my health be like?
- About how much will I weigh?
- What three characteristics will most describe my life?
- What will I be doing for fun, and how much fun will I be having?
- What kind of exercise will I be doing?
- What kinds of physical pain will I be experiencing?
- How sedentary will I be?
- What will my body look like?
- How much alcohol will I be drinking?
- How many cigarettes will I be smoking?
- How stressed will I be?

- How loved will I feel?
- How loving will I be?
- How much will I respect myself?

Now that you have clarified where you want to be (*created your vision*) and where you currently are, or will be if you don't change (*your reality check*), consider the following:

We all resist change. Even promises of better health, more money, or increased happiness don't cause lasting change. Yet, our brain readily embraces making progress toward a clearly envisioned goal. Once your new mindset is established, it will take on a life of its own.

The object of your One Day Personal Wellness Retreat is to define the result that you want to live for the rest of your life. The 28-Day Plan builds on this empowering day and spurs your progress toward your vision. This is much more powerful than problem-solving. It's about creating a new result. Enjoy!

Part Six

FOOD IS ENERGY:

A New Mindset and Plan for Permanent Weight
Loss and Balanced Energy Throughout the
Cycle of Life . . . The Blueprint

The Hardest Work Is Behind You

Before we get into Part Six, I would like to make a
strong suggestion. As soon as you finish reading the entire book,
please set your date for your Personal Wellness Retreat. Give yourself some planning time, but not too much. Don't put it off. Just do
it!

You have begun to dust away the cobwebs in your mind that have
tangled you up in unhealthful eating habits. Through what you've
read so far, you have learned about the nutritional needs of your
body throughout the cycle of life. You now can recognize how your
attitudes toward food have been shaped by Madison Avenue and
the multibillion-dollar foot and diet industries. Following the questionnaires you've already taken, you should take stock of your present state of wellness and weigh the strengths and weaknesses of

your Health Profile. Set your sights on reasonable, attainable weight goals. You are almost ready for your *personal action plan*. A plan so simple, it will keep you motivated, feeling energetic and alive—a plan that will take *diet* (that four-letter word!) out of your vocabulary forever.

Most of the hard work is already done. Identifying the sources of your misperceptions about food by determining your current Health Profile required great courage, honesty, and self-value. By this process, you have begun to ignite your will to *eat wise and live well*. You should feel empowered and motivated by what you've read so far!

The knowledge of where you have been, and where you are presently, will motivate you as you embark on a twenty-eight-day journey toward greater health and energy. But the journey doesn't end after twenty-eight days; that is just the beginning. If you follow the action plan described in this part of the book for *just 28 days*, you and your family will be firmly on the path toward your naturally desired weight and energy for the rest of your life.

Permanent weight loss comes from within, not from without. It doesn't come in a bottle, a jar, or even a book. Throughout this book, I aim to give you the resources, knowledge, and tools that will help strengthen the source of wellness within you. This *natural source* is your key to permanent weight loss and radiant energy. I will teach you simple guidelines to follow for twenty-eight days— guidelines that will allow you to tap into this natural healing source and stimulate its power to keep you physically and emotionally well.

As you prepare to begin your twenty-eight-day journey toward wellness, keep in mind that short-term weight loss is *not* your goal. You are reaching for much more, and it is all within your reach! During these twenty-eight days, you will establish the eating habits and tastes that will bring you and your family a lifetime of improved health and balanced weight. Your journey to wellness doesn't end after just four weeks—you are establishing a *blueprint* for wellness and a healthier weight *for life*.

Put Your Mind on the Meal

Now that you've cleaned out your mental refrigerator and tossed away all your harmful thoughts, feelings, and emotions about food, you have begun to create a new mindset toward food and nutrition. This mindset will guide you toward healthful choices about the foods that you eat and feed your family—*naturally*. This mindset will also free you from calorie-counting, restrictive diets, and the favorite weight-loss fad of the moment.

At this point, you may be saying to yourself, "Dr. Taub, quit worrying about what I think and get to the point: *What should I eat?*"

Dear reader, remember that *you eat only as well as you think*. You will not change the way you eat (at least not in a lasting way) until you change your mind. And that is exactly what you have been doing. What is in your mind directly guides what you choose to put in your mouth. What is in your mind affects *every single cell* of your body. Why? Because your body is more than the sum of its parts. It is a magnificent system of energy, and your mind is the motor. What you think, along with what you eat, either helps keep your energy in perfect balance, which is your *natural state of health*, or disrupts your energy, which is the *unnatural state of illness*.

The essential key to losing weight is to change the way you think about food. From reading earlier parts of this book, you are already beginning to break out of your old mindset and rebuild a new, healthful one. It is important that I work on your mindset for just a bit longer, so hang in there!

One of the leading reasons so many of us are overweight to begin with is that *we don't think about what we eat*. How can we? Most of us eat while engaged in some other activity. We eat breakfast in the car on the way to work; in fact, a whole range of breakfast foods has been created to accommodate the needs of the commuting eater! We grab lunch and take it back to our desk to eat while finishing that report that was supposed to be finished yesterday. When we do have dinner at home, it's often while reading the newspaper or watching television. Simply swallowing our food is commonplace, and chewing our food properly is rare!

Think about the last meal you ate. Was it really a meal? What did you eat? Where were you when you ate it? Were you sitting down? These may sound like peculiar questions, but so many people eat in a rush on their way to somewhere else. Where was your mind during that meal? On the newspaper? On the phone call you made while eating? On the meeting in the next hour? On what you have to do when you're done eating?

Perhaps your eating habits are not unlike Barbara's. Barbara is a young professional, works long hours, and seems to be always "on the go." When I met Barbara, she was on the first vacation she had taken since graduating college. She was on a cruise ship sailing through Mexico, and on her first day aboard she happened to walk into my seminar on wellness, a program I created for cruise ships around the globe to transform a regular vacation into a Voyage to Wellness. For Barbara, it was a long overdue week of restoring some control to her otherwise chaotic life.

Barbara had perfected the skill of eating on the run. On her morning commute to work, she'd munch a bagel and cream cheese and down her first of many cups of coffee for the day, paying more attention to the traffic than her food. For lunch, which really just meant any fifteen minutes she could sneak away from the office in the afternoon, she frequented fast-food places downtown near work, then inhaled her food during her quick walk back to the office. Dinner wasn't much better. She alternated between five restaurants on her path home from work, ordering the same takeout dinners week after week. Barbara ate her takeout in front of the television, watching the evening news, since she never had time to read a newspaper.

Barbara stayed to hear what the Voyage to Wellness was all about, and decided to stay with the course for the week. When we began to talk about mindful eating, eating with awareness, she was one of the first to resist. "I'm sorry, Dr. Taub, but I just don't have the time to sit down and linger over an enjoyable meal."

Then I asked Barbara, "When was the last time you really enjoyed what you ate?" She said it was that very morning. She was sitting on the deck, enjoying the early morning sun, eating a plate of fresh pineapple, mango, and kiwi. She said she'd forgotten how delicious fresh fruit was. I asked her how she was feeling then, at midmorning. "I feel wonderful, energetic, ready to go explore when we pull into port." She went on to say that in fact she could not remember the last time she felt so good. "Really, I usually feel like I'm dragging after a meal, or my stomach gets upset."

As Barbara evaluated her current health profile, it became apparent that the illnesses she experienced, the daily discomforts she endured, were all related to her eating habits. She complained of indigestion, constipation alternating with diarrhea, and fatigue. She was at least ten to fifteen pounds heavier than she should be and her cholesterol was much too high.

During the seven-day cruise, I asked Barbara to eat every meal mindfully. This can be difficult on a cruise ship, where a banquet of rich, decadent food is available around the clock. But Barbara did it! She ate her fruit breakfasts on the deck every morning. She enjoyed more fruit and vegetables for lunch. She dined each night with fellow passengers enrolled in the Voyage to Wellness. Here is a letter I received from Barbara a month after the cruise:

Dear Dr. Taub:

Thank you for taking me on a Voyage to Wellness. I had really forgotten what a true pleasure eating is. I took food for granted, and I took my health for granted. But after seven days of thinking about what I ate, taking the time to enjoy my meals and savoring all of the flavors, my eating habits have changed forever. I realized that in the time it took me to park, jump out of my car, then wait in line for a bagel and coffee, I could have sat peacefully at home enjoying my fresh fruit. And I can't eat watching the news at night anymore—it just upsets my stomach! Since I've been eating mindfully and staying on the top five steps of your Food Energy Ladder, I have not had one bout of indigestion, constipation, or diarrhea. And I have more energy than ever. Thank you!

Many of us are just like Barbara. We rarely have our minds on the meal, the food, the taste. When we're eating, we're seldom thinking about the food we put in our mouth; so many other things are going on. Other activities are distracting us. That isn't eating at all! It's ingesting, inhaling, consuming—our minds are elsewhere.

When your mind is elsewhere, you are likely to make poor food choices. And you're also much more likely to overeat. On the other hand, when you eat with awareness, as Barbara learned, you are likely to choose foods that are healthy and recognize when your body is telling you that your stomach is full. Not only do you appreciate the taste of food more, but you also eat less. This is a much better feeling than the impulse to loosen your belt buckle, swallow a few antacids, and lie down after a meal.

Think about what you eat. Awareness is so important. And when you eat with awareness, rather than on autopilot, you will enjoy the foods you are eating much more. When you eat with awareness, every mouthful becomes more pleasurable and satisfying. Every mouthful counts. Eating this way, you are less likely to overeat.

You Need a "Blueprint" for Action

Empowered with knowledge and understanding, you are ready to move forward. In Part Six of this book you will learn how to put your new mental blueprint into action for permanent weight loss and radiant energy. This blueprint is the foundation for achieving your naturally ideal weight and energy *for the rest of your life*. It will guide you to make the small changes in your eating habits and activities that your body is begging you to make, changes that will boost your energy, balance your weight, and enhance your body's innate ability to stay well.

I will not ask you to embark on any changes that seem unreasonable to you. Diets fail because they require changes that are impossible to sustain over the long haul. I will ask you to learn *a new way of eating for life.* The steps you will take during this month are so much simpler than the strict dietary regimens with which you are probably all too familiar and disillusioned. Yet the effect of these steps is profound and everlasting.

I urge you to follow the steps described for twenty-eight days. After that, you will be lighter, more energetic, and healthier. At the end of four weeks, your feelings of wellness and energy will motivate you to continue to eat this way for the rest of your life. It will seem like the most natural thing to do.

Think of an architect's blueprint for a house. It's the master plan, the foundation. Would you even consider building a new house with a temporary blueprint? Of course not. A blueprint has to be the foundation for a long-lasting, solid, sound structure. Think of your body and health in the same way. After all, you may move from house to house in your lifetime, but you only live in one body. Be the architect of your own health. Put into action a sound and solid blueprint that will ensure healthy weight and well-being.

During the twenty-eight days it will take to establish a solid blueprint for lifelong health and ideal weight, you will begin to feel more enthusiastic and more focused. Your body's own natural healing forces will thrive and you will experience a greater sense of well-being, self-esteem, and happiness. It will be exciting for you to experience firsthand how small improvements in your diet can reap such big benefits throughout your cycle of life.

You have read about the dynamic relationship between nutrition and health in previous parts of this book. Don't take lightly what dramatic improvements you can make in your health through the foods you eat. Weight loss is only one of the many significant health benefits you will experience through proper nutrition.

A nutritional strategy high in fruits and vegetables and low in animal fat and fake foods has the proven power to help prevent and even reverse heart disease, lower the risk of many types of cancer, control diabetes, and increase longevity.

In this 28-Day Plan, you will learn how to harness the power of food for weight loss and improved health. Why does it take twenty-eight days to put your new blueprint into action? You may think that sounds like a long time—actually twice as long as a two-week starvation diet. Let's put this into perspective. It took you a lifetime to develop the unhealthful eating habits you have now. If it takes you only twenty-eight days to dissolve these habits forever, isn't that a good return on your investment? Twenty-eight days in the span of a lifetime is just a drop in the bucket, but it is going to make an enormous splash for the rest of your life.

You might as well choose a two-week starvation diet regimen if all you want to do is lose a few pounds quickly and don't mind gaining them back within the next few months. However, if lifelong health and achieving your ideal weight is your goal, it takes only twenty-eight days to put the process permanently in motion. During that time, you will be teaching your body new tastes and learning new ways of preparing your foods. You are creating new, healthful eating habits. They are lessons in eating your body will respond to immediately. After twenty-eight days, you will be feeling so good, so energetic, and so much lighter that you will continue on your path to wellness for life.

Unlike a strict diet of two weeks of feeling deprived, hungry, and dissatisfied, these twenty-eight days are filled with delicious, appetizing, and filling foods. Why punish yourself for a few weeks when you can pamper yourself for four weeks and beyond? You will discover how simple it is to eat well. No diet foods. No diet pills. No diet drinks. No confusing formulas to remember. Just a sensible, natural approach to eating that will help you gain energy and health while losing weight. It doesn't get any better than that!

Food Is Energy . . . Or It's Not

Food is energy. This is the basic scientific principle underlying the way of eating that I advocate. Remember what you learned in the previous parts of this book: Your body is an energy system; every single process in your body requires energy to work. Circulation, metabolism, respiration, digestion—everything needs energy! Every muscle, every organ, every cell needs energy to function healthily. When your energy is low, your body doesn't have the resources it needs to function healthily, and that is when illness results. When your energy is high, health and ideal weight are in your hands. And, as you also learned earlier, food is the source of energy your body needs most.

Food either gives you energy or it takes energy away from you. Food is nature's medicine for nourishing your energy. What you eat either nourishes and helps balance your energy system or it eats away at that balance. In the pages that follow, you will learn a very simple, instinctive way of distinguishing high-energy foods from low-energy foods so that you can feed your body with the proper fuel to lose weight and be well.

If you feel sluggish throughout the day, if you have to drag yourself out of bed and to work, if you rely on coffee to keep you semi-alert, your energy supply is running dangerously low. If you feel down, unmotivated, as if you are just getting by, your energy is nearly drained. Rather than focus on losing weight, turn your pursuits toward increasing your energy and bringing it back into balance through the foods you eat. Good health, ideal weight, an optimistic outlook, and a peaceful mind will follow.

Nourish Your Body's Natural Capacity to Lose Weight

Yes, I've said it over and over and I will say it again: the best way to lose excess weight and burn fat is to eat foods bursting with nature's life-energy. When you feed your body foods that are high in energy, your body will naturally begin to burn excess fat and lose weight. Your body has more wisdom than all of the diet gurus and the nutritional scientists combined! You just need to eat foods that feed your body's innate wisdom and allow it to do its work.

Most of us don't eat enough "live" energy foods and eat too much food with "dead" energy. If you fill up on dead foods, you are actually starving your body of the energy it requires to be well. Dead food depletes your energy. When you feel sluggish or sleepy after a heavy meal, it's because your body must work overtime, using its life-energy to digest too many dead foods. You feel energy-less because you are.

Specialty diet foods do not give your body proper energy. You may feel as if you are eating something that is low in fat, but foods that are empty of live energy will not help you lose weight. When you lose energy, your body cannot lose weight over the long term in a healthy manner. Diets that restrict you from eating tend to restrict your energy. Your body can only do its natural work of burning your excess fat when it has abundant live energy to do so.

When you emphasize live, high-energy foods in your meals, eating will become an entirely different and more pleasurable experience. The pleasure extends beyond the meal, because after you eat a meal abundant in live foods, your body will thrive from the food's energy. Live food helps your body burn fat, stave off illness and disease, and makes homeostasis soar!

When we understand food as energy, we understand "convenience foods" in an entirely different way. Convenience doesn't come in a can or ready-made microwavable meal. Dead foods are a terrible inconvenience to your body. They give your body less than it needs, and they use up bodily energy to digest them. Digestion requires more energy than any other function your body performs, and digesting dead foods places an incredible burden on your digestive system. If you frequently eat foods marketed as "convenient," ask yourself, "How convenient is it to eat something that robs my body of energy, vitality, and health?"

If you are trying to lose weight, feel healthier, and more fit, the most convenient foods you can eat are alive with energy. Live foods give your body the energy it needs to burn its excess fat efficiently.

Your body certainly recognizes the difference between live and dead food. But remember that when it comes to food, your natural instincts have been suppressed; our culture has trapped your taste buds. You know this as well, even if it's hard to admit. There are no fields of flowing white bread, no potato chips sprouting under the soil, no rivers of soda pop. When was the last time you saw jelly doughnuts growing on trees?

The Food Energy Ladder

Here we are—you are ready! Thank you for your patience and let's go on. You need a ladder to help climb up and out of the traps our culture has set for your taste buds. Thus, I have created the Food Energy Ladder to help you climb back up to foods that are alive and filled with energy and avoid foods that weaken your energy. The Food Energy Ladder is an easy, common-sense tool to help you visualize foods that are alive and filled with energy, as well as foods that are dead and energy depleting. When you care for your body with high-level fuel, you have the highest potential for achieving *Total Health Rejuvenation* and natural weight loss permanently.

Look at the Food Energy Ladder. The food at the top of the ladder is high in energy. The food at the bottom is virtually *energy-less*. Foods at the top of the ladder are natural, while foods at the bottom of the ladder tend to be artificial, processed, and chemically engineered. Your goal for the next twenty-eight days is to stay on the top five steps of the ladder, eating foods that are highest in energy. The 28-Day Plan is as simple as that!

It doesn't mean that the foods at the bottom steps are forbidden.

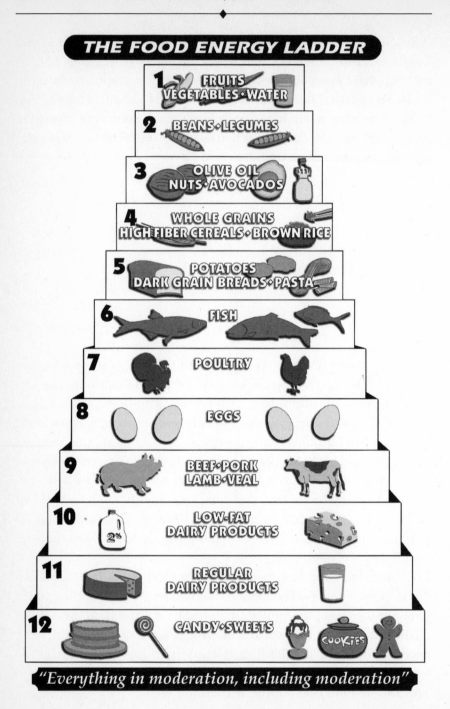

THE FOOD ENERGY LADDER

1 FRUITS VEGETABLES·WATER

2 BEANS·LEGUMES

3 OLIVE OIL NUTS·AVOCADOS

4 WHOLE GRAINS HIGH FIBER CEREALS·BROWN RICE

5 POTATOES DARK GRAIN BREADS·PASTA

6 FISH

7 POULTRY

8 EGGS

9 BEEF·PORK LAMB·VEAL

10 LOW-FAT DAIRY PRODUCTS

11 REGULAR DAIRY PRODUCTS

12 CANDY·SWEETS

"Everything in moderation, including moderation"

Indeed, some of the recipes that follow use small amounts of dairy or eggs. Remember, this is not about deprivation! If you feel deprived of something you want, you will only hunger for it more. That is why it is important to eat primarily foods at the top of the ladder, then *only occasionally* and *moderately* from the foods at the bottom of the ladder. If you slide down the ladder, all you have to do is climb right back up to where you were.

These twenty-eight days, along with your Personal Wellness Retreat, are going to jump-start your energy gain and weight loss. The twenty-eight days of eating high on the Food Energy Ladder will engrain these healthful habits within you and activate your will to continue to *eat wise and live well* beyond the twenty-eight days. **For maximum momentum, stay on the top five steps of the ladder as much as possible.** For most people, weekends are the most likely time for eating lower on the ladder. Allow yourself those moments, but in moderation. An occasional ice cream is not going to sabotage your energy. Where you need to be most diligent, however, is with flesh foods. Poultry and fish are fine, but not more than once every three days. There is even room in this nutritional strategy for a hamburger or steak, but *not* more than once a week. Any more than that and you will not gain the momentum and motivation you need to activate this blueprint for life.

Once you begin to eat the energy way, you will naturally be inclined to stay within the top five steps of the ladder because you will know and feel that these foods enhance your energy, while you will know and feel that the foods at the bottom sap your energy. You will know this by the end of twenty-eight days. When you climb to the top half of the Food Energy Ladder, you will leave your weight worries behind. When you eat at that level, enjoying all of those naturally energy-enhancing foods, your struggles with weight will come to an end—naturally. If you slip down the ladder from time to time, don't punish yourself or feel that you've failed. There is no pit of fire at the bottom of the ladder! If you find yourself at the bottom of the ladder, just climb right back up with your next meal.

To follow the Food Energy Ladder, the basic principles are simple and straightforward:

Eat foods from the top five steps
in abundance and variety.

◆

Before noon, eat mostly
fresh fruits and juices,
with whole grain breads and cereals.

◆

Eat flesh food in moderation:
Eat fish or poultry no more than once every three days;
limit red meat to no more than once a week.

◆

Eat with awareness
and remember this motto:

*"Everything in moderation . . .
including moderation!"*

Let's climb up the ladder together, step-by-step, so that you understand why the foods are categorized as they are. Remember that the higher on the ladder you eat, the higher the food's energy. And the greater the energy, the more fat you will lose.

At the bottom step of the ladder, *Step 12*, are refined sweets, including chocolate and sugar. The surge of energy you may feel after eating a candy bar is temporary. After the surge subsides, your energy is lower than it was before you ate the sweet. These foods provide a quick jolt but then make your energy dive. The sugar low that follows quickly after the sugar high earns these foods their place at the bottom rung of the Food Energy Ladder. To satisfy your sweet tooth, turn to nature. Nature's fruit is both sweet and sweet on energy.

Dairy foods are at *Steps 10* and *11*. Nearly every dairy food is now available in a low- or nonfat variety that is generally healthier for you. Cheddar, jack, mozzarella, cottage, and cream cheeses are available in reduced-fat versions. Yogurt from skim milk is almost entirely fat-free. These are more healthful than regular dairy products, not only because they contain less fat, but also because they are easier to digest and don't burden your mucous membranes as much. Still, these foods are difficult to digest, and impossible to digest for some. Remember, cow's milk is wonderful nourishment, if you're a baby cow.

You will find some dairy products in the recipes in this book because most of us are simply not ready to give dairy up completely; remember the motto, *Everything in moderation . . . including moderation*. It is important for you though to stop drinking all the glasses of milk you've been taught are so healthy. My favorite cartoon character, the witty but perennially misunderstood young Calvin of Bill Waterson's *"Calvin and Hobbes,"* showed that wonderful intelligence only children possess when he pondered the question of cow's milk. Calvin asked his animated, stuffed tiger Hobbes, "Who was the guy who first looked at a cow and said, 'I think I'll drink whatever comes out of these things when I squeeze 'em?' " Only humans believe they need the milk of another species to be healthy!

You may protest here, since you know dairy is a source of calcium which is necessary for healthy bones and body. Consider the following foods not only as alternative sources of calcium, but as full of life-energy: broccoli, spinach, brussel sprouts, celery, carrots, artichokes, lima beans, and swiss chard.

Eggs have taken a real beating in the last few years. You should eat eggs in moderation, not only because they are *the leading source of high cholesterol* in the American diet, but also because they are dead energy. That is why they are at *Step 8.*

Eggs are only energy when they grow into chickens. Whether you boil, fry, scramble, or poach them, eggs stay low on the ladder. Especially avoid eggs for breakfast—they do not provide the energy you need to begin your day. If you must eat eggs, most grocery stores carry fresh eggs from free-range chickens. And whenever possible, remove the yolks.

Energy eating doesn't mean you have to become a vegetarian, but flesh foods, especially red meat, have low energy. The foods on *Step 9* of the ladder should be downplayed in your diet. Because red meat takes so much energy to digest, it is a burden on your system. If you must eat red meat, then limit yourself to no more than once a week. This will at least give your body the ample time it usually requires to fully digest and eliminate red meat before challenging your system with more of it. The more you burden your body, the less energy you will have for burning fat and protecting yourself from illness.

The average American eats about 175 pounds of meat every year. Red meat is one of the leading sources of fat in the American diet. Remember what you've learned so far about all the health consequences of a diet heavy in meat: *Even just cutting down on how much red meat you eat, and choosing leaner cuts, will lower your animal fat intake and benefit your energy, weight and overall health.* Also keep in mind that when you eat red meat, you are being subjected to the hormones and antibiotics regularly injected into the animals we eat, and these substances are foreign energy to your body.

Poultry, on *Step 7*, is a better alternative than red meat, and many people are already substituting poultry for red meat at the dinner table. Of course, chicken deep-fried with the skin on is just as fatty as red meat. White, skinless chicken breast, grilled or broiled, is the healthier alternative. You can go a step further by eating chicken in smaller amounts, in a sauté of vegetables or with lots of rice. But remember, the concern here is not just about fat. While it is important for you to reduce fat in your diet, the emphasis in this plan is on *increasing your energy*. Poultry, as with other animal foods, is low in efficient live energy. When you do eat poultry, accompany it with lots of fresh vegetables.

Fish, *Step 6*, is the healthiest of flesh foods, higher in energy than red meat or poultry. But it is important to know where the fish comes from. In many parts of the United States, contaminated waters can lower the nutritional value of fish and, in some cases, pose dangerous health risks. If there are toxins in the fish, then that is toxic foreign energy to your body. Fresh fish, from healthy waters, are an excellent, low-fat source of protein. Enjoy fish in moderation, with generous amounts of vegetables!

In fact, whenever you eat red meat, poultry or fish, follow this same energy-wise guideline: Instead of serving vegetables on the side, make the vegetables as prominent as the flesh food part of your meal. You can even try serving vegetables, pasta, and rice as the main dish, with smaller amounts of flesh food on the side. This is the best way to "have your meat and eat it, too."

Remember: The foods between *Steps 6* and *12* should be eaten only on occasion. Flesh foods, such as poultry and fish, should not be eaten more often than once every three days during the next twenty-eight days. Fresh fish is best. Red meat, such as beef and pork, should not be eaten more often than once a week during the next twenty-eight days. Adding it up, that's about two or three meals of flesh food each week.

As for other foods on the lower steps of the ladder, it's okay to have a little cheese grated over your pasta, some slivers of chicken in your vegetable soup, some hard-boiled egg on your chef's salad, some cream in your coffee or milk in your cereal. Again, some of the recipes in this book use dairy products and eggs. These small amounts on occasion are inconsequential, as long as 90 percent of your meal consists of foods from the top five steps.

Potatoes, pasta and dark bread, the complex carbohydrates on *Step 5*, are a healthful source of energy. Seek out less processed bread and pasta. These slow-burning foods provide sustained energy, so they are ideal for dinner when accompanied by lots of fresh vegetables.

The whole grain foods on *Step 4* are filling and loaded with healthful fiber and energy. Brown rice is considerably more nutritious than white rice. Cereals made from whole or less-refined grains such as corn, wheat, rye, oats, and rice are a wonderful source of healthful, complex carbohydrates. These are much higher in fiber than refined, processed junk cereals. Recent studies demonstrate that a high fiber-diet is associated with as much as a 20 percent decrease in the risk of heart attack.

As you come to *Step 3* on the ladder—nuts, avocados, and olive oil—you may think you've climbed your way right to high-fat heaven! True, these foods are rich and high in fat, but they are also valuable sources of natural energy. They come from the earth, grow in the sun, and contain no cholesterol. The energy of the fat in an olive, a nut, or an avocado is not the same as the energy of the fat in a strip of bacon! Mediterranean cuisine is laden with olive oil, but people living in that region have some of the lowest rates of heart disease on earth. Also a handful of walnuts every other day seems to reduce, not increase, the risk of heart attack among Americans. But how can this be if fatty foods are supposedly in the danger zone? While these foods are high in plant-based fat, they are abundant in life-energy—and thus have a place high upon the Food Energy Ladder. Eat them in moderation and enjoy!

If you want to eat for healthy energy and to lose weight, there is simply no better source than an abundant daily supply of water, fresh fruits and vegetables, including beans and legumes, from *Step 1* and *Step 2*. Vegetables and fruits should be the leading foods in your diet. Every day you should eat more of these foods than any other. Plant foods are full of life-energy from the sun that nourishes them. Eating plenty of plant foods nourishes your body naturally and stimulates your body's innate healing abilities.

Drink and eat generously from the top two steps of the ladder, making fruits and vegetables the centerpiece of every meal. These plant-based foods are full of fiber. Four or five servings of fruits and vegetables each day will give your body the fiber it needs for proper elimination, which is vital for overall health as well as weight loss. Most Americans don't eat nearly the amounts of fruits and vegetables they need. In fact, most Americans don't even eat a single piece of fruit a day—not even an apple to keep the doctor away. No wonder Americans are so low in energy and overweight.

You've climbed the Food Energy Ladder. For the next twenty-eight days, your ultimate goal is to drink plenty of water and eat foods on the top five steps. When you eat on those top five steps, eating an abundance of fresh fruits and vegetables, your weight will gradually return to its *natural ideal*. That's how homeostasis works. Your body remembers wellness and strives toward balance. If you feed your body naturally, it will naturally achieve its balance. *And then you will not have to worry about excess weight.*

Remember, this is a ladder, not a law. If you eat something on the lower steps, you have not broken any law. We all know too well that restricting foods makes them more appealing, which is why diets drive us crazy. *The goal here is to reduce, not restrict.*

Let's Take the Confusion Out of Food Combining

More than a decade ago, I wrote the foreword to the #1 best-selling nutritional book, *Fit For Life*, a book that revolutionized the way millions of people around the world think about nutrition. The book proposed that, to obtain the most energy from the foods you eat, certain foods should be combined in certain ways. Many people swear by the combinations offered in *Fit For Life*. But others lost their way in the complicated guidelines of what food combinations to emphasize and what to avoid.

Nutritional science has progressed in the last ten years, and we now know that some of the combinations cautioned against in *Fit For Life* can be ignored. So, in a streamlined, scientific update of the principles set forward in that book, the following simple guidelines will help maximize your energy as you eat among the top five steps of the Food Energy Ladder. These guidelines take the confusion and complexities out of food combining.

BREAKFAST AND BEFORE LUNCH

Skipping breakfast is a sure path to sagging energy by lunch time. Your body needs energy to get started in the morning. For breakfast, the following foods will give you an abundant supply of long-lasting energy:

- *Fresh fruit and fruit juice—as much as you want*
- *Whole grain, low-fat cereals without added sugar*
- *Use nonfat, 2% milk, rice or soy milk*
- *Whole grain breads, muffins or bagels with little, if any, butter*
- *Limit coffee to two cups*

This breakfast menu departs from the strict principles of *Fit For Life*, which recommended that fruit be eaten alone, never in combination with other foods. The reasoning behind this rule is that fruit requires very little energy to digest, but when combined with other foods, fruit requires more energy to digest.

Some fruits, however, may actually assist in the process of digesting other foods. Also, combining fruit with other nutritious foods is much better for you than the typical American breakfast combination of eggs, bacon, and toast. If you want to eat fruit and whole grain toast or a bagel for breakfast, go right ahead. You can even enjoy a nutritious whole grain waffle with sliced strawberries (hold the whipped cream, and if you must have syrup, make sure it's real maple!). Eat as much fruit as you want before noon, but don't stuff yourself.

This breakfast may be different from what you now eat in the morning. Some of my patients have given up a thirty-year habit of eggs, toast, and bacon, and swear by a breakfast full of fresh fruit, fruit juice, and some whole grain cereals and breads. Just give it a try—the proof is in the experience! You'll love all the energy this breakfast gives you, and at about eleven o'clock at the office, when you'd typically be reaching for that third cup of coffee, you'll appreciate it even more.

LUNCHTIME TO DINNER

From lunch to dinner, emphasize vegetables, whole grains, and more fruit. If you are likely to have flesh food at dinner, be absolutely sure to avoid flesh at lunch. A lunch of soup, salad, and good bread will fill you with energy during the day and, unlike a heavy lunch, won't make you feel sluggish or in need of nap. The ideal lunch is loaded with raw, fresh vegetables. Eat a generous salad with low-fat dressing and a bowl of vegetable soup, or try layering fresh vegetables in a whole wheat pita or between two layers of fresh, crusty Italian bread. There are endless healthful possibilities, many of which you will find in the recipe section of this book.

DINNER AND BEYOND

For dinner, emphasize complex carbohydrates such as potatoes, rice, and pasta. Eat more vegetables and avoid animal foods. When you eat poultry or fish (not more than once every three days), eat it in smaller amounts, in a sauté of vegetables or accompanied by pasta or rice.

If you do eat red meat (not more than once a week), then on the following day try to eat only fruits and vegetables. This is because red meat is a shock to your energy system, and eating only fruits and vegetables the next day will help your body retain its energy balance.

It's important not to get fanatical about the above guidelines. Remember the Food Energy Ladder motto: *Everything in moderation—including moderation!* Fanaticism fuels failure. Just remember that fruits and vegetables should be in greatest abundance with most of your meals. If the only green you are seeing on your plate is the parsley being used for garnish, then you aren't eating enough vegetables!

Avoid eating after eight o'clock in the evening. By this time, you're gearing up for the rest and rejuvenation your body requires to begin its elimination cycle. Eating after 8:00 P.M., can divert the energy necessary for eliminating wastes from your body to ongoing digestion. You will also miss those vital hours of complete, internal rest so necessary for you to replenish your body with. People who eat late in the evening frequently complain of restless sleep. In great part, such restlessness comes from the new digestive work you've asked your body to perform when it should be doing otherwise: eliminating the unused food you've eaten during the day.

If you absolutely must eat later at night, then it's best to limit your food to a piece of fruit or some raw vegetables. Be assured that if you don't eat after eight at night, you will sleep much more soundly and feel more refreshed and energetic when you awake in the morning.

If you work the night or graveyard shift, the eight o'clock guideline will not work for you. That's okay. Just don't eat at least three hours before going to bed. Your body will adjust very soon and you will never feel dead on the graveyard shift again.

Let's review what and how you should be eating for the next twenty-eight days. First, keep your mind on your meal. When you eat with awareness, every mouthful is more satisfying, and you are much less likely to overeat. Then just follow the guidelines of the

Food Energy Ladder. Stay mainly on the top five steps. If you slide down, climb back up at your next meal. Eat an abundance of fresh fruit in the morning. Eat an abundance of vegetables, especially in soups and salads, along with good whole grain bread and fresh fruit for lunch. Emphasize green leafy vegetables, potatoes and beans, along with complex carbohydrates (rice or pasta) at dinner. Keep in mind that soybean products may be very beneficial in protecting against breast cancer and prostate cancer. Limit poultry and fish to not more often than once every three days. Eat fresh fish if it is available. Don't eat red meat more than once a week. And don't eat after eight o'clock (or three hours before going to bed).

During these twenty-eight days, you are putting into action your new blueprint for a lifetime of nutritional wellness, ideal weight, and balanced energy. In twenty-eight days, you will have imprinted this blueprint into every cell of your body. Remember, your goal isn't fast, temporary weight loss. Your goal is to increase your energy so that your body will burn more fat and your immune system will be stimulated to prevent illness and disease—weight loss will come naturally.

In Part Seven, you'll find a variety of recipes for delicious, satisfying meals that nourish your body with energy and nutrients without burdening your digestive system. Eating naturally for optimal energy doesn't mean you have to go out of your way to shop at a health-food store. Eating naturally actually streamlines your kitchen requirements. Your main ingredients are fresh fruits, fresh vegetables, potatoes, whole grains, pasta, and rice. All these foods should be readily available in your neighborhood supermarket. If not, it is worthwhile to go a little farther. Because the produce is fresh and locally grown, a trip to the local farmer's market is ideal in this regard. As you'll find out in Part Seven, if there is one rule to the recipes, it is this: they are made of easily acquired foods. There are no obstacles to eating well the natural way!

Behind Every Healthy Body Is a Strong Mind: Don't Let Stress Sidetrack Your Will to Eat Wise and Live Well!

Stress is a major obstacle to eating well. Stress affects what you eat. From time to time, as you reach for the top five steps of the ladder, the negative thoughts caused by stress may tug at your heels. You can shake off these thoughts and break free from stress, however, if you possess effective tools to strengthen your resilience. You can learn to surmount stress so that it doesn't sabotage your will to eat well.

Everyone has a certain amount of normal stress in his or her life. Managing this stress by disarming its power to divert you from your goals is especially important when making positive changes in your life, particularly in your attitude toward food and your eating patterns. Stress is the major trigger for overeating and for eating poorly. Because diets play on feelings of guilt, anxiety, and deprivation—all stressful emotions—they undermine your self-value and will to be well. Diets put you under so much mental and emotional stress, they have a built-in mechanism for failure!

Stress begins in your mind. That doesn't mean there aren't people and circumstances that ignite stress; it's your mental and emotional response to them that does the damage. Yes, our culture and environment trigger stress. But in response, you can cultivate a strong mind that will help protect you. That is why your new mental blueprint is such a vital foundation for the changes in nutrition you are making! The blueprint puts *you* in control, so that stress doesn't control you and what you eat.

Healthful, high-energy food can help you in dealing with stress. But if food is one of the ways you typically respond to stress, then understand why dead, low-energy food really is no escape. If a bag of fudge cookies is your common weapon against stress, you are losing the battle. On the other hand, if you nourish your body with live, high-energy foods during stressful times, you will remain in control and help give your body and mind the strength you need to resolve the stress you face.

When you are stressed out, your energy burns up. Most people greet a stressful situation with worry, anger, fear, and anxiety. As a result, you pour so much energy into the source of your stress that you feel drained. In fact, you *are* drained—drained of the vital energy that you need to keep body and mind well.

Stress, in fact, is a national epidemic. It is the leading factor that makes us susceptible to illness and disease. Stress diminishes your body's amazing ability to keep you well. Nonetheless, you have a tremendous healing force within you, a healing force with the wisdom to keep well and close to your naturally ideal weight. Stress burdens that healing force within you. At the same time, stress weakens your body's immune system, and if stress persists you may not be able to defend against infection and disease.

Stress is largely the result of feeling you have no options left, are at the end of your rope and ready to give in. It's easy to feel this way if you have little or no energy. But when you supercharge your energy, as you will when you eat high on the Food Energy Ladder, you will feel empowered instead of hopeless, bold instead of broken, and determined instead of depressed. That is why the nutritional ladder you are learning to climb is such a powerful tool for stress management. When you climb up the Food Energy Ladder, you boost your energy and your will to be well. You feel healthier, more vital, more energetic, and positive. These feelings of self-value protect you from the harmful effects of stress. *Feelings of self-esteem take the steam out of stress!*

You can vaccinate yourself against stress as you would against viruses. Yet it doesn't require a needle and it is perfectly painless. And the only side effects are wonderfully positive. Your protection against stress comes from inside of you. Balanced energy inoculates you against stress. Eating high on the Food Energy Ladder naturally bolsters your energy and stops your stress in its tracks, before it stops you in yours!

Eating high on the Food Energy Ladder will also help you stay out of the vicious stress/food cycle. People commonly react to stress by overeating, eating junk food, or both. Stress triggers eating, and eating triggers more stress. When stress causes you to be upset, depressed, sad, anxious, or worried, it leads you to indulge in poor eating habits. When under emotional distress, you are more likely to fall back down the ladder and indulge in the very eating habits you are currently trying to change.

The power of emotional distress to plunge you back into behaviors you are trying to inhibit is called the "stress disinhibition effect." I've seen this effect in many of my patients, who drink, smoke, and eat too much. Allen, a thirtysomething stockbroker, came to me with his blood pressure skyhigh. He was headed straight for a heart attack before he turned forty: He was fifty pounds overweight and his only exercise was waving his arms wildly on the stockmarket floor. If he was going to ward off the heart attack that was just around the corner, Allen knew lifestyle changes were absolutely necessary, and we both knew that the first place to begin was with his eating habits. He began to eat according to the principles of the Food Energy Ladder, and in just two months he looked remarkably healthier, felt better, and his blood pressure fell dramatically.

Allen's climb up the Food Energy Ladder was temporarily stymied when the stress of a sudden stockmarket decline crashed down upon him. He was terrified of losing everything: his clients, his job, his savings, his home. His emotional distress over the situation triggered his slide back into the very eating habits he was working so hard to overcome. Allen returned to my office again with his blood pressure dangerously high.

First I asked Allen to take several deep breaths. As he began to relax, I asked him to tell me about the sources of his stress. Like many people, he identified work as the main culprit. Worry over finances, time pressure, job security, and future prospects all heightened his stress. Once Allen identified his sources of stress, which also triggered his overeating, we were ready to discuss how to cope with it all. Overeating wasn't solving his stress. In fact, overeating caused him more stress in regard to his health.

In the questionnaire answered earlier, you identified what causes stress in your life. You, too, can now begin to control your response to the people, events, and circumstances you associate with stress. That doesn't mean you can lead a stress-free life just like that! But

♦

you can devise an action plan that will strengthen your energy to surmount stress and prevent you from overeating or eating poorly in response to your stress.

Extreme stress overwhelms the human body's energy system. It's a bit like turning on every light and appliance in your house at the same time. The fuse box or circuit breaker overloads and blows out. Stress robs your energy and leaves you out of balance and without the mental resources to make healthy eating choices. This is why it is so crucial to take stock of the stressful situations in your life and work to either change those that you can or change your reaction and response to those that you can't. Everyone has some level of stress in their life that cannot be avoided, and it's in those situations that you need positive, effective methods for conquering stress, so that it doesn't conquer you.

The good news is that you are already taking momentous steps to build up your resistance to stress! Climbing the Food Energy Ladder cultivates your inner strength and energy and your will to eat wise and live well. The higher you climb, the lower your chances of experiencing the negative impact of stress. During stressful times, it is especially important to stay among the top five steps of the ladder and especially to avoid sweets (the "sugar blues" is a poor state to be in under stress). Eating well is one of the best forms of stress prevention. The investment you make in your energy now will save you from stress in the future.

In all of my years working with patients one thing has become especially clear: If you are trying to make lifestyle changes involving food, alcohol, or nicotine, the key to your success is an effective way to manage stress. Your climb up the Food Energy Ladder will be permanently successful once you learn how to effectively deal with stressful situations that can cause you to give in to temptation.

Stress sidetracks your resolve. So much of your body's energy is mobilized to fight the harmful physical effects of stress that you are left with little energy to help maintain your will to eat wise and live well. Excessive stress consumes your energy, leaving you with a weakened ability to cope. But this 28-Day *Action* Plan will help you keep your mindset right on track.

Unless you have the resources and tools, psychological and emotional stress can create a downward spiral all too difficult to avoid.

Under stress, people turn to food for comfort. But indulging in the very behaviors you're trying to control just makes you feel more stressed out. You feel bad for eating poorly, for falling back on the old habits from which you are trying to free yourself. And when your self-value drops, your stress rises. One of the greatest benefits of climbing the Food Energy Ladder is that the longer you stay among the top five steps, the more powerful your resolve becomes, and the better able you are to fight the stress disinhibition effect.

According to the diet industry, failure to lose weight is a personal fault. How many times have we heard these "ifs": *If she only tried harder . . . If he only had more willpower . . . If she just had more determination* . . . These negative messages probably do more harm than the diets themselves—they are part of your mental blueprint and it's time to erase them. It is time for you to show yourself deep compassion and realize that it is not your lack of personal strength that has undermined your past efforts to lose weight. The underlying cause of a dieter's relapse is almost always the lack of effective skills for coping with stressful situations and demands. Without such skills, even a person with the strongest inner resolve is likely to lapse back into poor eating behaviors.

It is crucial to remember that if, during the twenty-eight days, you occasionally eat foods from the bottom of the Food Energy Ladder, *you have not failed*. This is *not* an all-or-nothing diet. This is not about deprivation. Moderation is your motto. Don't judge yourself if you have an occasional bowl of ice cream. You are not doomed to failure if you do. Don't beat yourself up for lacking willpower. Instead, ask yourself: Why do I want to eat ice cream? Is it a response to a stressful situation? Or do I simply want a little bit of something sweet? If stress is causing you to crave ice cream, remind yourself that it won't make the stress go away. And if the stress remains, you are likely to feel tempted again. If you just want a little ice cream, remind yourself of your long-term goals and try a low-fat variety or nonfat frozen yogurt. Or just have a *little bit* of ice cream. That's part of moderation.

For many people, food is a habitual escape from stress. Eating through a pint quart of ice cream, a chocolate cake, or a bag of fast-food hamburgers and fries may seem to offer a temporary escape from worries and troubles. For the moment, the act of eating takes your mind off your worries; it indulges your senses, giving you feelings of pleasure. But the effect is fleeting. Once the act of indulgence is over—the ice cream is gone, not a crumb of cake remains, the bag of fast food is empty—the feelings of stress return, and most people feel worse than they did before binging.

Should you find yourself in the above scenario, don't attribute your lapse to personal inadequacy or failure. Just recognize that you are learning how to develop the tools for effectively managing stress in the future. Don't berate yourself or judge yourself harshly. Feelings of low self-esteem just add fuel to the fire of stress. Show yourself some compassion and climb right back up the Food Energy Ladder at your next meal.

During the first twenty-eight days of eating high on the Food Energy Ladder, you are reprogramming your thoughts and your taste buds. Remember, you are putting a new blueprint into action. And, as you learn how to eat well, and continue to eat well over time, you will *unlearn* the negative habit of overeating in response to stress.

Regularly renewing your body's energy supply with fresh, live foods is one major step in combatting stress. Renewing your mental energy is equally important; reducing negative thoughts reduces your harmful responses to stress. Mental relaxation provides nourishment for your mind. You previously read about the mental relaxation exercises that bolster your will to eat wise and live well. Regularly practicing these exercises is a wonderful form of stress insurance. Unlike physical exercise, it's impossible to overdo it! (Just don't practice mental relaxation while driving!) The more timeouts you give your mind, the more opportunity you take for moments of peace and calm, the greater your ability to respond to stress effectively. Remember, regular mental relaxation builds a strong and healthy mind. And a strong and healthy mind won't be rattled by stress.

Keep practicing the mental relaxation exercises. Increase your practice when you feel stressed out. This is especially important when a stressful situation triggers emotional hungers for foods low on the Food Energy Ladder. Now that you have identified the situations that trigger stress in your life, prepare yourself for those moments with mental relaxation. If family visits are high on your list of stressors, be sure that during the visit you take your own personal timeout, ten minutes to practice your mental relaxation. I assure you, you will be able to cope with even the most tense family situations afterwards.

Shortly, in Parts Eight, Nine and Ten, respectively, you will learn how physical activity helps inoculate you against stress and about nutritional supplements that enhance your energy, which is especially important during stressful times. For now, understand that the new mindset you have created and are putting into action empowers you with knowledge that is essential to being well, losing weight, and beating stress. Twenty-eight days may seem like a lot right now, but what you do during those days will establish your blueprint for the rest of your life. Climbing the Food Energy Ladder will strengthen your ability to achieve your ideal weight and lead a healthy, stress-free life.

During these twenty-eight days, *don't* obsess about weight loss. *Don't* hop on the scale every morning after you shower. *Don't* be in a rush to see if your size eight jeans from five years ago fit again. Just relax and enjoy the process of taking good care of yourself. Think about the process itself, not the desired result. If you enjoy the process, and stay with it long enough so it becomes a natural habit to eat and mentally relax, the desired weight loss will naturally result. Keep your mind in the present and don't worry about the future. Feel good about yourself for taking such good care of your body. Put your best foot forward and climb up the ladder. Remember, this is not just about losing weight; it is about improving your health and energy forever! It is about enhancing homeostasis—the basis of *Total Health Rejuvenation*. Nature will take care of the rest.

The Power of the Written Word

In the twenty-eight days that it takes to turn energy eating into a natural habit, your progress will be visible in many ways. Your weight loss will show, your increased energy will shine through, your eyes will light up with radiant health, and your up-lifted outlook will be clear to all. Your feelings about yourself, your body, and your health should be soaring right now! You have already done the hardest work of all. That hard work of introspection, self-reflection, and personal evaluation has put you firmly on the path to natural weight loss and radiant energy. You are on the ladder toward *Total Health Rejuvenation*, upward bound!

Keep in mind that your eyes have been trained to see yourself in a certain way—probably much more critically than others actually see you. Many people who experience weight loss have a difficult time adjusting their self-image to their new, more slender, healthier self. Many of us look at ourselves as if through a funhouse mirror: Our self-image is distorted and out of perspective.

A positive self-image is vital to your motivation to continue to climb up the Food Energy Ladder. It is especially important to change your feelings about your body. Remember, as you have learned, your body image influences how well you care for your body. A poor body image encourages poor care in eating.

I don't want you to lose sight of all that you have already accomplished. Remember, changing your mindset is the most important step—it is the *key* to changing your diet. Believe it or not, you have already made tremendous efforts to establish a new mindset to support your new eating habits. Just by reading this book, you've proven that you are interested in change. What your eyes may not see in the mirror can be seen on paper, if you write it down. The

♦

best way to see all the progress you are making, all the important ways you are caring for your health, is to keep a daily journal.

Think of keeping your journal as if it was a love letter to yourself. Praise yourself for all the good you are doing. Congratulate yourself for eating high on the Food Energy Ladder. Every day, write down at least one thing you are proud of. For example, if you had a wonderful garden salad for lunch instead of a hamburger, write it down so that you can remember how good that made you feel. If you conquered a craving for chocolate by eating a naturally sweet piece of fruit instead, write that down!

Your journal is also a great place to note your responses to your daily meditations. Take some time after you finish your meditation and write down how you are feeling. Write down anything interesting or inspiring that came up during the meditation, an image or a feeling. Make notes about how you feel before and after meditating. What are the differences? Keeping a journal of these experiences leaves you with proof positive that you can see and touch, a record to remind you of the revolutionary steps you are personally taking to increase your energy, and achieve your naturally ideal weight. Total health rejuvenation!

Emphasize the positive in your journal, but don't ignore any hurdles you find yourself leaping. Writing down the difficulties is not to remind you of a weakness or to make you feel guilty if, for example, you fall down the ladder now and then. But it can help you overcome those hurdles the next time you face them. You will be infinitely more appreciative of the progress you are making when you see how far you have come.

Keeping a journal is a powerful strategy for stress management. When you feel stressed out, taking a moment just to write down how you feel, especially about whatever is making you stressed, has the same effect as a tea kettle that reaches the boiling point and then lets off steam. Writing it down helps relieve the pressure of stress before it reaches the boiling point—before *you* boil over. When stress triggers an emotional hunger to eat poorly or to overeat, sit down and begin writing. The process of writing it down may be just the pressure valve you need. Remember that food is only a fleeting escape from stress. Let your journal be a comforting and constructive source for blowing off stress.

Your journal is so important to your journey that I have included space for a "model therapeutic journal" and inspirational quotes for each of the days. Make sure to purchase a special journal or notebook that you will carry with you. Just follow the model provided. It is especially important that every day you note whether you stayed on the top five steps of the Food Energy Ladder. *You don't have to count the cream in your coffee, milk in your cereal or the small amounts of dairy and eggs in this book's recipes.*

In the upper righthand corner of the page of your journal, make a ✓ if all of your meals for that day came from the top five steps. If you ate below Step 5, mark the box with an ✗. At the end of the twenty-eight days, count up all of the ✗s. Hopefully, there are no more than ten because you need to stay among the top five steps for the majority of the twenty-eight days to jump-start the process of permanent weight loss. If you have more than twelve ✗s, begin the twenty-eight days again. Don't punish yourself. You are making big improvements. *Just begin again . . . and know that this time you will do it! Total Health Rejuvenation* is worth it!

At the end of the twenty-eight-day period, I want you to make a special entry in your journal. Give yourself tremendous praise for taking twenty-eight days to improve your weight and wellness for the rest of your life. Take a look back at the journey. It wasn't so difficult, was it? Don't you feel ready to continue eating this way for the rest of your life? *Pledge to yourself that you will continue to climb up—and stay on top of—the Food Energy Ladder.*

With your new mindset about food, your feet firmly on the Food Energy Ladder, and a journal in hand to track your progress, you are ready for action. You are in control. You have a blueprint and a ladder! That's all you need to climb up to new personal health and energy peaks. You will be amazed by how good you look and feel after just twenty-eight days. People will comment on how rested, radiant, light and energized you appear. *They will want to know what you are doing to look so great.*

Total Health Rejuvenation requires you to treat your body as a temple for your soul during the 28-Day Plan—meditating, exercising, staying high on the Food Energy Ladder, and keeping a therapeutic journal . . . *not a lot to ask of yourself!*

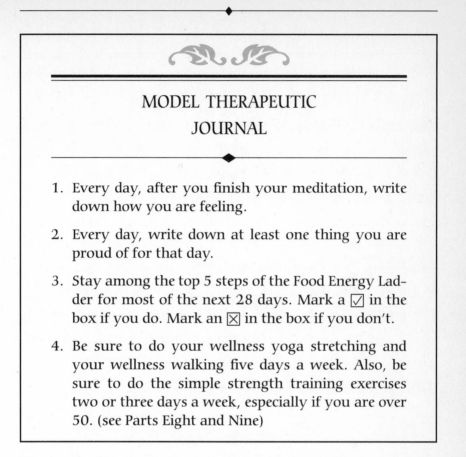

MODEL THERAPEUTIC
JOURNAL

1. Every day, after you finish your meditation, write down how you are feeling.

2. Every day, write down at least one thing you are proud of for that day.

3. Stay among the top 5 steps of the Food Energy Ladder for most of the next 28 days. Mark a ☑ in the box if you do. Mark an ☒ in the box if you don't.

4. Be sure to do your wellness yoga stretching and your wellness walking five days a week. Also, be sure to do the simple strength training exercises two or three days a week, especially if you are over 50. (see Parts Eight and Nine)

Please get a notebook. Just use the "Model Therapeutic Journal" on the following pages as a guide to what you should be writing down in your own notebook each day. Please take the time to reflect on each day's very special inspirational quote, which I have chosen to be part of your daily dose of self-administered TLC—*Tender Loving Care.*

DAY 1

I had an incredible meditation experience. I always pray a lot and ask God a lot of questions. But with my mind becoming so quiet, I felt that I could finally hear God's answers. They made me cry because I could see how much strength I really have and I could truly feel how much God loves me.

Before noon, I had a glass of fresh orange juice and I ate half of a cantaloupe as well as a banana, which made me feel great all day! I had a big salad and some good whole wheat bread for lunch. My family loved the vegetable lasagna I made for our Sunday dinner. No meat at all, today. That's amazing for me—for my kids and husband too.

Let's see . . . I did my yoga stretches and my wellness walk and I actually enjoyed it, which is no small matter for a couch potato like me. Where did I get all this energy? What a great start!

DAY 2

A wonderful meditation again! I felt like I did when I was a little girl and I used to lie on the grass during summer evenings and watch the stars. I must have drifted really deeply because when I opened my eyes, I felt like a child again!

Last night I slept great—maybe because I didn't eat after 8 PM. Also, I set the alarm for an hour earlier so I could meditate, exercise, and still have time to get to work.

I know I'll really sleep like a baby tonight because I did the entire set of strength training exercises— with 5 pound weights! Now I'm really proud of myself! Starting the day with so much fruit seems to be giving me an incredible amount of energy. I just love it.

DAY 1 ☐

_____
_____
_____
_____
_____
_____
_____
_____
_____
_____
_____

Look at a day when you are supremely
satisfied at the end. It's not a day when
you lounge around doing nothing, it's
when you've had everything to do, and
you've done it.

—MARGARET THATCHER

DAY 2 ☐

_____
_____
_____
_____
_____
_____
_____
_____
_____
_____
_____

Look after yourself every day and put
forth your best effort to love yourself
enough to do what's best.

—OPRAH WINFREY

DAY 3 ☐

_____
_____
_____
_____
_____
_____
_____
_____
_____
_____
_____

The world cares very little about what
a man or woman knows; it is what a
man or woman is able to do that
counts.

—BOOKER T. WASHINGTON

DAY 4 ☐

_____
_____
_____
_____
_____
_____
_____
_____
_____
_____
_____

It's okay to make mistakes. Mistakes
are our teachers—they help us to learn.

—JOHN BRADSHAW

DAY 5 ☐

If you want your dreams to come true,
don't sleep, act!

—YIDDISH PROVERB

DAY 6 ☐

The only place where your dream
becomes impossible is in your own
thinking.

—ROBERT H. SCHULLER

DAY 7 ☐

There is hunger for ordinary bread but
there is also hunger for love, for
kindness and for thoughtfulness. This
is the great poverty that makes people
suffer so much.

—MOTHER TERESA

DAY 8 ☐

If opportunity doesn't knock, build a
door.

—MILTON BERLE

∾ DAY 9 ❑

_____

Our greatest glory is not in never
falling, but in rising every time we fall.
—CONFUCIUS

∾ DAY 10 ❑

_____

You must do the very thing you think
you cannot do.
—ELEANOR ROOSEVELT

∾ DAY 11 ❑

_____

We all have ability. The difference is
how we use it.
—STEVIE WONDER

∾ DAY 12 ❑

_____

They can conquer who believe they
can. He has not learned the first lesson
of life who does not every day
surmount a fear.
—RALPH WALDO EMERSON

DAY 13 ❑

We can do anything we want if we
stick to it long enough.
—HELEN KELLER

DAY 14 ❑

If I'd known I was gonna live this long,
I'd have taken better care of myself.
—EUBIE BLAKE AT AGE 100

DAY 15 ❑

Dining is, after all, a spiritual
experience.
—NICOS KAZANTAKIS

DAY 16 ❑

Strength does not come from physical
capacity. It comes from an indomitable
will.
—MAHATMA GANDHI

DAY 17 ❑

When you win . . . you won't
remember the pain.
—JOE NAMATH

DAY 18 ❑

The ultimate measure of a man is not
where he stands in moments of
comfort and convenience, but where he
stands in times of challenge.
—MARTIN LUTHER KING

DAY 19 ❑

We write our own destiny. We become
what we do.
—MADAME CHIANG KAI-SHEK

DAY 20 ❑

Never wait for trouble. Be prepared
for it.
—CHUCK YAEGER

❧ DAY 21 ❑

The doctor of the future will give no
medicine, but will interest his patients
in the care of the human frame, in diet,
and in the cause of disease.
— THOMAS EDISON

❧ DAY 22 ❑

Every blade of grass has its Angel that
bends over it and whispers, *"Grow . . .
Grow."*
— THE TALMUD

❧ DAY 23 ❑

Resolve, and you are free!
— HENRY WADSWORTH LONGFELLOW

❧ DAY 24 ❑

Never let the fear of striking out get in
your way.
— BABE RUTH

ᔒ DAY 25 ❏

The journey of a thousand miles begins
with one step.

—LAO-TSZE

ᔒ DAY 26 ❏

The whole of science is nothing more
than a refinement of everyday
thinking.

—ALBERT EINSTEIN

ᔒ DAY 27 ❏

Everyone's life is a fairy tale written by
God's fingers.

—HANS CHRISTIAN ANDERSON

ᔒ DAY 28 ❏

Start the day with love. Fill the day
with love. End the day with love.

—SATHYA SAI BABA

DAY 28

I'm really proud of myself. . . . I feel like I've been living my life as a prayer for the past 28 days. I've meditated every day, exercised almost every day, eaten foods high on the Food Energy Ladder, and kept writing in my journal.

The exercise was truly fun but very surprising. As a former devoted couch potato, I still can't believe how well I'm doing with wellness yoga stretching, wellness walking and lifting weights.

I know that I'll never be able to look at food in the same way again. No milk for me means no gas. I love it! Also, when I add up my (checks) and my (x's) in the journal, I see that I've eaten turkey or chicken 4 times and fish 4 times. And no beef or pork . . . not bad for having spent my childhood growing up in Kansas City!

Also, I'm no longer so fearful and worried so much of the time—it's like my stress level is lower than it's been in years because now I know just how I can cope. After all, I have strength and God loves me!

One last thing. It has felt completely natural for me to continue living the way that I did during my one day Personal Wellness Retreat . . . in other words, no doing anything wrong and also being more loving. I feel great, I know I look good . . . and I'm really proud of myself!

Part Seven

THE COOKBOOK

*Recipes for Radiant Energy and
Weight Loss That Lasts*

A WORD FROM ANNELI TAUB

Many people have asked me how I cook for a wellnesss medical doctor. I reply in words attributed to Zorba the Greek that I once saw written on the ceiling of an old country inn in Corsica: "I have decided, after all, that dining is a spiritual experience."

I grew up in Europe with a mother who made everything from scratch. So it would never cross my mind to use a so-called ready-made meal from the supermarket freezer. I never hesitate to drive the extra miles to a farmer's market where I can pick through the freshest produce available, produce still clinging to vines, still dusted with soil. I'll splurge on a good olive oil and balsamic vine-gar to accent and bring out the flavors of these delicious foods. A good bakery is a must for the best bread. When I shop at the local supermarket, I especially look for fruits and vegetables that are in season and locally grown because I want foods that are ripened naturally by the sun. My extra efforts are rewarded with the joy of my husband (and our guests) eating foods full of energy that taste as if they originated from my own garden.

I used to be a big meat eater. But once I moved away from fatty, fleshy foods to cleaner, fresher, live-energy foods, I had very little need to go back to my old ways. Do the same and your body will thank you for it.

I'm happy to share with you some of our favorite recipes for delicious meals. I've also included a few recipes from *Seven Steps To Self-Healing* by Edward A. Taub, M.D., *The Low Fat Jewish Vegetarian Cookbook* by Debra Wasserman and *Great Tastes—Healthy Cooking From Canyon Ranch*. I believe you'll find all the recipes to be healthy, savory, and easy to prepare. Simplicity and common sense are the most important aspects of my cooking. I don't count calories or fat grams. I just try to stay among the top five steps of the Food Energy Ladder. Taste is subjective, so a recipe shouldn't be measured exactly by one teaspoon of this and two teaspoons of that. I encourage you to improvise—I'd much rather inspire you than direct you.

Here, then, is what and how we eat in our home. Hopefully, as it is for us, eating will become a spiritual experience for you. *L'Chaim—To Life.*

SALADS

Antipasto di Anneli

MAKES 4 SERVINGS

Serve this antipasto on a spring or summer evening, with your favorite red wine and fresh bread.

12 *stalks asparagus, steamed until tender, and halved*
1 *12-ounce jar artichoke hearts in water, drained*
1 *red bell pepper, sliced in thin strips*
1 *red onion, thinly sliced*
1 *cup sundried tomatoes (softened in a bowl of hot water,*
drained and chopped)
1 *8-ounce can Kalamata olives in water, drained*
8 *leaves fresh basil, chopped coarsely*
2 *tablespoons olive oil*
2 *tablespoons balsamic vinegar*
2 *tablespoons lemon juice*
1/2 *cup shaved asagio cheese*
Salt and pepper to taste

NOTE: To soften sundried tomatoes: place sun dried tomatoes in a bowl of scalding water and set aside for 15–20 minutes. Drain and chop.

1. On a large platter or serving plate, arrange asparagus, artichoke hearts, bell pepper, and onion.

2. Top with sundried tomatoes, olives, and basil.

3. Mix together olive oil, balsamic vinegar, and lemon juice. Drizzle over vegetables.

4. Top antipasto with asagio cheese and season to taste with salt and pepper.

♦

Traditional Italian antipasto salads are so high in fat and calories. The vegetables are drenched in oil and soggy, with layers of processed meats.

♦

This low-fat, vegetarian variety brings out the best flavors of an antipasto. It's filled with Italian delicacies, such as artichoke hearts and sumptuous olives, but goes light on the high-fat cheeses and unhealthy oils.

Caesar Salad

MAKES 2 SERVINGS

Our family and friends agree that this recipe has all of the goodness of a traditional Caesar salad without the unhealthy traditional raw egg.

½ cup Parmesan cheese, grated
1 tablespoon low-fat plain yogurt
4 garlic cloves, minced
Juice of half a lemon
1 tablespoon Worcestershire sauce
½ tablespoon Dijon mustard
Black pepper to taste
8 leaves romaine lettuce, washed and torn

1. To prepare the dressing, combine the first 6 ingredients in a medium-size mixing bowl and whisk well. Season dressing to taste with pepper.

2. Pour dressing over lettuce and toss to coat leaves thoroughly.

There are endless "healthful" variations on this timeless classic. Unfortunately, most lack the flavor of a true Caesar salad. Here's a variation that tastes just like a Caesar salad is supposed to taste!

Quick Noodle Salad

MAKES 2 SERVINGS

This cool salad is perfect for a warm summer day or evening. It's light and refreshing—the perfect salad for a picnic.

> 2 tablespoons lime juice
> 1 tablespoon soy sauce
> 1 tablespoon canola oil
> 2 cucumbers, peeled, halved, seeded, and sliced
> 1/2 red bell pepper, seeded and thinly sliced
> 6 ounces plain ramen, soba, or vermicelli noodles
> 2 cups water
> 2 tablespoons cilantro, chopped

1. Mix the lime juice, soy sauce, and oil. Add the cucumbers and bell peppers and toss well.

2. Put the ramen in a bowl and cover with boiling water. Let the noodles stand until al dente—about ten minutes—then strain. Let ramen cool, then combine with the vegetable mixture.

3. Garnish with cilantro and serve.

NOTE: If using soba or vermicelli noodles, follow cooking instructions on package.

For a delicious variation with added protein, top noodles with 1/2 cup of toasted peanuts or cashews, chopped coarsely.

◆

Be creative about adding more grains to your diet. Along with traditional pastas, other varieties of noodles are high in complex carbohydrates, fiber, and vitamins.

◆

Ramen or soba noodles are available in most supermarkets and natural food stores. If your store does not carry them, vermicelli pasta is a fine substitute.

◆

Most ramen noodles come in a package with a seasoning pack. Keep the noodles, but throw away the seasoning pack—most are loaded with high-fat tropical oils and animal products.

Tomato Mozzarella Salad

MAKES 2 SERVINGS

On warm evenings, we dine on this salad for dinner alone. With fresh bread for soaking up the zesty vinaigrette, it is a substantial and healthy meal.

2 tablespoons pine nuts, toasted (walnuts are suitable, too)
2 cloves garlic, mashed
¹/₂ tablespoon olive oil
¹/₂ cup Arugula, washed and torn in bite-size pieces
5 leaves Romaine lettuce, washed and torn in bite-size pieces
¹/₂ tablespoon balsamic vinegar
Salt and pepper to taste
1 tablespoon raisins, soaked in water for 10 minutes
2 large tomatoes, cut in wedges
8 ounces low-fat mozzarella cheese, cut in ¹/₄ inch slices

1. Combine nuts with garlic and olive oil. Spread on a foil-covered baking sheet and toast in 350° oven for 5 minutes, until golden brown. (Keep a close eye on this because it browns quickly).

2. In a large bowl, toss greens with vinegar and season to taste with salt and pepper. Stir in raisins and toasted nuts.

3. On a platter, arrange tomato wedges and cheese slices around the tossed greens.

4. Serve with crunchy Italian bread or fresh baguettes.

The fresh and tangy tastes of this salad make a delicious meal in itself. Wonderfully light and crisp, and easy to prepare, this salad is full of energy and protein.

◆

Pine nuts come from the cones of the stone pine and have a deep, rich flavor. Combined with low-fat mozzarella, this light salad packs a protein punch.

◆

For a lively variation, substitute small bits of apple for the raisins.

◆

Anneli's Tomato Salad

MAKES 4 SERVINGS

This is a simple yet sensational salad. The freshest vine-ripened tomatoes will create the most flavorful salad.

> 8 medium tomatoes, cut in small wedges
> 1 tablespoon rice vinegar, (seasoned)
> $1/2$ small onion, minced
> 1 tablespoon parsley, finely chopped
> $1/2$ teaspoon salt
> 1 teaspoon sugar
> Black pepper to taste

1. Place tomato wedges in a medium bowl. Set aside.

2. In another bowl, mix together vinegar, onion, parsley, salt, sugar, and pepper, beating well with a fork.

3. Pour mixture over tomatoes and toss lightly.

4. Try serving with Veggie Burgers and fresh corn.

Tomatoes are a versatile vegetable, high in vitamin C. To keep tomatoes fresh and flavorful, do not refrigerate them. This may seem counterintuitive, but it's true. The cold refrigerator not only destroys a fresh tomato's flavor, it may destroy its vitamins.

◆

When buying tomatoes, buy only as much as you can use in the next three or four days. The extra trip to the store or farmer's market will be well worth it.

◆

Rice vinegar gives this salad loads of flavor without loading it with the fat of traditional salad dressings. This salad is virtually fat free.

◆

For variety, use cucumbers instead of tomatoes, or try a combination of both.

Swabian Potato Salad

MAKES 4 SERVINGS

This salad originates from the southwestern region of Germany. When I was growing up, no Sunday meal was complete at my house without this salad (which we called Grossmutter's Kartoffel Salat). It's much more flavorful (and healthful!) than the traditional potato salad made with mayonnaise.

> 6 medium potatoes (Yukon Gold is best), peeled and
>   boiled until just soft, thinly sliced
> ½ small onion, finely grated
> 2 tablespoons white vinegar
> 2 tablespoons canola oil
> 1 tablespoon chopped chives
> ½ teaspoon salt
> ½ teaspoon pepper
> 1 teaspoon sugar
> 1 teaspoon Dijon mustard

1. Place sliced potatoes in a large bowl. Set aside.

2. Mix all remaining ingredients together in a small bowl, stirring vigorously till creamy.

3. Add mixture to potatoes. Stir gently. If too dry, add some hot water.

NOTE: If time allows, cook the potatoes a few hours before, so they are easier to slice very thin.

Potatoes are loaded with healthful complex carbohydrates and are a wonderful source of vitamin C, iron, and fiber. It's only how we prepare them that sometimes makes them high in fat and unhealthy. Unlike traditional potato salads doused in mayonnaise, this one gets its creamy texture from vinegar and Dijon mustard.

◆

When it comes to satisfying foods that fill you up without all the calories and fat, potatoes cannot be beat.

◆

◆

Accompany this dish with Swabian Cucumber Salad for a memorable summer picnic. You can even combine the two salads into one. Because it's free of mayonnaise, this potato salad will not spoil.

◆

For dinner, this salad marries wonderfully with Chicken Goulash or Turkey Patties.

Fast Green Bean Salad

MAKES 2 SERVINGS

Savory, tasty and tangy, this salad is a treat for the tastebuds and so easy to prepare. Use fresh green beans if they are in season.

I 14-ounce can French-cut green beans, drained
I tablespoon onion, finely grated
I tablespoon parsley, finely chopped
I tablespoon white vinegar
¼ teaspoon salt
½ teaspoon Maggi
Dash each of pepper and sugar
I tablespoon canola oil

1. Drain the water from the beans and empty them into a bowl. Add the remaining ingredients and mix well, so that all the beans are coated with dressing.

Green beans are a high-fiber vegetable. A great, tasty way to get most of the nutritional fiber you need in a day is to enjoy this salad.

♦

This is quick and simple but has a distinct flavor, thanks to the blend of Maggi, pepper and sugar. Maggi is a condiment which has a nutty, round taste and is widely used in Germany. It's also great for soups, instead of salt. Look for Maggi in the gourmet foods or condiment section at your market.

Mango Dressing

MAKES 2 CUPS

This delicious, aromatic dressing complements a fresh salad of spinach leaves or other greens. It's tropical flavors are perfect any time as long as mangos are available.

1 *small mango, peeled and cored*
1 *garlic clove, mashed*
2 *tablespoons nonfat yogurt or silken tofu*
1 *tablespoon cilantro*
1/2 *teaspoon pepper*
2 *teaspoons lemon juice*
Salt to taste

1. Put all ingredients in a blender or food processor and blend until creamy.

2. Chill well and serve over your favorite salad, or for something different, over rice.

Mangos are freshest and most flavorful in late spring and summer, when they are in season.

♦

This sweet-smelling and succulent fruit is a wonderful source of vitamin A and potassium.

♦

Be sure to pick mangos that are not overripe or bruised.

Tahini Dip or Dressing

MAKES APPROXIMATELY 1 CUP

Tahini and garlic are a tangy combination that liven up any sandwich or salad. For dip, follow the directions below. To thin dip for a salad dressing, add water until desired consistency.

> ¼ cup tahini (sesame seed paste)
> 1 tablespoon lemon juice
> 1 tablespoon soy sauce
> 1 tablespoon white vinegar
> 1 garlic clove, mashed
> 2 tablespoons water (more for a thinner dressing)

1. In a bowl, whisk together all ingredients. For a creamier texture, use a blender.

2. Add more water for dressing. If you add too much water and dressing is too runny, just add more tahini.

Tahini is a traditional middle-eastern ingredient used in dips and dressings. Tahini comes from sesame seeds and is a rich source of protein.

♦

Thick, this makes a wonderful sandwich spread or dip for fresh vegetables and pita bread. Thinned with additional water, this is the perfect dressing for a fresh spinach salad.

♦

SAUCES

♦

Simply Fresh Tomato Sauce

MAKES 2 SERVINGS

The best tomato sauce comes from the freshest ingredients—tomatoes and basil soaked with the energy of the sun. On the coast of the Italian Riviera, we asked the chef of our favorite restaurant what the secret to his great sauce was, and he exclaimed, *"Il sole! The sun!"*

> ½ tablespoon olive oil
> 1 small onion, finely diced
> 3 cloves garlic, crushed
> 1 small carrot, peeled and shredded
> 6 ripe tomatoes, diced
> 2 tablespoons fresh basil, chopped
> Salt and pepper to taste
> Dash of sugar

1. Heat oil in a medium-size pan and add onion, garlic, and carrot. Sauté over medium heat for about 8 minutes, until onion is soft but not brown.

2. Add the tomatoes and basil and simmer on low heat for 15 minutes, stirring often. Season to taste with salt, pepper, and sugar.

This sauce is so low in fat, and its ingredients come mainly from the very top of the Food Energy Ladder. Served with a plate of steaming pasta, this makes a low-fat, high-energy meal.

♦

Select fresh tomatoes carefully. Look for bruises or soft spots. Choose vine-ripened tomatoes if available.

♦

When basil is not in season, or for variation, use fresh parsley in the recipe.

♦

A little sugar helps bring out the taste in tomatoes.

♦

For a pure, healthy and easy to prepare tomato sauce, this recipe can't be beat.

♦

Lycopene gives tomatoes their red color and it is probably the substance that decreases prostate cancer significantly in men who eat lots of tomato sauce.

Best Basic Tomato Sauce

MAKES 2 SERVINGS

This simple, tasty sauce is better than any jar tomato sauce you'll find in the store—I assure you. And if you are in a hurry, this sauce will be ready in almost as little time as it takes your pasta to boil.

> 28-ounce can whole tomatoes with juice
> 1 tablespoon olive oil
> 5 garlic cloves, crushed
> 1/2 small yellow onion, finely diced
> 1/2 carrot peeled and sliced very thin
> 1 tablespoon Italian herbs (i.e., basil, parsley, oregano)
> Juice of 1 medium orange
> 1 teaspoon sugar
> 3/4 teaspoon salt
> Pepper to taste

1. Tear or cut tomatoes into small pieces, removing any hard stems. Set aside.

2. Heat oil in a medium pot and add garlic, onion, carrot, and Italian herbs. Sauté until garlic is golden, stirring well.

3. Add tomatoes, orange juice, sugar, salt, and pepper. Simmer on low heat for 20 minutes and serve over hot pasta.

When fresh tomatoes are unavailable, or you are short on time, terrific tomato sauce can start from canned tomatoes.

◆

Orange juice revitalizes canned tomatoes and brings out their flavor.

◆

Select whole canned tomatoes in juice. Some varieties contain added salt and other spices. Plain, simple whole tomatoes are all you need.

◆

Canning fresh tomatoes yourself is a wonderful summer activity and will guarantee you delicious tomato sauce throughout the year.

Mushroom Spinach Sauce for Baked Potatoes

MAKES ABOUT 2 CUPS

Turn a plain baked potato into a delicious low-fat meal. One taste and you will forget the high-fat butter and sour cream commonly served over baked potatoes.

> 4 baked potatoes
> 1 tablespoon canola oil
> 2 cups onions, minced
> 2 tablespoons all purpose flour
> 1½ cups water
> 2 cups mushrooms, chopped
> 1 cup frozen chopped spinach, thawed and drained, or 1
>   cup fresh spinach, washed and chopped
> Juice of ½ lemon
> Salt and pepper to taste

1. Bake potatoes in a 450° oven for approximately 1 hour, or until soft.

2. In a large skillet, heat oil and add onion. Sauté until translucent, stirring frequently. Add mushrooms and sauté 3–5 minutes (pan will become dry). Add flour and water and stir well until creamy.

3. Add spinach and lemon juice and stir well. Season to taste with salt and pepper.

4. Turn heat to low and simmer for 8 minutes, stirring frequently.

5. Slice open potatoes down the center and top with sauce.

Americans love potatoes, and one of the most popular ways to eat them is baked.

◆

Fresh baked potatoes are typically turned into a nutrition nightmare by smothering them with high-fat toppings. Two tablespoons of butter adds 24 grams of fat!

◆

Potatoes are super sources of potassium, vitamin C, and fiber. Their skins are especially nutritious—loaded with more fiber, iron, calcium, zinc, and B vitamins.

◆

Here is a delicious topping to enjoy over baked potatoes without adding fat and calories. The mushrooms are an excellent source of potassium and phosphorous.

◆

For variety, substitute swiss chard for spinach and add a few chopped walnuts.

◆

This sauce was created to top baked potatoes but it can also be enjoyed over steamed cauliflower.

◆

Serve with a fresh baguette.

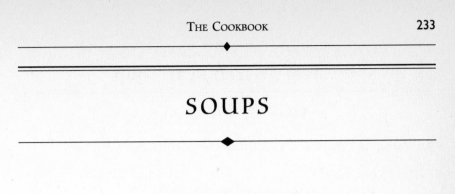

SOUPS

Cold Tsatziki Soup

MAKES 4 SERVINGS

Smooth and cool, this authentic Greek soup comes together in hardly any time. It's perfect for a light lunch, and tastes even better on the second day.

> 2 cucumbers, peeled and coarsely grated
> Salt and pepper to taste
> 1 pint low-fat plain yogurt
> Juice of ½ lemon
> 1 garlic clove, mashed
> 2 cups water
> 2 tablespoons fresh mint, finely chopped

1. Place cucumbers in a medium bowl and season to taste with salt and pepper. Set aside.

2. In another bowl, mix yogurt with lemon juice, garlic, and water.

3. Combine the cucumbers and yogurt mixture, add mint leaves, and stir well.

This soup is perfect for a hot summer day. The cool and crisp flavors of cucumber and mint are delicious and refreshing.

◆

Fresh mint gives this soup its distinct taste. Mint is easy to grow. If you don't have a garden, even a small container on the windowsill will produce amazing results.

◆

If mint is too strong for your tastes, substitute fresh parsley for a more subtle soup.

Savory Green Bean Soup

MAKES 4 SERVINGS

This soup is hearty and healthful, the perfect meal in itself.

> 5 cups water
> 1 teaspoon summer savory herb
> 3 cups green beans
> 2½ tablespoons canola oil (½ tablespoon for browning onions, 2 tablespoons for browning flour)
> 2 medium onions, finely diced
> 3 tablespoons all purpose flour
> 1 tablespoon vinegar
> 2 teaspoons salt
> 2 teaspoons sugar
> 1 pound wide egg noodles

1. Bring water to a boil with summer savory. Add beans to boiling water and cook for 20 minutes.

2. While beans cook, heat ½ tablespoon canola oil in a small skillet and sauté onions until brown. Transfer onions to a small bowl and set aside. In the same skillet, heat 2 tablespoons canola oil and add flour, stirring constantly to avoid clumping. Cook flour until golden brown and barely smoking. Watch carefully, flour turns from brown to burned very quickly!

3. Add onions and flour to the beans and water and stir. Add vinegar, salt, and sugar, and let simmer for 15 minutes.

4. While soup simmers, boil water for noodles. Cook noodles until al dente. Serve soup hot, over noodles.

Garden-fresh green beans are the key to this flavorful soup. Green beans picked from the garden are loaded with life-energy. Look for a local farmer's market for the freshest beans available. If fresh beans are not possible, frozen or canned beans are a good alternative.

◆

If you have children, involve them in the preparations. Children love the popping sound that beans make when they break off the ends!

Carrot and Orange Soup

MAKES 4 SERVINGS

This is a refreshing, light soup. Ginger, coriander, turmeric, chili powder, and cumin create a delightful palette of spices and herbs.

> 2 teaspoons olive oil
> 1 small onion, minced
> 1-inch slice of fresh ginger, peeled and minced (optional)
> 1 garlic clove, minced
> 1/2 teaspoon ground coriander
> 1/2 teaspoon ground cumin
> 1/2 teaspoon ground chili powder
> 1/4 teaspoon turmeric
> 1/4 pound carrots, thinly sliced (About 5 large carrots)
> Grated zest and juice of 1 large orange
> 1 large orange, peeled and chopped
> 3 cups fresh vegetable broth or bouillion
> 1–2 teaspoons fresh lemon juice
> Salt and pepper to taste
> Cilantro leaves or twists of orange zest for garnish
>   (optional)

1. Heat oil in a saucepan. Add onion, ginger, garlic, and spices. Sauté gently for 3–5 minutes. Add carrots and cook 8 more minutes, stirring frequently.

2. Add orange zest, chopped orange flesh, and broth to the pan. Bring to a boil, then reduce heat, cover, and simmer gently for 20 minutes.

3. Purée soup in a blender or food processor. Reheat gently, then stir in the orange and lemon juices and season to taste.

4. Serve garnished with cilantro leaves or twists of orange zest, if desired.

"Soup up" your energy and immune system with this delicious soup!

◆

◆

Carrots are an outstanding source of beta-carotene, which boosts the immune system and helps to prevent cataracts, cancer and heart disease.

◆

It's common knowledge that the vitamin C found in oranges boosts the immune system and helps relieve colds, but research also suggests that it may help guard against cancers of the breast, cervix, and gastrointestinal system.

Fresh Vegetable Broth

MAKES ABOUT 5 CUPS

The perfect way to use up vegetables in the fridge. This broth gives Vegetable Risotto a wonderful flavor.

2 *large carrots, sliced*
I *large onion, sliced*
2 *celery stalks, outer, sliced*
A *few celery leaves*
A *few parsley stems*
2 *sprigs each of fresh thyme and marjoram*
2 *bay leaves*
3 *garlic cloves, crushed with the side of a knife*
A *strip of lemon peel*
I0 *black peppercorns*
6 *cups water*

1. Put all ingredients in a large saucepan. Bring to a boil, then re-duce the heat, cover the pan, and simmer until vegetables are just soft but not mushy, about 45 minutes. Let cool.

2. Strain broth through a sieve into a large container, pressing the solids to extract as much liquid as possible. Keep covered in the refrigerator. Use broth within four days.

Vegetable broth is simple and satisfying to make. Homemade is much healthier, and lower in sodium, than store-bought broth. You will taste the difference!

♦

Broccoli Soup with Walnuts

MAKES 4 SERVINGS

This is a favorite autumn or winter soup, the perfect overture to a good meal, or a perfect meal, in itself. Serve with a loaf of crusty bread for dipping in this savory soup.

>1 medium onion, chopped
>4–5 cups fresh broccoli, stems sliced and florets separated
>1 tablespoon butter
>1 cup vegetable bouillion or water
>1 cup milk or plain soy or rice milk
>¼ cup half-and-half
>Salt and pepper to taste
>3 tablespoons walnuts, chopped and toasted

1. In a large pot sauté onion and broccoli in butter for 5 minutes.

2. Add bouillion (or water) and milk and simmer gently for 30 minutes, or until broccoli is tender.

3. Transfer to food processor or blender, purée until smooth, and return to pot.

4. Add half-and-half and walnuts. Season to taste with salt and pepper.

This soup provides plentiful amounts of fiber to your diet. Broccoli and nuts are both high in fiber. Fiber helps remove excess cholesterol from the blood, and thus helps keep your heart healthy.

♦

Broccoli may be the most maligned vegetable, but it is also one of the most healthful vegetables you can eat. Broccoli is loaded with compounds that help protect against cancer, as well as vitamin C and beta-carotene.

♦

Nuts are wonderful for your health when eaten regularly and in moderation. The monounsaturated fat and vitamin E in nuts helps protect against heart disease.

Wonderful Mushroom Soup

MAKES 2 SERVINGS

This soup is so simple to prepare and so flavorful. The complex tastes of fennel and anise liqueur will linger on your tongue long after the last spoonful has been eaten.

1 tablespoon canola oil
1 small onion, diced
1 clove garlic, minced
1 stalk celery, diced
2 tablespoons fennel, diced
3 cups vegetable bouillion or water
8 ounces mushrooms (a brown variety), sliced
2 tablespoons parsley, chopped very thin
1 teaspoon butter
2 tablespoons cream
1 tablespoon anise liqueur or Pernod (optional)
Salt and pepper to taste

1. Heat oil in a medium pot and add onion, garlic, celery, and fennel. Sauté on medium heat for 10 minutes, stirring often. Add mushrooms and sauté for 5 minutes, stirring often.

2. Add bouillion or water and simmer on low heat for 30 minutes.

3. Let cool and transfer to blender. Purée soup until smooth.

4. Return to pot and add butter, cream, parsley, and liqueur.

5. Serve with a fresh baguette and boiled or mashed potatoes.

Mushrooms are a staple of fall and winter cooking, especially for hearty soups and stews.

◆

This soup is best prepared with a good brown mushroom that has a deep flavor, such as cremini or porcini.

◆

Fennel is at its freshest in fall, and its delightfully sweet licorice flavor mingles well with strong mushrooms.

◆

Swabian Lentil Soup

MAKES 4 SERVINGS

When I was a child in Germany, many snowy, bitter-cold after-
noons were warmed by the fragrance of a big pot of lentil soup
simmering on the stove. This soup is especially flavorful the next
day.

6 cups water
1 cup brown lentils
1 cup celery, peeled and cut into ¹/₂ inch slices
1 carrot, peeled and cut into ¹/₂ inch slices
2 tablespoons canola oil
1 medium onion, diced
1 tablespoon all purpose flour
Salt and pepper to taste
1 tablespoon white vinegar
1 teaspoon sugar
4 cups wide noodles

1. Rinse lentils with fresh water through a fine strainer.

2. Boil water, add lentils, celery, and carrots, and cook over low
   heat, simmering for 45 minutes.

3. Meanwhile, heat oil and sauté onions until just light brown. Add
   flour and stir constantly until golden brown and just starting to
   smoke. Watch carefully to avoid burning.

4. After the lentils and vegetables have simmered for 45 minutes,
   add the flour-onion mixture and stir well. Simmer for 10 minutes.

5. Add vinegar, sugar and season to taste with salt and pepper.

6. While soup simmers, cook noodles following directions on
   package.

7. Pour soup over noodles in soup bowls.

◆

The nutty flavor of lentils combined with noodles makes a hearty winter soup.

◆

The combination of lentils and noodles create a satisfying soup filled with fiber and loaded with energy.

◆

Lentils were one of the very first crops to be cultured and they are now grown all over the planet. India produces more than fifty varieties of different colors and sizes to help provide adequate protein and Vitamin B_1 (thiamin) to its population in the traditional dish called "dahl."

◆

All of us would do well to eat more energy-rich lentils, and this delicious, savory soup is a wonderful way to do so because it is truly a meal in itself.

Chicken Soup with Savoy Cabbage

MAKES 4 SERVINGS

The scent of this soup cooking will fill your kitchen with a warm aroma in winter. When anyone in our family is feeling under the weather, this soup will boost his or her energy and help ward off a cold. This recipe combines my mother's favorite cabbage soup with Ed's mother's famous chicken soup. We think it's a perfect marriage of flavors and traditions.

> 6 cups water
> 4 skinless chicken breast fillets, sliced
> 1 small leek, cut in $^{1}/_{2}$ inch chunks
> 2 carrots, peeled and cut in 2-inch chunks
> 1 celery root, peeled and cut in $^{1}/_{2}$ inch chunks
> 1 bay leaf
> 1 small Savoy cabbage, cut in small pieces
> $^{1}/_{4}$ cup chives, cut very thin (optional)
> $^{1}/_{4}$ cup parsley, chopped
> Salt and pepper to taste

1. Bring water to a boil, and add chicken and leek. Cover and cook on medium heat for about 30 minutes.

2. Add carrots, celery root, bay leaf, and cabbage. Cover and cook for another 30 minutes on low heat.

3. Just before serving, add parsley or chives, and season to taste with salt and pepper.

4. Serve over rice, or just with some crusty fresh bread.

5. Remember to remove the bay leaf prior to eating the soup.

Wintertime is for soups, and this one is filled with hearty vegetables and chicken. Leftovers make a more flavorful soup the following day, and the broth can be used in many other recipes.

◆

Making a soup stock is a terrific way to use up the vegetables in your refrigerator. The vegetables fill the broth with a healthy supply of vitamins.

◆

This soup cooks fairly fast, in just an hour. The vegetables will be cooked but not soggy and flavorless. Overcooking vegetables in water or broth destroys their vitamins.

◆

Savoy cabbage, loaded with vitamin A and calcium, is dark and green with a tight and curly head and crinkly leaves.

◆

Celery root gives a delectable flavor to this hearty dish.

Potato Parsley Soup

MAKES 2 SERVINGS

Whenever I cook this soup, I am transported by its aroma to my mother's kitchen in Germany. At home in California, it reminds me of all the warmth and comfort I felt watching my mother cook.

5 cups cold water, lightly salted
4 medium potatoes, such as Idaho baking potatoes,
    peeled and cut in 2-inch pieces
6 cloves garlic, peeled and left whole
1 medium onion, quartered
½ cup low-fat milk
1 ½ cups parsley, chopped fine
Salt and pepper to taste

1. In a large pot, boil water and add potatoes, garlic, and onion. Cook until vegetables are very soft, about 30 minutes. Do not drain water.

2. Using a masher, mash potatoes, garlic and onion until smooth, creating a creamy soup. Add milk slowly, until desired consistency. Add parsley and stir well.

3. Simmer over low heat for 10 minutes. Add salt and pepper to taste and serve hot.

A creamy potato soup without the high-fat cream. This soup is actually almost entirely fat-free.

◆

Parsley comes off the sidelines in this recipes and plays a starring role. This soup proves that parsley has flavor worthy of more than just a garnish. For additional flavor, add chopped carrots or celery.

Mexican Chicken Soup

MAKES 4 SERVINGS

On our visits to Zhijuatenejo, Mexico, we encountered this tangy, satisfying soup. Each time I sit down to enjoy it now, I have the memory of the festive mariachi players singing and dancing to colorful music.

> 1 tablespoon canola oil
> 1 medium onion, finely diced
> 2 limes, juiced
> 4 skinless chicken breast filets, cut in 1/2 inch pieces
> 5 cups chicken broth
> 4 tomatoes, diced
> 1/2 bell pepper, diced
> 6 corn tortillas
> 2 tablespoons canola oil
> 1/2 cup cilantro, chopped
> Salt and pepper to taste

1. Heat 1 tablespoon oil in a large pot and sauté onions until translucent. Squeeze in juice of both limes, reduce heat, add chicken and sauté 3–5 minutes.

2. Add broth, tomatoes, and bell pepper. Cook about 45 minutes, until chicken is tender. Season to taste with salt and pepper.

3. In the meantime, cut 2 tortillas into small pieces. Heat 2 tablespoons oil and fry tortilla pieces until crisp and golden. Drain well on paper towels to remove excess oil.

4. Put chicken pieces in soup bowls, add tortilla pieces, and cover with broth. Sprinkle each bowl generously with cilantro.

5. Serve with steaming hot tortillas on the side and a dish of fresh salsa.

This Mexican soup sparkles with the tangy flavors of lime and cilantro. This is the perfect soup for a refreshing meal on a summer evening. Leftovers are even more delicious the second day, after the flavors have mingled overnight.

◆

Tomatoes, bell pepper, and cilantro give this soup wonderful color, a real celebration of summertime. This soup is simple to prepare but dazzling to the eyes and stomach.

APPETIZERS

Portobello Appetizer

MAKES 4 SERVINGS

This is a wonderful party appetizer. For a side dish, the rich flavors complement a crisp Caesar salad. And what a great sandwich it makes with a little lettuce and tomato!

2 tablespoons olive oil
2 large portobello mushrooms, stems removed, sliced thin
2 tablespoons balsamic vinegar
Salt and pepper to taste
1/2 tablespoon fresh thyme, chopped
1 teaspoon fresh rosemary, chopped
(Substitute 3 teaspoons dried Italian herbs, if fresh herbs unavailable)
2 garlic cloves, peeled
1/2 cup parmesan cheese, grated

1. In a medium skillet, heat 1 tablespoon oil and sauté portobellos until deep brown. Drain on paper towel.

2. Arrange mushrooms on a plate, sprinkle with balsamic vinegar, salt and pepper.

3. In the same skillet, combine chopped herbs and garlic together and add 1 tablespoon olive oil. Mix well. Cook for 5 minutes on low heat.

4. Drizzle herb mixture over mushrooms.

5. Sprinkle mushrooms with parmesan.

6. Serve mushrooms alone or on a baguette with sprigs of arugula and sliced tomatoes.

Rich, plump portobellos are our favorite variety of mushrooms. Once found only in specialty food stores, they are now common in most supermarket produce sections.

♦

This is a pleasing appetizer. For variation, serve the sautéed mushrooms over a bed of rice or pasta for a main dish.

♦

Portobello mushrooms are as meaty and satisfying as a great piece of beef!

Mock Chopped Liver

MAKES 6 SERVINGS

Chopped liver fans will rave about this healthy, low-fat variation of a traditional paté. Deborah Wasserman's recipe captures all the strong flavors of the original classic but is much lower in fat and completely vegetarian.

½ pound green beans, chopped in bite-size pieces
¾ pounds mushrooms, chopped
I small onion, peeled and finely chopped
I teaspoon canola oil
¼ cup walnuts, chopped
Salt and pepper to taste
¼ cup water

1. Sauté green beans, mushrooms, and onion in oil over medium-high heat for 10 minutes.

2. Pour mixture into food processor bowl, add remaining ingredients, and blend until creamy.

3. Chill and serve on a bed of lettuce with pita bread or raw vegetables.

Thanks to Deborah Wasserman's creative cooking, snacking before dinner doesn't have to throw you off the top of the Food Energy Ladder.

◆

Giving a dinner party? Going to a potluck? This is an excellent, easy-to-prepare, low-fat appetizer that will please vegetarians and non-vegetarians alike.

◆

For variation, this can be spread on bread for a delicious vegetarian sandwich.

Curry Zucchini Dip

MAKES APPROXIMATELY 1 CUP

Guests always love this appetizer. The refreshing flavors of yogurt and curry make this a perfect pre-dinner treat.

1 teaspoon canola oil
1 medium onion, cut in quarters
2 zucchini, cut in 2-inch cubes
3 tablespoons low-fat plain yogurt
1 teaspoon lemon juice
1 ½ teaspoons curry powder
Dash sugar
Salt and pepper to taste

1. Heat oil and sauté onion and zucchini for 5 minutes.

2. Purée the mixture in a food processor or blender with yogurt, lemon juice, curry, and a dash of sugar. Add salt and pepper to taste.

Curry adds intense flavor to vegetables. This smooth, creamy dip makes a memorable appetizer served with crackers, warmed pita bread, or fresh carrot and celery sticks. Unlike most dips, it is low in fat and calories.

♦

You can also use this dip to enliven any sandwich.

◆

French Salmon Spread

MAKES 4 SERVINGS

Many fans of French cuisine, like myself, have had to give up their favorite French dishes because they do not accommodate a low-fat lifestyle. Over the years, I have learned to transform traditionally rich French recipes into low-fat, high-energy variations that still maintain their distinct French flavors. This one is derived from an appetizer served in our favorite Parisian bistro. Bón appetit!

> 1 tablespoon mustard (preferably Dijon)
> 1 tablespoon olive oil
> 3 ounces smoked salmon, finely chopped
> 1 tablespoon onion, minced (optional)
> 1 tablespoon greens of spring onion, finely chopped (chives
>   can be substituted)
> Salt and pepper to taste

1. Mix mustard with oil until creamy.

2. Add salmon, onion, greens of spring onion or chives, season to taste with salt and pepper and mix well. Refrigerate for several hours before serving.

3. Simply tear off hunks of baguette and enjoy, or toast slices and top with spread.

Americans love appetizers. Unfortunately, most appetizers are high in fat and filled with meat. This dish is borrowed from the French and transformed into an intensely appetizing but not sinfully fattening spread.

◆

Traditional rillette is served throughout France, made of pork or rabbit. In this dish, salmon is substituted for a lighter, healthier spread, with terrific taste. If smoked salmon is unavailable, substitute another variety of smoked fish.

Rolled Salmon with Carrots

MAKES 4 SERVINGS

This is a favorite party appetizer. Splurge on a high-quality, very fresh smoked salmon—the added flavor is worth the extra cost!

8 slices smoked salmon
1 teaspoon horseradish or mustard
1 teaspoon honey
1 tablespoon fresh dill, chopped fine
Pepper
4 lettuce leaves, cut in thin strips
1 carrot, peeled and shredded with a potato peeler
½ lemon

1. Arrange slices of salmon next to each other on a plate.

2. Mix horseradish or mustard with honey, dill, and a dash of pepper. Spread evenly on each salmon slice. Top with lettuce strips and roll up.

3. Arrange carrot shavings on 4 plates and lay salmon rolls on top. Sprinkle lemon juice on top of each roll.

Seafood and vegetables combine to create a healthy meal rich in flavor, vitamins, and minerals.

♦

Smoked salmon is a wonderful source of omega-3 fatty acids, shown in research to reduce the risk of cardiac disease.

♦

Carrots add healthful beta-carotene and vitamin C to this dish.

♦

As a variation, substitute peeled cucumber slices for lettuce.

Black Olive Tapenade

Our visit to Nice was memorable in part because of this delicious appetizer. Each time I make it I am transported back to that fine little restaurant by the market where we enjoyed this tapenade on a fresh baguette with a glass of Beaujolais. C'est magnifique!

2 cups pitted black olives
2 tablespoons capers
2 anchovy fillets
2 garlic cloves, peeled
2 tablespoons fresh thyme (or 1 teaspoon dried thyme)
1 tablespoon Dijon mustard
1 teaspoon ground pepper
1 teaspoon Cognac (optional)

1. Mix all ingredients in a food processor until smooth.

2. Serve with crusty sourdough bread or a French baguette.

The intense flavors of olives, capers, and anchovies create a heavenly appetizer. Their strong flavor is perfect for a tapenade spread lightly on a French baguette.

◆

True, olives are high in fat, but of the mono-unsaturated type that is good for your heart!

◆

This is a wonderful appetizer to make ahead of time. Covered tightly, it will stay fresh in the refrigerator for days.

◆

Any strong olive will do, but I like Kalamata or Black Nicoise best. These are no longer just gourmet store delicacies, but can be found in cans in most supermarkets. You can easily pit olives yourself by pressing the olive with the bottom of a cup.

Hearty Garlic Spread

MAKES 1 1/2 CUPS

This delicious spread earns its name because garlic truly is good for your heart. This is staple fare in the French countryside and Mediterranean. Combined with their zest for life, no wonder people from both areas have such low rates of heart disease! Traditionally, the spread is served to flavor crusty bread, fish soup, and seafood.

> 1 cup silken tofu, firm
> 6 cloves garlic, peeled
> 1 tablespoon lemon juice
> 1 tablespoon olive oil
> Salt and pepper to taste

1. Combine all ingredients in a food processor and blend until smooth. Season to taste with salt and pepper.

2. Refrigerate until serving in an airtight container; freshness lasts up to a week.

Peeling garlic can be frustrating if you don't know this simple trick: place single cloves on a cutting board or counter. With the flat side of a large wooden spoon or a wide chef's knife, smash them. The peels just fall away.

♦

Garlic is wonderful for your health. Scientific studies have shown its preventive value in warding off bacteria viruses, fungi, and other organisms that cause human disease. Chemicals in garlic also protect the heart. Researchers have shown that garlic has a cholesterol-lowering effect, reduces blood pressure, and can help prevent blood clots.

♦

Enjoy this as a dip for raw or steamed vegetables, or as a zesty sandwich spread.

Lentil Paté

MAKES 6 SERVINGS

This vegetarian paté is an excellent alternative to liver paté. It transforms the humble lentil into an elegant appetizer.

1 cup lentils
2¼ cups water
1 onion, peeled and minced
4 cloves garlic, peeled and minced
2 teaspoons canola oil
1 teaspoon pepper
½ teaspoon white vinegar

1. Cook lentils in water over medium heat for 45 minutes. Meanwhile, sauté onion and garlic in oil for 2 minutes.

2. When lentils are cooked, drain and pour them into food processor bowl. Add sautéed onion and garlic, pepper, and vinegar.

3. Blend in food processor until creamy, adding a little water if necessary. Season to taste with salt and pepper.

4. Chill and serve with pita bread, crackers, or raw vegetables.

Lentils are an inexpensive and low-fat source of carbohydrates, fiber and protein.

◆

Unlike other legumes, lentils can be prepared in less than an hour. They can be cooked without pre-soaking but remember to rinse and drain them several times before cooking.

◆

Many thanks to Deborah Wasserman for this creative vegetarian appetizer.

SIDE DISHES

Stuffed Cucumbers Nany

MAKES 4 SERVINGS

Swiss friends introduced us to this savory dish. It's light but surprisingly filling, topped with the Best Basic Tomato Sauce.

1 cup brown rice
2 cups water
1 8-ounce package low-fat cream cheese
2 tablespoons raisins
Salt and pepper to taste
5 medium cucumbers, peeled, halved lengthwise and
*   seeded*
Best Basic or Simply Fresh Tomato Sauce (Recipe pages
*   228 and 230)*

1. Cook brown rice according to directions on package, but 10 minutes less than required cooking time.

2. Drain rice and mix with cream cheese and raisins. Add salt and pepper to taste.

3. Fill half of the cucumbers with the rice mixture. Top each stuffed cucumber with another half and secure with toothpick.

4. Place stuffed cucumbers in a casserole dish.

5. Make one recipe of Best Basic Tomato Sauce and pour over stuffed cucumbers. Cover and bake for 45 minutes at 300 degrees

---

We love vegetables in their natural, raw, fresh state. When we cook them, we favor recipes that draw out the naturally delicious flavors. It's easy to overcook vegetables and destroy not only their flavor but their nutritional value.

◆

This delicious dish combines the cool taste of cucumbers with the sweetness of raisins and nutty taste of brown rice.

◆

Yes, this recipe uses cream cheese (low fat), but remember our motto for healthy eating: "Everything in moderation . . . including moderation!"

◆

For variation, substitute turkey for brown rice.

Mashed Potatoes and Vegetables Italiano

MAKES 2 SERVINGS

This dish turns plain old mashed potatoes into something truly wonderful! a traditional American favorite combined with some Italian culinary pizzazz . . . *buon appetito!*

3 medium potatoes
½ tablespoon olive oil
1 small onion, minced
4 cloves garlic, mashed
¼ cup skim, soy, or rice milk, scalded
½ cup pine nuts, toasted
½ cup red bell pepper, diced
1 cup mushrooms (any variety), cut in half
½ tablespoon lemon juice
1 cup tomato sauce (Recipe page 230)
½ teaspoon fennel seeds
1 teaspoon Italian herbs (i.e. basil, oregano, parsley page 230)
Salt, pepper, and sugar to taste
Pat butter (optional)
Shredded Parmesan cheese (optional)

1. Peel potatoes, cut in quarters, and boil in salted water until soft, approximately 20–25 minutes.

2. While potatoes boil, heat ½ tablespoon olive oil in large pot and sauté onion until translucent and add garlic. Stir frequently to avoid burning.

3. Add to pot all vegetables, lemon juice, tomato sauce, fennel seeds, and Italian herbs. Season with salt, pepper, and sugar to taste. Simmer on low heat for about 20 minutes.

4. When potatoes are done, drain them well, add hot milk, and mash well. Add a pat of butter if you like. Stir in pine nuts and season with salt and pepper to taste.

5. Transfer mashed potatoes to plates and top with the vegetables. Sprinkle with shredded parmesan if desired.

It's easy to find vegetarian inspiration in many of our favorite American dishes, including the humble mashed potato! Potatoes are a super high-energy food. This complex carbohydrate provides long-lasting energy, as well as abundant amounts of fiber, vitamin C, potassium, and other minerals.

◆

Yukon Gold potatoes are great for this dish because of their natural buttery taste and creamy consistency.

◆

Feel free to vary the vegetables according to your tastes and what is in season: eggplant, cauliflower, and green peas are a delicious variation.

◆

Cooked Green Beans and Carrots

MAKES 2 SERVINGS

Want to create a quick vegetarian dish with just a few on-hand ingredients? This makes a great side dish.

> 2 cups vegetable bouillion or water
> 6 small carrots, peeled and sliced lengthwise in quarters
> 2 cups green beans, trimmed
> 1 teaspoon olive oil
> 1 small onion, diced
> 1 small orange, washed, zest and juice
> Salt and pepper to taste
> 2 tablespoons parsley, finely chopped

1. Boil bouillion or water and cook carrots for 8 minutes. Remove carrots, leaving liquid in pot.

2. Add beans to liquid and cook for about 12 minutes, until crisp tender. Remove from liquid.

3. Keep beans and carrots warm.

4. Heat oil in a small skillet and sauté onions until translucent. While onions cook, grate orange peel, then add peel and juice of orange to onions. Add salt and pepper and sauté 5 more minutes.

5. Pour orange juice mixture over carrots and beans and toss well. Transfer to plates and sprinkle with parsley before serving.

6. This is delicious with a plate of rice.

Green beans are a terrific source of fiber and vitamin C. We use green beans in a variety of dishes because they are available year-round.

◆

Vegetables are most nutritious raw. To preserve their vitamins and minerals, vegetables should be cooked gently, until crispy tender, not wilted.

◆

For variety, in place of beans use another high-fiber vegetable, such as broccoli or cauliflower.

Stewed Tomatoes and Cucumbers

MAKES 2 SERVINGS

Simplicity makes this combination of tomatoes and cucumbers work so well. The secret is in the sweetness of the tomatoes—fresh and vine-ripened are best.

> 1 teaspoon canola oil
> 2 medium cucumbers, peeled and sliced into $1/4$-inch pieces
> 2 large tomatoes, diced
> Salt and pepper to taste
> $1/4$ teaspoon sugar
> 2 tablespoons parsley, chopped
> 1 tablespoon Parmesan cheese, grated

1. Heat oil. Add cucumber and tomatoes and sauté on low heat for 15 minutes.

2. Add salt, pepper, and sugar to taste.

3. Sprinkle with parsley and parmesan cheese.

4. This is delicious served over brown rice or a light pasta, such as angel hair or cappellini.

Gently stewing tomatoes and cucumbers brings out the sweet flavors of these summer vegetables.

♦

This is an unusually tasty variation on a cool, crisp tomato-and-cucumber salad. This is a wonderfully light dish, perfect for a warm spring or summer evening.

♦

For variety, use this dish as a layer in a vegetarian lasagna.

Savory Red Cabbage

MAKES 4 SERVINGS

The beautiful color of red cabbage makes this a festive side dish for a special Thanksgiving meal. But it's wonderful anytime, served with potatoes for a strictly vegetarian meal, or with turkey or chicken.

> 2 tablespoons canola oil
> 1 medium onion, diced
> 1 large red cabbage, cut in very thin slices (Discard thick white stems)
> 1 large apple, peeled, cored, and cut in wedges
> 1/2 cup raisins
> 1/2 cup white vinegar
> 3/4 cups water
> Salt and pepper to taste

1. Heat oil in a large pot and sauté onions until translucent.

2. Add cabbage, apple, and raisins.

3. Immediately add vinegar and water.

4. Cover and cook for 45 minutes on low heat, stirring occasionally.

5. Add a little more water if cabbage gets too dry.

6. Add salt and pepper to taste.

Red cabbage is a super source of vitamin C. The most popular way of preparing cabbage is in a cole slaw, a typically high-fat, high-calorie dish.

◆

Here is a flavorful, low-fat way to enjoy the goodness of cabbage. If you only ever eat cabbage in cole slaw, you are in for a delightful surprise!

Leeks in Vinaigrette

MAKES 2 SERVINGS

Aromatic balsamic vinegar adds dazzle to leeks. This recipe seems very gourmet but is so simple to prepare.

> 5 cups water
> 1 teaspoon salt
> 4 medium leeks
> 1 1/2 tablespoons canola oil
> 1 tablespoon balsamic vinegar
> 1 teaspoon Dijon mustard
> 1 tablespoon orange juice
> Salt and pepper to taste

1. Heat water in medium-size pot and add a teaspoon of salt for boiling.

2. Cut off roots and tops of leeks, clean well, and cut in 4-inch lengths. Drop into boiling water for about 15 minutes, or until just tender. Drain and set aside.

3. Mix oil, vinegar, mustard, orange juice, and season to taste with salt and pepper to a creamy consistency.

4. Arrange leeks on a plate and drizzle with dressing.

Leeks are commonly used to flavor broth but have wonderful flavor served on their own as a side dish.

◆

Not only are leeks an excellent source of dietary fiber, they also contain a chemical called allium, which is receiving a lot of attention for its cholesterol-lowering effect.

◆

Enjoy this as a side dish, or as a main dish accompanied with any potato recipe, or simply with peeled, soft boiled potato wedges.

Mashed Potatoes with Basil and Pine Nuts

MAKES 2 SERVINGS

Mashed potato fans will love this dish. The addition of fresh basil and toasted pine nuts make a classic meal even better!

> 6 potatoes (Yukon Gold if available), peeled and boiled in
>   3–4 cups of water until soft
> ½ cup hot milk (skim or soy)
> 1 packed cup fresh basil, very finely chopped (Reserve a
>   few whole leaves for garnish)
> 3 tablespoons pine nuts, toasted
> 1 tablespoon butter (optional)
> Salt and pepper to taste

1. Mash potatoes together with hot milk until creamy.

2. Add basil, pine nuts and butter (optional), and season to taste with salt and pepper, and mix until smooth.

3. Serve this dish alone, garnished with a few leaves of basil, or accompany it with a fresh tomato salad.

Once again, mashed potatoes provide the beginnings of a memorable, flavorful dish.

◆

Puréed potatoes can be used as the basis for many variations on mashed potatoes that incorporate fresh vegetables and herbs.

◆

There is no reason for people trying to lose weight to stay away from mashed potatoes. It's all in the way they are prepared. Traditional recipes are heavy on cream and butter, but potatoes mashed with just skim milk are surprisingly creamy and smooth.

◆

This recipe calls for pine nuts, but you can substitute chopped hazelnuts. To toast the nuts, place them in a nonstick skillet on very low heat. Stir frequently, because they burn easily.

Nouveau Kale

MAKES 4 SERVINGS

This winter dish was a staple in my mother's house. Although she made a traditional dish with lots of meat and sausage, this new version is tastier, lower in fat and higher in energy. The toasted nuts bring out the nutty flavor of this wonderful winter green.

1 tablespoon olive oil
1 small onion, diced
4 cloves garlic, minced
1 ½ pounds kale, cleaned and chopped
½ cup water
¼ cup raisins
¼ cup walnuts or pine nuts, toasted
Salt and pepper to taste

1. Heat olive oil in medium pot. Add onion and garlic and sauté until translucent.

2. Add remaining ingredients to pot and stir well.

3. Cook for approximately 10 minutes, until kale is soft.

4. Serve with rice or mashed potatoes.

Kale is a nutritious winter green. Like other leafy greens, it is a superb source of calcium, vitamin A, and iron.

◆

For readers who like to garden, kale is easy to grow when started from seed in spring or fall. The plants will be ready in time for late fall and winter meals.

◆

When choosing kale at the market, avoid the larger leaves (more than 10 inches), which are tough. Smaller leaves are tender.

Roasted Vegetables

MAKES 2 SERVINGS

While these vegetables roast in a balsamic marinade, your kitchen will become remarkably fragrant. The vinegar draws out the vegetables' subtle flavors. Vegetables never tasted so good!

½ tablespoon balsamic vinegar
1 ½ tablespoons extra virgin olive oil
1 teaspoon salt
1 tablespoon rosemary
1 cup mushrooms, halved
1 cup green beans, broken in half
1 medium onion, sliced
1 medium sweet potato, peeled and cut in large chunks
1 large carrot, peeled and cut in large chunks
5 cloves garlic, peeled

1. Preheat oven to 450°.

2. Prepare marinade in a large bowl, combining vinegar, oil, salt, and rosemary.

3. Add vegetables (including garlic) to the marinade and coat evenly.

4. Spread vegetables out in a shallow baking pan and pour marinade on top.

5. Roast vegetables for 35–40 minutes (or until sweet potato is soft), stirring occasionally. Vegetables are done when they are a warm brown, caramel-like color.

There's nothing more delicious than the flavor of roasted fresh vegetables. Roasting vegetables brings out their naturally sweet juices.

◆

For variety, add other vegetables of your choice. Zucchini, red or green bell pepper, and Roma tomatoes roast very well.

◆

Enjoy roasted vegetables with fresh crusty bread, or spoon them over a plate of basmati rice.

Ciabatta Sandwich

MAKES 4 SERVINGS.

Radishes, oranges, and vinaigrette make this a spirited sandwich.

1 *loaf Ciabatta or French bread*
1 *bunch watercress, stems removed*
1 *bunch radishes, thinly sliced*
2 *small oranges, peeled and thinly sliced*
1 *small cucumber, peeled and thinly sliced*
1 *tablespoon olive oil*
1 *tablespoon balsamic vinegar*
1 *teaspoon Dijon mustard*
1 *garlic clove, mashed*

1. Cut bread lengthwise in half and divide into 4 pieces. Layer watercress, radishes, orange and cucumber slices on 4 halves.

2. Beat together olive oil, vinegar, mustard, and garlic with wire whisk until creamy.

3. Pour vinaigrette over vegetables and bread. Cover with remaining bread and serve.

Thin slices of radish give this sandwich punch. Radishes are high in vitamin C and are easily grown in a simple window box.

◆

Topped with a tangy vinaigrette, this makes a delicious high-energy lunch.

◆

Ciabatta, sometimes called "slipper bread" for its long flat shape, is our favorite Italian bread. It has a light and airy texture, sometimes we nibble on it so much there's very little left for a sandwich!

◆

For variety, substitute watercress with spinach or arugula and add tomato slices.

♦

Tomato Carrot Sandwich

MAKES 2 SERVINGS

This is the ultimate veggie sandwich. We always pack it when we take day hikes or spend the day at the beach.

> Four slices whole wheat bread, toasted
> ½ cup Dijon mustard
> 3 tablespoons, honey
> 2 tablespoons, lemon juice
> ½ avocado, mashed
> ½ cup carrots, peeled and grated
> 1 tablespoon parsley, chopped
> 1 spring green onion, diced
> 1 medium tomato, sliced
> 2 pieces romaine lettuce

1. To prepare honey mustard see #1 on page 272.

2. Spread honey mustard on one slice of bread, avocado on the other slice.

3. Layer carrots, onion, tomato, lettuce, and parsley and top each sandwich with remaining slice of bread.

This sandwich is high in fiber and bursting with vitamin C. Carrots, onions, and avocado are good sources of fiber. You should eat at least two high-fiber foods each day—this sandwich helps meet your daily fiber needs.

♦

For variety, stuff sandwich ingredients in a whole-wheat pita bread or wrap them up in a fresh tortilla.

Sardine Sandwich

MAKES 2 SERVINGS

Simple to prepare but so delicious you will savor every bite. Pumpernickel and sardines are two strong flavors that complement each other well. This is a perfect high-energy lunch, especially when served with a fresh raw vegetable salad.

4 slices Pumpernickel bread
3³/₄-ounce can brisling sardines
4 scallions, thinly sliced
Fresh lemon juice

1. Break off tails of sardines.

2. Arrange a layer of sardines on one slice of bread, top with scallions, and drizzle with lemon juice. Top with second slice of bread and serve.

Canned brisling sardines are more than just a delicacy, they are healthy for you.

◆

Sardines are one of the very best source of calcium to help prevent osteoporosis. They also provide special fatty acids (omega-3s) to help keep our arteries clean and prevent heart attacks and strokes. Sardines are also rich in selenium, zinc, chromium and iron.

◆

Sardines are obviously a wonderful addition to your regular diet and this tasty sardine sandwich will appeal even to those who have not been sardine lovers.

Arugula, Lettuce, and Tomato Sandwich

MAKES 2 SERVINGS

This is a favorite lunch in spring or summer, when arugula is in abundance. Parmesan and tomato make this a surprisingly substantial sandwich, flavored with aromatic balsamic vinegar.

> Baguette or any crusty bread
> 2 leafs lettuce
> 4 leafs arugula
> 1 medium tomato, sliced thin
> ½ teaspoon oil
> 1 teaspoon balsamic vinegar
> Parmesan cheese, grated

1. Cut bread lengthwise in half and top with layers of vegetables, beginning with lettuce, arugula, and tomatoes.

2. Sprinkle vegetables with oil, vinegar, and Parmesan cheese. Top with another slice of bread or serve open-faced.

Fresh greens bring distinct and unusual flavors to any "garden-variety" salad. This salad is anything but ordinary—we serve it on bread!

◆

One of the keys to eating a more vegetarian-based diet is learning how to turn salads from simple into spectacular.

◆

For variety, and extra iron, use spinach instead of lettuce leaves.

Ecumenical Bagel

MAKES 2 SERVINGS

We love bagels, lox, and cream cheese for Sunday brunch, or lunch anytime, but sometimes we prefer this vegetarian version of the classic.

> 1 medium green bell pepper, seeded and sliced
> 2 medium tomatoes, sliced ¼-inch thick
> 1 red onion, sliced ¼-inch thick
> 2 onion bagels, sliced in half
> Reduced fat cream cheese
> Lemon pepper

1. Preheat oven to 400°.

2. Spread bell pepper, tomatoes, and onions on a sheet of aluminum foil (shiny side up).

3. Roast vegetables for about 15 minutes. Remove from oven and wrap foil around vegetables to keep them warm.

4. Toast bagels. Spread a thin layer of cream cheese on each half, top with roasted vegetables. Sprinkle with a dash of lemon pepper and serve open-faced.

This traditional Jewish sandwich doesn't have to be high in fat and calories. It can even be converted to suit a vegetarian's tastes.

◆

There are many reduced-fat cream cheeses, or you can use just a thin spread of regular cream cheese.

◆

We like to use onion bagels because they are so flavorful, but you can use any variety, such as sesame or poppy seed, egg or plain.

Roasted Vegetable Sandwich

MAKES 2 SERVINGS

Whenever we picnic with friends, we always include roasted vegetables. They make a delicious sandwich on a baguette.

> 2 *red bell peppers, sliced*
> 1 *large zucchini, sliced*
> 1 *large onion, thinly sliced*
> 2 *garlic cloves, peeled and thinly sliced*
> 1 *fresh baguette*
> ½ *cup Parmesan cheese, grated*
>
> *Marinade:*
> 3 *tablespoons balsamic vinegar*
> 2 *tablespoons olive oil*
> 1 *tablespoon molasses*
> 1 *tablespoon fresh basil, chopped*
> 1 *tablespoon fresh thyme (or substitute 1 teaspoon Italian*
>   *herbs, dried)*

1. Combine marinade ingredients in a large bowl. Add cut vegetables and let stand for 60 minutes, then drain. Arrange peppers, zucchini, onion and garlic on a baking sheet covered with foil (shiny side up) and bake at 400° for approximately 30 minutes, until vegetables are golden brown.

2. For sandwiches, slice baguette in half and layer vegetables on bread. Sprinkle with Parmesan cheese.

3. As a dinner suggestion, serve grilled vegetables over brown rice and complement with fresh green salad.

Vegetables are easy to roast in the oven. But if you have the time, vegetables turn a summertime barbecue into a healthy, low-fat delight.

◆

Summer is the perfect time for grilling, and the season offers a variety of flavorful vegetables.

◆

Whether you prepare these vegetables in the oven or over the coals, you'll enjoy their succulent, smoky sweet flavors.

◆

Picnic Energy Sandwich

MAKES 2 SERVINGS

This sandwich has become legendary! We first encountered the original energy sandwich on St. John's Island, in The Caribbean, where we had the tangiest honey mustard ever! Back home, we tried infinite variations on this island favorite. Our friends and family say this one is the absolute best.

> ½ cup Dijon mustard
> 3 tablespoons honey
> 2 tablespoons lemon
> 2 small loaves of French bread
> Garlic cheese spread (such as Rondele)
> 2 slices Norwegian smoked salmon (optional)
> 1 avocado, peeled and sliced
> 1 tomato, sliced
> 1 cup alfalfa sprouts

1. To prepare honey mustard: Combine the Dijon mustard, honey, and lemon juice. Whisk well.

2. Cut bread lengthwise and spread honey mustard on two halves.

3. On top of honey mustard, spread a thin layer of garlic cheese spread. Top with smoked salmon if desired. Then begin adding layers of vegetables in this order: avocado, tomato, sprouts.

4. Serve with plenty of napkins!

Be creative with sandwiches. They can be a great high-energy lunch in the middle of your working day or on a weekend picnic.

◆

We love to use avocado in sandwiches. We know it is high in fat, but the fat in an avocado is not the same as the fat in a strip of bacon or slice of pastrami! Avocados are a wonderful source of vitamins.

◆

Very Veggie Burgers

MAKES 10 PATTIES

These burgers are delicious on fresh sourdough bread or a whole-wheat bun. Kids love them as much as adults.

1 tablespoon canola oil
½ pound mushrooms, quartered
1 small onion, diced
2 tablespoons walnuts or sunflower seeds
1 large carrot, coarsely grated
1 tablespoon apple peeled and grated
1 teaspoon marjoram
Salt and pepper to taste
1 cup green beans, cooked to crisp tender
1 cup Garbanzo beans, drained
1 tablespoon tahini or peanut butter
1 tablespoon Worcestershire sauce
3 tablespoons bread crumbs
1 egg white

1. Heat oil in a large skillet. Add mushrooms, onions, nuts, carrot, apple, and marjoram. Sauté until mushrooms appear golden brown. Add salt and pepper to taste.

2. Transfer vegetables to medium-size bowl and add green beans, garbanzos, tahini or peanut butter, Worcestershire sauce, and bread crumbs.

3. Combine everything well and put in a food processor. Pulse 3 or 4 times. Mixture should be a coarse consistency. Mix in egg white.

4. Form mixture into palm-sized patties.

5. Bake on a nonstick baking sheet in oven at 450° for 15 minutes; turn over patties and cook another 15 minutes. Alternatively, fry patties in a skillet with light coating of canola oil until golden brown.

◆

We've searched all over the world for the best veggie burger. Some taste too much like soy, some have a gummy texture, some simply fall apart!

◆

Veggie burgers are a healthy alternative to hamburgers, but unless they are pleasurable to eat and tasty, why would anyone switch?

◆

Some veggie burgers try too hard to resemble hamburgers. That's not our goal with this recipe. We've created a healthy and delicious, low-fat burger that is sure to win over even the toughest skeptics!

◆

For variety, use this recipe to make a veggie loaf.

ENTREES

White Cabbage and Potatoes

MAKES 4 SERVINGS

This dish is sure to warm hearts and bellies on a late autumn or cold winter's night. Cabbage and potatoes are a soothing and filling combination.

1 tablespoon canola oil
1 medium onion, diced
½ teaspoon sugar
1 small white cabbage, shredded finely
½ cup water
1 teaspoon caraway seeds
5 medium-size potatoes (Yukon Gold if available), peeled
   and cut in quarters
Salt and pepper to taste

1. Heat oil in large pot, add onion, and sauté until golden. Sprinkle with sugar.

2. Add cabbage and cook on high heat until cabbage is slightly browned (about 10 minutes), stirring often to prevent burning.

3. Add water and caraway seeds, cover, and cook on low heat for 40 minutes. Season to taste with salt and pepper, and add more water if too dry.

4. While cabbage cooks, in a separate kettle boil potatoes until soft.

5. Drain potatoes and combine with cabbage. Serve warm.

Potatoes are a superior source of complex carbohydrates, vitamins, and minerals. Eating more of this type of carbohydrate is a wonderful way to cut down on fat in your diet without feeling starved. Potatoes are one of the most filling foods, and are so good for you.

♦

Potatoes only become high-fat when topped with butter and sour cream, or whipped with milk and butter.

♦

Here is a delicious way to enjoy potatoes, mixed with the goodness of cabbage. The presence of caraway seeds in this recipe is a wonderful remedy for the gassiness some people experience from cabbage.

Mushroom-Stuffed Pasta Shells

MAKES 4 SERVINGS

Every shell is stuffed with a delightful surprise of mushrooms and cheese. This is a perfect substantial dinner that is delicious any time of the year.

> 2 teaspoons olive or canola oil
> 1 small onion, minced (½ cup)
> 1 garlic clove, minced
> 1¼ pounds mushrooms, chopped
> 2 tablespoons chopped fresh rosemary
> 1 tablespoon chopped fresh parsley
> 1 cup crumbled feta cheese
> ½ cup pine nuts
> ¼ cup raisins
> Salt and freshly ground black pepper
> 20 jumbo pasta shells
> 4 cups Simply Fresh or Best Basic Tomato Sauce (pages
>   228 and 230)
> Chopped parsley for garnish

1. Preheat oven to 350°.

2. Heat oil in a nonstick skillet, add the onion, and sauté 2–3 minutes. Add the garlic and mushrooms and sauté a few minutes more, stirring from time to time. Stir in the rosemary and parsley and continue to cook until the liquid from the mushrooms has evaporated. Remove from heat. Stir in half the cheese, the pine nuts, and the raisins, and season lightly. Let cool.

3. Cook the pasta shells in a large saucepan of boiling water until barely al dente. Drain well and dry on paper towels before filling.

4. Fill the pasta shells with the mushroom mixture. Arrange the filled shells in a large baking dish, pour the tomato sauce over and around them, and then sprinkle with the remaining cheese. Cover dish with foil and bake in the preheated oven for 30–40 minutes.

5. Sprinkle with chopped parsley.

◆

Pasta shells can be stuffed with virtually any ingredients. Fresh mushrooms and herbs are the tastiest filling we've tried. This recipe is always a hit, even with meat-and-potato types!

◆

The addition of fresh rosemary makes this dish especially flavorful and fragrant.

◆

This dish is unbelievably good the next day—even cold!

Farfalle with Beans and Tuna

MAKES 4 SERVINGS

This is a perfect dish to prepare when you have unexpected guests. It's simple but delicious and can be enjoyed year-round.

1 tablespoon olive oil
1 large onion, finely diced
4 cloves garlic, mashed
2 tablespoons Vermouth Rosso (optional)
8 fresh tomatoes, peeled and diced, or 1 28-ounce can
   crushed tomatoes
1 10-ounce package frozen lima beans, defrosted
1 teaspoon sugar
Salt and pepper to taste
1 tablespoon oregano
1 can tuna in water, drained and cut into small chunks
1 pound farfalle (bowtie pasta)

1. Heat olive oil in large pot. Add onion and garlic and sauté until translucent. Add vermouth.

2. Add tomatoes, beans, sugar, and oregano. Season to taste with salt and pepper. Cook on medium-low heat for 15 minutes.

3. Mix tuna into sauce and simmer for about 3 minutes, until tuna is just warm.

4. While sauce is simmering, cook pasta to al dente and, mix together with sauce, and serve.

This dish proves there are delicious ways to eat high-protein meals without relying on high-fat red meat.

◆

Pasta, beans, and tuna combine to create a dish packed with energy but low in fat. This is a classic italian combination, where beans play a prominent role in cooking.

◆

Not only are beans a super source of protein, they are also high in fiber, iron and other minerals.

Spaghetti with Tomatoes and Arugula

MAKES 4 SERVINGS

The freshness of spring or summertime comes alive in this light but satisfying dish. It takes less than a half hour to prepare—perfect if you'd rather sit down and enjoy a beautiful sunset instead of toiling over a hot stove.

> 1 pound spaghetti
> 2 tablespoons balsamic vinegar
> 2 tablespoons orange juice
> 1/2 teaspoon Dijon mustard
> 1 tablespoon olive oil
> Salt and pepper to taste
> 8 medium tomatoes, diced
> 1 bunch arugula, chopped

1. Cook spaghetti in boiling water until al dente.

2. While spaghetti cooks, mix vinegar, orange juice, and mustard in a medium bowl. Whisk together well.

3. Slowly add oil, and season with salt, and pepper. Add tomatoes and arugula and mix well.

4. Pour tomato mixture over spaghetti and gently toss.

Arugu-what? *Arugula . . . This flavorful leafy green has only recently made it into mainstream cooking. It is now a staple in California cuisine, and because it is rich in calcium and vitamins, we think it deserves its place in all healthy cooking.*

◆

If you garden, arugula is simple to grow. With a little care, one plant will thrive throughout the summer.

Vegetable Risotto

MAKES 2 SERVINGS

This risotto is rich and creamy but very low in fat. Asparagus and asagio cheese are a memorable combination. Look for the freshest, most tender stalks of asparagus available.

2 cups trimmed asparagus tips
3 cups water
1 tablespoon olive or canola oil
2 shallots, chopped (about ¼ cup)
1 garlic clove, minced
1½ cups short-grain or Arborio rice
Vegetable broth recipe (page 237)
Pinch of saffron threads (optional)
Strip of lemon peel
1 tablespoon lemon juice
2 cups sliced button mushrooms
8 sundried tomatoes packed in oil, well drained and
   chopped
½ cup chopped walnuts or cashew nuts, toasted
Salt and freshly ground black pepper
Roughly chopped flat-leaf parsley and large shavings of
   Asagio cheese (optional) for garnish

1. Put asparagus in a small saucepan of boiling water and cook until barely tender, 2–3 minutes. Drain, reserving cooking liquid. Refresh the asparagus in ice water and set aside.

2. Heat oil in a heavy saucepan. Add shallots and garlic and sauté 2–3 minutes. Stir in rice and cook 3 minutes, stirring occasionally.

3. Add enough vegetable broth to the reserved asparagus cooking liquid to make 3 cups. Add to the pan the saffron threads, if using, and lemon peel and juice. Bring to a boil, then reduce heat, cover, and simmer 10 minutes.

4. Add mushrooms and sundried tomatoes and cook, covered, until rice is tender—another 10 minutes. Stir in asparagus and nuts for the last few minutes of cooking.

5. Remove lemon peel, season to taste, and transfer to a warm dish. Sprinkle with chopped parsley and large shavings of Asagio cheese, if using. Serve risotto at once.

Risotto is a wonderfully creamy Italian rice. It has a texture and flavor that is simply out of this world. This dish takes a little longer to prepare, but it is well worth the extra time.

◆

An endless variety of ingredients can be added to the basic risotto. Asparagus is a particularly delicious variation, but you can substitute radicchio, green peas, spring onions, mushrooms, or beans.

Rigatoni with Asparagus and Parsley

MAKES 4 SERVINGS

This is a delicious springtime pasta, when asparagus is abundant. We buy huge bunches of it at the farmer's market on Saturday mornings and enjoy it throughout the week. This is our favorite recipe, filled with the freshness and sweet flavors of spring.

½ pound asparagus, cut into 2-inch pieces
2 cups water
1 teaspoon salt
1 teaspoon olive oil
2 cloves garlic, mashed
2 tomatoes, peeled, cut in wedges
2 tablespoons parsley, finely chopped
Salt and pepper to taste
Shaved parmesan cheese
1 pound rigatoni

1. Put asparagus in medium-size pot. Add just enough water to cover asparagus. Add salt and cook for approximately 12 minutes (depending on size) until asparagus is crisp tender.

2. Heat oil and sauté garlic until just fragrant.

3. Add asparagus, tomatoes and parsley. Season to taste with salt, and pepper. Stir well. Cover and turn heat to lowest setting.

4. Cook pasta to al dente.

5. Drain pasta and combine with asparagus mixture. Divide onto four plates and top with shaved parmesan.

6. Serve with a fresh green salad.

Asparagus is our favorite spring vegetable, at its peak between April and July. Especially in California, where 70 percent of the country's asparagus is grown, we can even find it fresh in the stores between February and July.

◆

♦

When selecting asparagus, choose firm stalks with tightly closed tips.

♦

Asparagus is best served the day you buy it, but will keep in the refrigerator for four or five days. If fresh asparagus is not available, frozen stalks or canned asparagus will do.

♦

Asparagus is a wonderful source of vitamin A, which is beneficial for eyesight.

Pasta with Bread Crumbs and Spinach

MAKES 4 SERVINGS

This Sicilian dish harmonizes the distinct flavors of garlic, lemon, and spinach with the sweetness of basil and raisins. Enjoy it with a glass of Chianti for a deeply pleasing meal.

> 1 tablespoon olive oil
> 1/2 yellow onion, diced
> 5 cloves garlic, minced
> 4 cups fresh spinach, stemmed and chopped; or one 10 ounce package frozen, chopped spinach, thawed and drained
> 2 tablespoons canola oil
> 1 cup plain bread crumbs
> 1/2 cup shredded parmesan cheese
> 1 cup fresh basil chopped, or 1 tablespoon dried basil
> 1 tablespoon grated lemon or orange zest
> 1/4 cup raisins
> 1 pound farfalle (bowtie pasta)
> Salt and pepper to taste

1. In a large sauté pan or skillet heat 1 tablespoon olive oil and sauté onion and garlic until golden brown. Add spinach and cook until just wilted. Season to taste with salt and pepper. Transfer spinach to a bowl and set aside.

2. In the *same pan* heat 2 tablespoons canola oil and stir in bread crumbs.

3. Add breadcrumbs, parmesan cheese, basil, lemon or orange zest, and raisins. Sauté over *low* heat 3–5 minutes, stirring frequently. Remove from heat.

4. Cook pasta al dente, drain, and transfer to large serving bowl. Combine pasta with spinach and bread crumb mixture and serve immediately.

♦

This dish has its origins in Sicily and fits perfectly with the new low-fat tastes of more and more Americans.

♦

Greens and grains make this a healthful dinner, high in fiber and vitamins and low in calories and animal fat.

♦

Enjoy variations on this dish by substituting any winter green, such as Swiss chard or kale. These winter greens are abundant sources of vitamins and iron.

Healthy Lasagna or Roll–ups

MAKES 6 SERVINGS

This wonderful pasta dish inspired by our very good friend Debbie Oliphant is absolutely delicious. You'll fill up on a healthy dish and look forward to leftovers the next day.

> 2 pounds fresh spinach, blanched
> 1 cup pine nuts, toasted (or substitute chopped walnuts)
> 2 cloves garlic, mashed
> 1 cup low-fat mozzarella cheese, shredded
> $\frac{1}{2}$ cup raisins
> 1 egg white
> Salt and pepper to taste
> 9–12 lasagna noodles, cooked al dente
> Tomato sauce (according to season, use Simply Fresh or
>   Best Basic recipes on pages 228 and 230)

1. Drain blanched spinach, let cool down, and squeeze out all liquid. Chop fine.

2. Add toasted nuts, garlic, mozzarella, raisins and egg white to the spinach. Season to taste with salt and pepper.

3. Cover bottom of 9-inch × 9-inch baking dish with a little tomato sauce.

4. Place one layer of lasagna noodles, then one layer of spinach mixture. Add another layer of sauce, then noodles, then spinach mixture and repeat using remaining noodles, spinach mixture and sauce, making 3–4 layers total. Top with tomato sauce.

5. Cover with foil and bake at 350° for 30 minutes. Remove foil and bake another 15 minutes.

6. To make roll-ups, lay lasagna noodles on a flat surface and spread about 2 tablespoons of spinach mixture on top of each noodle. Roll noodles up and place them seam-side down in the baking dish. Top with tomato sauce, cover with foil and bake.

7. Serve with Caesar salad.

◆

One variation to try: make your mixture using half spinach and half kale, which packs a healthy punch of vitamins and anti-oxidants.

◆

A handful of nuts a few times a week, such as in this recipe, seems to make for a healthier heart, and this is a great way to have them. Along with the sauce of your choice, you can also add sliced mushrooms and red peppers.

◆

You will only need about 9 noodles, but in cooking some will break so be sure to cook more if you are making roll-ups.

Spaghetti with Lentil Tomato Sauce

MAKES 2 SERVINGS

Even spaghetti and meatball lovers will rave about this dish! Lentils give this recipe great flavor and texture.

   2 teaspoons olive oil
   1 medium carrot, thinly sliced
   1 medium onion, diced
   3 garlic cloves, minced
   1 28-ounce can whole peeled tomatoes
   1 teaspoon Italian herbs (i.e., basil, parsley, oregano)
   3/4 cup dried brown or green lentils
   Salt, pepper, and sugar to taste
   1 16-ounce package spaghetti

1. Heat oil in medium-size pot and sauté carrot, onion, and garlic over medium heat for about 5 minutes. Stir frequently so garlic doesn't burn.

2. Empty the canned tomatoes together with liquid into a medium-size bowl and mash with potato masher.

3. Add mashed tomatoes, Italian herbs, and lentils to sautéed vegetables and stir well. Simmer over low to medium heat for about 40 minutes, adding water if necessary to keep the sauce from becoming too thick. Sauce should be the consistency of a meat or bolognese sauce. Season to taste with salt and pepper.

4. Cook spaghetti in boiling water until al dente. Combine pasta with sauce and serve.

This creative combination of grains and lentils provides plenty of carbohydrates, fiber, and protein.

◆

◆

This meal will give your body long-lasting energy and satisfy your taste buds and hunger.

◆

Lentils are easy to prepare. They are the only legume that does not have to be pre-soaked before cooking.

◆

This makes a wonderful filling for lasagna. It tastes even better than ground up meat!

Pasta with Buckwheat

MAKES 2 SERVINGS AS A MAIN DISH,
4 AS A SIDE DISH

The simplicity of this dish is the key to its good taste. Pasta and buckwheat blend in a wonderful texture. Our family calls this traditional dish, Kasha Varnishkes.

> 2 cups water
> 2 cups farfalle pasta (bowtie pasta)
> 1 cup kasha (roasted buckwheat groats)
> 1 teaspoon butter
> 1 medium onion, minced
> Salt and pepper to taste

1. Boil 2 cups of water in medium saucepan. Add the kasha and return to a boil. Reduce heat, cover and simmer gently until tender, about 10–15 minutes.

2. Cook the pasta until al dente.

3. Melt butter in a small skillet, add the onion, and sauté until lightly browned, stirring frequently.

4. Add the onion to the cooked kasha. Drain the pasta and lightly toss with the kasha and onion mixture. Serve immediately. Tastes great with cucumber salad as a side dish.

Buckwheat, also known as kasha, is a high-fiber grain. It also provides good supplies of magnesium, vitamin B_6, zinc, copper, and iron.

◆

This is a simple dish, combining pasta and kasha, for a filling high-fiber, high-energy meal.

Eggplant Rollatini

MAKES 4 SERVINGS

Thanks to the magnificent chefs at Canyon Ranch, this delicious and healthy meal is low in calories and fat. For variety, we sometimes substitute fresh garden zucchini for eggplant.

2/3 cup bread crumbs
1 tablespoon parmesan cheese
1/4 teaspoon dried ground basil
1/4 teaspoon dried ground rosemary
1/4 teaspoon dried ground parsley
1/4 teaspoon dried ground thyme
3/4 cup part-skim ricotta cheese
1 pound eggplant, cut into 12 slices about 1/4-inch thick
1 cup tomato sauce
2 tablespoons gratred part-skim mozzarella cheese
4 ounces spaghetti or linguini

1. Preheat oven to 350°.

2. Combine bread crumbs, parmesan cheese, and half of herbs in a small bowl and set aside.

3. In small bowl, mix remaining half of herbs into ricotta cheese and set aside.

4. Steam eggplant slices until pliable, about 3 to 5 minutes.

5. Lay each eggplant slice in bread crumbs, patting to be assured the coating will stick.

6. Spoon 1 tablespoon of ricotta cheese mixture near edge of each slice of eggplant and roll to form a tube.

7. Arrange eggplant rolls in shallow 8-inch × 11-inch baking dish. Sprinkle extra crumbs over them and top evenly with tomato sauce and mozzarella cheese. Bake until heated through, about 30 minutes.

8. While rollatini are baking, cook pasta, drain, and divide evenly among 4 plates.

9. Place 3 eggplant rollatini over pasta and serve immediately.

Italian cooking makes the most of fresh seasonal vegetables. Italian home cooking entails a daily trip to the market, where fresh vegetables fill the stands. One of the most enjoyable pastimes on our Italian vacations is to sit at a sidewalk café and watch the animated conversations between grocers and customers as they compare the size and color of fresh bell peppers, smell the fragrance of freshly picked basil, and select the firmest, reddest vine-ripened Roma tomatoes.

◆

Eggplant is a staple of Italian cooking. In Italy, eggplant is rarely fried, as it is here in the states. In this low-fat recipe (only 8 grams of fat per serving), the unique flavor of eggplant is enhanced with Italian herbs and tomatoes.

◆

Pasta with Tomatoes and Cheese

MAKES 4 SERVINGS

This is a delicious dish in late summer, when tomatoes are at their ripest. The delicate cottage cheese balances the flavors of tomatoes, fresh basil, and garlic.

4 large beefsteak tomatoes, diced
3/4 cup low-fat cottage cheese, large curd
1/4 cup fresh basil chopped
1 large garlic clove, minced
2 tablespoons olive oil
Salt and pepper to taste
1 pound penne or fusilli pasta
Freshly grated Romano cheese for garnish (optional)

1. Combine tomatoes, cottage cheese, basil, garlic, oil, salt, and pepper in bowl. Mix together gently. Time permitting, let stand for about 15 minutes so the flavors mingle.

2. Cook pasta until al dente. Drain and return to saucepan. Add tomato mixture and fold together gently.

3. Taste and adjust seasoning. Sprinkle with Romano cheese, if desired, and serve immediately.

4. Makes a great lunch the next day, served cold.

You can enjoy a creamy pasta sauce without the high fat. Instead of cream and butter, this sauce uses low-fat cottage cheese, which gives this recipe great texture.

◆

Cottage cheese comes in both 1 percent and 2 percent low-fat varieties, with 1 and 2 grams of fat per 4 ounce serving, respectively. Either is a small fraction of the fat content from the heavy creams that are usually the basis for a creamy pasta sauce.

Orange Couscous with Vegetables

MAKES 2 SERVINGS

As the couscous cooks, it soaks up the orange juice and garlic and becomes intensely aromatic and tasty. This meal is a delight for all your senses.

> 1 tablespoon canola oil
> Medium onion, finely diced
> 2 cloves garlic, minced
> ½ red pepper, cut into ½″ slices
> 2 tablespoons raisins
> 1 cup orange juice
> ½ cup frozen lima beans, defrosted and blanched (fresh
>   lima beans, blanched if available)
> 1 cup water
> ¾ cup couscous, uncooked
> Salt and pepper to taste

1. Heat oil in a medium pot. Add onion and garlic and sauté until translucent.

2. Add red pepper, raisins, and orange juice. Sauté for 15 minutes.

3. Add lima beans and water. Stir and bring to a boil.

4. Stir in couscous. Remove from heat and let stand for 5 minutes without stirring.

5. Fluff with fork and serve with crispy cucumber or tomato salad.

Couscous is a nutty, aromatic grain. Combined with vegetables, it is an excellent source of energy and a delicious way to lower fat in your diet.

◆

This grain is a staple of Middle Eastern cooking. It is a hard wheat semolina, cracked, ground and rolled in flour.

◆

Among the grains, this is one of the easiest and fastest to prepare. Overcooked couscous will lose its light and fluffy texture.

Asparagus Chicken

MAKES 4 SERVINGS

The appealing and unusual flavors of this dish consistently draw
raves from family and friends. Delicate asparagus and mushrooms
are dazzled with capers and lemon juice.

1 ½ tablespoon canola oil
1 onion, finely chopped
2 cups mushrooms, sliced
2 whole skinless chicken breasts, cut into chunks
(1 pound tofu for vegetarian version, drained and cut into
    chunks)
3 tablespoons all purpose flour
1 cup water
2 pounds fresh asparagus tips or one 15-ounce can (save
    liquid)
2 tablespoons capers
Juice of ½ lemon
½ tablespoon sugar
½ tablespoon salt
½ teaspoon pepper
2 cups Basmati rice
4 cups water
1 tablespoon fresh parsley, chopped

1. Heat oil in a medium pot and sauté onions until translucent.
   Add mushrooms and sauté until they turn light brown.

2. Add chicken and sauté until it appears white on all sides, about
   10 minutes.

3. Sprinkle flour over chicken and stir well. Add water, asparagus
   and its juice, capers, lemon juice, sugar, salt and pepper. Cover.
   Cook on low heat for 35 to 40 minutes, stirring occasionally.

4. In the meantime, cook Basmati rice in water; follow directions
   on package.

5. Serve the asparagus chicken mixture over rice and sprinkle it with parsley.

The festivity of traditional German cooking is captured in this low-fat chicken dish. Capers and asparagus add unmistakable flavor.

◆

Try serving over halved puff pastry shells. Guests love it.

◆

This entrée is easily transformed into a vegetarian meal by substituting tofu for chicken.

Turkey Meatloaf

MAKES 4 SERVINGS

Canyon Ranch has taken the high-fat American standard meatloaf and turned it into a healthful, low-fat meal—not your average, ho-hum meatloaf!

$^1\!/_4$ cup diced onion
$^3\!/_4$ pound ground skinless turkey breast
$^3\!/_4$ cup dry whole-wheat bread crumbs
1 egg white
Pinch salt
Pinch black pepper
$^1\!/_2$ cup tomato sauce
$1^1\!/_2$ teaspoons Worcestershire sauce

1. Preheat oven to 350°. Lightly spray baking sheet or loaf pan with nonstick vegetable coating and set aside.

2. Combine all ingredients in large bowl and mix well.

3. Form meat into loaf shape on baking sheet or put in loaf pan. Bake about 40 minutes or until loaf is firm to the touch.

This is a perfect meal for you and your family if you are making the transition away from red meat to a more vegetarian-based diet.

♦

Turkey is much lower in fat than red meat. In fact, one serving of this meatloaf has only 4 grams of fat.

♦

Breaded Chicken

MAKES 2 SERVINGS

In Germany, we call this Schnitzel. But instead of pork or veal, traditionally found in most restaurants, this recipe uses chicken. When we are in the mood for a flesh-based meal, this is one of our favorites.

> 2 skinless chicken breast fillets, pounded thin
> Salt and pepper
> 2 tablespoons all purpose flour
> 1 egg white, beaten lightly
> 2 tablespoons bread crumbs
> 3 tablespoons canola oil
> Juice of 1/2 lemon (optional)

1. Sprinkle chicken with salt and pepper. Dip chicken first, in flour to coat evenly, then dip in egg whites, followed by bread crumbs.

2. Heat oil in a large skillet and fry chicken on both sides on medium heat for about 15 minutes, until golden brown and well done. Shake skillet occasionally to prevent burning.

3. Drain chicken on paper towels to remove excess oil. Squeeze lemon juice over chicken and serve with Potato Salad, noodles and brown gravy.

Poultry, in moderation, can be part of a low-fat, high-energy diet. Many traditional meat dishes can be lightened up by substituting chicken for red meat.

♦

When chicken or other flesh food is a part of your meal, accompany it with lots of vegetables for energy balance. This recipe harmonizes well with Potato Cucumber Salad.

♦

Enjoy this dish hot for dinner, or cold on a sandwich the next day, with some Dijon mustard and sauerkraut. This makes an unusual and delicious sandwich.

Chicken Goulash

MAKES 4 SERVINGS

This was the traditional Sunday meal in my house when I was growing up, but my mother prepared it with pork and beef. I created this healthier version so that I can still enjoy the wonderful fragrance and memories of this meal.

2 tablespoons canola oil

2 medium onions, diced

2 skinless chicken breast fillets, cut into 2-inch chunks

16 ounces of mushrooms (brown if available) cut in half

4 cloves garlic, sliced

1 tablespoon tomato paste

4 cups water

1/2 cup beer (optional)

1 teaspoon sugar

1 teaspoon paprika

Salt and pepper to taste

1 lb. wide noodles

1. Heat oil in a large pot and add onions. Sauté until golden.

2. Add chicken. Stir frequently until chicken is golden brown, being careful not to burn.

3. Add mushrooms and garlic. Stir well. Cook for 10 minutes.

4. Add tomato paste and stir well for about 5 minutes.

5. Turn heat to medium/low. Slowly begin adding water, 1 cup at a time (also add beer). Let each cup cook down a bit before adding more (this creates a nice, strong gravy).

6. Cover and simmer for 45 minutes, stirring occasionally. Add sugar and paprika, then salt and pepper to taste.

7. Serve over wide noodles, with Swabian Cucumber Salad and Swabian Potato Salad for an authentic German dinner.

◆

Traditional goulash is filled with pork and beef—a dish so high in fat it can make your heart race just thinking about it! But this low-fat version replaces red meat with poultry for a hearty and heart-healthy goulash.

◆

Poultry is a good source of protein. To reduce fat from chicken, be sure to remove all skin and any visible fat.

◆

For a strictly vegetarian version, use portobello mushrooms instead of chicken. Portobellos are "meaty" and flavorful, and make a perfect vegetarian goulash.

Halibut on Vegetables

MAKES 2 SERVINGS

Fish and vegetables are a winning high-energy combination. You won't believe how tasty this is.

> 2 halibut steaks
> Salt and pepper to taste
> Juice of 1 lemon
> 1 cup water
> 2 cups carrots, cut in 2-inch slices
> 2 medium potatoes, cut in 2-inch cubes
> 2 cups green peas
> 2 tablespoons Crème Fraîche or low-fat sour cream
> ³/₄ tablespoon Dijon mustard
> 1 teaspoon Worcestershire sauce
> 2 tablespoons parsley, chopped

1. Preheat oven to 350°.

2. Clean and wash fish. Sprinkle with salt and lemon juice.

3. In a large pot, pour 1 cup water and add carrots and potatoes. Boil about 10 minutes, until vegetables are crisp tender, but not mushy. Reserve water.

4. While vegetables cook, mix crème fraîche with mustard and Worcestershire sauce until smooth. Add salt and pepper to taste.

5. Add crème fraîche mixture and parsley to pot with water and vegetables and stir well.

6. Transfer vegetable mixture to a 9″ × 9″ casserole dish. Lay halibut on top of vegetables. Cover with foil and bake in the oven on low heat for about 20–30 minutes, until fish is opaque and flaky.

7. Transfer vegetables and fish to plates and serve hot.

Fish has many nutritional and health benefits. We try to eat fish each week.

♦

Fish contains omega-3 fatty acids, the unsaturated fats that may help lower choles-terol levels in the blood. Fish also provides niacin, riboflavin, vitamins B_6 and B_{12}, and at least a dozen important minerals, including calcium, magnesium, and potassium.

◆

Halibut is very lean and nutritious. If halibut is unavailable, select any other fresh, light fish, such as sea bass. This recipe also works with swordfish, shrimp or scallops. Also experiment with other seasonal vegetables, such as cauliflower and red pepper.

Turkey Burgers

MAKES 4 SERVINGS

These patties are delicious as an entrée, served with red cabbage, potatoes and gravy, or served between a whole-wheat bun or sourdough bread with mustard, ketchup, and thinly sliced pickles.

> 2 *slices bread*
> 1 *medium onion, minced*
> 2 *tablespoons canola oil*
> 24 *ounces ground turkey, extra lean*
> 1 *tablespoon parsley, minced*
> 1 *egg*
> 1 *teaspoon salt*
> *Pepper to taste*
> 1 *tablespoon Maggi seasoning*

1. Soak bread in water for 5 minutes, then squeeze out all water, completely.

2. In a large skillet, sauté onion in 1 teaspoon oil until browned, stirring frequently.

3. In a large bowl mix sautéed onion with turkey and bread, parsley, egg, salt, pepper, and Maggi. Add a little water if too dry.

4. Form palm-sized patties and fry in remaining tablespoon oil until golden brown on each side until well done. Use a nonstick pan if possible. Drain on paper towel.

Ground turkey makes a much lighter and lower fat burger than ground red meat. Be certain to choose extra lean turkey.

♦

This is a great meal for families making the transition away from red meat toward a more vegetarian-based diet.

♦

The fat content of regular hamburgers gets even higher when cheese and high-fat condiments such as mayonnaise are added. These burgers are so flavorful, they don't need those high-fat extras.

Tin Foil Salmon and Vegetables

MAKES 4 SERVINGS

This is our absolute favorite fish dish. It is easy, fast, and actually fun to prepare, and even more fun to eat. We've experimented with the ingredients from thyme to thyme, but this original recipe is the winning combination.

> 4–6 stalks celery, diced
> 4 spring onions, diced (or regular onions)
> 4 medium carrots, peeled and cut in ¼ inch pieces
> ½ tablespoon canola oil
> 2 pounds salmon fillet, cut into 4 pieces
> 2 ripe tomatoes, sliced
> 1 lemon, sliced
> 4 basil leaves
> ¼ teaspoon fresh thyme, or a pinch dried
> Salt and fresh-ground pepper to taste
> 4 squares (12 × 12 each) aluminum foil

1. Preheat oven to 450°.

2. In a medium skillet, sauté celery, onions, and carrots in ½ table-spoon canola oil for 5 minutes, or until just tender—don't over-cook. Season with salt and pepper to taste.

3. On each foil sheet, layer one-fourth of the ingredients in the fol-lowing order:
   Sautéed vegetables
   Salmon fillets
   Salt and pepper
   Tomato slices
   Lemon slices
   Bay leaf
   Thyme

4. Fold the packets securely, tucking edges carefully, and place on a baking sheet.

5. Bake 20 minutes. Slit packets before serving and transfer to plates, or allow guests to open their own (be careful of the escaping steam).

6. Serve with basmati rice.

Salmon is frequently disparaged as a high-fat fish. It is higher in fat than halibut or catfish, but it is still very heart healthy. Salmon has plenty of omega-3 fatty acids, which have been identified as a potential agent in lowering cholesterol levels in the blood.

◆

Often it is the cooking method that adds high amounts of fat to seafood. In this dish, the salmon is oven-baked with just a small amount of added oil for sautéing the vegetables.

Crab Cakes

MAKES 12 PATTIES OR 6 SERVINGS

These are always a favorite at dinner parties. We have to double the recipe to satisfy hungry guests!

> ⅔ cup drained silken tofu
> 2 teaspoons canola oil
> 4 teaspoons freshly squeezed lemon juice
> 3 tablespoons Worcestershire sauce
> Pinch celery salt
> Pinch white pepper
> Pinch ginger
> Pinch paprika
> Dash tabasco sauce, or to taste
> 2 lightly beaten egg whites
> 1 cup soft whole-wheat bread crumbs
> 3 cups canned crab meat, flaked and drained well (about
>   6 ounces)
> ¼ cup minced onion
> 2 tablespoons minced celery

1. Using a food processor with a metal blade, blend tofu, oil, lemon juice, Worcestershire sauce, seasonings, and Tabasco sauce until smooth. Transfer mixture to bowl and add all other ingredients. Mix well. Cover tightly and refrigerate until well chilled.

2. Divide chilled mixture into 12 patties. Cook in nonstick skillet over medium heat until brown on both sides.

Traditional crab cakes, fried in lots of oil, are loaded with fat. But it's easy to transform this high-fat favorite into a heart-healthy dish.

♦

Simply use a nonstick skillet and leave out the egg yolks, and you will have a delicious crab cake with half the fat of the traditional recipe (just 5 grams) and a healthy 27 grams of protein.

♦

We use canned crab in this recipe. Be sure to pick crab canned in water, not oil. To lower the sodium content, the Canyon Ranch chefs who created this recipe recommend soaking the crab meat in skim milk for 30 minutes in the refrigerator and draining with a colander before using.

Salmon Tomato Rigatoni

MAKES 2 SERVINGS

This quintessential Italian dish was inspired by a meal we had in northern Italy, where the lakes in the region bring fresh fish to the restaurant tables every night.

> 1 tablespoon olive oil
> 1 medium onion, finely diced
> 2 cloves garlic, mashed
> 1/2 pound fresh salmon fillet, cut in 2-inch pieces
> 1/2 tablespoon Italian herbs (i.e. basil, parsley, oregano)
> 2 tablespoons tomato paste
> 1 cup water
> 1/2 cup walnuts, chopped
> Juice of 1 small lemon
> 1 teaspoon sugar
> Sugar, salt and pepper to taste
> 1/2 pound rigatoni

1. Heat oil in a large frying pan. Add onion and garlic and sauté until translucent.

2. Add salmon pieces, herbs, and tomato paste to the pan and stir very well for 5 minutes.

3. Add water, walnuts, lemon juice, sugar, and season with salt and pepper to taste. Sir well and cover.

4. Simmer on low heat for 20 minutes. Meanwhile, boil pasta, and cook to al dente.

5. Be sure to check the taste of the sauce while it cooks. Remember—add salt and pepper slowly. You can always add more, but you can't take it out.

6. Serve sauce over plates of rigatoni. *Mangia bene!*

Variation: if salmon is not available, you can use canned tuna. Be sure to use tuna packed in water, not oil. If you use canned tuna, do not cook the fish, just mix it in once all the other ingredients are thoroughly cooked.

♦

For heightened flavor and pizzazz, add a handful of capers.

♦

Tips for cooking pasta: boiling water is easy, but the perfect pasta requires a few tricks. Use a large pot filled with water; too little water doesn't give pasta enough room to expand and results in sticky pasta.

♦

Don't add oil to the water. It's not necessary and will make pasta so slippery your sauce won't mix well.

◆

Catfish with Tomatoes

MAKES 2 SERVINGS

Catfish is one of the healthiest types of seafood available. We eat it regularly.

Juice of ½ lemon
2 catfish fillets, cleaned
1 teaspoon canola oil
1 medium onion, finely diced
1 green bell pepper, cut in thin rings
10 medium fresh tomatoes, sliced, or one 28-ounce can
   whole peeled tomatoes, mashed
Salt and pepper to taste
2 tablespoons parsley, chopped fine

1. Preheat oven to 350°.

2. Squeeze lemon juice over catfish fillets and sprinkle with salt and pepper.

3. Heat oil in medium-size pot. Add onion; sauté until translucent. Add bell peppers and tomatoes. Season to taste with salt and pepper. Cook on low for 10 minutes.

4. Spread half of the bell pepper and tomato-mixture across the bottom of a small ovenproof cassserole dish. Lay catfish fillets on top and cover with remaining mixture.

5. Cover with foil and bake in a preheated 350° oven until fish is opaque in the center, approximately 30 minutes.

6. Remove foil. Sprinkle with parsley and serve hot from the oven with mashed potatoes or rice.

Catfish is our preferred seafood because it is farm-raised, which guarantees that fish are raised in a quality controlled environment. They are raised in water from underground wells and are fed a high protein mixture of soybean, wheat, corn, vitamins, and minerals.

Salmon Croquettes

MAKES 2 SERVINGS

This recipe always pleased the hungry Taub boys when they were growing up. These croquettes are light and taste so good.

> 2 6-ounce cans salmon, skinned and boneless
> Juice of $\frac{1}{2}$ medium-size lemon
> 1 tablespoon parsley, finely chopped
> 1 egg white
> $\frac{3}{4}$ cup matzoh meal or plain bread crumbs
> 1 $\frac{1}{2}$ tablespoons canola oil for frying

1. Mix salmon in a medium bowl with the lemon juice, parsley, egg white, and matzoh meal (or bread crumbs). If mixture is too wet, add more bread crumbs. Season to taste with salt and pepper.

2. Form flat patties, the size of your palm.

3. Heat oil in a frying pan and fry patties until medium golden brown on each side.

4. Serve with a light cucumber salad, or between two slices of crusty sourdough bread.

Salmon is one of the best sources of omega-3 fatty acids, which have recently been shown to be very beneficial to your health.

◆

This recipe is a wonderful substitute for hamburgers, and makes great leftovers for sandwiches the next day.

◆

Sue's Jambalaya

MAKES 4 SERVINGS

Our good friend Sue Myers served this flavorful dish to us and brought good old Southern hospitality to a New York city high-rise apartment! The meal inspired the same celebratory spirit characteristic of Mardi Gras in New Orleans . . . We nearly forgot we were in the Big Apple!

> 4 skinless chicken breasts, cut into strips
> 1 tablespoon canola oil
> 1 medium onion, diced
> 2 ribs celery, diced
> ½ green bell pepper, diced
> 2 cloves garlic, minced
> 2 teaspoons paprika
> 1 cup tomato juice
> ½ cup vegetable broth
> 1 teaspoon Creole seasoning
> ¾ cup long grain rice
> ¼ cup scallions, sliced
> Salt and fresh ground pepper to taste

1. Season chicken with salt and pepper. Heat oil in large skillet or stock pot and fry chicken on high heat until brown on both sides. Remove chicken from pot and set aside.

2. Reduce heat to medium and add vegetables, garlic, and 1 teaspoon paprika. Sauté for 3 to 5 minutes, or until just tender. Return chicken to pot and add tomato juice, vegetable broth, 1 teaspoon paprika, and creole seasoning.

3. Bring mixture to a boil and add rice. Stir thoroughly to distribute rice evenly. Return to a boil, cover, reduce heat and simmer for 10 minutes.

4. Remove cover and stir well to turn the rice from top to bottom. Cover and continue cooking for another 15 minutes.

5. Uncover, stir well, add scallions, and serve.

Traditional Southern food is typically high fat and heavy on meat. But with a little imagination, the spicy, smoky flavors of the South can be captured in variations that reduce the meat and fat.

◆

This healthful, light variation on a Creole classic highlights fresh vegetables and authentic Southern seasonings.

◆

For a strictly vegetarian and absolutely delicious variation, simply omit the chicken.

◆

Stuffed Bell Peppers

MAKES 4 SERVINGS

These peppers take little time to prepare but will impress your taste buds and your family.

1 cup vegetable bouillon or vegetable broth (see recipe
    page 237)
2 red or green bell peppers, cut in half lengthwise and
    seeded
1 medium onion, finely diced
1 teaspoon butter
5 medium potatoes, cooked, peeled, and mashed
1 tablespoon parsley, finely chopped
2 tablespoons sundried tomatoes, chopped
1 pinch marjoram
1 cup green peas, fresh or frozen, defrosted
Salt, pepper and nutmeg to taste
1 cup low-fat plain yogurt
4 tablespoons chives, finely chopped (or spring onion
    greens)

1. Pour vegetable bouillon into a casserole dish and place pepper halves in dish.

2. Sauté onions in butter until golden brown.

3. Mix with mashed potatoes, then add parsley sundried tomatoes, marjoram, green peas, nutmeg, salt and pepper, and mix well. If filling is too dry or stiff, add a bit of hot water.

4. Spoon filling into peppers and cover with tin foil.

5. Bake on lowest oven rack for 40 minutes at 350°.

6. While peppers bake, mix yogurt and chives and season with salt and pepper.

7. Top baked peppers with yogurt mixture and serve hot.

◆

A savory stuffing transforms these bell peppers into a satisfying and tasty main dish.

◆

Look for plump, fresh red peppers. Red peppers are sweeter than green varieties, and easier to digest. They are also loaded with vitamin C.

◆

Give this unusual medley of tastes a try. Even the most "confirmed" meat-eaters will be in for a nice surprise!

◆

For a variation lower in fat and dairy free, omit the yogurt and accompany peppers with brown rice on the side.

Turkish Black-eyed Peas Over Rice

MAKES 5 SERVINGS

This delicious recipe uses black-eyed peas creatively.

2 cups brown rice
8 cups water
2 large onions, peeled and finely chopped
1 tablespoon olive oil
2 10-ounce boxes of frozen black-eyed peas
1 cup lemon juice
6 ripe tomatoes, chopped
Salt and pepper to taste

1. Cook rice in 5 cups water in a large pot until done. Meanwhile, stir-fry onions in oil for 2 minutes in a large pot.

2. Add black-eyed peas, 3 cups water and lemon juice.

3. Cover pot and simmer for 30 minutes, stirring occasionally.

4. Add tomatoes and seasonings and simmer 10 minutes longer, stirring occasionally.

5. Serve hot over cooked rice.

Many thanks to Deborah Wasserman for this high-energy dish.

◆

It is also a wonderful source of dietary fiber, with 12 grams per serving.

Fast Cuban Beans

MAKES 4 SERVINGS

This dish is so healthy and bursting with the flavors of Cuba.

1 tablespoon canola oil
1 medium onion, diced
4 cloves garlic, mashed
2 green bell peppers, cubed
2 tomatoes, ripe and quartered
1/2 teaspoon cumin
2 15-ounce cans black beans, drained
1/2 cup of water
1 tablespoon Cilantro, chopped
Juice of 1 small lime
Salt and pepper to taste
1 teaspoon sugar

1. Heat oil in large pot. Add onion, garlic, and bell pepper. Sauté on medium heat until onion is translucent, stirring often.

2. Add tomatoes, beans, cumin, and water. Stir well. Simmer on low 20 minutes. While cooking, add cilantro, lime juice, salt and pepper to taste, and sugar.

3. Serve with Basmati or simple white rice.

This dish will delight your taste buds and ignite your energy.

◆

Black beans are a rich source of protein. Combined with lots of fresh vegetables, this is a healthy, high-fiber meal.

Tomato and Lima Bean Stew

MAKES 4 SERVINGS

An autumn afternoon in the French countryside, surrounded by vineyards . . . that's what this delightful stew, created by my French sister-in-law, always brings to mind.

1 cup lima beans, dried. Soaked for 6 hours or overnight
5 cups water
1 tablespoon olive oil
6 garlic cloves, mashed
½ teaspoon Rosemary
Salt and pepper to taste

The sauce:
1 28-ounce can whole peeled tomatoes, stems removed
½ tablespoon sugar
Juice of 1 medium orange
Salt and pepper to taste

1. Rinse beans after soaking. In 3 cups fresh water bring beans to boiling point. Remove beans from heat, drain, and rinse. Pour beans into medium casserole dish. Add 2 cups water, olive oil, garlic, rosemary, salt, and pepper to taste. Stir together well. Cover tightly with aluminum foil and bake at 175° for 2½ hours.

2. While the beans bake, prepare the tomato sauce. In a medium pot add tomatoes, orange juice, salt, pepper, and sugar. Mash together and cook for 10 minutes.

3. When the beans are done, add them to the tomato sauce.

4. Serve with crusty French bread . . . et voila! Bon appetit!

One bowl of this hearty stew contains tremendous amounts of soluble fiber. Even small servings of cooked beans appear to have have a cholesterol-lowering effect.

♦

♦

Soaking beans and rinsing them with plenty of fresh water decreases the gas-producing elements and makes them easier to digest.

♦

If you don't have time to cook dried beans, frozen or canned beans are a fine alternative but bake only for one hour. Choose a brand with no salt added and rinse them well.

◆

Vegetable Chili

MAKES 6 SERVINGS

This chili has great character! I like to make it in abundance so there will be leftovers. After the spices and vegetables mingle overnight, the chili is even more tasty.

> 1 tablespoon olive oil
> 1 large onion, finely diced
> 5 carrots, peeled and sliced
> 2 red bell peppers, cored, seeded, and diced
> 3 stalks celery, diced
> 3 cloves garlic, finely minced
> 1 teaspoon cumin
> 1½ tablespoons chili powder
> 1 small jalapeño pepper, minced (optional)
> Salt and pepper to taste
> 1 cup water
> 1 28-ounce can chopped tomatoes
> 2 tablespoons sherry, or ¼ cup beer (optional)
> 1 15-ounce can black beans
> 1 15-ounce can red kidney beans
> Nonfat plain yogurt, chopped scallions, shredded cheddar
>   cheese (optional) for garnish

1. Coat the inside bottom of a large, heavy saucepan with olive oil and heat over medium-high heat. Add onion, carrots, red bell pepper, celery, and garlic. Cook, stirring frequently, for 10 minutes, or until the onion is transluscent.

2. Stir in cumin, chili powder, jalapeño pepper, water, tomatoes, and sherry or beer. Season to taste with salt and pepper. Bring to a boil.

3. Lower heat and cover. Simmer for 15 minutes.

4. Add beans, cover, and cook for 5 minutes. Uncover the pan and continue cooking until the liquid has thickened slightly.

5. Top each serving with a spoonful of yogurt, chopped scallions, and shredded cheese.

A good, hearty vegetable chili provides a high-energy, healthful meal. This chili contains only healthy monounsaturated fat and is loaded with fiber, protein, and vitamins.

◆

Chili is a versatile dish. Served over brown rice, you'll get even more fiber. Alternatively, this is delicious over couscous or noodles. Kids love to eat this chili wrapped up in a tortilla.

◆

However you serve it, vegetable chili is spicy and satisfying.

DESSERTS

Apple Pie Nany

MAKES 6 SERVINGS

This pie is easy to prepare and tastes heavenly. It proves you can indulge in dessert without loading up on fat and calories.

One half of a 17¼-ounce package frozen puff pastry
 (Pepperidge Farm is excellent; use 1 sheet)
3 large apples, peeled and shredded
2 tablespoons honey
2 tablespoons raisins, rinsed with water
3 tablespoons walnuts or pecans, chopped and toasted

1. Preheat oven to 400°.

2. Thaw puff pastry sheet until it unfolds easily without breaking. Lay it in a round 9- or 10-inch glass pie plate.

3. Combine apples, honey, raisins, and nuts. Spread evenly over pastry sheet.

4. Bake pie on lower oven rack for 20 minutes or until sides are just turning brown.

5. Let cool and serve.

Apple pie is an American classic, but most traditional recipes are heavy with butter and sugar.

♦

Instead of a high-fat, buttery crust, this recipe uses a light puff pastry. A bit of honey enhances the natural sweetness of apples without adding lots of sugar.

◆

◆

Enjoy this treat especially in fall, when apple orchards are overflowing with fresh fruit.

◆

For a tart variation, use raspberries instead of apples. In summertime, use fresh strawberries.

◆

This low-fat apple pie will satisfy even the sweetest tooth!

♦

Orange Raisin Muffins

MAKES 1 DOZEN MUFFINS

These muffins are fast and simple to prepare. Serve them fresh out of the oven for a delightful, healthy breakfast.

1 1/2 cups all-purpose flour
1 teaspoon baking powder
1 teaspoon baking soda
1/8 teaspoon salt
2 egg whites
1/2 cup low-fat buttermilk
2 tablespoons canola oil
3 tablespoons honey
2 tablespoons apple sauce, unsweetened
1 large orange, juice and zest
1/2 cup raisins

1. Preheat oven to 350°. Lightly coat a 12 cup muffin tin with vegetable spray, or fill with paper liners.

2. Sit flour, baking powder, baking soda, and salt into a medium bowl and set aside.

3. In another bowl, using a whisk, beat egg whites until very foamy. Add buttermilk, canola oil, honey and applesauce and beat well.

4. Add dry ingredients and raisins to wet ingredients and stir *just* until flour is combined. *Do not* overmix.

5. Fill muffin cups about 3/4 full.

6. Bake approximately 12–15 minutes or until muffins are golden brown.

7. Remove muffins and cool on wire rack.

Most muffins in cafes and bakeries are really just breakfast cakes—high in fat and sugar.

♦

"Healthy" muffins tend to be so dry and flavorless they are no fun to eat.

♦

Here is a healthy muffin that is moist and tasty, and very good for you. The applesauce and orange juice give this muffin moisture, adding fat and a natural sweetness without adding sugar.

♦

Variation: Soy milk can be substituted for buttermilk to reduce fat even more.

Baked Apples with Dried Plums

MAKES 4 SERVINGS

The aroma of baked apples always reminds me of autumn and winter weekends in Germany, when the fragrance of apples, honey, and brown sugar seemed to linger in the kitchen all day long.

4 *large apples*
3 *tablespoons rolled oats*
2 *tablespoons corn flakes*
2 *tablespoons raisins*
3 *tablespoons honey*
1 *teaspoon cardamom (optional*
6 *dried plums, finely chopped*
1 *tablespoon brown sugar*

1. Preheat oven to 350°.

2. Core apples. Make a large opening at the top and leave a bit of core at the bottom of each apple to hold in filling. Place apples in casserole dish.

3. Combine oats, corn flakes, raisins, honey, cardamom, and dried plums. Spoon filling into apples and top with a sprinkle of brown sugar.

4. Bake apples at 350° for approximately 35 minutes until they are soft. Check for softness with tip of a knife. Remove from oven and spoon some baking juice over apples before serving.

This delicious, homey dish is perfect for breakfast or for dessert. It is especially good in the fall when apples are at their best.

♦

Choose a tart, flavorful baking apple. Braeburn or Granny Smith are good because as they bake they become tender but not mushy.

♦

Apples are a superb source of nutritional fiber.

♦

As a dessert variation, top with a spoonful of low-fat whipped cream or low-fat vanilla ice cream.

Toasted English Muffins with Fruit Topping

MAKES 4 SERVINGS

This is a nourishing high-energy breakfast. Fresh fruit is delicious spread on toast. For an especially wholesome breakfast, use whole-wheat English muffins.

4 English muffins
1 banana, mashed with 2 teaspoons lemon juice
1 tablespoon honey or maple syrup
1 small inner tender celery stalk, finely minced
1 apple, peeled and minced or shredded

1. Split and toast English muffins.

2. While muffins toast, mix mashed banana with honey or maple syrup.

3. Add celery and apple bits and mix well.

4. Spread evenly on each muffin and serve warm.

Mom was right—breakfast *is* the most important meal of the day. Especially if you are trying to lose weight. People who skip breakfast tend to eat more later on in the day.

♦

You need energy in the morning. A cup of coffee is not enough. If you think skipping breakfast will help cut down your daily calorie intake, think again. When you skip breakfast, you rob your body of the energy it needs to gear up for the day ahead. You will be more likely to crave high-fat junk foods later, when your energy in running on empty.

♦

This simple breakfast is fast to prepare and loaded with nutritional goodness. Parents and kids alike will enjoy it!

♦

For a variation, substitute pears, strawberries, or walnuts.

Fresh Fruit Freeze

MAKES 4 SERVINGS

Children and adults alike will devour this dessert. This is especially refreshing on a hot summer night.

> 6 *frozen bananas (Peel bananas and wrap in plastic wrap*
>   *before freezing), cut into chunks*
> *or*
> 2 *cups any frozen fruit, cut into chunks*
> 1 *tablespoon honey (optional)*
> ½ *cup vanilla soy milk (optional)*

1. Place frozen fruit in a food processor or blender. Add honey and soy milk (if desired) and process or blend until creamy but some small chunks of fruit remain.

2. Transfer to bowls and serve immediately.

There are many wonderful, low-fat as well as non-dairy alternatives to ice cream. Our favorite is this pure fruit dessert. It is so simple and it's sweetened by nature.

◆

Frozen bananas make an especially creamy fruit freeze, but you can try this recipe with all of your favorite fruits—strawberries, peaches, raspberries . . . Use your imagination!

◆

Honey and soy milk make a creamier dessert but are optional.

Part Eight

EXERCISE-WISE

I have mulled over the best way to approach the subject of exercise now for days. Should I list all the health benefits derived from exercise? Should I shock you with the damaging side effects of not exercising at all? Or should I simply encourage nonexercisers to get up on their feet and out the door?

The longer I debated how to begin, the more aware I became of the ache spreading across my back. After three days of sitting in my desk chair with little more than a few fifteen-minute breaks to answer phone calls, my lower back was so sore I could barely sit still.

That back pain made me aware that, in trying to think and write about exercise, I had neglected my own regular exercise. Each time my wife invited me out for beach walks and wellness yoga stretching, I insisted I could not interrupt my work then, and that she should enjoy the walk and stretching in the sunshine on her own.

Now the pain in my lower back forced me to remember that, even at the busiest moments in life, it is crucial to get up out of your chair, put on your walking shoes or sneakers, and get in motion. After thirty minutes of walking on the beach, my back pain subsided—and I knew exactly how to open this part of the book!

Most of us probably *think* about exercise more often than we *do* exercise. Indeed, we spend lots of time thinking our way *out* of exercising. Do any of these statements sound familiar to you?

- It's too cold.
- It's too hot.
- I'm too busy.
- I'm running late.

- I'm too tired and really need a nap.
- It can wait until tomorrow.

How easy it is to fall into these traps. Even as I was thinking about how to persuade readers to start exercising regularly, I let my own daily exercise fall to the wayside. It took intense back pain for me to become aware of this irony. I put the computer to sleep, pushed back my chair, grabbed my walking shoes, and headed for the beach. Even the smallest dose of exercise is powerful medicine!

I called my brother on the phone to tell him about my experience. "Guess what cured my writer's block on the exercise chapter? *Exercise!*" My brother, who has been a physician almost as long as I have, said, "Ed, if exercise can cure your writer's block, it can probably cure *anything!*"

Although my brother was innocently exaggerating, there is some truth to his statement. Even small amounts of regular exercise encourage a healthy body and mind as well as help protect against and treat many chronic illnesses and diseases. You have almost certainly heard news reports or seen headlines about the health benefits of exercise. Perhaps you paid attention, perhaps you didn't pay attention. Either way, after learning about your body's energy system and the cycles of your life, you can now truly appreciate the information and use it to your best health advantage.

To be exercise-wise, you need to understand the exercise *whys*. Why is exercise so important to your health? Why is it absolutely essential that you begin exercising now? Consider these facts:

- Exercise is effective prevention and treatment for coronary heart disease. Brisk walking and other aerobic exercises strengthen and reduce strain on the heart muscles. People who exercise regularly have an amazingly lower risk of heart attack compared to people who lead sedentary lives. A study of forty male runners between the ages of fifty and eighty showed that most of them had hearts as healthy as athletes half their age. In fact, research at the National Institutes of Health has shown that the heart of an older person, when free of disease, functions comparably to that of a much younger person. Exercise helps protect against coronary heart disease while inactivity ranks fourth as a major risk factor for heart disease just behind overweight, hypertension, and smoking, as determined by the American Heart Association.

- The *New England Journal of Medicine* has reported that regular exercise is an essential factor in the treatment of high cholesterol. Researchers at Stanford tracked the cholesterol levels of 197 men and 180 postmenopausal women for one year. At the beginning of the study, all the men had moderately high blood levels of LDL cholesterol (the cholesterol that damages the heart) and were considered at high risk for coronary heart disease. Participants were divided into four groups: one group followed a low-fat, low-cholesterol diet and did weekly aerobic exercise; the second group followed the low-fat diet but did not exercise; the third group did regular exercise but ate as they normally did; the last group made no changes, continuing with their regular lifestyle. After a year, the study found that there were no significant reductions in LDL cholesterol levels for those who followed a low-fat diet alone. In fact, the only group that showed any improvement was the group that combined a low-fat diet with exercise.
- Studies have shown a link between exercise and a lower risk of colon cancer. At Harvard Medical School, a study of Harvard alumni found that those who took brisk thirty-minute walks five times a week had half the incidence of colon cancer than a group of less-active alumni.
- Studies have also shown that women who exercised one to three hours per week had 20 percent to 30 percent fewer cases of breast cancer. *Women who exercised at least four hours a week demonstrated a 37 percent decrease in the incidence of breast cancer!*
- Exercise helps create and maintain healthy bones and is essential for preventing bone mass loss as we advance in the cycle

of life. Small doses of regular exercise are the best medicine for preventing osteoporosis, or slowing down its progress if it has already set in. Research has shown that just thirty minutes of exercise three times a week slows bone mass loss among women. While calcium consumption is essential to preventing and treating osteoporosis, exercise combined with calcium strengthens bones and makes them more dense. Weight-bearing activities (such as walking), in which you use your bones and muscles against gravity, increase bone density. Resistance activities, such as light weight lifting, strengthen the bones. In fact, research has shown that postmenopausal women who did forty minutes of resistance activity twice a week gained 1 percent in bone density after one year, compared to a group of sedentary women, who lost between 2 and 2½ percent during that same period. Studies have found that people who do light weight-lifting activities have as much as 10 percent greater bone density compared to people who do not exercise.

- As we advance in the cycle of life, not only our bones but also our muscles become more frail. Frailty contributes to a number of health problems among older adults, such as falls and hip fractures. A frail body has a harder time recovering from even minor spills or stumbles. But even in the mature stages of the life cycle, physical frailty can be reversed with small doses of exercise. Regular physical activity strengthens muscles and improves mobility. A physically active ninety-year-old may be less frail than a sedentary sixty-year-old. In a study of men and women between the ages of eighty-six and ninety conducted by the National Institutes of Health, those who exercised with light weights increased the strength of their leg muscles threefold! With greater leg strength and knee and hip flexibility, this group was proactive in preventing weakness-related injuries that commonly occur among older adults.

- As the process of entropy unfolds in the later years of the human lifecycle, it is not uncommon for the body to lose its ability to utilize glucose efficiently and normally. This results in what we call non-insulin dependent, or adult-onset, diabetes. Active people are less likely to develop this form of diabetes than sedentary people. Even after the onset of this disease, however, regular physical activity helps in treatment by improving the body's insulin sensitivity and blood glucose level.

- It's no secret that physical activity is necessary for achieving and maintaining your optimal weight; not only by burning excess calories, but by increasing your energy and bringing it back into balance. Exercise is a magic key!

- Perhaps the most important benefit of exercise is the effect it has on your psychological and spiritual outlook. Exercise makes your feelings of self-value and self-esteem soar. When you feel better about yourself, when you feel empowered and energetic, you make healthier choices in your eating and lifestyle habits.

Those are some of the most important exercise *whys*. Generally speaking, exercise is a naturally powerful medicine. Exercise empowers people to *prevent disease before it occurs because exercise helps to prevent energy imbalance*. Especially as individuals advance in the cycle of life (as the force of entropy gains momentum), exercise becomes a key to slowing down this process. The American College of Sports Medicine and the Centers for Disease Control and Prevention recently sent out a call to action: For optimal health, every adult should do moderate physical activity for thirty minutes most, if not all, days of the week.

As a physician, one of the most important prescriptions I can give my patients is an "Exercise Rx."* The combination of a healthful diet and regular physical activity stimulates your own internal pharmacy to help prevent the majority of illnesses and diseases related to being overweight. You see, this is not just another "diet book"—there are plenty of those already available. Perhaps losing weight is your goal. But as I have emphasized throughout, if you do not address the actual factors that are *causing* you to be overweight, you will never lose weight healthily and permanently. If you are overweight, your energy is out of balance. My goal is to help you increase and balance your energy—so you will lose weight naturally and permanently. *This is Total Health Rejuvenation.*

---

*The "Exercise Rx" has been expanded in this revised edition to include "Simple Strength Training." Please see Part Nine.

Exercise is one of the most powerful tools for creating more energy in your life. It is just as important as eating well. Starting to exercise is just as important, from an energy wellness perspective, as quitting smoking. With more energy, through a combination of exercising and eating wisely, you will extend your life, slow the process of entropy, and live a more fulfilling, productive life, even at the most advanced stages of the lifecycle.

We cannot defy age—aging is natural, healthy, and necessary. In many cultures, age is associated with strength, beauty, wisdom, and esteem. But in our culture, advertising-driven standards of beauty and strength emphasize youth and encourage us to fight aging tooth and nail, as if age itself was a disease! The approach I advocate is much different. Aging is not a disease, but a natural process. It's how we live and the choices we make that are catalysts for either the premature onset and speedy progress of entropy, or for extending and enhancing nature's cycles of life.

Especially as we reach the later stages of our lifecycle, what we don't use we are more prone to lose. For example, as older adults become less active, and as bone and muscle mass naturally decrease, the hip muscles and joints become more fragile. Hip fractures are among the most common injuries for seventy- to ninety-year-olds. Adults in this age group however, who use their hip muscles and joints through gentle stretching, light weight lifting, walking, and swimming, greatly improve their bone density and strengthen their muscles.

Entropy and its effects on the body are natural. But exercise is the best tool for countering the negative effects of entropy. I recently received a letter from a seventy-four-year-old woman who is so convinced of the benefits of regular walking that she formed a wellness walking club in the retirement community where she lives.

Dear Dr. Taub,

I thought you would be proud to know what a positive impact you have had on my life and health, as well as on my community. I never thought exercise was possible because of nagging arthritis in my knees and hips that developed about five years ago. Since that time, I'd spent most of my days sitting in a chair, enjoying the sunshine and company of dear friends. But now I know that all of that sitting around just made the stiffness and pain worse! After reading one of

◆

your books, I adopted your "use it or lose it" attitude and now I walk
twenty minutes every day. The pain in my hips and knees comes back
only when I skip my walks.

   All it took was one step, then another; it was as easy as that. Six
months later, I'm leading a group of ladies in daily walks around our
community, and all of us feel younger and more energetic than ever
before! Tell your patients that we found the secret fountain of
youth—in our feet!

Thanks from all of us,
Greta M.

Greta discovered what so many people are learning: Regular exercise, especially walking and simple stretching, is the best tool for achieving optimal health, no matter your cycle of life, and *especially* if you are upwards of fifty. Remember that chronological age influences but *does not determine* your health and energy. Greta, as an active seventy-four-year-old, is chronologically older than a fifty-year-old inactive woman, but she is more physiologically fit than her younger counterpart.

Indeed, there is a difference between your body's age in actual years and your body's age in terms of energy and fitness. Greta's body is much younger than her seventy-four years. Regular exercise has slowed the process of entropy and elevated her energy and fitness. Science still hasn't found a way to turn back the clocks, but exercise is, as Greta says, the closest thing to a fountain of youth. Regular physical activity is a fountain of energy. The more you drink from it, the younger you will feel in body and mind. And, the more you drink from it, the thirstier you will be for more exercise and the energy it imparts.

Is your physical age in or out of sync with your chronological age? Do you think your body is older or younger than your chronological years? Flexibility, strength, and energy are the keys to building a fit body. A fit body is one that is at least as young as, if not younger than, your chronological age. Here are some simple questions to help you determine your fitness level:

1. Most days, I feel _____ flexible.
   (a) very
   (b) somewhat
   (c) not very

2. Standing up, I can bend from the waist and touch _____.
   (a) the floor
   (b) my toes
   (c) my knees
   (d) I can hardly bend from the waist

3. Most days, I feel _____ energetic.
   (a) extremely
   (b) very
   (c) moderately
   (d) not very

4. Walking up a flight of stairs makes me feel _____.
   (a) energized
   (b) a little huffy and puffy, but I could make one more flight
   (c) exhausted

5. Most days, I feel _____ strong.
   (a) very
   (b) pretty
   (c) not very

6. I can carry a few bags of groceries into the house without feeling exhausted.
   Yes   No

7. I can rake the leaves in the yard without feeling like I need to sit down.
   Yes   No

8. I can play with my kids or grandkids without getting too tired.
   Yes   No

What is most important is that you have the energy and vitality to accomplish your daily tasks productively and with enthusiasm. If you can run 10 kilometers, that's wonderful. But what matters more is that you are getting the most out of your daily activities so they don't get the best of you.

People commonly give up on exercise for one or all of these reasons:

- They choose an exercise they don't like.
- They set unrealistic goals.
- They don't stick with it long enough to experience the benefits.

For many people, beginning to exercise is so difficult and quitting is so simple. If, however, you choose an exercise that you enjoy, one you can stick with and that produces visible benefits, you will not be discouraged and give up.

Of all the exercises and sports activities commonly practiced, brisk walking is the simplest and has the lowest drop-out rate. I advocate walking because it is so easy to do and so easy to stick with. Other activities may burn more calories faster, and may produce more muscle mass or lower body fat more quickly. But if it is difficult to stick with over time, its benefits will be limited. People start and stop exercise programs every day. Walking has the staying power to produce long-term health benefits, especially permanent weight loss!

Walking is the oldest form of exercise. Unlike other activities, such as running, swimming, skiing, and tennis, participation does not decline among people in their mid and later years. Almost everyone can walk. The only lessons you need in walking are those you received when you were a toddler. It doesn't cost an arm and a leg to participate, and the only gear you really need is a good pair of walking shoes. Walking is easy to do almost anytime and anywhere; you don't have to rely on a team, and even inclement weather doesn't have to stop you. You can walk alone or in a group like Greta's.

Because walking is so easy to do, it is much easier to stick with over time than other forms of exercise. Think about it this way: You are already walking; now it's just a matter of increasing the amount of time and the pace of your walk. It's easy to turn a stroll into a workout. Just pick up the pace and sustain it.

Unlike many kinds of exercise, there are virtually no health risks associated with walking. Walking does not strain your muscles or bones the way jogging and high-impact aerobics do. It's easy on your arms, legs, and back. In fact, it's so easy to do, you may be wondering, *how can it be a serious form of exercise?* Just because walking is easy does not mean it is ineffective. Walking briskly and regularly promotes all the health benefits associated with exercise, but without the injuries commonly suffered. Walking regularly strengthens the heart and lungs while improving the body's ability to consume oxygen, and it reduces blood pressure. By lowering blood pressure and burning excess calories through walking, you are taking preventive measures against heart attack and stroke.

If your goal is to lose weight, there is nothing to lose with walking except pounds. When you walk, you burn just about the same number of calories per mile as if you were jogging. Since walking is a weight-bearing activity, a person who weighs more will burn more calories than a lighter person walking the same distance at the same pace. The dropout rate for new joggers is much higher than the rate for brisk walkers, which makes it more effective for your health over the long haul.

The fact that walking is easy is the very reason why walking works. Walking completely satisfies the body's need for movement and energy. Walking is a simple but surprisingly effective way to lift us out of the sedentary lifestyle into which so many of us have settled. It's no wonder that, in 1996, the Surgeon General of the United States declared such sedentary habits the cause of a rising public epidemic. Most people know that physical activity will improve their health, but many still struggle against that truth or are not motivated to put it into action in their own lives. That is partly because the first steps seem so hard.

Actually, walking makes the first steps quite easy. Many of us have been misled to believe in the "no pain, no gain" slogan of the 1980s. Exercise does not, indeed *should not*, hurt your body. Even the most moderate physical activity will have a tremendous positive impact on those who have led a lifetime of inactivity. Walking just twenty to thirty minutes, at a steady clip, five times a week will reduce your risk of falling prey to obesity, heart disease, hypertension, breast cancer, colon cancer, osteoporosis, diabetes, and many other illnesses.

In her letter to me, Greta also indicated another health benefit of walking: Regular walking helped relieve the chronic pain associated with arthritis in her joints. I've heard from many readers who find that even after a few days of walking, the pain associated with all kinds of illnesses subsided. Walking has helped many of my own patients reduce the number of medications they depended on for years. My own mother has made a remarkable recovery from triple bypass heart surgery with the help of daily walks in the sunshine. Walking lifted her spirits and increased her energy while strengthening her body and attitude. Her doctors were amazed by her will to get well. She literally walked herself to wellness! Although they cautioned her that too much activity might sap her energy, she demonstrated to them how sensible walking was, and it made her energy soar!

The Surgeon General emphasizes the important health benefits of exercise in preventing risk of many major diseases. Just as important, however, are the benefits of walking for your mood and outlook. In fact, one way that walking benefits your health is by its capacity to reduce stress. Many people walk to lose weight but discover they're shedding stress as well as pounds. Remember that stress is the leading cause of illness. When you are stressed, your energy is out of balance, and that's when illness strikes.

One of my patients, Jerry, invited me to share his story with readers. Jerry is a business executive whose physiological age was much older than his chronological age of forty-five.

Dr. Taub,

A year ago, I dragged myself into your office overweight, stressed out, chain-smoking—literally hopeless. The best advice you gave me was to leave my car at home and start walking to work. Eager to rid myself of the stress of rush-hour traffic, I complied. You assured me it would be worth leaving an hour early in the morning. Doc, that change actually saved me time. It turned out that walking was faster than sitting in rush-hour traffic! But it saved me more than just time—it truly saved my life.

I was on a collision course with a heart attack; my blood pressure was already through the roof. As I began walking, everything fell into balance. I began to lose weight, not just because of the exercise, but because as I started to feel better about myself, I made smarter, healthier choices about what I ate, what I did. Even quitting smoking was much easier than I thought it would be. It was keeping me from enjoying my walks, so it naturally felt good to stop.

I smoked and overate because I was so stressed. The level of stress in my life did not change (except for eliminating the stress of rush hour), but my ability to deal with it changed. Walking proved to be incredibly effective for releasing stress. Even if I began my walk with a wrinkled brow, tight shoulders, and a scowl, after only a few blocks I couldn't resist feeling better. I began to appreciate my surroundings, the trees, people who smiled as they passed. I stopped worrying about the pile of work waiting for me on my desk, the phone calls that had to be made and the e-mail that needed a response. When I arrive at work, I can now tackle those things more productively, and without all of the stress and anxiety. Walking truly did wonders!

Oh, and how can I forget? I lost twenty pounds. I have so much more energy, strength and stamina. Little things that exhausted me before are no big deal now. I am forty-five but feel physically better and more optimistic than I did when I was twenty.

Jerry's letter goes on to describe how he met the love of his life on one of his morning walks to work! Walking helped eliminate the stress in his life, and when that happened, a world of opportunities was just a few steps away. Jerry gained a partner in walking, and in life.

Why does walking help eliminate stress? Walking, like other exercise, triggers the release of substances known as endorphins. These substances are what produce the "runner's high." The good news is, you don't have to be a runner to experience the beneficial rush of endorphins from the brain. When you walk, your brain releases endorphins that naturally flow to the parts of your body in need of repair or rejuvenation. Endorphins are the brain's natural healers that not only stimulate physical healing but mental outlook as well. A walk in the sunshine (with sunscreen) is even better, because the light of the sun boosts the level of serotonin in the brain. Nothing cures a sad heart or brooding mood like a walk outdoors (except, perhaps, a walk outdoors with a companion!).

Endorphins soothe your stress and let your positive side shine through. This is why walking has proven so beneficial to relationships at work and at home. Groups of co-workers who walk together at lunch or before or after work interact better with each other during the day. Walking together positively influences the way coworkers relate to each other. The same is true with couples. My wife and I walk together daily and both feel our communication with each other reaches exceptional clarity during and after our walks. Walking, and the release of endorphins, makes us feel so good about ourselves and each other.

Walking also soothes stress on another level. When you walk outside, in nature, you can see the issues and events that trigger your stress anew. Spending time in nature reminds you that you are part of something much bigger, that life has greater meaning than, you are able to see while you work. When you feel connected with nature, you make choices that are more in tune with nature, including what you eat. New walkers always tell me that they feel better about their bodies, about themselves, and have a more positive mental outlook. Such feelings inspire your will to be well, and continue to be well in every aspect of your life.

Remember that you are only as well as you feel. In other words, your feelings and attitude have a profound effect on your health, energy, and weight. Physical and mental health are deeply intertwined. When your mental energy is out of balance, for example, because of negative feelings or stress, your physical energy will be shaken out of balance. Therefore, you need an exercise program that inspires total wellness, in body and mind.

The best workout for body and mind combines walking with stretching and strength training. Both walking and stretching generate greater energy and help restore energy balance. Combined, walking, stretching and strength training play a tremendous role in slowing down the process of entropy and reducing the negative effects of premature aging. While walking provides the weight-bearing activity so important to strengthening bones and muscles, stretching and weight lifting contributes to bone strength and density.

Stretching is a gentle form of resistance exercise for everyone, but weight lifting is especially important as you age. Instead of using free weights or barbells, however, stretching uses the weight of your own body. Regular stretching complements walking. The increased flexibility and relaxation that stretching provides protects you against straining muscles during walking. Furthermore, serious walkers sometimes become inflexible as the muscles in the back and legs become tighter and stronger. Stretching helps prevent stiffness and inflexibility, and keeps your stride long and smooth. So, ideally, it is preferable to do some stretching before you do your walking. I am personally an advocate of what I call "wellness yoga stretching." We will address that shortly.

Early in life, from the time you are an infant through about age thirty, your body builds its bones. Your bone mass is at its peak between ages twenty and thirty. Exercise is essential for children to achieve their optimal growth and to establish good bone health early on. Yet today, young people are more inactive than ever before. Inactivity among children already contributes to poor bone health in later life, putting them at risk for osteoporosis and other degenerative bone diseases.

As we progress through the cycle of life, our bone mass begins to diminish. By the time we are thirty or forty, bone mass loss begins to occur, sometimes at the rate of 1 percent each year. The rate of bone mass loss depends largely on how active we were as children, current physical activity, and calcium consumption. At this age, a minimum of thirty minutes of weight-bearing activity, such as walking, stretching, and strength training at least every other day is essential.

For women, loss of bone density speeds up during menopause. Some women eventually lose as much as 20 percent of their bone mass. The best steps to slow down bone mass loss are those you take with your own two feet. Plenty of brisk walking, combined with stretching and strength training, will slow down bone mass loss and strengthen your bones significantly. Arm yourself against osteoporosis: *Use your legs!*

At the age of sixty and beyond, both men and women continue to lose bone mass. At this age, it is especially important to combine walking, stretching and strength training. In addition to these bone strengthening exercises, men and women at this age should increase their intake of calcium and vitamin D. Exercise and supplements are your best tools for preventing the loss of height, or "dowager's hump," that results from bone mass loss. It is never too late to begin exercising. Even in the later stages of your lifecycle, exercise imparts major health benefits.

Now that you are wise to the exercise *whys*, and have a clear understanding of the benefits exercise imparts to body, mind, and spirit, your motivation to begin exercising is hopefully at a peak. You're ready to begin; you just need a sensible, enjoyable, and effective program to help you attain your health and weight goals. In the remainder of this part of the book, you will learn a simple but powerful combination of walking, stretching and strength training—my "Exercise Rx": a prescription for energy that will make entropy smooth sailing through *Total Health Rejuvenation*. So, before you lace up your walking shoes, read on!

As long as you have no serious health conditions that prevent you from walking, there are only a few basics to cover before you begin. (If you have any concerns, check with your primary care physician before you start.) First, when you walk or do any other form of exercise, keeping yourself hydrated with water is essential. Even if it's cold outside, as your body heats up inside, it requires water to move efficiently. Drink water before, during and after your walk. If you are walking outdoors in sunlight, be sure to wear a cap and/or protective sunscreen. If you are walking in cold weather, wear layers of clothing instead of a heavy coat so that you are warm but can remove layers and tie them around your waist as your body heats up. A warm wool cap will keep your head warm and protect you from the cold.

Your common sense may tell you to avoid walking outdoors in cold weather, but regular walking has been shown to actually help reduce the risk of catching the common cold. In my experience, people who walk at least twenty minutes a day, five days a week, have cold symptoms half as frequently as non-walkers. Walking also boosts immune cell activity and empowers the body to protect itself from bacteria and viruses.

Shoes that fit right are essential. If your shoes are too tight, your feet will ache. When purchasing walking shoes, remember that your feet are smaller at the beginning of the day and larger at the end of the day. Just as your car runs best when it has good tires, your body walks best when there are good, comfortable shoes on your feet.

Remember, it is preferable to do some stretching before you begin walking. When you set out on your walk, spend the first few minutes walking at a leisurely pace to warm up and loosen your muscles. After you've walked for a few minutes, stop at a curb or beside a tree to do a brief stretch. Use the tree for support and stretch one leg back and press your heel toward the ground, feeling the stretch in your calf. Stretch the other leg and then continue with your walk.

You learned everything you needed to know about walking when you were a child. A few reminders will help you get the most out of your walk and help minimize the risk of straining muscles. The basic things to remember are:

1. Begin with good posture. Walk with a straight spine. Lift your chest; relax your shoulders and pull them back slightly. Gently contract your abdominal muscles to support the muscles of your lower back. Keep your chin parallel to the ground and look straight ahead. If you stare at the ground as you walk, you may end up with a stiff neck.

2. Loosen up your arms and relax your shoulders. Let your arms swing loosely by your side at first. Shake out your hands and wrists, wiggle your fingers, and release any tension in your arms and hands. To increase the flow of energy, bend your arms at the elbow and let them pump at your side as you walk. Relax your hands in loose fists. Boost your heart rate and speed by swinging your arms, bent at the elbow, in an arc from waist to chest.

3. Relax your knees and keep them slightly flexed. If you walk with locked knees, you are more likely to develop soreness. Walk with short, fast, gliding steps, heel to toe. Let your heel naturally touch the ground first, then roll along your foot and lift off your toes. People who walk on their toes tend to experience shin splints, or pain in their lower front legs. Glide from heel to toe and avoid a choppy step.

4. Remember to breathe. As you walk with good posture, your chest and rib cage are open and expanding, allowing you to take full, deep breaths.

5. When walking and stretching, always wear comfortable clothing that is loose but not too baggy. Anything that restricts your movement limits the benefits of your workout.

6. Smile and have fun! Exercise is most beneficial when you are enjoying yourself.

Now, just when you think you're finally ready to start, you may find yourself up against the "walker's wall." The walker's wall refers to the million and one reasons your mind will erect to block your walk. Especially if you have been leading an inactive life for a while, your mind and body have settled comfortably into inertia and may resist attempts to break out and work out. Pay attention to the messages your mind is sending your body. Recognize your mind's resistance, and then determine that your will to be well is infinitely stronger than your mind's stubborn resolve to stay at rest. Maggie Spilner, the walking editor of *Prevention* Magazine's Healthy Ideas website (www.healthyideas.com), suggests the following exercise: Repeat a word or phrase that is meaningful to you and has the power to propel you out the door. Some examples she gives are: "I love how I feel when I'm walking"; "I am strong and healthy"; "walking works wonders." My favorite is, "I am walking to wellness." Such affirmations have the power to raise your energy and lift your spirits. The hardest part is getting out the door—once you are walking, the good feelings the activity generates take care of the rest.

Wellness Walking Week-by-Week

WEEK ONE

For the first week, walk at least four times. If you are new to fitness, begin with just three times a week. During the first week, walk as long and as briskly as you can while still feeling good about it. Try at least ten minutes each walk but just do whatever you can. No excuses! The aim this week is to gradually begin integrating exercise into your daily life. The key is to build walking into a habit, as integral to your day as brushing your teeth. If you start gradually, walking will become a highlight of your day, not a drag. Getting started may be hard at first, but as it becomes a habit, your exercise will seem as essential to you as the air you breathe.

It is especially important during this first week that walking be enjoyable. Remind yourself that each walk is a time out you are taking for your health and happiness. If you enjoy and value the time spent walking, you will stick with it.

WEEK TWO

Gradually increase the frequency and duration of your walks. Add five minutes to each walk you take, and be sure to take at least four walks this week. So, for Week Two, walk a minimum of fifteen minutes on four days, and spread the days out if you can.

As you walk, be aware of your posture and pace. If you find that your eyes are fixed on the sidewalk, lift your chin. Put a smile on your face and enjoy the scenery. Correct shrugged shoulders. Focus on walking heel to toe. How is your pace? Increase your speed by taking short, fast steps, rather than big, gaping steps.

WEEK THREE

You've been walking almost every day for two weeks. Congratulations! You should be feeling great, enjoying more energy throughout the day, and sleeping more soundly through the night. This week, increase your walking time to at least twenty minutes a day for at least four days.

If you find it hard to set aside twenty straight minutes each day, it is fine to occasionally split your walking time in half, walking ten minutes in the morning and the remaining ten in the afternoon or evening. Twenty consecutive minutes is optimal, because it takes about ten minutes to get your heart rate up to the point that you are a little huffy and puffy. Even if you don't have twenty consecutive minutes, however, ten minutes here and ten minutes there is much, much better than not walking at all.

And remember, the goal is to find ways of integrating physical activity into your daily life. As walking becomes a habit, you will find it increasingly easy to set aside your exercise time. In time, it will become the activity around which you schedule other things.

WEEK FOUR

You are steps away from a full month of regular walking. Congratulations on our resolve and dedication! By now you are probably finding that walking has become its own reward. You look and feel great, your skin glows, your attitude is improved, and stress affects

♦

you less and less. Even those who have never exercised until now have begun to experience the benefits of physical activity.

For this week, increase the duration of your walk by another five minutes and boost the frequency of your walks one more day. Your goal this week is to walk a minimum of twenty-five minutes on at least five days. In any case, just do the best that you can.

Have you hit the walker's wall? If excuses spring to mind before you set out on a walk, take a long, hard look at them. Is it a legitimate excuse? In other words, should it really stand between you and your walk? Unless you are truly sick or injured, overcome the excuse by repeating an affirmation such as, "I am walking to wellness." Repeat it over and over until your walking shoes are on, your laces are tied, and you are out the door, arms pumping, feet gliding, energy soaring!

If at any point the prescribed pace begins to feel uncomfortable and you are feeling exhausted, reduce the duration of your walk by five minutes. While you are establishing the exercise habit, the frequency of your walks is much more important than the length of time you walk. Frequency is also more important than pace. If you are getting huffy and puffy in the first five minutes of your walk, feeling breathless and unable to speak comfortably, you are walking too fast. Make your pace as brisk as feels comfortable given your current state of fitness. If you are moving so fast that you are uncomfortable, you will not enjoy your walk and will be missing out on one of the greatest benefits of exercise. Use the "talk test" to determine the right speed. If you are too huffy and puffy to be able to speak, you are walking too fast. Walking almost every day is essential, especially in the beginning. It's the habit of actually getting motivated, putting your walking shoes on and getting yourself out the door, that is most important to ingrain in your mind and body right now.

If at any point you are feeling more ambitious than the program prescribes, there are many enjoyable ways to increase the intensity of your walk. Find a path that includes hills. Slight grades will work muscles harder, burn calories faster, and get your heart pumping more vigorously. If you live near the beach, walk barefoot in the sand. Walking in sand adds a level of resistance that works your calf muscles especially well. At one time, fitness experts encouraged the use of small hand or ankle weights to increase workout intensity, but now most agree that even the lightest weights invite injury to the joints and muscles.

The most common reason people get waylaid on their walk to wellness is lack of time. I cannot count the number of times people have told me, "I'm too busy to exercise." In fact, I cannot count the number of times I've said this to myself! There are some creative ways around that particular walker's wall, as I know from firsthand experience. The exercise program can easily be integrated into even the busiest schedule with just a little bit of imagination and flexibility.

Remember Jerry's story, told earlier? Jerry found room for walking in his hectic life by leaving the car in the garage and trading tires for a pair of walking shoes with good treads. He walked thirty minutes to and from work each day. At first, when he was just starting out, he woke up an hour early to give himself enough time to walk to work. He was very out of shape and needed extra time to walk at a very moderate pace. Within two weeks, however, walking at a comfortable pace, the walk to work took only twenty minutes.

If you live too far from work to walk the entire way, continue to drive but park three or four blocks from your workplace. Alternately, spend half of your lunch hour walking. Just bring a pair of walking shoes to work with you. You will be amazed at how much energy you have after lunch, and how much more focused and productive you are in those afternoon hours.

There are other excellent ways to integrate a workout into your work day. Skip the elevator and take the stairs. Climbing stairs, like walking, is a weight-bearing activity that builds stronger muscles and bones. This is true of both walking up and down the stairs. This healthy habit will probably save you time as you no longer wait for the elevator to arrive.

Throughout the day, be aware of your posture. Both sitting and standing, your spine should be elongated, your chest open, and your shoulders relaxed. So many shoulder, neck, and backaches are the result of poor posture at work. Slouching in your chair puts tremendous pressure on your lower back, and hunching over your desk strains the muscles of the back, neck, and shoulders. Poor posture is usually a manifestation of stress. When stress makes you feel tired and sluggish, it shows in your shoulders. When stress makes you feel constrained and under pressure, your chest tends to collapse inward and literally does constrain your breathing capacity. Remember, you are learning to prevent stress and all of the manifestations of stress, especially overweight and illness.

Small corrections in your posture at work can help relieve tension and discomfort and help you have more productive workdays. My patients often tell me that as they became aware of correct posture, they felt less tense and pressured. By learning to sit straight and lift up out of your hips, elongating your spine, you will breathe deeper, feel taller and lighter, have more energy, and experience pain and discomfort much less frequently.

Simple Wellness Yoga Stretching Is Simply Essential

As I mentioned previously, walking is most beneficial when combined with simple stretching. The combination of walking and stretching has a powerful impact on your health, weight, and energy. Like walking, stretching is an activity suitable for all fitness types, no matter how flexible you are right now.

Before introducing you to nine easy wellness yoga stretches that you can easily and joyfully incorporate into your daily activities, it is important that you understand how stretching fits into the overall health and weight goals you are ready to achieve. The stretches included in this program are especially beneficial because they are based on yoga, an ancient art and science that has become so popular in the West because it balances body, mind, and spirit.

Let's stick with stress for a moment. Remember, stress is the trigger that sets off energy imbalance. Being overweight is one of the most common effects of energy imbalance. Stretching is an ideal strategy for relieving stress. Freeing yourself of harmful stress is the first and most important step to freeing yourself of excess weight.

Physical and psychological health are deeply intertwined. Only an exercise program that works out your body and mind will be effective. Physical energy imbalance affects your mood and attitude. When your energy is low, self-esteem and body image tend to plummet. Similarly, when your self-esteem is waning and you feel bad about yourself, you tend to make less than optimal choices about what you eat and what you do. The health of the body and mind go hand in hand.

The regular practice of stretching helps strengthen and tone muscles, increases flexibility, and relaxes both body and mind. Stretching makes the joints more loose and supple, and it relaxes the large muscle groups in your legs and back. Slow, gentle stretching relieves stress in the body and in the mind, improving your mental focus and clarity, reducing worry and anxiety, strengthening your overall well-being. Remember: Mental well-being is necessary for a **well being**.

Stretching also incorporates methods of breathing that help increase the capacity of the lungs. Not only does this strengthen your respiratory system, but improving the flow of oxygen throughout your body also helps bring essential nutrients to the muscles. After stretching, most people experience a surge of energy and feel refreshed. That feeling results because stretching enhances the circulation of blood throughout your entire body.

For adults in the later stages of the cycle of life, wellness yoga stretching has another major benefit: The regular practice of stretching improves your balance and equilibrium. As we age and entropy speeds up, balance begins to decline. In 1997, the *Journal of the American Geriatrics Society* published a study showing that for adults over age sixty, poor balance contributed to a more than 50 percent increase in their risk of a fall-related injury.

Just as exercise strengthens bones and slows bone mass loss, regular physical activity can improve balance. Stretches that build balance are especially important for women forty and over, who experience the most rapid loss of balance. In her book, *Strong Women Stay Young*, Miriam Nelson writes that most women in this age group can hold their balance on one leg for less than fifteen seconds. Men, she says, because of their tendency to have more physical strength, don't begin to lose balance until about age fifty.

Remember that chronological age is usually different from physiological age. Very active older adults have greater balance than inactive younger people. The more physical activity you get, the more balance you will have.

Test your own balance now: Stand firmly on both feet, eyes focused straight ahead on a point that is not moving. Slowly shift your weight onto what you consider to be your strongest leg. Slowly lift your other foot off the floor. Count the number of seconds you remain balanced. Dr. James Rippe, a cardiologist at Tufts University School of Medicine in Boston, gives the following formula to assess your equilibrium: If you can stand on one leg for twenty-two seconds or more, you have the equilibrium of a twenty-year-old; fifteen seconds compares to a thirty-year-old; 7.2 seconds to a forty-year-old; 3.7 seconds to a fifty-year-old; and 2.5 seconds to a sixty-year-old.

No matter what age you are, you can develop the equilibrium of a twenty- or thirty-year-old. Exercises such as walking and stretching strengthen and tone the muscles in your legs and back which give you balance. Greater balance reduces your risk of falls and fall-related injuries.

Stretching has all the wonderful attributes of walking. It's enjoyable, you move at your own pace, and it encourages physical well-being as well as peace of mind. Like walking, stretching stimulates the flow of energy throughout your body. This energy is vital for weight loss. Many patients tell me that after struggling to lose weight for years, the breakthrough came, surprisingly, with stretching. Gentle stretching calms and balances your energy, and when energy is balanced, weight loss occurs naturally.

Like walking, stretching is meant to be enjoyed. Never strain, pull, or bounce while you stretch. Everybody, depending on their level of flexibility, has a different comfort zone. Whether your body is limber or stiff, all you have to do is find your point of comfort and stay there. Stretching is a challenging but noncompetitive activity. As long as you enjoy it, you will continue to practice it.

Let's cover some basics before introducing you to wellness yoga stretches.

1. Stretching will be easier and more comfortable if you do not eat a meal just before you begin. If you stretch in the morning,

a piece of fruit beforehand is fine. But consuming a large meal will make you sluggish, and much of the energy you generate will be diverted to the process of digestion.

2. Try to pick a regular time to stretch. If possible, stretch just before your wellness walk. Stretching at a regular time will help create the habit of stretching in your daily life.

3. Wear loose and comfortable clothing, but nothing too baggy that will interfere with your range of movement. Use an exercise mat or blanket if the floor is hard or cold. Preferably, stretch with bare feet or socks only.

4. Find a quiet place with fresh air to practice your stretching. If weather permits, outdoor stretching is ideal—you get the benefits of stretching, sunlight, and fresh air. Indoors is fine, as long as it is mostly free of distracting noises and smells. If possible, stretch near an open window.

5. Honor your body. The purpose of stretching is to relax. Many people have a tremendously difficult time succumbing to relaxation. The more you relax in your stretches, the greater the health benefits. Remember that the goal is to relieve stress in the body, so don't push yourself too hard. Be comfortable and enjoy.

6. Breathe. Many people tend to hold their breath during stretching, which adds tension and strain to the activity. As you stretch, breathe freely and smoothly. The point is to unwind, not get yourself all wound up. How can you decompress if you are holding in all of that stale air?

Breathing is so important to your health and energy. Because we breathe naturally, you may think a breathing practice is unnecessary. Most of us, however, do not breathe to our full capacity because stress and tension get in the way. Try this simple breathing exercise, which will help you breathe more fully and deeply:

Lie down on your back with your legs outstretched and your feet relaxed. Place your hands on each side of your rib cage. Now, inhale slowly and deeply, and feel your breath rise up through your abdomen, then your lower lungs, then your upper lungs and entire chest. Exhale slowly and feel your chest, ribs, and abdomen relax as the breath goes out. You can also do this while sitting up comfortably with good posture while gently relaxing your shoulders.

This may be the opposite of how you presently breathe. To get into the habit of breathing this way, place your hands on your abdomen and feel it expand when you inhale and constrict when you exhale. If it helps, you can also imagine your lungs and abdomen as a balloon that fills with air as you inhale and releases air as you exhale. Repeat this breathing practice three more times, each time following the breath as it expands up through the body as you inhale, relaxing the body as you exhale.

Practice this basic full breath during and between each stretch. Breathing deeply and slowly will help you relax into each stretching position. In between stretches, deep, full breathing will heighten your awareness of the wonderful feeling of energy flowing through your body.

This breath is also excellent to practice in situations or moments when you feel inundated by stress. No one even has to know you are doing anything out of the ordinary. Just focus on your breath, breathe deeply, and feel the breath rise and fall in your chest and torso. This breathing exercise will loosen up a tight chest, relax pinched shoulders, calm nerves, and cool body temperature.

Now you are ready to learn the wellness yoga stretches. Many may feel familiar to you. Just keep in mind that the goal here is to relax and restore your energy. Practice the stretches in the order described below, as the sequence takes the body through a deliberate range of motions and movements. This series of stretches will give your body a thorough and balanced workout. Like walking, stretching is easily adaptable to all body types and fitness levels. People at all ages and fitness levels can benefit from these stretches. To increase the intensity of a stretch, hold it longer. Each stretch can be modified for those with less flexibility. Listen to your own body's limits and keep the stretches comfortable. This entire cycle of wellness yoga stretches requires a minimum of fifteen minutes to complete. As your flexibility and strength improve, as well as your ability to relax, you will find yourself taking more time, holding stretches longer, relaxing more deeply. You can spend fifteen minutes or an hour with this cycle. Its up to you. But take at least the necessary fifteen minutes, at least five times a week, to get the full benefits of stretching.

Leg Stretches

As walking builds and strengthens your leg muscles, it is important to do stretching that keeps these muscles limber and loose. These stretches promote flexibility, which balances the strength-building effects of walking. Strong and flexible legs improve your balance and provide protection for your lower back.

1. Lie on your back and let the muscles of your back relax against the floor. Bend your knees so that both feet rest on the floor beneath your knees. Let your arms relax by your sides with palms upturned. Wiggle your fingers to relax them. Breathe deeply and relax.

2. Begin drawing your knees toward your chest. Wrap your arms around your knees and slowly hug your legs to your chest while taking full, deep breaths. Each time you exhale, allow your legs to relax further toward your chest. As you relax into this stretch, let your lower back raise slightly off the floor.

3. Continue breathing deeply and lower your left foot to the floor with your knee bent. Now gently stretch the right leg by raising your foot toward the sky. Use your hands to support your leg if necessary, and if your legs are stiff, keep the knee slightly bent. Hold this stretch for a while, remembering to breath deeply. Lower the leg and repeat with your left leg.

4. After stretching your right and left legs, bend your knees and pull both legs to your chest once more. Feel the stretch in the lower back while breathing and relaxing After several deep breaths, lower your feet to the floor and stretch out your legs fully. Let your legs and back relax.

The Cobra

With this position, you stretch the chest and strengthen the muscles of the lower back. The Cobra improves flexibility in your spine, which is essential for balance. It also unties the knots of tension that tend to build up in your back, allowing you to move more freely and comfortably in all your daily activities. The Cobra is excellent therapy if you suffer from low back pain.

1. Roll over on your belly, legs outstretched. Place the palms of your hands on the floor just beneath your shoulders. Keep your elbows tucked in close to your sides. Lift your head gently so your chin rests lightly on the floor. (For a gentler stretch, turn your fingers toward each other with your elbows turned out.)

2. While slowly inhaling, begin raising your chin and upper chest off the floor. Focus on using your back muscles, not your arms, to lift yourself. Your palms should be resting lightly against the floor, not pressing against it. Take a deep, full breath and, as you exhale, relax your shoulders and pull them away from your ears. Hold this stretch, while taking several breaths, only for as long as it is comfortable.

3. Gently lower your chest back to the floor. Turn your head and rest your cheek against the floor, and let your arms relax loosely at your sides. Continue breathing, nice and deep.

4. Return your palms to the floor beneath your shoulders. Lengthen your legs out behind you. Lift your head and rest your chin on the floor. This time, as you inhale, press your palms against the floor as if you are doing a push-up (unless you are doing the gentler stretch). Now tighten your buttocks, lift up your torso, and extend the arch in your back, keeping your stomach and hips on the floor. You should feel a gentle stretching of the muscles in your middle and lower back. Arch your back only as far as it is comfortable and without straining. Remember to take slow, deep breaths.

5. As you exhale, begin slowly lowering your body to the floor. Rest your cheek on the floor, breathe deeply, and relax your entire body.

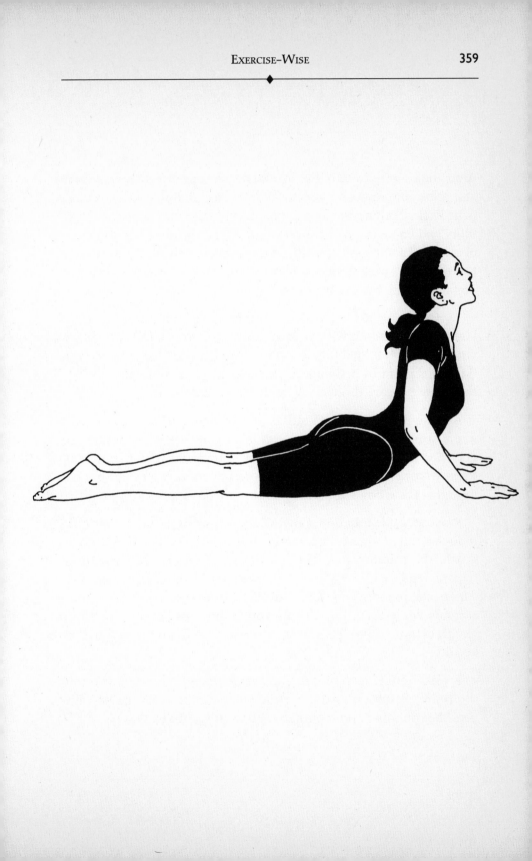

The Cat

After the Cobra stretch, it is important to continue to fully stretch and relax your spine and back. The Cat stretch flexes and stretches your back all along the length of your spine, building greater flexibility and encouraging healthy alignment. This stretch is also especially good for people with tight or sore lower backs. If you wake up in the morning with a stiff back, this is a wonderful stretch to do first thing, even before stepping into the shower.

1. Kneel on the floor with your knees just under your hips and your hands lined up with your shoulders. If your knees are stiff or tender, place a folded blanket under them. Turn the palms so your fingertips point directly ahead. Straighten your spine and neck so that your eyes are directed at the floor beneath you.

2. Take a deep breath, and as you exhale, curl your back, just like a stretching cat. Tuck your chin to your chest to round your neck and upper back, and gently tuck your pelvis under your hips. Press your palms against the floor so your arms are straight but not locked at the elbows. Take several slow, deep breaths.

3. Now, while inhaling, slowly flatten your back, raise your chin to look straight ahead, and gently arch your spine to create a small dip in the middle back. Stretch the front of your neck without hyperextending it and allow your shoulders to pull away from your ears to create more length in your neck. Hold the stretch for several seconds while breathing deeply and feeling the stretch down the length of your spine. Keep your elbows straight and your head relaxed.

4. Take a full, deep breath and, as you exhale, slowly move into the rounded stretch again, curling your back toward the sky. Repeat the rounding and arching sequence three times slowly.

Seated Shoulder Stretch

Now that you have stretched your legs and spine, the shoulders and upper body need attention. Many people carry a good deal of tension in their shoulders and upper back. Tension in the upper spine can throw your whole back out of balance.

1. Sit comfortably on the floor with your legs crossed. First concentrate on good posture, lifting up out of your hips and elongating the spine. Rest your palms in your lap, fingers intertwined. Inhale deeply and raise your arms above your head, turning the palms towards the sky. As you slowly exhale, pull your shoulders down away from your ears.

2. Continue to breathe deeply and gently press your arms back behind your head, feeling the stretch down the inside of the arms and in the shoulders. While exhaling, slowly lower your arms and return your palms back to your lap.

3. Shake your arms out by your side, wiggling the fingers, shaking out the wrists. Rest your palms back in your lap and feel the energy in your shoulders.

4. Intertwine your fingers again. This time, as you inhale, stretch your arms out in front of you and lift your hands to chest level. Turn your palms away from you and press them outwards, and round your upper back gently, creating a stretch down the upper back and shoulders, down the length of your arms. To create a deeper stretch, pull your shoulders down away from your ears. Hold the stretch for several breaths, exhale, and release.

5. Shake your arms out by your side again, releasing any tension in your upper back and shoulders. Finally, wrap your arms around your shoulders as if you are giving yourself a hug. Sit up with good posture and gently tuck your chin into your chest. Pull your shoulders away from your ears and feel the stretch in your neck and shoulders. Take several deep breaths, then relax.

The Rag Doll

A great way to relieve tension in the back is to let gravity do its magic. The Rag Doll works with the flow of gravity to stretch and relax your entire spine, neck, and shoulders. The stretch is also wonderful for flexibility in the legs. If you have a history of dizziness or high blood pressure, be cautious and hold this stretch only briefly.

1. Stand upright, feet together and firmly planted on the floor. Lift your chest, pull your shoulders down and back, tuck in your pelvis, and keep your knees fairly firm but relaxed bent about 2–4 inches. Your chin should be level with the floor, your eyes focused straight ahead. Let your arms dangle loosely by your sides.

2. Begin with a slow deep breath. As you exhale, tuck your chin gently into your chest and begin to slowly round your upper body from the waist, while curling your chest over your legs. Let your arms swing loosely in front of you, without tension.

3. As you breathe, bend over as far as is comfortable for you. If your legs are stiff or if you feel strain in your hamstrings or shins, bend your knees a little bit more. Continue breathing fully and deeply, relaxing further with each exhalation.

4. While inhaling, very slowly come back up to a standing and upright position. Make sure to keep your knees soft, while tucking in your pelvis and keeping your chin pressed toward your chest until you are standing upright in order to avoid dizziness.

5. Stand still and with good posture for a while. As you breathe, release any lingering tension or tightness in your back and legs.

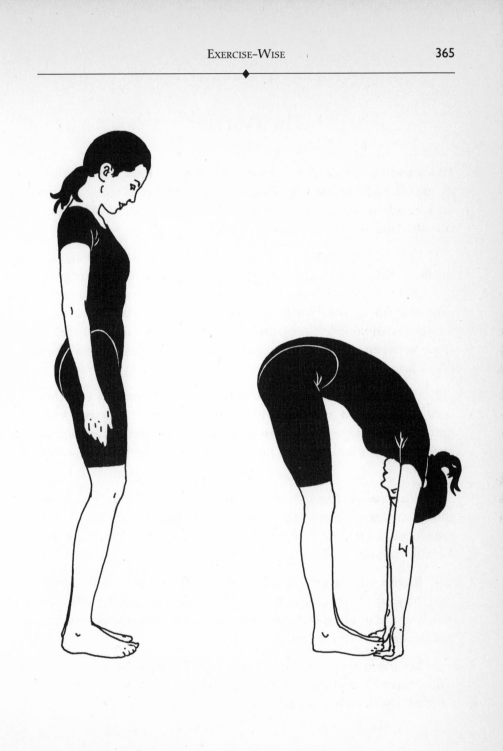

The Warrior

This standing stretch strengthens the legs while improving flexibility in your back. While stretching the upper back, this stretch opens up your chest area, improving your breathing capacity. The Warrior also improves your balance.

1. Stand upright with good posture, feet firmly pressing against the floor. Bring your palms together at your chest, in a prayer position, and relax your shoulders. Inhale deeply, expanding your ribcage and filling your lungs with air. As you exhale, take a step forward with your left foot, creating between one and two feet of space between your feet. Keep your hips squared forward and your knees firm but not locked.

2. Continue breathing deeply and fully while bending your left knee until it is just over your ankle (not your toes). Bend your knee only to the point you are comfortable—do not strain your leg or knee. Stretch your right leg firmly behind you, heel pressing into the floor.

3. With palms together, lift your arms above your head and gently back, creating a slight arch in the upper back. Keep your eyes focused forward and hold the stretch for as long as it is comfortable for you.

4. Breath deeply again, and as you exhale, lower your hands back to your chest, step your right foot forward to your left, and slowly come to an upright, standing position. Breathe deeply and relax your arms to your sides.

5. Let the muscles in your legs and back relax. When you are ready, repeat the stretch with your right leg coming forward and your left leg stretched behind you.

The Half Moon

It is important during stretching to use your back's full range of motion to promote maximum flexibility. Arching and bending stretches need to be balanced with sideways bending stretches. The Half Moon stretches the sides of your back and promotes suppleness in the spine. This stretch is also wonderful for increasing circulation and strengthening your breath. Moreover, it tones the muscles of the waist and abdomen.

1. Stand upright with good posture, feet firmly together with your knees relaxed. Inhale deeply and raise your arms above your head until your palms meet lightly.

2. Exhale slowly and bend your upper body to the right. Bend from the waist and keep your hips squared straight ahead. Hold your head relaxed and centered in between your arms and be sure you are not hunching your shoulders to your ears.

3. Hold the stretch for as long as it is comfortable—hopefully for at least three complete breaths. Now inhale as you come back to the center, rising up onto your toes and stretching the soles of your feet with your arms reaching toward the sky. Exhale as you lower yourself back down onto your feet while relaxing your arms by your side. Relax.

4. Repeat the stretch again, this time bending to the left. Focus on your lower back, making sure it is not swaying and that it is gently tucked forward. As you hold the sideways stretch, roll your shoulders gently backward so that your rib cage expands.

Gentle Spinal Stretch

Having stretched the spine forward and back and side to side, now it is important to gently twist the spine. Twisting stretches restore suppleness to the disks between each vertebrae and help keep your spine in proper alignment. A limber spine is truly the backbone of health and fitness. If your spine is inflexible, it effects all of the muscles in your back and hips. Twisting stretches also stimulate energy in the digestive area and help promote healthy digestion.

1. Stretch out on your back on your floor. Stretch your legs out in front of you with your arms at your side. Inhale deeply and use your abdominal muscles to pull both knees up to your chest. Hug them gently there for a moment and then, keeping your legs bent and your knees together, lower your legs to the right side. Let your legs rest against the floor, or, if they don't reach the floor, rest them on a pillow beside you.

2. Outstretch your arms at shoulder height and flatten your upper back and shoulders against the floor. With your legs resting to the right, turn your head gently to the left to increase the twist. Continue breathing deeply and fully, relaxing more into the twist each time you exhale.

3. Take a deep breath and use your abdominal muscles to help draw your knees back to your chest. Now slowly lower your feet to the ground and stretch out your legs. Relax your arms by your side and consciously let go of any tension you are holding in your back or legs.

4. Repeat this stretch, twisting your legs to the left and gently turning your head to the right.

Relaxation Stretch

In stretching it is important to combine rigor with relaxation. The benefits of stretching are deepened and more fully felt when you take a few moments after stretching to consciously relax the entire body. As you relax, you can feel all the energy generated from your stretching coursing through every muscle of your body. This is also a wonderful time to reaffirm your commitment to wellness to yourself. Relaxed and refreshed, your body and mind are receptive to such positive input.

1. Lie on your back, legs stretched out before you. Let your legs and feet relax, toes pointing comfortably outward. Rest your arms easily by your sides, palms upward, fingers free of tension. Gently close your eyes so that you are not distracted by anything in your environment. If you are cold, cover yourself with a warm blanket.

2. If your back is sore in this position, modify the stretch by placing a chair in front of you and resting your lower legs on the seat of the chair. The chair will help support your lower back.

3. Lie still in this position, being aware of how your body feels. Find any tension lingering in the body and imagine that as you exhale, you release the tension. Breathe slowly and deeply, letting the slow smooth rhythm of your breath relax you further.

4. Remain in the Relaxation stretch for at least five minutes, giving your body a chance to experience all of the effects of stretching. Slowly open your eyes and come to a seated position, and feel how refreshed and energetic you are.

Summing Up Exercise

Whether you practice your walking, stretching and strength training together, or do them at separate times of the day, the combination of activities is a powerful prescription for health, energy, and weight loss. As you notice your progress, you will be motivated to continue and make exercise an essential part of your daily life, as natural as getting dressed in the morning.

To help make your progress visible, take the time each day to note a few things about your exercise and how you are feeling in the journal you are keeping about your eating patterns. These notes are important reminders to yourself of how much you are learning, growing, achieving, and gaining (or, in most cases, losing!). If you skip a day of exercise, write down how you feel then, too. Do you notice a change in your energy level? How about your sleep? Take note of all your changes. After a month of walking, or other exercise, stretching and strength training, turn back the pages and read your notes in those early days and weeks. See how far you have come!

If you are ill, physically disabled, or for any reason unable to walk, stretch or lift weights as much as I have suggested, then just do as much as you can. Just do it and please remember that there should be no excuses.

Before going on to Simple Strength Training (Part Nine of this revised book), I want to alert you to a new scientific report: a study of 72,000 nurses published in the August 26, 1999 issue of *The New England Journal of Medicine,* indicated that the women who walked briskly for just three hours a week reduced their risk of heart disease by more than a third!

Part Nine

SIMPLE STRENGTH TRAINING

In 1999, since the first edition of *Balance Your Body, Balance Your Life* was published, the American College of Sports Medicine issued an official recommendation urging people over 50 to do strength training two to three days a week.

Now that I've reached 60 and I can feel and see the positive results of strength training, I sure wish I had started at 50. But like many people my age, I didn't because I thought it would be too tedious, complicated, and frankly not necessary for better health. I was wrong! Strength training is easy, enjoyable and beneficial—*especially because the results occur so simply.*

Moreover, strength training is the only type of exercise that substantially slows down and even reverses the loss of muscle, bone density and overall strength that used to be considered inevitable in the second half of our personal human life cycle. A study in the prestigious *New England Journal of Medicine* reported that in just 10 weeks of a strength training program, 50 frail men and women were able to increase their weight-lifting ability by more than 100 percent! *There's no way to stop time—but you can help to make entropy smooth sailing.*

Don't worry if you're not athletic. Don't worry if you have never done anything like this before. You should be comforted by the fact that this is an ideal form of exercise because it doesn't require athletic prowess—*just a willingness to concentrate on what you are doing and a commitment to stick with it.* Strength training reshapes your body, makes you feel younger, and helps you lose weight naturally and permanently. It's ideal for women, not only to help prevent and reverse osteoporosis, but also to help decrease symptoms of **PMS** and menopause. After strength training for just six months, women as well as men are extremely likely to stay with it forever!

The eight exercises featured in this chapter are perfect for beginners and non-beginners. Motivation is the biggest challenge until you establish a routine, so designate a specific time of the day— preferably before breakfast or before lunch.

You may wish to start your strength training at a gym or, if you can afford it, hire a personal trainer to help get you into a routine and keep you motivated. You may also decide to work out with a friend. But all you really need to get started, working out in the comfort and convenience of your own home, is three sets of weights!

Purchase Three Sets of Two Weights
SMALL FRAME: Fair Strength (most women)
3 pounds • 5 pounds • 8 pounds
LARGER FRAME: More Strength (most men)
5 pounds • 8 pounds • 10 pounds

The goal is to condition your major muscles by lifting weights heavy enough to achieve two to three sets of 10–15 repetitions before the muscles become fatigued. Two or three days a week for 20 to 30 minutes a session is ideal. Take a day or two off between strength training sessions to give your muscles a rest. *Just enjoy your increased energy!*

It's very important to do at least a few stretches to get limber before strength training, so try doing your wellness yoga stretches. Also, it's best to get your heart beating faster and work up a little bit of a sweat, so try some brisk "wellness walking" before starting.

Whether you are a beginner or not, you should start slowly and progress gradually. Women especially should choose lighter weights and go easy on themselves, rather than experience too much exertion.

- Start with what really feels like a light weight for you.
- Breathe properly by exhaling . . . *slowly* . . . while lifting weights, and inhaling while returning weights to the starting position.
- Do the exercise slowly, 15 times in a perfect form, by concentrating on the involved muscles.
- If it was no challenge at all, then move up to the next heavier weight for the next set.
- If it was too heavy for you to be comfortable, then move down to the lower weight.
- If it was challenging but something you were able to accomplish, then that is your weight!
- From now on, do three sets of 10–15 repetitions with this weight until it becomes way too easy. You may wish to purchase two heavier weight in a month or two.

STRENGTH TRAINING AT HOME

- Lunges—for your buttocks, thighs and legs
- One Arm Row—for your back
- Pectoral Fly—for your chest
- Lateral Raise—for your upper arms
- Upright Row—for your shoulders
- Biceps Concentration Curl—for front of your upper arms
- Triceps Extension—for back of your upper arms
- Abdominal Crunches—for your abdomen

Lunges: Stand up straight with your feet slightly apart and your abdominal muscles tightened. Take a large step forward with your right foot, while bending both of your knees. Keep your right foot flat while your left knee is pointing towards the floor. It's very important that the knee of your forward leg is over your foot, not in front of it. Pause for a moment and then push back with your right leg, raising yourself upright again. Do this 10–15 times and then repeat the exercise with your left leg in front of you. If you have difficulty balancing, you can always hold onto a chair by your side with one hand for support.

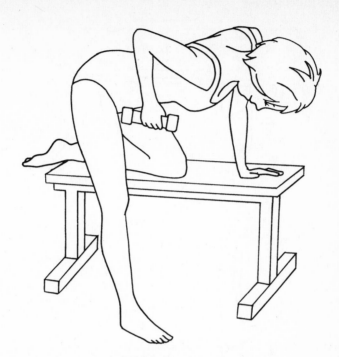

One Arm Row (Use medium weights.): Start with your right foot on the floor and your left knee on a bench or a chair seat. Keep your back parallel to the floor rather than hunching up, and let your right hand hang down while holding the weight. Tighten your abdominal muscles, bend your right elbow and pull your upper arm as far back as it will comfortably go. Keep your palm facing your body and don't swing your elbow out to the side. Pause and slowly lower the weight. Except for the arm raising the weight, keep the rest of your body still. After you do this 10–15 times with one arm, repeat with your other arm. Do two or three sets with each arm, pausing briefly between sets.

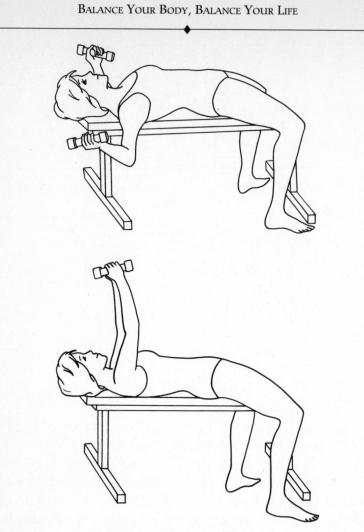

Pectoral Fly (Use medium weights.): Keep your feet flat and your hips and shoulders on the bench. Tighten your abdominal muscles and push your arms up until your elbows are almost straight with your palms facing each other. Pause and slowly lower your arms. Move your arms up and then back in a smooth arc as if you were wrapping and then unwrapping your arms around someone. Don't lower your arms much below the level of the bench. Make sure to visualize your pectoral muscles doing all the work. Do 10–15 repetitions of this exercise. Do two or three sets.

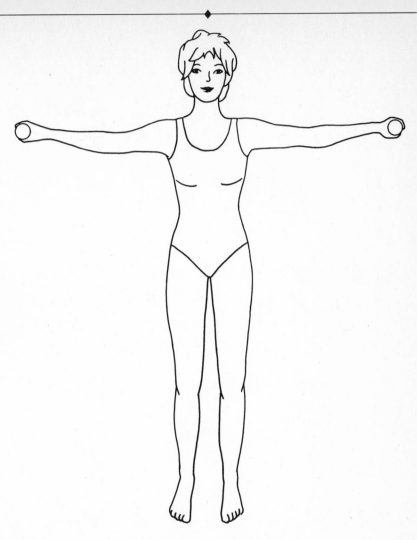

Lateral Raise (Use light or medium weights.): Start with your feet at hip-width apart, your knees slightly bent, your abdominal muscles tightened and both hands hanging down at your sides while holding the weights. Now straighten (but don't lock) your elbows and lift both arms simultaneously away from your sides until they reach shoulder level. Pause and slowly lower your arms back to your sides. Don't lean forward during this exercise and make sure to keep your palms turned downwards as your lift. Do 10–15 repetitions of this exercise. Do two or three sets.

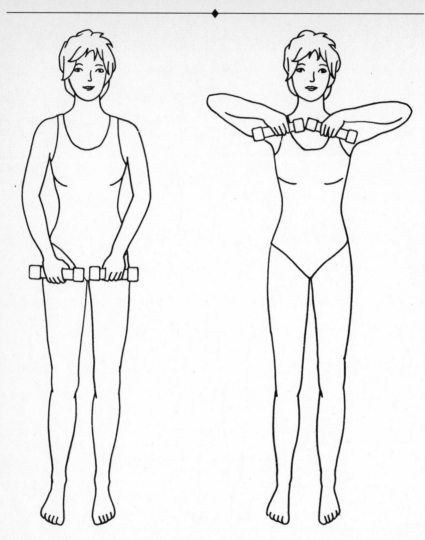

Upright Row (Use light or medium weights.): Start with your feet hip-width apart, your knees slightly bent and your abdominal muscles tightened. Both hands should be holding the weights and let them hang down in front of your thighs with your palms facing in. Now slowly lift your arms up until the weights are slightly higher than your shoulders. Pause and slowly lower the weights back down. Don't lean back or forward as you lift and don't swing the weights around. Do 10–15 repetitions of this exercise. Do two or three sets.

Biceps Concentration Curl (Use medium to heavy weights.): Sit on a bench or a chair with your feet more than shoulder-width apart. Holding a weight in your right hand, lean forward and place your right elbow against the inside of your right knee. Tighten your abdominal muscles and slowly curl the weight toward your shoulder as if you were cracking a walnut between your elbow. Focus on squeezing your biceps at the top of the curl and lower the weight at the same speed that you lifted it. Do this exercise 10–15 times before switching sides. Do two or three sets with each arm.

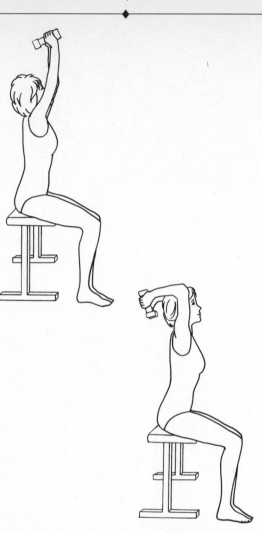

Triceps Extension (Use medium weights.): Sit comfortably with your feet flat on the floor. Tighten your abdominal muscles. Push the weights up until your arms are straight and your palms are facing each other. Pause and slowly bend your elbows while keeping your upper arm straight. Lower the weights until you feel a stretch in your triceps (or the weights are close to touching your shoulders). Pause and straighten your elbows, keeping your upper arms still while slowly lifting the weights back up in an arc so you don't hit your head. Keep your elbows pointed up so they don't flare out to your sides during the movement. Do 10–15 repetitions of this exercise. Do two to three sets.

Abdominal Crunches: Keep your knees bent and feet flat on the floor. Imagine that you are pushing the small of your back into the floor. Place your hands behind your head with your elbows comfortably out to your sides. Use your hands only to keep your neck supported, not to lift it or push your chin up or forward. Tighten your abdominal muscles and raise your head, shoulders and upper back just a few inches off the floor. Come up about 30 degrees, hold for a moment while squeezing your abdominal muscles, and then slowly lower your shoulders all the way back down. Keep going until you do three sets of 10–15 crunches, pausing very briefly in between sets.

Part Ten

NUTRITIONAL
SUPPLEMENTS . . .
BEYOND DEFICIENCY

Descartes Was Wrong!

Scientific progress took a wrong turn during the seventeenth century, when philosopher Rene Descartes claimed that good science consisted only of those things that could be measured objectively. The impact of Descartes's pronouncement has been profound. Based on this paradigm, medical students are trained to see the body as a collection of cells and organs constantly in need of repair. From the paradigm of wellness, I view the body as an energy system always seeking balance and remembering wellness. The treatments I prescribe for patients assist their body's own efforts to restore balance and remember wellness. I prescribe treatments that assist the body's natural internal pharmacy—the healing force known as homeostasis. Homeostasis is the key to *Total Health Rejuvenation* and permanent weight loss.

Homeostasis baffles the traditional scientific paradigm because it is difficult to observe and measure. Keep in mind, however, that just because something cannot be measured or observed under a microscope does not disprove its existence.

Homeostasis is always at work in your body, even as youth eventually gives way to entropy. Constant changes encoded in your DNA began in your body from the moment your father's sperm united with your mother's egg. Every minute, hour, day, month, and season of your life has reflected this incredible journey. Even as you approach the last stage of your lifecycle, you'll be powered by the very same energy that first breathed life into you. When used properly, vitamins and minerals stimulate homeostasis and permanent weight loss. It may sometimes be difficult to measure such factors, but they do exist. *Descartes was wrong.*

Vitamins and minerals are some of nature's best catalysts for energy balance. Your body uses the chemicals in these substances to build, maintain, and repair your tissues and organs. Unfortunately, the medically recommended uses of vitamins and minerals established years ago no longer address our modern understanding of energy and total wellness.

There is an entirely new and evolving science of nutritional supplementation—much of it beyond the scope of this book—that addresses many everyday but significant problems: "Social drinkers" require more vitamins C, B_6, B_{12}, and zinc; smokers require extra vitamin C and folic acid; sexually active men need more zinc; people regularly using antacids need more thiamin and calcium; antibiotics may deplete the body of vitamin C, riboflavin, and zinc; cholesterol-lowering medicine may lower blood levels of vitamins A, B_{12}, D, K, and folic acid; even regular laxative use can deplete the body of vitamins A, C, D, E, and K.

Medical doctors have been trained to recommend supplemental vitamins and minerals only for infants, children, pregnant women, chronic alcoholics, and very ill adults. Additionally, physicians have been trained to diagnose and treat the diseases caused by vitamin deficiency, such as beriberi (thiamin deficiency), scurvy (vitamin C deficiency), and pellegra (vitamin B_6 deficiency). In the meantime, hundreds of studies have emerged documenting that nutritional supplements can help prevent congenital abnormalities of the spine, cataracts, heart disease, stroke, and cancer. *It's obviously gone way beyond deficiency!*

How many vitamins and minerals should you take? Which kinds? Why? How do you compensate for special circumstances? Here, I hope to make you aware of the importance of vitamins and minerals and to motivate you to take them every day. You rely on manuals for the proper operation of your car, computer, VCR, microwave oven, and much more. Why not refer to one for the most important pieces of equipment you'll ever operate—your body?

What follows is a road map for the sensible use of vitamins and minerals to keep your energy in balance. I believe the best way for me to guide you is to share what I personally take, and what I recommend to my family and patients. First, however, I'll tell you about vitamins and minerals.

The "Vital Amines"

The term *vitamins* originated in the beginning of the twentieth century, when medical scientists discovered that the body couldn't manufacture proteins from amino acids that were necessary to life without the presence of certain substances. These substances, which were found only in foods, were called "vital amines." Eventually the term was shortened to *vitamins*.

Vitamins are organic substances that nature supplies to support human life. They carry out their specific functions by supplying certain life-giving codes that regulate the metabolism within our cells. They are responsible for efficiently converting food into energy and are necessary for good vision, healthy blood, and strong bones and teeth. They ensure the proper functioning of the heart, the nervous system, and the reproductive system. These vital amines indeed contribute to our vitality!

Minerals are also essential to life and vitality. These are single-chemical elements found concentrated in all parts of the body. Some are present in abundance, like calcium and magnesium; others are found in mere traces, such as zinc and copper. Most are essential to life, and because our bodies are unable to manufacture them, we must obtain them through the foods or supplements we ingest.

Free Radicals and Antioxidants

Free radicals are highly reactive, unstable oxygen molecules. They possess an unpaired electron that causes them to search out more balanced molecules, snatch their electrons, and leave them unstable in return. This is the chemical process called *oxidation*. Oxidation is the scientific term for *rust*.

Every cell in the human body is constantly exposed to the oxidation process from free radicals normally generated by our daily metabolism and natural aging process. Problems only occur when there are too many of these renegade electron-thieves. You can't see them or feel them, but modern life tends to cause an explosion of free radicals because of inner influences such as stress, anxiety, and depression, and outside influences such as cigarette smoke, air pollution, pesticides, contaminants, and unhealthy food. In these times, it's estimated that each of our cells experience many thousands of free radical "hits" a day!

Antioxidants are chemicals that protect our bodies against the harmful effects of free radical damage. They inhibit free radicals and impede the damage they cause. Naturally occurring antioxidants help prevent or repair oxidative damage, but once the amount of rust we accumulate exceeds our body's ability to repair it, degeneration and disease occur—free radicals accelerate aging, weaken immunity, and cause cancer. Your body makes many of its own antioxidants to combat free radical damage, but it also depends on you to ingest sufficient amounts of antioxidants such as vitamin C, vitamin E, vitamin A, beta-carotene, and selenium.

Vitamin C: Cancer, Cataracts, and Colds

Vitamin C possesses a remarkable ability to reduce the havoc caused by free radicals. It plays a vital role in building healthy bones and teeth, promotes wound healing and tissue repair, and appears to be particularly effective in cleaning up some of the damage from cigarette smoke. Moreover, vitamin C helps to maintain a healthy heart by working in synergy with vitamin E and other antioxidants to prevent atherosclerotic plaque in the coronary arteries.

More than thirty scientific studies have demonstrated that vitamin C has a protective effect against cancer. People with low vitamin C intakes have significantly more cancer of the mouth, larynx, esophagus, breast, lung, stomach, colon, rectum, and cervix than people with higher vitamin C intakes. One large study of people ingesting more than 200 mg. per day showed a 60 percent decreased risk of salivary gland cancer.

There is also very strong evidence that vitamin C, along with vitamin E and beta-carotene, protects against cataracts. Vitamin C is normally sixty times more concentrated in the lens of the eyes than in the blood. It has been estimated that the number of cataract operations in the United States would decrease by at least 50 percent if people took adequate amounts of antioxidant vitamins. The Harvard Nurses' Study of over eighty-thousand women demonstrated an 83 percent decrease in the incidence of cataracts among those consuming at least 250 mg. of vitamin C for ten years as compared to those who were not taking supplements.

What about the common cold? The body's natural response, when it senses a cold coming on, is to crave foods rich in vitamin C, such as fresh orange juice. An entire book could be written on the controversy over whether vitamin C protects against the common cold, but that is not my purpose here. However, my strong belief, after practicing pediatrics and family medicine for over three decades, is simply: Yes, vitamin C protects against colds. I take 750 to 1,000 mg. vitamin C every day, and I usually double or even triple my daily vitamin C intake when I feel I am "coming down with something"—*and it helps*.

Vitamin E: The Miracle Antioxidant

Vitamin E is required for the formation of DNA and blood cells. It also prevents premature aging by reducing oxidation. Vitamin E is found naturally in green leafy vegetables, as well as nuts and vegetable oils. Strong evidence also suggests that vitamin E supplementation helps prevent heart disease, cataracts, strokes, and cancer. In a major study involving over four hundred colon cancer patients and a similar number of healthy individuals, it was found that the use of multivitamins containing 200 IU of vitamin E for ten years was associated with a 57 percent reduction in the risk of colon cancer. Finally, vitamin E also appears to improve immunity, especially in the elderly. In a study of over eleven thousand elderly people conducted by the National Institute on Aging, it was found that users of both vitamin E and vitamin C supplements had a 53 percent decreased risk of mortality from heart disease and a 42 percent decreased risk of mortality from all causes, compared to those who did not take supplements. No wonder vitamin E is called the miracle antioxidant!

The Harvard Nurses' Study demonstrates a 41 percent reduction in heart disease for women ingesting at least 200 IU of vitamin E for more than two years. The Cambridge Heart Antioxidant Study of men with heart disease showed that those who ingested 400 to 800 IU of vitamin E every day for eighteen months reduced their risk of heart attack by 75 percent compared to those men who didn't take a vitamin E supplement. Almost all studies show that people with high intakes of vitamin E, taken as a nutritional supplement, have lower risks of heart disease. Supplements are an extremely important means of increasing vitamin E consumption because most foods provide just small amounts of vitamin E. A cup of almonds contains about 20 IU of vitamin E; a cup of hazelnuts has about 30 IU. We would need to ingest more than four quarts of olive oil a day to provide 400 IU of vitamin E!

Beta-carotene and Vitamin A

Vitamin A and beta-carotene, called carotenoids, are required for healthy mucous membranes, skin, bones, and teeth. Beta-carotene is converted into vitamin A in the body. Carotenoids are also essential for general and night vision. Vitamin A deficiency is one of the five major malnutrition problems in the world, most commonly found in children who consequently develop infections, pneumonia, and diarrhea, and who tend to die prematurely. Deficiency in adults can cause general and night blindness, rough, scaly skin, and increased susceptibility to infections. Beta-carotene is found naturally in yellow and green vegetables and fruits: carrots, pumpkins, spinach, corn, turnips, apricots, cantaloupe, mangoes, papaya, and sweet potatoes. Vitamin A is found mostly in dairy products, eggs, and fish liver oil. These potent and effective antioxidants help our body to defend itself against free radical activity and, while doing so, help protect us against cataracts, stroke, heart disease, and many types of cancer.

Carotenoids are also essential for the prevention of age-related macular degeneration (AMD), which is the most common cause of visual impairment and legal blindness in the United States. AMD occurs in about 20 percent of the population above the age of sixty-five. No treatment is available for most people, and their ability to read, drive a car, or even recognize familiar faces may be lost. The effect on the quality of life is so severe that we should be doing everything we can to prevent this condition. Since our body does not synthesize carotenoids, we are dependent on food sources and nutritional supplements. For this reason, beta-carotene and vitamin A supplementation is highly recommended. While beta-carotene can be used in larger doses, the dose of vitamin A should be limited to 5,000 IU a day.

Selenium: Team Player and Cancer Knockout

Selenium is a mineral and a highly effective antioxidant found naturally in seafood, as well as in grains and seeds grown in soil containing selenium. A deficiency of selenium weakens the effect of some of the antioxidants that the body itself produces to counter free radical damage. Selenium actually helps protect other antioxidants, such as vitamin C, vitamin E, and beta-carotene, while working right alongside them to combat free radicals.

A stunning thing happened in scientific research on selenium recently. While studying the effects of selenium, researchers halted the study prematurely when they discovered the results were so important that they had to be announced to the public without delay. The research found a dramatic lowering of rates of cancer in people who were taking 200 mcg of selenium for up to ten years, compared to those who were not taking selenium. In the group taking selenium, rates of prostate cancer were 69 percent lower, rates of colorectal cancer were 64 percent lower, and there was a 30 percent lower incidence of lung cancer.

Calcium, Vitamin D, and Osteoporosis

Calcium and vitamin D work in remarkable synergy. The mineral calcium is necessary for healthy bone growth and essential for the heart and proper nerve and muscle function. We obtain vitamin D, which our body requires to absorb calcium, from our intestines, primarily from our being exposed to sunlight.

Increased intakes of calcium and vitamin D help to build healthy bones during childhood and adolescence and slow the bone loss that comes with aging and entropy. The combined effects of calcium and vitamin D are crucial for helping to prevent osteoporosis and the bone fractures associated with this condition. Research indicates that adequate calcium and vitamin D supplementation in premenopausal women can prevent the loss of more than 1 percent of bone mass per year. That can amount to a substantial decrease of bone loss by the onset of menopause. The right combination of calcium and vitamin D dramatically reduces the risk of nonvertebral fractures among men as well as women. The incidence of hip fractures can be reduced by as much as 50 percent.

In light of abundant new evidence linking calcium and vitamin D intakes to bone health, the prestigious Institute of Medicine recently increased its calcium and vitamin D recommendations for adults. The recommendations for vitamin D were doubled to 400 IU daily for people aged fifty-one to seventy and tripled to 800 IU daily for people over the age of seventy. It is now recommended that people over the age of fifty consume 1,200 mg. of calcium daily, compared to the previous recommendation of 800 mg. daily for this age group.

Most people don't ingest anywhere near these amounts of calcium. And while most people identify cow's milk and dairy products as sources of calcium, these foods, as we've learned, are not ideal. Green leafy vegetables, peas, beans, nuts, whole grain bread, and fish are much healthier sources of calcium. At the same time, most people do not get enough vitamin D because they are sunlight deprived. Although some vitamin D is present in oily fish (sardines, salmon), fortified cereals, and milk, our body depends primarily on sunlight to manufacture this vitamin. The destruction of the ozone, which necessitates avoiding direct sunlight, and all the daylight hours spent indoors, is an evolutionary surprise that our bodies are ill-equipped to handle.

Our skin contains a chemical that changes to vitamin D when exposed to the ultraviolet rays of sunlight. That's why our bone mass actually decreases during winter and spring and rises in summer and fall. Vitamin D supplementation is especially helpful to people who always wear sunscreen or sit in the shade while outside, because they don't synthesize adequate amounts of vitamin D. Finally, with age and entropy, the amount of vitamin D the stomach can absorb decreases while simultaneously people tend to be outdoors even less. Studies demonstrate that approximately 50 percent of Americans and Europeans over the age of sixty are vitamin D deficient.

Here's the bottom line: The key to preventing one of the worst problems occurring during the later stages of the human lifecycle is to *begin the process of prevention earlier*. Osteoporosis, characterized by a serious loss of bone material, predisposes us to softened, easily breakable bones. Osteoporosis is so common that about 50 percent of women over age fifty experience broken bones because of it, including fractured vertebrae. About 30 percent of men also experience broken bones from osteoporosis. Thus, it is crucial for you to know that the proper use of calcium, vitamin D, and magnesium supplements can potentially decrease the rate of osteoporotic fractures almost by half.

Magnesium: A Very Essential Mineral

Magnesium, found in green leafy vegetables, nuts, soybeans, whole grain cereals, bananas, and fish, helps ensure the strength of our bones and the proper functioning of our heart, muscles, and nerves. It is necessary for strengthening our immunity and is also a crucial catalyst for the body's entire energy production system. Diuretic medications used for high blood pressure may cause the body to lose magnesium through the urine. Diets that are deficient in magnesium may lead to osteoporosis, diabetes, kidney and heart disease, as well as cause feelings of low energy and a general lack of vitality. Several excellent clinical studies demonstrate that magnesium supplementation may be useful for the treatment and prevention of cardiac arrhythmia, asthma, chronic obstructive pulmonary disease, and migraine headaches.

The science of nutritional supplementation requires an understanding of the underlying nutrient interrelationships within the body. Proper *balance* is necessary. The balance between magnesium and calcium is especially crucial. Magnesium is instrumental in keeping calcium in solution within our bloodstream, as well as converting vitamin D into a form the body can utilize. Thus, calcium and vitamin D increase our daily magnesium requirements. Studies demonstrate a steady rise in the rate of cardiovascular disease in countries where people ingest small amounts of magnesium in relation to their amounts of calcium intake. As your calcium intake increases, your magnesium intake should also increase. The optimum calcium/magnesium ratio appears to be between 2 and 2½ to 1. Thus, a 1,000 mg. calcium supplement should be balanced with 400 to 500 mg. of magnesium.

Iron: A Double-Edged Sword

The mineral iron plays an essential role in building healthy blood, enhancing our immunity, and supporting the complicated metabolism of virtually all our cells. Besides red meat, excellent food sources for iron include green leafy vegetables (such as spinach), peas, nuts, soybeans, and whole grain cereals. Well-balanced, mostly vegetarian diets are perfectly compatible with adequate iron intake. Moreover, it is important to be aware of the fact that milk and dairy products may seriously interfere with the ability of our intestines to absorb iron from foods.

Iron deficiency is a prevalent nutritional condition in the United States in women of child-bearing age. Recent national surveys indicate that about 10 percent of adolescent girls and menstruating women in the United States are iron deficient. This translates to about 10 million adolescent girls and women of child-bearing age who would benefit from more green vegetables as well as iron supplementation! On the other hand, too much iron in the body may increase the risk of liver and heart disease and cancer. Thus, men and postmenopausal women should generally avoid nutritional supplements containing iron.

Zinc: Just a Little Bit Does a Lot

Zinc is an indispensable mineral. It is required for the synthesis of DNA, protein, and insulin, and it is vital for the proper functioning of our eyes, liver, kidneys, muscles, and testicles. Yet only 2 to 3 grams of zinc are present in the entire body, where it concentrates mostly in the bones, eyes, and prostate gland. Zinc deficiency leads to infertility, impaired immunity, abnormal night vision, and delayed healing of wounds. Men require more zinc than women.

It is important also to be aware that an excess of zinc may lead to serious problems, including nausea, vomiting, diarrhea, lethargy, and fatigue. It may also lead to a deficiency of copper in the body. Thus, it's important to be careful about the amount of zinc contained in nutritional supplements. Besides red meat, zinc is found naturally in nuts (Brazil nuts, cashews, pecans, and peanuts), whole grains, sesame seeds, black-eyed peas, garbanzo beans, poultry, and seafood. Oysters contain an incredibly high amount of zinc.

As a result of a study at the prestigious Cleveland Clinic, zinc has been enjoying wide popularity in the form of a throat lozenge to lessen the severity and shorten the duration of colds. Unfortunately, the study was conducted with an unusually small amount of people, the beneficial results were not very dramatic, and other researchers have not been able to consistently replicate the findings. We need to wait for confirming studies. It reminds me of the old adage I tell my patients: *I can treat your cold with medicine and it will go away in a week—or we can do nothing and it will take seven days.*

Vitamin B_{12}: The Great Masquerade

Vitamin B_{12} is necessary for our body to release energy from the food we eat. It is required for cell growth, healthy blood, a well-functioning nervous system, and reproduction. Remarkable as it seems, about 50 percent of people over the age of sixty in North America and Europe may be deficient in vitamin B_{12}. We used to think the major reason was that older people lose the ability to secrete gastric acid in their stomachs. Now we know that is not so.

Vitamin B_{12} deficiency causes damage to the sheath that surrounds nerves so that electrical impulses cannot travel along them. When the nerve sheath falls into disrepair, it can cause mental confusion, memory loss, dementia, and various psychiatric problems. Older people with significant memory loss should have their vitamin B_{12} blood levels checked. Vitamin B_{12} deficiency can also cause neurological deficits that lead to a lack of balance, a stumbling walk, and numbness in the body and limbs. In general, vitamin B_{12} deficiency can result in severe, health-destroying pernicious anemia.

The signs and symptoms of vitamin B_{12} deficiency are seldom correctly diagnosed because they mimic the findings of so many other mental and physical illnesses. To further complicate the diagnosis of vitamin B_{12} deficiency, the common blood tests that medical doctors perform to establish this diagnosis are usually not helpful. (The proper test to perform is a specific serum B_{12} level or a test of a certain B_{12} derivative.)

It's important to know that folic acid supplementation, now common in breads and cereals, tends to mask the symptoms of pernicious anemia. Consequently, the National Academy of Sciences has recommended that people over the age of fifty should be taking vitamin B_{12} supplements—orally! American and Western European physicians traditionally have been taught that B_{12} could only be given by injection. Now it is common knowledge that, in appropriate dosages, *oral B_{12} works just fine.*

Vitamin B_{12} is truly an all-purpose vitamin, and it requires only a microscopic amount to do the job. I strongly urge all adolescents and adults to take this remarkable substance as a nutritional supplement each day.

Preventing Congenital Birth Defects and Living Healthfully with Folic Acid

The human body requires folic acid to regulate cell division and maintain a healthy immune system. Folic acid is a B vitamin found in green leafy vegetables, nuts, peas, and beans. One of the most surprising breakthroughs in nutritional science in the last fifty years has been the discovery that folic acid supplementation helps prevent several types of serious birth defects. Women who ingest nutritional supplements containing 400 mcg. of folic acid within one to three months of becoming pregnant and during the first trimester of their pregnancy will dramatically lower their risk of having babies with neural tube birth defects such as spina bifida (an opening in the spine, which leads to paralysis or a severe handicap) or anencephaly (partial or complete absence of the brain). The degree of protection against these catastrophic defects is remarkable—up to an 80 percent reduction!

The neural tube of the fetus is the earliest phase of the spinal cord and brain. It develops within the first month of pregnancy, when many women are not even aware they are pregnant. The scientific evidence is strong—all women who are capable of becoming pregnant should consume 400 mcg. of folic acid throughout their child-bearing years to reduce the risk of having a baby with spina bifida or anencephaly.

It's important to note that in all the scientific studies, the risk reduction has been seen when a supplement of 400 mcg. of folic acid was consumed *in addition to* the usual diet. Thus, the effective level of folic acid is not a total of 400 mcg. but *an increase of 400 mcg.* over the amount of folic acid consumed naturally.

There is also evidence that women who take folic acid as part of a comprehensive multivitamin formula help protect their infants against other birth defects, including cleft lip, cleft palate, urinary tract defects and defects, involving the arms and legs. Additionally, it has been demonstrated that women ingesting multivitamins with minerals during pregnancy are less likely to deliver premature or low birth weight infants.

Important new scientific data indicates that multivitamins containing folic acid may not only protect against birth defects, but may also substantially reduce your risk of cancer, heart disease and stroke. This groundbreaking information is discussed in the following pages.

Understanding Homocysteine

It is important that you read this again, even though we've touched upon it in Part Four. You have the opportunity to launch a preemptive strike against a major enemy: atherosclerosis. Atherosclerosis refers to the buildup of fatty deposits in your blood vessels that could trigger heart attacks and strokes. The current scientific understanding of atherosclerosis is based upon the very simplistic notion that the cholesterol we ingest is somehow deposited on the walls of our heart and brain arteries, eventually causing an obstruction and subsequent heart attack or stroke. I do not believe this simple explanation. It is much more likely that injury to the inner linings of our blood vessels allows the fatty deposits to build up that then lead to heart attacks and strokes. The health of our heart and brain vessels has to be compromised before plaque builds up and obstructs them.

But there is something much larger to consider: The human body isn't so poorly constructed that it would just deposit excess fat on the inner linings of the very blood vessels that support life by nourishing its brain and heart. Indeed, mounting scientific evidence supports the notion that the fatal buildup of atherosclerosis occurs *after* the inner linings of our arteries have become thickened and damaged. Moreover, I believe that the deposition of fatty material upon these injured cells represents our body's ill-fated attempt to protect the injury and halt the damage—an inadequate Band-Aid for the ravages of civilization.

Stress, hypertension, smoking, and elevated homocysteine, a toxic amino acid, appear to be the major causes of injury to the inner linings of our blood vessels. Recent findings indicate that stress and stress-related high blood pressure promote injury to the endothelium of the arteries feeding blood to our brain and heart. It has been demonstrated that "type A" individuals who have blood pressure rises in response to mental stress also have the most atherosclerosis and thickening of the inner lining of their carotid arteries.

Homocysteine has a direct toxic effect on the inner lining of human blood vessels. It appears to cause coronary artery disease and strokes by injuring the lining of the arteries *regardless* of the level of cholesterol in the blood. Actually, the *majority* of people with significant coronary artery disease have been found to have normal cholesterol levels.

Widespread interest in the United States regarding homocysteine began with the 1992 publication of a Harvard study of nearly fourteen thousand male physicians. A striking three-fold increase in the rate of heart attack was found in the men with elevated homocysteine levels. More recently, the 1998 publication of the Harvard study of female nurses found that those consuming 400 mcg. of folic acid and 3 mg. of vitamin B_6 a day lowered their incidence of coronary artery disease and heart attack almost by half!

Homocysteine seems to interfere with the ways that endothelial cells use oxygen and results in an excess of damaging free radicals in the lining of the arteries. It also promotes deposition of collagen between the cells, which causes a thickening and hardening of the arterial walls. Additionally, it seems to increase the potential for platelets to aggregate together, which can lead to clot formation.

What causes homocysteine levels to build up? The most important factor causing elevated blood homocysteine levels appears to be the inadequate intake of B vitamins, including folic acid, B_6, and B_{12}, which are required to break down homocysteine in the body.

It is important to be aware of the fact that homocysteine is mostly a by-product of the body's metabolism of red meat, cheese, and other dairy products. Other factors proven to increase homocysteine are cigarette smoking, lack of exercise, and coffee consumption. Extensive research carried out in Holland indicates that merely the combination of smoking, coffee consumption, and low folic acid intake can increase the rate of cardiovascular disease by 40 percent!

Age and hormones also matter. Premenopausal women have homocysteine levels about 20 percent lower than men of the same age. After menopause, the levels approach that of men of the same age. Homocysteine levels then continue to increase with age in both sexes. Moreover, deficiency of the thyroid hormone also causes a rise in homocysteine levels.

How can you best prevent the buildup of homocysteine in your blood? Take a daily nutritional supplement with 400 mcg. of folic acid. I also recommend a *minimum* of 6 mg. a day of B_6 for all adults, a *minimum* of 40 mcg. a day of B_{12} for adults under the age of fifty, and a *minimum* of 400 mcg. a day of B_{12} for those over fifty years old.

Also, as you read earlier in this book, regular exercise is extremely important. Of course, quitting smoking is crucial. It makes sense to limit coffee to no more than two cups a day. Finally, limiting your red meat and dairy intake should have a significant impact on keeping your homocysteine level within a normal range.

European scientists have never been as convinced about the importance of dietary cholesterol in heart disease and stroke as American scientists. Now there is ample evidence that first our most important blood vessels are injured, and then our body responds by coating the injury with fat. *Isn't that enough reason to take your vitamins and minerals every single day?*

Recipe for Wellness

Many studies show the wonderful benefits of vitamins and minerals for the efficient functioning of our bodies throughout our human lifecycle. One consistent finding stands out in all the research: Taking a daily comprehensive nutritional supplement, proper daily exercise, and eating foods that are filled with life-energy are the keys to maintaining optimal health and wellness.

The following formula is what I take every day and recommend to my family and patients, both adolescents and adults:

- vitamin A
  (as beta-carotene)   10,000 IU
- vitamin B_1 20 mg.
- vitamin B_2 20 mg.
- vitamin B_6 20 mg.
- vitamin B_{12} 100–1,000 mcg. *(increase with age)*
- niacin   20 mg.
- biotin   30 mg.
- pantothenic acid   30 mg.
- folic acid   400 mcg.
- vitamin C   750 mg.
- vitamin D   400–600 IU *(increase with age)*
- vitamin E   400 IU
- vitamin K   25–80 mcg.
- calcium   500–1,200 mg. *(men/women, increase with age)*
- selenium   200 mcg.
- magnesium   250–500 mg. *(men/women)*
- iron   18 mg. *(only menstruating women)*

- copper   2 mg.
- zinc   15–40 mg. *(women/men)*
- manganese   5 mg.
- chromium   100 mcg.
- molybdenum   75 mcg.
- iodine   75 mcg.
- boron   3 mg.

A Vitamin and Mineral Update

Since the first edition of this book was published, there has been a major explosion of new scientific data that validates the information as well as the underlying concept in Part Ten: *A scientifically-based formula of vitamins and minerals can help your body prevent cataracts, osteoporosis, heart disease, stroke, and cancer!*

So it is now more important than ever for you to keep in mind that your body doesn't manufacture vitamins and minerals (except for tiny amounts such as vitamin B-12). Therefore, the only way for you to get the vitamins and minerals your body requires is through the food you ingest, nutritional supplements, and sunshine (vitamin D). However, even if you eat properly, it is *highly unlikely* that you will get the amounts of vitamins and minerals that your body requires to maintain it's energy balance—*The key to total health rejuvenation and permanent weight loss.*

Data in an important Finnish study recently published in the *Journal of the National Cancer Institute* strongly suggests that vitamin E supplementation greatly reduced the risk of prostate cancer: Finnish men taking vitamin E supplements demonstrated a 36 percent lower incidence of prostate cancer than men who took a placebo!

Moreover, data in a study of women nurses recently published in the *Annals of Internal Medicine* has provided the strongest evidence yet that folic acid might help prevent colon cancer—our nation's second largest cancer killer. *Only lung cancer kills more Americans.* The study of more than 80,000 nurses being followed by researchers from Harvard Medical School suggests that the women who took multivitamins containing folic acid for at least 15 years had a 75 percent decrease in their risk of colon cancer!

Dr. Edward Giovannucci, the head researcher, commented that, although only women were studied, other research suggests that folic acid has similar effects in men. He also pointed out that supplements aren't a panacea. Exercise and a diet rich with fruits and vegetables remain essential to colon cancer prevention. *I wholeheartedly agree!*

It is also noteworthy that the decrease in colon cancer was considerably less in women who were taking multivitamins for only a short time. This supports a previous finding in the same nurses' study showing an 83 percent decrease in cataracts among the women who were taking Vitamin C supplements for *over ten years.* So it's important for you to realize that there are no "quick fixes." In other words, it's crucial to take a comprehensive formula that contains sensible amounts of high quality ingredients in the proper balance, over an extended period of time, to build up your immunity to disease. *This plea for your good health cannot be overemphasized.*

Part Eleven

PREVENTIVE THEOLOGY

"BEHIND EVERY BLADE OF GRASS IS ITS VERY OWN
ANGEL THAT FOREVER WHISPERS . . . 'GROW, GROW'"
(The Talmud)

I believe there is only one religion: *the religion of love.* The point was made clearer to me this morning when my wife Anneli, who is Christian, came into my office wearing a Jewish "Star of David" around her neck. I thought to myself, *"What an honor for Judaism!"* It clarified what Dr. Robert H. Schuller, minister of the Crystal Cathedral, meant when he said to me during an interview on his "Hour Of Power" television show: "Dr. Taub, like Jesus, you are a Jew, and I believe you and He are on the same wavelength." Afterwards, he took me aside and said, beaming, "You are developing 'Preventive Theology' . . . *what an honor for Christianity!"*

Preventive Theology constitutes the beginning of what I hope will be a true "Healing Testament" for this new millennium. It's for everyone seeking health and well-being as well as permanent weight loss. It's generally based on the principles of Judaism and Christianity because both faiths would be so much better served by living with each other's wisdom. Christians might well consider the special covenant between the Jews and God, which after more than five thousand years remains very much alive and is still mentioned daily in prayers throughout the world! Jewish contributions in science, medicine, philosophy, psychology, literature, music, and charity have been enormous as a result of this special covenant, which requires Jews to live ethical lives, be charitable, seek justice, and walk humbly before God. On the other hand, Jewish people might well consider the magnificence of the Sermon on the Mount preached by Jesus. It is the essence of Christianity, yet the beauty and wisdom radiating from it can inspire all of us to seek new vistas of personal health and healing.

In the Twenty-third Psalm, perhaps the most beloved part of the Jewish Torah (first five books of the Old Testament), King David shares an epiphany: God is *accessible* to us:

"The Lord is my shepherd: I shall not want.
He makes me lie down in green pastures.
He leads me beside the still waters. He restores my soul.
He guides me in straight paths for His name's sake.
Yea, though I walk through the valley of the shadow of death,
I will fear no evil, for *Thou art with me* . . .

To this, the New Testament adds the essence of the greatest story that has ever been told: *Love one another.* The Bible is indeed a *good* book!

Now that I have become a physician with Jewish roots and Christian wings (and a Buddhist and Hindu outlook), I can see that healing miracles are occurring every moment! No wonder Saint Augustine wrote 1,700 years ago: *"Miracles never contradict nature. Miracles only contradict what we know about nature."* And no wonder, more recently, the French scientist and Christian theologian Teilhard De Chardin was inspired to write:

"Some day, after we have mastered the winds, the waves, the tides and gravity, we shall harness the energies of love. Then for the second time in the history of the world, Man will have discovered fire."

I believe I learned everything I needed to know about God before I went to kindergarten. I recall asking my mother, as she was giving me a bath one evening when I was about three years old, "Where is

God?" I vividly remember her reply: "God is everywhere." I also remember asking: "Do you mean God is right here?" and her reply: "*Sure* . . . just put your toes up against the water where it's running into the bathtub and feel how good it feels . . . *God is in that water.*" I still recall how delighted I was with this *terrific* bit of information—*as well as how wonderful my toes felt just wriggling around in that water!* Then I remember asking my mother, "Is it ever possible to see God?" "Absolutely," she said, "You can see God wherever you see love, because God is love."

By the time I did get to kindergarten, I knew I wanted to be either a fireman, a policeman, or a doctor, so I could help take care of people. I felt God would appreciate that, since after all, as my mother had said, God was love. Then, while preparing for my Bar Mitzvah at 13 years-old, I began feeling that God would also appreciate my being a good Jew . . . especially the way that Rabbi Maimonides, a major theologian as well as the greatest Jewish physician of all time, described being Jewish. Referring to Micah in the Old Testament, he said: "To be a good Jew is to do charity, seek justice, love goodness and walk humbly before God." Then the great rabbi and physician went on to say: "Everything else is mere commentary." *That sparked my decision to go to medical school.*

I also went to medical school because I felt driven to serve as an educator and a healer. I wanted to help keep my patients well in the first place and, if they became ill, to help get them well as quickly as possible. It was 1960, when iron lungs for polio victims were fortunately being wheeled into storage and penicillin was rapidly evolving into a whole new group of antibiotics. We students, as well as our teachers, were enthralled with developing more vaccines and more antibiotics for preventing and treating disease. Indeed, we anticipated making special "magic bullets" for every major illness. Who could have imagined then that the major epidemic we'd have to confront in the new millennium would be obesity and its related diseases? Being overweight certainly causes more illness and death than smallpox or polio ever did! Thus, while we were searching for magic bullets, modern physicians steadily lost sight of the importance of stimulating in our patients an abiding will to be well.

I am reminded of Sandra, a young woman who was diagnosed with cancer at the age of 27. She described her initial experiences with doctors at a teaching hospital in New York City as being "poked, stabbed and poisoned . . . *and they just referred to me as 'the neck mass.'* " "The treatment was so horrible and I felt so unloved by the doctors that I wanted to die," she said. After a relapse one year later, she moved to California where she found a new group of doctors, and a new attitude. She told me she knew she was going to be OK when her oncologist said to her, "Medical science can only do so much. *You have to help, too.* I want you to beat this cancer. You have to want to beat it, too." He prescribed surgery and radiation therapy along with good nutrition, less stress, happiness and prayer. *Sandra has been healthy ever since.*

By now you know what is in my heart. So I will share something I have discovered after 35 years of being a physician, without softening it or pulling any punches: *It's absolutely ridiculous for physicians to ignore the fact that their patients' spiritual outlook and behavior can profoundly affect their capacity for health and healing!* People who love God and who live ethical lives are happier, less fearful, and far less likely to become sick from stress. And when they are ill, they also get better more quickly. Finally, people who believe in a completely loving supreme being are able to conquer their addictions more successfully—*including urges to eat and cravings for junk food.*

As a matter of fact, miracles of healing occur thousands of times everyday in America. We physicians call this phenomenon an *"idiopathic spontaneous remission,"* which means that we haven't got the slightest idea what happened! But I have asked hundreds of patients with idiopathic spontaneous remissions, especially involving serious diseases (lupus erythematosis, periarteritis nodosa, rheumatoid arthritis, leukemia, cancer), to tell me what happened. Virtually every patient says the same thing, *"I just prayed and put myself totally in God's hands."*

*LOVE THE LORD THY GOD WITH ALL THY HEART, AND
WITH ALL THY SOUL, AND WITH ALL THY MIND"*
(The New Testament)

Preventive Theology entails loving God with a totally trusting heart, which requires us to be loving, kind, charitable and ethical human beings . . . *for Jews, this means listening to Jehovah; for Christians, it means following the teachings of Jesus. For Jews and Christians alike . . . it means following the Ten Commandments.*

Preventive Theology is also based on the notion that your health is primarily determined by our own personal responsibility, self-value and reverence for life. This means it is necessary to do whatever *you* can do to help make your body a healthier environment for your soul to flourish in. You see, Preventive Theology is a verb as well as a noun; its goal is to make you feel completely *worthy* of saying *"I Love You God."*

When you begin naturally changing the silent refrain in the meditation introduced in Part One of this book from *"I Have Strength"* and *"God loves me,"* to *"I Love You God,"* with a sense of total surrender, then you will truly know in your heart how much you can really determine your own health destiny . . . *and by doing so, you release God's Healing Force in you.*

You see, God *already* loves you, since God is love. What it all boils down to is that *you* need to feel completely worthy to love God. There is no question about it, your spiritual outlook and behavior is a very significant factor in determining whether you will stay healthy or become ill, and certainly whether you'll lose weight permanently. Furthermore, most people are seriously questioning the deeper purpose of their existence. A *USA Today* article during 1999 reported that when Americans were polled about what they would ask God if they were allowed just one question, the majority answered, *"What is my purpose here on earth."* So please, would you, *just for a moment,* imagine God's presence everywhere and in every living thing? Would you also, *just for a moment,* imagine that all life emanates from God's heart? *Good,* now please take some time to reflect upon your purpose in life.

All human beings are on a spiritual pilgrimage back to the source of infinite energy—*God's heart.* Our purpose is to love one another, and strive always towards goodness. Human beings are most reminded of their purpose when they are extolling the divinity of life through charity, meditation, prayer, and ingesting life-energy food from the top steps of the Food Energy Ladder in Part Six of this book.

Your spiritual pilgrimage back to the heart of God can be a glorious experience if you assist nature by nourishing your mind while also supporting your body with regular exercise and good food. Or you can subject yourself to the effects of stress by lacking love in your heart and neglecting your body. Remember, I.L.L. is often equivalent to *I Lack Love*. To love one another while striving always towards goodness . . . this is the ultimate spiritual effect. *Can you imagine how wonderful the world would be if each person lived by this ideal?* Ethics and integrity emanate from the whispers of your heart—the voice of truth propelling you toward goodness. When you listen to the whispers through meditation and prayer, you are making a major spiritual effort. We truly reap what we sow and our life is a consequence of our actions. Remember, beliefs are not spiritual unless they are manifested by spiritual conduct. Actions speak louder than words and virtue moves our soul towards God. Therefore, our health and well-being flowers only when it is watered by personal responsibility, self-value and reverence for life. ***This is Preventive Theology.***

If you are ill or obese it means *your energy is out of balance.* Therefore, any efforts to preserve or restore your health, or to lose weight permanently, should logically be efforts to bring that energy back into balance. Since your body and your mind are a complete and total ensemble, what is in your heart and on your mind can help keep you well or make you sick. Toxic emotions such as fear, loneliness, or anger hurt your body, while love, hope and forgiveness are transformed into natural medicines that *balance your body and balance your life.*

I'm sure you would agree with me that the basis of health care should be as *spiritual* as it is *scientific.* Therefore, if you will allow me the privilege of being your Wellness Medical Doctor, I want to remind you about the spiritual essence of *Total Health Rejuvenation*: If you are willing to take one genuine, heartfelt step towards God, then God will take a thousand steps toward you. *With this in mind, I wish to respectfully ask you to consider signing the following contract, as your genuine and heartfelt step . . . **To-Life.***

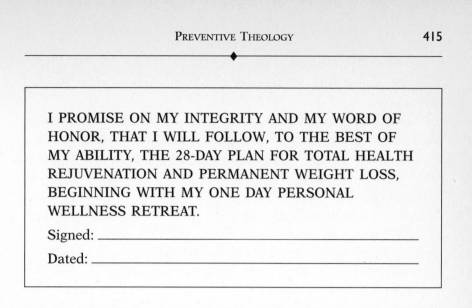

> I PROMISE ON MY INTEGRITY AND MY WORD OF
> HONOR, THAT I WILL FOLLOW, TO THE BEST OF
> MY ABILITY, THE 28-DAY PLAN FOR TOTAL HEALTH
> REJUVENATION AND PERMANENT WEIGHT LOSS,
> BEGINNING WITH MY ONE DAY PERSONAL
> WELLNESS RETREAT.
>
> Signed: _____
>
> Dated: _____

"START THE DAY WITH LOVE, FILL THE DAY WITH
LOVE, END THE DAY WITH LOVE . . . THIS IS THE WAY
TO GOD."
(Sathya Sai Baba)

There is only one religion and that is the religion of love . . . love for ourselves, others, and God. *This inspiration is the basis of all our major faiths: Judaism, Christianity, Buddhism, Hinduism, and Islam.* Do you have to be religious to experience health, well-being and permanent weight loss? Perhaps not, but in my experience there are very few atheists in emergency rooms or coronary care units! This was very recently brought home to me. It began with a phone call I received at 4 A.M.

I almost lost my mother.

"I'm sorry to wake you up son, but I've got chest pain and I'm really scared."

"Mother, I want you to call 911 and then take a baby aspirin. I'll see you at the hospital."

By the time I arrived at the emergency room, she was already hooked up to a heart monitor, breathing oxygen, and receiving intravenous nitroglycerine and morphine. *But she was still having severe pain.*

The ER physician said to me, "It sure looks like a coronary, or at least unstable angina, even though the EKGs and vital signs are normal. We've got an IV morphine drip going now so we'll see what happens with the pain."

He asked my mother, "On a scale of 1–10, with 10 being the worst pain you've ever experienced, including childbirth, what is the level of pain you're having now?"

"It's the worst pain I've ever had. Ten plus!"

Finally, with more morphine, her pain diminished. The ER doctor reviewed the situation with me: "Her EKG looks perfectly normal, which is amazing considering her pain. Plus her X-rays and blood tests are normal. But I still can't believe it's not a coronary artery problem. Sometimes a dissecting aorta could do this, but her aorta looks normal on the chest film. I suppose we should consider esophageal spasm because it can wake people up with this type of crushing chest pain too—it's called "The Great Imitator" because everyone thinks it's a coronary. *But no, I don't think it's that.* Until we have evidence to the contrary, it's a myocardial infarct or a threatened myocardial infarct. The cardiologist has been called and is on the way."

Later, the cardiologist explained to my mother, "You have three major coronary arteries and I believe one or more of them is significantly blocked even though your EKG is normal. This means your heart muscle is struggling for oxygen to keep itself alive. Fortunately, I don't think you've damaged any heart muscle yet."

"Can I just go home then?" my mother said, "on nitroglycerin or maybe some beta-blocker pills like some of my friends take for their angina?"

"Oh no!" the cardiologist replied. "We need to monitor you constantly because you are not at all out of the woods. I also propose doing a cardiac catheterization—threating a tube up your femoral artery in your groin, and then injecting dye into your coronaries. If they are OK, then we'll put you on the proper medications and send you home. If there's a blockage, then we'll inflate the artery with a balloon or a plastic device. The procedure has very few complications and it's very safe."

Twenty-four hours later, I stood in front of a video screen reviewing the cardiac catheterization results with the cardiologist. My own heart raced as he explained, "There's at least a 70 percent blockage in each of your mom's three main coronary arteries, and I'm afraid I might dislodge a calcium deposit if I go in there with a balloon—it could cause a catastrophic event such as a myocardial infarction, an embolism, or even a stroke—who knows."

Already knowing, yet dreading the answer, I asked, *"What's the bottom line?"* "Open heart surgery," he replied, "probably at least a triple bypass. Your mother's heart muscle is still perfectly healthy, so we could decide to wait . . . but if we do it now, then we avoid the possibility of having to do it later when it's an emergency and her heart has already been damaged by an infarct."

What would you do if this was your mother? Well, what I did was call two other cardiologists who were old friends of mine. I needed reassurance because my mother had been perfectly healthy just yesterday! I posed the same question to each of them: "What would you do if this was your mother?" *"Operate now,"* each of them said.

Our family prayed together the night before open heart surgery. My brother and son, who are also medical doctors, my daughter, who has a Ph.D. and with whom I have a very close relationship, and my wonderful father joined hands with my wife and I as we formed a circle around my mother in her bed, each of us asking for God's help, and each of us remembering what she had written to all of us, for what seemed almost forever, on all our birthday cards—*"Love is all there is."* That was all there was in her hospital room that night. I knew more than ever that there was only one true religion . . . the religion of Love, so I prayed in the simplest, purest, most meaningful way I have ever experienced: *I Love You, God . . . I Love You God . . . I Love You God.*

After a seven hour surgical procedure the next day, my heart sank when I saw the heart surgeon's exhausted expression as he came into the family waiting room. After all, a decision had been made to take my mother through an unforeseen and dangerous journey, when just two days ago she was perfectly fine. *Should we have just done nothing? Did we make the wrong choice?*

"She's fine," the doctor said. Simply. Exquisitely. *"She's fine."*

I Love You, God.

MEET DR. TAUB

◆

Edward A. Taub, M.D., is an accomplished author and esteemed physician. After graduating from the State University of New York Medical School in Syracuse in 1963, Dr. Taub completed his internship at the University of California Medical School at Irvine and then served two years with the United States Public Health Service and the United States Coast Guard, achieving the rank of lieutenant commander. His pediatrics residency was served at the University of Southern California—Los Angeles County General Hospital, and he completed National Institutes of Health fellowships in Community Psychiatry and Adolescent Medicine. He is a Fellow of the Academy of Pediatrics. Dr. Taub has been a family doctor and pediatrician for over thirty-five years, served as a member of the clinical faculty of the University of California Medical School at Irvine for two decades, and is a member of the American Medical Association.

From 1968 to 1983, Dr. Taub was the President and Medical Director of the Tustin-Irvine Pediatric Medical Group, Inc., in California, caring for over a hundred thousand children. He also served as Director for the Chapman University Health Center, and has been studying and developing weight loss programs for his patients since 1979. In addition, he founded a clinic for troubled adolescents and received a Disneyland Distinguished Community Service Award.

Currently, Dr. Taub directs the Wellness Medicine Institute. He was the first physician ever to hold the position of wellness medicine director at a major hospital in the United States. In this capacity, Dr. Taub teaches physicians, as well as patients, about

Integrative Medicine. In the United States, he is pioneer in this field.

In May 1997, Dr. Taub became the Wellness Medical Doctor for QVC, Inc., America's largest home shopping channel, which reaches over 65 million homes—live, seven days a week, twenty-four hours a day. As chairman of a joint venture company with QVC called Health Ventures Partners, Dr. Taub develops wellness products, programs, and books for QVC viewers. Dr. Taub's *Nature's Code* **Multivitamin Nutritional System** received QVC's treasured Q Star Award for "Most Innovative Product of the Year" in 1998.

In addition, Dr. Taub has been a leader in the battle against cigarette addiction. He was the national spokesperson, team leader, and stress management consultant for **HOW TO QUIT**, the National Wellness Stop Smoking Campaign. For achieving a remarkably high success rate of 95.6 percent, Dr. Taub's is the only smoking cessation program to date ever to be reviewed, approved, and supported by the prestigious American Medical Association.

Dr. Taub has broadcast his teachings widely among diverse audiences. He became organized labor's first Wellness Director for the AFL-CIO and Teamsters unions (1981–85). He has addressed the American Medical Association, the President's Association of the American Management Association, the California Medical Association, the American Academy of Pediatrics, and the National Education Association. Dr. Taub has been featured on "The Today Show," "Good Morning America," "CBS This Morning," CNN, and numerous television and radio shows across the nation. He has delivered many keynote speeches and currently conducts Integrative Medicine seminars for physicians, nurses, businesses, and educational organizations. He also has provided consulting services for NBC-TV; James River, Inc.; Fit For Life, Inc.; and the General Nutrition Company. Additionally, he has directed more than fifty "Voyage to Wellness" programs for Cunard, Carnival, and Windstar cruise lines.

Among Dr. Taub's literary accomplishments are four other

books: *Voyage to Wellness, Prescription for Life, The Wellness Rx,* and the *Seven Steps to Self-Healing* Pack (recent winner of Golden Book Award from *Body, Mind, Spirit* Magazine).

Dr. Taub has also authored the path-breaking foreword to *Fit For Life,* the best-selling nutritional book of all time.

RESOURCES

◆

INTRODUCTION

Skinner, J.D., et al. Fruit juice intake is not related to children's growth. *Pediatrics* 1999; 103: 58–63.

Smythe J.M., et al. Effects of writing about stressful experiences on symptom reduction in patients with asthma and rheumatoid arthritis. *Journal of the American Medical Association* 1999; 281:1304–1309.

Wolk A., et al. Long-term intake of dietary fiber and decreased risk of coronary heart disease among women. *Journal of the American Medical Association* 1999; 281:1998–2004.

Wootan, M. "USDA's food guide pyramid for children should promote healthful food choices, not heart disease." *Center For Science in the Public Interest Press Release*: March 25, 1999.

PART ONE

The American Dietetic Association, 1997 Nutrition Trends Survey.

Fraser, Laura. *Losing It: America's Obsession With Weight and the Industry That Feeds On It*. NY: Dutton, 1997.

"Heavy Losses: New study shows that you can keep weight off." *Washington Post*, Monday, September 8, 1997.

Iggers, Jeremy. *The Garden of Eating: Food, Sex, and the Hunger for Meaning*. NY: Basic Books, 1996.

1996 Surgeon General's Report on Physical Activity and Health, www.cdc.gov/nccdphp/sgr

"Number of overweight children doubles." *USA Today*, February 2, 1998.

PART THREE

Chronic Care In America, A 21st Century Challenge. The Robert Wood Johnson Foundation, Princeton, NJ; November 1996.

Eisenberg, D. M., et al. Unconventional medicine in the United States; prevalence, costs, and patterns of use. *New England Journal of Medicine* 1993; 328; 246–52.

For Our Patients, Not for Profits: A Call to Action. The Ad Hoc Committee to Defend Health Care. *Journal of the American Medical Association* 1997; 278:1733–34.

Herrick, J.B., Clinical features of sudden obstruction of the coronary arteries. *Journal of the American Medical Association* 1912; 59:2015–2020.

Hill, J. O., et al. Environmental Contributions to the Obesity Epidemic. *Science* 1998; 280:1371–74.

Landmark Report on Public Health Perceptions of Alternative Care. Landmark Healthcare Company. Sacramento, CA; November 1997.

Munoz, K. A., Food intakes of U.S. children and adolescents compared with recommendations. *Pediatrics*, 1997; 100:323–29.

Troiano, R. P., et al. Overweight prevalence and trends for children and adolescents: the National Health and Nutrition Examination Surveys, 1963 to 1991. *Archives of Pediatrics & Adolescent Medicine* 1995; 149:1085–91.

PART FOUR

Bahna, S. Common Manifestations of Cow's Milk Allergy in Children, *Lancet* 1978; 1:304–22.

Beeson, W. L., et al. Chronic disease among Seventh-day Adventists, a low-risk group. *Cancer*, 1989; 64:57–81.

Cheskin, L. J., et al. Gastrointestinal symptoms following consumption of Olestra or regular triglyceride potato chips; a controlled comparison. *Journal of the American Medical Association* 1998; 279:150–52.

Cryan, J., Johnson, R. K., Should the current recommendations for energy intake in infants and young children be lowered? *Nutrition Today* 1997; 17:69–72.

Cumming, R. G., et al. Breastfeeding and other reproductive factors and the risk of hip fractures in elderly women. *International Journal of Epidemiology* 1993; 22:684–91.

Cunningham, A. S. Morbidity in breast-fed and artificially fed infants. *Journal of Pediatrics* 1977; 90 (5):726–29.

Davis, M. K., et al. Infant feeding and childhood cancer. *Lancet* 1988; 2:365–68.

Dershowitz, R. A. *Ambulatory Petiatric Care*. New York: J. B. Lippincott, 1993.

Dewey, K. G., et al. Differences in morbidity between breast-fed and formula-fed infants. *Journal of Pediatrics* 1995; 126:696–702.

Duncan, B., et al. Exclusive breast-feeding for at least four months protects against otitis media. *Pediatrics* 1993; 91:867–72.

Feskanich, D., et al. Milk, dietary calcium, and bone fractures in women: a 12-year prospective study. *American Journal of Public Health* 1997; 87:992–97.

Ford, R. P. K., et al. Breastfeeding and the risk of sudden infant death syndrome. *International Journal of Epidemiology* 1993; 22:885–90.

Frank, A. L., et al. Breast-feeding and respiratory virus infection. *Pediatrics* 1982; 70:239–45

Gerstein, H. C. Cow's milk exposure and type 1 diabetes mellitus. *Diabetes Care* 1994; 17:13–19.

Goran, M. I., et al. Energy requirements across the life span: New findings based on measurement of total energy expenditure with doubly labeled water. *Nutrition Today* 1995; 15:115–50.

Gortmaker, S. I., et al. Television viewing as a cause of increasing obesity among children in the United States, 1986–90. *Archives of Pediatric and Adolescent Medicine* 1996; 150:356–62.

Harvard Report on Cancer Prevention. Volume 2: Prevention of Human Cancer. Published as supplement of *Journal of Cancer Causes & Control* 1998.

Howie, P. W., et al. Protective effect of breast feeding against infection. *British Medical Journal* 1990; 300:11–16.

Kassirer, J. P., Angell, M. Losing Weight—An Ill-fated New Year's Resolution. *New England Journal of Medicine* 1998; 338: 52–54.

Kovar, M. G., et al. Review of the epidemiologic evidence for an association between infant feeding and infant health. *Pediatrics* 1984; 74:S615–38.

Melton, L. J., et al. Influence of breastfeeding and other reproductive factors on bone mass later in life. *Osteoporosis International* 1993; 3:76–83.

Meridia advertisement. *Journal of the American Medical Association* 1998 279; 640 AQ–AX.

Meridia advertisement. *New England Journal of Medicine* 1998; 338: 14 (last nine pages).

Morrow-Tlucak, M., et al. Breastfeeding and cognitive development in the first two years of life. *Social Science in Medicine* 1988; 26:635–39.

Newcomb, P. A., et al. Lactation and a reduced risk of pre-menopausal breast cancer. *New England Journal of Medicine* 1994; 330:81–87

Oski, F. A., et al. Don't discount breast-feeding. *New England Journal of Medicine* 1991; 325: 60–61.

———. Don't drink your milk. Teach Services, Inc. 1996.

———. Infant nutrition, physical growth, breast-feeding, and general nutrition. *Current Opinions in Pediatrics* 1994; 361–64.

———. Is bovine milk a health hazard? *Pediatrics* 1985; 75:182–86.

Pisacane, A., et al. Breast-feeding and urinary tract infection. *Journal of Pediatrics* 1992; 120:87–89.

Popkin, B. M., et al. Breast-feeding and diarrheal morbidity. *Pediatrics* 1990; 86:874–82.

Riggs, B. L., et al. Dietary calcium intake and rate of bone loss in women. *Journal of Clinical Investigation* 1987; 80979–82.

Rosenblatt, K. A., et al. WHO Collaborative Study of Neoplasia and Steroid Contraceptives. *International Journal of Epidemiology* 1993; 22:192–97

Saarinen, U. M., et.al. Breastfeeding as prophylaxis against allergic disease: prospective follow-up study until 17 years old. *Lancet* 1995; 346:1065–69.

Sabaté, J., et al. Nuts: a new protective food against coronary heart disease. *Current Opinion in Lipidology*, 1994; 5:11–16.

Sanchez, T. V., et al. Bone mineral in elderly vegetarian and omnivorous females. *Proceedings of the Fourth International Conference on Bone Measurement*. Bethesda, MD: NIAMDD (NIH Publication #80–1938), 1980: 94–98.

Scholl, T. O., et al. Use of multivitamin/mineral prenatal supplements: influence on the outcome of pregnancy. *American Journal of Epidemiology*, 1997; 146(2):134–41.

Spock, Benjamin and Parker, Steven J. Dr. Spock's Baby and Child Care. Pocket Books, 1998.

Thune, I., et al. Physical Activity and the Risk of Breast Cancer. *New England Journal of Medicine* 1997; 336:1269–75.

U.S. Department of Health Education and Welfare. Healthy People: The Surgeon General's Report on Health Promotion and Disease Prevention, 1995.

Wang, Y. S., Wu, S. Y., The effect of exclusive breast feeding on development and incidence of infection in infants. *Journal of Human Lactation* 1996; 12:27–30.

PART FIVE

Camargo, C. A., et al. Prospective study of moderate alcohol consumption and mortality in U.S. male physicians. *Archives of Internal Medicine* 1997; 157:79–85.

Fritz, Robert. *The Path of Least Resistance*. Fawcett, 1984.

Klem, M. L., et al. Patterns of weight loss maintenance. *The American Journal of Clinical Nutrition* 1997; 66:239–46.

Prochaska, James, Norcross, John, and Diclemente, Carlo. *Changing For Good*. Avon, 1994.

Sklare, J. H. *The Inner Diet*. Roswell, GA: Inner Resource, Inc., 1993.

Smith-Warner, S. A., et al. Alcohol and breast cancer in women: a pooled analysis of cohort studies. *Journal of the American Medical Association* 1998; 279:535–40.

PART SIX

Barnard, Neil D. *Food For Life*. NY: Crown Books, 1993.

Heatherton and Renn, Stress and the Disinhibition of Behavior. *Mind/Body Medicine: A Journal of Clinical Behavioral Medicine*, Vol. 1, No. 2, pp. 72–81.

Taub, Edward A. Commentary: Wellness paradigm shift. *Mind/Body Medicine: A Journal of Clinical Behavioral Medicine*, Vol. 1, No. 2, pp. 82–84.

PART EIGHT

Era, P., et al. Postural balance and self-repeated functional ability in 75 year old men and women. *Journal of the American Geriatric Society*, 1997; 45:80–92.

Nelson, Miriam E. Strong Women Stay Slim. Bantam, 1998.

Stefanick M. L., et al. Effects of diet and exercise in men and postmenopausal women with low levels of HDL cholesterol and high levels of LDL cholesterol. *New England Journal of Medicine*, 1998; 339:12–20.

"Recommendations from the Centers for Disease Control and Prevention and the American College of Sports Medicine." *Journal of the American Medical Association*, 273, 402 (1995).

PART TEN

Bales, C. W., Micronutrient deficiencies in nursing homes: should clinical intervention await a research consensus? *Journal of the American College of Nutrition* 1995; 6:563–64.

Block, G. Vitamin C and cancer prevention: the epidemiologic evidence. *American Journal of Clinical Nutrition* 1991 Supplement; 53:270S–82S.

Boucher, B. J. Vitamin D, glucose intolerance and insulinemia in elderly men. *Diabetologia* 1997; 40:344–47.

Chandra, R. K.. Graying of the immune system: can nutrient supplements improve immunity in the elderly? *Journal of the American Medical Association*; 277:1398–99.

Dickinson, V. A., et al. Supplement use, other dietary and demographic variables, and serum vitamin C in NHANES II. *Journal of the American College of Nutrition* 1994; 13:22–32.

Giovannucci, Edward. Multivitamin use, folate and colon cancer in women. *Annals of Internal Medicine* 1998; 129: 517–524.

Graham, I. M., Daly, L. E., et al. Plasma homocysteine as a risk factor for vascular disease: the European concerted action project. *Journal of the American Medical Association* 1997; 277:1775–81.

Hathcock, J. N. Vitamins and minerals: efficacy and safety. *American Journal of Clinical Nutrition* 1997b; 66:427–37.

Looker, A. C., et al. Prevalence of iron deficiency in the United States. *Journal of the American Medical Association* 1997; 277:973–76.

Macknin, M. L. Zinc Gluconate Lozenges for treatment of the common cold: A randomized, double blind, placebo-controlled study. *Annals of Internal Medicine* 1996; 125:81–88.

McCully, Kilmer S. *The Homocysteine Revolution*. CT: Keats Publishing, 1997.

Meydani, S. N., et al. Vitamin E supplementation and in vivo immune response in healthy elderly subjects: a randomized controlled trial. *Journal of the American Medical Association* 1997; 277:1380–86.

Milunsky, A., et al. Multivitamin/folic acid supplementation in early pregnancy reduces the prevalence of neural tube defects. *Journal of the American Medical Association* 1989; 262:2847–52.

Olson, K.B., Pienta, K.J. Further clues for prostate cancer prevention. *Journal of the National Cancer Institute* 1999; 90: 414–415.

Pitkin, R. M. Dietary reference intakes for thiamin, riboflavin, niacin, vitamin B_6, folate, vitamin B_{12}, pantothenic acid, biotin and choline. *National Academy of Sciences; Institute Of Medicine*; April 7, 1998.

Rimm, E. B., Willett, W. C., et al. Folate and vitamin B-6 from diet and supplements in relation to risk of coronary heart disease among women. *Journal of the American Medical Association* 1998; 279:359–64.

———, Stampfer, M. J., et al. Vitamin E consumption and the risk of coronary heart disease in men. *New England Journal of Medicine* 1993; 328:1450–56.

Seddon, J. M., et al. Dietary carotenoids, vitamins A, C, and E and advanced age-related macular degeneration. *Journal of the American Medical Association* 1994; 272:1413–20.

Shaw, G. M., et al. Risks of orofacial clefts in children of women using multivitamins containing folic acid periconceptionally. *Lancet* 1995; 346:393–96.

Snodderly, D. M. Evidence for protection against age-related macular degeneration by carotenoids and antioxidant vitamins. *American Journal of Clinical Nutrition* 1995; 62 (suppl):1448S–61S.

Stampfer, M. J., et al. Vitamin E consumption and the risk of coronary disease in women. *New England Journal Of Medicine* 1993; 328:1444–49.

Stampfer, M. J., Malinow, M. R., Willett, W. C., et al. A prospective study of plasma homocysteine and risk of myocardial infarction in U.S. physicians. *Journal Of The American Medical Association* 1992; 268:877–81.

Stephens, N. G., et al. Randomised controlled trial of vitamin E in patients with coronary disease: Cambridge Heart Antioxidant Study (CHAOS). *Lancet* 1996; 347:781–86.

Thomas, M. K., et al. Hypovitaminosis D in medical inpatients. *New England Journal of Medicine* 1998; 338:777–83.

Welten, D. C., et al. A meta-analysis of the effect of calcium intake on bone mass in young and middle-aged females and males. *Journal of Nutrition* 1995; 125:2802–13.

PART ELEVEN

Eddy, Mary Baker. *Science and Health with Key to the Scriptures.* The First Church of Christ, Scientist, 1994.

Carlson, Paul, R. *O Christian! O Jew!* David C. Cook, 1974.

Gomes, Peter J. *The Good Book.* William Morrow, 1996.

Schneerson, Menachem M. *Toward a Meaningful Life.* William Morrow, 1995.

Teilhard De Chardin, Pierre. Phenomenon of Man. HarperCollins, 1980.

USA Snapshots. Going to a higher authority. *Yankelovitch Partners for Lutheran Brotherhood. USA Today* December 30, 1998.

BIBLIOGRAPHY

Atkinson, Brooks (Editor). *Selected Writings of Ralph Waldo Emerson*. Modern Library, 1992.

Benson, Herbert. *Timeless Healing*. Scribner, 1996

Barnard, Neil D. *Food For Life*. Crown Books, 1993.

Bohm, David. *Wholeness and Implicate Order*. Routledge, Kegan and Paul, 1980.

Buber, Martin. *I and Thou*. Scribner, 1958.

Chopra, Deepak. *Ageless Body, Timless Mind*. Harmony, 1993

Cousins, Norman. *Anatomy of an Illness*. Norton, 1979.

Damasio, Antonio R. *Descartes' Error*. Grosset/Putman, 1994

Diamond, Harvey and Marilyn. *Fit For Life*. Warner Books, 1985.

Einstein, Albert. *The World As I See It*. Citadel, 1978

Frankl, Victor E. *Man's Search For Meaning*. Washington Square Press, 1959

Fritz, Robert. *The Path of Least Resistance*. Fawcett, 1984.

Greben, Stanley E. *Love's Labor*. Schocken Books, 1984

Lown, Bernard. *The Lost Art of Healing*. Houghton Mifflin, 1996.

O'Hara, Valerie. *Five Weeks to Healing Stress*. New Harbinger, 1996.

Pellitier, Kenneth R. *Mind As Healer, Mind As Slayer*. Delacorte Press, 1977

Robbins, John. *Diet For a New America*. Stillpoint Publishing, 1987.

Sandweiss, Samuel H. *Sai Baba, the Holy Man and the Psychiatrist*. Birthday Press, 1995

Sarno, John E. *The Mind Body Prescription*. Warner Books, 1998.

Schuller, Robert H. *Self-Esteem: The New Reformation*. Word Books, 1982

Sklare, J. H. *The Inner Diet*. Roswell, GA: Inner Resource, Inc. 1993.

Taub, Edward A. *The Seven Steps To Self-Healing*. DK Publishing, 1996

———. *The Wellness Rx*. Prentice Hall, 1995.

Valliant, George E. *The Wisdom of the Ego*. Harvard, 1993

Wilson, Edward O. *Consilience: The Unity of Knowledge*. Alfred A. Knopf, 1998.

INDEX

RECIPE INDEX

◆

DESSERTS